Pointing the Way to Reasoning

POINTING THE WAY TO REASONING

Commentaries to

COMPENDIUM OF DEBATES

[བསྡུས་གྲྭ་]

TYPES OF MIND

[བློ་རིག་]

ANALYSIS OF REASONS

[རྟགས་རིགས་]

---

by

SERMEY KHENSUR LOBSANG THARCHIN RINPOCHE

with

Vincent Montenegro

ORAL COMMENTARY SERIES

MAHAYANA SUTRA AND TANTRA PRESS

Mahayana Sutra and Tantra Press
112 West Second Street
Howell, New Jersey 07731

Library of Congress Cataloging-in-Publication Data

Tharchin, Sermey Geshe Lobsang, 1921–
Pointing the way to reasoning : commentaries to compendium of debates, types of mind, analysis of reasons / Sermey Khensur Lobsang Tharchin Rinpoche with Vincent Montenegro.
p. cm. - - (Oral commentary series)
ISBN 0-918753-18-X
1. Buddhist logic. 2. Knowledge, Theory of (Buddhism)
3. Buddhism--China--Tibet--Doctrines. I. Title: Commentaries to compendium of debates, types of mind, analysis of reasons. II. Montenegro, Vincent 1954–
III. Title. IV. Series.
BC25.T53 2005
160--dc22

2005000004

Cover: Image of Glorious Dharmakīrti courtesy of Venerable Yongyal Rinpoche.

།སེར་སྨད་མཁན་ཟུར་བློ་བཟང་མཐར་ཕྱིན་རིན་པོ་ཆེ།

Sermey Khensur Lobsang Tharchin Rinpoche

About Khensur Rinpoche

Sermey Khensur Lobsang Tharchin Rinpoche (1921–2004) was born in Lhasa, Tibet. He entered the Mey College of Sera Monastery at an early age and proceeded through the rigorous twenty-three-year program of Buddhist monastic and philosophical studies. Upon successful completion of the public examination by the best scholars of the day, Rinpoche was awarded the highest degree of Hlarampa Geshe with honors.

In 1954, he entered Gyu-me Tantric College. In 1959, Rinpoche went into exile. While in India, he was actively involved in Tibetan resettlement and education. He developed a series of textbooks for the Tibetan curriculum and taught at several refugee schools, including those at Darjeeling, Simla, and Mussoorie.

In 1972, Khensur Rinpoche came to the United States to participate in the translation of various Buddhist scriptures. After the completion of this project, he was invited to serve as Abbot of Rashi Gempil Ling, a Buddhist temple established by Kalmuk Mongolians, in Howell, New Jersey. Rinpoche also founded the Mahayana Sutra and Tantra Center, with branches in Washington, D.C. and New York. Over the years he offered a vast range of Buddhist teachings on both Sutra and Tantra. In particular, every spring he would impart Lam Rim teachings for several weeks to accompany the Highest Yoga Tantra initiations he gave in the summer, followed by extensive explanations in the fall.

In 1991, Rinpoche was asked by His Holiness the Dalai Lama to serve as Abbot of Sera Mey Monastery in South India. After his appointment there, where he accomplished a monumental work to improve the lives of the monks, he returned to the United States to resume the teaching of Mahayana Dharma, while continuing to help Sera Mey Monastery from afar.

On December 1st, 2004, on the 20th day of the 10th month of the Wood Monkey year 2131, Rinpoche passed and remained in his final meditation for five days. His holy body was cremated on Je Tsong Khapa Day, December 7th, 2004, at Rashi Gempil Ling, First Kalmuk Buddhist Temple in Howell, New Jersey.

~ CONTENTS ~

~ Contents ~

~ CONTENTS ~

Editor's Note

Source

The material presented here is from a series of teachings on logic given by Khensur Rinpoche primarily to a small group of students over a period of twelve years from 1992–2004. The transcripts were drawn from approximately 50 audio cassette tapes, consisting of roughly 100 hours of teachings.

The main source materials Rinpoche used for these teachings are: for Part I, *Compendium of Debates*, selections from Yongdzin Purbuchok Lobsang Tsultrim Jampa Gyatso's (***Yongs 'dzin phur lcog pa blo bzang tshul khrim byams pa rgya mtsho***) (1825–1901) *Magic Key to the Path of Reasoning: A Presentation of the Compendium of Debates [Types of] Mind, and [Analysis of] Reasons that Discloses the Meaning of the Great Scriptures on Valid Cognition* (known as "*Yongdzin Dura*") (***Tshad ma'i gzhung don 'byed pa'i bsdus grwa dang blo rtags kyi rnam gzhag rigs lam 'phrul gyi lde mig***); for Part II, *Types of Mind*, a selection from *Analysis of the Perfection of Wisdom* (***Phar phyin mtha' spyod spyi don***), a monastic commentarial textbook used by Sera Mey Monastery, written by Kedrup Tenpa Dargye (***mKhas grub chen po dge 'dun bstan dar ba***) (1493–1568); for Part III, selections of *Analysis of Reasons, The Essence of Scriptural Authority and Logical Reasoning: A Presentation of Reasoning to Delight Scholars* (***rTags rigs kyi rnam gzhag lung rigs kyi snying po bsdus pa mkhas pa dgyes byed***) by Chone Lama Drakpa Shedrup (***Co ne bla ma grags pa bshad sgrub***) (1675–1748).

Pronunciation

In order to help students of the Tibetan language, we have included the original texts accompanied by a simplified romanization. It is our purpose to make pronunciation as easy as possible and expect that the serious reader will seek guidance from someone knowledgeable in the language to clarify linguistic subtleties. Below is a brief pronunciation guide.

a as in "f**a**ther"
e as in "w**e**t"
i either short, as in "**i**t" or long, as in "m**ee**t"
u as in "b**oo**t"

(Umlauted vowel) **ö**, similar to the **e** sound in the word "h**e**rb"

STYLE

In an attempt to render Rinpoche's teaching style in written form we have chosen to retain repetitions, anecdotes, and often humorous instructions integral to his teaching method. As the interweaving of English with Tibetan is an important facet of Rinpoche's style, to capture as accurately as possible the flow of his teachings we have given an approximate pronunciation in roman italics, directly followed by an English translation of the word or phrase set off by commas. Whenever the actual spelling of the Tibetan is required, such words are set in boldface italics in parentheses (using the Wylie spelling system).

Actual debates between Rinpoche and the students are marked off by three asterisks and a rule. All translated material is indented and given first in Tibetan, followed by a simplified romanization, and then the English translation. We include the root texts that form the basis for these teachings, as well as a glossary of terms, and list of definitions to facilitate practice in debate.

SELECTIONS

Those passages Rinpoche did not emphasize or cover in the commentary have been left untranslated.

IMPORTANT NOTE

Any errors that may appear in this work are solely the responsibility of the editor-translator.

ACKNOWLEDGMENTS

We acknowledge the infinite kindness of our holy Lama, Khensur Lobsang Tharchin Rinpoche, for his supreme generosity and patience in teaching us over the years and bestowing upon us the priceless jewels from his inexhaustible treasury of wisdom and compassion. In particular we wish to express our gratitude for his teachings on logic, the basis of Buddhist knowledge.

We also wish to thank Venerable Achok Rinpoche for his kind presence and generous help.

PART I

བསྡུས་གྲྭ་

COMPENDIUM OF DEBATES

༄༅། །ཚད་མའི་གཞུང་དོན་འབྱེད་པའི་བསྡུས་གྲྭ་དང་བློ་རྟགས་ཀྱི་རྣམ་
གཞག་རིགས་ལམ་འཕྲུལ་གྱི་ལྡེ་མིག་ཅེས་བྱ་བ་བཞུགས་སོ། །

ཡོངས་འཛིན་ཕུར་ལྕོག་པ་བློ་བཟང་ཚུལ་ཁྲིམས་བྱམས་པ་རྒྱ་མཚོས་བརྩམས་

Commentary to selections of

Yongdzin Purbuchok Lobsang Tsultrim Jampa Gyatso's

MAGIC KEY TO THE PATH OF REASONING: A PRESENTATION OF THE COMPENDIUM OF DEBATES, [TYPES OF] MIND, AND [ANALYSIS OF] REASONS THAT DISCLOSES THE MEANING OF THE GREAT SCRIPTURES ON VALID COGNITION

༄༅། །བླ་མ་དང་མགོན་པོ་རྗེ་བཙུན་འཇམ་པའི་དབྱངས་ལ་ཕྱག་འཚལ་ལོ།།

།གང་གི་བློ་གྲོས་སྒྲིབ་གཉིས་སྤྲིན་བྲལ་ཉི་ལྟར་རྣམ་དག་རབ་གསལ་བས།
།ཇི་སྙེད་དོན་ཀུན་ཇི་བཞིན་གཟིགས་ཕྱིར་ཉིད་ཀྱི་ཐུགས་ཀར་གླེགས་བམ་འཛིན།
།གང་དག་སྲིད་པའི་བཙོན་རར་མ་རིག་མུན་འཐོམས་སྡུག་བསྔལ་གྱིས་གཟིར་བའི།
།འགྲོ་ཚོགས་ཀུན་ལ་བུ་གཅིག་ལྟར་བརྩེ་ཡན་ལག་དྲུག་ཅུའི་དབྱངས་ལྡན་གསུང་།

།འབྲུག་ལྟར་ཆེར་སྒྲོག་ཉོན་མོངས་གཉིད་སློང་ལས་ཀྱི་ལྕགས་སྒྲོག་སྒྲོལ་མཛད་ཅིང་།
།མ་རིག་མུན་སེལ་སྡུག་བསྔལ་མྱུ་གུ་ཇི་སྙེད་གཅོད་མཛད་རལ་གྲི་བསྣམས།
།གདོད་ནས་དག་ཅིང་ས་བཅུའི་མཐར་སོན་ཡོན་ཏན་ལུས་རྫོགས་རྒྱལ་སྲས་ཐུ་བོའི་སྐུ།
།བཅུ་ཕྲག་བཅུ་དང་བཅུ་གཉིས་རྒྱན་སྤྲས་བདག་བློའི་མུན་སེལ་འཇམ་པའི་དབྱངས་ལ་འདུད། །

།ཨོཾ་ཨ་ར་པ་ཙ་ན་དྷཱིཿ།

།བརྩེ་ལྡན་ཁྱོད་ཀྱི་མཁྱེན་རབ་འོད་ཟེར་གྱིས།
།བདག་བློའི་གཏི་མུག་མུན་པ་རབ་བསལ་ནས།
།བཀའ་དང་བསྟན་བཅོས་གཞུང་ལུགས་རྟོགས་པ་ཡི།
།བློ་གྲོས་སྤོབས་པའི་སྣང་བ་སྩལ་དུ་གསོལ། །།

I PROSTRATE TO YOU, Holy Mañjushrī, my Lama and Protector,
Whose intelligence like a dazzling wash of sun
Dissolves the clouds of ignorance and
Dissipates the two obscurations.

The volumes of scripture pressed close to Your heart
Bespeak Your mind's unmatched knowledge
    of all things true and their extent.
And Your love for beings, like a mother's for her only child,
Swells on seeing us tormented by suffering and ignorance
As we grope our dim way in this spiral of cyclic existence.

I bow down to You, Lord Mañjushrī,
Dispeller of mental darkness,
Whose wisdom frees us from the iron shackles
    of our former bad deeds,
And whose speech, a treasure of sixty pure qualities,
    like a dragon's roar
Jars this groggy mind astonished from its sleep of mental affliction.

You, who hold Your sword aloft to rout the dark of ignorance
And lay waste the roots of suffering,
Reveal Your pristine body with one hundred and twelve marks
    adorned,
Ornaments of a prince Bodhisattva,
Sure sign of attainment of the tenth *bhūmi*.

OM AH RA PA TSA NA DHI

May the light of Your loving wisdom
Banish forever the gloom of my mental stupor and
Inspire me with quick intelligence and insight to penetrate
The profundity of the scriptures and their commentaries.

EXPLANATION OF THE TITLE AND HOMAGE

༄༅། །ཚད་མའི་གཞུང་དོན་འབྱེད་པའི་བསྡུས་གྲྭ་དང་བློ་རྟགས་ཀྱི་རྣམ་གཞག་རིགས་ལམ་འཕྲུལ་གྱི་ལྡེ་མིག་ཅེས་བྱ་བ་བཞུགས་སོ། །

tse me shung dön je pe du ra dang lo tak kyi
nam shak rik lam trul gi de mik che ja wa shuk so

Magic Key to the Path of Reasoning: A Presentation of the Compendium of Debates, [Types of] Mind, and [Analysis of] Reasons that Discloses the Meaning of the Great Scriptures on Valid Cognition

༄༅ । །བླ་མ་དང་མགོན་པོ་འཇམ་དཔལ་དབྱངས་ལ་ཕྱག་འཚལ་ལོ།

la ma dang gön po jam pel yang la chak tsel lo

I make prostrations to my Lama and Glorious Protector Mañjushrī!

THE MORE WIDELY KNOWN TITLE of this book on logic, which includes the *Compendium of Debates*, (a selection of which follows) is *Yongdzin Dura. Yongdzin* means tutor, referring to the author who was a very great Lama belonging to Purbuchok Monastery in Tibet and who served as the tutor of the Thirteenth Dalai Lama. This formidable scholar, a tall, dignified man, was known as Purchok Jampa Rinpoche. While teaching logic to the Thirteenth Dalai Lama, he composed this textbook expressly to help him in his studies. It is for this reason that the title of the book carries his name.

Tse me shung dön je pe in the title means opening or disclosing the meaning of the great volumes on valid cognition; that is, the material presented here opens our logic wisdom. Among the many kinds of wisdom our logic wisdom is the best. How is it going to open our wisdom? *Du ra kyi nam shak*, By presenting this collection of topics on logic. Since the pronunciation of this word has become corrupted, nowadays it is pronounced "*du ra*" instead of "*du dra*." *Rik lam*, Path of reasoning, refers to this system of logic. This is not just a general presentation of this material but an essential explanation that acts like *trul gyi de mik*, a magic key for performing miracles. This entire work is a miraculous book of logic because the subjects collected here are the key to unlocking the meaning of those more extensive and detailed texts on *tse ma*, valid cognition.

Chak tsel means making prostrations. Before composing this work the author pays homage by way of making prostrations to the combination of his Lama and the Savior Mañjushrī. Making prostrations at the beginning of a text as a preliminary to its composition is a way to collect an unbelievably great amount of virtue, which will assist the author in composing such a great work and help him to bring it to completion. This is the temporary purpose; the ultimate purpose, of course, is to achieve Buddhahood.

INTRODUCTION

Sakya Paṇḍiṭa said:

Scholars are the ones who do hard work and
face many difficulties.
Those who wish to take it easy and
stay comfortably without working
Cannot become scholars at all.

KYABJE PABONGKA RINPOCHE DECHEN NYINGPO and his classmate, Gyelrong Sharpa Chöje—known as Jangsem Chöje Lobsang Nyima[1]—went together very often to debate when they were at their monastery. Indeed, both of them became Geshes.[2] Later Jangsem Chöje Lobsang Nyima entered Gyu Me Tantric College and became a great scholar. He proceeded to become *gi gö*,[3] an administrator, as I did, then Lama Umdze,[4] then Abbot, and finally almost reached the position of Ganden Tripa. Pabongka Rinpoche Kyabje Dechen Nyingpo's life proceeded in another direction such that he was later to become a very famous teacher of Sutra and Tantra, especially of the *Lam Rim* (Stages of the Path to Enlightenment) tradition. Whenever he taught, many people came from miles and miles around to attend his teachings. Everybody said he was an unbelievable expert on all subjects.

Later, when Lobsang Nyima had learned that Kyabje Dechen Nyingpo was going to be in nearby Chusang Ritrö (***chu bzang ri khrod***), his curiousity piqued from having heard so much relating to Kyabje Pabongka's fame coming from all quarters, he decided to visit him and so he brought along a pot of excellent yogurt as a gift

---

[1] It is from this great logician that Rinpoche received instruction on the basics of logic.

[2] An abbreviation of ***dge ba'i shes gnyen*** (*ge we she nyen*), literally meaning "spiritual friend," referring to the degree acquired at some monasteries upon the completion of a specified curriculum of religious studies.

[3] *Gi gö* (***dge bskos***) is a disciplinarian or monitor in a monastery.

[4] *Umdze* (***dbu mdzad***) is a chanting leader for religious ceremonies.

for Rinpoche. During that visit they met for a long time discussing many points on numerous topics. Since Kyabje Pabongka had answered every one of his questions so thoroughly, Lobsang Nyima couldn't argue with him at all on any of the points. Upon his return, when others asked about the visit he remarked: "When we were on the debate ground at Sera Mey, Kyabje Dechen Nyingpo wasn't an expert at debate by any means. At the time I didn't think he had learned very much. But now I understand that his way of studying and mine went in different directions. For instance, when we debated, I for my part, would apply reasons and quotations to back up my arguments, all the time focusing on the other debater. But Kyabje Pabongka, for his part, when studying, asking questions, giving answers, reciting quotations, giving reasons, everything, would focus all of these on himself, applying them to his own mind. Therefore, by using such a method, there is no way to argue with him on any of the points since he has mastered them all."

In a similar way you, too, have to use the material presented here as a way to advance in your practice, applying the logic to your own mind. This is by far the most important technique for studying. The crucial point is that you have to learn to apply everything in logic to your own condition, to your own situation. For instance, when we make the statement: *dra chö chen, mi tak te, che pa yin pe chir*, consider sound, it is impermanent, because it is produced, this is *tak yang dak,* a perfect reason. Such a statement can be either *rang dön kab kyi tak yang dak*, a perfect reason of proof for oneself, or *shen dön kab kyi tak yang dak,* a perfect reason of proof for others. This latter kind of proof is used for the purpose of teaching others, especially in debate. For *rang dön kab kyi tak yang dak*, a perfect reason of proof for oneself, you don't need an opponent in debate; the opponent is you yourself, your own mind. You are the one to whom you are addressing logical statements. This is how to use logic for one's own benefit as a practitioner. Ostensibly you are using *dra*, sound, as the subject of debate. However, you should think of you yourself as the *chö chen*, subject of the debate. What are you trying to prove about *dra*, sound? "I'm trying to prove that sound is impermanent." How? "By making the logical statement, *dra chö chen, mi tak te, che pa yin pe chir*, consider sound, it is impermanent, because it is produced." When using *che pa*, produced, as a reason, you can use both *mi tak pa*, impermanent, and *ke chik ma*, momentary, as the *drup che chö*, quality to be proved, in that statement. What is *ke chik ma*, momentary? "It is *mi tak pe tsen nyi*, the definition of impermanence." Impermanence is a quality that refers to something that cannot stay the same for more than a moment. "How is that?" It cannot stay for more than a moment because it is disintegrating with each passing instant.

Now, does this nature of *mi tak pa*, impermanence, only apply to sound or does it also apply to you as well? Have you thought about it? Have you meditated on it? Have you gained a realization of this nature? You have to think: "I am *mi tak pa*, impermanent, because I am *che pa*, produced. I should apply logic in such a way while focusing on the nature of my own mind, of my own heaps, of my own life. All of these are impermanent because they are produced. Why? *Gyu kyen kyi kye pe na che pa*, If something arises from causes and conditions it is a product. *Gyu* means main causes; *kyen* means secondary causes. When these came together they made my heaps. It is for this reason that I am impermanent." We can apply the logic rule of positive pervasion, *che pa yin na mi tak pa yin pe kyap*, whatever is produced must be impermanent or changing; and the counter pervasion, *tak na ma che pe kyap*, whatever is permanent cannot be produced. This means that if it is a permanent entity, *gyu kyen kyi ma che pa*, it cannot have been produced by any causes or conditions.

With this knowledge we can come to realize that our life also is changing from moment to moment and cannot remain for more than an instant. Are we getting younger or older? Of course we are getting older. Can anybody stop this process? No, nobody can since our nature is *mi tak pa*, impermanent. As we get older and older, without a doubt eventually we will reach our final destination. When we reach it what will happen to us? What can we do? At that time the only thing that will help us is our Dharma knowledge. Nothing else will be of the slightest help. This is the specific purpose for teaching about *dra mi tak pa*, the impermanence of sound. The practitioner has to apply this knowledge to himself, to prove to himself that he is changing with each passing second, that his life is *ke chik ma*, momentary, and that this process cannot be stopped. This is precisely where one's Dharma knowledge begins; this is Dharma's starting point. The practitioner who gains a realization of his nature as *mi tak pa*, impermanent, with valid cognition, of course will desist from acting foolishly, and will endeavor to do something beneficial for his future. The only way to benefit one's future is to practice Dharma.

This is why you should learn this system nicely. If you do, you will have gained a kind of knowledge known as *je pak tse ma*, inferential valid cognition, about your impermanent nature. Once you realize this by your inferential valid cognition your knowledge becomes infallible. If you realize infallibly through inferential valid cognition that you yourself are impermanent and have that nature, this is the main key for study, for practice, for meditation, and for achieving the ultimate goal. If you don't have that specific kind of knowledge, no matter what Dharma knowledge you do have, it will just dissipate. The main point of the knowledge learned in these debates is to prove the real nature of the practitioner himself or herself through using correct reasons. Such knowledge makes you a real practitioner, a real scholar, a real logician.

These are not just some statements made up by certain logicians to pass the long summer days. They have a big meaning. The original logic comes from Buddha. In order to be able to comprehend this system, however, you must learn the rules of logic so that they can guide you. You must also know how the arguments go, what the quotations are referring to, how to fill in the proper subjects and reasons, so that later you will be able to read them by yourself and understand them. If you don't learn the rules you will remain in the same position without advancing; but if you do, they will act as your guide, like a teacher pointing the way.

Once a certain nomad on a pilgrimage arrived in Lhasa City. When he went to the marketplace somehow he got completely lost. Since he kept seeing the same Ani [Buddhist nun] again and again selling bread at a stand there, he thought to himself, "Umm, that's very strange! No matter which way I go I keep seeing that same Ani selling her bread." Of course, since he had become totally bewildered he was just walking round and round in circles. Similarly, in the logic field you can get completely lost if you cannot understand the logic rules and are not able to follow the debates properly. Therefore, you have to think of extra explanations and extra reasons to try to clarify the meanings to yourself so that you don't lose your way in the argument.

This system most likely is very similar to the system of mathematics that you learned in school. Not only does it stir your brain but sometimes you will need a bottle of extra-strength aspirin. If you learn this system from beginning to end, it will make everything else you read related to Dharma very clear.

Of the five volumes we have to study in the monastery, the most difficult subject is pramāṇa, the study of logic and valid cognition. However, not everybody can be an expert in logic. In the three great monasteries, we had six colleges. Every year each college produced two or three *hlarampa geshes*—making a total of sixteen to seventeen altogether—after twenty-four to twenty-five years of study. In all, we had one hundred and sixty monks in our class. Of these, only our monitor, the great scholar Gyentsa Shakya from Lhasa, my friend Geshe Jampel Senge, who later lived in Italy and passed away there, and myself became *hlarampa geshes*. Only this small handful gained that degree. So, as you can imagine, this logic text is very useful and helps to produce a different kind of scholar, yet it is not a subject that is easy to learn well. Because of that I started to teach only two people since they requested it. Later the class increased to four people. Among the four one of them disappeared. Where did she go? Eventually the rumor got around that I was teaching this material to a small group and so people began asking me what the requirements were for listening to these teachings. Finally, after the rumor spread too widely I opened up the class to everyone. For the first class last Sunday, many people came. But today, as you can see, most of those who came last time have disappeared...maybe they went to the place of those great Indian logic masters—Acharyas Dignāga and Dharmakīrti. Or maybe they just got a sour taste.

Dialogue One

Below is a template used for identifying the various parts of a logical statement. Since reference will be made to this template later on when giving examples for different logical points, it will be helpful to become familiar with it from the outset.

སྒྲ་ཆོས་ཅན། མི་རྟག་སྟེ། བྱས་པའི་ཕྱིར་ཞེས་བཀོད་པའི་ཚེ་སྒྲ་རྩོད་གཞི། མི་རྟག་པ་བསྒྲུབ་བྱའི་ཆོས། སྒྲ་མི་རྟག་པ་བསྒྲུབ་བྱ། བྱས་པ་རྟགས་ཡང་དག །རྟག་པ་དགག་བྱའི་ཆོས། སྒྲ་རྟག་པ་དགག་བྱར་འཇོག་སྟེ། གཞན་ལ་སྦྱོར་ཚུལ་རིགས་འགྲེ །

dra chö chen mi tak te che pe chir she gö pe tse dra tsö shi mi tak pa drup che chö dra mi tak pa drup ja che pa tak yang dak tak pa gak che chö dra tak pa gak jar jok te shen la jor tsul ring dre

Consider sound, it is impermanent, because it is produced. When making this statement, sound is the basis of debate. Impermanence is the quality to be proved. [That] sound is impermanent is the thesis. [That it is] produced is a perfect reason. Permanent sound is the object of refutation. [That] sound is permanent is the thesis to be refuted. [The elements] of this syllogism can be applied similarly to other cases.

Dra, Sound, is *tsö shi*, the basis of debate. *Mi tak pa*, Impermanence, is *drup che chö*, the quality to be proved. What is this statement trying to prove? *Dra mi tak pa drup ja*, The thesis, which is that sound is impermanent. This is the main thesis that we are trying to prove. How are we going to try to prove it? By using *che pa*, product or produced, as a reason. How and by what was sound produced? *Gyu dang kyen gyi che pa*, It was produced by causes and conditions. In this case, *che pa*, produced, is *tak yang dak*, which means a perfect reason. *Tak*, in general, means reason, like a clue, a reasonable clue. *Yang dak* means perfect or correct. For example, when a murder is committed, the police begin looking for clues to discover who did the crime. Until they find the perfect clue that leads them to the criminal, they have to gather a lot of evidence. However, when a crime is committed, the police know that not all clues are good clues and that some may even lead them astray, so they try to avoid false clues. Once they find the correct clue, *tak yang dak*, a perfect reason or sign, that perfect clue proves the thesis. "From the evidence and these perfect clues it looks like so and so did the crime in question. We have perfect evidence to prove that this person is in fact the one who killed him!" In the template above, *che pa*, produced, is a perfect reason to prove that *dra*, sound, is *mi tak pa*, impermanent.

Now, it is not enough to just make a statement to somebody in order to prove something. To whom are you going to prove that sound is impermanent? The person to whom you make such a statement has to be an appropriate recipient of that reason. First, it is important to understand that there is someone who presents an argument and someone who receives it. In the case above, who is proving what to whom? *Nga göl*, The questioner or challenger, should be *rang luk*, [a proponent of] our own system; and *chir göl*, the respondent or one answering the challenges, is the one to whom the argument is presented. In our example, *nga göl* and *chir göl* are debating about whether or not sound is impermanent.

If someone is *chir göl*, a respondent, that person is not necessarily *chir göl yang dak*, an appropriate respondent, with whom to debate. In order to qualify as an appropriate respondent in a particular debate, specific qualifications are required. These qualifications are identified in the definition of *chir göl yang dak*, an appropriate respondent, as follows: *tak chö dön sum tse me nge shing drup ja la shen dö shuk pe göl wa kab kyi chir göl yang dak kyi tsen nyi*,[5] the definition of an appropriate opponent in a debate is someone who has ascertained by valid cognition the reason, the quality to be proved, and the subject [that is, he has ascertained each of the components of the syllogism individually] but has doubt about the thesis of the statement. If such a person satisfies all of these requirements, then he is an appropriate respondent with whom to debate. *Tak*, in this definition, refers to the reason; *chö* refers to *drup che chö*, the quality to be proved; and *dön* refers to *shen dö chö chen*, or the subject about which the respondent has doubt.

Chir göl, The respondent, has perceived *tak*, the reason, which is *che pa*, produced, by his inferential valid cognition. This means that he understands the nature of production through using valid inferential reasoning and, as a consequence, he doesn't have any doubt about sound's being a product. Inferential valid cognition is known in Tibetan as *je pak tse ma.* How does one gain *je pak tse ma* oneself? This is explained by its definition: *rang gi tak yang dak la ten ne rang gi shel ja gok gyur wa la sar du mi lu we rik pa* [or *shen rik*] *je pak tse me tsen nyi*,[6] the definition of inferential valid cognition is a new, infallible awareness [other knower] in regard to a hidden phenomenon, its object of comprehension, based on perfect reasons. This is the definition according to the Sautrāntika school, and therefore the term *sar du*, newly, is included in this definition. According to the definition used in the Prāsaṅgika school, it is not necessary to use this term. *Sar du* means newly or fresh, not "Sadhu," or those people with long hair and a big stomach painted different colors as you see in southern India.

Che pa, Product, is *rang gi shel ja*, its object of comprehension. *Tse ma*, Valid mind, is the subject or consciousness that is doing the perceiving. The respondent knows that if something is a product it

---

[5] རྟགས་ཆོས་དོན་གསུམ་ཚད་མས་ངེས་ཤིང་གྲུབ་བྱ་ལ་ཤེས་འདོད་བཞུག་པའི་རྒོལ་བ་སྐབས་ཀྱི་ཕྱི་རྒོལ་ཡང་དག་གི་མཚན་ཉིད།

[6] རང་གི་རྟགས་ཡང་དག་ལ་བརྟེན་ནས་རང་གི་གཞལ་བྱ་ལྐོག་གྱུར་བ་ལ་གསར་དུ་མི་བླུ་བའི་རིག་པ་ [གཞན་རིག་] རྗེས་དཔག་ཚད་མའི་མཚན་ཉིད།

has arisen through causes and conditions. Such a respondent can easily understand, for instance, that sprouts arise from seeds and that smoke comes from fire, and so forth. Therefore, he knows that a product is created from its causes. *Rang gi tak yang dak*, Its perfect reason, is that a product is made by *gyu dang kyen*, causes and conditions. *Che pa*, Product, is the object of the respondent's *je pak tse ma*, inferential valid cognition. *La ten ne* means relies upon. *Gok gyur wa la* means that it is hidden or concealed from his direct perception. For example, when you look at this table, the table itself is *ngön gyur*, directly perceptible, to your eye consciousness; however, the causes and conditions that produced it are not directly perceptible but *gok gyur*, hidden or concealed, from your direct perception. So *che pa*, produced, [the production of the table] is *gok gyur*, a hidden phenomenon. *Sar du mi lu we rik pa* means that the person perceived "product" newly with his reasoning; that is, he had an initial realization of the nature of sound being produced from causes and conditions. *Mi lu wa* means infallible; *rik pa* means a kind of mind.

Chir göl yang dak, An appropriate respondent, should have all of these qualities. We say that this appropriate respondent *kor sum ke len pa*, which means he accepts the three factors. What are these three factors?[7] 1) *Dra che pa tse me nge*, He perceives by inferential valid cognition that sound is a product; 2) *che na mi tak pe kyap pa tse me nge*, his inferential valid cognition perceives that whatever is produced must be impermanent; 3) *dra mi tak pa yin min la shen dö shuk*, he has doubt about whether or not sound is impermanent. In brief, since the respondent has inferential valid cognition about [sound's] being produced, inferential valid cognition about impermanence, and inferential valid cognition about sound, he understands all of these perfectly.

Shen dö is a logic term equivalent to *te tsom* meaning doubt. What is the definition of *te tsom*? *Rang yul la ta nyi su dok pe sem jung te tsom gyi tsen nyi*,[8] The definition of doubt is a mental derivative [as opposed to a primary consciousness] that oscillates

---

7 རྟགས་བསལ་ཁྱབ་གསུམ་

8 རང་ཡུལ་ལ་མཐའ་གཉིས་སུ་དོགས་པའི་སེམས་བྱུང་ཐེ་ཚོམ་གྱི་མཚན་ཉིད།

between two views with respect to a single object. So the respondent is doubtful about sound in so far as he is not sure whether its nature is permanent or impermanent.

It is important to understand that not everybody is *chir göl yang dak*, an appropriate respondent. One is an appropriate respondent only relative to a certain *tsö shi*, subject of debate, and state of understanding. If a respondent has *kor sum*, those three factors, in his mind relative to a specific subject, then he qualifies as an appropriate opponent in debate.

One of the masters of logic was Palden Chökyi Drakpa, Glorious Dharmakīrti, who wrote several famous texts on logic. If you were to present this logical statement to him, would he qualify as an appropriate respondent? Would this be a perfect reason for him? No. Why not? Because the author of these logic books doesn't have any doubt about whether or not sound is impermanent. If you were to present this statement to him, he would be *chir göl*, a respondent, but not *chir göl yang dak*, an appropriate respondent. If you were to make this statement to a person who perceives sound by valid cognition, but doesn't perceive that whatever is produced must be impermanent, he likewise would be *chir göl*, a respondent, but not *chir göl yang dak*, an appropriate respondent, because he doesn't have all the qualifications mentioned in the definition of an appropriate respondent.

At this point we can check our understanding by employing the method used in debate as follows:

***

—*Chir göl yang dak gyi tsen nyi shak gyu me pe chir*, It's obvious you can't state the definition of an appropriate respondent.

—*Tak ma drup*, That's not true. (In effect, you are saying, *me pa tak ma drup*, It's not true that I don't have the definition of an appropriate respondent.)

—*Chir göl yang dak gyi tsen nyi shak gyu yö par tel*, So it follows that you can state the definition of an appropriate respondent? (If you don't have the definition in your mind, you

can say: *chir tang yö, nga la me*, generally there is one, but I don't know what it is!)
—*Dö*, Yes, I can.

(According to the rules of debate you can only answer two ways to a *tel*,[9] logical consequence: either with *dö*,[10] I agree with your assertion, or *chi chir*,[11] I disagree.)

—*Sho*, Then tell me what it is!

(*Sho*[12] means to posit something or give an example. Literally, the term means put or place something somewhere.)

—*Tak chö dön sum tse me nge shing drup ja la shen dö shuk pe göl wa kab kyi chir göl yang dak kyi tsen nyi*, The definition of an appropriate respondent in a debate is one who has ascertained by valid cognition the reason, the quality to be proved, and the subject [that is, each of the components of the syllogism individually] but has doubt about the thesis of the statement.
—*Je pak tse me tsen nyi shak gyu me pe chir*, I bet you can't tell me the definition of inferential valid cognition.
—*Tak ma drup*, That's not true.
—*Je pak tse me tsen nyi shak gyu yö par tel*, So you can tell me the definition of inferential valid cognition?
—*Dö*, Yes, I can.
—*Sho*, Tell me!
—*Rang gi ten tak yang dak la ten ne rang gi shel ja gok gyur wa la sar du mi lu we rik pa je pak tse me tsen nyi*, The definition of inferential valid cognition is a new, infallible awareness with

9 ཐལ་

10 འདོད་

11 ཅིའི་ཕྱིར་

12 ཞོག་

regard to a hidden phenomenon, its object of comprehension, based on perfect reasons.

Now, in relation to the model statement:

Dra chö chen, mi tak te, che pe chir she gö pe tse dra tsö shi, mi tak pa drup che chö, dra mi tak pa drup ja, che pa tak yang dak, tak pa gak che chö, dra tak pa gak jar jok te shen la jor tsul ring dre, Consider sound, it is impermanent, because it is produced. When making this statement, sound is the basis of debate. Impermanence is the quality to be proved [about sound]. [That] sound is impermanent is the thesis. Produced is a perfect reason. Permanent sound is the object of refutation. [That] sound is permanent is the thesis to be refuted. [The elements] of this syllogism can be applied similarly in other cases.

—*Gak ja shak gyu me pe chir*, There is no object of refutation.
—*Yö*, There is. *Tak pa shak*, [That sound is] permanent.
—*Tsö shi shak gyu me pe chir*, There is no basis of debate.
—*Yö*, There is. *Dra shak*, Sound is that.
—*Drup che chö shak gyu me pe chir*, There is no quality to be proved.
—*Yö*, There is. *Mi tak pa shak*, Impermanence [is that quality you wish to prove about sound].
—*Tak yang dak shak gyu me pe chir*, I guess there's no perfect reason in this statement.
—*Tak ma drup*, That's not correct.
—*Ka re shak*, Well then, what is it?
—*Che pa shak*, "Product" is a perfect reason in that statement.
—*Gak che chö shak gyu me pe chir*, Well, there's no quality to be refuted then.
—*Yö*, Where did you get that idea? Of course there is. *Tak pa shak*, Permanence [of sound] is that.
—*Gak ja shak gyu me pe chir*, There must certainly be no thesis to be refuted.
—*Tak ma drup*, That's not so either. *Dra tak pa shak*, Permanent sound [is the thesis to be refuted].

—*Kor sum ka re shak*, What are the three factors [in regard to this statement]?

—1) *Dra che pa yin pa tse me nge*, [The opponent] perceives by his valid cognition that sound is something produced; 2) *che na mi tak pe kyap pa tse me nge*, [the opponent] perceives by his valid cognition that whatever is produced is impermanent; and 3) *dra mi tak pa yin min la shen dö shuk pa*, [the opponent] has doubt about whether or not sound is impermanent.

All perfect reasons make use of this same system of *kor sum*, the three factors, to prove them.

Now, if I were to make the following statement: *dra chö chen, mi tak te, dra yin pe chir, she gö pe tse, dra te dra mi tak par drup pe tak yang dak yin pe chir*, "consider sound, it is impermanent, because it is sound, sound in that statement is a perfect reason proving that sound is impermanent," such a statement would be incorrect. The kind of reason used here is known as *de drup kyi tak tar nang*, a false reason in a proof. In general there are two kinds of reasons: *tak yang dak*, perfect reasons, and *tak tar nang*, false reasons. Additionally, there are three principal types of false reasons: 1) *ma drup pe tak*, unestablished false reasons or reasons that are false because their validity cannot be established; 2) *ma nge pe tak*, indefinite false reasons or reasons that are false because of not applying accurately; and 3) *gel tak*, contradictory false reasons or reasons that are false because they entail a logical contradiction. Together we call them simply *de drup kyi gel ma nge ma drup pe tak*, contradictory, indefinite, and unestablished reasons in a particular proof.

The reason stated above—that sound is impermanent because it is sound—is an example of *ma drup pe tak*, an unestablished reason, one of the nine principal kinds of unestablished reasons. More specifically, this statement is an example of *shi tak ta te me ne ma drup pa*, an unestablished reason wherein *tsö shi*, the basis of debate, and *tak*, the reason, are the same.

Definitions are especially important in the study of logic. They give a very sharp and exact meaning. When debating you have to have the definitions and answers ready. This way you can get the precise meaning of the debate and gain a clear idea of the system being used in logic. First you have to memorize the definitions, then you can check them using the method of debate. For example, *ma she dön go wa mi'i tsen nyi*,[13] the definition of a human being is that which knows how to speak and understands meaning. *Tsön ja*, The object to be defined, in this case is *mi*, human being, which has that *tsen nyi*, definition. The definition (*tsen*) and the object it defines (*tsön*) have a relationship known as *kyap pa nam pa go gye*,[14] "Eight Doors of Pervasion."

We will examine this relationship below.

***

eight doors of pervasion
kyap pa nam pa go gye

—*Mi'i tsen nyi shak gyu me pe chir*, You can't posit the definition of a human being.

—*Tak ma drup*, That's not so.

—*Mi'i tsen nyi shak gyu yö par tel*, So then you can posit the definition of a human being?

—*Dö*, Yes, of course.

—*Sho*, Well, tell me what it is!

—*Ma she dön go wa mi'i tsen nyi*, That which knows how to speak and understands meaning.

—*Ma she dön go wa chö chen, mi'i tsen nyi yin par tel*, Consider that which knows how to speak and understands meaning, it follows that this is the definition of a human being?

—*Dö*, Yes, that's right.

—*Ma she dön go wa dang mi nyi la tsen tsön kyi kyap pa nam pa go gye nge par tel*, Then it follows that what knows how to speak and understands meaning definitely has a relationship of the Eight Doors of Pervasion between the object to be defined and its definition?

---

13 སྨྲ་ཤེས་དོན་གོ་བ་མིའི་མཚན་ཉིད།

14 ཁྱབ་པ་རྣམ་པ་སྒོ་བརྒྱད་

—*Dö*, Yes.

—*Kyap pa nam pa go gye trang shok*, Count out the eight ways in which they pervade each other!

1) *Mi* yin na *ma she dön go wa* yin *pe kyap*, If it is a human being, then it must know how to speak and understand meaning.
2) *Ma she dön go wa* yin *na mi* yin *pe kyap*, If it knows how to speak and understand meaning, then it must be a human being.
3) *Mi* ma yin *na ma she dön go wa* ma yin *pe kyap*, If it is not a human being, then it does not know how to speak or understand meaning.
4) *Ma she dön go wa* ma yin *na mi* ma yin *pe kyap*, If it does not know how to speak or understand meaning, then it must not be a human being.
5) *Mi* yö na *ma she dön go wa* yö *pe kyap*, If there exists a human being, then it is that which knows how to speak and understands meaning.
6) *Ma she dön go wa* yö na *mi* yö *pe kyap*, If there exists something that knows how to speak and understands meaning, then there exists a human being.
7) *Mi* me na *ma she dön go wa* me *pe kyap*, If there does not exist a human being, then there doesn't exist what knows how to speak and understands meaning.
8) *Ma she dön go wa* me na *mi* me *pe kyap*, If there doesn't exist what knows how to speak and understands meaning, then there doesn't exist a human being.

Now, what about the following:

—*Mi yin na ma she dön go wa yin pe kyap par tel*, If it is a human being, then it follows that it must know how to speak and understand meaning?

—*Dö*, Yes, that's true.

—*Kyap na kye ma tak pe chi pa chö chen*, If such must be the case, what about a newborn baby? *Ma she dön go wa yin par tel*, You're going to tell me that it knows how to speak and understands meaning?

—*Dö*, Yes.

—*Ma she par tel*, So it knows how to speak? *Go war tel*, And you're trying to convince me that it can understand meaning? What about an unconscious person? *Dön go wa yin par tel*, Does he understand meaning, too? And I suppose he can speak as well? In fact, there's really not much difference between an unconscious person and a corpse. Also, what about the gods Indra and Brahma? You're going to convince me that they too are *mi*, human beings, because they can speak and understand meaning? Are they humans or not? *Gya jin dang tsang pa chö chen, mi yin par tel*, Indra, the king of the gods of the desire realm, and Brahma, the king of the form realm, it follows from what you say that they are human beings then?
—*Chi chir*, No, Indra and Brahma are not humans.
—*Mi ma yin par tel*, You're telling me they're not humans? *Ma she dön go wa yin pe chir*, [They are humans], because they know how to speak and understand meaning!

The beings of the six realms must be completely different from one another: humans are humans, gods are gods, and so forth. *Mi dang hla gel wa yin*, Humans and gods are contradictory. [If a being is a god it cannot be human; if a being is human it cannot be a god.] They correspond to the definition of contradictory, which is *ta te gang shik shi tun mi si pa*,[15] two things that are different and not possible to be one. [This definition has two parts: the first reveals that whatever two things are contradictory must be *ta te*, different; and the second, if two things are contradictory, it is impossible for there to be one thing that is both of them.]

—*Tak ma drup*, That's not true. [This is the correct answer. If you don't say *tak ma drup*, you are accepting Indra and Brahma as *mi*, humans.]
—*Mi ma yin par tel, hla yin pe chir*, They are not human beings, because they are gods. *Gya jin chö chen, ma she dön go wa ma yin par tel*, Consider Indra, it follows from what you say that he doesn't know how to speak and understand meaning?

---

[15] ཐ་དད་གང་ཞིག་གཞི་མཐུན་མི་སྲིད་པ་འགལ་བའི་མཚན་ཉིད།

—*Dö*, Yes, that's correct. (You have to say *dö*, I agree, with what you said above.)
—*Ma mi she par tel*, How is it that he doesn't know how to speak? What about when he made a request to the Buddha saying: "Please teach us Dharma"? Didn't Indra and Brahma come down and offer a golden Dharma wheel and a conch shell and request Buddha to teach beings? Of course they can speak and understand meaning. Wasn't Buddha Shākyamuni *mi*, a human? If that's the case, then are not Indra and Brahma *mi*, humans?

You don't know how to answer? If you don't know, then I don't know either. Determining which class they belong to is your problem. As they say on TV, "That's your problem, pard'ner!" Nevertheless, when debating on the debate ground you can't just sit there in dead silence. You have to have an answer ready immediately.

[In this case you have to answer with:]

—*Re re ne yin, dom*[16] *tak ma drup*, Each is true, but when combined they are not true. It is very important to know this response because there are many cases in which such an answer is needed. *Dom* means combined together. You can say: *re re ne yin, ma she pa yin, dön go wa yin*, each is true [separately]: they know how to speak and they know how to understand meaning.
—*Ma she pa yin, dön go wa yin, ma she dön go wa yin par tel*, It is in fact the case that they know how to speak and that they understand meaning, so they must understand meaning and know how to speak?
—*Chi chir*, No, that's not so.
—*Ma mi she par tel*, Then you're saying they don't know how to speak?
—*Chi chir*, Why would I say that?
—*Dön ma go war tel*, And you're saying they don't understand meaning?

---

16 སྡོམས་

—*Chi chir*, Why, I never said that.

—*Ma she dön go wa yin par tel*, Then they know how to speak and understand meaning?

—*Chi chir*, Why?

—*Ma she par tel*, Don't they know how to speak?

—*Dö*, Yes, sure they do.

—*Dön go war tel*, And don't they understand meaning?

—*Dö*, Yes, of course.

—*Ma she dön go wa yin par tel*, Therefore, according to what you say they know how to speak and understand meaning?

—*Chi chir*, Why is that?

This is why you can only respond to the reason given above [*ma she dön go wa yin pe chir*] with *dom tak ma drup, re re ne yin*, Combined this is not true, yet individually they do have each one of these qualities; that is, *ma she pa gang shik dön go wa yin pe chir*, because they have one quality of knowing how to speak and another of understanding meaning. Nevertheless, *ma she pa gang shik dön go wa yin na, ma she dön go wa yin pe ma kyap*, if someone is potentially able to speak and potentially capable of understanding meaning, he is not necessarily someone who by definition speaks and understands meaning. That is the meaning of *dom tak ma drup*, something that is the combination of both is not established.

[The point at issue here is to demonstrate how *tsen*, a definition, and *tsön*, the object it defines, must have the Eight Doors of Pervasion, and that there is nothing besides that object being defined that can qualify as having that definition, even though there may be some things that potentially possess those qualities without having them as their distinguishing and overriding characteristics. The purpose of such a debate may be looked upon as a way of refining the mind of the one who holds the definition, of incurring precision of expression in the face of potential confusion with regard to mixing certain defining characteristics. In the case above, speaking and understanding meaning are the defining characteristics of one class of being i.e., humans, whereas speaking and understanding meaning are not the overriding defining characteristics of the gods.]

Dialogue Two

We have to approach the next subject this way. *Tsul sum yin pa tak yang dak gyi tsen nyi*, The definition of a perfect reason is that which is the three modes. *Shi drup na tak yang dak yin pe kyap*, If it exists, then it must be a perfect reason.

***

When I make the following statement, what will you respond?

—*Shi drup na tak yang dak yin pe kyap par tel*, It follows that whatever exists must be a perfect reason?
—*Dö*, Yes, that seems true.
—*Kyap na, tak tar nang chö chen, tak yang dak yin par tel*, If that's the case, what about false reasons, so they too must be perfect reasons?
—*Chi chir*, No. Why would you say that?
—*Yin par tel, shi drup pe chir*, It follows [that such is the case] because false reasons exist.
—*Tak tar nang chö chen, tak yang dak ma yin par tel*, Consider false reasons, then they aren't perfect reasons?
—*Dö*, Of course they're not.
—*Yin par tel, shi drup pe chir*, But they [must be] perfect reasons, because they exist.
(What will you answer in this case?)
—*Tak ma drup*, That's not true.
—*Tak tar nang chö chen, shi ma drup par tel*, Consider false reasons, you're saying that they aren't perfect reasons?
—*Dö*, That's right, they're not.
—*Tak tar nang chö chen, me par tel*, Consider false reasons, it follows from what you say that false reasons don't even exist?

—*Chi chir*, Why? Of course they exist.

—*Tak tar nang chö chen, yö par tel*, Consider false reasons, then they exist?

—*Dö*, Yes.

—*Shi drup na tak yang dak yin pe ma kyap par tel*, If you say that, it would follow that if something exists it doesn't necessarily have to be a perfect reason?

—*Chi chir*, No, that's not true.

—*Per na, mi yin na pö pa yin pe ma kyap par tel*, For example, if someone is a human being, it follows that he does not necessarily have to be a Tibetan?

—*Dö*, That's right.

—*Sho*, Give me an example!

—American *chö chen*, An American.

—American *chö chen, mi yin par tel*, Consider an American, is he a human being?

—*Dö*, Yes.

—*Pö pa ma yin par tel*, Yet he's not a Tibetan?

—*Dö*, Correct.

—Then, *mi yin na pö pa yin pe ma kyap par tel*, if someone is a human being, it follows that he is not necessarily a Tibetan?

—*Dö*, Yes.

—*Dö na, shi drup na tak yang dak yin pe ma kyap par tel*, If you agree with that, if something exists, it follows that it is not necessarily a perfect reason? *Shi drup na tak yang dak ma kyap na...*, If it's the case that what exists is not necessarily a perfect reason... What about *tsul sum yin pa tak yang dak kyi tsen nyi*, the definition of a perfect reason is that which is the three modes; and the rule: *shi drup na tak yang dak yin pe kyap*, if it exists it must be a perfect reason? *Shi drup na tak yang dak yin pe kyap par tel*, Does it follow that whatever exists must be a perfect reason?

—*Dö*, Yes, it does.

—*Tak tar nang chö chen, tak yang dak yin par tel*, All right, what about false reasons, are they perfect reasons, too?

—*Chi chir*, No. Why? This is similar to saying that the two *tse me mik pa yö pe tsen nyi*,[17] the definition of an existent is that which is observed by valid cognition, and *tse me ma mik pe me pe tsen nyi*,[18] the definition of a non-existent is that which is not observed by valid cognition, are the same. Why would this be? Because *yö pa dang me pa gel wa yin pe chir*, existents and non-existents are mutually contradictory, or opposites, as are false reasons and perfect reasons.

Again:

—*Gel wa yin na te nyi yö pa yin par tel*, If two things are contradictory, it follows that they are both existents?
—*Chi chir*, No. Why?
—*Te nyi yö pa ma yin par tel*, Then it follows that the two are not existents?
—*Dö*, Yes, that's right.
—*Dö na, yö pa dang me pa nyi gel wa ma yin par tel*, If you agree with that, then you must agree that the two, existents and non-existents, are not contradictory?
—*Chi chir*, Why?
—*Gel wa yin par tel*, You say they are contradictory?
—*Dö*, Yes.
—*Gel wa yin na te nyi yö pa yin par tel, yö pa dang me pa nyi gel wa yin par tel*, If they are contradictory, it follows that they must both be existents, even though existents and non-existents are contradictory?
—*Dö*, Yes.
—*Yö pa dang me pa nyi yö par tel*, Then existents and non-existents are both existents?
—*Chi chir*, Why?
—*Gel wa ma yin par tel*, Well, then it follows that they are not contradictory?

---

[17] ཚད་མས་དམིགས་པ་ཡོད་པའི་མཚན་ཉིད།

[18] ཚད་མས་མ་དམིགས་པ་མེད་པའི་མཚན་ཉིད།

—*Chi chir*, No, they are contradictory.

—*Ta te gang shik shi tun mi si pa gel we tsen nyi*, But the definition of contradictory is two things that are different yet not possible to be one thing that is both of them. *Yö pa dang me pa nyi gel wa yin par tel*, The two, existent and non-existent, are contradictory, isn't that so?

—*Dö*, Yes.

—*Yö pa dang me pa nyi ta te yin par tel*, And the two, existent and non-existent, are also different?

—*Dö*, Yes, they are.

—*Yö pa dang me pa nyi shi tun mi si pa yin par tel*, Isn't it also true that it is impossible for one thing to be both an existent and a non-existent?

—*Dö*, Yes.

—*Yö pa dang me pa nyi gel wa yin par tel*, Therefore, from what you say you should agree that an existent and a non-existent are contradictory?

—*Dö*, Yes, I agree.

—*Ta te tsul kyi sho*, Okay, show how they are different!

There is a method for proving how two things are different known as *ta te tsul*, a method for distinguishing differences. Following is an example using the two, pot and pillar, to show how they are different.

method for distinguishing differences
ta te tsul

—*Ka wa dang bum pa nyi gel wa yin par tel*, Isn't it so that the two, a pillar and a pot, are contradictory?

—*Dö*, Yes, that is so.

—*Ka wa dang bum pa nyi shi tun mi si par tel*, Isn't it also the case that it is impossible for one thing to be both a pillar and a pot?

—*Dö*, Yes, of course.

—*Ka wa dang bum pa nyi ta te yin par tel*, Surely a pillar and a pot are different entities?
—*Dö*, Yes, they are.
—*Ka wa dang bum pa nyi ta te tsul kyi sho*, Show how a pillar and a pot are different!
—*Ka wa bum pa dang ta te, bum pa ka wa dang ta te, te nyi yö pa gang shik chik ma yin pe chir*, Pillar is different from pot; pot is different from pillar; whenever there are two existents, they cannot be one and the same.

If two entities are different, then they must comply with these points. Therefore…

—*Tak yang dak dang tak tar nang nyi gel wa yin par tel*, So isn't it the case that perfect reasons and false reasons are contradictory?
—*Dö*, Yes, that must be so.
—*Tak yang dak dang tak tar nang nyi ta te yin par tel*, Are perfect reasons and false reasons different?
—*Dö*, Yes. (If they are contradictory, then they must necessarily be different. That is the first part of *ta te tsul*. There is no way to escape this argument.)
—*Dö na, ta te tsul kyi sho*, If you agree with this, show how they are different!
—*Tak yang dak tak tar nang dang ta te, tak tar nang tak yang dak dang ta te, te nyi yö pa gang shik chik ma yin pe chir*, A perfect reason is different from a false reason; a false reason is different from a perfect reason; those two being existents, they cannot be one and the same thing.
—*Tak yang dak dang tak tar nang nyi yö pa yin par tel*, Does it follow that perfect reasons and false reasons are both existents? (If you say: *De nyi yö pa ma yin*, "Those two are not existents," when you've just got done showing how they are different existents using the method for distinguishing differences [*ta te tsul*] used above, as in *te nyi yö pa gang shik*, "they are both existents …" then you've lost the debate.) *Te nyi yö pa yin par tel*, Then they are both existents?
—*Dö*, Yes, I suppose they would have to be.

—*Dö na, tak tar nang chö chen, yö pa yin par tel*, If you agree that they are both existents, what about false reasons, they are existents?
—*Dö*, Yes.
—*Dö na, shi drup na tak yang dak yin pe ma kyap par tel*, If you agree with this, it looks like the logic rule must be untrue because from what you say, if something exists it does not necessarily have to be a perfect reason.
—*Chi chir*, Why?
—*Shi drup na tak yang dak yin pe kyap par tel*, Now you're saying that if something exists it must be a perfect reason?
—*Dö*, Yes, that's true. (You have to agree with this since it is the logic rule.)
—*Dö na, tak tar nang chö chen, tak yang dak yin par tel*, If you accept that, what about false reasons, I suppose they too are perfect reasons?
—*Chi chir*, No.
—*Tak tar nang chö chen, tak yang dak ma yin par tel*, Let's see, it follows from what you're saying that false reasons are not perfect reasons?
—*Dö*, I accept that.
—*Yin par tel, shi drup pe chir*, Surely false reasons must be perfect reasons because they exist.
—*Chi chir*, Why would you say that?
—*Tak tar nang chö chen, shi ma drup par tel*, Let's consider false reasons, then they don't exist?
—*Chi chir*, I don't agree.
—*Shi drup par tel*, Then false reasons do exist?
—*Dö*, Yes.
—*Tak tar nang chö chen, tak yang dak yin par tel*, Let's take false reasons, it follows that they are perfect reasons?
—*Chi chir*, No.
—*Tak tar nang chö chen, yö pa ma yin par tel*, Consider false reasons, then they aren't existents?
—*Chi chir*, No, that's not true.

—*Tak yang dak dang tak tar nang nyi ta te ma yin par tel,* So it must be the case that perfect reasons and false reasons are not different?

—*Chi chir,* Why? How can that be?

—*Ta te tsul kyi sho,* Demonstrate how they are in fact different!

—*Tak yang dak tak tar nang dang ta te, tak tar nang tak yang dak dang ta te, te nyi yö pa gang shik chik ma yin pe chir,* A perfect reason is different from a false reason; a false reason is different from a perfect reason; those two being existents, they cannot be one thing.

—*Te nyi yö par tel,* So isn't it the case that those two are existents as you just indicated?

—*Dö,* Yes, it seems so.

—*Tak yang dak dang tak tar nang nyi ka yö pa yin par tel,* Well then, perfect reasons and false reasons are both existents?

—*Dö,* I guess so.

—*Tak tar nang yö pa yin par tel,* So we can safely say that a false reason is an existent?

—*Dö,* Yes.

—*Yö pa yin na, shi drup par tel,* Isn't it also true that if something exists, it is a basic existent, since these are synonyms?

—*Dö,* Yes, that has to be so.

—*Tak tar nang chö chen, shi drup par tel,* Okay, what about a false reason, it would have to be an existent?

—*Dö,* Yes, I imagine so.

—*Dö na, shi drup na tak yang dak yin pe ma kyap par tel,* If you agree, then it follows that if something exists it is not necessarily a perfect reason?

—*Chi chir,* No, that's not true.

—*Shi drup na tak yang dak yin pe kyap par tel,* Isn't it so that if it exists it must be a perfect reason [since that is the logic rule]?

—*Dö,* Yes.

—*Tak tar nang chö chen, tak yang dak yin par tel,* Okay then, what about a false reason, it must be a perfect reason judging from what you just said?

—*Chi chir,* Why?

—*Shi drup na tak yang dak yin pe ma kyap par tel*, If it exists, then it is not necessarily a perfect reason?
—*Chi chir*, No, that's not the case.
—*Tak yang dak dang tak tar nang nyi gel wa ma yin par tel*, Wouldn't it also follow from what you say that a perfect reason and a false reason are not contradictory?
—*Chi chir*, No, that doesn't follow.
—*Gel wa yin par tel*, Then they are contradictory?
—*Dö*, Yes, they are.
—*Tsa trang nyi chö chen, gel wa yin par tel*, Consider both hot and cold, it follows that they are contradictory?
—*Dö*, Yes.
—*Tsa drang nyi chö chen, ta te gang shik shi tun mi si pa yin par tel*, Consider both hot and cold, it follows that they are different and it is impossible for one thing to be both of them?
—*Dö*, Yes, that's correct.
—*Te nyi ta te yin par tel*, And those two are different from one another?
—*Dö*, Yes.
—*Ta te tsul kyi sho*, Show how they are different!
—*Tsa wa trang wa dang ta te, trang wa tsa wa dang ta te, te nyi yö pa gang shik chik ma yin pe chir*, Hot is different from cold; cold is different from hot; since both are existents, they cannot be one and the same thing. [Perfect reasons and false reasons are in fact contradictory since they are different from one another and it is impossible for one thing to be both of them.]

Now, to clarify:

—*Te drup gyi tsul sum yin pa tak yang dak gyi tsen nyi*, The definition of a perfect reason is that which is the three modes <u>in a [particular] proof</u>. Moreover, *shi drup na tak yang dak yin pe kyap*, whatever exists must be a perfect reason in a proof. From the debate above you can understand the necessity of specifying the context of the argument by saying "*te drup gyi*," which means "in a particular proof."

In *Analysis of Reasons* (Part III of the present text), where the nature of reasons is discussed, it says:

གཉིས་པ་རྟགས་ཡང་དག་གི་ལོག་ཕྱོགས་གཏན་ཚིགས་ལྟར་སྣང་
བཤད་པ་ལ། མཚན་ཉིད་དང་། དབྱེ་བ་གཉིས། དང་པོ་ལ། ཁ་ཅིག་
གིས། ཚུལ་གསུམ་མ་ཡིན་པ། གཏན་ཚིགས་ལྟར་སྣང་གི་མཚན་ཉིད་
ཟེར་ན། མི་འཐད་དེ། གཏན་ཚིགས་ལྟར་སྣང་མེད་པའི་ཕྱིར་ཏེ།
གཞི་གྲུབ་ན། རྟགས་ཡང་དག་ཡིན་པས་ཁྱབ་པའི་ཕྱིར།

nyi pa tak yang dak gi lok chok ten tsik tar nang she pa la, tsen nyi dang ye wa nyi, dang po la, ka chik gi, tsul sum ma yin pa ten tsik tar nang gi tsen nyi ser na, mi te de, ten tsik tar nang me pe chir te, shi drup na, tak yang dak yin pe kyap pe chir

The second part: regarding the explanation of false reasons, that is, those that are the opposite of perfect reasons, there are two sections consisting of the definition and classifications.

If someone says: "That which is not the three modes is the definition of a false reason," this is not correct, because false reasons do not exist. Why? This is the case because if something exists it must be a perfect reason.

Tak yang dak gyi lok chok means the opposite of a perfect reason. *Tak tar nang she pa la* means discussing false reasons. *Tsen nyi* means the definition; *ye wa* means the various classifications of false reasons. *Ka chik* means some debater who puts forth his definition of a false reason. *Ser na* means when he says that. What definition does he give? *Tsul sum ma yin pa ten tsik tar nang gyi tsen nyi*, That which is not the three modes is the definition of a false reason. However, this cannot be the correct definition. *Mi te* means that's not correct. *Te* shows why. *Ten tsik tar nang me pe chir*, Because a false reason doesn't exist. *Te*, Why is that? Here one reason is given: *shi drup na tak yang dak yin pe kyap pe chir*, Because whatever exists must be a perfect reason.

In the following section, again from *Analysis of Reasons*, a second reason is given for why false reasons don't exist outside of the syllogistic context.

OUR OWN SYSTEM (from the section on *Analysis of Reasons*)
RANG LUK

གཉིས་པ་རང་ལུགས་ནི། དེ་སྒྲུབ་ཀྱི་ཚུལ་གསུམ་མ་ཡིན་པ། དེ་སྒྲུབ་ཀྱི་
གཏན་ཚིགས་ལྟར་སྣང་གི་མཚན་ཉིད། གཉིས་པ་དབྱེ་བ་བཤད་པ་ནི།
ཕྱིར་གཏན་ཚིགས་ལྟར་སྣང་མེད་ཀྱང་། གཞི་ལ་སྦྱར་ན། དེ་སྒྲུབ་ཀྱི་
འགལ་བའི་གཏན་ཚིགས། མ་ངེས་པའི་གཏན་ཚིགས། མ་གྲུབ་པའི་
གཏན་ཚིགས་དང་གསུམ།

nyi pa rang luk ni, de drup kyi tsul sum ma yin pa, de drup kyi ten tsik tar nang gi tsen nyi, nyi pa ye wa she pa ni, chir ten tsik tar nang me kyang, shi la jar na, de drup kyi gel we ten tsik, ma nge pe ten tsik, ma drup pe ten tsik dang sum

The second part consists of [the view of] our own system: the definition of a false reason in a proof is that which is not the three modes in that proof. The second part concerns an explanation of the various classifications [of false reasons in a proof]. Although, in general, false reasons do not exist, when applied to an existent within a specific context, there are three possible kinds of false reasons in a proof. They are: contradictory false reasons, indefinite false reasons, and unestablished false reasons.

THE SECTION CONSISTING OF *rang luk*, the views of "our own system," puts forth its beliefs in order to dispel doubts about the subject. *Tak tar nang, ten tsik tar nang*, and *gyu tsen tar nang* are synonyms meaning a false or pseudo reason. Sometimes this is stated as *ten gyur tar nang*, a false consequential reason, when the style of debate changes. To resolve the debate presented above, the reason is clearly stated as: *chir ten tsik tar nang me kyang*, although, in general, false reasons do not exist, *shi la jar na*, if you use a false reason in a specific statement, it does exist. Those can be of three kinds relative to specific statements: 1) *gel we ten tsik*, a contradictory false reason, 2) *ma nge pe ten tsik*, an indefinite false reason, and 3) *ma drup pe ten tsik*, an unestablished false reason. In general, these three divisions of false reasons don't exist unless they are used in a specific statement. Therefore, it is critical to add *de drup kyi*, in a specific proof, when making a statement, for example: *de drup kyi gel we ten tsik*, a false contradictory reason in a proof; *de drup kyi ma nge pe ten tsik*, a false indefinite reason in a proof; and *de drup kyi ma drup pe ten tsik*, a false unestablished reason in a proof. If you use a false reason in a proof, it may be any one of these three wrong reasons. *Ma drup pe ten tsik*, A false unestablished reason, does not exist, but *de drup kyi ma drup pe ten tsik*, a false unestablished reason in a proof, does exist. The same applies to the other two kinds of false reasons.

Examples of these are as follows. In relation to the model statement: *dra chö chen, mi tak te, che pe chir*, consider sound, it is impermanent, because it is produced, if I were to make the statement: *dra chö chen, tak te, che pe chir*, consider sound, it is permanent, because it is produced, using *che pa*, produced, as a reason, this is an example of *de drup gyi gel tak*, a contradictory false reason in a proof. Or again, if I were to make the statement: *dra chö chen, mi tak te, nyen ja yin pe chir*, consider sound, it is impermanent, because it is an object of hearing, using such a reason is an example of *de drup kyi ma nge pe ten tsik*, a false indefinite reason in a proof. Finally, if I were to make the statement: *dra chö chen, mi tak te, dra yin pe chir*, consider sound, it is impermanent, because it is sound, using such a reason is an example of *de drup kyi ma drup pe ten tsik*, a false unestablished reason in a proof.

Do you understand? Or do you need some aspirin? It should be stirring your brain. This method is very important. It will open your wisdom completely and make it sharp and clear.

Dialogue Three

Now, if I were to say:

***

—*Ngö po yin na bum pa yin pe kyap*, Whatever is a causally effective thing must be a pot, what would you answer?

—*Ma kyap*, That does not pervade.

—*Ka wa chö chen, bum pa yin par tel, ngö po yin pe chir*, Take a pillar, it would logically follow that it is a pot, because it is also a causally effective thing. *Tak kyap ke*, You've accepted that pervasion. [That is, in continuation of the debate above, if you accept the pervasion that if it is a basic existent it must be a perfect reason, then you are forced to accept that if a false reason exists it must be a perfect reason.]

So, if we apply the logic rule of pervasion to the statements below; that is, *shi drup na tak yang dak yin pe kyap*, whatever is a basic existent is a perfect reason, we must pursue the argument as follows:

—*Kyap na, tak tar nang chö chen, tak yang dak yin par tel*, If that pervades, what about a false reason, wouldn't it follow from what you assert that it too is a perfect reason?

—*Chi chir*, No, why would you say that?

—*Yin par tel, shi drup pe chir*, That follows precisely because a false reason is an existent.

—*Tak ma drup*, That's not so. (When answering with "*tak ma drup*," you are saying that a false reason does not exist.)

—*Tak tar nang chö chen, shi ma drup par tel*, Consider a false reason, it doesn't exist?

—*Dö*, That's right, it doesn't exist.

—*Tak kyi tsen nyi shak gyu me pe chir*, From what you say it's obvious you can't tell me the definition of a reason.
—*Tak ma drup*, That's not so. I can tell you the definition of a reason.
—*Sho* (or) *kyi sho*, Tell me what it is then!
—*Tak su gö pa chö chen*, Take anything you posit as a reason.
—*Tak su gö pa chö chen, tak kyi tsen nyi yin par tel*, You're saying that anything you posit as a reason is the definition of a reason?
—*Dö*, Yes.
—*Yin na, tak la ye na, tak yang dak dang tak tar nang nyi me par tel*, If that's so, what about when classifying reasons, then there aren't two divisions consisting of perfect reasons and false reasons?
—*Chi chir*, Why is that?
—*Tak la ye na, ka tsö yö*, Well, how many types of reasons are there?
—*Nyi yö*, There are two.
—*Nyi me par tel, nyi po te re re ne trang gyu me pe chir*, I don't think there are two. But if there are, you probably won't be able to list each one individually.
—*Tak yang dak dang tak tar nang nyi chö chen*, The subject, the two: perfect reasons and false reasons.
—*Tak la ye na, tak yang dak dang tak tar nang nyi yö par tel*, So, when classifying reasons, there are two divisions consisting of perfect reasons and false reasons?
—*Dö*, Yes.
—*Tak tar nang chö chen, tak yin par tel*, Okay, what about a false reason, wouldn't that too qualify as a reason?
—*Dö*, Yes, it would.
—*Tak tar nang chö chen, yö par tel*, So a false reason exists?
—*Chi chir*, Why on earth would you say that?
—*Me par tel*, It doesn't exist?
—*Dö*, That's right.
—*Tak la ye na nyi me par tel*, Then when you classify reasons, there are not two types but only one?
—*Chi chir*, Why do you say that?

—*Tak la ye na nyi yö par tel*, So it follows that when classifying reasons there are two?
—*Dö*, Correct.
—*Tak la ye na nyi yö na, tak tar nang yö par tel*, So if there are two divisions of reasons when classifying them, then a false reason, being one of the two, must exist?
—*Dö*, I guess so.
—*Yö na, tak tar nang chö chen, yö pa yin par tel*, If it exists, then it follows from what you say that a false reason must be an existent?
Chi chir, Why?
—*Tak tar nang chö chen, tak yin par tel*, Consider a false reason, isn't it a reason?
—*Dö*, Yes, it is.
—*Tak yin par tel, yö me gang rung yin pe chir*, It's a reason because a false reason can be either an existent or a non-existent. *Tak tar nang chö chen, yö me gang rung yin par tel*, Consider a false reason, then it can be either an existent or a non-existent?
—*Dö*, Yes, it can be either of them.
—*Yö me gang rung yin na, tak su gö pa yin pe kyap pe chir*, This is so because whether it exists or not, it can still be stated as a reason. *Kyap te, ri bong ra te, te chö chen, mi tak te, ri bong ra yin pe chir, she pe tak su gö pe chir*, This is necessarily so because you can even give a hare's horn as a reason. For example, you can say, "Consider anything, it is impermanent, because it's a hare's horn." This means that you can use any reason in a proof regardless of whether it exists or not. This is like the "freedom of speech" in the First Amendment, which allows you to say anything you want. Drölma[19] *chö chen, kyi yin te, ri bong ra yin pe chir*, Consider Drölma, she's a dog, because she is a hare's horn. Just because you give a reason doesn't mean it is true or *tak yang dak*, a perfect reason.

This is clarified by the following from the section on *Analysis of Reasons*:

[19] Drölma is the name of Rinpoche's dog.

རྟགས་སུ་བཀོད་པ། རྟགས་ཀྱི་མཚན་ཉིད། དེ་སྒྲུབ་ཀྱི་རྟགས་སུ་བཀོད་པ། དེ་སྒྲུབ་ཀྱི་རྟགས་ཀྱི་མཚན་ཉིད། ཡོད་མེད་གང་རུང་ཡིན་ན། དེ་སྒྲུབ་ཀྱི་རྟགས་ཡིན་པས་ཁྱབ་སྟེ། དེ་ཡིན་ན། དེ་སྒྲུབ་ཀྱི་རྟགས་སུ་བཀོད་པས་ཁྱབ་པའི་ཕྱིར་ཏེ། རི་བོང་རྭ་དེ། དེ་ཆོས་ཅན། མི་རྟག་སྟེ། རི་བོང་རྭ་ཡིན་པའི་ཕྱིར་ཞེས་པའི་རྟགས་སུ་བཀོད་པའི་ཕྱིར།

tak su gö pa, tak kyi tsen nyi, te drup kyi tak su gö pa, de drup kyi tak kyi tsen nyi, yö me gang rung yin na, de drup kyi tak yin pe kyap te, de yin na, de drup kyi tak su gö pe kyap pe chir te, ri bong ra te, te chö chen, mi tak te, ri bong ra yin pe chir she pe tak su gö pe chir

The definition of a reason is that which you put forth as a reason. The definition of a reason in a specific proof is that which you put forth as a reason in a specific proof. Whether the reason exists or not, it is necessarily a reason in that proof. That is so, because it is what you stated as the reason in that proof. Take a hare's horn in the following example: consider anything, it is impermanent, because it is a hare's horn, in making that statement, a hare's horn is what you state as the reason in that proof.

Now you have to understand the distinction being made in the following:

—*Shi drup na, tak yang dak yin pe kyap te*, If it exists, it must be a perfect reason, because s*hi drup na, kyö tak su gö pe kyap pe chir*, if it exists, it can necessarily be stated as a reason. However, *shi drup na, de drup kyi tak yang dak yin pe ma kyap*, if it exists, it is not necessarily a perfect reason in a specific proof. To state it more simply: *de drup kyi tak yin na, de drup kyi*

tak yang dak yin pe ma kyap, if it is a reason in a specific proof, it is not necessarily a correct reason in that proof.
—*Sho*, Give me an example!
—*De drup kyi tak tar nang chö chen*, Consider the subject, a false reason in a specific proof.

We can also state it this way: *de drup kyi tak yin kyang, de drup kyi tak yang dak yin pe ma kyap,* even though it is a reason in a specific proof, it is not necessarily a correct reason in that proof. This implies that we can use anything as a reason in a proof, since here we are not talking about correct reasons, only about reasons in general. There is a logic phrase that is very useful: *gang dren dren yin pe chir*, which means, if there is no rule you can say anything about anything.

Now, if I say:

—*De drup kyi tak yin na, de drup kyi tak yang dak yin pe ma kyap par tel*, If it is a reason in a proof, does it follow that it is not necessarily a correct reason in that proof?
—*Dö*, Yes.
—*Sho*, Give me an example!
—*Dra chö chen, mi tak te, mik she kyi sung ja yin pe chir, she gö pe tse, mik she kyi sung ja chö chen, de drup kyi tak yin, de drup kyi tak yang dak ma yin*, Consider sound, it is impermanent, because it is an object held by the eye consciousness; when making this statement, what is held as an object of the eye consciousness is a reason given in this statement, but it is not a correct reason in this proof [since sound, of course, is the object of the ear consciousness and not of the eye consciousness].

It is very important to learn the Tibetan language so that you can better understand this logic system.

OUR OWN SYSTEM

RANG LUK

general (category) and particular (instances)
chi che drak

གཉིས་པ་རང་ལུགས་ལ། སྤྱིའི་མཚན་ཉིད་ཡོད་དེ། རང་གི་གསལ་བ་
ལ་རྗེས་སུ་འགྲོ་བའི་ཆོས་དེ་དེ་ཡིན་པའི་ཕྱིར། སྤྱི་ལ་སྒྲས་བརྗོད་རིགས་
ཀྱི་སྒོ་ནས་དབྱེ་ན་གསུམ་ཡོད་དེ། རིགས་སྤྱི། དོན་སྤྱི། ཚོགས་སྤྱི་དང་
གསུམ་ཡོད་པའི་ཕྱིར།

nyi pa rang luk la, chi'i tsen nyi yö te, rang gi sel wa la je su dro we chö te te yin pe chir, chi la dre jö rik gi go ne ye na sum yö de, rik chi, dön chi, tsok chi dang sum yö pe chir

In our system, there is a definition of general (category), because that which covers its particular instances is that definition. When general (category) is nominally divided there are three kinds: class generality, meaning generality, and collection generality.

WHEN CLASSIFYING GENERAL categories you have to say *chi la dre jö rik gi go ne ye na*, which means that when describing these three, you are merely classifying them nominally, making verbal distinctions; that is, such distinctions do not comprise real classifications. If someone were to ask you how many classifications of general categories there are, you would have to answer with *dre jö rik gi go ne ye na sum yö*, *rik chi, dön chi, tsok chi dang sum yö*, when nominally divided, there are three kinds: class generality, meaning generality, and collection generality.

རིགས་སྤྱིའི་མཚན་ཉིད་ཡོད་དེ། རང་གི་རིགས་ཅན་དུ་མ་ལ་རྗེས་སུ་འགྲོ་བའི་ཆོས་དེ་དེ་ཡིན་པའི་ཕྱིར། མཚན་གཞི་ཡོད་དེ། ཤེས་བྱ་དེ་དེ་ཡིན་པའི་ཕྱིར།

rik chi tsen nyi yö de, rang gi rik chen du ma la je su dro we chö de de yin pe chir, tsen shi yö de, she ja de de yin pe chir

There is a definition of class generality; that phenomenon which covers many things of the same class is the definition of class generality. There is an illustration of class generality; an object of knowledge is just that.

Rik means kind or class. For example, *dro we rik druk* means the six classes of beings in samsara. Therefore, *chi*, general, and *rik chi*, class generality, must be synonymous. The other two—*dön chi*, meaning generality and *tsok chi*, collection generality—are nominal categories; that is, they are just called "general categories" but are not real general categories. *Rik chen* means instance or particular. For example, *ka wa*, pillar, and *bum pa*, pot, are *ngö pö rik chen*, the particulars of the class generality of causally effective thing. Usually *je su dro wa* means "following" or "going after," but here it has the special meaning of "covering" its many particular instances.

She ja, Object of knowledge, is an example of a class generality because it covers all permanent and impermanent entities. *Shi drup na she ja yin pe kyap*, Whatever is a basic existent must be an object of knowledge. What does *she ja* mean? *She* means knowledge; *ja* means its object; that is, an object of knowledge or that which is knowable. What is the definition of *she ja*? *Lö'i yul du cha rung wa she je tsen nyi*,[20] A suitable object of the mind is the definition of an object of knowledge. Does *ri bong ra*, a hare's horn, exist? No. How do you know? *Lö'i yul du cha rung wa ma yin pe chir*, Because it is not a suitable object of the mind. *Lo* means the subject or mind that holds an object. *Yul* means [its] object. *Cha rung wa ma yin* means it

[20] བློའི་ཡུལ་དུ་ཆ་རུང་བ་ཤེས་བྱའི་མཚན་ཉིད།

is not a suitable object. If it is an existent then it must be an object of someone's perception. Therefore, *ri bong ra*, a hare's horn, can be neither *rik chi*, a class generality, nor *rik chen*, a particular [of such a class because it is not a suitable object of anyone's perception].

> བུམ་པའི་དོན་སྤྱིའི་མཚན་ཉིད་ཡོད་དེ། བུམ་འཛིན་རྟོག་པ་ལ་བུམ་པ་མ་ཡིན་བཞིན་དུ་བུམ་པ་ལྟ་བུར་སྣང་བའི་སྒྲོ་བཏགས་ཀྱི་ཆ་དེ་དེ་ཡིན་པའི་ཕྱིར།
>
> *bum pe dön chi tsen nyi yö de, bum dzin tok pa la bum pa ma yin shin du bum pa ta bur nang we dro tak kyi cha de de yin pe chir*
>
> There is a definition of the meaning generality of a pot; the superimposed factor that, while not being a pot, appears like a pot to the conceptual mind apprehending a pot, is such a definition.

Dön chi, A meaning mental image or general mental image, has to be used in regard to something specific. One cannot just have a general mental image, but rather one has to have a general mental image *of* something; for example, *bum pe dön chi*, the general mental image of a pot, given in the definition above. We usually use another definition of a general mental image of a pot, which is: *bum dzin tok pa la bum pa ma yin pa le lok par nang wa bum pe dön chi'i tsen nyi*,[21] the definition of the general mental image of a pot is what appears as opposite of not being a pot to the conceptual mind apprehending a pot. Even though it is not a pot, it appears to the mind as a pot. *Dro tak* means what is just ascribed as opposed to the actual thing. What is the definition of *tok pa*, conceptual mind? *Dra*

---

[21] བུམ་འཛིན་རྟོག་པ་ལ་བུམ་པ་མ་ཡིན་པ་ལས་ལོག་པར་སྣང་བ་བུམ་པའི་དོན་སྤྱིའི་མཚན་ཉིད།

dön dre rung du dzin pe lo tok pe tsen nyi,[22] The definition of conceptual mind is a mind that finds it suitable to mix a meaning mental image with a sound mental image. *Dön chi*, A meaning mental image, of a pot is just the appearance of the image of a pot to your mind. *Dra chi*, A sound mental image, means that when somebody says the word "*bum pa*," "pot," an image of pot appears in your mind. When these two are mixed in such a way that they appear to become almost the same object, this is an example of a conceptual mind.

We can use the mental image of President Clinton as an example. We can have a mental image of the President while sitting here in New Jersey, but if we go to visit him in the White House in Washington, we can see him directly and thereby gain direct cognition of him. With regard to the definition: *bum pe dön chi tsen nyi yö de, bum dzin tok pa la bum pa ma yin shin du bum pa ta bur nang we dro tak kyi cha*: *bum dzin tok pa* means a concept of a pot; that is, an indirect cognition or general mental image of a pot that appears to our conceptual cognition indirectly. The appearance of this object to our conceptual mind is not the real thing but just an image of the real thing. *Bum pa ta bur nang wa* means appears to that conceptual mind as a real pot. *Dro tak* refers to that object's being just ascribed to that appearance. *Cha* means part or just that thing.

མཚན་གཞི་ཡོད་དེ། བུམ་འཛིན་རྟོག་པ་སྐད་ཅིག་མ་གཉིས་པ་ལ་བུམ་པ་སྐད་ཅིག་གཉིས་པ་མ་ཡིན་པ་ལས་ལོག་པར་སྣང་བ་དེ་དེ་ཡིན་པའི་ཕྱིར།

tsen shi yö de, bum dzin tok pa ke chik ma nyi pa la bum pa ke chik nyi pa ma yin pa le lok par nang wa de de yin pe chir

There is an illustration of a meaning mental image of a pot; that which appears as opposite of not being a second-

---

[22] སྒྲ་དོན་འདྲེས་རུང་དུ་འཛིན་པའི་བློ་རྟོག་པའི་མཚན་ཉིད།

moment pot to the second-moment conceptual mind apprehending a pot is that.

Bum dzin, Apprehending a pot, refers to the eye consciousness perceiving a pot directly. First you can see a pot directly; you see its shape, its color, other characteristics, and so forth. But when you go somewhere where there is no pot, you can have *bum dzin tok pa*, a conception of a pot, which is not the direct perception of a pot. How then do you perceive the pot? *Dön chi gyu ne*, Through a general mental image, and therefore, indirectly. You can retain an image of the pot in your mind after your first initial perception of it; this is the meaning of *ke chik nyi pa*, the second moment of that pot's image appearing to your mind. Now, to give another example. Did you see a teapot on my table in the temple last night? Yes. Just that very first moment of seeing the teapot last night was the direct visual perception of the teapot. Immediately after that initial direct perception of the teapot a mental image of the teapot appeared in your mind. The first moment of that mental image of a pot is referred to as *bum dzin tok pe ke chik dang po*. Remembering that teapot again, for example, at this moment when talking about it, is the second moment of the image of the teapot or *bum dzin tok pe ke chik nyi pa*. The second moment is also conceptual, although it is a little more removed and calls for further imagination to elicit it.

Bum pa ma yin pa le lok pa, The opposite of non-pot, is pot. *Bum dzin tok pa la bum pa ma yin pa le lok par nang wa bum pe dön chi tsen nyi*, The appearance of the opposite of non-pot to the conceptual mind conceiving a pot is the definition of the meaning mental image of a pot. You have to remember the definition of a meaning mental image in relation to one object, as we did with a pot, so that you can apply it to all other cases.

In debate there is a way of determining whether one is talking about a positive entity or a negative entity, and that is by counting the number of negatives used in a statement. If an even number of negatives is used, then the subject is a positive entity; if an odd number is used, the subject is a negative entity. For example, *bum pa* ma *yin pa le* lok *pa* has two negatives, and so refers to a positive entity, a pot; *bum pa* ma *yin pa*, has one negative and so refers to a negative entity, or non-pot. Again, *bum pa yin pa le* lok *pa* is non-pot, while *bum pa* ma *yin pa le* lok *pa* is pot. This is explained briefly in *rang luk*, our system, as follows:

མ་ཡིན་པ་ལས་ལོག་པ་དང་། ཡིན་པ་གཉིས་དོན་གཅིག །ཡིན་པ་ལས་ལོག་པ་དང་། མ་ཡིན་པ་གཉིས་དོན་གཅིག

ma yin pa le lok pa dang, yin pa nyi dön chik, yin pa le lok pa dang, ma yin pa nyi dön chik

Opposite of not being something and being something are synonymous. Opposite of being something and not being something are synonymous.

མ་ཡིན་པ་ལས་ལོག་པ་དུ་བརྩེགས་ཀྱང་། མ་ཡིན་པ་ལས་ལོག་པ་གཅིག་པུ་དང་དོན་གཅིག །ཡིན་པ་ལས་ལོག་པ་ཆ་དང་། མ་ཡིན་པ་ལས་ལོག་པ་དོན་གཅིག

ma yin pa le lok pa du tsek kyang, ma yin pa le lok pa chik pu dang dön chik, yin pa le lok pa cha dang, ma yin pa le lok pa dön chik

No matter how many times you stack up the opposite of not being that thing, it is equivalent to simply being that thing. When saying the opposite of being that thing an even number of times, it is equivalent to the opposite of not being that thing [that is, being that thing].

ཡིན་པ་ལས་ལོག་པ་ཡ་དང་བཅས་ན། ཡིན་པ་ལས་ལོག་པ་གཅིག་པུ་དང་དོན་གཅིག་ཡིན་པའི་ཕྱིར་རོ།

yin pa le lok pa ya dang che na, yin pa le lok pa chik pu dang dön chik yin pe chir ro

> If we say the opposite of being that thing an odd number of times, it is equivalent to saying simply the opposite of being that thing [that is, not being that thing].

In the classification of general categories as mentioned above, there is also what is known as *dra chi*, a sound generality, which is an image induced by sound. Whenever you hear a word and an image of that object comes to mind as a result of hearing that sound, this is is what is known as a sound generality. *Dön chi*, A meaning generality, does not necessarily arise from hearing a sound; such an image can just appear to the mind without being induced by words.

> ཚོགས་སྤྱིའི་མཚན་ཉིད་ཡོད་དེ། རང་གི་ཆ་ཤས་དུ་མ་འདུས་པའི་
> གཟུགས་རགས་པ་དེ་དེ་ཡིན་པའི་ཕྱིར།
>
> *tsok chi tsen nyi yö de, rang gi cha she du ma du pe suk rak pa de de yin pe chir*
>
> There is a definition of a collection generality; a rough form that consists of many parts gathered together is that.

Tsok chi, A collection generality, means something that comes about by having many parts put together such as this microphone. Anything that consists of many parts gathered together and has its own function is a collection generality. *Rang gi cha she* means its parts. This can refer to anything of that nature, for example, a clock, a house, the body, the General Assembly in the UN, the United States Congress, and so forth. Every one of the members is a part of a whole that has many parts coming together to create one object. *Tsok* means a collection; *chi* means general. *Du pa* means gathering or meeting together. *Suk rak pa* means rough form. Of course, the more parts it has, the less subtle is the object.

Generally, *rak pa*, rough, *tra wa*, subtle, and *shin tu tra wa*, most subtle, are relative. For example, grain belongs to the general category of crops. When many kernels of grain gather together to form crops, this is *tsok chi*, a collection generality. Even a single grain of rice, although it appears to be simple and without parts, when smashed will reveal that it has parts. Relative to the general category of grain it is *tra wa*, subtle. But relative to its own parts it is *rak pa*, rough, because it can be further broken down into parts. *Suk* means form. What is the definition of *suk*, form? *Suk su rung wa suk kyi tsen nyi*,[23] The definition of form is what is suitable as form. Some of the monastic logic texts say that *suk*, form, and *pem po*, matter, are synonymous. However, *suk yin na pem po yin pe ma kyap, pem po yin na suk yin pe kyap*, whatever is form is not necessarily matter, yet whatever is matter is necessarily form.

There can be a lot of debate concerning whether or not something must have form in order for it to be *tsok chi*, a collection generality. For example, *she pa*, consciousness, even though it is not form can also be *tsok chi* since it has many parts consisting of many different kinds of consciousnesses.

***

—*Suk la ye na ka tsö yö*, When classifying form, how many kinds are there?

—*Chu chik yö, chi suk nga, nang gi suk nga, nam par rik che ma yin pe suk chik*, There are eleven: five outer forms, five inner forms, and one non-indicative form.

What are these? The five outer forms consist of *suk, dra, dri, ro, rek ja*, visible form (shape and color), sound, smell, taste, and tangibles; the five inner forms consist of *mik gi wang po, na we wang po, ne'i wang po, che'i wang po,* and *lu ki wang po*; eye sense power, ear sense power, nose sense power, tongue sense power, and body sense power. *Nam par rik che ma yin pe suk*,[24] Non-indicative form or form for the mental consciousness,[25] the eleventh kind of form mentioned here, can be explained as follows. When we first take vows, we have *nam par rik che kyi suk*, indicative form [that is,

---

[23] གཟུགས་སུ་རུང་བ་གཟུགས་ཀྱི་མཚན་ཉིད།

[24] T: ***rnam par rig byed ma yin pa'i gzugs***; S: *avijñaptirūpa*

[25] T: ***chos kyi skye mched***; S: *dharmāyatana*

perceptible inner and outer form]. At this time we repeat the vows after our Lama and make prostrations in front of him with a very good physical manner. The virtue that comes as a result of taking these vows at the time of taking them endows the taker of the vows with *nam par rik che kyi suk*, indicative form. If someone were watching the entire process—witnessing the repetition of vows and our making prostrations—they would think, "Oh, they are doing something very virtuous!" Therefore, this kind of "form" can be seen by others. However, once we have finished taking the vows, we still retain them continuously; we do not lose them. Although others may not be able to see them, we still have them. Such form is known as *nam par rik che ma yin pe suk*, non-indicative form.

ཚོགས་སྤྱི་དང་། རིགས་སྤྱིའི་གཞི་མཐུན་ཡོད་དེ། བུམ་པ་དེ་དེ་ཡིན་པའི་ཕྱིར།

tsok chi dang rik chi shi tun yö de, bum pa de de yin pe chir

> There exists something that is a combination of both a collection generality and a class generality; a pot is just that.

Shi tun means something that is a combination of both things. If there is something that can be both a collection generality and a class generality, this implies that the two, *tsok chi* and *rik chi*, are not *gel wa*, contradictory.

What is an example of something that is both? A pot. A pot is *tsok chi*, a collection generality, because *rang gi cha she du ma du pe suk rak pa*, it is a rough form that consists of many parts gathered together, such as its spout, base, lip, belly, and so forth. Additionally, *bum pa rik chi yin te, rang gi rik chen du ma la je su dro we chö yin pe chir*, a pot is a class generality because it is a phenomenon that covers its many particular instances. How many *rik chen*, particular instances, or kinds of pots are there? Many. For example there are golden pots, clay pots, silver ones, tall ones, many kinds of pots.

ཚོགས་སྤྱི་མ་ཡིན་པ་དང་། རིགས་སྤྱིའི་གཞི་མཐུན་ཡོད་དེ། ཤེས་
བྱ་དེ་དེ་ཡིན་པའི་ཕྱིར།

tsok chi ma yin pa dang rik chi shi tun yö de, she ja de de yin pe chir

There exists something that is not a collection generality but is a class generality; that is what an object of knowledge is.

Tsok chi ma yin na, rik chi ma yin pe ma kyap, If it's not a collection generality, it's not necessarily not a class generality, because object of knowledge is just that. Why is *she ja*, object of knowledge, not a collection generality? Since every phenomenon is an object of knowledge there is nothing that is not an object of knowledge. Also, because object of knowledge as a general category of objects of knowledge is *tak pa*, a permanent entity, it cannot be *suk rak pa*, rough form [in compliance with the definition of a collection generality]. Only impermanent entities can be rough form.

She ja tak pa yin, she ja yin na tak pa yin pe ma kyap, Object of knowledge is a permanent entity, however, whatever is an object of knowledge is not necessarily a permanent entity. *Kye rang gi go chö chen*, Take your head, for example, *she ja yin, tak pa ma yin*, although an object of knowledge, it's not a permanent entity.

***

—*Kye rang gi go chö chen, she ja yin par tel*, What about your head, isn't it an object of knowledge?

—*Dö*, Yes.

—*Tak pa ma yin par tel*, So it isn't a permanent entity?

—*Dö*, That's right.

—*She ja yin na tak pa yin pe ma kyap par tel*, Then it follows that if something is an object of knowledge, it is not necessarily permanent?

—*Dö*, Yes.

—*Sho*, Give me an example!

—*Nga rang gi go chö chen*, My head, for example.

If *she ja*, object of knowledge, is *tak pa*, permanent, it cannot be form. If it cannot be form, then it cannot be *suk rak pa*, rough form. If it cannot be *suk rak pa*, rough form, then it cannot be *tsok chi*, a collection generality. The philosophical idea here is that *tsok chi*, a collection generality, is only established relative to physical objects.

—*She ja chö chen, tak pa yin par tel*, Consider object of knowledge, it logically follows that it is a permanent entity?

—*Dö*, Yes.

—*Kye rang chö chen, tak pa yin par tel*, What about you, are you a permanent entity, too?

—*Chi chir*, No, why?

—*Kye rang chö chen, tak pa ma yin par tel*, So you're not a permanent entity?

—*Dö*, Yes, that's right.

—*Kye rang chö chen, she ja ma yin par tel*, Well then, aren't you an object of knowledge?

—*Chi chir*, Sure, I am.

—*She ja chö chen, tak pa yin par tel*, Now consider object of knowledge, didn't we just get done saying that it was a permanent entity?

—*Dö*, Yes, we did.

—*She ja sa gyu me par tel*, What about an object of knowledge, it's not something that can be eaten?

—*Chi chir*, No, why?

—What, you can't eat bread? Bread is an object of knowledge, isn't it?!

On the debate ground we call this "*she ja gok tsok*." *Gok* means garlic; before you eat it you have to smash it. Can you smash garlic? Isn't garlic an object of knowledge? You cannot smash an object of knowledge? When someone gets involved in such a circular argument, we say, "Ahhh, that's just *she ja gok tsok*!" Everybody knows the rules of logic, so when this happens we all just laugh and finish the debate right there.

རིགས་སྤྱི་མ་ཡིན་པ་དང་། ཚོགས་སྤྱིའི་གཞི་མཐུན་ཡོད་དེ། ཀ་བུམ་གཉིས་དེ་ཡིན་པའི་ཕྱིར།

rik chi ma yin pa dang tsok chi shi tun yö de, ka bum nyi de yin pe chir

There exists that which is not a class generality, but is a collection generality; that is just what (the two) pillar-pot is.

Above we said that *she ja*, an object of knowledge, is an example of something that is a class generality but not a collection generality. Here it gives an example of something that is a collection generality but not a class generality—(the two) pillar-pot.

***

—*Ka bum nyi chö chen, rik chi ma yin par tel*, Consider pillar-pot, it follows that it is not a class generality?
—*Dö*, Yes, that's correct.
—*Tsok chi yin par tel*, But it is a collection generality?
—*Dö*, Yes.
—*Rik chi ma yin te,* It's not a class generality, because if it were, *rang gi sel wa du ma la je su dro we chö*, [it would have to be] a phenomenon that covers many particulars of its own type. [*Sel wa*, *che drak*, and *rik chen* are synonyms meaning particular instances.]
—*Ka bum nyi chö chen, rang gi rik chen du ma yö par tel*, What about pillar-pot, doesn't pillar-pot have many of its own particular instances? (This kind of reasoning is similar to *she ja gok tsok*.)
—*Chi chir*, Why would you say that?
—*Bum pa chö chen, rang gi sel wa du ma yö par tel*, Consider a pot, does it follow that it has many particulars belonging to it?
—*Dö*, Yes.
—*Sho*, Give me an example!

—A silver pot, a clay pot, a golden pot, and so forth, are all types of pots and as such are particular instances of "pot."

In the field of logic *ka bum nyi*, the two—pillar-pot, is known as *yin pa mi si pa she ja*, an object of knowledge that is not possible to be it. You cannot find a single thing that comprises both of them. [Furthermore, this is why the text qualifies such a classification by saying *dre jö rik kyi go ne ye na*, when nominally classified.] We can explain it this way. *Ka wa yin na bum pa ma yin pe kyap; bum pa yin na ka wa ma yin pe kyap*, If it is a pillar then it cannot be a pot; if it is a pot then it cannot be a pillar. Therefore, *ka bum nyi*, the two—pillar-pot, cannot be *rik chi*, a class generality. If you were to give *ka bum nyi yin pa*, something that is a pillar-pot, as an example, that would be a very big mistake on the debate ground. Everybody would say, "Ah, what a rookie. He doesn't know the first thing about logic!"

རིགས་སྤྱི་མ་ཡིན་པ་དང་། ཚོགས་སྤྱི་མ་ཡིན་པའི་གཞི་མཐུན་ཡོད་དེ།
རྟག་དངོས་གཉིས་དེ་ཡིན་པའི་ཕྱིར།

rik chi ma yin pa dang tsok chi ma yin pe shi tun yö de, tak ngö nyi de yin pe chir

There exists that which is neither a class generality nor a collection generality; the two—permanent-impermanent entity—is just that.

Rik chi ma yin pa dang tsok chi ma yin pe shi tun yö de, There is some kind of phenomenon that cannot be either a class generality or a collection generality: *tak ngö nyi ke de yin pe chir*, the two—permanent entity and causally effective thing is that. Such a thing could not be a class generality, because if it were, its *rik chen*, particular instances, would have to be something that is *tak ngö nyi ka*, both a permanent entity and a causally effective thing. To say that would be a big mistake. We also cannot say that such a thing is a collection generality, because this would imply that the two—permanent entity and causally effective thing, could be form, which it couldn't possibly be.

བྱེ་བྲག་གི་མཚན་ཉིད་ཡོད་དེ། ཁྱབ་བྱེད་དུ་འཇུག་པའི་རང་གི་རིགས་ཡོད་པ་ཅན་གྱི་ཆོས་དེ། རང་ཉིད་བྱེ་བྲག་ཡིན་པའི་མཚན་ཉིད་ཡིན་པའི་ཕྱིར།

che drak gi tsen nyi yö de, kyap che du juk pe rang gi rik yö pa chen gyi chö de, rang nyi che drak yin pe tsen nyi yin pe chir

There is a definition of a particular instance; a phenomenon that is of the same class as the entity covering it is that.

Kyap je means that which covers. *Chi*, A general category, covers its particular instances. *Du ma juk pa* means you can find many general categories that cover it. (*Juk pa* is a verb that means "to cover," similar to *je su dro wa*.)

Is a pot an example of a phenomenon that has many general categories covering it? Yes. Why? Because a pot is both *ngö pö che drak*, a particular instance of causally effective thing, and *she je che drak*, a particular instance of object of knowledge, and so forth. Therefore, pot is an example of something that is both a general category and a particular instance.

As mentioned above, when you classify *chi*, general category, you have to add *dre jö rik gi go ne*, nominally classified. If you don't add this, you will have problems. If you say *chi la ye na sum yö*, when general categories are classified there are three kinds, someone might reply with: *ka bum nyi chö chen, chi yin par tel*, What about (the two) pillar-pot, you're telling me that that is a general category? [Again, this is an example of something that is only nominally designated a "general category," since there is no object of knowledge, no one thing that is both of these.]

Such arguments appear in the section that follows *rang luk*, our own system, known as *tsö pa pong wa*, dispelling remaining doubts (which will not be dealt with in this present text).

You have to practice saying these definitions very quickly. It is easier if you break them into parts and repeat them. You must also learn the rules of logic, the way the arguments go, so that later when you read them by yourself you will understand them since these rules will serve as your guides. This method is like a teacher pointing the way. If you don't learn the rules and the method of reading these arguments, you will stay in the same position without any improvement.

The method and philosophy in the other *ka chik ma*'s, debates, are the same. Therefore, if you gain a thorough understanding of the first one, you will more easily come to understand the others. However, even if you were to memorize all of these without understanding the main key, they will just be blah blah. Okay? If you go pretty far learning this material, at some point you will become experts. In the future it will help a lot. You won't have another occasion like this to learn this material in detail. The subject, object, and action all have to come together nicely.

Debate One

general (categories) and particular (instances)
chi che drak

ཁ་ཅིག་ན་རེ། སྤྱི་ཡིན་ན་བྱེ་བྲག་མ་ཡིན་པས་ཁྱབ་ཟེར་ན། དངོས་པོ་ཆོས་ཅན། བྱེ་བྲག་མ་ཡིན་པར་ཐལ། སྤྱི་ཡིན་པའི་ཕྱིར། ཁྱབ་པ་ཁས།

ka chik na re, chi yin na che drak ma yin pe kyap ser na, ngö po chö chen, che drak ma yin par tel, chi yin pe chir, kyap pa ke

If *KA CHIK MA* [someone] says: Whatever is a general category necessarily cannot be a particular instance. *RANG LUK* [Our system] responds with: Consider a causally effective thing, it would logically follow that it is not a particular instance, because it is a general category. You asserted that pervasion.

IF AN OPPONENT IN DEBATE, whom we call *KA CHIK MA*, should assert that whatever is a general category necessarily cannot be a particular instance, *RANG LUK*, our system, counters with: What about causally effective thing, [according to your view] it could not be a particular instance because it is a general category. *KA CHIK MA* cannot maintain that a general category can also be a particular instance because he has already accepted that it couldn't be. *Kyap pa ke* means "you already accepted the pervasion," which is: if something is a general category it necessarily cannot be a particular instance.

མ་གྲུབ་ན། དངོས་པོ་ཆོས་ཅན། སྤྱི་ཡིན་པར་ཐལ། ཁྱོད་ཀྱི་བྱེ་བྲག་ཡོད་པའི་ཕྱིར།

> *ma drup na, ngö po chö chen, chi yin par tel, kyö kyi che drak yö pe chir*
>
> If KA CHIK MA responds with: That's not true. RANG LUK says: Consider causally effective thing, it logically follows that it is a general category, because it has its own particular instances belonging to it.

If KA CHIK MA says: *Tak ma drup*, It's not true, this means that the opponent does not believe that causally effective thing could be a general category.

We call this a "consequence" *sel wa*[26] or *ten gyur*[27] (S: *prasaṅga*) in the Prāsaṅgika system. *Sel wa* is the method used in debate whereby the second part of a three-part statement is made to the opponent such that he is not able to accept the consequence of the retort since it would harm his own thesis or assertion. It actually establishes by valid cognition the opposite of the thesis. Here, *ngö po*, causally effective thing, is *chö chen*, the subject of debate; *che drak ma yin pa*, not being a particular instance, is *sel wa*, the consequence; and *chi yin pe chir*, because it is a general category, is *tak*, the reason. This is *ten gyur*, the [absurd] consequence, system. However, there is another system used in debate in which only statements of belief, rather than statements of absurdity, are put forth. These are known as *jor wa*,[28] syllogisms or formal arguments. An example is *ngö po chö chen, che drak yin te, ke chik ma yin pe chir*, consider causally effective thing, it is a particular instance, because it is momentary. This reveals that such is the belief of the speaker. In the *ten gyur* system, for the *sel wa*, or second part of the three-part statement only *tel* is used, which means it follows as a(n absurd) consequence of what the opponent asserts.

---

[26] *Sel ba* (***bsal ba***) or false thesis is what is established by valid cognition to be the opposite of that which is proposed. The thesis and what is used to prove it are contradictory. Therefore, when presented with such a statement in debate, the defendant cannot accept the thesis.

[27] ཐལ་འགྱུར་

[28] སྦྱོར་བ་

What is *kyap*, the pervasion, in the statement presented above? *Chi yin na che drak ma yin pe kyap pa*, Whatever is a general category cannot be a particular instance. Since this is KA CHIK MA's main belief, he cannot see how *ngö po*, causally effective thing, can possibly be a general category. Therefore, he responds with: [*Chi yin pa*] *tak ma drup*, I don't accept that causally effective thing is a general category. So RANG LUK, in response, qualifies his statement with: *Ngö po chö chen, chi yin par tel, kyö kyi che drak yö pe chir*, Consider causally effective thing, it is too a general category, because it has its own particular instances.

Kyö, generally meaning "you," is an indefinite relative pronoun that relates back to the subject of the original statement. Here it refers to *ngö po*, causally effective thing. It is like saying: "You, *ngö po*, are a general category because you have your own particular instances." Or, "You, causally effective thing, are like a supreme general, because you have many troops under you." Does it make sense? Particular instances are related to the general category to which they belong.

མ་གྲུབ་ན། དངོས་པོ་ཆོས་ཅན། ཁྱོད་ཀྱི་བྱེ་བྲག་ཡོད་པར་ཐལ།
བུམ་པ་དེ་དེ་ཡིན་པའི་ཕྱིར།

ma drup na, ngö po chö chen, kyö kyi che drak yö par tel,
bum pa de de yin pe chir

If KA CHIK MA responds with: That's not true, RANG LUK says: Consider causally effective thing, it follows that it does have its own particular instances, because a pot is just one of those particular instances.

What does *tak ma drup* imply? [*Kyö kyi che drak yö pa*] *tak ma drup*, It is not true that causally effective thing has its own particular instances. To this, RANG LUK offers "pot" as an example of a particular instance within the category of causally effective thing, saying: *ngö po chö chen, kyö kyi che drak yö par tel, bum pa de de yin pe chir*, consider [the category of] causally effective thing, indeed it does have its own particular instances, because pot is one of them. This is only one example, but in fact, there are many, such as pillars, human beings, form, consciousness, non-associated formations,[29] and so forth, which are all the particular instances belonging to [the general category of] causally effective thing.

The main idea is that *chi*, general category, and *che drak*, particular instance, are not contradictory or mutually exclusive. That is why RANG LUK is using causally effective thing to prove that a particular instance can also be a general category. Once that is proved, later RANG LUK can proceed to prove that causally effective thing can be both a general category and a particular instance [of another category].

མ་གྲུབ་ན། བུམ་པ་ཆོས་ཅན། ཁྱོད་དངོས་པོའི་བྱེ་བྲག་ཡིན་པར་ཐལ།
ཁྱོད་དངོས་པོ་ཡིན། ཁྱོད་དངོས་པོ་དང་བདག་གཅིག་ཏུ་འབྲེལ། ཁྱོད་
མ་ཡིན་ཞིང་དངོས་པོ་ཡང་ཡིན་པའི་གཞི་མཐུན་པ་དུ་མ་གྲུབ་པའི་ཕྱིར།

ma drup na, bum pa chö chen, kyö ngö pö che drak yin par tel, kyö ngö po yin, kyö ngö po dang dak chik tu drel, kyö ma yin shing ngö po yang yin pe shi tun pa du ma drup pe chir

If KA CHIK MA responds with: That's not true, RANG LUK says: Consider a pot, it logically follows that a pot is a particular instance of [the category of] causally effective thing, because 1) a pot is a causally effective thing, 2) a pot has a relationship of same nature with causally effective thing, and 3) there are many causally effective things that are not a pot.

Tak ma drup na means if he doesn't accept a pot as a particular instance of *ngö po*, causally effective thing, then RANG LUK specifies why it is in fact a particular instance of causally effective thing. *Kyö* (referring to *bum pa*, pot) *ngö pö che drak yin par tel*, It follows that you (pot) are a particular instance of causally effective thing. *Tak*, The reason, is given in three parts as follows: 1) *kyö ngö po yin*, first,

[29] *Den min du che* (**ldan min 'du byed**) is a causally effective thing that is neither matter nor mind.

a pot is a causally effective thing, 2) *kyö ngö po dang dak chik tu drel*, a pot and causally effective thing have a relationship of same nature, and 3) *kyö ma yin shing ngö po yang yin pe shi tun pa du ma drup pe chir*, there are many other bases [or existents] that are causally effective things but are not a pot.

It's not necessary to prove the first part of this reason, that is, that a pot is a causally effective thing, because the opponent has already accepted that. However, the other two parts do require further proof.

རྟགས་གཉིས་པ་མ་གྲུབ་ན། བུམ་པ་ཆོས་ཅན། དངོས་པོ་དང་བདག་གཅིག་འབྲེལ་ཡིན་པར་ཐལ། དངོས་པོ་དང་བདག་ཉིད་གཅིག་ཡིན་པ་གང་ཞིག དངོས་པོ་དང་ཐ་དད་ཀྱང་ཡིན། དངོས་པོ་མེད་ན་ཁྱོད་མེད་དགོས་པའི་ཕྱིར།

tak nyi pa ma drup na, bum pa chö chen, ngö po dang dak chik drel yin par tel, ngö po dang dak nyi chik yin pa gang shik, ngö po dang ta te kyang yin, ngö po me na kyö me gö pe chir

If *KA CHIK MA* responds with: The second part of your reason is not true, *RANG LUK* says: Consider a pot, it logically follows that it has the relationship of being of the same nature with causally effective thing, because it is the same nature as causally effective thing, it is different from causally effective thing, and, if the general category of causally effective thing did not exist, a pot could not possibly exist.

Tak nyi pa ma drup na means that if he doesn't accept the second part of that reason, which is *kyö ngö po dang dak chik tu drel wa yin*, that pot is related to causally effective thing through being of the same nature, then *RANG LUK* responds by giving the reason in three parts as stated above. This method of establishing the particular instances of a general category is called *che drak drup tsul*, the method for determining particular instances. *Ngö po*, Causally effective thing, is *chi*, a general category, and *bum pa*, a pot, is *che drak*, a particular instance, of the general category of causally effective thing. *Ngö po*, Causally effective thing, is *bum pe chi*, a general category to which a pot belongs. *Bum pa*, A pot, is *ngö pö che drak*, a particular instance of causally effective thing.

You should learn this method so that you are able to establish the particular instance of any general category.

method for determining particular instances
che drak drup tsul

***

—*Bum pa chö chen, ngö pö che drak yin par tel*, Consider a pot, does it follow that it is a particular instance of causally effective thing?

—*Dö*, Yes, it does. (*KA CHIK MA* will say that it is not a particular instance, but if you are *RANG LUK*, you will approve.)

—*Che drak drup tsul kyi sho*, Show me how pot is a particular instance of causally effective thing! What is the relationship between a pot and causally effective thing?

—*Bum pa chö chen, kyö che drak yin par tel, kyö ngö po yin, kyö ngö po dang dak chik tu drel, kyö ma yin shing ngö po yang yin pe shi tun pa du ma drup pe chir*, Consider a pot, it follows that it is a particular instance, because a pot is a causally effective thing, a pot has the same nature as causally effective thing, and there are many things that are causally effective things but are not a pot. These three parts, *che drak drup tsul*, the method for determining particular instances, has three qualities: 1) if two things have the relationship of general category and particular instance, for example, if something is a particular instance of causally effective thing, it must necessarily be a causally effective thing; 2) it must have the same nature as causally effective thing; and 3) there must be many causally effective things that have that nature but are not a pot.

You should memorize this method. Repeat it by counting on your mala each repetition at least twenty-one times.

If your subject is not *ngö po*, a causally effective thing, in the first place, it would be useless to try to prove the other parts of the reason. When debating about a pot, of course both parties in the debate should agree that a pot is a causally effective thing.

The second part of the reason can be expressed in three ways: *dak nyi chik tu drel*, *ngo wo chik du drel*, and *rang shin chik tu drel*, all meaning "being of the same nature." There are two kinds of relationships: *dak chik tu drel wa*, a relationship of same nature, class, or quality, and *te jung gi drel wa*, a causal relationship.

An example of the first kind of relationship is found in the statement: *dra chö chen, mi tak te, che pe chir*, consider sound, it is impermanent, because it is produced; *che pa*, produced, is *tak*, the reason; *mi tak pa*, impermanent, is *drup che chö*, the quality to be proved. *Tak chö kyi drel wa*, The relationship between the reason and the quality to be proved, is one of same nature, or *dak nyi chik pe drel wa*, since sound has the nature of impermanence.

An example of the second is the relationship found in the statement: *du den gyi la la chö chen, me yö te, du wa yö pe chir*, consider smoke on a mountain pass, there must be fire, because there is smoke. What is *tak*, the reason? *Du wa yö pe chir*, Because there is smoke. What is *drup che chö*, the quality to be proved? *Me yö*, [That] there is fire. Why? We know this because *du wa te me le jung wa*, smoke arises from fire. Such a relationship is *de jung gyi drel wa*, a relationship of cause and effect.

What does relationship of same nature mean? For example, when *bum pa*, a pot, exists, it exists as *ngö po*, a causally effective thing, since it has the nature of a causally effective thing. It is very important that you understand this. When a pot comes into being, it comes into being as a causally effective thing. Whenever a pot exists, it exists as a causally effective thing. If there were no *ngö po*, causally effective things, then a pot could not exist either. If the general category doesn't exist, its particular instances, in this case a pot, cannot exist.

རྟགས་དང་པོ་མ་གྲུབ་ན། བུམ་པ་ཆོས་ཅན། དངོས་པོ་དང་བདག་ཉིད་
གཅིག་ཡིན་པར་ཐལ། དངོས་པོ་དང་རང་བཞིན་གཅིག་ཡིན་པའི་ཕྱིར།

tak dang po ma drup na, bum pa chö chen, ngö po dang dak nyi chik yin par tel, ngö po dang rang shin chik yin pe chir

If *KA CHIK MA* responds with: The first part of your reason is not true, *RANG LUK* says: Consider a pot, it logically follows that it is of one nature with causally effective thing, because it has the same essence.

Tak dang po ma drup na refers to the first part of the reason, which expressed in full is: *ngö po dang dak nyi chik yin pa tak ma drup* meaning the opponent maintains that a pot is not of one nature with causally effective thing.

རྟགས་གཉིས་པ་མ་གྲུབ་ན། བུམ་པ་ཆོས་ཅན། དངོས་པོ་དང་ཐ་དད་
ཡིན་པར་ཐལ། གཟུགས་ཡིན་པའི་ཕྱིར།

tak nyi pa ma drup na, bum pa chö chen, ngö po dang ta te yin par tel, suk yin pe chir

If *KA CHIK MA* responds with: The second part of your reason is not true, *RANG LUK* says: Consider a pot, it logically follows that it is different from causally effective thing, because it is form.

If *KA CHIK MA* does not agree with the second part of the reason, which is *ngö po dang ta te kyang yin*, [that a pot] is different from [is not identical with] causally effective thing, *RANG LUK* responds by saying that a pot is form [implying that that which has form cannot be an abstract, permanent general category, and as such must be a specific concrete entity]. General *ngö po*, "causally effective thing," cannot be *suk*, form, because *suk*, form, and *ngö po*, the general category of "causally effective thing," are *ta te*, different entities. You cannot pick up a general "causally effective thing" because general "causally effective thing" is an abstract and not a concrete entity.

You should be able to establish a pot as a particular instance of causally effective thing by using the three points of *ngö po drup tsul*, establishing [the relationship of general and particular] with regard to a causally effective thing.

The structure of these debates should guide you. You have to try to understand how this system of logic works and become familiar with what each part of these statements is referring to. If you learn this system from the outset, it will make things very clean and clear-cut. We call each of these sections one *ka chik ma*. If you learn one *ka chik ma* nicely, then the next one becomes easier. If you read each one over several times, gradually you will come to understand them. Of course it is difficult at the very beginning. If you eat *pak*, barley dough, it is also very difficult to swallow at first, since it goes down reluctantly and just sticks there in your throat. Even so, just try and recite these debates over and over. Then, after reciting for some time, you can hang outside to dry. Don't worry, you won't blow away.

རྟགས་གསུམ་པ་མ་གྲུབ་ན། བུམ་པ་ཆོས་ཅན། དངོས་པོ་མེད་ན་ཁྱོད་མེད་དགོས་པར་ཐལ། དངོས་པོ་མེད་ན་གང་དྲན་དྲན་ཡིན་དགོས་པའི་ཕྱིར།

tak sum pa ma drup na, bum pa chö chen, ngö po me na kyö me gö par tel, ngö po me na, gang dren dren yin gö pe chir

If KA CHIK MA responds with: The third part of your reason is not true, RANG LUK says: Consider a pot, if causally effective things did not exist, it logically follows that a pot could not exist because, if causally effective things did not exist [and yet pots existed], then you could say anything about anything.

གང་གི་རྟགས་གསུམ་པ་མ་གྲུབ་ན། བུམ་པ་ཆོས་ཅན། ཁྱོད་མ་ཡིན་ཞིང་དངོས་པོ་ཡང་ཡིན་པའི་གཞི་མཐུན་པ་དུ་མ་གྲུབ་པར་ཐལ། ཙན་དན་གྱི་ཀ་བ་དེ་ཡང་དེ་ཡིན། ཤུག་པའི་ཀ་བ་དེ་ཡང་དེ་ཡིན་པའི་ཕྱིར།

gang gi tak sum pa ma drup na, bum pa chö chen, kyö ma yin shing ngö po yang yin pe shi tun pa du ma drup par tel, tsen den gyi ka wa de yang de yin, shuk pe ka wa de yang de yin pe chir

If *KA CHIK MA* responds with: The third part of the reason above [referring to the third part of *che drak drup tsul*] is not true, *RANG LUK* says: Consider a pot, it logically follows that there are many things that belong to the general category of causally effective thing, yet are not a pot, since sandalwood pillars belong to that general category as do pillars made of juniper.

རྩ་བར་འདོད་ན། དངོས་པོ་ཆོས་ཅན། བྱེ་བྲག་ཡིན་པར་ཐལ། ཤེས་བྱའི་བྱེ་བྲག་ཡིན་པའི་ཕྱིར།

tsa war dö na, ngö po chö chen che drak yin par tel, she je che drak yin pe chir

If *KA CHIK MA* still holds to the basic consequence [that a causally effective thing cannot be a particular instance], *RANG LUK* now responds with: Consider causally effective thing, it follows that it is a particular instance, because it is a particular instance of the general category of objects of knowledge.

མ་གྲུབ་ན། དངོས་པོ་ཆོས་ཅན། ཤེས་བྱའི་བྱེ་བྲག་ཡིན་པར་ཐལ། ཁྱོད་ཤེས་བྱ་ཡིན། ཁྱོད་ཤེས་བྱ་དང་བདག་གཅིག་ཏུ་འབྲེལ། ཁྱོད་མ་ཡིན་ཞིང་ཤེས་བྱ་ཡང་ཡིན་པའི་གཞི་མཐུན་པ་དུ་མ་གྲུབ་པའི་ཕྱིར།

ma drup na, ngö po chö chen, she je che drak yin par tel, kyö she ja yin, kyö she ja dang dak chik tu drel, kyö ma yin shing she ja yang yin pe shi tun pa du ma drup pe chir

If *KA CHIK MA* responds with: That is not true, *RANG LUK* says: Consider a causally effective thing, it follows that it is a particular instance of objects of knowledge, because a causally effective thing is an object of knowledge, it is related to object of knowledge through being of the same nature, and there are many objects of knowledge that are not causally effective things.

You have to learn *chi che drak*, general (category) and particular (instances), so that no matter what you see you will be able to determine what is a general category and what is a particular instance. You will know such and such is a general category because it has its own particular instances, or that it is a particular instance because it has a general category covering it. If it is *che drak*, a particular instance, you have to know how it qualifies as a particular instance and know the relationship between a particular instance and the general category to which it belongs.

We know that something is *dak chik gyi drel wa*, related by same nature, through applying the following examination. For example, *bum pa dang dak chik drel yin par tel, ngö po dang dak nyi chik yin pa gang shik, ngö po dang ta te kyang yin, ngö po me na kyö me gö pe chir*, it follows that pot is related to [causally effective thing] through being of the same nature because, first, pot and causally effective thing have the same nature, pot and causally effective thing are different entities, and if the general category of causally effective thing did not exist, pot could not exist.

***

—*Bum pa chö chen, ngö po dang ta te yin par tel,* Consider pot, it follows that it is different from causally effective thing?

—*Dö,* Yes.

–*Ta te tsul kyi shok,* Explain how they are different! Indicate how *bum pa,* pot, is *ngö po dang ta te,* different from causally effective thing.

—*Bum pa ngö po dang ta te, ngö po bum pa dang ta te, te nyi yö pa gang shik chik ma yin pe chir,* Pot is different from causally effective thing; causally effective thing is different from pot; whenever you have two existents, they cannot be one and the same thing. (If pot is *dak nyi chik,* of the same nature, as *ngö po,* causally effective thing, then it must be *ngö po dang ta te,* different from causally effective thing.)

Now what's the relationship between *she ja,* object of knowledge, and *ri bong ra,* a hare's horn? Are they *ta te,* different, or not? Are *yö pa,* existents, and *me pa,* non-existents, *gel wa,* contradictory, or not? They are *gel wa,* contradictory. Therefore, they should be *ta te,* different, of course.

Another example of two contradictory phenomena is *tak pa dang mi tak pa,* permanent and impermanent entities.

—*Gel wa yin te, gel wa tsen nyi kyi shok,* To indicate that they are contradictory give the definition of contradictory!

—*Ta te gang shik shi tun mi si pa gel we tsen nyi,* Two different entities that cannot have a common basis is the definition of contradictory.

—*Ta te gang shik shi tun mi si pa gel we tsen nyi yin par tel,* Then it follows that two different entities that cannot have a common basis is the definition of contradictory?

—*Dö,* Yes.

—*Gel wa yin na, ta te gang shik shi tun mi si pa yin pe kyap,* If something is contradictory, then it must necessarily be two different entities that cannot have a common basis?

—*Kyap,* Yes, that is what it entails.

—*Kyap pa nam pa go gye yö par tel,* Then it follows that they have the Eight Doors of Pervasion, that is, each one—the object defined and its definition—mutually pervade each other?
—*Dö,* Yes, that's so. (A summary of the Eight Doors of Pervasion can be stated as follows: *yin na yin pe kyap, ma yin na ma yin pe kyap, yö na yö pe kyap, me na me pe kyap pe chir,* if it is the one it must also be the other; if it is not the one, then it must not be the other; if the one exists, then the other must exist; if the one does not exist, then the other must not exist.)
—*Gel wa yin na, ta te gang shik shi tun mi si pa yin pe kyap par tel,* If two things are contradictory, then they must be two separate entities that cannot have a common basis?
—*Dö,* Yes, that's right.
—*Kyap na, yö pa dang me pa nyi gel wa yin par tel,* If there is such entailment, then it's possible to say that existents and non-existents are contradictory?
—*Dö,* Yes, of course.
—*Dö na, yö pa dang me pa nyi ta te yin par tel,* If you accept that, then existents and non-existents are different?
—*Dö,* Yes, they are.
—*Ta te yin na, ta te tsul kyi shok,* If they are in fact different, indicate the manner in which they are different!
—*Yö pa yin na yö pa me pa dang ta te, me pa yö pa dang ta te, te nyi yö pa gang shik chik ma yin pe chir,* If something is an existent, that existent must be different from the non-existent, and the non-existent must be different from that existent; those two being existents they cannot have a common basis.
—*Te nyi yö pa yin par tel,* From what you just said it logically follows that those two—the existent and the non-existent—are existents? [In the definition it says *te nyi yö pa,* those two things being existents. If that were the case, then *me pa,* a non-existent, would also have to be *yö pa,* an existent.]

What is the definition of *yö pa,* an existent? *Tse me mik pa yö pe tsen nyi,* The definition of an existent is that which is perceived by valid cognition; and *tse me ma mik pa me pe tsen nyi,* the definition of a non-existent is that which is not perceived by valid cognition.

This is how you get stuck in a debate. On the debate ground sometimes they use the term *ham pa she*, which means a kind of boldness or bravado in spite of everything. You can see this kind of behavior sometimes in the courts when two lawyers are arguing and one of them happens to argue more forcefully than the other, and, through sheer bravado the bullheaded one wins the case. Innocent people often have to go to jail as a result of this kind of blustering, or the reverse happens where the criminal gets off free. In the same way, sometimes on the debate ground when some debaters know that they're holding a weak position in the debate yet wish to avoid looking silly, just by sheer bravado they act like they know what they're talking about and convince the other debater of their view even if it is not accurate. Therefore, if you cannot prove your case with good reasons on the debate ground, your opponent may win by his boldness just to show you that you have not clarified the points in your own mind.

DEBATE TWO

general (category) and particular (instances)
chi che drak

ཁ་ཅིག་ན་རེ། དངོས་པོའི་སྤྱི་ཡིན་ན། དོན་བྱེད་ནུས་པའི་སྤྱི་ཡིན་པས་
ཁྱབ་ཟེར་ན། མཚོན་བྱ་ཆོས་ཅན། དོན་བྱེད་ནུས་པའི་སྤྱི་ཡིན་པར་
ཐལ། དངོས་པོའི་སྤྱི་ཡིན་པའི་ཕྱིར། ཁྱབ་པ་ཁས།

ka chik na re, ngö pö chi yin na, dön che nu pe chi yin pe kyap ser na, tsön ja chö chen, dön che nu pe chi yin par tel, ngö pö chi yin pe chir, kyap pa ke

If *KA CHIK MA* makes the statement: If it is the general category of causally effective thing, it must also be the general category of that which is able to effect something, *RANG LUK* responds with: Consider an object to be defined, from what you say it would absurdly follow that such is the general category of that which is able to effect something, because it is the general category of causally effective thing. You asserted that pervasion.

IN ORDER TO UNDERSTAND THIS assertion first you have to know the definition of *ngö po*, causally effective thing. *Dön che nu pa ngö pö tsen nyi*,[30] The definition of causally effective thing is that which is able to effect something. The Eight Doors of Pervasion apply to an object to be defined and its definition. Therefore, *RANG LUK* says: *tsön ja chö chen, dön che nu pe chi yin par tel*, consider an object to be defined, it follows that such is the general category of that which is able to effect something.

---

[30] དོན་བྱེད་ནུས་པ་དངོས་པོའི་མཚན་ཉིད།

If something is an object to be defined it must also be its definition and if something is a definition it must also be its object to be defined, and so forth.

RANG LUK accepts that *tsön ja ngö pö chi yin*, object to be defined is the general category covering causally effective thing, but not that object to be defined is the general category covering *dön che nu pa*, that which is able to effect something, because it is a definition and not an object to be defined. Therefore, he says: *tsön ja ngö pö chi yin, dön che nu pe chi ma yin*, object to be defined is the general category covering causally effective thing, but not the general category covering the definition "that which is able to effect something."

What is the logical idea being expressed in this debate? Aren't a definition and its object to be defined *yin kyap nyam*,[31] equally pervasive; that is, (*yin na yin pe kyap, yin na yin pe kyap*, if it is the one then it must equally be the other), and so forth? If so, then why isn't *tsön ja*, object to be defined, the general category covering the definition "that which is able to effect something"?

Ngö po, Causally effective thing, is *tsön ja*, an object to be defined; *dön che nu pa*, that which is able to effect something, is *tsen nyi*, its definition. Therefore, causally effective thing is a particular of the general category of *tsön ja*, objects to be defined, which covers all phenomena, since everything existent can be defined. *Tsön ja* is the general category covering causally effective things, and consequently causally effective thing is a particular of the general category of objects to be defined. How is that? *Tak yö chö sum tsang wa tsön je'i tsen nyi*,[32] The definition of object to be defined is that which satisfies the three characteristics of being an ascribed existent. What are these three characteristics? The first characteristic is *chir tsön ja yin pa*, in general it should be an object to be defined. Second, *rang gi tsen shi teng du drup pa*, that thing to be defined should cover its examples; for instance, *ngö pö tsen shi ka re shak*, what can you posit as an example of a causally effective thing? *Bum*

[31] ཡིན་ཁྱབ་མཉམ་

[32] བཏགས་ཡོད་ཆོས་གསུམ་ཚང་བ་མཚོན་བྱའི་མཚན་ཉིད།

pa shak, A pot is an example. Third, if it is an object to be defined *rang gi tsen nyi gang yin pa te le tsen gyi shen gyi tsön ja mi che pa*, it is an object to be defined that has only that definition [defining it] and no other. Every object to be defined has its own definition. *Ngö po*, Causally effective thing, is *tsön ja*, the object to be defined, and *dön che nu pa*, that which is able to effect something, is its definition and only its definition.

Dze yö chö sum tsang wa tsen nyi kyi tsen nyi,[33] The definition of a definition is that which satisfies the three characteristics of being a substantial existent. Here, the same criteria apply except that instead of being an ascribed existent[34] a definition is a substantial existent.[35]

Generally, *ngö po*, causally effective thing, and *dön che nu pa*, that which is able to effect something, are *yin kyap nyam*, equally pervasive. Why? Because they are *tsön ja*, an object to be defined, and *tsen nyi*, its definition. But *tsön ja*, object to be defined, is the general category to which causally effective thing belongs, and not the general category to which *dön che nu pa*, "that which is able to effect something," belongs, even though they are *yin kyap nyam*, equally pervasive. Why? This is so because the general category to which "that which is able to effect something," belongs is *tsen nyi*, definition, and not *tsön ja*, object to be defined.

མ་གྲུབ་ན། མཚོན་བྱ་ཆོས་ཅན། ཁྱོད་དངོས་པོའི་སྤྱི་ཡིན་པར་ཐལ།
དངོས་པོ་ཁྱོད་ཀྱི་བྱེ་བྲག་ཡིན་པའི་ཕྱིར།

ma drup na, tsön ja chö chen, kyö ngö pö chi yin par tel, ngö po kyö kyi che drak yin pe chir

If *KA CHIK MA* responds with: That's not true, *RANG LUK* says: Consider object to be defined, it follows that it is the general

---

33 རྫས་ཡོད་ཆོས་གསུམ་ཚང་བ་མཚན་ཉིད་ཀྱི་མཚན་ཉིད།

34 བཏགས་ཡོད་

35 རྫས་ཡོད་

> category of causally effective thing, because causally effective thing is a particular instance belonging to the general category of objects to be defined.

(This is the main key.) When KA CHIK MA says *tak ma drup*, in full this implies *tsön ja ngö pö chi yin pa tak ma drup*, it is not true that object to be defined is a general category to which causally effective thing belongs.

> མ་གྲུབ་ན། དངོས་པོ་ཆོས་ཅན། མཚོན་བྱའི་བྱེ་བྲག་ཡིན་པར་ཐལ། ཁྱོད་མཚོན་བྱ་ཡིན། ཁྱོད་མཚོན་བྱ་དང་བདག་གཅིག་ཏུ་འབྲེལ། ཁྱོད་མ་ཡིན་ཞིང་མཚོན་བྱ་ཡང་ཡིན་པའི་གཞི་མཐུན་པ་དུ་མ་གྲུབ་པའི་ཕྱིར།
>
> *ma drup na, ngö po chö chen, tsön je che drak yin par tel, kyö tsön ja yin, kyö tsön ja dang dak chik tu drel, kyö ma yin shing tsön ja yang yin pe shi tun pa du ma drup pe chir*
>
> If KA CHIK MA responds with: That's not true, RANG LUK says: Consider causally effective thing, it follows that it is the particular of the general category of objects to be defined, because 1) causally effective thing is an object to be defined, 2) causally effective thing is related to the general category of objects to be defined by being of the same nature, and 3) there are many things that are objects to be defined that are not a causally effective thing.

If he says *tak ma drup*, this stated in full is *ngö po kyö kyi che drak yin pa tak ma drup*, it is not true that causally effective thing is a particular of the general category of objects to be defined. The debate proceeds with the same structure as before using *chi che drak drup tsul*, the method for determining general categories and particular instances, as a way to prove how something is a particular belonging to a general category.

If someone were to say to you: *che drak drup tsul kyi sho*, show me how something is a particular instance belonging to a general category in this context, you can say: *ngö po chö chen, tsön je che drak yin par tel, kyö tsön ja yin, kyö tsön ja dang dak chik tu drel, kyö ma yin shing tsön ja yang yin pe shi tun pa du ma drup pe chir*, consider causally effective thing, it follows that it is a particular instance of object to be defined, because causally effective thing is an object to be defined; causally effective thing is related to the general category of objects to be defined through a relationship of same nature; and even if causally effective thing did not exist, there would still be many other objects to be defined.

རྩ་བར་འདོད་ན། དོན་བྱེད་ནུས་པ་ཆོས་ཅན། ཁྱོད་མཚོན་བྱའི་བྱེ་བྲག་མ་ཡིན་པར་ཐལ། མཚན་ཉིད་ཡིན་པའི་ཕྱིར་ཏེ། དངོས་པོའི་མཚན་ཉིད་ཡིན་པའི་ཕྱིར།

tsa war dö na, dön che nu pa chö chen, kyö tsön je che drak ma yin par tel, tsen nyi yin pe chir te, ngö pö tsen nyi yin pe chir

If *KA CHIK MA* still holds to the basic consequence [that object to be defined is the general category of "that which is able to effect something"], *RANG LUK* responds with: Consider "that which is able to effect something," it logically follows that such is not a particular instance of the general category of objects to be defined, because it is the definition of causally effective thing [i.e., it is a definition and not an object to be defined].

Tsa war dö na, If the opponent holds to the basic consequence, is a phrase that refers to the very first *tel*, consequence, within this debate. This can be stated as: *tsön ja chö chen, dön che nu pe chi yin par dö na*, consider object to be defined, [if the opponent accepts that] it is the general category covering "that which is able to effect something...," and so forth.

"That which is able to effect something" is not a particular instance of object to be defined, because it is a definition. This follows the logic rule: *tsen nyi yin na tsön ja ma yin pe kyap, tsön ja yin na tsen nyi ma yin pe kyap*, whatever is a definition cannot be an object to be defined, and whatever is an object to be defined cannot be a definition. If it is *gyu tsen yang dak*, a correct reason, then it should have *kyap pa*, pervasion, such that *tsen nyi yin na tsön je che drak ma yin pe kyap*, whatever is a definition cannot be a particular instance of object to be defined. Why? If it is *tsön je che drak*, a particular instance of object to be defined, it must itself be an object to be defined.

Te at the end of the last assertion shows that another reason is going to be given to prove that "that which is able to effect something" is a definition. *Ngö pö tsen nyi yin pe chir*, Because "that which is able to effect something" is the definition of causally effective thing. *Ngö pö tsen nyi yin na tsen nyi yin pe kyap*, If it is the definition of causally effective thing, then obviously it must be a definition. *Tsen nyi yin na tsön ja ma yin pe kyap*, If it is a definition, [according to the logic rule given above] it cannot be an object to be defined. Therefore, *tsön je che drak yin na tsön ja yin gö*, if it is a particular instance of object to be defined, it itself must be an object to be defined.

Is it clear so far? Are you sure?

Now what decision have you made in your philosophy? If I say, *tsön ja chö chen, dön che nu pe chi yin par tel*, consider object to be defined, it follows that it is the general category of "that which is able to effect something," what do you have in your mind, "Yes, that's true" or "Uh-uh, that's not true"? You have to answer with *chi chir*, No, it's not true. The logic in your philosophy should tell you this: *tsen nyi yin na tsön je che drak ma yin pe kyap*, if it is a definition, it definitely cannot be a particular instance of object to be defined.

***

—*Ka re shak*, What are you going to posit as an example of a definition?

—*Dön che nu pa chö chen*, The subject "that which is able to effect something."

—*Dön che nu pa chö chen, tsen nyi yin par tel*, Consider "that which is able to effect something," it follows that this is a definition?

—*Dö*, Yes, it does.

—*Tsön je che drak ma yin par tel*, And it's not a particular instance of object to be defined?

—*Dö*, That's right.

—*Dön che nu pa chö chen, tsön je che drak ma yin par tel*, Consider "that which is able to effect something," it follows that it is not a particular instance of object to be defined?

—*Dö*, Yes.

—*Tsön je che drak ma yin te, tsen nyi yin pe chir te*, It is not a particular instance of object to be defined, because it is a definition. Why?

—*Tsen nyi yin te, ngö pö tsen nyi yin pe chir*, It is a definition, because it is the definition of causally effective thing.

—*Ngö pö tsen nyi yin na tsen nyi yin pe kyap*, Then, if it is the definition of causally effective thing it must be a definition?

—(You have to say) *kyap pa*, that is necessarily so.

This can be clarified by examining our system's belief as given below.

OUR OWN SYSTEM

RANG LUK

definition and object to be defined
tsen tsön

གཉིས་པ་རང་ལུགས་ལ། མཚོན་བྱའི་མཚན་ཉིད་ཡོད་དེ། །བཏགས་ཡོད་ཆོས་གསུམ་ཚང་བ་དེ་དེ་ཡིན་པའི་ཕྱིར། བཏགས་ཡོད་ཆོས་གསུམ་འདྲེན་ཚུལ་ཡོད་དེ། སྤྱིར་མཚོན་བྱ་ཡིན་པ། རང་གི་མཚན་གཞིའི་སྟེང་དུ་གྲུབ་པ། རང་གི་མཚན་ཉིད་གང་ཡིན་པ་གཅིག་པོ་དེ་ལས་གཞན་པ་གང་གི་ཡང་མཚོན་བྱ་མ་ཡིན་པ་དང་གསུམ་པོ་དེ་འདྲེན་རིགས་པའི་ཕྱིར།

nyi pa rang luk la, tsön je tsen nyi yö de, tak yö chö sum tsang wa de de yin pe chir, tak yö chö sum dren tsul yö de, chir tsön ja yin pa, rang gi tsen shi teng du drup pa, rang gi tsen nyi gang yin pa chik po de le shen pa gang gi yang tsön ja ma yin pa dang sum po de dren rik pe chir

The second section: our own system. There is a definition of object to be defined, because that which fulfills the three characteristics of an ascribed existent is that. There is a way to elicit those three characteristics: 1) generally it is an object to be defined, 2) there is a basic existent that serves as its illustration, and 3) it doesn't serve as an object to be defined for any other definition.

CHÖ SUM, THREE QUALITIES, should all be present. What are these three qualities? 1) *Chir tsön ja yin pa*, Generally it must be an object to be defined, 2) *rang gi tsen shi teng du drup pa*, an illustration or example of it exists, 3) *rang gi tsen nyi gang yin pa te le tsen nyi shen gyi tsön ja mi che pa*, it is not the object to be defined for any other definition.

For example, *ngö po*, causally effective thing, is *tsön ja*, an object to be defined, because *tak yö chö sum tsang wa*, it fulfills the three characteristics of ascription. First, it is an object to be defined. Second, an illustration or example of it exists. For example, *ngö po*, causally effective thing, is a general classification that includes a pot, which is a particular instance of causally effective thing. Third, *ngö po*, causally effective thing, acts as *tsön ja*, an object to be defined, and not as *tsen nyi*, a definition, and does not serve as an object to be defined for any other definition. Even though definition and object to be defined are *yin kyap nyam*, equally pervasive, and causally effective thing is an object to be defined for the definition *dön che nu pa*, that which is able to effect something, nevertheless, causally effective thing is not the object to be defined for *ke chik ma*, momentariness, for example, although it itself is in fact momentary.

མཚན་ཉིད་ཀྱི་མཚན་ཉིད་ཡོད་དེ། རྫས་ཡོད་ཆོས་གསུམ་ཚང་བ་དེ་
དེ་ཡིན་པའི་ཕྱིར། རྫས་ཡོད་ཀྱི་ཆོས་གསུམ་འདྲེན་ཚུལ་ཡོད་དེ། སྤྱིར་
མཚན་ཉིད་ཡིན་པ། རང་གི་མཚན་གཞིའི་སྟེང་དུ་གྲུབ་པ། རང་གི་
མཚོན་བྱ་གང་ཡིན་པ་དེ་ལས་གཞན་པ་གང་གི་ཡང་མཚན་ཉིད་མ་ཡིན་
པ་དང་གསུམ་པོ་དེ་འདྲེན་རིགས་པའི་ཕྱིར།

tsen nyi kyi tsen nyi yö de, dze yö chö sum tsang wa de de yin pe chir, dze yö kyi chö sum dren tsul yö de, chir tsen nyi yin pa, rang gi tsen shi teng du drup pa, rang gi tsön ja gang yin pa de le shen pa gang gi yang tsen nyi ma yin pa dang sum po de dren rik pe chir

There is a definition of definition, because that which fulfills the three characteristics of a substantial existent is that. There is a way to elicit these three characteristics: 1) generally it is a definition, 2) there exists a basic existent that illustrates it, and 3) it doesn't serve as a definition for any other object to be defined.

The structure is the same as that for an object to be defined described above.

Debate Three

general (category) and particular (instances)
chi che drak

ཁ་ཅིག་ན་རེ། དངོས་པོའི་སྤྱི་ཡིན་ན། མི་རྟག་པའི་སྤྱི་ཡིན་པས་ཁྱབ་ཟེར་ན། མི་རྟག་པ་དང་ཐ་དད་ཆོས་ཅན། མི་རྟག་པའི་སྤྱི་ཡིན་པར་ཐལ། དངོས་པོའི་སྤྱི་ཡིན་པའི་ཕྱིར། ཁྱབ་པ་ཁས།

ka chik na re, ngö pö chi yin na, mi tak pe chi yin pe kyap ser na, mi tak pa dang ta te chö chen, mi tak pe chi yin par tel, ngö pö chi yin pe chir, kyap pa ke

One scholar states: If something is the general category of causally effective thing, it must necessarily be the general category of the impermanent. *RANG LUK* responds with: Consider what is different from the impermanent, it would follow from what you say that it is the general category of the impermanent, because it is the general category of causally effective thing. That is what you asserted.

WHAT DOES *KE CHIK MA* MEAN? *Ke chik ma mi tak pe tsen nyi*,[36] That which is momentary is the definition of the impermanent. This means that whatever is impermanent has a continuum that changes from moment to moment. *Mi tak pa*, The impermanent, in this case, is *tsön ja*, the object to be defined, and *ke chik ma*, momentary, is *tsen nyi*, the definition.

---

[36] སྐད་ཅིག་མ་མི་རྟག་པའི་མཚན་ཉིད།

***

—*Mi tak pe tsen nyi shak gyu me pe chir*, I bet you don't know the definition of impermanence.

—*Tak ma drup*, That's not true.

—*Mi tak pe tsen nyi shak gyu yö par tel*, Then you do know the definition?

—*Dö*, Yes.

—*Sho*, Tell me!

—*Ke chik ma chö chen*, That which is momentary is the definition.

—*Ke chik ma chö chen, mi tak pe tsen nyi yin par tel*, Then that which is momentary is the definition of impermanece?

—*Dö*, Yes.

Mi tak pa dang ta te, Different from that which is impermanent, can be a general category and it can be *tak pa*, a permanent entity. *Ke chik ma*, That which is momentary, itself as the definition of *mi tak pa*, impermanent, is also *ta te*, different from, *mi tak pa* since it is not identical with *mi tak pa*; that is, only *mi tak pa* is not different from *mi tak pa*. The idea of "difference" can be described this way. For example, *am jo ye pa dang yön pa ta te, te nyi yö pa gang shik chik ma yin pe chir*, the right ear is different from the left ear, those two being existents are not one and the same thing.

When KA CHIK MA makes the statement: *ngö pö chi yin na mi tak pe chi yin pe kyap*, if it is the general category of causally effective thing, it must be the general category of impermanent thing, *RANG LUK* responds with: *mi tak pa dang ta te chö chen*, what about that which is different from the impermanent, it would [absurdly] follow that this is the general category covering the impermanent.

Generally, we say *mi tak pa yin na ngö po yin pe kyap*, whatever is impermanent must be a causally effective thing, and conversely, *ngö po yin na mi tak pa yin pe kyap*, whatever is a causally effective thing must be impermanent. Although impermanent and causally effective thing are synonyms, they each have their own definitions defining them. *Dön che nu pa ngö pö tsen nyi*, The definition of a causally effective thing is what is able to effect something, and *ke chik ma mi tak pe tsen nyi*, the definition of impermanent is that which is momentary.

***

—*Mi tak pa dang ta te chö chen, mi tak pe chi yin par tel*, Consider different from the impermanent, it follows from what you say that it is the general category of the impermanent?
—*Chi chir*, No, that's not so.
—*Yin par tel* (when debating, verbally you have to say this to make the connection to what was previously said), *ngö pö chi yin pe chir, kyap pa ke*, it does follow from what you say (that it is the general category covering the impermanent), because it is the general category of causally effective thing, since you have already asserted that pervasion.

མ་གྲུབ་ན། མི་རྟག་པ་དང་ཐ་དད་ཆོས་ཅན། ཁྱོད་དངོས་པོའི་སྤྱི་ཡིན་པར་ཐལ། དངོས་པོ་ཁྱོད་ཀྱི་བྱེ་བྲག་ཡིན་པའི་ཕྱིར།

ma drup na, mi tak pa dang ta te chö chen, kyö ngö pö chi yin par tel, ngö po kyö kyi che drak yin pe chir

If KA CHIK MA says: That's not true, RANG LUK responds with: Consider that which is different from the impermanent, it follows that it is the general category of causally effective thing, because causally effective thing is one of its particular instances.

Ma drup na expressed in full is *ngö pö chi yin pa tak ma drup na*, which means if KA CHIK MA says that it is not true that that which is different from the impermanent is the general category of causally effective thing.

***

—*Mi tak pa dang ta te chö chen, mi tak pe chi yin par tel*, Consider that which is different from the impermanent, it follows that it is the general category of the impermanent?

—*Chi chir*, No, that's not correct.

—*Yin par tel, ngö pö chi yin pe chir*, It logically follows from what you say that it is the case because it [that which is different from the impermanent] is the general category of causally effective thing.

—*Tak ma drup*, It's not true [that that which is different from the impermanent is the general category covering causally effective thing].

—*Mi tak pa dang ta te chö chen, kyö ngö pö chi yin par tel, ngö pö kyö kyi che drak yin pe chir*, Consider different from the impermanent, it follows that it *is* the general category of causally effective thing, because causally effective thing is a particular instance of different from the impermanent.

Here it is applying the same reason as before, that is, if something is a particular instance of a general category, that general category covers it. In brief, in order to belong to a specific general category, that subject under discussion must be something that is one of the particular instances belonging to that general category.

If you digest one debate nicely, you will be able to understand the other ones very easily.

རྩ་བར་འདོད་ན། མི་རྟག་པ་དང་ཐ་དད་ཆོས་ཅན། མི་རྟག་པའི་སྤྱི་མ་ཡིན་པར་ཐལ། མི་རྟག་པ་ཁྱོད་ཀྱི་བྱེ་བྲག་མ་ཡིན་པའི་ཕྱིར།

tsa war dö na, mi tak pa dang ta te chö chen, mi tak pe chi ma yin par tel, mi tak pa kyö kyi che drak ma yin pe chir

If KA CHIK MA accepts the basic consequence, RANG LUK responds with: Consider that which is different from the impermanent, it follows that it is not the general category of the impermanent, because the impermanent is not one of its particular instances.

Tsa war dö na means if *KA CHIK MA* accepts the basic consequence, which is *mi tak pa dang ta te chö chen, mi tak pe chi yin par tel,* consider that which is different from the impermanent, it follows that it is the general category of the impermanent. (It is important not to forget the basic premise that is stated at the beginning of the argument and the basic consequences elicited form it. You have to keep them in your mind so that you can follow the debate throughout.) If *KA CHIK MA* agrees, in order to refute this, *RANG LUK* counters with the reason: "This is not the case because the impermanent cannot be a particular instance of different from the impermanent," [since different from the impermanent must be *different from* the impermanent and can neither be the same as, nor a particular instance of, the impermanent].

མ་གྲུབ་ན། མི་རྟག་པ་ཆོས་ཅན། མི་རྟག་པ་དང་ཐ་དད་ཀྱི་བྱེ་བྲག་མ་ཡིན་པར་ཐལ། མི་རྟག་པ་དང་ཐ་དད་མ་ཡིན་པའི་ཕྱིར།

ma drup na, mi tak pa chö chen, mi tak pa dang ta te kyi che drak ma yin par tel, mi tak pa dang ta te ma yin pe chir

If *KA CHIK MA* says: That's not true, *RANG LUK* responds with: Consider the impermanent, it is not a particular instance of different from the impermanent, because the impermanent is *not* different from the impermanent.

If *KA CHIK MA* says *tak ma drup*, stated in full this means *mi tak pa kyö kyi che drak ma yin pa tak ma drup*, it is not the case that the impermanent is not a particular instance of different from the impermanent. This means that if different from the impermanent were the general category of the impermanent, then the impermanent would have to be one of the particular instances of different from the impermanent. This cannot possibly be because if something is the particular instance of different from the impermanent, it must be *different from* the impermanent. The impermanent *is* the impermanent, just as a nose *is* a nose. Nose is *chik*, one, and not *ta te*, different, from itself. A nose is the same as a nose; you only have one nose, so your nose is the same as your own nose. However, the right ear and the left ear are two or *ta te*, different. This is a very good philosophical system.

If something is *ngö pö che drak*, a particular instance of causally effective thing, it must be a causally effective thing. If something is *mi tak pa dang ta te kyi che drak*, a particular instance of different from the impermanent, it must be different from the impermanent. Above, KA CHIK MA is asserting that the impermanent is *different from* the impermanent, which of course it is not.

Did you get it? You have to digest it.

མ་གྲུབ་ན། མི་རྟག་པ་ཆོས་ཅན། ཁྱོད་ཁྱོད་དང་ཐ་དད་མ་ཡིན་པར་ཐལ། ཁྱོད་གང་ཟག་གི་བདག་མེད་ཡིན་པའི་ཕྱིར།

ma drup na, mi tak pa chö chen, kyö kyö dang ta te ma yin par tel, kyö gang sak gi dak me yin pe chir

If KA CHIK MA says: That's not true, RANG LUK responds with: Consider the impermanent, it follows that it is not different from the impermanent, because the impermanent lacks a self of person.

The reason RANG LUK gives in this case, *kyö gang sak kyi dak me yin pe chir*, because the impermanent lacks a self of person, is a very famous *rik lam*, path of reasoning. This can be explained using the following logical rule: *shi drup na, gang sak kyi dak me yin pe kyap*, whatever is a basic existent must be void of a self of person. [This implies that if something is impermanent it cannot be different from the impermanent because as something that lacks the self of person, it is something that belongs to existents. As an existent it cannot be *different from* itself but must be *the same as* or *one with* itself.]

What is the meaning of *gang sak kyi dak me*? This varies according to the different schools. In the Prāsaṅgika school system this refers to *tong nyi*, *shūnyatā* or emptiness. Here in the lower school system [Sautrāntika] *dak me*, selflessness, refers to the selflessness of person [as a self-sufficient independent controller of the aggregates].

Why is it the case that *shi drup na, gang sak kyi dak me yin pe kyap*, whatever is a basic existent must be void of a self of person? *Dak du drup pa mi si pe chir*, Because it is not possible to establish an inherently existent self. No such self could exist. *Dak du drup pa*, Inherently existent self, is *gak ja*, the object being refuted here. If something exists, its existence can be validated through being perceived by *tse ma*, valid cognition. There is no way to perceive an inherently existent self by valid cognition, because no such self exists. If something is perceived by one valid cognition, it cannot be rejected by the valid cognition of another. That is the system of logic. Did you understand?

GREATER PATH OF CAUSE AND EFFECT

GYU[N] DRE CHE WA

THIS SECTION IS VERY IMPORTANT.

བཞི་པ་རྒྱུ་འབྲས་ཆེ་བའི་རྣམ་གཞག་བཤད་པ་ལ།

shi pa gyun dre che we nam shak she pa la

The fourth section: regarding the presentation of the greater path of cause and effect.

Gyu means cause; *dre* means result. *Che wa* means great, referring to the more difficult topics. *Nam shak* means presentation. *She pa* means an explanation about this topic. *Gyun dre chung ngu*, The lesser or beginning presentation of cause and result, which is a little easier, comes earlier in this text but will not be discussed here.

དགག་གཞག་སྤོང་གསུམ་ལས།

gak shak pong sum le

The three: refuting others' views, positing our own views, and dispelling remaining doubts.

These terms are an abbreviation of the following: *shen luk* <u>*gak*</u> *pa, rang luk* <u>*shak*</u> *pa, tsö pa* <u>*pong*</u> *wa* <u>*sum*</u>. *Gak* means to reject or refute. What is being refuted is *KA CHIK MA*'s wrong idea. If you reject an opponent's wrong idea by saying, "You're wrong; that's not correct," he will respond with: "Well, if this is wrong, tell me the correct idea!" Consequently, we have the second section wherein the author states the views of his own system, which is the meaning of *rang luk shak pa*, establishing our own system's views. Now, since *KA CHIK MA*, the person stating these views, is not stupid, but most often is a very learned scholar, after establishing *RANG LUK*'s idea, which is the correct one, he might respond with: "Yes, your view may very well be correct, but there are still some problems with it." This is the purpose of the third section, *tsö pa pong wa*, dispelling remaining doubts. In this section the two parties debate the views presented by *RANG LUK*. Here certain points of contention are taken up wherein *RANG LUK* has to defend his view. In this section, *KA CHIK MA* is the one arguing the points, *tsö pa*, while *RANG LUK* is the one rejecting, *pong wa*, those new objections. However, as mentioned before, this third section will not be included in this present text.

OUR OWN SYSTEM

RANG LUK

greater path of cause and effect
gyu(n) dre che wa

གཉིས་པ་རང་ལུགས་གཞག་པ་ལ། རྒྱུ་བཤད་པ། རྐྱེན་བཤད་པ།
འབྲས་བུ་བཤད་པ། ཞར་བྱུང་འདུས་མ་འོངས་ཡོད་མེད་ལ་དཔྱད་པ་
དང་བཞི། དང་པོ་ལ་མཚན་ཉིད་བཤད་པ་དང་དབྱེ་བ་བཤད་པ་
གཉིས། དང་པོ་ནི། སྐྱེད་བྱེད་རྒྱུའི་མཚན་ཉིད། ཡང་ན། ཕན་
འདོགས་བྱེད་རྒྱུའི་མཚན་ཉིད། གཉིས་པ་དབྱེ་བ་བཤད་པ་ལ། རྒྱུ་ལ་
དངོས་རྒྱུ་དང་། བརྒྱུད་རྒྱུ་གཉིས་སུ་དབྱེ་བ། ཉེར་ལེན་དང་། ལྷན་
ཅིག་བྱེད་རྐྱེན་གཉིས་སུ་དབྱེ་བ། སྒྲས་བརྗོད་རིགས་ཀྱི་སྒོ་ནས་དྲུག་ཏུ་
དབྱེ་བ་དང་གསུམ། དང་པོ་ནི། དངོས་སུ་སྐྱེད་བྱེད། དངོས་རྒྱུའི་
མཚན་ཉིད། བརྒྱུད་ནས་སྐྱེད་བྱེད། བརྒྱུད་རྒྱུའི་མཚན་ཉིད། གཞི་
ལ་སྦྱར་ན། དུ་བའི་དངོས་སུ་སྐྱེད་བྱེད་དུ་བའི་དངོས་རྒྱུའི་མཚན་ཉིད།
ཡང་ན། དུ་བའི་དངོས་སུ་ཕན་འདོགས་བྱེད། དུ་བའི་དངོས་རྒྱུའི་
མཚན་ཉིད། མཚན་གཞི་ནི། མེ་ལྟ་བུ་ལ་བྱེད་དེ། མེ་མཚན་གཞི།
དུ་བའི་དངོས་རྒྱུ་ཡིན་པར་མཚོན། དུ་བའི་དངོས་སུ་སྐྱེད་བྱེད་ཡིན་པ་
ཞེས་པའི་མཚོན་སྦྱོར་འདི། མཚོན་སྦྱོར་རྣམ་དག་ཡིན་པའི་ཕྱིར།

nyi pa rang luk shak pa la, gyu she pa, kyen she pa, dre bu she pa, shar jung de ma ong yö me la che pa dang shi, dang po la tsen nyi she pa dang ye wa she pa nyi, dang po ni, kye che gyu'i tsen nyi, yang na pen dok che gyi'i tsen nyi, nyi pa ye wa she pa la, gyu la ngö gyu dang, gyu gyu nyi su ye wa, nyer len dang, hlen chik che kyen nyi su ye wa, dre jö rik kyi go ne druk tu ye wa dang sum, dang po ni, ngö su kye che, ngö gyi'i tsen nyi, gyu ne kye che gyu gyu'i tsen nyi, shi la jar na, du we ngö su kye che du we ngö gyu'i tsen nyi, yang na, du we ngö su pen dok che, du we ngö gyu'i tsen nyi, tsen shi ni, me ta bu la che de, me tsen shi, du we ngö gyu yin par tsön, du we ngö su kye che yin pa she pe tsön jor di, tsön jor nam dak yin pe chir

The second part: [the philosophy] according to our system. This has four sections: an explanation on causes, an explanation on conditions, an explanation on effects, and an incidental analysis on whether or not past and future time exist. Regarding the first there are two parts: an explanation on the definition of cause and its classifications. The first, the definition of cause is a producer. Another definition of cause is that which acts as a helper. The second, an explanation of its classifications has three parts: first, is the dual division of cause into direct cause and indirect cause; second, is another dual division into substantial cause and co-operating condition; and third, there is a way of nominally classifying causes into six kinds. Regarding the first, the definition of direct cause is that which produces directly. The definition of indirect cause is that which produces indirectly. When applying these definitions to specific examples, the definition of the direct cause of smoke is that which is the direct producer of smoke. Additionally, that which is a direct helper in producing smoke is the definition of the direct cause of smoke. Fire serves as an example of the direct cause of smoke. It serves as an example because it is a perfect illustration of something that is the direct producer of smoke.

RANG LUK SHAK PA MEANS A presentation of the views of our own system. *Gyu she pa* means explaining causes; *kyen she pa*, means explaining conditions; *dre bu she pa* means explaining effects; *shar jung* means "incidental," referring to the explanation of *de pa*, past time, *ma ong*, future time, but more specifically, being an examination into whether or not they exist.

There are two ways of stating the definition of cause: *kye che gyu'i tsen nyi*, a producer is the definition of a cause, or *pen dok che gyu'i tsen nyi*, what acts to help something come about is the definition of cause. For example, fire is *pen dok pa*, the helper of cooking, in that it assists in the cooking of food. Food itself is *pen dok pa*, a helper, in so far as it is used to keep people alive. If people don't have food, they will die.

In the root text *Commentary to (Dignāga's) "Compendium of Valid Cognition"*[37] it says: "*pen dok gang yin kye pa yin*, [cause] is anything that assists in or causes production." This is virtually the definition of cause. If it helps, then it assists in bringing something about. If it doesn't help, then it cannot assist in making anything come about.

***

—*Gyu she pa la sa che ka tsö yö*, How many categories are there regarding the explanation of cause?

—*Nyi yö*, Two.

—*Nyi po te ka re ka re re*? What are each of those two?

—*Tsen nyi she pa dang ye wa she pa nyi*, The two, an explanation on the definition and an explanation on the classifications [of causes].

—*Dang po tsen nyi she pa la gyu'i tsen nyi kyi shok*, Tell me the first category, an explanation on the definition of cause!

---

[37] (T: ***tshad ma rnam 'grel***; S: *Pramāṇavārttika*) is one of the seven treatises (***tshad ma sde bdun***) on logic by the great logician Dharmakīrti; a commentary to Master Dignāga's *Compendium of Valid Cognition* (T: ***tshad ma kun las btus pa***; S: *Pramāṇasamuccaya*).

—*Kye che gyu'i tsen nyi, yang na, pen dok che gyu'i tsen nyi,* That which produces [something], or that which assists in the production [of something] is the definition of cause.

—*Nyi pa ye wa she pa la gyu la ye na ka tsö yö,* Regarding the explanation of the second part, how many classifications of cause are there?

—*Gyu la ngö gyu dang gyu gyu nyi su ye wa, nyer len dang hlen chik che kyen nyi su ye wa, dre jö rik kyi go ne druk du ye wa sum yö,* There are three separate ways of classifying cause: first, it can be classified into the two, direct cause and indirect cause; second, it can be classified into substantial cause and co-operating condition; and third, there is a way of nominally dividing it into six classifications.

Dre jö rik kyi go ne ye na druk du ye wa means that you only nominally classify causes into these six divisions.

Ngö su kye che ngö gyu'i tsen nyi, The definition of direct cause is that which produces directly. *Gyu ne kye che gyu gyu'i tsen nyi,* The definition of an indirect cause is that which produces indirectly. An illustration of *ngö gyu,* direct cause, is a seed, together with *sa, chu, me, lung,* [the four great elements] earth, water, fire, and air. For example, when these causes gather together under proper conditions, and a sprout is ready to be produced, just before the arising of the sprout, these causes are *ngö gyu,* direct causes, because they are the direct producers of the sprout. By saying "just before the sprout" this implies that such causes are *nyu gu'i nga lok su jung wa* or *nyu gyu'i nga lok de ma tak tu jung wa,* which means that just prior or immediately before the arising of a sprout those elements and seeds are the direct producers of that sprout.

Gyu gyu, Indirect cause, means before that in time, implying some temporal distance. For example, if you have a seed that hasn't reached the field yet, perhaps because it is sitting in a drawer in your house, it is a sprout's *gyu gyu,* indirect producer. It is not the direct producer due to a separation in time and because the proper conditions have not gathered together to produce a sprout. Later, if the proper conditions arise, then it can turn into the sprout's direct cause.

Gyu (**brgyud**) means continually [that is, indirect causes are the same continuum as a direct cause]. *Gyu* (**rgyu**) means cause. Therefore, *gyu gyu* means causes that [although they are potential direct causes] are generally temporally removed from being the direct producers of their effects. *Gyu ne* means [acting as a helper] through something or by means of something, for example, a message is passed via a messenger. Since an indirect cause is a continuum, it is described as *gyu* (**brgyud**), "indirect" or "through something."

Shi la jar na means explaining these definitions by way of using specific illustrations to which they can be applied.

Du we ngö su kye che du we ngö gyu'i tsen nyi, The definition of the direct cause of smoke is that which directly produces smoke. *Du wa* means smoke. The implication is that fire is the direct cause of smoke. *Yang na* means or; that is, we can also say *du we ngö su pen dok che du we ngö gyu'i tsen nyi*, the definition of the direct cause of smoke is that which directly assists in the production of smoke.

Tsen shi ni, An example is, *me ta bu*, like fire. This is *tsön jor*, or an illustrative example. When a statement ends with one of the three "*de*" particles, this shows *jor wa*, a statement of proof that implies belief in its correctness, rather than an absurd consequence, which is indicated by the use of the word "*tel*" meaning it [absurdly] follows that....

Me ta bu la che de, me tsen shi, du we ngö gyu yin par tsön, Fire is used since it represents an example of smoke's direct producer.

Du we ngö su kye che yin pa she pe tsön jor di, tsön jor nam dak yin pe chir, This statement that shows how fire acts as the direct producer of smoke is a perfect statement of proof. How can you prove that fire is *du we ngö gyu*, the direct cause of smoke? *Du we ngö gyu yin par tsön den, du we ngö su kye che tsön yin pe chir*, Because [fire] is something that directly produces smoke, it is representative of the direct cause of smoke. Therefore, it is *tsön jor nam dak*, a perfect representative example or reason. *Tsön jor, jor wa yang dak*, and *tak yang dak* are synonyms all meaning a perfect reason.

The main purpose of this proof statment is to prove that fire is the direct cause of smoke in order to illustrate an example of a direct cause. Examples of *gyu gyu*, the indirect cause, of smoke may be kinds of fuel such as wood, gasoline, kerosene, and the like.

A typical discussion you might have after having studied this section on the *Compendium of Debates* should go something like this:

***

"Did you study *Dura*?"

"Yes, I did."

"Did you learn about causes?"

"Yes, of course.

"What did you learn?"

"Oh, well, *kye che gyu'i tsen nyi*, the definition of cause is that which is a producer, or you can say *pen dok che gyu'i tsen nyi*, the definition of cause is that which assists in production."

"Yeah, that's correct. Now, what about cause's classifications?"

"Well, you can classify causes in three ways: *ngö gyu dang gyu gyu*, direct cause and indirect cause; or *nyer len dang hlen chik che kyen*, substantial cause and co-operating condition; or *dre jö rik kyi go ne druk*, nominally you can classify them into six kinds. You can say it that way."

"It seems you learned it pretty well. Can you tell me what the definition of *ngö gyu* is?"

"Sure. *Ngö su kye che ngö gyu'i tsen nyi*, The definition of direct cause is that which produces directly. And *gyu ne kye che gyu gyu'i tsen nyi*, the definition of indirect cause is that which produces indirectly."

"What do they mean? Can you give me an example of a direct cause?"

"Well, you can use fire as an example of a direct cause."

"How can fire be an example of direct cause?"

"Fire is an example of direct cause because it is the direct producer of smoke. That example is *tsön jor nam dak*, a perfect representative reason."

"I'm amazed. You really did learn about direct and indirect causes."

After studying this material you should be able to express yourself that way.

གཉིས་པ་ཉེར་ལེན་དང་ལྷན་ཅིག་བྱེད་རྐྱེན་འཆད་པ་ནི། རང་གི་ཉེར་འབྲས། རང་གི་རྫས་རྒྱུན་དུ་གཙོ་བོར་སྐྱེད་བྱེད། རང་ཉིད་ཉེར་ལེན་ཡིན་པའི་མཚན་ཉིད། གོ་བ་བྱས་ན། ཉེར་ལེན་གྱི་མཚན་ཉིད་དུ་ཡང་འཇོག མཚན་གཞི་ནི། ཟག་བཅས་ཀྱི་ཕུང་པོ་ལྔ་ལྟ་བུ། རང་གི་ལྷན་ཅིག་བྱེད་འབྲས།རང་གི་རྫས་རྒྱུན་མ་ཡིན་པར་གཙོ་བོར་སྐྱེད་བྱེད། རང་ཉིད་ལྷན་ཅིག་བྱེད་རྐྱེན་གྱི་མཚན་ཉིད། དངོས་པོ་ཡིན་ན། ལྷན་ཅིག་བྱེད་རྐྱེན་ཡིན་པས་ཁྱབ། རྒྱུན་དང་བཅས་པའི་དངོས་པོ་ཡིན་ན། ཉེར་ལེན་ཡིན་པས་ཁྱབ།

nyi pa nyer len dang hlen chik che kyen che pa ni, rang gi nyern dre, rang gi dze gyun du tso wor kye che, rang nyi nyer len yin pe tsen nyi, go wa che na, nyer len gyi tsen nyi du yang jok tsen shi ni, sak che kyi pung po nga ta bu, rang gi hlen chik chen dre, rang gi dze gyun ma yin par tso wor kye che, rang nyi hlen chik che kyen gyi tsen nyi, ngö po yin na, hlen chik che kyen yin pe kyap, gyun dang che pe ngö po yin na, nyer len yin pe kyap

The second: an explanation of substantial cause and co-operating condition. The definition of something that is a substantial cause is that which is the principal producer of an effect in its substantial continuum. In order to have a better understanding of what a substantial cause is, let us use an example such as our five contaminated appropriated heaps. The definition of something that is a co-operating condition is that which principally produces its co-operating effect not present in its own substantial continuum. If something is a causally effective thing it must necessarily be a co-operating condition. If something is a causally effective thing accompanying a continuum it must necessarily be a substantial cause.

Rang gi nyer dre rang gi dze gyun du tso wor kye che, rang nyi nyer len yin pe tsen nyi, The definition of something that is a substantial cause is that which is the principal producer of an effect in its substantial continuum.

Dze means substance. For example, fertilizer cannot turn into a sprout, nor can heat, water, earth, or air, and so forth. Only a seed can turn into a sprout. Therefore, a sprout is *dze gyun du,* of the substantial continuum, of a seed.

Seeds turn into sprouts and become plants, which in turn produce more seeds that likewise can be planted to produce other plants, and so on. *Dze gyun* means a substantial continuum. *Rang gi nyer dre* means substantial effect, that is, both the cause and its effect are of the same substance.

If *rang* refers to a seed, its *nyer dre,* substantial effect, is a sprout. *Tso wor kye che* means principal producer or cause. Principal cause and *nyer len* are very close in meaning. Secondary causes are *hlen chik che kyen,* co-operating conditions, such as earth, water, air, and fertilizer, which gather together and help seeds produce a sprout. The principal cause is the seed.

Go wa che na means an easy way to help one understand. *Nyer len gyi tsen nyi du yang jok tsen shi* means you can make a proof statement for that definition of substantial cause—as was done with the example of fire used above—and give an example: *sak che kyi pung po nga ta bu,* like samsara's five contaminated heaps. In this case we can say that karma is *nyer len,* the principal substantial cause of our next life, while the five heaps are *hlen chik che kyen,* the co-operating conditions of that life. Why are these five heaps *hlen chik che kyen,* the co-operating conditions? Because they produce what is similar to them—that is, the next life's contaminated five heaps—without being present in their own substantial continuum. This relationship goes on continually. However, the five heaps themselves cannot turn into a sentient being.

As for *nyer len*, substantial cause, in relation to the consciousness of our future life, a quotation from the *Commentary to (Dignāga's) "Compendium of Valid Cognition"* states:

།རྣམ་ཤེས་མིན་པ་རྣམ་ཤེས་ཀྱི།
།ཉེར་ལེན་མིན་པའི་ཕྱིར་ཡང་གྲུབ།

nam she min pe nam she gyi
nyer len min chir chir yang drup

What is not consciousness cannot be
the substantial cause of consciousness.

A principal belief in the philosophy of Buddhism is that we have previous and future lives. If something is *nam she*, consciousness, its *nyer len*, substantial cause, must be *nam she*, consciousness, as well. Four of the five heaps of a newborn baby are not the result of consciousness; only *nam she gyi pung po*, the consciousness heap, is the substantial result of consciousness. So the very first moment of a newborn baby's consciousness should have consciousness as its *nyer len gyi gyu*, substantial cause. That consciousness cannot have parents. The parents are only responsible for producing the other four heaps, but they cannot produce the consciousness heap, since that heap is a continuum extending from beginningless time. Consciousness arises from the substantial cause of consciousness. The consciousness of an individual's former life is what produced the consciousness of this life. Therefore, the very last moment of this present life's consciousness will produce, and as such be the substantial cause of, the first moment of the next life's consciousness. This goes on continually. It is for this reason that we as Buddhists believe in former and future lives. In non-Buddhist schools, they believe, for example, that beings arise just from the gathering of the four elements or some such.

Nyer len, The substantial cause, of *nam she gyi pung po*, the consciousness heap, is steady. The substantial cause of *suk kyi pung po*, the form heap, is the combined egg and sperm of our parents. The substantial cause of the other three heaps, *tsor we pung po*, feeling heap, *du she kyi pung po*, conception heap, and *du che kyi pung po*, mental formation heap, are unsteady.

Ngö po yin na, hlen chik che kyen yin pe kyap, Whatever is a causally effective thing must be a co-operating condition. *Gyun dang che pe ngö po yin na nyer len yin pe kyap*, Whatever is a causally effective thing accompanying a continuum must be a substantial cause. What does this mean? Does every *ngö po*, causally effective thing, have *gyun*, a continuum? *Suk*, Form, has a continuum, but *dra*, sound, (one kind of causally effective thing), however, does not have a continuum. In scripture it says: *dra la ring dre gyun me pe chir*, because those things like sound don't have a continuum. Even though it is *ngö po*, a causally effective thing, it is *ring dre gyun me*, of such a nature that it lacks a continuum. Any *ngö po*, causally effective thing, can be *hlen chik che kyen*, a co-operating condition, because it helps its results [to come about]. However, there is a lot of debate about this.

གསུམ་པ་རྒྱུ་ལ་སྒྲས་བརྗོད་རིགས་ཀྱི་སྒོ་ནས་དབྱེ་ན་དྲུག་ཡོད་དེ། མཛོད་ལས། བྱེད་རྒྱུ་ལྷན་ཅིག་འབྱུང་བ་དང་། །སྐལ་མཉམ་མཚུངས་པར་ལྡན་པ་དང་། །ཀུན་ཏུ་འགྲོ་དང་རྣམ་སྨིན་ཏེ། །རྒྱུ་ནི་རྣམ་པ་དྲུག་ཏུ་འདོད། །ཅེས་གསུངས་པ་ལྟར་དྲུག་ཡོད་པའི་ཕྱིར། སོ་སོའི་མཚན་ཉིད་དང་། མཚན་གཞི་ནི། བུམ་པ་དང་རྫས་ཐ་དད་ཀྱང་ཡིན། བུམ་པ་སྐྱེ་བ་ལ་གེགས་མི་བྱེད་པ་ཡང་ཡིན་པའི་གཞི་མཐུན་དུ་དམིགས་པ། བུམ་པའི་བྱེད་རྒྱུའི་མཚན་ཉིད། མཚན་གཞི། ཀ་བ་ལྟ་བུ། བྱེད་རྒྱུ་ལ། སྒྲས་བརྗོད་རིགས་ཀྱི་སྒོ་ནས་དབྱེ་ན། བྱེད་རྒྱུ་ནུས་ལྡན་དང་། ནུས་མེད་གཉིས།

> *sum pa gyu la dre jö rik kyi go ne ye na druk yö de, dzö le, che gyu hlen chik jung wa dang, kel nyam tsung par den pa dang, kun tu dro dang nam min te, gyu ni nam pa druk tu dö, che sung pa tar druk yö pe chir, so sö tsen nyi dang, tsen shi ni, bum pa dang dze ta te kyang yin, bum pa kye wa la gek mi che pa yang yin pe shi tun du mik pa, bum pe che gyu'i tsen nyi, tsen shi ka wa ta bu, che gyu la, dre jö rik kyi go ne ye na, che gyu nu(n) den dang nu me nyi*
>
> The third: when nominally classified there are six types of causes. *The Treasury of Higher Knowledge*,[38] mentions six causes as follows: "Non-interfering active cause, co-arising cause, cause of similar fortune, concomitant cause, omnipresent cause, and ripening cause, these six kinds of causes are those accepted [by the Vaibhāṣhika school]. The definitions of each of these and their illustrations follow. The definition of a non-interfering active cause of a pot is something that is both a substance different from pot and what does nothing to impede the pot's existence. A pillar is an example of such a cause. When non-interfering active cause is nominally classified there are two kinds: a non-interfering active cause that has power [to cause results] and a non-interfering active cause that lacks power [to cause results].

One may describe *che gyu*, non-interfering active cause, this way. *Ka wa bum pa dang dze ta te kyang yin* means a pillar is one kind of substance and a pot is another. A pillar's substance is not a pot's substance. Therefore, *bum pa kye pa la gek mi che pa yang yin pe shi tun du mik pa* means it [a pillar] is something that doesn't harm or impede the production or existence of a pot. *Shi tun pa* means one object that has both qualities mentioned in the definition. *Bum pe che gyu'i tsen shi ka wa ta bu*, An illustration of a non-interfering active cause of pot is a pillar; 1) a pillar has a different substance, and 2) it won't impede the arising of a pot.

---

[38] (T: ***chos mgnon pa mdzod***; S: *Abhidharmakośa*), a text composed by the great scholar Vasubandhu.

Gyu kyen refers to five of the six causes mentioned above, the sixth being *che gyu*, non-interfering active cause, which is merely a nominal cause, or in name only. We say all are causes *che gyu ma tok*, except for non-interfering active cause. *Che gyu* cannot be a cause because of being *tak pa*, a permanent entity. Why is non-interfering active cause considered a permanent entity? *Ka re pi*, Why did it get kicked out, of the group of causes? We use this expression when we say *pu gu ngen pa te nang ne pi*, the bad kid was kicked out of the house, or simply, *pi pa yin*, he got kicked out. *Kyen gyi nang ne che gyu pi pa ka re yin*, Why has non-interfering active cause been kicked out of the class of causes? Because it is a permanent entity. *Gang yin ser na che gyu tak pa re*, Why do you say that non-interfering active cause is a permanent entity, since *kyen yin na ngö po yin gö*, whatever is a condition must be a causally effective thing? Because *che gyu tak pa re*, non-interfering active cause is a permanent entity. *Che tsang*, That's why, *pi pa re*, it got kicked out. *Che gyu tak pa yin pe gyu tsen ka re yo*, Well then, why is non-interfering active cause a permanent entity?

At this point you have to say, *ha ha dure nang gyi pu gu chung chung de tsö shing gyi re*, which means, Ha! Ha! Even the little kids in the *Dura* class know that! The logic rule is: *tak ngö nyi ke cha yö pe chö yin na tak pa yin pe kyap*, whatever phenomenon can be classified into causally effective thing and permanent entity, that phenomenon itself must be classified as a permanent entity. *Tsen shi*, An example, is *she ja*, object of knowledge. *She ja tak pa yin, she ja yin na tak pa yin pe ma kyap*, Object of knowledge is a permanent entity, but whatever is an object of knowledge is not necessarily a permanent entity. Also, *she ja yin na ngö po yin pe ma kyap*, whatever is an object of knowledge is not necessarily a causally effective thing. *She ja*, Object of knowledge, is permanent because it can be classified generally into both kinds of entities: causally effective things and permanent entities.

Therefore, *rang le shen pa che gyu gyu*, non-interfering active cause is any cause that is other than itself. *Che gyu chö chen, tak pa yin te, tak ngö nyi ke cha yö pe chö yin pe chir*, Consider non-interfering active cause, it is a permanent entity, because [it complies with the logic rule that states] if any phenomenon can be classified into permanent entities and causally effective things it itself must be permanent. *Bum pa le shen pe chö bum pe che gyu*, The non-interfering active causes of a pot are those phenomena that are other than the pot. *Ngö po le shen pe chö ngö pö che gyu*, The non-interfering active causes of a causally effective thing are those phenomena that are other than causally effective thing. Also, either causally effective things or permanent entities can be considered the non-interfering active cause of a pot. For example, *nam ka*, space, is *bum pa le shen pe chö*, a phenomenon that is other than a pot, as is *ka wa*, a pillar. All phenomena, including mental causes, which are other than a pot are pot's non-interfering active cause.

The two kinds of non-interfering active causes are mentioned and illustrated below.

དང་པོ་ནི། བུམ་པ་དང་ཀ་བ་སོགས་འདུས་བྱས་མཐའ་དག་ལ་བྱེད། གཉིས་པ་ནི། ཤེས་བྱ། རྟག་པ། སྤྱི་མཚན་སོགས་འདུས་མ་བྱས་ཀྱི་ཆོས་རྣམས་ལ་བྱེད། སྒྲས་བརྗོད་རིགས་ཤེས་བརྗོད་པའི་རྒྱུ་མཚན་ཡོད་དེ། བྱེད་རྒྱུ་ནུས་མེད་ཡིན་ན། བྱེད་རྒྱུ་མ་ཡིན་པས་ཁྱབ་པ་ཤེས་པའི་ཆེད་དུ་ཡིན་པའི་ཕྱིར།

dang po ni, bum pa dang ka wa sok du che ta dak la che, nyi pa ni, she ja, tak pa, chi tsen sok du ma che kyi chö nam la che, dre jö rik she jö pe gyu tsen yö de, che gyu nu me yin na, che gyu ma yin pe kyap pa she pe che du yin pe chir

Examples of the first (a non-interfering active cause that has power) [to bring about a result] consists of all composed things such as a pot and a pillar. Examples of the second (a non-interfering active cause that has no power) [to bring about a result] consist of such phenomena as "object of knowledge" and permanent entities [in general]; that is, uncomposed phenomena such as general abstract entities. There is a reason for saying these are only nominal causes. Why? It is specified this way so that one knows that if something is a non-interfering active cause that has no power it is necessarily not the kind of cause that brings about a result.

An example of *che gyu nu(n) den*, a non-interfering active cause that has power, is *bum pa dang ka wa sok du che ta dak la che*, pot, pillar, and the like, in effect, every causally effective thing is an example. Examples of the second, *che gyu nu me*, a non-interfering active cause that has no power, are *she ja*, object of knowledge, *tak pa*, permanent entity, *chi tsen*, general abstract phenomenon, and all *du ma che kyi chö*, uncomposed phenomena. What is the definition of *she ja*? *Lo'i yul du cha rung wa*, That which is suitable as an object of the mind, which means any phenomenon that can be perceived by a perceiving subject. *Lo*, Mind, is the subject. *Yul* is the object. *Cha rung wa* means an appropriate object. An example of *cha mi rung*, an inappropriate object, is *ri bong ra*, a hare's horn. What is the definition of *tak pa*, permanent entity? *Chö dang ke chik ma ma yin pe shi tun pa tak pe tsen nyi*,[39] That which is both a phenomenon and non-momentary is the definition of permanent entity. What is *chi tsen*? Usually *chi tsen*, general abstract phenomenon, is *tok pe nang wa*, an object that appears to the conceptual mind. *Ngön sum gyi nang wa*, An object that appears to direct perception, is *rang tsen*, a specific concrete phenomenon. This is the view that accords with the Sautrāntika school system.

Ngö po, Causally effective thing, *rang tsen*, a specific concrete phenomenon, and *du che*, composed entity, are synonyms. *Chi tsen*, General abstract phenomenon, *tak pa*, permanent phenomenon, and *tok pe nang wa*, an object that appears to the conceptual mind, are synonyms.

Why does it say *dre jö rik gi go ne*, nominally? This next sentence gives the reason as follows: *che gyu nu me yin na, che gyu ma yin pe kyap pe che du yin pe chir*, in order to make it understood that if something is a non-interfering active cause without power, it is not a cause that acts and brings about effects. You can just call it a "cause" but it is not a real cause.

---

[39] ཆོས་དང་སྐད་ཅིག་མ་མ་ཡིན་པའི་གཞི་མཐུན་པ་རྟག་པའི་མཚན་ཉིད།

The Treasury of Higher Knowledge describes *che gyu*, non-interfering acting cause, as *rang le shen pa che gyu'i gyu*, a cause that is everything other than that object itself. This is according to the Vaibhāṣhika school system's view. This means that those phenomena that are not a given thing are that thing's cause; that is, everything that is not that thing is a cause of that thing. However, this belief creates difficulties when taken up in the higher schools. What's the definition of cause? *Kye che gyu'i tsen nyi*, The definition of cause is a producer. *Gyu ngö po dre bu sum dön chik*, Cause, causally effective thing, and effect are synonyms according to the belief of the Sautrāntika school system and higher tenet systems. However, this is not accepted by the Vaibhāṣhika school. Why? Because if *che gyu*, non-interfering acting cause, is *rang le shen pa che gyu gyu*, a cause that is everything other than itself, *ka wa le shen pe chö tam che ka we gyu yin par tel*, it would logically follow that every phenomenon that is other than a pillar is the cause of that pillar; that is, anything that is not a pillar is a non-interfering active cause of a pillar [including permanent entities, such as space, for instance, which is not a causally effective thing and therefore cannot qualify as a cause].

***

So, if someone were to say:

—*Ka wa le shen pe chö tam che ka we gyu yin par tel*, Do you agree that the non-interfering active cause of a pillar is all phenomena other than that pillar? (You have to respond with)...

—*Dö*, Yes, I agree.

—*Nam ka chö chen, ka we gyu yin par tel*, What about space, is that a non-interfering active cause of a pillar as well?

—*Dö*, Yes, it would have to be.

—*Nam ka chö chen, ngö po yin par tel*, Consider space, you would agree then that it's a causally effective thing?

—*Chi chir*, No, why on earth would I think that?

—*Nam ka chö chen, ngö po ma yin par tel*, Consider space, so you're saying that it's not a causally effective thing?

—*Dö*, I accept that it's not.

—*Nam ka chö chen, bum pe chi gyu yin par tel,* Consider space, it follows that it's still the non-interfering active cause of a pot?
—*Dö,* That's right.
—*Nam ka chö chen, rang le shen pe chö yin par tel,* Consider space, so it's a phenomenon that is other than a pot? (*Rang* refers to *bum pa*, a pot.)
—*Dö,* I accept that.
—*Nam ka chö chen, bum pa ma yin par tel,* Well then, consider space, you're telling me it's not a pot?
—*Dö,* Of course it's not.
—*Bum pa ma yin na nam ka bum pa le shen pe chö yin par tel,* If space is not a pot, doesn't it follow that space is a phenomenon that is other than a pot?
—*Dö,* Yes.
—*Bum pe gyu yin par tel,* It follows that it [space] is the cause of a pot?
—*Dö,* Yes, that would follow.
—*Ngö po yin par tel,* Then you accept that space is a causally effective thing?
—*Chi chir,* No, that's not so.
—*Ngö po ma yin na,* If it's not a causally effective thing, *nam ka chö chen, gyu ma yin par tel,* consider space, so it's not a cause?
—*Chi chir,* Why? That's not true either.
—*Ngö po ma yin pe chir,* Because it's not a causally effective thing.
—*Kyap pa ma jung,* There is no pervasion [meaning that just because it is not a causally effective thing doesn't mean that it is not a cause].
—*Nam ka chö chen, gyu yin par tel,* Consider space, it's a cause then?
—*Dö,* Yes, it is.
—*Nam ka chö chen, chi gyu ma yin par tel,* Consider space, so it's not a non-interfering active cause?
—*Chi chir,* Why?
—*Nam ka chö chen, chi gyu yin par tel,* Then space *is* a non-interfering active cause?
—*Dö,* Yes, I'll accept that

From the above argument, you can see why it is necessary to add certain points when we debate in order to accommodate this Vaibhāṣhika school belief.

The idea behind *che gyu*, a non-interfering active cause, is this. Let's take a pot, for example. While other things exist but are not a pot they do not hinder the arising of the pot in any way; it is as if they remain quietly letting the pot arise and exist without harming it. All phenomena that are not the pot are that pot's non-interfering active cause because they don't obstruct it. When debating about this cause, we have to qualify our statements with the phrases: *che gyu nu(n) den*, non-interfering active causes that have power, and *che gyu nu me*, non-interfering active causes that lack power. In the debate above we used *nam ka*, space, as an example of a non-interfering active cause that doesn't have any power to produce effects because it is a permanent entity. Nevertheless, such entities are still *bum pe che gyu*, the non-interfering active causes of a pot, since they don't hinder the pot from arising and disintegrating.

The Vaibhāṣhika school uses the following example to illustrate non-interfering active cause. They say, "It is like our king who allows us to stay very comfortably without bothering or interfering with us." [In this sense he acts passively as a cause by not hindering our actions.] In the same way, other things don't bother a pot; they don't prevent it from existing, but rather allow it to exist, as if they were helping it. That is the idea.

On the debate ground this idea often sparks unbelievable debates. Someone might say, "You're telling me that when the sun rises the sunlight doesn't hurt the shining of the stars?" Or, "Don't obstacles obstruct the paths from growing in one's mind? In order to achieve the Path of Insight it's necessary to get rid of obstacles. The main function of the obstacles of the mental afflictions (*nyön drip*) is to obstruct the achievement of nirvana. Now, if these *nyön drip*, obstacles of the mental afflictions, are *che gyu*, non-interfering active causes, don't they hurt the achievement of nirvana? Don't *she drip*, the obstacles to omniscience, obstruct the path to Buddhahood?" As one might imagine there can be no end to debates such as these.

Is it getting a little bit better? If you continue with these debates, proceeding slowly as you go, digesting each one before you go on to the next one, that's very good. But if you just keep racing forward all the time, hungry for more, without establishing a firm basis, that isn't good. Just reading more and more and more isn't good at all; what is good is to make your understanding go deeper and deeper.

ཕན་ཚུན་དུས་མཉམ། རྫས་ཐ་དད་ཀྱང་ཡིན། ཕན་ཚུན་སྐྱེ་བ་ལ་གེགས་མི་བྱེད་པ་ཡང་ཡིན་པའི་གཞི་མཐུན་པར་དམིགས་པ། ལྷན་ཅིག་འབྱུང་བའི་རྒྱུའི་མཚན་ཉིད། མཚན་གཞི་ནི། ལྷན་ཅིག་དུ་སྐྱེས་པའི་འབྱུང་བ་བཞི་དང་། དངོས་རྒྱུ་ཚོགས་པ་གཅིག་པའི་མིག་སོགས་དབང་པོ་ལྔ་དང་། དངོས་རྒྱུ་ཚོགས་པ་གཅིག་པའི་བུ་རམ་གྱི་རོ་གཟུགས་གཉིས་ལྟ་བུའོ།

pen tsun du nyam, dze ta te kyang yin, pen tsun kye wa la gek mi che pa yang yin pe shi tun par mik pa, hlen chik jung we gyu'i tsen nyi, tsen shi ni, hlen chik du kye pe jung wa shi dang, ngö gyu tsok pa chik pe mik sok wang po nga dang, ngö gyu tsok pa chik pe bu ram gyi ro suk nyi ta bu'o

The definition of a co-arising cause is a combination of being different substances and what arises at the same time without harming the production of each other. An illustration of such a cause is the four elements [earth, water, fire, and air] that arise together, or the five sense powers such as the eye [sense power], which are a single collection of direct causes, or the two—taste and form—of a lump of brown sugar that are likewise a single collection of direct causes.

An explanation of *hlen chik jung we gyu*, co-arising cause, is as follows. *Pen tsun du nyam*, Mutual time, meaning these causes exist at the same time, is one of the qualities of this kind of cause. For example, the four elements—earth, water, fire, and air—are qualities that are present simultaneously in one cause. *Dze ta te kyang yin* means they have different substances. For example, water has a different substance from air; fire has a different substance from earth, and so forth. *Pen tsun kye wa la gek mi che pa yang yin pe shi tun par mik pa* means that they are different substances that exist together at the same time and same place, but neither impedes the existence of the other.

Tsen shi, An example, is *hlen chik du kye we jung wa shi*, the simultaneous occurrence of the four elements [in a single cause], as well as *ngö gyu tsok pa chik pe mik sok wang po nga*, which means the gathering together of direct causes such as the five sense powers at the same time and place. *Chi jung wa* means the four outer elements, and *nang gi jung wa* means the four inner elements. For example, although the eye sense power is the unique governing condition for the eye sense consiousness, it alone cannot produce eye consciousness but requires other causes, the presence of the four elements, for instance, to bring about the resultant apprehension of an object.

Bu ram gyi ro suk means the taste and form (shape) of sugar. When you eat a cube of brown sugar, the experience of both the taste and the shape are simultaneously accompanied by the presence of the four elements. Before the sugar reaches your mouth it consists of the outer [four] elements. When it reaches your mouth and tongue the contact causes the occurrence of the inner four elements related to the tongue sense power. The power of these elements is not always equal, for sometimes your tongue is dry, which indicates that it is lacking the water element, such that it is difficult to talk. If there is no air element, the tongue cannot move and remains still like a rock.

In regard to this cause a verse in *The Treasury of Higher Knowledge* states: *hlen chik jung gang pen tsun dre*,[40] that which arises together to produce a mutual result. *Hlen chik* means together; *jung* means arise; therefore, they exist together at the same time. *Gang* is an indefinite pronoun meaning whatever. *Pen tsun* means mutually. *Dre* means result. This refers to those things that come

---

[40] ལྷན་ཅིག་འབྱུང་གང་ཕན་ཚུན་འབྲས།

together and mutually serve to create a mutual result. There are mutual causes and mutual results. For example, although all four elements—earth, fire, water, and air—are present in every object, whenever any one of them is the stronger of the four, that element predominates causing that nature to become more evident in the object. Also, *kye sok ga wa shi*[41] means *kye wa*, birth or arising; *sok*, and the rest, referring to *ga wa*, old age, *na wa*, sickness, and *chi wa*, death.[42] *Shi* means four. These four, being co-arising causes, also contribute their qualities to any given cause. These qualities serve as both causes and results. Since these four qualities are likewise present both in main mind as well as its mental derivatives, they even accompany *dom nyi*, the two vows, consisting of *so tar gyi dom pa*, the Pratimoksha vows, and *chang sem kyi dom pa*, the Bodhisattva vows. If something is *hlen chik jung we gyu*, a co-arising cause, it must be *ngö po*, a causally effective thing. Therefore, this kind of cause has a very wide meaning, which includes both physical matter and mind.

> རང་གི་རིགས་འདྲ་ཕྱི་མ་རང་དང་འདྲ་བ་སྐྱེད་བྱེད། རང་ཉིད་སྐལ་
> མཉམ་གྱི་རྒྱུའི་མཚན་ཉིད། མཚན་གཞི་ནི་བུམ་པ་ལྟ་བུ།
>
> *rang gi ring dra chi ma rang dang dra wa kye che, rang nyi kel nyam gyi gyu'i tsen nyi, tsen shi ni bum pa ta bu*
>
> The definition of something that is a cause of similar fortune is what later produces something that is of its own class; a pot for example.

Kel nyam gyi gyu, cause of similar fortune, is the third among the six kinds of nominal causes. *The Treasury of Higher Knowledge* describes this cause as follows:

---

41 སྐྱེ་སོགས་རྒ་བ་བཞི་

42 སྐྱེ་རྒ་ན་འཆི་

།སྐལ་མཉམ་རྒྱུ་ནི་འདྲ་བ་འོ།

kel nyam gyu ni dra wa o

Causes of similar fortune are alike.

This refers to *ge we kel nyam dang mi ge we kel nyam pa*, fortunes that are similar in virtue and similar in non-virtue. This means that the result and cause are of the same class or kind. This kind of cause can be either form or consciousness. *Kel* means fortune or class; *nyam pa* means equal; that is, equal in so far as they pertain to the same realm: the desire realm, form realm, or formless realm. *Ge wa*, Virtue, cannot produce *mi ge wa*, non-virtue; nor can *ge wa*, virtue, be *kel nyam gyi gyu mi ge wa*, of a similar or equal fortune with non-virtue. Further, that which belongs to the desire realm is not *kel nyam gyi gyu*, the cause of similar fortune, for what belongs to the form realm and vice versa. Additionally, if a cause has the nature of contaminated virtue, the result also has the nature of contaminated virtue. Conversely, if a cause is *ge wa sak me*, uncontaminated virtue, its result likewise will be *ge wa sak me*, uncontaminated virtue. If causes are *nyön mong chen*, afflictive, so are the results. If the causes are *ma drip lung ma ten*, neutral and unobscured, so too are the results. This implies that some causes may be *lung ma ten*, neutral or unspecified, yet still be *drip pa*, obstacles, while others being neutral may be *ma drip*, without the influence of obstacles.

Further, we can say that *pung po nga po te kel nyam gyi gyu*, the five heaps are a kind of cause of similar fortune. That is, if one has *sak che gyi pung po*, samsara's five heaps, they by nature belong to the class of contaminated heaps, because causes and effects are of the same class. However, the aggregates pertaining to Aryas and Arhats are *sak me gyi pung po nga*, five uncontaminated heaps.

The Vaibhāṣhika school system is unbelievable. In the monastery we had to recite *The Treasury of Higher Knowledge* and its commentary in class for one year. Following that, we debated the important points until we finished the entire text. We were very lucky to be able to learn it in such great detail. That was an incredibly fortunate time.

ཕན་ཚུན་མཚུངས་ལྡན་རྣམ་པ་ལྔ་མཚུངས་ཀྱང་ཡིན། ཕན་ཚུན་སྐྱེ་བ་ལ་གེགས་མི་བྱེད་པ་ཡང་ཡིན་པའི་གཞི་མཐུན་དུ་དམིགས་པ། མཚུངས་ལྡན་གྱི་རྒྱུའི་མཚན་ཉིད། མཚན་གཞི་ནི། མིག་གི་རྣམ་པར་ཤེས་པ་དང་དེའི་འཁོར་དུ་བྱུང་བའི་ཚོར་བ་ལྟ་བུ།

pen tsun tsung den nam pa nga tsung kyang yin, pen tsun kye wa la gek mi che pa yang yin pe shi tun du mik pa, tsung den gyi gyu'i tsen nyi, tsen shi ni, mik gi nam par she pa dang de'i kor du jung we tsor wa nyi ta bu

The definition of concomitant cause is that which is a combination of the mutually shared five concomitant aspects and what doesn't impede their mutual arising. An illustration is the eye consciousness and whatever feeling that arises accompanying it.

Tsung den gyi gyu, Concomitant cause, is the fourth among the nominal causes. This cause is described in *The Treasury of Higher Knowledge* as follows:

།མཚུངས་ལྡན་རྒྱུ་ནི་སེམས་དག་དང་།
།སེམས་བྱུང་རྟེན་མཚུངས་ཅན་རྣམས་སོ།

tsung den gyu ni sem dak dang
sem jung ten tsung chen nam so

Concomitant cause is mind and the
mental derivatives that have a similar basis.

This means that mind and its mental derivatives are mutually associated. Therefore, this kind of cause refers only to consciousness. *Sem*, Main mind, and *sem jung*, mental derivatives, work together. This can be likened to having a dinner party where you cook a lot of food and lay it out on the table for everybody to enjoy, which they do, finishing all the food that you have prepared. One person cannot finish it all by himself. Everybody has to do hard work together in order to eat it. Similarly, if a large group of people goes on a trip together, going camping for example, each person has to load everything they need, their own belongings, on their back. This way everybody pitches in and combines their strength in order to carry what is needed by the group as a whole.

རང་གི་འབྲས་བུར་གྱུར་པའི་རང་དང་ས་གཅིག་པའི་ཉོན་མོངས་ཅན་ཕྱི་མ་སྐྱེད་བྱེད་ཀྱི་ཉོན་མོངས་ཅན་དེ། རང་ཉིད་ཀུན་འགྲོའི་རྒྱུའི་མཚན་ཉིད། མཚན་གཞི་ནི། འདོད་ཆགས་ལྟ་བུ།

rang gi dre bur gyur pe rang dang sa chik pe nyön mong chen chi ma kye che kyi nyön mong chen de, rang nyi kun drö'i gyu'i tsen nyi, tsen shi ni, dö chak ta bu

The definition of something that is an omnipresent cause is that which possesses mental afflictions and produces a later mental affliction of the same level as its effect. An illustration is desire.

The fifth of the nominal causes is *kun drö'i gyu*, omnipresent cause. *Nyön mong chen* means what is related to the mental afflictions. Trees, for example, are *lung ma ten*, neutral, as are the four elements generally; that is, they are neither virtuous nor non-virtuous. Therefore, an omnipresent cause can only be mental.

མི་དགེ་བ་དང་། དགེ་བ་ཟག་བཅས་གང་རུང་གིས་བསྡུས་པ། རྣམ་སྨིན་གྱི་རྒྱུའི་མཚན་ཉིད། མཚན་གཞི་ནི། སྲོག་གཅོད་ཀྱི་ལས་ལྟ་བུ།

mi ge wa dang, ge wa sak che gang rung gi du pa, nam min gyi gyu'i tsen nyi, tsen shi ni, sok chö kyi le ta bu

> The definition of ripening cause is that which is gathered by either non-virtue or contaminated virtue. An illustration is the karma of killing.

Nam min kyi gyu, ripening cause, is the sixth nominal cause. This cause is referred to in *The Treasury of Higher Knowledge* as follows:

> །རྣམ་སྨིན་རྒྱུ་ནི་མི་དགེ་དང་།
> །དགེ་བ་ཟག་བཅས་རྣམས་ཁོ་ན།
>
> *nam min gyu ni mi ge dang*
> *ge wa sak che nam ko na*
>
> A ripening cause is only either
> non-virtue or contaminated virtue.

This passage means that our body, for example, is a ripening effect of *ge wa sak che*, contaminated virtue, and *nyön mong*, mental afflictions. Why is this? Because we are in samsara, and consequently our body is samsara's body and so its quality is afflicted. A dog's body, for instance, is *mi ge we dre bu*, the effect of non-virtue. Although our body is the effect of virtue, nevertheless, this virtue is *ge wa sak che*, contaminated virtue, not *ge wa sak me*, uncontaminated virtue. *Le mi ge wa* means bad karma, which is *ngen drö nam min gyi gyu*, the ripening karma of bad realms. In contrast, *ge wa sak che*, contaminated virtue, means virtue that has been collected by *nyön mong*, mental afflictions, and as such is *den drö nam min gyi gyu*, a ripening cause of the fortunate (higher) realms. The life experienced by each of the higher realm beings—gods, demigods, and humans—is *ge wa sak che nam min kyi dre bu*, the ripened result of contaminated virtue; and the life experienced by each of the lower realm beings is *mi ge we nam min gyi dre bu*, the ripened result of non-virtue. *Sak*, Contaminated, refers to *nyön mong*, the mental afflictions. *Che*, Possessing, refers to collecting the causes with mental afflictions. A ripening cause by nature must have the quality of contaminated virtue or non-virtue. If it is *nam min gyi gyu*, a ripening cause, then it must be *ge wa sak che dang mi ge wa gang rung*, either contaminated virtue or non-virtue; there is no exception. One karma cannot be both kinds of cause; it has to be either the one or the other. This accords with *ten drel yen lak chu nyi*, the twelve limbs of dependent origination. The first limb is *ma rik pa*, ignorance. Ignorance cannot be abandoned until one has achieved the status of *dra chom pa*, an Arhat. Due to that ignorance, you collect *le*, karma. This karma that you collect through ignorance is *sak che kyi le*, contaminated karma, which must be either *ge wa sak che*, contaminated virtue, or *mi ge wa*, non-virtue.

According to the Vaibhāṣhika school system in order to collect *ge wa sak me*, uncontaminated virtue, you have to first achieve *tong lam*, the Path of Insight. But according to the Vajrayāna system, through achieving *de tong nyi su me pe ye she*, inseparable bliss-wisdom, you can collect virtue that is strong enough to become *ge wa sak me*, uncontaminated virtue.

ལུང་མ་བསྟན་རྣམས་རྣམ་སྨིན་གྱི་རྒྱུ་མ་ཡིན་ཏེ། དེ་རྣམས་ཀྱིས་རྣམ་སྨིན་གྱི་འབྲས་བུ་འབྱིན་མི་ནུས་པའི་ཕྱིར་ཏེ། ས་བོན་རུལ་པས་མྱུ་གུ་མི་བསྐྱེད་པ་ལྟ་བུ་ཡིན་པའི་ཕྱིར།

lung ma ten nam nam min gyi gyu ma yin te, de nam kyi nam min gyi dre bu jin mi nu pe chir te, sa bön rul pe nyu gu mi kye pa ta bu yin pe chir

Neutral (or unspecified) things are not a ripening cause because neutral things are incapable of creating ripening effects, just as a rotten seed is incapable of yielding a sprout.

དགེ་བ་ཟག་མེད་ཀྱིས་རྣམ་སྨིན་གྱི་འབྲས་བུ་མི་འབྱིན་ཏེ། དེ་ཉོན་མོངས་ཀྱི་ལྷན་དང་བྲལ་བའི་ཕྱིར། དཔེར་ན། ལྷན་དང་བྲལ་བའི་ནས་རྗོག་སྐམ་རྡིལ་བས་མྱུ་གུ་མི་བསྐྱེད་པ་ལྟ་བུ་ཡིན་པའི་ཕྱིར།

ge wa sak me kyi nam min gyi dre bu mi jin te, de nyön mong kyi len dang drel we chir, per na, len dang drel we ne dok kam hril we nyu gu mi kye pa ta bu yin pe chir

Additionally, uncontaminated virtues do not yield effects because they are free of being watered by the mental afflictions. For example, when a barley seed is completely dried up, since it lacks moisture, it is utterly incapable of producing a sprout.

རྣམ་སྨིན་གྱི་རྒྱུ་ཡིན་ན། མི་དགེ་བ་དང་དགེ་བ་ཟག་བཅས་གང་རུང་ཡིན་པས་མ་ཁྱབ་སྟེ། མི་དགེ་བ་དང་དགེ་བ་ཟག་བཅས་གཉིས་རྣམ་སྨིན་གྱི་རྒྱུ་ཡིན་ཀྱང་། དེ་གཉིས་གང་རུང་མ་ཡིན་པའི་ཕྱིར།

nam min gyi gyu yin na, mi ge wa dang ge wa sak che gang rung yin pe ma kyap te, mi ge wa dang ge wa sak che nyi nam min gyi gyu yin kyang, de nyi gang rung ma yin pe chir

If something is a ripening cause, it is not necessarily something that is either non-virtue or contaminated virtue. Although non-virtue and contaminated virtue are both a ripening cause, what is either of those two is neither [non-virtue or contaminated virtue].

Why is this? *Suk chö chen, ge mi ge gang rung gi du pa ma yin par tel, lung ma ten yin pe chir*, Consider form, it does not consist of either virtue or non-virute, because it itself is neutral or unspecified.

This system is amazing. If you learn it well, at some point you won't even need a teacher. You can make yourself some *maté* and then sit there sipping it while you read and think about it.

རྒྱུ་དྲུག་གི་ཡིན་པ་ཡོད་དེ། ཀུན་འགྲོ་མི་དགེ་བར་གྱུར་བའི་སེམས་དང་། དེའི་འཁོར་དུ་གྱུར་པའི་ཚོར་བ་སོགས་ཀུན་འགྲོ་ལྔ་པོ་དེ་དེ་ཡིན་པའི་ཕྱིར།

gyu druk gi yin pa yö de, kun dro mi ge war gyur we sem dang de'i kor du gyur pe tsor wa sok kun dro nga po de de yin pe chir

There exists something that is that sixth cause, because a non-virtuous mind as well as the five omnipresent factors that accompany that non-virtuous mind such as feeling[43] is that.

[43] The five omnipresent factors are: 1) *sem pa* (***sems pa***) intention; 2) *tsor wa* (***tshor ba***) feeling; 3) *du she* (***'du shes***) discrimination; 4) *yi la che pa* (***yid la byed pa***) attention; and 5) *rek pa* (***reg pa***) contact.

Debate Four

cause and effect
gyu(n) dre

དང་པོ་ནི། ཁ་ཅིག་ན་རེ། རྒྱུ་ཡིན་ན་རྒྱུ་དྲུག་ཀ་ཡིན་པས་ཁྱབ་ཟེར་ན།

dang po ni, ka chik na re, gyu yin na gyu druk ka yin pe kyap ser na

The first; if *KA CHIK MA* says: If something is a cause it must be all six causes.

DRUK KA, ALL SIX, REFERS TO THE six kinds of causes, which are mentioned in *The Treasury of Higher Knowledge* above. In response to this pervasion *RANG LUK* replies:

གཟུགས་ཆོས་ཅན། རྒྱུ་དྲུག་ཀ་ཡིན་པར་ཐལ། རྒྱུ་ཡིན་པའི་ཕྱིར། ཁྱབ་པ་ཁས།

suk chö chen, gyu druk ka yin par tel, gyu yin pe chir, kyap pa ke

What about form, from what you say it would logically follow that it must be those six causes, because it is a cause. You asserted that pervasion.

What is the definition of *suk*, form? *Suk su rung wa suk gyi tsen nyi*, That which is suitable as form is the definition of form. *Suk* implies form in general, but here requires further explanation. This *suk* is visible form, which consists of both color and shape; that is, it is a visible object of the eye consciousness. Since you cannot smell or hear color but only see it, *suk* in this case is the unique object of the eye consciousness.

Now, although such a form is a cause, is it all six causes? No, obviously not *all* six causes can be form; however, it can be *some* of these six causes. How many fingers do you have on one hand? Five. Does this entail that your right index finger is all your five fingers? "Finger" is a general term. One finger is not *all* of your five fingers. Each one of them is a finger, but one finger is not all of them. This is the main idea being presented here.

འདོད་ན། གཟུགས་ཆོས་ཅན། རྣམ་སྨིན་གྱི་རྒྱུ་དང་། མཚུངས་ལྡན་གྱི་རྒྱུ་དང་། ཀུན་འགྲོའི་རྒྱུ་གསུམ་རེ་རེ་ནས་ཡིན་པར་ཐལ། རྒྱུ་དྲུག་ཀ་ཡིན་པའི་ཕྱིར།

dö na, suk chö chen, nam min gyi gyu dang tsung den gyi gyu dang, kun drö'i gyu sum re re ne yin par tel, gyu druk ka yin pe chir

If KA CHIK MA agrees [with the previous consequence], RANG LUK responds with: Consider form, it would follow that it is each of the three causes—a ripening cause, a concomitant cause, and an omnipresent cause, since [according to you] it is all six causes.

Dö na means if KA CHIK MA agrees with this statement, or expressed in full, *gyu druk ka yin par dö na*, if he accepts that form must be all six causes [since it is a cause], RANG LUK responds by listing three of those six causes. If any cause must be all six causes, then it would entail that form is a ripening cause, a concomitant cause, and an omnipresent cause. What would you answer to this "*tel*," consequence? *Chi chir*, No, that's not the case.

འདོད་ན། གཟུགས་ཆོས་ཅན། དགེ་མི་དགེ་གང་རུང་གིས་བསྡུས་པ་ཡིན་པར་ཐལ། རྣམ་སྨིན་གྱི་རྒྱུ་ཡིན་པའི་ཕྱིར།

dö na, suk chö chen, ge mi ge gang rung gi du pa yin par tel, nam min gyi gyu yin pe chir

If *KA CHIK MA* accepts [that form must be each of these three kinds of causes], *RANG LUK* responds with: Consider form, it follows [from what you assert] that it is collected by either [contaminated] virtuous or non-virtuous karma, because it is a ripening cause [since according to you it must be all six causes].

What is an example of *nam min gyi gyu*, a ripening cause? The suffering lives of the three lower realms are a result of *mi ge we gyu*, non-virtuous ripening causes. *Ge wa sak che*, Contaminated virtue, produces the lives of the three higher realms of samsara. As mentioned before, our *pung po nga*, five aggregates, are *nam min gyi pung po*, ripened aggregates, or aggregates that are a result of contaminated virtue. This is the nature and function of *nam min gyi gyu*, a ripening cause.

མ་ཁྱབ་ན་ཁྱབ་པ་ཡོད་པར་ཐལ། རྣམ་སྨིན་གྱི་རྒྱུ་ཡིན་ན་དགེ་མི་དགེ་གང་རུང་གིས་བསྡུས་པས་ཁྱབ་པའི་ཕྱིར་ཏེ།

ma kyap na kyap pa yö par tel, nam min gyi gyu yin na ge mi ge gang rung gi du pe kyap pe chir te

If *KA CHIK MA* says there is no pervasion, *RANG LUK* responds with: It follows that there is pervasion, because if something is a ripening cause it includes either virtue or non-virtue.

What pervasion does *KA CHIK MA* disagree with? That it is necessarily the case that whatever is a ripening cause must be either non-virtue or contaminated virtue. One karma cannot be both kinds of cause, virtue and non-virtue; it must be either the one or the other.

Te means "why?" showing that a reason follows. *RANG LUK* cites *The Treasury of Higher Knowledge* to substantiate this argument:

> མཛོད་ལས། །རྣམ་སྨིན་རྒྱུ་ནི་མི་དགེ་དང་། །དགེ་བ་ཟག་བཅས་
> རྣམས་ཁོ་ན། །ཞེས་གསུངས་པ་ཡིན་པའི་ཕྱིར།
>
> *dzö le, nam min gyu ni mi ge dang, ge wa sak che nam ko na, she sung pa yin pe chir*
>
> *The Treasury of Higher Knowledge* says: "A ripening cause consists only of either non-virtue or contaminated virtue."

Ko na, Only, in the verse means it is exclusively either of these two. *Le mi ge wa* means bad karma, which is *ngen drö nam min gyi gyu*, the ripening karma of bad realms. *Ge wa sak che* means virtues that were collected by *nyön mong*, mental afflictions. This latter kind of ripening karma is *den drö nam min gyi gyu*, a ripening cause of the higher realms.

Now, we can gain some understanding from this assertion. What about Buddhas and Arhats, don't they also have *suk*, form? However, their form is not *nam min gyi gyu*, a ripening cause, since it is collected neither by non-virtue nor contaminated virtue. These are very important points in the philosophy of the different tenets.

> གོང་དུ་འདོད་ན། གཟུགས་ཆོས་ཅན། དགེ་མི་དགེ་གང་རུང་གིས་
> བསྡུས་པ་མ་ཡིན་པར་ཐལ། ལུང་མ་བསྟན་ཡིན་པའི་ཕྱིར།
>
> *gong du dö na, suk chö chen, ge mi ge gang rung gi du pa ma yin par tel, lung ma ten yin pe chir*
>
> If *KA CHIK MA* accepts the above statement, *RANG LUK* responds with: Consider form, it follows that form is not comprised of either virtue or non-virtue, because it [form] is neutral [unspecified].

What does *gong du dö na*, if he agrees with the above, refer to? It refers to the previous assertion, which is: *suk chö chen, ge mi ge gang rung gi du pa yin par tel*, consider form, it follows that it consists of either virtue or non-virtue. Here KA CHIK MA agrees with that assertion. *RANG LUK*, however, refutes this by saying that form is unspecified or not designated in scripture. This refers to Buddha's designating various things as either virtuous or non-virtuous. Since Buddha didn't designate whether form is virtuous or non-virtuous, consequently it is neutral or undesignated. We often say *ge sok sum*, the three—virtue, and so forth, which refers to *ge mi ge lung ma ten*, virtuous, non-virtuous, and unspecified. You have to digest these words. *Ge wa*, Virtue, can be either *sak che kyi ge wa*, contaminated virtue, or *sak me kyi ge wa*, uncontaminated virtue. With regard to ripening cause, the kind of virtue implied is *ge wa sak che*, contaminated virtue.

གཞན་ཡང་། གཟུགས་ཆོས་ཅན། ཤེས་པ་ཡིན་པར་ཐལ།
མཚུངས་ལྡན་གྱི་རྒྱུ་ཡིན་པའི་ཕྱིར།

shen yang, suk chö chen, she pa yin par tel, tsung den gyi gyu yin pe chir

Furthermore, consider form, it would absurdly follow that form is consciousness, because it would have to be a concomitant cause [if, according to you, it must be all six causes].

Shen yang, Furthermore, is equivalent to saying "it's not over yet." *She pa* means consciousness. What is the definition of *she pa*? *Sel shing rik pa she pe tsen nyi*,[44] Clear and aware (that is, perceiving its own object clearly) is the definition of consciousness. Again, the definition of form is that which is suitable as form. What is the definition of *den min du che*, a non-associated formation? *Suk she*

---

[44] གསལ་ཞིང་རིག་པ་ཤེས་པའི་མཚན་ཉིད།

gang rung ma yin pe ngö po,[45] That causally effective thing which is neither form nor consciousness.

If something is *tsung den gyi gyu*, a concomitant cause, it must be either *sem*, a main mind, or *sem jung*, one of the mental derivatives. From this description we can understand how *suk*, form, could not be *tsung den gyi gyu*, a concomitant cause, because it would have to be consciousness, which of course it is not. *Sem dang sem jung*, Main mind and mental derivatives, are *she pa*, consciousness. *Nyi ka yin pa me, suk dang she pa shi tun mi si pa*, What is both of them [form and consciousness] doesn't exist, for it is impossible to have a combination of something that is both form and consciousness. *Tsung den gyi gyu yin na, sem sem jung gang rung yin pa*, If something is a concomitant cause, it must be either main mind or a mental derivative. Therefore, *tsung den gyi gyu yin na she pa yin pe kyap*, whatever is a concomitant cause is necessarily consciousness. This is upheld by another quotation from *The Treasury of Higher Knowledge* cited below:

> མ་ཁྱབ་ན་ཁྱབ་པ་ཡོད་པར་ཐལ། མཚུངས་ལྡན་གྱི་རྒྱུ་ལ་རྫས་སྤྱི་
> གཉིས་མགོ་སོགས་བཅད་ནས་སེམས་དང་སེམས་བྱུང་གཉིས་སུ་
> གྲངས་ངེས་པའི་ཕྱིར་ཏེ། མཚུངས་ལྡན་རྒྱུ་ནི་སེམས་དག་དང་།
> །སེམས་བྱུང་བརྟེན་མཚུངས་ཅན་རྣམས་སོ། །ཞེས་གསུངས་པའི་ཕྱིར།
>
> *ma kyap na kyap pa yö par tel, tsung den gyi gyu la dze chi nyi go sok che ne sem dang sem jung nyi su trang nge pe chir te, tsung den gyu ni sem dak dang, sem sems jung ten tsung chen nam so, she sung pe chir*
>
> If KA CHIK MA says there is no pervasion, RANG LUK responds with: It follows that there is pervasion, because a concomitant cause is only designated as being one of two kinds: a main mind or a mental derivative, which eliminates

---

[45] གཟུགས་ཤེས་གང་རུང་མ་ཡིན་པའི་དངོས་པོ་ལྡན་མིན་འདུས་བྱེད་ཀྱི་མཚན་ཉིད།

> the possibility of confusing it with anything else. As it says in *The Treasury of Higher Knowledge*: "A concomitant cause has those elements that are concomitant with the mind and its mental derivatives."

In the text above the phrase *dze chi nyi go* is used for clarification during debate to indicate that the debater has mixed up two separate things.

What is *kyap*, the pervasion? *Tsung den gyi gyu yin na, she pa yin pe kyap*, Whatever is a concomitant cause must necessarily be consciousness. *Sem dak* means consciousnesses, indicated by the pluralizer "*dak*." This is referring to the six kinds of consciousness [main minds]. *Sem jung* means the mental derivatives [secondary minds]. *Ten tsung chen nam* refers to *kye sok ga wa shi*, the four: birth, old age, and so forth mentioned previously. That is, when the six consciousnesses arise they arise together with these four qualities. It is for this reason that the subject, *suk*, form, is neither *sem*, mind, nor *sem jung*, mental derivative. Why is this cause called *tsung den*? *Tsung* means similar; *den* means having. What does it have that is similar? There are five things shared by main mind and its mental derivatives. These are known as *tsung den nam pa nga*,[46]

---

[46] མཚུངས་ལྡན་རྣམ་པ་ལྔ། རྟེན་མཚུངས་པ། དམིགས་པ་མཚུངས་པ། རྣམ་པ་མཚུངས་པ། དུས་མཚུངས་པ། རྫས་མཚུངས་པ།

The five shared factors are: common basis [sense power], common object of focus, common aspect, common time, and common substantial entity. These are described in Yongdzin Yeshe Gyaltsen's text *A Necklace for the Lucid* (***sems dang sems byung gi tshul gsal bar ston pa blo gros mgul rgyan***) as follows: "Similar basis, similar object of focus, similar aspect, similar time, and similar substance. The meaning of each of these are given individually: 1) since main mind and its mental derivatives rely upon the same sense faculty (***rten***), they have a similar basis; 2) since any object of focus of the main mind also serves as the object of focus of the mental derivatives, they have a similar object of focus (***dmigs pa***); 3) when main mind focuses on the color blue, for example, causing a blue aspect to arise, since those mental derivatives accompanying that main mind also have that blue aspect, they have a similar aspect (***rnam pa***); 4) since both main mind and its the five shared factors: *ten tsung pa, mik pa tsung pa, nam pa tsung pa, du tsung pa,* and *dze tsung pa. Tsung den* means that mind and mental derivatives share these five qualities in one mental event.

གཞན་ཡང་། གཟུགས་ཆོས་ཅན། ཉོན་མོངས་ཅན་ཡིན་པར་ཐལ།
ཀུན་འགྲོའི་རྒྱུ་ཡིན་པའི་ཕྱིར། མ་ཁྱབ་ན་ཁྱབ་པ་ཡོད་པར་ཐལ།
ཀུན་འགྲོའི་རྒྱུ་ཡིན་ན་ཉོན་མོངས་ཅན་ཡིན་པས་ཁྱབ་པའི་ཕྱིར་ཏེ།
མཛོད་ལས། ཀུན་འགྲོ་ཞེས་བྱ་ཉོན་མོངས་ཅན། །ཞེས་གསུངས་པ་
ཡིན་པའི་ཕྱིར།

shen yang, suk chö chen, nyön mong chen yin par tel, kun drö'i gyu yin pe chir, ma kyap na kyap pa yö par tel, kun drö'i gyu yin na nyön mong chen yin pe kyap pe chir te, dzö le, kun dro she ja nyön mong chen, she sung pa yin pe chir

Furthermore, consider form, it would follow [from what you assert] that it consists of mental afflictions, because it is an omnipresent cause. If *KA CHIK MA* says there is no pervasion, *RANG LUK* responds with: It follows that there is pervasion, because if something is an omnipresent cause, it must consist of mental afflictions. Also, *The Treasury of Higher Knowledge* states: "Omnipresent cause is so called [because] it consists of mental afflictions."

Shen yang means there is still more to be discussed, since the third point has to be made regarding *kun drö'i gyu*, omnipresent cause. *KA CHIK MA* responds with *ma kyap*, there is no pervasion, to

---

mental derivatives arise, abide, and cease simultaneously, they have a similar time (***dus***); and 5) since each mind is accompanied by a mental derivative having a substance of a similar class, the mental derivative "feeling," for example, they are explained as having a similar substance (***rdzas***).

the assertion: *kun drö'i gyu yin na nyön mong chen yin pe kyap*, whatever is an omnipresent cause is necessarily something that consists of mental afflictions.

Kun dro, ching wa, tra gye, and *nyön mong* are synonyms meaning mental affliction. How can we describe *kun drö'i gyu*, omnipresent cause? We can say that it consists of mental afflictions, and so it is a kind of mind. If it is mind, then it cannot be *suk*, form.

In the Abhidharma system *nyön mong chen*, those that have mental afflictions, are called *ma rik pa*, ignorance, but are neither real ignorance nor real mental afflictions. Why? Because even Arhats have them. For example, when the mother of Mogalgyipu,[47] one of Buddha's disciples, passed away, this disciple meditated very deeply in order to find out where she had taken rebirth. Although he meditated for a long time, he still couldn't determine where it was she had been reborn. So he asked Buddha, saying: "Even though I've checked for a long time, I still cannot discover where my mother has taken rebirth." Then Buddha, seeing that he wasn't having much success, himself checked and discovered that she had been reborn very far away, on the north side of one of the several million planets. Of course, that planet also has its own set of three higher and three lower realms. His mother had taken rebirth as a hell being in the hell of that very distant planet.

This example reveals how without the Buddha's help that Arhat wasn't able to perceive such a subtle occurrence since there was something blocking his perception. Nevertheless, that obstacle to his perception is not real *ma rik pa*, ignorance; that is, it is not *nyön mong*, a mental affliction, and therefore is called *nyön mong chen ma yin pe ma rik pa*, an "ignorance" that is without mental afflictions.

So when it says above: *suk chö chen, nam min gyi gyu dang tsung den gyi gyu dang, kun drö'i gyu sum re re ne yin par tel,* consider form, it follows [from what you say] that it is each of these—a ripening cause, a concomitant cause, and an omnipresent cause—you would have to answer with, *Chi chir*, No, that's not the case, since as form, it could not be a combination of these three kinds of mental causes.

---

[47] T: ***mo'u 'gal gyi bu***; S: *Maudgalyāyanaputra*

ཙ་བར་འདོད་མི་ནུས་ཏེ། ཁྱོད་དུ་གྱུར་པའི་ཉོན་མོངས་ཅན་མ་ཡིན་པ་མཐའ་ཡས་པ་ཡོད་པའི་ཕྱིར།

tsa war dö mi nu te, kyö du gyur pe nyön mong chen ma yin pa ta ye pa yö pe chir

KA CHIK MA cannot accept the root consequence, because there exist limitless forms that do not possess mental afflictions.

What is the root consequence? *Suk chö chen, nyön mong chen yin par tel,* Consider form, it follows that it consists of mental afflictions. *Dö mi nu te* means KA CHIK MA cannot say he accepts this statement. Why? Because there are many forms that do not consist of mental afflictions. *Kyö* here refers to the subject "form." As I mentioned before, since Buddhas and Arhats have form, we cannot say that their forms consist of mental afflictions.

Up to this point you have got a lot to think about already. Is it making you dizzy?

If it is *nam min gyi gyu*, a ripening cause, what should it be? *Ge wa sak che mi ge wa gang rung yin gö,* It must be either contaminated virtue or non-virtue. This means that the result of contaminated virtue is a higher realm's rebirth—as a human, a demigod, or a god. The suffering that is unique to the human realm is that they have to undergo the four kinds of suffering of birth, old age, sickness, and death. The specific suffering for the worldly gods is *chi po kye she kyi dung ngel*, the consciousness of where they will be reborn in the future after they die. They also have to experience one week of suffering of the lower gods' realm. In relative time, twenty-four hours of their time is equal to fifty years of a human being's life. One week of their time equals 350 human years. That is an unbelievably long time. When they are born, they arise through *dzö kye*, miraculous birth. This is similar to the arrival of a new guest. When they arrive everything has already been prepared for them.

Also the gods have a special *ngön she*, clairvoyance, which induces them to think: "Now I have been born in a very good, happy place. Why was I born here?" When they check with their clairvoyance they see their previous life and how they collected virtue to gain their present life. However, that thought immediately disappears and they begin doing nothing but thoroughly enjoying themselves, entertaining themselves, like some people do in the bars of New York. They don't even have to change their clothes since their garments always remain new and clean and their bodies are continuously adorned with flower garlands that retain their sweet fragrance and freshness. The gods and goddesses get together and do little else but sport and enjoy themselves the entire time they are in that realm.

Finally, for at least one week, they begin seeing signs of their imminent death. What signs are these? Their flower garlands begin to wilt and lose their fragrance and give off a foul odor, so much so that the other gods and goddesses start avoiding them and run away as soon as they see them. Naturally, this sets them to wondering: "What happened? When I came here everything was very pleasant and beautiful. But all that is fading now." They take this as a definite sign that they are about to die very soon. This is the meaning of *chi po wa*.

Their clairvoyance is such that they can check where it is they will be reborn in samsara after their death. Most of them will be reborn in the lowest hot hell because they had been spending all of their time only enjoying themselves rather than collecting any new virtue. This means that they have almost bankrupted their virtue bank account so that their virtue is almost exhausted; the only thing left is the result of their bad deeds. Soon they realize that they are about to go to a hell realm, because they begin to see the hell beings who are suffering there. They begin to reflect: "My enjoyments have almost finished. In one week I will become a hell being and have to undergo inconceivably terrible suffering." That is the gods' unique suffering.

For humans, their unique suffering is to have to be born, get sick, get old, and then die.

The unique suffering of the demigods is that they have to continually fight with the worldly gods. This fighting goes on for a long, long time, most often resulting in the demigods' defeat.

***

When *KA CHIK MA* says:

—*Gyu yin na gyu druk ka yin pe kyap*, If something is a cause it must be all six causes, what is wrong with this assertion? You can't just say "It's not true!" You have to give a reason why it's not true. If you don't have any reason to back it up, you have to say: "I swear it's wrong. It's just gotta be wrong. I don't know why, but I swear it's wrong!"

Ser na means if you say that. You should have a subject (*chö chen*) ready immediately in response to such an assertion.

—*Suk chö chen, gyu druk ka yin par tel*, Consider form, you're saying that it too is all six causes?

—*Chi chir*, No, why?

—*Gyu yin pe chir, kyap pa ke*, Because it's a cause. That's what you just asserted.

If you say *tak ma drup*, that's not true, this is like saying that *suk*, form, is not *gyu*, a cause! If you were to say *tak ma drup* on the debate ground, they would laugh and jeer at you and say: "Can you believe that? He doesn't even know that form is a cause!!"

What is *kyap pa*, the pervasion, being made? *Gyu yin na gyu druk ka yin pe kyap*, If it's a cause it must be all six causes.

—*Suk chö chen, gyu druk ka yin par tel*, Consider form, it would follow from what you assert that it is all six causes then?

—*Chi chir*, Why?

—*Gyu druk ka yin par tel, gyu yin pe chir*, It would logically follow from what you say that [form] is all those six causes, because [form] is a cause.

[Here, *KA CHIK MA* contradicts his own assertion.]

—*Kyap pa ma jung*, That does not pervade, (which expressed in full is, *suk yin na gyu druk ka yin pe ma kyap*, whatever is a cause is not necessarily all six causes).

—*Gyu yin na gyu druk ka yin pe ma kyap par tel*, If it's a cause, then it follows that it must not be all six causes?

—*Dö*, That's correct.
—*Sho*, Give me an example!
—*Suk chö chen*, Take form, for example.
—*Suk chö chen, gyu yin par tel*, Consider form, it's a cause?
—*Dö*, Yes, it is.
—*Gyu yin te*, It's a cause because...
—*Ngö po yin pe chir*, It's a causally effective thing. Why? *Gyu dang ngö po dön chik*, [Because] cause and causally effective thing are synonymous.
—*Suk chö chen, gyu yin par tel*, Consider form, it follows that it's a cause?
—*Dö*, Yes, that's right.
—*Suk chö chen, gyu druk ka ma yin par tel*, Consider form, then it's not all six causes?
—*Dö*, Yes, that's right.
—*Gyu druk ka ma yin te*, Form is not all six causes because...
—(If you have the knowledge you can respond with:) *Nam min gyi gyu yang ma yin, tsung den gyi gyu yang ma yin, kun drö'i gyu yang ma yin pe chir*, Form is neither a ripening cause, a concomitant cause, nor an omnipresent cause. We can enumerate reasons just like coaches often do on TV during football games when they say for example, "That team doesn't have the power, they don't have the determination, and they don't have the drive to win...," as a way of counting qualities. Therefore, if *suk*, form, is all of those six causes, it would certainly have to include these three kinds of causes as well.
—*Suk chö chen, nam min gyi gyu ma yin par tel*, Consider form, it follows that it is not a ripening cause?
—*Dö*, Correct.
—*Ma yin te*, It's not a ripening cause because...
—*Ge mi ge gang rung ma yin pe chir*, [Form] is neither contaminated virtue nor non-virtue. Why? If it is necessary to cite a reference to back up your statement you can quote the passage from *The Treasury of Higher Knowledge* given before.

What is the purpose of citing a quotation? If the person accepts Acharya Vasubandhu as a great scholar and second Buddha, he has to accept his quotations as well. That is the purpose. After citing a passage from such a text, your opponent will think: "Oh, now I believe what you're saying, since you gave me that quotation."

—*Suk chö chen, tsung den gyi gyu ma yin par tel*, Consider form, so it follows that it is not a concomitant cause?
—*Dö*, Yes.
—*Ma yin te,* It's not a concomitant cause because...
—*Sem sem jung gang rung ma yin pe chir*, Form is neither main mind nor a mental derivative.
—*Suk chö chen, kun drö'i gyu ma yin par tel*, Consider form, it also follows that it is not an omnipresent cause?
—*Dö*, Yes, that's right.
—*Ma yin te*, It's not an omnipresent cause because...
—*Nyön mong ma yin pe chir*, It is not a mental affliction. (This means that if it is *nyön mong*, a mental affliction, it must be mental. If it is mental it cannot be form. Form and mind are completely different. If it is form, it cannot be mind; if it is mind it cannot be form.)

You have to learn the debate pattern "*der tel, de chir*, it follows that that is the case, because of such and such." Once you learn the system, it will be very good. You should also know that saying *yin pa tak ma drup*, it's not the case that it is..., is the same as saying *ma yin*, it is not..., and that saying, *ma yin pa tak ma drup*, it is not the case that it is not..., is the same as saying *yin*, it is.... Logicians have to follow the logic system. If someone doesn't follow that system, they will say, "Go away." That is the reason it says in the text, "You cannot say you accept such a statement." This is not arbitrary, since the debaters are following specific rules to comply with the established debate system.

You have to learn the philosophy of logic this way. Its system is completely different from that of other fields of study. If you learn this system it will become very easy for you to read and understand other Dharma texts. If you finish this *Compendium of Debates* (*Dura*), it will make it easier to understand the higher school systems, which use this system of *gak shak pong sum*, refuting others' views, positing our own views, and dispelling further doubts, like this one.

Now, we have just completed one *ka chik ma*, the longest one so far. You should try your best to memorize it so that you can repeat it automatically without stumbling or hesitating.

OUR OWN SYSTEM

RANG LUK

conditions

kyen

གཉིས་པ་རྐྱེན་འཆད་པ་ལ། མཚན་ཉིད་དང་དབྱེ་བ་གཉིས། དང་པོ་ནི། གྲོགས་བྱེད་པ། རྐྱེན་གྱི་མཚན་ཉིད། གཉིས་པ་དེ་ལ་དབྱེ་ན། རྒྱུ་རྐྱེན། དམིགས་རྐྱེན། བདག་རྐྱེན། དེ་མ་ཐག་རྐྱེན་དང་བཞི། དང་པོ་ནི། རྐྱེན་དང་དོན་གཅིག གཉིས་པ་ནི། སྔོན་འཛིན་མངོན་སུམ་སྔོན་པོའི་རྣམ་ལྡན་དུ་གཙོ་བོར་དངོས་སུ་སྐྱེད་བྱེད། སྔོན་འཛིན་མངོན་སུམ་གྱི་དམིགས་རྐྱེན་གྱི་མཚན་ཉིད། ཡང་ན། སྔོན་འཛིན་མངོན་སུམ་རང་གི་རྣམ་ལྡན་དུ་གཙོ་བོར་དངོས་སུ་སྐྱེད་བྱེད། རང་ཉིད་སྔོན་འཛིན་མངོན་སུམ་གྱི་དམིགས་རྐྱེན་གྱི་མཚན་ཉིད། མཚན་གཞི་ནི། སྔོན་པོ་ལྟ་བུ། མདོར་ན། སྔོན་པོ་དང་ཡུལ་དུས་རང་བཞིན་གང་ལ་ལྟོས་ཏེ། གྲུབ་བདེ་རྫས་གཅིག་ཡིན་ན། སྔོན་འཛིན་མངོན་སུམ་གྱི་དམིགས་རྐྱེན་ཡིན་པས་ཁྱབ། གསུམ་པ་ནི། སྔོན་འཛིན་མངོན་སུམ་རང་དབང་དུ་གཙོ་བོར་དངོས་སུ་སྐྱེད་བྱེད། སྔོན་འཛིན་མངོན་སུམ་གྱི་བདག་རྐྱེན་གྱི་མཚན་ཉིད། མཚན་གཞི་ནི། སྔོན་འཛིན་དབང་པོའི་མངོན་སུམ་གྱི་ཐུན་མོང་མ་

ཡིན་པའི་བདག་རྐྱེན་དུ་གྱུར་པའི་མིག་དབང་དང་། དེའི་ཐུན་མོང་བའི་བདག་རྐྱེན་དུ་གྱུར་པའི་ཡིད་དབང་ལྟ་བུ།

nyi pa kyen che pa la, tsen nyi dang ye wa nyi, dang po ni, trok che pa, kyen gyi tsen nyi, nyi pa de la ye na, gyu kyen, mik kyen, dak kyen, de ma tak kyen dang shi, dang po ni, kyen dang dön chik, nyi pa ni, ngön dzin ngön sum ngön pö nam den du tso wor ngö su kye che, ngön dzin ngön sum gyi mik kyen gyi tsen nyi, yang na, ngön dzin ngön sum rang gi nam den du tso wor ngö su kye che, rang nyi ngön dzin ngön sum gyi mik kyen gyi tsen nyi, tsen shi ni, ngön po ta bu, dor na, ngön po dang yul du rang shin gang la tö te, drup de dze chik yin na, ngön dzin ngön sum gyi mik kyen yin pe kyap, sum pa ni, ngön dzin ngön sum rang wang du tso wor ngö su kye che, ngön dzin ngön sum gyi dak kyen gyi tsen nyi, tsen shi ni, ngön dzin wang pö ngön sum gyi tun mong ma yin pe dak kyen du gyur pe mik wang dang, de tun mong we dak kyen du gyur pe yi wang ta bu

The second section, regarding an explanation of conditions. This has two parts: its definitions and classifications. The first: the definition of a condition is that which acts as a helper. When conditions are classified, there are four kinds: causal condition, object condition, governing condition, and immediately preceding condition. First, causal condition and condition are synonymous. Second, the definition of an object condition of a direct perception perceiving blue is that which is the principal direct producer of a direct perception perceiving blue in the aspect of blue. Additionally, the definition of something that is an object condition of a direct perception perceiving blue is that which is the principal direct producer of a direct perception perceiving blue in its aspect. An example is the color blue. Briefly, if something is the same as blue in terms of its establishment and abiding, in relation to object, time, and nature, it must necessarily be the object condition of a direct perception perceiving blue. Third, the definition of a governing condition of a direct

> perception perceiving blue is that principal direct producer [acting] as a sense power for a direct perception perceiving blue. Examples are the eye sense power that becomes the unique governing condition of a direct sense consciousness perceiving blue and the mental sense power that becomes the common governing condition of that consciousness. [The fourth follows.]

EXAMPLES OF *KYEN*, CONDITIONS, for a sprout are *sa, chu, me, lung*, earth, water, fire, air, [the four great elements], whereas a seed is its *nyer len gyi gyu*, main cause.

Ngön[48] *dzin mik she* means an eye consciousness that perceives the color blue. That blue color is *mik kyen*, an object condition, or unique cause of that eye consciousness perceiving blue. When you look here at this paper you see a white color; that is not *ngön dzin mik she*, an eye consciousness perceiving blue. What kind of perception is it then? It is *kar pö nam pa chen*, an eye consciousness perceiving a white color. *Nam pa* means aspect or perception. *Nam den* means perceiving *as* or having that aspect. Color is the unique *mik kyen*, object condition, for an eye consciousness.

Ngön dzin ngön[49] *sum* means a direct perception apprehending blue. Your eye consciousness, in this case, is *ngön dzin ngön sum*, a direct perceiver perceiving blue. What is its perception? It is *ngön pö nam pa*, the aspect of blue or perceiving *as* blue, and as no other color. Nevertheless, when your focus changes, you have different *mik kyen*, object conditions, which in turn produce different eye consciousnesses. *Tso wor* means principally, referring to the principal cause, which is that blue color.

Ngön dzin mik she, An eye consciousness apprehending blue, and *ngön por nang we mik she*, an eye consciousness to which something appears as blue, are different. For example, if someone has a wind ailment whereby that person's air element is defective in some way, this may create faulty vision such that things appear to that person as blue to their eye consciousness; for example, they may see snowy mountains as blue [when the common healthy eye sees them as

---

48 ***sngon***; blue

49 ***mngon***; direct

white]. Such a consciousness is not *ngön dzin mik she*, an eye consciousness apprehending blue, but rather *trul she*, a mistaken consciousness. Why? *Ngön por nang wa gang shik ngön po ma yin pe chir*, Because it is something that *appears* as blue, not something that *is* blue. This implies that what one perceives and the object perceived are different.

Ngön dzin ngön sum ngön pö nam den du tso wor ngö su kye che ngön dzin ngön sum gyi mik kyen gyi tsen nyi, The definition of an object condition of a direct perception apprehending blue is that which is the principal direct producer of a direct perception perceiving blue in the aspect of blue. *Ngön sum* means perceiving its object directly. *Ngön pö nam den du* means perceiving its object as having the aspect of blue, and not red or white, for instance. Why do we perceive the color blue? Because the object is blue. The color blue produces a blue perception in the eye consciousness. *Tso wor ngö su kye che*, its principal direct producer, is *mik kyen*, that object condition, which is the color blue; *ngö su* means directly; *kye che* means produces. From this explanation we can understand that whenever the object changes the eye consciousness also changes accordingly.

The definition is expressed twice. The first one pertains to the subject; the second, to the object. The second one is *ngön dzin ngön sum rang gi nam den du tso wor ngö su kye che rang nyi ngön sum gyi mik kyen gyi tsen nyi*, the definition of an object condition directly apprehending blue is that which principally produces the direct apprehension of blue in its aspect. For example, a blue color is *mik kyen*, the object condition, of *ngön dzin mik she*, the eye consciousness apprehending blue. Why does this occur? Because the color blue produces this consciousness. What is the main function of an object condition? To produce its own subject or mind. What is *tsen shi*, the illustration, that is given here for an object condition? *Ngön po*, The color blue. *Ta bu* means like.

Ngön po dang yul du rang shin gang la tö te drup de dze chik yin na ngön dzin ngön sum gyi mik kyen yin pe kyap, If something is one substantial entity with blue in its establishment and abiding, in relation to object, time, and nature, it must necessarily be the object condition of a direct perception apprehending blue. *Drup de dze chik,*[50] One substantial entity of establishment and abiding, is an expression unique to the field of logic. Let me give you an example of what this means. Look over there at the blanket on my bed. When looking over there, you see a specific color at a specific time in a specific place. When you focus on something else you are also changing *mik kyen*, the object condition. Therefore, the color blue is *drub de dze chik*, one substantial entity in its establishment and abiding; these qualities are one with the object condition of the eye consciousness apprehending blue.

Rang shin, Nature, here is referring to that blue color's nature. *Gang la tö te* means relying on them, that is, on the color, the time, and the location, all of the qualities that turn into *mik kyen*, the object condition, of *ngön dzin mik she*, the eye consciousness apprehending blue.

Now *dak kyen*, governing condition, refers to the six sense powers or faculties: eye sense power, ear sense power, nose sense power, tongue sense power, body sense power, and mental sense power. They are called *dak pö kyen*, sense powers as conditions, implying that these sense powers have the power to produce the sense consciousnesses. *Wang po* means power. *Mik gi wang po*, Eye sense power, is *dak kyen*, the governing condition, for *mik kyi nam she*, the eye sense consciousness. The external color blue, for example, is *mik kyen*, the object condition, for that sense consciousness. The text defines a governing condition as follows: *ngön dzin ngön sum rang wang du tso wor ngö su kye che ngön dzin ngön sum gyi dak kyen gyi tsen nyi*, the definition of the governing condition for a direct apprehension of blue is what principally produces through its own power the direct perception of blue. This means it possesses the power to produce a consciousness. Eye consciousness is related to the sense power. The eye sense power is related to the eye organ or eyeball. If you hurt the eyeball, it will automatically hurt your eye sense power as well as your eye sense consciousness.

Tsen shi ni, ngön dzin wang pö ngön sum gyi tun mong ma yin pe dak kyen du gyur pe mik wang dang de'i tun mong we dak kyen du

---

[50] སྒྲུབ་བདེ་རྫས་གཅིག་

gyur pe yi wang ta bu, An illustration is, for instance, an eye sense power that becomes the unique governing condition of a direct sense power apprehending blue as well as a mental sense power that becomes the common governing condition.

How many *ngön sum*, direct (sense powers), are there? There are six. The first five are *wang pö ngön sum*, direct sense powers, and the sixth is *yi kyi ngön sum*, direct mental "sense" power. The first five unique sense powers are form or physical; the sixth one is mental. What do you see here? A blue color. Now, what did you see just now? Blue. The recollection of the perception of blue made possible by *de ma tak kyen*, an immediately preceding condition, becomes *yi wang*, the mental sense power, for the mind consciousness.

Even though you are looking at the color blue, you are still producing *yi wang*, a mental sense power. How do you know that is the case? You may be comparing the look of the blue now with the way you remember it a moment ago with respect to the changing light, for instance. You might think, "Now it's more clear or darker," and so forth. Once the first consciousness has disappeared, as a result it produces *yi kyi nam she*, the mind consciousness.

Yi wang, A mental sense power, occurs just upon the disappearance of any of the six consciousnesses. That is the meaning of the root text that says: *druk po de ma tak pa yi, nam she gang yin te yi do*, any of the six consciousnesses acts as the immediately preceding condition for the mental sense power.

བཞི་པ་ནི། སྔོན་འཛིན་མངོན་སུམ་མྱོང་བ་གསལ་རིག་ཙམ་དུ་གཙོ་བོར་དངོས་སུ་སྐྱེད་བྱེད་ཀྱི་རིག་པ། སྔོན་འཛིན་མངོན་སུམ་གྱི་དེ་མ་ཐག་རྐྱེན་གྱི་མཚན་ཉིད། མཚན་གཞི་ནི། སྔོན་འཛིན་མངོན་སུམ་གྱི་སྔ་ལོགས་དེ་མ་ཐག་ཏུ་བྱུང་བའི་སྔོན་པོ་ཡིད་ལ་བྱེད་པའི་ཤེས་པ་ལྟ་བུ།

shi pa ni ngön dzin ngön sum nyong wa sel rik tsam du tso wor ngö su kye che kyi rik pa, ngön dzin ngön sum gyi de ma tak kyen gyi tsen nyi, tsen shi ni, ngön dzin ngö sum gyi nga lok de ma tak tu jung we ngön po yi la che pe she pa ta bu

> The fourth, the definition of an immediately preceding condition of a direct [sense] perception perceiving blue is the principal direct producer as just clear mind experiencing that direct perception perceiving blue. An example of this kind of condition is a consciousness that mentally engages a blue color that arises immediately before the direct perception [by that eye consciousness] apprehending blue.

Nyong wa, Experiencing, means just producing it as it feels, like a memory (*dren pa*), which occurs just before that consciousness perceives blue. Since *ngön dzin mik she*, eye consciousness apprehending blue, is *ngö po*, a causally effective thing, it changes with each fingersnap, with each passing moment. The first moment of consciousness turns into *de ma tak kyen*, the immediately preceding condition, for the second moment of consciousness of that object; the second one becomes *de ma tak kyen*, the immediately preceding condition, for the third one, and so on. *De ma tak* means just immediately before, whereas *nga lok su jung wa*, also meaning before, can be long before and not necessarily immediately before.

> མདོར་ན། དབང་ཤེས་ཡིན་ན། ཁྱོད་ཀྱི་རྐྱེན་གསུམ་ག་ཡོད་པས་ཁྱབ།
> ཤེས་པ་ཡིན་ན། ཁྱོད་ཀྱི་དེ་མ་ཐག་རྐྱེན་དང་། ཁྱོད་ཀྱི་བདག་རྐྱེན་
> གཉིས་ཀ་ཡོད་པས་ཁྱབ། དབང་ཤེས་ཡིན་ན། ཁྱོད་ཀྱི་ཐུན་མོང་མ་
> ཡིན་པའི་བདག་རྐྱེན་དུ་གྱུར་པའི་དབང་པོ་གཟུགས་ཅན་པ་ཡོད་པས་
> ཁྱབ་སྟེ།
>
> *dor na, wang she yin na, kyö kyi kyen sum ga yö pe kyap, she pa yin na, kyö kyi de ma tak kyen dang, kyö kyi dak kyen nyi ka yö pe kyap, wang she yin na, kyö kyi tun mong ma yin pe dak kyen du gyur pe wang po suk chen pa yö pe kyap te*

In summary, whatever is a sense consciousness must have all three conditions. Whatever is a consciousness must have both an immediately preceding condition and a governing condition. Whatever is a sense consciousness must have a physical sense power that becomes the unique governing condition for that consciousness.

Dor na means briefly, something like "what's the bottom line?" indicating that here a concise explanation will be given.

Whatever is a sense consciousness must have three kinds of conditions: *mik kyen*, object condition, *dak kyen*, governing condition, and *de ma tak kyen*, an immediately preceding condition. Now, when it says above, *she pa yin na kyö kyi de ma tak kyen dang, kyö kyi dak kyen nyi ka yö pe kyap*, whatever is a consciousness must have both an immediately preceding condition and a governing condition, which condition is being excluded? *Mik kyen*, Object condition. *Mik kyen* is a direct object. It is not necessary for every consciousness to have a direct object. Now, when it says, "Whatever is a sense consciousness must have a physical sense power that becomes the unique governing condition for that consciousness," what is being excluded? *Yi kyi nam she*, Mind consciousness, the sixth of the six consciousnesses. Why? Because it doesn't have *tun mong ma yin pe dak kyen du gyur pe wang po suk chen pa*, a unique physical sense power that becomes its object condition, but instead has a mental power that occurs immediately after any of those consciousnesses.

ཚད་མ་མདོ་ལས། དེ་ཡི་ཐ་སྙད་དབང་པོས་བྱས། །ཞེས་གསུངས་
པའི་ཕྱིར། ཡིད་ཤེས་ཡིན་ན། ཁྱོད་ཀྱི་ཐུན་མོང་མ་ཡིན་པའི་བདག་
རྐྱེན་དུ་གྱུར་པའི་ཡིད་དབང་ཡོད་པས་ཁྱབ་སྟེ། ཚད་མ་མདོ་ལས།
གཟུགས་ཤེས་པ་ནི་རྣམ་གཉིས་ཏེ། མིག་དང་ཡིད་ལ་བརྟེན་པའོ།

།ཞེས་པའི་ནང་ཚན་དུ་གྱུར་པའི་ཡིད་ལ་བརྟེན་པའོ་ཞེས་པའི་གཞུང་དོན་གྲུབ་པའི་ཕྱིར།

tse ma do le, de yi ta nye wang pö che, she sung pe chir, yi she yin na, kyö kyi tun mong ma yin pe dak kyen du gyur pe yi wang yö pe kyap te, tse ma do le, suk she pa ni nam nyi te, mik dang yi la ten pa'o, she pe nang tsen du gyur pe yi la ten pa'o she pe shung dön drup pe chir

In *Compendium of Valid Cognition*[51] by Acharya Dignāga, it says: "'Sense power' is a term that is applied to that [mental sense power]." If something is a mind consciousness it must have a mind sense power that becomes its unique governing condition. Again, from the same text: "For a consciousness [apprehending] form there are two distinct [powers upon which that consciousness relies]: the first is an eye sense power, the second is a mind sense power." This is the meaning of the phrase that says, "Relying on the mind."

[51] T: ***tshad ma kun las btus pa***; S: *Pramāṇasamuccaya*

Debate Five

cause and effect
gyu(n) dre

ཁ་ཅིག་ན་རེ། དངོས་པོ་ཡིན་ན་ཁྱོད་ཀྱི་རྐྱེན་བཞི་ག་ཡོད་པས་ཁྱབ་ཟེར་ན། གཟུགས་ཆོས་ཅན། དེར་ཐལ། དེའི་ཕྱིར། ཁྱབ་པ་ཁས། འདོད་ན། གཟུགས་ཆོས་ཅན། ཁྱོད་ཀྱི་དམིགས་རྐྱེན་དང་། དེ་མ་ཐག་རྐྱེན་གཉིས་རེ་རེ་ནས་ཡོད་པར་ཐལ། ཁྱོད་ཀྱི་རྐྱེན་བཞི་ག་ཡོད་པའི་ཕྱིར། འདོད་ན། གཟུགས་ཆོས་ཅན། ཁྱོད་ཀྱི་དམིགས་རྐྱེན་དང་། དེ་མ་ཐག་རྐྱེན་གཉིས་རེ་རེ་ནས་མེད་པར་ཐལ། ཁྱོད་ཀྱི་དམིགས་རྐྱེན་མེད་པ་གང་ཞིག དེ་མ་ཐག་རྐྱེན་མེད་པའི་ཕྱིར། རྟགས་རེ་རེ་ནས་གྲུབ་སྟེ། ཁྱོད་བེམ་པོ་ཡིན་པའི་ཕྱིར།

ka chik na re, ngö po yin na kyö kyi kyen shi ga yö pe kyap ser na, suk chö chen, der tel, de chir, kyap pa ke, dö na, suk chö chen, kyö kyi mik kyen dang, de ma tak kyen nyi re re ne yö par tel, kyö kyi kyen shi ga yö pe chir, dö na, suk chö chen, kyö kyi mik kyen dang, de ma tak kyen nyi re re ne me par tel, kyö kyi mik kyen me pa gang shik, de ma tak kyen me pe chir, tak re re ne drup te, kyö bem po yin pe chir

If *KA CHIK MA* says, If something is a causally effective thing it must have all four conditions, *RANG LUK* responds with, Consider form, it would follow that it has all four conditions, because it is a causally effective thing, since that is what you asserted. If *KA CHIK MA* accepts the consequence, *RANG LUK* replies with, Consider form, it logically follows that it would have to have an object condition and an immediately preceding condition, because [according to you it is supposed] to have all four conditions. If KA CHIK MA agrees with this consequence, RANG LUK responds with, Consider form, it follows that it does not have either an object condition or an immediately preceding condition, because form does not have either an object condition or an immediately preceding condition. Both of these statements are true, because form is matter [and not consciousness].

IN A PREVIOUS DEBATE, *GYU DRUK KA*, all six causes, was used in an assertion made about form. Here, similarly, *kyen shi ka*, all four conditions, is being posited about a causally effective thing.

What does *kyap pa ke*, you asserted that pervasion, refer to above? It refers to the assertion, *ngö po yin na, kyö kyi kyen shi ka yö pe kyap*, whatever is a causally effective thing must have all four conditions.

If KA CHIK MA agrees with the consequence, which expressed in full is *suk chö chen, kyö kyi kyen shi ka yö*, consider form, it has all four conditions, RANG LUK responds with, *suk chö chen, kyö kyi mik kyen dang de ma tak kyen nyi re re ne yö par tel, kyö kyi kyen shi ka yö pe chir*, consider form, it follows that it has each of those two conditions, i.e., object condition and immediately preceding condition, because [according to you, as a causally effective thing] it [form] must have those four conditions.

Again, *suk chö chen, kyö kyi mik kyen dang de ma tak kyen nyi re re ne yö par dö na*, If he accepts this consequence that form has an object condition and an immediately preceding condition, RANG LUK responds with, *suk chö chen, kyö kyi mik kyen dang de ma tak kyen nyi re re ne me par tel, kyö kyi mik kyen me pa gang shik, de ma tak kyen me pe chir*, consider form, it does not have either an object condition or an immediately preceding condition.

If KA CHIK MA replies with, *tak ma drup*, that's not the case, to each part of this statement (divided by *gang shik*), RANG LUK responds with, *tak re re ne drup te*, each of these statements individually is in fact true. Why are they true? Here RANG LUK negates the previous assertion in two parts. *Tak re re ne drup te* means there are two reasons given, one for each part. The first you find by going to what precedes *gang shik* in the statement above, which is: *suk chö chen, kyö kyi mik kyen me par tel, kyö pem po yin pe chir*, consider form, it has no object condition, because form is matter. And *suk chö chen, kyö kyi de ma tak kyen me par tel, kyö pem po yin pe chir*, consider form, it has no immediately preceding condition, because form is matter. This implies that only what is mental can have an object condition or an immediately preceding condition, whereas form, not being mental, cannot.

In some *yik cha*, monastic debate manuals, they say that *suk*, form, and *pem po*, matter, are *dön chik*, synonymous. *Dul du drup pa pem pö tsen nyi*,[52] The definition of matter is that which is atomically established. This definition is accepted by the lower tenet systems; however, for the higher schools, there is some debate about it. When debating, sometimes it is very difficult to accept *pem po*, matter, as equivalent to *suk*, form. For example, *sang gye gyi sa*, the Buddha's status, has *suk ku*, form body, but this cannot be considered *pem po*, matter.

De ma tak kyen, An immediately preceding condition, only refers to what is mental and arises immediately after any of the sense consciousnesses. Any *wang she*, sense consciousness, can serve as *de ma tak kyen*, the immediately preceding condition, for *yi kyi nam she*, mind consciousness. *De ma tak* means after sense consciousness and immediately preceding mind consciousness; *kyen*, condition, means it occurs as a condition for that mind consciousness such that it arises just prior to it. Additionally, an immediately preceding condition is itself *dak kyen*, a governing condition, for mind consciousness.

Dak kyen, The governing condition, or sense power, for eye consciousness is subtle form. Eye consciousness itself is *de ma tak kyen*, the immediately preceding condition, for the first moment of *yi kyi nam par she pa*, mind consciousness. For example: "I saw something and I remember it." "When did you see it?" "I saw it on the table just now." Seeing something is eye consciousness;

---

[52] རྡུལ་དུ་གྲུབ་པ་བེམ་པོའི་མཚན་ཉིད།

remembering something is mind consciousness. The unique governing condition of the eye consciousness is *mik gi wang po*, a [physical] eye sense power. An example of *mik kyen*, an object condition, is represented by the colors and shapes that you see. That eye consciousness is *de ma tak kyen*, the immediately preceding condition, for the memory of what you just saw, producing the mind consciousness. The object appears to the mind consciousness through *yi kyi wang po*, the mental sense power. Each moment consists of a different sense power [or rather, different moments of that sense power]. *Yul wang nam she sum*, The object, sense power, and consciousness, all three come together to produce the experience of an object.

Rang gi tun mong ma yin pe dak kyen mik wang suk chen pa la ten ne kye pe nam she mik gi nam she kyi tsen nyi,[53] The definition of eye consciousness is a consciousness that is generated in reliance upon a physical eye sense power, its unique governing condition. *Per na, ngön dzin mik she ta bu*, For example an eye consciousness perceiving blue. Each one of the sense powers is unique to each of those sense consciousnesses. But *yi wang*, mental sense power, is mental and not *suk chen pa*, physical.

Mik wang, Eye sense power, produces an eye consciousness. That eye consciousness itself subsequently becomes *yi wang*, a mind power, and not a sense power, in that it has no form. Again, in succession, first you have an eye sense power, then an eye consciousness, then a mind consciousness. When the eye sense power perceives a blue color, it produces *ngön dzin mik she*, eye consciousness perceiving blue. That eye consciousness perceiving blue produces *ngön dzin yi kyi she pa*, mind consciousness apprehending blue. *Ngön po*, A blue color, is *mik kyen*, the object condition. *Mik kyi nam she*, Eye sense consciousness, itself turns into *yi wang*, the mind power, by producing *dren she*, a recollection consciousness. This is what is described in *The Treasury of Higher Knowledge* as:

---

[53] རང་གི་ཐུན་མོང་མ་ཡིན་པའི་བདག་རྐྱེན་དམིགས་དབང་གཟུགས་ཅན་པ་ལ་བརྟེན་ནས་སྐྱེས་པའི་རྣམ་ཤེས་མིག་གི་རྣམ་ཤེས་ཀྱི་མཚན་ཉིད།

> Any of the six consciousnesses are the immediately preceding condition for the mental faculty.

Any of the six consciousnesses becomes *yi wang*, the mental faculty, for *yi kyi nam par she pa*, mind consciousness. *Mik wang* means eye sense power. The eye sense consciousness relies upon the eye sense power. The eye sense power relies upon the main body. Generally, *yul wang nam she sum*, the three—an object, a sense power, and consciousness—need to be present for there to be any experience of an object.

Ngön pö nam pa means perceiving as a blue color. How many causes does *ngön dzin mik she*, eye consciousness perceiving blue, have? Three: *mik kyen*, object condition, *dak kyen*, governing condition, and *de ma tak kyen*, immediately preceding condition. What is *mik kyen*, the object condition, in this case? The color blue. What is *de ma tak kyen*, the immediately preceding condition? It consists of both *sem*, main mind, and *sem jung*, the mental derivatives. *Mik kyen*, The object condition, is external form; *mik wang*, the eye sense power, is internal form; *tsung pa de ma tak kyen*, those immediately preceding conditions associated with mind, are mental.

In the term "*dak kyen*," governing condition, *dak* means owner, indicating that the owner of the sense power (which is internal form) and the owner of that consciousness are the same. The main function of the sense power, in this case, is to produce eye consciousness, which is its result. What kind of eye consciousness? There can be many different kinds, depending upon the external *mik kyen*, object condition. Thus, a blue color is *mik kyen*, the object condition, for *ngön dzin mik she*, eye consciousness perceiving blue. The sense power that holds that blue is *tun mong ma yin pe dak kyen*, the unique governing condition, for that eye consciousness. The main producer of *ngön dzin mik she*, eye consciousness perceiving blue, is that blue color, which is its object. Its main producer is not white, or a mixture of many colors, but blue. The same is true for the other consciousnesses as well.

Is *ngön dzin wang po*, the sense power apprehending a blue color, *tun mong ma yin pe dak kyen*, the unique governing condition, for *ngön dzin mik she*, an eye consciousness perceiving blue? Yes.

However, that sense power itself is not *tso wo kye che*, the prinicipal producer, of that consciousness in the aspect of blue. The blue color, in this case, as *mik kyen*, an object condition, is the principal producer of that consciousness.

What is *mik kyen*, the object condition, of *ngön dzin mik she*, an eye consciousness apprehending blue? A blue color. *Mik kyen*, Object condition, means *nam den du tso wor kye pa*, the principal cause [of the eye consciousness perceiving blue] in that aspect of blue. That *wang po*, sense power, which is *dak kyen*, the governing condition, has the function of producing *wang she*, sense consciousness. Nevertheless, that sense power itself is not the principal cause for producing *ngön dzin mik she*, an eye consciousness apprehending blue.

Each *mik kyen*, object condition, and *dak kyen*, governing condition, has a unique ability. If *wang po*, the sense power, is present, its unique ability can produce *wang she*, sense consciousness, with each kind of sense consciousness being dependent upon its unique object. Generally speaking, if it is consciousness, it must be either *wang she*, sense consciousness, or *yi she*, mind consciousness.

Is it getting a little bit better? Is this crystal clear now, or still a little bit cloudy? Not very *kyir ra mur kyi*, making you more dizzy? In order to catch the meaning, you have to read the sentences carefully to grasp the continuity of the argument. Later you will become used to the style and eventually become self-sufficient at reading and understanding this material.

The flow of the previous debate can be outlined as follows:

> *Ngö po yin na, kyö kyi kyen shi ka yö pe kyap ser na*, If someone says, Whatever is a causally effective thing must have those four conditions, [what would you respond?]
>
> *Suk chö chen, kyö kyi kyen shi ka yö par tel, ngö po yin pe chir, kyap pa ke*, Consider form, it would follow that it has those four conditions, because it is a causally effective thing. That is what you asserted.

Suk chö chen, kyö kyi kyen shi ka yö par do na, If [the other party] agrees with the consequence that form has those four conditions, you might reply with: *Suk chö chen, kyö kyi mik kyen dang, de ma tak kyen nyi re re ne yö par tel, kyö kyi kyen shi ka yö pe chir*, Consider form, so you're telling me that it has both an object condition and an immediately preceding condition, because [according to you] it [is supposed to have] those four conditions?

Suk chö chen, kyö kyi mik kyen dang, de ma tak kyen nyi re re ne yö par do na, If [the other party] agrees with this as well...(you counter this with): *Suk chö chen, kyö kyi mik kyen dang, de ma tak kyen nyi re re ne me par tel*, Consider form, it follows that it has neither an object condition nor an immediately preceding condition. [The voice goes up to show that it is a statement and not a question. When the inflection of the voice drops, this signifies a question of non-belief possibly colored with some sarcasm. On the debate ground, if the inflection of your voice drops, the opponent has to answer; when the inflection of your voice goes up, the opponent has to wait to hear what you have to say, while you make a statement and not a question]. *Kyö kyi mik kyen me pa gang shik de ma tak kyen me pe chir*, First, [form] doesn't have an object condition, and second, it doesn't have an immediately preceding condition. *Tak re re ne drup te*, Each of these is true because... *Suk chö chen, kyö kyi mik kyen me te, kyö pem po yin pe chir*, Consider form, it doesn't have an object condition, because it is matter [and not mind]. *Suk chö chen, kyö kyi de ma tak kyen me te, kyö pem po yin pe chir*, Consider form, it doesn't have an immediately preceding condition, because it is matter [and not mind].

If you don't learn this way, repeating and filling in each part of the debate pattern, you won't be able to learn nicely. If you have thoroughly digested the previous debate, you can exchange the *chö chen*, subject of debate, and use this same pattern with any other subject.

DEBATE

SIX

cause and effect
gyu(n) dre

ཁ་ཅིག་ན་རེ། བེམ་པོ་ཡིན་ན་ཁྱོད་ཀྱི་དམིགས་རྐྱེན་དང་དེ་མ་ཐག་རྐྱེན་གཉིས་རེ་རེ་ནས་མེད་པས་མ་ཁྱབ་པར་ཐལ། བུམ་པའི་དེ་མ་ཐག་རྐྱེན་ཡོད་པའི་ཕྱིར། མ་གྲུབ་ན། བུམ་པའི་དེ་མ་ཐག་རྐྱེན་ཡོད་པར་ཐལ། བུམ་པའི་དངོས་ཀྱི་ཉེར་ལེན་དེ་དེ་ཡིན་པའི་ཕྱིར། མ་གྲུབ་ན། བུམ་པའི་དངོས་ཀྱི་ཉེར་ལེན་ཆོས་ཅན། བུམ་པའི་དེ་མ་ཐག་རྐྱེན་ཡིན་པར་ཐལ། བུམ་པའི་རྐྱེན་ཡིན་པ་གང་ཞིག བུམ་པའི་སྔ་རོལ་དེ་མ་ཐག་ཏུ་བྱུང་བ་ཡིན་པའི་ཕྱིར་ཟེར་ན་མ་ཁྱབ། བུམ་པ་ཆོས་ཅན། ཁྱོད་ཀྱི་དེ་མ་ཐག་རྐྱེན་མེད་པར་ཐལ། ཁྱོད་ཀྱི་མཚུངས་པ་དེ་མ་ཐག་རྐྱེན་མེད་པའི་ཕྱིར། མ་གྲུབ་ན། བུམ་པ་ཆོས་ཅན། ཁྱོད་ཀྱི་མཚུངས་པ་དེ་མ་ཐག་རྐྱེན་མེད་པར་ཐལ། ཁྱོད་གསལ་རིག་ཡིན་པར་བསྐྱེད་པའི་རྐྱེན་མེད་པའི་ཕྱིར། མ་ཁྱབ་ན་ཁྱབ་པ་ཡོད་པར་ཐལ། ཆོས་དེའི་མཚུངས་པ་དེ་མ་ཐག་རྐྱེན་ཞེས་པའི་མཚུངས་པའི་དོན་ནི་རྐྱེན་དེ་དང་འབྲས་བུ་དེ་གཉིས་གསལ་རིག་མཚུངས་པ་ལ་བྱེད་དགོས་ཤིང་། དེ་མ་ཐག་རྐྱེན་ཞེས་པ་རྐྱེན་དེས་འབྲས་བུ་དེ་གསལ་རིག་ཏུ་སྐྱེད་བྱེད་

ལ་བྱེད་པ་གང་ཞིག ཤེས་པ་མ་ཡིན་པ་ལ་དེ་མི་འཐད་པ་ཡིན་པའི་ཕྱིར།

ka chik na re, pem po yin na kyö kyi mik kyen dang de ma tak kyen nyi re re ne me pe ma kyap par tel, bum pe de ma tak kyen yö pe chir, ma drup na, bum pe de ma tak kyen yö par tel, bum pe ngö kyi nyer len de de yin pe chir, ma drup na, bum pe ngö kyi nyer len chö chen, bum pe de ma tak kyen yin par tel, bum pe kyen yin pa gang shik, bum pe nga röl de ma tak tu jung wa yin pe chir ser na ma kyap, bum pa chö chen, kyö kyi de ma tak kyen me par tel, kyö kyi tsung pa de ma tak kyen me pe chir, ma drup na, bum pa chö chen, kyö kyi tsung pa de ma tak kyen me par tel, kyö sel rik yin par kye pe kyen me pe chir, ma kyap na, kyap pa yö par tel, chö de tsung pa de ma tak kyen she pe tsung pe dön ni kyen de dang dre bu de nyi sel rik tsung pa la che gö shing, de ma tak kyen she pa kyen de dre bu de sel rik tu kye che la che pa gang shik, she pa ma yin pa la de mi te pa yin pe chir

If someone [KA CHIK MA in refutation to the previous debate] says, It doesn't follow that if something is matter it does not have an object condition or an immediately preceding condition, because there exists a condition that immediately precedes a pot. [If RANG LUK responds with] That is not the case, KA CHIK MA replies with, It does follow that there is an immediately preceding condition of a pot, because that is just what the direct substantial cause of a pot is. [If RANG LUK responds again with] That's not the case, KA CHIK MA replies with, Let's consider the direct substantial cause of a pot, it follows that it is a condition that immediately precedes a pot, because it is both a [causal] condition of a pot and something that occurs immediately prior to that pot. RANG LUK responds to this assertion with, There is no pervasion, [and now takes on the role of challenger]. [RANG LUK] says, Consider a pot, it doesn't have an immediately preceding condition, because there doesn't exist an immediately preceding condition that is associated with a pot. [If KA CHIK MA responds with],

That's not true, *RANG LUK* replies with, Consider a pot, there doesn't exist an immediately preceding condition associated with a pot, because it doesn't have a condition [associated with it] that generates it in the quality of clarity and awareness. If *KA CHIK MA* responds with, There is no pervasion, [that is, that whatever has the nature of clarity and awareness must be associated with an immediately preceding condition], *RANG LUK* upholds his position as follows. It is true that there is pervasion, because the meaning of "associated" in the phrase "being associated with the immediately preceding condition of that phenomenon," first of all necessitates that both the condition and its effect be similar in having the quality of clarity and awarenesss, and, the phrase "immediately preceding condition" is to be understood as that condition which serves to create its effect in the nature of what has clarity and awareness, since it would be incorrect that it should be anything other than consciousness.

THIS DEBATE IS TEACHING WHAT was taught above in reverse fashion. That is, above we decided that *suk yin na kyö kyi mik kyen dang de ma tak kyen nyi re re ne me pe kyap*, whatever is form must not have either an object condition or an immediately preceding condition. Here, on the contrary, *KA CHIK MA* reaffirms his position by asserting *pem po yin na kyö kyi mik kyen dang de ma tak kyen nyi re re ne me pe ma kyap par tel*, it does not necessarily follow that whatever is matter does not have an object condition or an immediately preceding condition. This means one cannot say *kyap par tel*, that it follows that it must pervade. A subject is put forth to prove that there must be pervasion: *bum pe de ma tak kyen yö pe chir*, because pot has an immediately preceding condition. However, if someone were to make this statement to you, *pem po yin na kyö kyi mik kyen dang de ma tak kyen nyi re re ne me pe kyap par tel*, it necessarily follows that whatever is matter does not have an object condition or an immediately preceding condition...? you would have to respond with "*dö*," I agree.

In this debate KA CHIK MA is fighting back with RANG LUK, like a tenant fighting back with his landlord. Previously, the landlord was fighting with his tenant, but now the tenant is defending himself against the landlord.

To the above statement RANG LUK has to answer with the correct response: *tak ma drup*, that's not true. *Bum pa*, Pot, is form. If something is form *kyö kyi de ma tak kyen me pe kyap*, it necessarily must not have an immediately preceding condition. Why? *Kyö pem po yin pe chir*, Because form is matter [and not mind]. *De ma dak kyen*, An immediately preceding condition, can only be consciousness and not matter.

RANG LUK gives the same reason for both, saying, *suk yin na kyö kyi mik kyen dang de ma tak kyen me pe kyap par tel, kyö pem po yin pe chir*, if something is form, it follows that it can't have an object condition or an immediately preceding condition, because it is matter.

KA CHIK MA says, You cannot say that, because *bum pe de ma tak kyen yö pe chir*, a pot [is something that] has a condition immediately preceding it.

When RANG LUK responds with, *ma drup*, that's not true, this is expressed in full as *bum pe de ma tak kyen yö pa tak ma drup na*, if he says that it isn't true that a pot has an immediately preceding condition. KA CHIK MA responds with, *bum pe de ma tak kyen yö par tel*, it does surely follow that a pot has a condition immediately preceding it (here the inflection of the voice rises because a statement of belief is being made and not an absurd consequence), *bum pe ngö kyi nyer len de de (bum pe de ma tak kyen) yin pe chir*, because the direct substantial cause of a pot is just that [condition immediately preceding it].

RANG LUK says, *bum pe ngö kyi nyer len de bum pe de ma tak kyen yin pa tak ma drup na*, which means, if he [RANG LUK] responds to this statement saying that it is not true that the direct substantial cause of a pot is the immediately preceding condition of a pot. KA CHIK MA replies by saying, *bum pe ngö kyi nyer len chö chen, bum pe de ma tak kyen yin par tel, bum pe kyen yin pa gang shik*, consider the direct substantial cause of a pot, it follows that it is a condition that immediately precedes it since first of all it is a [causal] condition, (the words "*gang shik*" divide the statement into two parts), *bum pe nga röl de ma tak tu jung wa yin pe chir*, and it is that which occurs immediately prior to the pot. *Ser na* means if he says that, *RANG LUK* responds with, *kyap pa ma jung*, there is no pervasion, meaning that just because something arises immediately prior to the pot doesn't mean that it is pot's immediately preceding condition.

What is this debate trying to express? This can be explained as follows. If you were to make a pitcher out of some material such as metal or clay, it would also require some water, tools, skill, and a lot of effort. Although all of these conditions are *bum pe kyen*, causes or conditions of a pot, they are not *bum pe nyer len*, the material cause of a pot, since neither water nor tools nor any other condition can turn into a pot. The only thing that can turn into a pot is that metal or clay [the substantial material]. These alone are *bum pe nyer len gyi gyu*, the material cause of a pot. We can express it this way. *Bum pe kyen yin na bum pe nyer len yin pe ma kyap*, Whatever is a cause of a pot isn't necessarily the substantial cause of a pot.

Similarly, earth, water, heat, and air are all *kyen* (*gyu-kyen*), causes of a sprout, but these four elements are not *nyer len*, the material cause, of a sprout, because these four elements themselves cannot turn into a sprout. What is *nyer len*, the substantial cause, then? The seed that directly produces the sprout is the substantial cause of a sprout. *Nyer len*, Substantial cause, and *kyen*, condition, are different.

We can clarify these terms by using an example. When we gather together things like dirt, water, fertilizer, seeds, and so forth, in order to plant a garden in the spring, everything we have gathered for this purpose may be considered those sprouts' *gyu* and *kyen*, causes and conditions. The seeds themselves are *nyer len gyi gyu*, the substantial cause, of those sprouts, but not *ngö kyi nyer len*, the direct substantial cause, of those sprouts, because it will take a long time before those sprouts grow from their seeds. Since you are only getting ready to plant seeds in your garden, after you plant them, you will have to tend them, making sure that they get sunlight, air, water, dirt, fertilizer, and so forth. The seed that is just planted is a future sprout's *nyer len*, substantial cause of a sprout, but not *ngö kyi nyer len*, the direct substantial cause of a sprout.

However, just when a sprout is about to come out the seed becomes *ngö kyi nyer len kyi gyu*, the direct substantial cause of that sprout. *Ngö gyu*, Directly, means just getting ready to produce, indicating that the causes are just ready to produce their result. Therefore, all those things gathered together when planting a seed are *gyu*, causes, and *kyen*, conditions, but not *ngö kyi gyu*, the direct cause, or *ngö kyi nyer len*, the direct substantial cause, which exist just immediately prior to the arising of a sprout. The fertilizer becomes *ngö gyu*, a direct cause, because there is no gap between the seed and the sprouting of that seed, but of course it does not become *ngö kyi nyer len*, the direct substantial cause, because the fertilizer cannot turn into a sprout.

Therefore, the causes that occur just before their result are not necessarily *de ma tak kyen*, immediately preceding conditions, even though they are *kyen*, conditions. *Nga röl du* means just before or prior to. You have to learn this way. Otherwise you cannot understand *de ma tak kyen*, immediately preceding condition.

What is *bum pe ngö kyi nyer len gyi gyu*, the direct substantial cause of a pot? The material from which the pot is made just before it becomes a pot. *Nyer len*, A substantial cause, can exist a long time before its result, but *ngö kyi nyer len*, direct substantial cause, means existing just immediately before its result. That is why in this debate *RANG LUK* responds with *tak ma drup*, that's not true, even though it may be a cause or a condition.

Bum pe ngö kyi nyer len chö chen, bum pe de ma tak kyen yin par tel, bum pe kyen yin pa gang shik, Consider the direct substantial cause of a pot, it follows that it immediately precedes that pot, because it is a condition. Here *KA CHIK MA* is trying to prove one by one each of its qualities. This is like saying, "It's okay to say *kyen*, condition; it's also okay to say *bum pe nga röl de ma tak tu jung wa yin*, it is what arises prior to a pot." However, *RANG LUK's* position holds that even though it did occur immediately before the pot, it is not *bum pe de ma tak kyen*, the immediately preceding condition of a pot. Also, even though it is *bum pe kyen*, the cause of pot, of course it occurred before the pot, but it is not necessarily the immediately preceding condition of a pot.

Bum pa chö chen, kyö kyi de ma tak kyen me par tel, Consider pot, it follows that it doesn't have an immediately preceding condition. If a pot has an immediately preceding condition, what quality should it have? That is, *bum pe de ma tak kyen yö na*, if pot has an immediately preceding condition, *kyö kyi tsung pa de ma tak kyen*, that immediately preceding condition is associated with it [implying that it must be mental]. *Tsung den*, Having association, means being only mental or having the quality of mind. Therefore, the quality of that immediately preceding condition can only be mental and not physical. This is referring to *tsung den nam pa nga*, the five factors associated with mind, consisting of time, object, substance, and so forth mentioned earlier. This means that when you use the phrase "*tsung pa de ma tak kyen*, the immediately preceding associated condition," it is not correct to use this in relation to a pot or any other material thing.

At this point in the debate, the debaters switch sides once again from the tenant [*KA CHIK MA*] back to the landlord [*RANG LUK*], who responds to the tenant's complaints by saying, *tak ma drup*, that's not true, and proceeds with, *bum pa chö chen, kyö kyi tsung pa de ma tak kyen me par tel, kyö kyi tsung pa de ma tak kyen me pe chir*, consider a pot, it follows that it doesn't have an associated immediately preceding condition, because there is no immediately preceding condition that is associated with pot. If you have *de ma tak kyen*, an immediately preceding condition, you must have *tsung pa de ma tak kyen*, an immediately preceding condition associated [with those five shared mental qualities].

Now if the tenant, *KA CHIK MA*, says *tak ma drup*, that's not true, or expressed in full, *kyö kyi tsung pa de ma tak kyen me pa tak ma drup na*, if he says that it's not true that there is no immediately preceding condition associated with mind for that pot, *RANG LUK* replies with, *bum pa chö chen, kyö kyi tsung pa de ma tak kyen me par tel, kyö sel rik yin par kye pe kyen me pe chir*, consider a pot, it does follow that there is no immediately preceding condition associated with mind for that pot, because there is no condition that generates something that is clear and aware.

Here it is necessary to recall the definition of conciousness (or mind). *Sel shing rik pa she pe'i tsen nyi*,[54] The definition of

---

[54] གསལ་ཞིང་རིག་པ་ཤེས་པའི་མཚན་ཉིད།

conciousness (or mind) is that which is clear and aware. *Sel rik* is short for *sel shing rik pa. Bum pa*, Pot, is form. Form cannot turn into mind; mind cannot turn into form. So a pot doesn't have *tsung pa de ma tak kyen*, an immediately preceding condition that is associated with mind. If it did, it must have a kind of *kyen*, condition, which can turn into mind possessing the qualities of clarity and awareness. But a pot does not have such qualities. Only mind produces mind. *De ma tak kyen*, An immediately preceding condition, must be mental. Even though a pot has preceding causes that came just before the pot, still they cannot be *de ma tak kyen*, an immediately preceding condition, because they are not mental.

KA CHIK MA responds to this with, *ma kyap*, which expressed in full is, *kyö sel rik yin par kye pe kyen me na, kyö kyi tsung pa de ma tak kyen me pe ma kyap*, if it is not a condition that generates something as clear and aware [mind], it is not necessarily not an immediately preceding condition that is mental.

RANG LUK responds with, *kyap pa yö par tel*, of course there is pervasion, and explains the meaning of *tsung pa*, associated [with mind]. *Tsung pe dön ni*, The meaning of associated, is that both causes and their results must be mind. Its function is to produce a result that is *sel rik*, clear and aware, or mind.

She pa ma yin pa la de mi te pa yin pe chir means that it is not correct for such a thing not to be consciousness; that is, it wouldn't be possible for such mental causes not to produce their results as having the nature of consciousness.

Okay! Whew! Finally! Next time you should know the pattern of these debates and be able to recite them almost automatically, like saying OM MANI PADME HUM, so you don't have to ponder over them every time.

OUR OWN SYSTEM

RANG LUK

effects

dre bu

གསུམ་པ་འབྲས་བུ་བཤད་པ་ལ། མཚན་ཉིད་དང་། དབྱེ་བ་དངོས།
སྒྲས་བརྗོད་རིགས་ཀྱི་སྒོ་ནས་དབྱེ་བ་དང་གསུམ། དང་པོ་ནི། བསྐྱེད་
བྱ་འབྲས་བུའི་མཚན་ཉིད། ཡང་ན། ཕན་འདོགས་བྱ་འབྲས་བུའི་
མཚན་ཉིད། གཞི་ལ་སྦྱར་ན། མེའི་ཕན་འདོགས་བྱ་མེའི་འབྲས་
བུའི་མཚན་ཉིད། གཉིས་པ་དབྱེ་བ་ནི། དངོས་འབྲས་དང་། བརྒྱུད་
འབྲས་གཉིས། དངོས་པོ་ཡིན་ན། དངོས་འབྲས་དང་བརྒྱུད་འབྲས་
གཉིས་ཀ་ཡིན་པས་ཁྱབ། གཞི་ལ་སྦྱར་ན། བུམ་པའི་དངོས་འབྲས་
དང་། བུམ་པའི་བརྒྱུད་འབྲས་གཉིས་འགལ་བ་ཡིན་ནོ། །དེས་འདུས་
བྱས་ཐམས་ཅད་ལ་རིགས་འགྲེ།

sum pa dre bu she pa la, tsen nyi dang ye wa ngö, dre jö rik kyi go ne dang sum, dang po ni, kye ja dre bu'i tsen nyi, yang na, pen dok ja dre bu'i tsen nyi, shi la jar na, me pen dok ja me dre bu'i tsen nyi, nyi pa ye wa ni, ngön dre dang gyun dre nyi, ngö po yin na, ngön dre dang gyun dre nyi ka yin pe kyap, shi la jar na, bum pe ngön dre dang, bum pe gyun dre nyi gel wa yin no, de du che tam che la ring dre

The third section, regarding an explanation of effects, consists of three parts: the definition, actual classifications, and nominal classifications. The first, the definition of an effect is that which is produced. Also, another definition is

> that which is assisted in its production. When applying this to an actual existent, the definition of the effect of fire is that which has been helped to be produced from fire [i.e., smoke].
>
> Second, the classifications: the two, direct effect and indirect effect. If something is a causally effective thing it must be both a direct effect and an indirect effect. However, when applied to an actual existent, [being] the direct effect of a pot and the indirect effect of a pot are contradictory. The same applies to all composed entities.

WHAT IS THE DEFINITION OF CAUSE? *Kye che gyu'i tsen nyi*, That which acts as a producer is the definition of a cause; or *pen dok che*, that which helps to produce. So the definition of an effect reflects these definitions when saying: *kye ja*, that which is produced, and *pen dok ja*, that which has been helped to be produced. This is an easy way to understand it.

Shi la jar na means when applying the definition to a specific example to illustrate it. *Me pen dok ja me'i dre bu'i tsen nyi*, That which has been helped to be produced from fire is the definition of the result of fire. Obviously this is smoke.

The two classifications of effect are *ngön dre*, direct effect, and *gyun dre*, indirect effect. Again, this reflects the dual division of cause into *ngö gyu*, direct cause, and *gyu gyu*, indirect cause.

Ngö po yin na ngön dre dang gyun dre nyi ka yin pe kyap, Whatever is a causally effective thing must be both a direct effect and an indirect effect. However, *shi la jar na*, when applied to a concrete example, *bum pe ngön dre dang bum pe gyun dre nyi gel wa yin no*, being both the direct effect of a pot and the indirect effect of a pot is contradictory. In the system [Sautrāntika] pertaining to the *Compendium of Debates* (*Dura*), generally *ngö po*, *gyu*, *dre bu*, *du che dön chik*, causally effective thing, cause, effect, and composed entity are synonymous in so far as they have the same nature. You can say, *ngö po yin na gyu yin pe kyap*, whatever is a causally effective thing must be a cause, and so forth. You can also say *ngö po yin na ngön dre dang gyun dre yin pe kyap*, whatever is a causally effective thing must be both a direct effect and an indirect effect.

However, when you apply this rule to a specific thing, these are considered to be contradictory [that is, there cannot be one thing that is both a direct effect and an indirect effect simultaneously of the same object]. As it says above, the direct effect of a pot cannot also be the indirect effect of the same pot and vice versa.

De du che tam che la ring dre means the same rule applies to all composed entities.

***

One way to examine this concept is as follows:

—*Bum pa chö chen, bum pe ngön dre dang bum pe gyun dre nyi gel wa yin par tel,* Consider a pot, it follows that the direct effect of pot and indirect effect of a pot are contradictory?
—*Dö*, Yes.
—*Bum pe ngön dre ka re shak,* Give an example of the direct effect of a pot!
—*Bum pe chi lok de ma tak su jung we dre bu,* An effect that arises immediately after a pot (this is the direct effect of a pot).
—*Bum pe chi lok de ma tak du jung we dre bu, bum pe ngön dre yin par tel,* Then an effect that arises just after a pot is the direct effect of a pot?
—*Dö*, Yes, that's correct.
—*Bum pe gyun dre ma yin par tel,* Then such an effect is not an indirect effect of a pot?
—*Dö*, That's correct.
—*Ngö po yin na gyun dre yin pe ma kyap par tel,* So it follows that whatever is a causally effective thing is not necessarily an indirect effect?
—*Chi chir*, No, why would you say that?
—*Ngö po yin na ngön dre dang gyun dre nyi ka ma kyap par tel,* Well, does it follow that whatever is a causally effective thing is not necessarily both a direct effect and an indirect effect?
—*Chi chir*, Why?
—*Ngö po yin na ngön dre dang gyun dre nyi ka kyap par tel,* Well is it not the case that whatever is a causally effective thing must be both a direct effect and an indirect effect?

—*Dö*, Yes.

—*Bum pe chi lok de ma tak du jung we ngö po te chö chen, bum pe ngön dre yin par tel*, All right, let's consider a causally effective thing that arises immediately after a pot, is this the direct effect of a pot?

—*Dö*, Yes.

—*Bum pe gyun dre ma yin par tel*, And it follows that it is not an indirect effect of a pot?

—*Dö*, Yes, that's right.

—*Bum pe ngön dre dang bum pe gyun dre nyi gel wa yin par tel*, And it would follow that the two, the direct effect of a pot and the indirect effect of a pot, are contradictory?

—*Dö*, Yes.

—*Shi tun me par tel*, There is not one thing that is both of them?

—*Dö*, Correct.

—*Bum pe ngön dre chö chen, bum pe gyun dre ma yin par tel*, Consider the direct effect of a pot, it's not the indirect effect of a pot?

—*Dö*, Yes.

—*Ngö gyu'i tsen nyi ka re shak*, Now, tell me, what is the definition of direct cause?

—*Ngö su kye che ngö gyu'i tsen nyi*, That which acts as a direct producer is the definition of a direct cause. For example, applying the definition to a specific phenomenon, *du we ngö su kye che du we ngö gyu'i tsen nyi*, the definition of the direct cause of smoke is the direct producer of smoke, which is fire. *Yang na, du we ngö su pen dok che du we ngö gyu'i tsen nyi*, Alternatively, that which directly helps to produce smoke is the definition of the direct cause of smoke. *Tsen shi me ta bu che te, du we ngö su kye che yin pa she pe tsön jor di, tsön jor nam dak yin pe chir*, Saying that fire acts as the direct producer of smoke is a perfect reason. *Tsön jor nam dak* and *tak yang dak* both mean a perfect reason.

—*Ngö po yin na ngön dre dang gyun dre yin pe kyap*, Whatever is a causally effective thing must be both a direct effect and an indirect effect. *Kyap na, bum pe ngön dre chö chen, bum pe gyun dre yin par tel*, If there is pervasion, let's consider the direct effect of a pot, doesn't it follow that it would have to be the indirect effect of a pot as well?

—*Chi chir*, No.

—*Bum pe gyun dre ma yin par tel*, Then it's not the indirect effect of a pot?

—*Dö*, Yes, that's true.

—*Gyun dre ma yin par tel*, It's not an indirect effect?

—*Chi chir*, That's not so.

—*Gyun dre yin par tel*, So it *is* an indirect effect?

—*Dö*, Yes.

—*Bum pe ngön dre chö chen, bum pe gyun dre yin par tel*, Let's consider the direct effect of a pot, it follows that it is an indirect effect of a pot?

—*Chi chir*, No.

—*Ngö po yin na gyun dre yin pe ma kyap par tel*, Then it would follow that whatever is a causally effective thing is not an indirect effect?

—*Chi chir*, No, that's not so.

—*Ngö po yin na gyun dre yin pe kyap par tel*, Whatever is a causally effective thing is necessarily an indirect effect?

—*Dö*, Yes.

—*Bum pe ngön dre chö chen, bum pe gyun dre yin par tel*, Let's consider the direct effect of a pot, then it follows that it is the indirect effect of a pot [as well]?

—*Chi chir*, No.

Why is this? Because as it says, *shi la jar na bum pe ngön dre dang bum pe gyun dre nyi gel wa yin no*, when applied to a specific existent there is no one thing that can be both a direct effect and an indirect effect of the same object because they are complete opposites. If it is the direct effect of a pot, it cannot also be its indirect effect.

The key is,

—*Bum pe ngön dre chö chen, bum pe ngön dre yin*, Let's consider the direct effect of a pot, [although] it is the direct effect of a pot, *bum pe gyun dre ma yin*, it is not the indirect effect of [that same] pot. *Gyun dre yin*, It is an indirect effect; however, *bum pe gyun dre ma yin*, it is just not the indirect effect of that same pot of which it is a direct effect. *Shi la jar na*, When it is applied to a specific [single] case, it cannot be both a direct effect and an indirect effect.

So, as it mentions above, you have to apply this same reasoning to all composed things, since *gyu, dre bu, ngö po, du che dön chik yin*, cause, effect, causally effective thing, and composed entity are synonymous.

OUR OWN SYSTEM

RANG LUK

effects (continued)

dre bu

འབྲས་བུ་ལ་སྒྲས་བརྗོད་རིགས་ཀྱི་སྒོ་ནས་དབྱེ་ན། རྣམ་སྨིན་གྱི་འབྲས་བུ། བདག་པོའི་འབྲས་བུ། རྒྱུ་མཐུན་གྱི་འབྲས་བུ། སྐྱེས་བུ་བྱེད་པའི་འབྲས་བུ། བྲལ་བའི་འབྲས་བུ་དང་ལྔ། དང་པོ་ཡོད་དེ། ཟག་བཅས་ཉེར་ལེན་གྱི་ཕུང་པོ་ལྔ་ལྟ་བུ་ལ་བྱེད་པའི་ཕྱིར། རྣམ་སྨིན་གྱི་འབྲས་བུ་དང་། རྣམ་གཉིས་དོན་གཅིག གཉིས་པ་བདག་པོའི་འབྲས་བུ་ཡོད་དེ། མ་དག་པའི་སྣོད་ཀྱི་འཇིག་རྟེན་ལྟ་བུ་ལ་བྱེད་པའི་ཕྱིར། གསུམ་པ། རྒྱུ་མཐུན་གྱི་འབྲས་བུ་ལ་གཉིས་ཡོད་དེ། མྱོང་བ་རྒྱུ་མཐུན་གྱི་འབྲས་བུ་དང་། བྱེད་པ་རྒྱུ་མཐུན་གྱི་འབྲས་བུ་གཉིས་ཡོད་པའི་ཕྱིར། དང་པོ་ཡོད་དེ། བདེ་འགྲོར་སྐྱེས་ཀྱང་ཚེ་ཐུང་བ་ལྟ་བུ་ལ་བྱེད་པའི་ཕྱིར། གཉིས་པ་ཡོད་དེ། བདེ་འགྲོར་སྐྱེས་ཀྱང་སྲོག་གཅོད་པ་ལ་དགའ་བ་ལྟ་བུ་ལ་བྱེད་པའི་ཕྱིར། བཞི་པ་སྐྱེས་བུ་བྱེད་པའི་འབྲས་བུ་ཡོད་དེ། ཞིང་པས་རྩོལ་བས་བསྒྲུབས་པའི་ལོ་ཏོག་ལྟ་བུ་ལ་བྱེད་པའི་ཕྱིར། མངོན་པ་ཀུན་བཏུས་ཀྱི་འགྲེལ་བ་རྒྱལ་སྲས་མ་ལས། སྐྱེས་བུ་བྱེད་པའི་འབྲས་བུ་ནི། འདི་ལྟ་སྟེ། ལོ་ཏོག་ལ་སོགས་པའོ། །ཞེས་

གསུངས་པའི་ཕྱིར། ལྔ་པ་བྲལ་བའི་འབྲས་བུ་ཡོད་དེ། སོ་སོར་
བརྟགས་འགོག་རྣམས་ལ་བྱེད་པའི་ཕྱིར།

dre bu la dre jö rik kyi go ne ye na, nam min gyi dre bu, dak pö'i dre bu, gyu tun kyi dre bu, kye bu che pe dre bu, drel we dre bu dang nga, dang po yö de, sak che nyer len gyi pung po nga ta bu la che pe chir, nam min gyi dre bu dang, nam nyi dön chik, nyi pa dak pö'i dre bu yö de, ma dak pe nö kyi jik ten ta bu la che pe chir, sum pa, gyu tun gyi dre bu la nyi yö de, nyong wa gyu tun gyi dre bu dang, che pa gyu tun gyi dre bu nyi yö pe chir, dang po yö de, den dror kye kyang tse tung wa ta bu la che pe chir, nyi pa yö de den dror kye kyang sok chö pa la ga wa ta bu la che pe chir, shi pa kye bu che pe dre bu yö de, shing pe tsöl we drup pe lo tok ta bu la che pe chir, ngön pa kun tu kyi drel wa gyel se ma le, kye bu che pe dre bu ni, di ta te, lo tok la sok pa'o, she sung pe chir, nga pa drel we dre bu yö de, so sor tang gok nam la che pe chir

When effects are nominally classified there are five kinds: 1) a ripened effect, 2) a dominant effect, 3) an effect correspondent with its cause, 4) an effect of human effort, and 5) an effect of liberation. The five contaminated appropriated heaps serve as an example of the first, a ripened effect. The terms "*nam min gyi dre bu*" and "*nam*" are synonymous. The impure world serves as an example of the second, a dominant effect. Regarding the third effect, an effect correspondent with its cause, there are two kinds: an effect whose experience is correspondent with its cause and an effect of correspondent actions. An example of the first of these is a being that, although having taken birth in one of the higher realms, has a very short life. An example of the second is a being that, although having taken birth in one of the higher realms, takes delight in killing other beings.

An example of the fourth, an effect of human effort, is illustrated by crops that have been produced through a farmer's effort. As it says in the commentary to the

Compendium of Valid Cognition[55] by Lobön Gyelbu Se: "Crops are an example of an effect that arises from effort." Analytical cessations are an example of the fifth, an effect of liberation.

WHEN NOMINALLY CLASSIFIED there are five kinds of effects: a ripened effect, a dominant effect, an effect correspondent with its cause, an effect of human effort, and an effect of liberation.

What is an example of *nam min gyi dre bu*, a ripened effect? *Sak che nyer len gyi pung po nga*, The five contaminated appropriated heaps, that were acquired through the influence of karma and mental afflictions. Our body is an example of this kind of effect, as is also *shu gu yö be dre bu*, an effect that has a tail (a dog). These are *nam min gyi dre bu*, ripened effects. *Nam min gyi dre bu yin te, nam min gyi gyu'i dre bu yin pe chir*, Whatever is a ripened effect, is the effect of a ripening cause. How many *nam min gyi gyu*, ripening causes, are there? There are two kinds as the verse states: *nam min gyu ni mi ge dang ge wa sak che nam ko na*, a ripening cause is exclusively either non-virtue or contaminated virtue. Drölma's ripening causes are *mi ge wa*, ripening non-virtuous causes; ours are *ge wa sak che*, afflicted or impure virtuous causes.

Nam min gyi dre bu dang nam min nyi dön chik, The two, ripened effect and thoroughly ripened, are synonymous. *Nam par min pa* means to ripen nicely, in terms of being the result of contaminated virtue or non-virtue. It is in this sense that our heaps are *nam min gyi pung po*, ripened heaps.

Nyi pa dak pö dre bu yö te, ma dak pe nö gyi jik ten ta bu la che pe chir, The second; there exists a dominant result, because the impure worldly vessel serves as an illustration. *Suk kam, suk me kam, dang dö kam*, The form realm, formless realm, and desire realm, are considered to be *ma dak pe nö kyi jik ten*, impure worldly vessels. *Nö jö*[56] is a term you should know. *Nö* means container, specifically the

---

[55] T: ***tshad ma kun btus***; S: *Abhidharmasamucchaya*

[56] སྣོད་བཅུད་

environment; *jö* means contained, specifically what animates that environment. The main worldly container is the three realms. What is contained therein are the beings living in those three realms. This term, *nö jö*, implies something that was created by the power of mental afflictions and karma. *Ma dak pa* means impure; consequently, the three realms are impure places. *Dak shing, tak pa ka chö, gan den, yi ge chön dzin*, often called pure lands, are *dak pö dre bu*, dominant results, as well. The beings who inhabit those lands possess the results of a common karma. Those beings can use those lands equally because they produced that karma in common. You, however, have to pay rent. These are what we call *tun mong yin pe dak dre*, a common dominant result, produced through a common karma, and *tun mong ma yin pe dak dre*, a unique dominant result. *Dak pö dre*, Dominant result, refers to the karma and mental afflictions of the owners of those places who produced them. We say *dak dre yul la min pa*, ripening in a place of dominant result. We can see many such results. For example, some landlords are very good and some not so good; some keep their environment very clean, while others allow their environment to become very dirty. There is good *dak dre* and bad *dak dre*; these are *tun mong ma yin pe dak dre*, unique dominant results. So there is a general dominant result and a unique dominant result, like the difference between having a house infested by lizards and Queen Elizabeth's palace where lizards are nowhere to be found.[57]

Now, *gyu tun gyi dre bu la nyi yö*, there are two kinds of effect corresponding to their cause: *nyong wa gyu tun gyi dre bu*, effects whose experience corresponds with their cause, and *che pa gyu tun gyi dre bu*, an effect of correspondent actions [that is, effects evident in habitual behaviour]. For example, if you pour hot water on those lizards they will experience very terrible suffering and die. The result of such an action will be that you experience a result in the future similar to the cause. Again, butchers kill animals. If there were no butchers, those animals would be able to continue living. When eaters and butchers come together those creatures experience the suffering of having their lifespan cut. Similarly, in the future, the

---

[57] Rinpoche is referring here to the house of a relative of one of the students, which was infested with lizards, and the actions (described above) that this relative took to get rid of them.

butcher will have to undergo the same kind of experience, such as having to die prematurely, among many other kinds of suffering. These are examples of a corresponding experiential result.

Che pa gyu tun gyi dre bu, An effect of corresponding actions, means how you act toward other beings, whether those actions are good or bad. In the future you will experience a result corresponding to the nature of that action. An example the text gives for the first one, *nyong wa gyu tun gyi dre bu*, experiential effects corresponding to their cause, is *den dror kye kyang tse tung wa*, although born as a being in the higher realms they will experience a short life and die at a young age. An example given for *che pa gyu tun gyi dre bu*, an effect of corresponding actions, is *den dror kye kyang sok chö pa la ga wa*, although born in one of the higher realms one delights in killing other creatures. This means that the actions you perform toward other beings will cause you to act in a similar manner or have the same behavior in the future. Some people feel that it is only natural to kill bugs, and birds, and fish, and even other people; this behavior gradually gets worse and worse with the object getting bigger and bigger [in terms of the field]. Furthermore, there are some people who, every time they move their mouth are prone to tell lies. This effect has to do with habit. Here it describes behavior in terms of bad habits, but this can also be in terms of good habits. Such habits, whether good or bad, come naturally, that is, as a natural result of former behavior. It is very important to know this.

The fourth kind of effect is a little easier to understand. *Shi pa kye bu che pe dre bu yö de, shing pe tsöl we drup pe lo tok ta bu la che pe chir*, An example of this fourth type of effect, an effect of human effort, is the effort of a farmer planting his crops; this refers to anything made by a person on purpose. *Dak, kye bu, gang sak* are synonyms for person. *Shing pe* means by a farmer; *tso we* means by effort; *lo tok* means crops; *ta bu* means example. There are many examples of this kind of effect.

Nga pa drel we dre bu, The fifth one, an effect of liberation, is very important. *Drel(n) dre* means cessations, synonymous with *gok den*, true cessations, which are achieved as a result of the paths. What are those paths? *Tsok lam*, Path of Accumulation; *jor lam*, Path of Preparation; *tong lam*, Path of Insight; *gom lam*, Path of Meditation; and *mi lob lam*, Path of No More Learning. *Drel(n) dre*,

Effect of liberation, implies that the meditator achieved *tong lam bar che me lam*, the uninterrupted path of insight [one of the four levels of the third path], by doing very hard work and thereby abandoned the obstacles to be abandoned while on that path. As a result he achieved *pang pe gok den*, true cessation of abandonment, or *drel(n) dre*, effect of liberation. The achievement of *nam dröl lam*, path of release, and achieving cessation is simultaneous. That cessation is *drel(n) dre*, an effect of liberation; however, it is not a real *dre bu*, effect.

Nam dröl lam, The path of release, is *lam*, a wisdom, and *dre bu*, effect. *Drel(n) dre gok den*, True cessation as an effect of liberation, is *tak pa*, a permanent entity, which implies that it is not *ngö po*, a causally effective thing. How could this possibly be? For example, doctors abandon the obstacle of six years of college study and, once having achieved that cessation, they receive their diploma. Even though that diploma can be burned or discarded, that doesn't change their situation in regard to their status of achievement. They still have that learning, which cannot be discarded or destroyed. It is somewhat similar to this.

Our own system

Rang luk

the three times

du sum

བཞི་པ་འདས་མ་འོངས་ཡོད་མེད་ལ་དཔྱད་པ་ནི། ཕྱིར་འདས་པ་དང་མ་འོངས་པའི་མཚན་ཉིད་མེད་དེ། འདས་པ་དང་མ་འོངས་པ་མེད་པའི་ཕྱིར་ཏེ། གཞི་གྲུབ་ན། ད་ལྟར་བ་ཡིན་པས་ཁྱབ་པའི་ཕྱིར། གཞི་ལ་ལྟོས་ནས་འཇོག་ན། བུམ་པའི་དུས་སུ་སྐྱེས་ཟིན་པ་ཡང་ཡིན། བུམ་པའི་དུས་སུ་འགགས་ཟིན་པ་ཡང་ཡིན་པའི་གཞི་མཐུན་པ། བུམ་པའི་དུས་སུ་འདས་པའི་མཚན་ཉིད། དེ་དང་བུམ་པའི་སྔ་ལོགས་སུ་བྱུང་བ་དོན་གཅིག བུམ་པའི་དུས་སུ་གྲུབ་ཟིན་པ་ཡང་ཡིན། བུམ་པ་དང་དུས་མཉམ་པ་ཡང་ཡིན་པའི་གཞི་མཐུན་པར་དམིགས་པ། བུམ་པའི་དུས་སུ་ད་ལྟར་བའི་མཚན་ཉིད། བུམ་པའི་དུས་སུ་སྐྱེ་བཞིན་པ་ཡང་ཡིན། བུམ་པའི་དུས་སུ་མ་སྐྱེས་པ་ཡང་ཡིན་པའི་གཞི་མཐུན་པར་དམིགས་པ། བུམ་པའི་དུས་སུ་མ་འོངས་པའི་མཚན་ཉིད།

shi pa de ma ong yö me la che pa ni, chir de pa dang ma ong pe tsen nyi me de, de pa dang ma ong pa me pe chir te, shi drup na, da tar wa yin pe kyap pe chir, shi la tö ne jok na, bum pe du su kye sin pa yang yin, bum pe du su gak sin pa yang yin pe shi tun pa, bum pe du su de pe tsen nyi, de dang bum pe nga lok su jung wa dön chik, bum pe du su drup sin pa yang yin, bum pa dang du nyam pa yang yin pe shi tun par mik pa, bum pe du su da tar we tsen nyi, bum pe du su kye shin pa yang yin, bum pe du su ma kye pa yang yin pe shi tun par mik pa, bum pe du su ma ong pe tsen nyi

The fourth section is an examination concerning whether or not past and future time exist. Generally speaking, there is no definition for either the past or the future, because neither the past nor the future exists. Why is this? If something exists it must necessarily be the present. If we apply a definition relative to an existent, we can posit the definition of the past at the time of a pot as that which is a combination of what has already arisen at the time of a pot and what has already ceased at the time of the pot. That and prior pot are synonymous. The definition of the present at the time of a pot is a combination of what is already established at the time of a pot and what is simultaneous with the pot. The definition of the future at the time of a pot is a combination of the continuous arising of the pot at the time of the pot and what has not yet arisen at the time of the pot.

IN GENERAL, THERE IS NO definition of past time or future time. In the logic system the rule is, *shi drup na da ta we yin pe kyap*, whatever exists must exist in the present.

Is everything that you experience in the present? Past? Or future? Everything you experience is in the present. Now, can you show me anything in this room that is in the past? No, because you cannot perceive anything in its previous moment. What about this teapot, is it *da ta wa, ma ong pa*, or *de pa*, present, future, or past? It is *da ta wa*, the present. The future of this teapot will be here and its past has already been here. Anything you can touch, see, hear, smell, taste is in the present. That is why it says here, *chir de pa dang ma ong pe tsen nyi me de*, generally there is no definition of the past or the future. If there is *tsön ja*, an object to be defined, it must have *tsen nyi*, a definition. If there is no *tsen nyi*, definition, there can be no *tsön ja*, object to be defined. Why do past and future time not exist in general? *Shi drup na da tar wa yin pe kyap pe chir*, Because if it exists it must be a present existent. Nevertheless, *shi la tö ne jok na*, if we use it in relation to an actual example, with a pot, for instance, we can give a definition as was given above.

Bum pe du su kye sin pa yang yin, bum pe du su gak sin pa yang yin pe shi tun pa bum pe du su de pe tsen nyi, The definition of the past at the time of a pot is a combination of what has already arisen at the time of a pot and what has already ceased at the time of the pot. *Kye sin pa* means arisen from causes. *Gak sin pa* means perished already when the pot is there.

Bum pe nga lok su jung wa, The previous moment of a pot, and *bum pe de pa*, past of a pot, are *dön chik*, synonymous. When the pot exists, the previous moment of the pot and the past of the pot have already gone.

Bum pe du su drup sin pe yang yin, bum pa dang du nyam pa yang yin pe shi tun par mik pa, bum pe du su da tar we tsen nyi, The definition of the present at the time of a pot is a combination of what has already been established at the time of a pot and what is simultaneous with the pot.

Bum pe du su kye shin pa yang yin, bum pe du su ma kye pa yang yin pe shi tun par mik pa, bum pe du su ma ong pe tsen nyi, The definition of the future at the time of a pot is a combination of the continuous arising of the pot at the time of the pot and what has not yet arisen at the time of the pot.

Here it is teaching past, present, and future time for rookies. We can examine this in a little more detail as follows.

Ke chik ma, Momentary, means being made of moments; that is, what is momentary cannot stay longer than an instant, implying that it disappears with each passing moment like the flowing of a river. When one moment of time finishes, the next time comes; when that one finishes, the following one comes, and so on. Therefore, at the time of the establishment of a sprout, for example—the present—can it [the sprout] stay until *ke chik nyi pa*, its next moment? Let's see. At the first moment when the sprout exists, at that time the sprout is there. However, at the second moment, that first moment's sprout has finished since the sprout is *ke chik ma*, momentary. *Ke chik ke chik kyi jik pe na ke chik ma*, If something disintegrates moment by moment, it is momentary. This is what it means to be *ke chik ma*, momentary. The first moment's sprout has already disintegrated at the time of the second moment of that sprout. Therefore, a sprout cannot still exist at the time of the second moment relative to the establishment of that sprout, because a sprout is momentary.

How can what is momentary be like that? When you buy a house, for example, are you buying thousands of houses at the same time [one house for every moment]? Obviously it's not like that. You are buying and paying for only one house. After you have signed the papers and bought the house, by the time you are ready to move in, the house that belonged to you at the time you bought it is already finished. You cannot move into *that* first moment's house. Furthermore, the house you moved into is finished by the time you are sitting in the living room. When you are eating breakfast in your kitchen, the house of the time in which you were sitting in the living room is finished. When you are sleeping in your bed, the house of the time you were eating is finished, and so on. That is the meaning of *ke chik ke chik kyi jik pa*, disintegrating moment by moment.

Why does it function this way? Because causally effective things are *gyun* (***rgyun***), a continuum. A continuum is a series of moments that go together. It is difficult for many people to understand this. The mind likewise is *gyu* (***rgyud***), a continuum. That is why it is called "a mental continuum." Sometimes extra words are added to clarify this, such as *she gyu* or *sem gyu*, both indicating this continuum of mind.

If we examine it as follows it may be easier to understand. We have the first moment, second moment, third moment, with each *se göl*, fingersnap. The first one cannot remain at the moment of the second snap nor can the second one remain at the time of the third snap of my fingers, and so forth. Why? Because the first one is *ngö po*, a causally effective thing, whose nature is *ke chik ma*, momentary. With each moment it perishes. If a sprout has started at the time of the first snap, that sprout of the first moment will disappear at the time of the sprout of the next moment, or *ke chik nyi pa*.

Is *bum pa*, pot, a general category or a particular instance? You can say it is both. For example, it is a general category because it covers such particular instances as golden pots, clay pots, etc. Yet, a pot is also a particular instance because there are particular pots belonging to the three times; i.e., today's pot, tomorrow's pot, yesterday's pot. Pot may also be categorized as a particular instance because it is the particular instance of the general category of *ngö po*, causally effective thing. Similarly, *nyu gu*, a sprout, can be a general category for the many kinds of sprouts, as well as for the sprouts of the three times—today's sprout, tomorrow's sprout, and yesterday's sprout. Since a sprout has its own particular instances of the three times, it is a general category. If it did not cover those sprouts of the three times, *nyu gu*, sprout, could not qualify as a general category.

This material may serve as a basis for study in the future. Make sure not to keep the meanings you learned in your mind so that if you lose your notebooks you will lose everything, okay? Sometimes it can be like that. Keep your notes without losing them and remember what I taught you. I lost my books fifty years ago, but I can still recite the texts without missing any of the words. Like that. You have to cook all of this and think about it.

In Tibet there are yaks. They spend the entire day grazing. When they come home from the fields, they regurgitate what they've eaten, and try to eat it again. In the logic field if you don't eat much, *de pa*, faith, won't come. If you eat a lot, eventually faith will come, and then you'll have to chew it all over again.

We'll stop here. That way you can learn slowly and digest everything. If I put a lot of atoms in your mind, at some point it may explode...boom...boom...bah...and there will be nothing left!

The words and the structure given here are new and not like those given in the regular kinds of classes. Learning logic is completely different from other subjects. You have to stir your brain all the time even until you get a headache. Ponder the meanings, memorize as much as you can, and review. It will gradually get better and better. Drölma, do you understand what I mean? Sometimes she listens to me. She even sits there and watches TV.

These *ka chik ma*'s are like a teacher. If you don't practice them you won't change your color. If you practice them you will change your color. Even small birds such as baby crows change their color. When they are small they are a grayish color; yet, by eating and drinking day after day, little by little their color begins to change. At some point their feathers turn very black and shiny. If you practice these debates little by little you too will change your color and become very shiny.

PART II

བློ་རིག་

TYPES OF MIND

[This initial section of Part II is taken from the portion of *Compendium of Debates* treating *lo rik*, types of mind.]

Our own system

Rang luk

object and object possessor

yul yul chen

In this section the views of this tenet system [Sautrāntika][1] are presented. The topic under examination is the nature of *yul*, object, and *yul chen*, subject or that which possesses an object.

རང་གི་ལུགས་ལ། ཡུལ་དང་ཡུལ་ཅན་གཉིས་ལས། དང་པོ་ནི།
བློས་རིག་པར་བྱ་བ། ཡུལ་གྱི་མཚན་ཉིད་དུ་འཇོག

rang gi luk la, yul dang yul chen nyi le, dang po ni, lö rik par ja wa, yul gyi tsen nyi du jok

According to our system there are two: object and subject. Of these two, regarding the first one, object. That which is to be cognized by the mind is put forth as the definition of an object.

Rang luk shak pa means putting forth the beliefs of our own system concerning *yul yul chen*, object and subject. In the definition for "object," given as *lö rik par ja wa*, that which is to be cognized by the mind, *lö*, by the mind, indicates the agent, in this case what is doing the perceiving; *rik par ja wa*, what is to be cognized, is the object of that perceiver, specifically, an object that is perceived by its subject.

[1] Sautrāntika school (***mdo sde pa***), a Hinayāna school of philosophy referring here to the Proponents of Sūtra Following Reasoning.

ཡུལ་ལ་དབྱེ་ན། སྣང་ཡུལ། ཞེན་ཡུལ། འཇུག་ཡུལ་དང་བཅས་པ་
རྣམས་སུ་ཡོད།

yul la ye na, nang yul, shen yul, juk yul dang che pa nam su yö

When objects are classified there are three kinds: appearing object, conceived object, and engaged object.

These classifications can be explained as follows. *Tse ma*, Valid cognition, can be classified into two kinds: *ngön sum tse ma*, direct valid cognition, and *je pak tse ma*, inferential valid cognition. The first one is a kind of mind that perceives its object directly, as when we are prompted to say, for example: "I see it," or "I hear it," and so forth. This implies that the object is being apprehended directly by a subject. When you look at these flowers you perceive them through *ngön sum tse ma*, direct valid cognition, specifically, by means of your direct valid eye cognition. Now, look over here at me. Don't move your eyes, okay? What did you see just a few seconds ago? Flowers. Do you remember those flowers? Yes. That kind of mind is *je pak*, which means indirect, since it is a kind of mind that does not perceive its object directly but indirectly through *tok pa*, conceptual mind. Therefore, *ngön sum* is direct cognition, and *je pak* is indirect cognition.

Nang yul, Appearing object, means the appearance of the object to the subject. *Shen yul*, Conceived object, means you perceive an object via that appearance; the appearing object turns into the object conceived by the mind. *Juk yul*, Engaged object, means the object you are focusing on.

བློ་དེའི་སྣང་ཡུལ་དང་བློ་དེའི་གཟུང་ཡུལ་དོན་གཅིག

lo de nang yul dang lo de sung yul dön chik

The appearing object of the mind and the object apprehended by the mind are equivalent in meaning.

These flowers appear to your eyes directly. Also, your eyes apprehend them directly. This is the meaning of *sung yul*, apprehended object. As you look at them these flowers serve as both the appearing object and the apprehended object of your eye consciousness and so in this sense they have the same meaning. *Lo de* means of any mind. Any appearing object of the mind must be the apprehended object of that mind.

> གཞི་གྲུབ་ན། སྣང་ཡུལ་ཡིན་པས་ཁྱབ་སྟེ། དངོས་པོ་ཡིན་ན་མངོན་སུམ་གྱི་སྣང་ཡུལ་ཡིན་པས་ཁྱབ་པ་གང་ཞིག རྟག་པ་ཡིན་ན། རྟོག་པའི་སྣང་ཡུལ་ཡིན་པས་ཁྱབ་པའི་ཕྱིར།
>
> *shi drup na, nang yul yin pe kyap te, ngö po yin na ngön sum gyi nang yul yin pe kyap pa gang shik, tak pa yin na, tok pe nang yul yin pe kyap pe chir*
>
> If it exists it must be an appearing object. Why? Because if it is a causally effective thing it must be the appearing object of a direct cognition, and if it is a permanent entity it must be the appearing object of a conceptual mind.

Kyap, It pervades, means it must be that way without any exceptions. *Te* shows that a reason is to follow. *Gang shik* indicates that what precedes is one quality of the definition. Again, using these flowers as an example, when you look at them, since they are *ngö po*, causally effective things, they appear to your eyes directly. Now, look at me. What did you see a moment ago? Flowers. Can you think of those flowers now? That kind of mind is *tok pa*, conceptual mind, and not direct perception because you are looking at me…that is, unless you are sneaking looks at those flowers like this. In this sense, *tok pe nang yul*, the appearing object of a conceptual mind, is not *ngö po*, a causally effective thing, but *tak pa*, a permanent entity. This implies that the flowers are not directly appearing to your eye sense consciousness but rather to your conceptual mind.

དང་པོ་གྲུབ་སྟེ། མངོན་སུམ་གྱི་སྣང་ཡུལ། གཟུང་ཡུལ། དངོས་པོ་
རྣམས་དོན་གཅིག་ཡིན་པའི་ཕྱིར།

dang po drup te, ngön sum gyi nang yul, sung yul, ngö po nam dön chik yin pe chir

The first statement [if it is a causally effective thing it must be the appearing object to a direct perception] is established because the object appearing to direct perception, the apprehended object, and causally effective thing are equivalent in meaning.

The first statement referred to is the pervasion: *ngö po yin na ngön sum gyi nang yul yin pe kyap*, whatever is a causally effective thing must be the appearing object of direct perception. On the debate ground we say *ngön sum gyi nang yul, ngö po, rang tsen sum dön chik*, the three—appearing object of direct perception, causally effective thing, and a specific concrete phenomenon—are synonymous or equivalent in meaning. Here the text uses *sung yul*, apprehended object, instead. Nevertheless, whenever we refer to an object of *tok pa*, conceptual mind, we have to use the term *shen yul*, conceived object. Therefore, *ngön sum gyi nang yul*, the appearing object of direct perception, and *ngön sum gyi sung yul*, the object apprehended by direct perception, must be *ngö po*, causally effective things. *Rang tsen*, A specific concrete phenomenon, must also be a causally effective thing. That these are synonyms is a rule of logic.

གཞན་ཡང་། དངོས་པོ་ཡིན་ན་མངོན་སུམ་གྱི་སྣང་ཡུལ་ཡིན་དགོས་
པར་ཐལ། དངོས་པོ་ཡིན་ན་མངོན་སུམ་གྱིས་མངོན་དུ་གྱུར་པའི་ཚུལ་
གྱི་རྟོགས་པར་བྱ་བ་ཡིན་དགོས་པའི་ཕྱིར།

shen yang, ngö po yin na ngön sum gyi nang yul yin gö par tel, ngö po yin na ngön sum gyi ngön du gyur pe tsul gyi tok par ja wa yin gö pe chir

Not only that, if it is a causally effective thing it follows that it must be the appearing object of direct perception, because if it is a causally effective thing it must be what is realized directly by direct perception.

Gö par tel, It follows that it is necessary, is showing the necessity of the reason for the previous statement. *Ngön du gyur pe* means directly, as in seeing something directly, hearing something directly, and so forth. *Tsul gyi* means way or manner. How? Directly, that is, in the process of perceiving there is no obstacle between subject and object. *Tok par ja wa* means the object must be perceived that way.

རྩ་རྟགས་གཉིས་པ་གྲུབ་སྟེ། རྟོག་པའི་སྣང་ཡུལ། གཟུང་ཡུལ།
རྟག་པ་རྣམས་དོན་གཅིག་ཡིན་པའི་ཕྱིར།

tsa tak nyi pa drup te, tok pe nang yul, sung yul, tak pa nam dön chik yin pe chir

The second root reason is established because the appearing object of a conceptual mind, the apprehended object, and permanent entity are synonymous.

Tsa tak nyi pa, The second root reason, is another pervasion that states, *tak pa yin na tok pe nang yul yin pe kyap*, if it is a permanent entity it must be the appearing object of a conceptual mind.

ཡང་མངོན་སུམ་གྱི་འཇུག་ཡུལ་དང་མངོན་སུམ་གྱི་འཛིན་སྟངས་ཀྱི་
ཡུལ་དོན་གཅིག

yang ngön sum gyi juk yul dang ngön sum gyi dzin tang gyi yul dön chik

Furthermore, the engaged object of direct perception and the mode of mentally holding an object of direct perception are synonymous.

Yang means not only that, showing that this discussion on types of objects has not concluded. These flowers are *ngön sum gyi juk yul*, the engaged object of the direct perception, of your eye consciousness. Your eye consciousness perceives them *as* flowers. Right now you are perceiving a teapot *as* a teapot coming through the doorway and tea *as* tea as it is being poured into your cup. Now you are perceiving the tea deliverer laughing. While perceiving him doing these things, he is *juk yul*, the engaged object, of your eye consciousness, and *dzin tang kyi yul*, the object of the way of mentally holding him *as* that object. Now you can see your tea directly. When you drink it it will turn into your *juk yul*, an "entering" object, because it is entering your throat. [Generally, *juk* means to enter. Here Rinpoche is making a play on words in the Tibetan.]

Dzin tang and *dzin tang kyi yul*, which have different meanings, are very important terms that you should know. *Dzin tang* refers to the mind or subjective mental attitude; that is, the mind that perceives something *as* something. *Dzin tang kyi yul*, on the other hand, refers to the object; that is, to the way the object is mentally held. In addition, there is wisdom's *dzin tang*, or wisdom's way of mentally holding something, and there is that pertaining to the way ignorance holds something, which is *dak dzin gyi dzin tang*, the way of mentally holding an object *as* inherently existent.

This is only a brief introduction. You can study this later when you have more time. Now, drink your tea down the way great Vasubandhu, *sang gye nyi pa*, the second Buddha, drank down the essence of the ocean of all the big volumes on *Abhidharma*, in one gulp (*hoop chik*).

རྟོག་པའི་ཞེན་ཡུལ། འཇུག་ཡུལ། དེའི་འཛིན་སྟངས་ཀྱི་ཡུལ་རྣམས་དོན་གཅིག

tok pe shen yul, juk yul de'i dzin tang kyi yul nam dön chik
The conceived object of a conceptual mind, the engaged object [of a conceptual mind], and the mode of apprehension of [a conceptual mind] are synonymous.

De'i, Of that, refers to *tok pa*, conceptual mind. The term *shen yul*, conceived object, is not used with *ngön sum*, direct perception, but only with *tok pa*, conceptual mind. *Juk yul* in this case refers to the object of perception of a conceptual mind.

གཞི་གྲུབ་ན། རྟོག་པ་དང་རྟོག་མེད་ཀྱི་ཤེས་པ་གཉིས་ཀའི་འཛིན་
སྟངས་ཀྱི་ཡུལ་ཡིན་པས་ཁྱབ་པོ།

shi drup na tok pa dang tok me kyi she pa nyi ke dzin tang kyi yul yin pe kyap po

If it exists it must be the object of the way it is mentally held by both a conceptual and non-conceptual consciousness.

An example of *tok pa*, conceptual mind, is *je pak tse ma*, inferential valid cognition. *Tok me*, Non-conceptual mind, refers to *ngön sum tse ma*, direct valid perception. *She pa* means consciousness. Two kinds of mind are being distinguished here: conceptual and non-conceptual. If it exists it can be perceived either by *je pak tse ma*, a conceptual mind, or by *ngön sum tse ma*, a non-conceptual mind. We can state it this way: *shi drup na je pak tse me shel ja yin pe kyap*, if it exists it must be an object of comprehension perceptible by inferential valid cognition; and, *shi drup na ngön sum tse me shel ja yin pe kyap*, if it exists it must be an object of comprehension perceptible by direct valid cognition.

How does something exist? Do elephants exist in the world or not? They exist. Do lions exist or not? They too exist. How can you prove that they exist? If you go to where they live, you can see them directly with your eye consciousness. Even if you don't go to where they live, you can still perceive them inferentially; that is, by *je pak tse ma*, indirect valid cognition, through using good reasons.

རང་འཛིན་རྟོག་པའི་འཛིན་སྟངས་ཀྱི་ཡུལ་ཡིན་ན། རྟོག་པའི་འཛིན་སྟངས་ཀྱི་ཡུལ་ཡིན་པས་མ་ཁྱབ་སྟེ། རི་བོང་རྭ་དེ་རྟོག་པའི་འཛིན་སྟངས་ཀྱི་ཡུལ་མ་ཡིན་པའི་ཕྱིར།

rang dzin tok pe dzin tang kyi yul yin na, tok pe dzin tang kyi yul yin pe ma kyap te, ri bong ra de tok pe dzin tang kyi yul ma yin pe chir

If something is an object of the mode of apprehension of the conceptual mind apprehending it, it is not necessarily an object of the mode of apprehension of the conceptual mind, because a hare's horn is not an object of the mode of apprehension of the conceptual mind.

If something is *dzin tang kyi yul*, an object of the mode of apprehension, it must exist. But *rang dzin tok pe dzin tang kyi yul*, an object of the mode of apprehension of the conceptual mind holding it, does not necessarily exist; take *ri bong ra*, a hare's horn, for example. Why is this? Because *rang dzin tok pa*, the conceptual mind apprehending it, is *lok she*,[2] a wrong consciousness. *Lok she* also has its own categories consisting of *lok pe yul*, an object of wrong consciousness, and *lok pe nang wa*, an appearing object of wrong consciousness, and so forth.

དེར་ཐལ། དེ་རྟོག་པའི་ཡུལ་མ་ཡིན་པའི་ཕྱིར་ཏེ། དེ་བློའི་ཡུལ་མ་ཡིན་པའི་ཕྱིར་ཏེ། དེ་བློའི་ཡུལ་དུ་བྱ་རུང་མ་ཡིན་པའི་ཕྱིར།

der tel, de tok pe yul ma yin pe chir te, de lo'i yul ma yin pe chir te, de lo'i yul du cha rung ma yin pe chir

---

[2] རང་གི་འཇུག་ཡུལ་ལ་འཁྲུལ་བའི་རིག་པ། ལོག་ཤེས་ཀྱི་མཚན་ཉིད།
The definition of wrong conciousness is a mind that is mistaken with regard to its engaged object.

Such is the case because that [a hare's horn] is not an object of the conceptual mind. [A hare's horn] is not an object of the conceptual mind because it is not an object of the mind. This is true because it is not a suitable object of the mind.

Der tel, It follows that, here refers to *ri bong ra de tok pe dzin tang kyi yul ma yin*, a hare's horn is not an object of the mode of apprehension of the conceptual mind. Why? *De tok pe yul ma yin pe chir*, Because it [a hare's horn] is not an object of the conceptual mind. Why is this? *Tok pe dzin tang kyi yul yin na tok pe yul yin gö*, If something is an object of the mode of apprehension of the conceptual mind, it must be an object of the conceptual mind. However, *de lö'i yul ma yin pe chir te*, it [a hare's horn] is not an object of the mind. *Te* is a particle that indicates a reason is to follow and means, "Why is this?" Because *tok pe yul yin na, she ja yin pe kyap*, if it is an object of the conceptual mind, it must be an object of knowledge [that is, it must exist]. Why? *Lö'i yul du ja rung wa she je tsen nyi*,[3] That which is suitable as an object of the mind is the definition of object of knowledge. However, *de lö'i yul du cha rung ma yin*, It [a hare's horn] is not a suitable object of the mind. It is not a proper object of the mind because it does not suit the definition of an object of knowledge.

དེ་ཆོས་ཅན། རང་འཛིན་རྟོག་པའི་འཛིན་སྟངས་ཀྱི་ཡུལ་ཡིན་པར་ཐལ།
བདག་མེད་ཡིན་པའི་ཕྱིར།

de chö chen, rang dzin tok pe dzin tang kyi yul yin par tel, dak me yin pe chir

Consider a hare's horn, it follows that it is an object of the mode of apprehension of the conceptual mind holding it, because it is selfless.

[3] བློའི་ཡུལ་དུ་ཆ་རུང་བ་ཤེས་བྱའི་མཚན་ཉིད།

De refers to a hare's horn. Here the text gives a very broad reason in the logic field to substantiate the statement, i.e., because it is selfless. Although there is a logic rule that states: *shi drup na dak me yin pe kyap*, whatever exists is selfless [void of self-existence], the pervasion above can be stated as follows: *dak me yin na rang dzin tok pe dzin tang kyi yul yin pe kyap*, if it is selfless it must be an object of the mode of apprehension of the conceptual mind holding it. That is, *dak me yin na yö pe ma kyab*, if it is selfless it does not necessarily have to be an existent; *ri bong ra chö chen*, take a hare's horn, for instance. This rule, *dak me yin na yö pe ma kyap*, if it is selfless it does not necessarily have to be an existent, is a little bit difficult for rookies. You may think, "Since it is selfless it must be a very good object of the mind!" or something like that. However, that is not the case. This logic rule means that anything, existent or non-existent, still lacks a self-existent nature. Why? Because there is no such self-existence and consequently, even that which does not exist, naturally, is not self-existent. Therefore, whether existent or non-existent, it is still selfless. So everything is selfless, even non-existents such as a hare's horn.

A Brief Synopsis of Types of Mind [4]

the seven types of mind

lo rik dun

In general there are four main *drup ta*,[5] tenet systems or philosophical schools, which include the Vaibhāṣhika, Sautrāntika, Yogāchāra, and Mādhyamika. Each of these schools has its own classifications as well. The *Compendium of Debates* (*dura*), *Types of Mind* (*lo rik*), and *Analysis of Reasons* (*tak rik*), belong mostly to the Sautrāntika and Yogāchāra school systems. However, we study all of these in the monastery. While studying them individually we have to know which tenet system we are presently in. If someone should ask, "What's your tenet system?" We would answer, "Mine is the Mādhyamika-Prāsaṅgika," for example. In order to understand the highest tenet system, of course we have to learn the lower ones very well first so that we can have a thorough understanding and a solid foundation of all of them before embarking on the study of the higher tenet systems.

Since *dura*, *lo rik*, and *tak rik* are among the initial studies at the monastery and pertain primarily to the Sautrāntika system, it is a rule that while studying these subjects we have to remain in that system and have to establish everything within that view. If we should happen to use reasoning belonging to the higher systems during a debate and employ their unique tenets, everybody will make fun of us and say, "Now you're wearing a Mādhyamika's hat!" This means that we have failed to maintain the views of the lower school system nicely and are not upholding the distinction between those four main systems. When we study pramāṇa, or valid reasoning, we also have to stay within the view of the Sautrāntika school system.

---

[4] This section on the "Seven Types of Mind" follows the summary of *lo rik* (***blo rig***) or *Types of Mind* as found in the General Monastic Commentarial Textbook (***phar phyin mtha' spyod spyi don***), by *Ke Drup Chen Po Gen Dun Ten Dar Wa* (***mkhas grub chen po dge 'dun bstan dar ba***) on Maitreya-nātha's *Abhisamayālaṃkāra*.

[5] གྲུབ་མཐའ་

[Main] Mind

དང་པོ་ལ། གསལ་ཞིང་རིག་པ། བློའི་མཚན་ཉིད།

dang po la, sel shing rik pa, lö'i tsen nyi

Regarding the first, clear and aware is the definition of mind.

Sel means clear; that is, the object is clear to the subject. *Rik pa*, as a noun, means mind. *Rik pa*, as a verb, means the action of the mind, which is to be aware and to perceive. This refers to the subject's action in regard to its object. What is perceiving the object? A mental subject or *rik pa*. Although *lo* and *rik pa* in general are synonyms, here *lo* is being used as *tsön ja*, an object to be defined, with *rik pa* as part of its *tsen nyi*, definition. [This is also often used as the definition of consciousness (***shes pa***).]

Where am I? Can you see me clearly? *Sel* means clear. *Lo*, Mind, in this case, is eye consciousness, your eye consciousness that is holding me clearly.

Alternatively, this definition can be expressed as follows:

རིག་པ་བློའི་མཚན་ཉིད། གསལ་ཞིང་རིག་པ་ཤེས་པའི་མཚན་ཉིད།
བློ་རིག་པ་ཤེས་པ་གསུམ་དོན་གཅིག

rik pa lö'i tsen nyi, sel shing rik pa she pe tsen nyi, lo rik pa she pa sum dön chik

The definition of mind is awareness. The definition of consciousness is that which is clear and aware. Mind, awareness, and consciousness are equivalent in meaning.

two classifications

དེ་ལ་དབྱེ་ན། ཚད་མ་དང་། ཚད་མིན་གྱི་བློ་གཉིས།

de la ye na, tse ma dang, tse min gyi lo nyi

When classifying mind there are two main types: valid mind and non-valid mind.

Lo la ye na ka tsö yö, How many classifications of mind are there? In general there are two main categories: valid mind and non-valid mind. *Tse ma* means right or valid cognition. *Tse min gyi lo* means incorrect or non-valid cognition. These two can be further classifed. *Lo la ye na lo rik dun,* When mind is classified there are seven types. These seven minds make up the two general categories: *tse ma nyi*, two types of valid cognition, and *tse min gyi lo nga* (or *tse min gyi she pa nga*), five types of non-valid cognition. The two valid cognitions are: *ngön sum tse ma*, direct valid cognition, and *je pak tse ma*, inferential valid cognition.

གསར་དུ་མི་སླུ་བའི་རིག་པ། ཚད་མའི་མཚན་ཉིད།

sar du mi lu we rik pa, tse me tsen nyi

The definition of valid mind is a new, infallible cognition.

Sar du means newly. *Mi lu wa* means infallible. *Rik pa* means awareness. We can use an example. When you look at the colors and shapes of flowers, you have to perceive them through your eye sense power. Without the eye sense power and the eyeballs, you would not be able to see objects. However, the eye sense power and the eyeballs are not themselves the subjective cognizer since they are form or physical and not mind or *rik pa*, awareness. Therefore, if something is *tse ma*, right cognition, the three characteristics in the definition must be present. First, it must be *sar du*, new, that is, perceiving its object freshly; second, it must be *mi lu wa* or infallible in relation to its object; and third, it must be *rik pa*, a mental subject.

With these three qualities it complies with the definition of *tse ma*, valid cognition, and hence qualifies as that kind of mind.

This is further clarified by an analysis of each part of the definition in the following passage from *Yongdzin Dura*:

> རང་ལུགས་ལ། གསར་དུ་མི་སླུ་བའི་རིག་པ་ཚད་མའི་མཚན་ཉིད།
> ཚད་མའི་མཚན་ཉིད་ཀྱི་ཟུར་དུ་གསར་དུ་དང་། མི་སླུ་བ་དང་། རིག་པ་
> ཞེས་གསུམ་སྨོས་པ་ལ་དགོས་པ་ཡོད་དེ། གསར་དུ་ཞེས་པས་དཔྱད་
> ཤེས་ཚད་མ་ཡིན་པ་གཅོད། མི་སླུ་བ་ཞེས་པས་ཡིད་དཔྱོད་ཚད་མ་
> ཡིན་པ་གཅོད། རིག་པ་ཞེས་པས་དབང་པོ་གཟུགས་ཅན་པ་ཚད་མ་
> ཡིན་པ་གཅོད་པ་ཡིན་པའི་ཕྱིར།
>
> *rang luk la, sar du mi lu we rik pa tse me tsen nyi, tse me tsen nyi kyi sur du sar du dang, mi lu wa dang, rik pa she sum mö pa la gö pa yö de, sar du she pe che she tse ma yin pa jö, mi lu wa she pe yi chö tse ma yin pa jö, rik pa she pe wang po suk chen pa tse ma yin pa jö pa yin pe chir*
>
> According to our system's view the definition of valid cognition is a new, infallible mind. There is a purpose for mentioning each of these three parts of this definition: 1) "new," 2) "infallible," and 3) "mind." Saying that it is "new" excludes valid cognition from being a subsequent mind. Saying that it is "infallible" excludes valid cognition from being speculative assumption. Saying that it is "mind" excludes valid cognition from being a physical sense power.

Rang luk la means according to our view. Do you have a *rang luk*? For *tsen nyi pa*'s, philosopher/debaters, not to have a *rang luk* would be terrible. Among the three sections of a traditional logic text—*shen luk gak pa, rang luk shak pa, tsö pa pong wa*—the first section consists of rejecting others' views; the second consists of putting forth one's own views; and the third involves eliminating remaining doubts that have been raised in opposition to our view. *La* means in or according to, so "in our system... we say such and such." This is the presentation of the student's own view. One must not forget that when studying texts propounding the Sautrāntika view, we have to uphold the beliefs and debate according to that view.

As we see from the explanation given above, each part of the definition of valid cognition has its own function: *sar du*, newly; *mi lu wa*, infallible; and *tse ma*, mind. Valid cognition is a kind of mind that perceives its object newly and infallibly. *Sur du* means one part at a time. *Mö pa* means indicating or making a statement. Therefore, it is stating what *sar du* means in the context of the definition of valid cognition. *Gö pa yö te* means there is a purpose for saying each of these. *She pe* means by saying such and such. *Jö* means to exclude or eliminate. Literally, *jö* means "to cut," like a weapon that cuts it off from that possibility. In other words, each part of this definition eliminates the possibility of valid cognition's being confused with other kinds of mind. For example, if it is *sar du*, new mind, then it must be *tse ma*, valid cognition. *Che she*, Subsequent cognition [according to the Sautrāntika school system], cannot be valid mind. So, by saying "new," this eliminates the possibility of valid mind's being a subsequent cognition. If it is new, it cannot be subsequent.

Rik pa, Awareness, excludes valid cognition from being one of the sense powers. *Wang po* means sense power. Among the six sense powers, the first five are clear physical form, and the last one is mental. *Suk chen pa*, Having physical form, excludes the first five powers from being *rik pa*, mental. If it is valid cognition it must be something that is mental and not physical.

A. Valid Cognition

two classifications

direct valid cognition and inferential valid cognition

དབྱེ་ན་མངོན་སུམ་གྱི་ཚད་མ་དང་རྗེས་སུ་དཔག་པའི་ཚད་མ་གཉིས།

ye na ngön sum gyi tse ma dang je su pak pe tse ma nyi

There are two classifications of valid cognition: direct valid cognition and inferential valid cognition.

Ye na, If you classify, is referring to the two classifications of valid cognition: *ngön sum gyi tse ma*, direct valid cognition, and *je su pak pe tse ma*, inferential valid cognition. *Ngön sum gyi tse ma* means that cognition which perceives its object directly. *Je su pak pe tse ma* means perceiving its object indirectly, by following something. For example, you can perceive the colors and shapes of these flowers directly. This is direct cognition. Now, where does a flower come from? From its seed. Can you see that flower's seed now? If you cannot see its seed, how do you know that the flower came from that seed? You know because you have observed stages of this process in the world; but more important, because this flower is a perishable entity that sprouts, grows, and then perishes. Why? Because it comes from a seed, which is its main cause. Why will it disappear? Because such is its nature.

Finding good reasons to substantiate something is an example of the way one gains inferential valid cognition. You can see these flowers but you cannot see the act of their growing from seeds. We can understand this because a flower is a particular instance belonging to the general category of causally effective thing, and consequently has an impermanent nature. If it is a thing, it must arise from causes. Every "thing" has its own unique causes. For example, hot peppers grow from their own unique seeds and as a result are hot to the taste.

Je su in the term *je su pak pe tse ma*, inferential valid cognition, means following after something, in this case, a reason or a sign. *Pak pa* means to guess; for instance, after doing some reasoning we come to a conclusion: "I guess it grows from a seed." That is a correct, accurate form of guessing. This is a brief explanation of inferential valid cognition. A more detailed explanation will be given later on in this text.

I. Direct valid cognition

རང་གི་རྟེན་རྟགས་ལ་མ་བརྟེན་པར་རང་གི་གཞལ་བྱ་ལ་རྟོག་པ་དང་
བྲལ་བའི་གསར་དུ་མི་སླུ་བའི་རིག་པ། དང་པོའི་མཚན་ཉིད།

rang gi ten tak la ma ten par rang gi shel ja la tok pa dang drel we sar du mi lu we rik pa, dang pö tsen nyi

> The definition of the first (direct valid cognition) is a new, infallible non-conceptual awareness that perceives its object of comprehension without relying upon perfect reasons as its basis.

Rang gi means "its" and refers to direct cognition. *Ten* generally means supporter but here refers to the main cause. You have to know the difference between *ten* (***rten***) and *ten* (***brten***); the first means supporter and the second is what it supports. This table, for instance, is a supporter and this cup is what is supported. What kind of main supporter is being referred to in this case? *Tak yang dak*, A perfect reason. *La ma ten par*, which here is employing the negative particle "*ma*," means that direct valid cognition doesn't rely upon perfect reasons as a supporter. For example, what's coming out of this incense holder? Smoke. Why is there smoke coming out of it? Because something must be burning inside. What is the cause of that burning? Fire. Because there is smoke coming out of the incense holder, there must be fire in there causing something to burn. That smoke could not possibly be coming out of there without relying upon fire as its cause. For this reason you guessed that there must be fire in that holder. This guess is correct. How do you know there is fire in this incense holder? Because smoke is coming out of it. Smoke is serving as a reason. Although you cannot see the fire directly from where you are sitting you can still perceive it through guessing correctly that it is in there, since smoke must rely upon fire as a cause for its production. Therefore, smoke is *tak*, a sign. Indirect cognition must rely upon a sign to get at its object. However, contrarily, *ngön sum tse ma*, direct valid cognition, does not have to rely upon a sign to get at its object, and so the definition says "*tak la ma ten par*," without having to rely upon a [correct] sign.

Rang gi shel ja means its object of direct cognition. *Tok pa dang drel wa* means free from conception. To have a better understanding of *tok pa*, conceptual cognition, we need to recall its definition. *Dra dön dre rung du dzin pe lo tok pe tsen nyi,*[6] The definition of conceptual cognition is a mind that finds it suitable to mix a general sound image and a general meaning image. This definition describes the nature of an object that appears to the conceptual mind. *Dra* refers to *dra chi*, general sound image, and *dön* refers to *dön chi*, a general meaning image. *Dre* means to mix. *Dre rung* means they are almost inseparable.

When a mental image comes to mind, this can happen in two ways. This can arise from *dön chi*, a general mental image arising from a meaning or from knowing the function of something, or *dra chi*, a general mental image arising from a sound. They are virtually the same. An example of the first is as follows. When you see smoke rising up from somewhere, an image of fire appears to your mind. Without words, when you are thinking about fire and an image of fire appears to your mind, that appearance of fire is *dön chi*, a general mental image arising from meaning, since it arises on the basis of knowing the qualities of fire from experience.

An example of the second, *dra chi*, a general sound image, is as follows. If I say the word "fire" to you [being an English speaker], this word causes an image of fire to appear to your mind. If I say, "Look, there's a fire over there," since you have heard the word "fire" and are familiar with the object it indicates, an image of fire appears in your mind on the basis of hearing that word spoken. That word indicates its object, which is fire. The appearance of fire to your mind at that time is *dra chi*, a general mental image arising from sound.

---

[6] སྒྲ་དོན་འདྲེས་རུང་དུ་འཛིན་པའི་བློ་རྟོག་པའི་མཚན་ཉིད།

Now, this can be examined a little further. *Me yin pa le lok pa* means the opposite of being fire. *Me ma yin pa le lok pa* means the opposite of not being fire, which is fire. However, there is a difference between the positive, fire, and the negative, the opposite of not being fire. The fire that you see outside is a positive fire. What appears to your mind as fire, however, is negative fire, or *me ma yin pa le lok pe nang wa*, the appearance of the opposite of non-fire, to your mind. This latter image of fire is *dön chi*, a general mental image arising from a meaning. That mental image doesn't perceive its object directly but just imagines what it is by following that word or image.

Ngön sum tse ma, Direct valid cognition, (the mind we are dealing with here) on the contrary, is not like that since it does not make use of mental images [or reasons] but rather gets at its object directly without any intermediary. Therefore, the definition states that it is free from conceptualization and so is lacking that characteristic.

Sar du means newly. *Mi lu wa* means infallible. For example, did you see some flowers in my room? Yes. What color were they? What shape did they have? You can tell exactly what you saw because you previously had a new, vivid impression of those flowers with your eye consciousness. That is what it means to be infallible or unerring, since it is correct. *Rik pa* means mind or cognition.

four classifications

དེ་ལ་དབྱེ་ན་དབང་པོའི་མངོན་སུམ་གྱི་ཚད་མ། ཡིད་ཀྱི་མངོན་སུམ་གྱི་ཚད་མ། རང་རིག་མངོན་སུམ་གྱི་ཚད་མ། རྣལ་འབྱོར་མངོན་སུམ་གྱི་ཚད་མ་དང་བཞི།

de la ye na wang pö ngön sum gyi tse ma, yi kyi ngön sum gyi tse ma, rang rik ngön sum gyi tse ma, neln jor ngön sum gyi tse ma dang shi

> When valid cognition is classified there are four: direct valid sense cognition, direct valid mental cognition, direct valid self-cognizing cognition, and direct valid yogic cognition.

a) DIRECT VALID SENSE COGNITION

In order to understand direct valid sense cognition it is necessary to have an understanding of what a sense power is. *Wang po* means sense power or sense faculty. There are six sense powers. The first five are *wang po suk chen pa*, physical sense powers, consisting of clear physical form; the sixth, *yi kyi wang po*, mental sense power, is not physical but mental, yet it is still called a "sense power." Using eye sense power as an example its definition is given as follows. *Rang dre mik she kyi ten nam tun mong ma yin pe dak kyen che pe rik su ne pe nang gi suk chen dang pa, mik gi wang pö tsen nyi,*[7] The definition of eye sense power is a clear, internal physical form that acts as the unique governing condition or basis for the eye consciousness, its effect. The body supports the eyeball, the eyeball supports the eye sense power, and the eye sense power supports the eye consciousness. In short, the eye sense power is the unique support for the eye consciousness since, based on that sense power, an eye consciousness is produced.

According to *The Treasury of Higher Knowledge*, each of these physical sense powers has a specific shape. For example, the eye sense power is described as having the shape of a Zarma flower, the tongue sense power as having the shape of half moons, and so forth.

The text now gives the definition of general direct valid sense cognition.

---

[7] རང་འབྲས་མིག་ཤེས་ཀྱི་རྟེན་ནམ་ཐུན་མོང་མ་ཡིན་པའི་བདག་རྐྱེན་བྱེད་པའི་རིགས་སུ་གནས་པའི་ནང་གི་གཟུགས་ཅན་དྭངས་པ་མིག་གི་དབང་པོའི་མཚན་ཉིད།

རང་གི་ཐུན་མོང་མ་ཡིན་པའི་བདག་རྐྱེན་དབང་པོ་གཟུགས་ཅན་པ་ལ་
བརྟེན་ནས་སྐྱེས་པའི་རང་གི་གཞལ་བྱ་ལ་རྟོག་པ་དང་བྲལ་བའི་མངོན་
སུམ་གྱི་ཚད་མ། དང་པོའི་མཚན་ཉིད།

rang gi tun mong ma yin pe dak kyen wang po suk chen pa la ten ne kye pe rang gi shel ja la tok pa dang drel we ngön sum gyi tse ma, dang pö tsen nyi

> The definition of the first one, (direct valid sense cognition), is a direct valid cognition that is free from conception with regard to its valid object, generated in reliance upon a physical sense power, its unique governing condition.

Rang gi means its, referring to direct valid sense cognition. *Tun mong ma yin pe dak kyen* means its unique governing condition or unique cause. The term "unique" refers to the fact that each sense power is specific to the consciousness it serves to produce. For example, when you see something, the unique governing condition is your eye sense power, and when you hear something, the unique governing condition for ear consciousness is your ear sense power, and so on. The ear sense power cannot serve to produce eye consciousness, just as the eye sense power cannot serve to produce an ear consciousness. *Dak kyen*, Governing condition, applies to each of the six consciousnesses. Your body, however, is the common support or cause for your consciousnesses to arise, but not *tun mong ma yin pe dak kyen*, the unique govering cause, for each of these consciousnesses.

The sense powers act as unique governing conditions serving to produce different consciousnesses in relation to their unique objects, which are called *mik kyen*, object conditions. The unique object of the eye consciouness is shapes and colors; for the ear consciousness it is sound; for the nose consciousness it is odors; for the tongue consciousness it is taste; and for the body consciousness it is tangible objects. Even though mind "sense" power is not physical, we have to describe it as being one of the sense faculties. The mind sense power for the mental consciousness, however, is a previous moment of any of the six consciousnesses.

Suk chen pa means physical form. *La ten ne* means relying upon that form. *Kye pe* means to arise or come out of. *Rang gi shel ja* means its object, the object unique to that particular faculty and consciousness. *Tok pa dang drel wa* means they are free from any kind of conception. *Ngön sum gyi tse ma* shows that they are direct valid cognition.

five classifications

དབྱེ་ན། གཟུགས་འཛིན་དབང་པོའི་མངོན་སུམ་གྱི་ཚད་མ་ནས།
རེག་འཛིན་དབང་པོའི་མངོན་སུམ་གྱི་ཚད་མའི་བར་ལྔ་ཡོད།

ye na, suk dzin wang pö ngön sum gyi tse ma ne, rek dzin wang pö ngön sum gyi tse me bar nga yö

> When classifying direct valid sense cognition there are five kinds beginning with direct valid sense cognition that apprehends visible forms [shape and color] up to direct valid sense cognition that apprehends tangible objects.

The individual objects of the consciousnesses are *suk, dra, dri, ro, rek ja*, visible form, sound, smell, taste, and tangible objects. *Suk* in this case refers to shapes and colors; that is, visible form, which is the object of the eye consciousness. *Ne* means from or beginning with. *Dzin* means perceiving. *Wang po* means the unique faculty. *Bar* means up to and including the fifth consciousness, which is the body consciousness whose object is any tangible thing.

རང་གི་ཐུན་མོང་མ་ཡིན་པའི་བདག་རྐྱེན་མིག་དབང་ལ་བརྟེན་ནས་རང་
གི་གཞལ་བྱ་ལ་རྟོག་པ་དང་བྲལ་བའི་གསར་དུ་མི་སླུ་བའི་དབང་པོའི་
མངོན་སུམ་གྱི་ཚད་མ། དང་པོའི་མཚན་ཉིད།

> *rang gi tun mong ma yin pe dak kyen mik wang la ten ne rang gi shel ja la tok pa dang drel we sar du mi lu we wang pö ngön sum gyi tse ma, dang pö tsen nyi*
>
> The definition of the first (direct valid sense cognition apprehending visible form) is a new, infallible direct valid cognition that is free from conception with regard to its object, generated in reliance upon the eye sense faculty, its unique governing condition.

Rang gi tun mong ma yin pe dak kyen means its unique governing condition, referring to *mik wang*, the eye faculty, whose unique object is visible form, consisting of shapes and colors. *Rang gi shel ja* means its [valid] object, which in this case is shapes and colors. *Tok pa dang drel we* means free from conception. *Sar du mi lu we* means new and infallible. *Dang po*, The first, refers to 1) *suk dzin wang pö ngön sum gyi tse ma*, direct valid sense cognition apprehending [visual] form. The second sense cognition is 2) *na we wang pö ngön sum gyi tse ma*, auditory direct valid sense cognition. The third is 3) *ne'i wang pö ngön sum gyi tse ma*, olfactory direct valid sense cognition. The fourth is 4) *je'i wang pö ngön sum gyi tse ma*, gustatory direct valid sense cognition. The fifth is 5) *lu kyi wang pö ngön sum gyi tse ma*, tactile direct valid sense cognition. The sense powers and the unique objects of each vary according to each individual consciousness.

> དེ་བཞིན་དུ་འོག་མ་རྣམས་ལ་ཤེས་པར་བྱའོ།
>
> *de shin du wok ma nam la she par ja'o*
>
> In a similar manner you should understand the definitions of the other consciousnesses that follow.

This means that you can apply the above definition to the other four sense cognitions by substituting the unique object and sense power appropriate to each one.

b) DIRECT VALID MENTAL COGNITION

རང་གི་ཐུན་མོང་མ་ཡིན་པའི་བདག་རྐྱེན་ཡིད་དབང་ལ་བརྟེན་ནས་རང་
གི་གཞལ་བྱ་ལ་རྟོག་པ་དང་བྲལ་ཞིང་གསར་དུ་མི་སླུ་བའི་མངོན་སུམ་
གྱི་ཚད་མ། ཡིད་ཀྱི་མངོན་སུམ་ཚད་མའི་མཚན་ཉིད།

rang gi tun mong ma yin pe dak kyen yi wang la ten ne rang gi shel ja la tok pa dang drel shing sar du mi lu we ngön sum gyi tse ma, yi kyi ngön sum tse me tsen nyi

The definition of direct valid mental cognition is a new, infallible direct valid cognition that is free from conception with regard to its object, generated in reliance upon the mental sense faculty, its unique governing condition.

Yi wang, The mental sense power, lacking physical form, is described by the great scholar Vasubandhu in *The Treasury of Higher Knowledge*:

> Any of the six consciousnesses acts as the immediately preceding condition for the mental sense power.

Druk po means those six, referring to the six consciousnesses. *De ma tak* means what arises immediately after those consciousnesses have disappeared. *Nam she* means consciousness. The six consciousnesses are: *mik kyi nam she*, eye consciousness, *na we nam she*, ear consciousness, *ne'i nam she*, nose consciousness, *je'i nam she*, tongue consciousness, *lu kyi nam she*, body consciousness, and *yi kyi nam she*, mind consciousness. These are mentioned in the *Heart Sutra* as: "*mik me, na wa me, na me, che me, lu me, yi me*, no [self-existent] eye, no ear, no nose, no tongue, no body, no mind."

Yi, Mind, in the quotation above refers to mental sense power. The mental sense power is a mind that occurs the moment immediately after any of these six consciousnesses. For example, when you plant seeds in a field, the crops will grow later. When the sprouts come, what happens to the seeds? They have disappeared once they've turned into the sprout's nature. Those seeds are the causes of those sprouts. In a similar manner, when those six consciousnesses have just disappeared, they turn into or produce mind consciousness. That is the meaning of *yi wang*, mental faculty. How then is it mental? Since it arises just before mind consciousness, its unique cause is mental. The mental faculty, which arises in reliance upon any one of the six consciousnesses, is a cause of mind consciousness. Of course, as a rule, causes come before their effects. Is there any variation in this rule? Which came first the chicken or the egg? You have to have certain rules when you debate. If you don't, you will go crazy.

Mind consciousness is very easy to understand. For example, what are those? Flowers. Now close your eyes. Do you remember those flowers? That memory is mental, a mind consciousness. It was produced just before that specific eye consciousness perceiving the flowers disappeared. If you hadn't seen the flowers in the first place, you would not have been able to remember those flowers.

It is necessary to imagine different situations like this for which to apply these definitions. Although you can be given an explanation countless times, without thinking about it for yourself you won't really understand it.

There are logical rules that say: *ngö po yin na gyu yin pe kyap*, whatever is a causally effective thing must be a cause; and *ngö po yin na dre bu yin pe kyap*, whatever is a causally effective thing must be a result. If it is a causally effective thing, it must be produced by something. If it it is produced by something, it must be a result. If it is a result, it must have a cause. Now, is a seed a cause or a result? It is both a cause and a result. Seeds are the cause of next year's crops. They rely upon different causes. There is no contradiction in this logic rule. It's very important that you learn all of these logic rules.

Yi wang, Mental sense power, must be one of the three kinds of *ngö po*, causally effective thing, because it has a cause. These three are: *suk, she pa, den min du che sum*, form, consciousness, and non-associated formations. Of the three, mind sense power is *she pa*, consciousness. Even though the mind sense power functions the same as the other five sense powers, its quality is different.

c) DIRECT VALID SELF-COGNIZING COGNITION

རང་གི་གཞལ་བྱ་ལ་རྟོག་པ་དང་བྲལ་ཞིང་མ་འཁྲུལ་བའི་གསར་དུ་མི་
སླུ་བའི་འཛིན་རྣམ། རང་རིག་མངོན་སུམ་གྱི་ཚད་མའི་མཚན་ཉིད།

rang gi shel ja la tok pa dang drel shing ma trul we sar du mi lu we dzin nam, rang rik ngön sum gyi tse me tsen nyi

The definition of direct valid self-cognizing cognition is a new, infallible unmistaken subjective apprehender that is free from conception with regard to its object.

Rang gi shel ja la means to its own unique object. *Tok pa dang drel shing* means free from conception. *Ma trul we* means unerring or unmistaken. *Sar du mi lu wa* means perceiving its object newly and infallibly. What is the meaning of *nam pa*, aspect? To use an example. What is this color? Red. When you look at this color your eye consciousness is said to take on *mar pö nam pa*, the aspect of [the color] red; that is, an object causes the consciousness to take on its aspect.

What is the meaning of *dzin nam*, subjective apprehender? *Dzin nam* means holding only a mental object in the manner of a subjective apprehender, and to be distinguished from *sung nam*, an outer or external object. *Dzin* and *nam* are often paired with other words as in *sung nam*, *sung dzin*, and so forth. *Sung* refers to outer objects, that is, to those objects that are not mental. *Sung nam*, Held or perceived aspect, refers to external objects held by the mind. On the other hand, *dzin nam*, an aspect of the apprehender or perceiver, is any object held by the mind that itself is mental. The perceiving subject, or mind, that holds that mental object is known as *rang rik*, self-cognizing consciousness. The object of *rang rik* is only mental and therefore *dzin nam* and not *sung nam.*

Again, do you see flowers on this table? "Yes." The eye consciousness that perceives these flowers is *sung nam* because it is holding an external object. Do you still remember those flowers? "Yes, I remember seeing them." Therefore, you had an eye consciousness that formerly perceived those flowers on the table.

Does that eye consciousness exist or not? "Yes, it exists." How can you prove that it exists? Because it has its own subject or perceiver, which is *rang rik*, self-cognizing awareness. That subject is perceiving its own eye consciousness with valid cognition.

Is there an elephant in front of this table? "No...but maybe something similar to an elephant...." Drölma, did you finish all your tea? So there is no elephant. If you say there is an elephant in front of the table, you would have to prove it by using correct cognition. If you have any kind of correct cognition of its existence, then it must be there; it is provable. Now, is there a clock on this table? "Yes." Can you prove it? "Yes, because I can see it directly with my eye consciousness." This means that you can prove it with *tse ma*, the valid cognition, of your eye consciousness. Now, I'm hiding the clock under the table. Do you still remember it? "Yes." This *dren she*, recollecting consciousness, is an awareness that arises in the mind just after perceiving something directly, for instance, after your eye consciousness has experienced an object. That eye consciousness is *dzin pa*, a holder, of an object, which in this case is a perception itself. *Rang rik*, Self-cognizing awareness, is the subject or mental apprehender, *dzin nam*, of that eye consciousness, which is itself the mental object of that awareness. That is why *rang rik ngön sum*, direct valid self-cognizing cognition, can prove it.

The short definition of self-cognizing cognition is *dzin nam*, subjective apprehender [whose object is only mental]. There is also a definition used in the higher schools as follows:

།ཁ་ནང་ཁོ་ནར་ཕྱོགས་ཤིང་འཛིན་པ་ཡན་གར་བར་གྱུར་པའི་རྟོག་པ་
དང་བྲལ་ཞིང་གསར་དུ་མི་སླུ་བའི་རིག་པ།

ka nang ko nar chok shing dzin pa yen gar war gyur pe tok pa dang drel shing sar du mi lu we rik pa

The definition of [self-cognizing direct valid cognition] is a new, infallible non-conceptual mind, a discrete apprehender, that is directed only inwardly.

Ka shows the direction; *nang* means inside; that is, the object is only an inner object. *Chok shing* means focusing or facing that direction, i.e., inside. *Dzin pa*, Holding, implies that the object is mental, referring to internal things. If it is not a person, then it can't have a mental object. *Dzin pa* shows that both the subject and the object are mental. *Yen gar wa* means to isolate, referring here to isolating mental things and rejecting any other kind of object as its object of perception. *Tok pa dang drel shing* means that it is not conceptual. *Sar du mi lu we rik pa* means a new, infallible mind.

Self-cognizing cognition, nevertheless, is not accepted by the Mādhyamika-Prāsaṅgika school, since according to this view, to accept such a cognition would require an endless regress of one mind verifying the next and so on ad infinitum.

d) DIRECT VALID YOGIC COGNITION

རང་གི་ཐུན་མོང་མ་ཡིན་པའི་བདག་རྐྱེན་ཞི་ལྷག་ཟུང་འབྲེལ་གྱི་ཏིང་ངེ་
འཛིན་ལ་བརྟེན་ནས་རང་གི་གཞལ་བྱ་ཡང་དག་པའི་དོན་ལ་རྟོག་པ་
དང་བྲལ་ཞིང་གསར་དུ་མི་སླུ་བའི་མངོན་སུམ་ཚད་མ། རྣལ་འབྱོར་
མངོན་སུམ་གྱི་ཚད་མའི་མཚན་ཉིད།

rang gi tun mong ma yin pe dak kyen shi hlak sung drel gyi ting ngen dzin la ten ne rang gi shel ja yang dak pe dön la tok pa dang drel shing sar du mi lu we ngön sum tse ma, neln jor ngön sum gyi tse me tsen nyi

The definition of direct valid yogic cognition is a new, infallible, non-conceptual direct valid awareness with regard to its perfect object based on single-pointed concentration that alternates between calm abiding and penetrative insight, its unique governing condition.

The unique cause or condition of this kind of mind is *ting ngen dzin*, single-pointed concentration (*samādhi*), alternating between *shi ne*, calm abiding (*shamatha*), and *hlak tong*, penetrative insight (*vipashyanā*), which has the quality of wisdom. *Shi ne*, Calm abiding, is a form of concentration; *hlak tong*, penetrative insight is wisdom. *Sung drel* means alternating and implies that one maintains *ting ngen dzin*, concentration, in meditation while alternating between these two. *La ten ne* means based on these. *Rang gi shel ja* means its object. *Yang dak pe dön* means a pure object, referring here to *dak me tra rak sum*, [one of] the three kinds of selflessness, which are: *gang sak gi dak me tra mo*, *chö kyi dak me rak pa*, and *chö kyi dak me tra mo*, subtle selflessness of person, rough selflessness of phenomena, and subtle selflessness of phenomena (referring to the aggregates). *Dak*, Inherently existent self, is the object to be refuted; *me* is a negative particle meaning "less," which negates the word that precedes it. Therefore, this is what you reject while you are meditating. [The kind of selflessness that is rejected varies according to the school. This will be briefly explained below.] Having rejected this, you have to perceive *yang dak pe dön*, a pure object. How do you perceive it? *Tok pa dang drel*, Without conception, and *sar du*, newly.

Rang gi mik pa la tse chik du nyam par shak pe tob kyi shin jang gi de wa kye par chen gyi sin pe ting nge dzin shi ne gyi tsen nyi,[8] The definition of calm abiding—the king of concentration—is a concentration induced by the power of meditative equipoise that, while fixed single-pointedly upon its object, is influenced by the extraordinary bliss of mental and physical ease.

There is another definition of direct valid yogic cognition given in the *Yongdzin Dura* as follows:

།རང་གི་ཐུན་མོང་མ་ཡིན་པའི་བདག་རྐྱེན་དུ་གྱུར་པའི་ཞི་ལྷག་ཟུང་
འབྲེལ་གྱི་ཏིང་ངེ་འཛིན་ལ་བརྟེན་ནས་སྐྱེས་པ་གང་ཞིག་རྟོག་པ་དང་

[8] རང་གི་དམིགས་པ་ལ་རྩེ་གཅིག་ཏུ་མཉམ་པར་བཞག་པའི་སྟོབས་ཀྱིས་ཤིན་སྦྱངས་ཀྱི་
བདེ་བ་ཁྱད་པར་ཅན་གྱིས་ཟིན་པའི་ཏིང་ངེ་འཛིན་ཞི་གནས་ཀྱི་མཚན་ཉིད།

བྲལ་ཞིང་མ་འཁྲུལ་བའི་འཕགས་རྒྱུད་ཀྱི་གཞན་རིག་གི་མཁྱེན་པ་དེ།
རྣལ་འབྱོར་མངོན་སུམ་གྱི་མཚན་ཉིད།

rang gi tun mong ma yin pe dak kyen du gyur pe shi hlak sung drel gyi ting nge dzin la ten ne kye pa gang shik tok pa dang drel shing ma trul we pak gyu kyi shen rik gi kyen pa de, nel(n) jor ngön sum gyi tsen nyi

The definition of direct [valid] yogic cognition is an exalted non-conceptual, unmistaken non-apperceptive awareness in the mind of an Arya that arises in dependence upon meditative concentration, its unique governing condition, which alternates between calm abiding and penetrative insight.

Nel(n) jor means yoga. What does that mean? A person who eats yogurt? *Nel ma* means nicely, perfectly, referring to a perfect object. For example, *lam nel ma* means a perfect path or perfect wisdom. *Jor* means putting together or joining, referring to a perfect subject or perceiving mind. Therefore, we can say good yogurt-eaters practice with their yogurt nicely! This kind of practice of a perfect subject with a perfect object is *nel(n) jor ngön sum tse ma*, direct valid yogic cognition. *Ngön sum*, Direct, implies that it is non-conceptual. *Rang gi* means its and refers to any of three kinds of direct yogic cognition. *Tun mong ma yin pe dak kyen* means its unique cause or governing condition. *Shi* is short for *shi ne*, (*shamatha*) or calm abiding. *Hlak*, means extraordinary and is short for *hlak tong*, penetrative insight or wisdom. What is the definition of *hlak tong*, penetrative insight? *Rang gi ten tu gyur pe shi ne la ten ne rang gi mik pe chö la so sor che tob kyi shin jang kyi de wa kye par chen gyi sin pe she rab hlak tong gi tsen nyi*,[9] The definition of penetrative insight is a wisdom influenced by the extraordinary bliss of (mental and physical) pliability [induced] by the power of individual analysis of phenomena, its object of focus, relying on calm abiding as its basis. *Tong* means seeing or perceiving, that is, an extraordianry mode of perceiving. Ordinary beings cannot perceive their objects in such a manner, but only *pak pa*, Aryas, can. *Shi ne* is a kind of meditative concentration, whereas *hlak tong*, penetrative insight, is a kind of wisdom. *Sung drel* means practicing these two together. *Ting ngen dzin la ten ne* means their basis is single-pointed concentration. *Kye pa*, Arises, implies that one achieves that knowledge or makes that direct yogic cognition arise through concentration. *Gang shik* indicates one quality of the definition that precedes these words. *Tok pa dang drel wa* means being free from conception. *Ma trul wa* means unerring or something that is not *trul she*, a mistaken consciousness.

Trul she, Mistaken consciousness, can be explained as follows. *Nang yul*, Appearing object, and *shen yul*, conceived object or object of a conceptual mind, as objects of *tok pa*, conceptual mind, are *trul wa*, mistaken, but not *lu wa*, erroneous. In fact, they can be *tse ma*, valid cognition. This point is a little bit delicate in the Mādyamika-Prāsaṅgika school system. However, in the Sautrāntika system, *je pak tse ma*, inferential valid cognition, is also *trul she*, mistaken consciousness; that is, *nang yul la trul she*, mistaken with regard to its appearing object, although it is not mistaken with regard to its *shen yul*, conceived or main object, since it is a kind of cognition that conceives its object perfectly and unerringly. Why is this? Because *dra dön dre rung du dzin pe shen rik*, it is a conceiving cognition that finds it suitable to mix a general sound image and a general meaning image, which is the definition of *tok pa*, a conceptual mind. As mentioned previously conceptual mind perceives its object by mixing these two. *Dön* means main object; however, *dön chi*, a

[9] རང་གི་རྟེན་ཏུ་གྱུར་པའི་ཞི་གནས་ལ་བརྟེན་ནས་རང་གི་དམིགས་པའི་ཆོས་ལ་སོ་སོར་དཔྱད་སྟོབས་ཀྱིས་ཤིན་སྦྱངས་ཀྱི་བདེ་བ་ཁྱད་པར་ཅན་གྱིས་ཟིན་པའི་ཤེས་རབ་ལྷག་མཐོང་གི་མཚན་ཉིད།

general meaning image, is not the actual main object but rather only the *appearance* of the main object.

An example of *dön chi*, a general meaning image, is *ka wa ma yin pa le lok pa*, the opposite of non-pillar. *Yin pa le lok pa*, The opposite of being something, is *ma yin pa*, not being that thing. *Ma yin pa le lok pa*, The opposite of not being something, is being that thing. *Ka wa ma yin pa le lok par nang wa*, Appearing as the opposite of non-pillar, is not a pillar, but is just the appearance of a pillar to the mind that perceives it. When the main object appears to the mind as *dön chi*, a general meaning image, that is a conceptual mind. The appearing object and the main object of perception are different. The objects of direct perception have no need of conceptions since the subject can perceive its object directly. This is why it states in the definition of direct valid yogic cognition, *tok pa dang drel shing ma trul we*, free from conceptions and unmistaken.

Pak gyu kyi means in the mind of an Arya or realized being. *Shen rik kyi kyen pa* means knowing other things than mind itself. This is mentioned in order to distinguish this kind of mind from *rang rik*, self-cognizing mind. *Kyen pa* means wisdom and is generally synonymous with *yum*, "the mother of wisdom," which is *The Perfection of Wisdom*,[10] *ngön tok*, direct realization, and *lam*, path.

The complete definition means the Arya's path, an unerring non-conceptual mind generated through concentration, which is a combination of calm abiding and penetrative insight in reliance upon concentration as its unique governing condition. Therefore, in order to qualify as direct valid yogic cognition all of these elements must be present.

What kind of *shi*, peace, is being referred to in *shi ne*? This is the peace relative to two major obstacles: *ching wa*, mental sinking, and *gö pa*, mental scattering. If your mind is not free from these two main obstacles, you cannot achieve concentration. Other obstacles that are very close to these are the two kinds of *dun dzi*, busyness: *lu kyi dun dzi*, being busy by body, and *sem kyi dun dzi*, being busy by mind. In order to gain this concentration your mind has to be free of these obstructions as well. *Lu kyi dun dzi* means rushing around from place to place or staying in a very busy place with many people coming and going around you. It also implies the sort of activity

[10] S: *Prajñāpāramitā*

referent to a practitioner's body while meditating. *Sem kyi dun dzi*, Being busy by mind, is referring to *nam tok*, which means having many meaningless thoughts going through your mind all the time while meditating, without holding the mind firmly in concentration on its object. This is a very powerful obstacle.

The main object of these two kinds of knowledge—*shi ne* and *hlak tong*—should be shūnyatā, emptiness, the lack of self-existence, the real nature of phenomena, which are synonyms. As there are many synonyms for emptiness, one can use whichever of these is most helpful to induce understanding of the meaning.

If you achieve penetrative insight through calm abiding, that meditation can abandon the mental afflictions. However, in order to achieve penetrative insight, first you have to achieve calm abiding. So, to achieve calm abiding everything must be properly arranged to practice it without obstacles.

Rang gi mik pa means its main object, which should be *tong nyi*, emptiness. *Tse chik tu* means one-pointedly. *Nam par shak tu* means meditating upon emptiness. While meditating upon shūnyatā, at some point your mind becomes used to that object. When it becomes used to perceiving shūnyatā, both your body and mind gradually become more and more suitable to that meditation, and you become more comfortable and have less physical and mental problems. At some point it gives you a great sense of pleasure and happiness both in mind and body; you feel a great ease and your body becomes very relaxed such that it becomes quite easy for you to practice. This state is known as *shin jang*, extremely well tamed or extraordinary ease, and applies to both the body and mind, which gain that quality through practice. This extraordinary ease helps your concentration and even makes it possible for you to stay in meditation as long as you wish. This is the meaning of the part of the definition of penetrative insight that states, *shin jang gyi de wa kye par chen gyi sin pe*, influenced by the extraordinary bliss of extreme ease. While being influenced by this extreme ease with your mind steadily concentrated on shūnyatā, you can achieve *shi ne*, calm abiding. This is one of the main causes of *nel(n) jor ngön sum*, direct [valid] yogic cognition.

Meanwhile, you have to check to make sure that you are holding your mind on shūnyatā, its object, and examining its nature or freedom from self-existence. Self-existence, the object to be refuted, is what we call *gak ja*. You have to examine how it is free of this object to be refuted. "Why has it become pure shūnyatā?" As you continue checking, at some point during the meditation you will find the exact meaning of emptiness. When you find it you have achieved *hlak tong*, penetrative insight. With that penetrative insight you have to continue to practice the concentration of calm abiding. Again, after achieving calm abiding, you have to examine your real nature, your mind's real nature, and so forth. When you find that real nature, you have to hold that understanding with calm abiding. This is how you should practice.

Tok pa dang drel shing, Free from conceptual mind, means that achieving an Arya's path perceiving shūnyatā is only direct perception and not conceptual, since it perceives shūnyatā directly. Such a direct perception is perfect wisdom without any error and is therefore *ma trul wa*, unmistaken. Who can have that kind of wisdom? Only Aryas. *Pak gyu kyi shen rik gi kyen pa* means the wisdom in the mind of an Arya. The first moment that you achieve this kind of wisdom of yogic direct cognition you become an Arya. As mentioned before, *shen rik*, cognition of those things other than mind itself, is mentioned to distinguish this from *rang rik*, self-cognizing mind, which is accepted by this lower school system. *Kyen pa* means path of wisdom.

four classifications by way of the basis

དེ་ལ་རྟེན་གྱི་སྒོ་ནས་དབྱེ་ན། ཉན་ཐོས་འཕགས་པ། རང་རྒྱལ་འཕགས་
པ། བྱང་སེམས་འཕགས་པ། སངས་འཕགས་ཀྱི་རྒྱུད་ཀྱི་རྣལ་འབྱོར་
མངོན་སུམ་དང་བཞི་ཡོད།

de la ten gyi go ne ye na, nyen tö pak pa, rang gyel pak pa, chang sem pak pa, sang pak kyi gyu kyi neln jor ngön sum dang shi yö

> When classifying direct valid yogic cognition by way of its basis there are four kinds: the yogic cognition in the mind of a Listener Arya, the yogic cognition in the mind of a Solitary Realizer Arya, the yogic cognition in the mind of a Bodhisattva Arya, and the yogic cognition in the mind of a Buddha Arya.

These classifications reveal the kinds of beings who are capable of having such a cognition and, by implication, reveals those who are incapable. Only Aryas can have a direct valid yogic cognition; not ordinary persons. Why? Because according to the definition given above, its unique governing condition is single-pointed concentration alternating between calm abiding and penetrative insight. Who can have this kind of mind? Listener Aryas, Solitary-Realizer Aryas, Bodhisattva Aryas, and Buddha Aryas.

If it is direct valid yogic cognition, its object must be *yang dak pe dön*, a perfect or supreme object. With regard to this supreme object —whether the selflessness of person or phenomena, in different degrees of subtlety or roughness—it varies according to the different schools.

For instance, neither Vaibhāṣhikas nor Sautrāntikas accept rough or subtle selflessness of phenomena. On the contrary, they assert that whatever exists must have a self of phenomena. Nevertheless, they posit the selflessness of person, both rough and subtle. Except for the Prāsaṅgikas, all the other schools—Vaibhāṣhika, Sautrāntika, Chittamātra, and Svātantrika—posit subtle and rough selflessness of person in a similar way. Rough selflessness of person is the emptiness [or absence] of a permanent, single, independent person;[11] subtle selflessness of person is the emptiness [or absence] of a self-sufficient, substantially existent person.[12] For Prāsaṅgikas, the rough selflessness of person is the emptiness [or absence] of a self-sufficient, substantially existent person; and subtle selflessness of

---

11 གང་ཟག་རྟག་གཅིག་རང་དབང་ཅན་གྱིས་སྟོང་པ་

12 གང་ཟག་རང་རྐྱ་ཐུབ་པའི་རྫས་ཡོད་ཀྱིས་སྟོང་པ་

person is the emptiness [or absence] of an inherently existent person.[13]

Although it is important that you learn this subject in detail, it is very difficult for brand new rookies to understand, and therefore only mentioned briefly here with the expectation that you will pursue it later.

direct valid yogic cognition in relation to subsequent cognition and non-ascertaining perception

Now, when outlining the various classifications of direct valid yogic cognition in the *Yongdzin Dura*, the following passages indicate that such a mind cannot be either subsequent cognition nor non-ascertaining perception. It states:

རྣལ་འབྱོར་མངོན་སུམ་དུ་གྱུར་བའི་སྣང་ལ་མ་ངེས་པའི་བློ་ནི་མེད་དེ།

རྣལ་འབྱོར་མངོན་སུམ་ཡིན་ན་རང་གི་གཞལ་བྱ་ངེས་པས་ཁྱབ་པའི་

ཕྱིར་ཏེ།

nel(n) jor ngön sum du gyur we nang la ma nge pe lo ni me de,
nel(n) jor ngön sum yin na rang gi shel ja nge pe kyap pe chir te

There doesn't exist an inattentive form of direct valid yogic cognition, because if it is a direct valid yogic cognition it must necessarily ascertain its object of comprehension.

In this regard, below is a quotation by the great Dharmakīrti:

ཚད་མ་རྣམ་འགྲེལ་ལས། བློ་གྲོས་ཆེན་པོས་མཐོང་ཉིད་ལས།

།རྣམ་པ་ཐམས་ཅད་ངེས་པར་བྱེད། །ཅེས་གསུངས་པའི་ཕྱིར།

---

13 གང་ཟག་རང་ངོས་ནས་གྲུབ་པའི་སྟོང་པ་

tse ma nam drel le, lo drö chen pö tong nyi le, nam pa tam che nge par che, che sung pe chir

In the *Commentary to (Dignāga's) "Compendium of Valid Cognition,"* it says: "Their great wisdom perceives all objects with perfect ascertainment."

Lo drö chen po means great wisdom. What is this great wisdom? *Nel(n) jor ngön sum*, Direct valid yogic cognition, the perception pertaining to Aryas. *Tong nyi le* means they perceive their object. *Nam pa tam che* means all of them. Therefore, such a mind cannot possibly be *nang la ma nge pa*, inattentive perception.

རྣལ་འབྱོར་མངོན་སུམ་དུ་གྱུར་པའི་བཅད་ཤེས་ཡོད་ཀྱང་། ཀུན་མཁྱེན་
ཡེ་ཤེས་སྐད་ཅིག་གཉིས་པ་ལྟ་བུ་ནི་བཅད་ཤེས་མ་ཡིན་ཏེ། ཀུན་
མཁྱེན་ཡེ་ཤེས་ཡིན་ན། ཚད་མ་ཡིན་པས་ཁྱབ་པའི་ཕྱིར་ཏེ།

nel(n) jor ngön sum du gyur pe che she yö kyang, kun kyen ye she ke chik nyi pa ta bu ni che she ma yin te, kun kyen ye she yin na, tse ma yin pe kyap pe chir te

Although there exists a subsequent cognition of yogic direct perception, the second moment, for example, of omniscient wisdom is not subsequent cognition because, what is omniscient wisdom must be valid cognition.

Kun kyen ye she means omniscient wisdom. *Kun kyen che she* means the subsequent moments of a Buddha's omniscience.

Among the four different levels of *nel(n) jor ngön sum*, direct valid yogic cognition, namely of a Listener Arya, a Solitary-Realizer Arya, a Bodhisattva Arya, and a Buddha Arya, the highest direct yogic cognition is that pertaining to a Buddha's omniscience. Above it says that whatever is a Buddha's omniscience must be valid cognition and not *che she*, subsequent mind. If it is *che she*, subsequent cognition, it must be *tse min gyi she pa*, non-valid cognition. *Te* here shows the reason why this is so and qualifies that reason by the following quotation:

> རྣམ་བཤད་ཐར་ལམ་གསལ་བྱེད་ལས། ཁོ་བོས་ནི་ཁ་ནང་དུ་ཕྱོགས་
> ནས་ཇི་ཙམ་བསམས་ཀྱང་། ཀུན་མཁྱེན་ཡེ་ཤེས་ལ་གསར་རྟོགས་
> ཀྱིས་མ་ཁྱབ་པ་མ་ཚོར་རོ། །ཞེས་པ་དང་།
>
> ***nam she tar lam sel che le, ko wö ni ka nang du chok ne ji tsam sam kyang, kun kyen ye she la sar tok kyi ma kyap pa ma tsor ro, she pa dang***
>
> This is subtantiated by a passage from *Explanations Clearing the Path to Liberation,*[14] in which it states: "No matter how much I ponder this subject deeply in my mind, I cannot find anything related to omniscient wisdom that is not valid cognition."

The great scholar and main disciple of Je Tsong Khapa, Gyeltsab Je, is referring to this kind of cognition in his commentary to the *Commentary to (Dignāga's) "Compendium of Valid Cognition." Ko wö ni* means I myself (i.e., the author, Gyeltsab Je Dharma Rinchen). *Ka nang du chok ne* literally means looking inwardly and implies that he was thinking very deeply. *Ji tsam sam kyang* means no matter how much I think about it. *Kun kyen ye she la sar tok kyi ma kyap pa ma tsor ro*, I never perceived anything related to omniscience that is not valid cognition. *Sar tok*, Newly realized, refers to *tse ma*, valid cognition. *Ma tsor* means cannot find.

Whatever is omniscience must be valid cognition and cannot be non-valid. *Kun kyen ye she* and *nam kyen* are synonyms meaning Buddha's omniscience. What is the definition of omniscience? *Chö*

---

[14] T: ***tshad ma rnam 'grel gyi tshig le'ur byas pa'i rnam bshad thar lam phyin ci ma log par gsal bar byed pa***

tam che ngön sum du tok pe ye she tar tuk nam kyen gyi tsen nyi,[15] The definition of omniscience is an ultimate wisdom that directly perceives all phenomena.

In this regard, the author of *Yongdzin Dura* offers a quotation of Kedrup Je, another principal disciple of Je Tsong Khapa, from his work *Clearing Away the Darkness from the Mind; Ornament of the Seven Treatises on Valid Cognition,*[16] another commentary to the *Commentary to (Dignāga's) "Compendium of Valid Cognition"*:

> ཚད་མ་ཡིད་ཀྱི་མུན་སེལ་ལས། ཚད་མ་སྔ་མས་བཟུང་བ་ཙམ་གྱིས་
> བཅད་ཤེས་སུ་འགྱུར་ན། ཀུན་མཁྱེན་ཡེ་ཤེས་སྐད་ཅིག་གཉིས་པ་ཡན་
> ཆད་བཅད་ཤེས་སུ་ཐལ་བ་སོགས་མཐའ་ཡས་པའི་གནོད་བྱེད་ཡོད་
> ཀྱང་འོག་ཏུ་བསྟན་པར་བྱའོ། །ཞེས་གསུངས་པའི་ཕྱིར།
>
> *tse ma yi kyi mun sel le, tse ma nga me sung wa tsam gyi che she su gyur na, kun kyen ye she ke chik nyi pa yen che che she su tel wa sok ta ye pe nö che yö kyang wok tu ten par ja'o, she sung pe chir*
>
> Just by the mere fact of being held by a previous valid cognition, if [direct yogic cognition] were to have subsequent moments of mind [implying that they are not valid], asserting such would cause limitless harm, since it would follow that everything from the second moment of direct yogic cognition all the way up to omniscience would have to qualify as subsequent mind [and consequently be invalid]. It is for this reason that I am going to take up this subject below.

---

15 ཆོས་ཐམས་ཅད་མངོན་སུམ་དུ་རྟོགས་པས་ཡེ་ཤེས་མཐར་ཐུག་རྣམ་མཁྱེན་གྱི་མཚན་ཉིད།

16 T: ***sde bdun la 'jug pa'i sgo don gnyer yid kyi mun sel***

What is the definition of *che she*, subsequent cognition? *Rang gi nyer len du gyur pe tse ma nga me tok sin tok pe dön la nen ne dzin pe rik pa che she kyi tsen nyi*, The definition of subsequent cognition is a mind that holds firmly to an object that has been previously realized by valid cognition, which serves as its cause. *Tse ma nga me sung wa tsam gyi* means, if you have just had a valid cognition a moment previously, it does not necessarily have to be subsequent cognition. Therefore, if you accept this, you also have to accept that the second moment of omniscience is a form of valid cognition as well, because omniscience is always valid cognition. Kedrup Je is saying here that since many wrong reasons can come as a result of failing to understand this point, he is going to describe these [wrong reasons and their refutations] later in his book.

Another classification is as follows.

two classifications by way of the object

ཡུལ་གྱི་སྒོ་ནས་དབྱེ་ན་ཇི་སྙེད་པ་རྟོགས་པའི་དེ། ཇི་ལྟ་བ་རྟོགས་པའི་རྣལ་འབྱོར་མངོན་སུམ་གཉིས་ཡོད།

yul gyi go ne ye na ji nye pa tok pe de, ji ta wa tok pe neln jor ngön sum nyi yö

> When classified by way of their object, direct valid yogic cognition can be classified into two kinds: that which realizes conventional truth objects and that which realizes ultimate truth objects.

If you classify direct valid yogic cognition in relation to its object, there are two kinds: *ji nye pa*, the multiplicity of things, and *ji ta wa*, things as they are, i.e., their true nature. This is a reference mainly to the Mādhyamika-Svātantrika school system. *Ji nye pa* means relative truth. For example, houses, furniture, people, the body, the mind, and so forth are all *ji nye pe chö*, relative truth objects. *Ji ta wa* means their real nature, referring to their non-inherent existence or voidness of self-existence.

The real nature of all things is *ji ta wa*, profound emptiness. We can use similar terms to express this profound emptiness, such as *tong nyi*, shūnyatā, or *dön dam pe chö*, ultimate truth phenomena, and so forth. The conventional nature of phenomena, however, is *ji nye pa*, what we call *kun dzob pe chö*, relative truth phenomena. All phenomena are comprised of both *ji nye pa*, relative truth, and *ji ta wa*, absolute truth.

Ji nye pa tok pe nel(n) jor ngön sum tse ma means direct valid yogic cognition realizing relative truth objects. *Ji nye pe chö*, Relative truth phenomena, can be classified into two kinds: *tak pa*, permanent phenomena, and *ngö po*, causally effective things or impermanent phenomena. Causally effective things are also classified into three kinds: form, consciousness, and those things that are neither form nor consciousness called *den min du che*, non-associated formations. There are many examples of this latter kind of causally effective thing. For example, what year is this? 1998. Is 1998 form or mental? You think it is mental? If it's mental can 1998 go crazy sometimes? If it is a mental phenomenon then it should potentially be able to go crazy. Is it form or mental? It is neither. Yet isn't it a causally effective thing? Yes, of course it's a thing. This is an example of *den min du che*, non-associated formation. Its definition is *suk she gang rung ma yin pe ngö po*,[17] a causally effective thing that is neither form nor consciousness.

In the Svatāntrika school, *gang sak gyi dak me tra mo*, subtle selflessness of person, is not profound. It is only *ji ta we chö*, a relative truth phenomenon. This refers to *gang sak den par me pa*, non-truly existent person, or *gang sak den par ma drup pa*, non-truly established person, which are synonyms. This is *tong nyi*, emptiness, according to the Svatāntrika school system. The profound object in their school system is *chö kyi dak me tra mo*, subtle selflessness of phenomena. *Chö kyi dak me rak pa*, rough selflessness of phenomena, for them is also not a profound object, since it is *ji nye pe chö*, a relative truth phenomenon. Therefore, among these three objects, according to the view of their system, two are relative truth objects, and the last one, *chö kyi dak me tra mo*, subtle selflessness

---

[17] གཟུགས་ཤེས་གང་རུང་མ་ཡིན་པའི་དངོས་པོ་ལྡན་མིན་འདུས་བྱེད་ཀྱི་མཚན་ཉིད།

of phenomena, is *ji ta wa*, ultimate truth. So, some of the objects of direct valid yogic cognitions are relative truth objects and some are absolute truth objects.

II. Inferential valid cognition

རང་གི་རྟེན་རྟགས་ཡང་དག་ལ་བརྟེན་ནས་རང་གི་གཞལ་བྱ་ལྐོག་གྱུར་བ་ལ་གསར་དུ་མི་སླུ་བའི་ཞེན་རིག །རྗེས་སུ་དཔག་པའི་ཚད་མའི་མཚན་ཉིད།

rang gi ten tak yang dak la ten ne rang gi shel ja gok gyur wa la sar du mi lu we shen rik, je su pak pe tse me tsen nyi

> The definition of inferential valid cognition is a new, infallible conceptual cognition with regard to a hidden object, its object of comprehension, based on a perfect reason.

Rang gi ten means its basis or supporter, referring to the cause by which to gain this type of mind. What is that basis? *Tak yang dak la ten ne* means based on a perfect reason. One gains inferential valid cognition only with perfect reasons. *Rang gi shel ja* means its object. *Gok gyur wa la* means with respect to a hidden object. *Rang dzin tok pe gok du gyur pe tsul gyi tok par ja wa gok gyur gyi tsen nyi,*[18] The definition of a hidden phenomenon is that object realized in a hidden manner by the conceptual mind grasping it. In general, *gok gyur*, hidden phenomenon, and *ngön gyur,*[19] manifest phenomenon, are not contradictory, and can often be one object that is both of them. *Gok gyur* means some subjects cannot perceive it directly because it is hidden to them. Is your real nature *gok gyur*, hidden, or *ngön gyur*, manifest to you? *Gok gyur*, Hidden. Why? Because you cannot

---

[18] རང་འཛིན་རྟོག་པས་ལྐོག་ཏུ་གྱུར་པའི་ཚུལ་གྱིས་རྟོགས་པར་བྱ་བ་ལྐོག་གྱུར་གྱི་མཚན་ཉིད།

[19] མངོན་སུམ་གྱི་ཚད་མས་དངོས་སུ་རྟོགས་པར་བྱ་བ་མངོན་གྱུར་གྱི་མཚན་ཉིད།
The definition of a manifest phenomenon is an object realized directly by direct valid cognition.

perceive it directly. If you could perceive it that way, this definition would also have to incorporate the definition of *nel(n) jor ngön sum tse ma*, direct valid yogic cognition. Even though your real nature is *gok gyur* to you, nevertheless, your real nature can be perceived by the direct valid yogic cognition of many Arhats, Aryas, and Buddhas. So for them your real nature is not *gok gyur*, hidden, but rather *ngön gyur*, manifest. This indicates that for some subjects something is hidden, while for others that same thing is manifest. Therefore, whether something is hidden or not is dependent upon the perceiver.

Sar du mi lu we means newly and infallibly. *Shen rik*, Other cognizing, means the opposite of *rang rik*, self-cognizing, and refers to the perception of outer objects or those objects other than one's own mind. *Je su* means after or following. After what? After realizing something through good reasons. *Pak pa*, To infer, means even if you cannot see that object directly, you guess that something must be there by using your reason.

Smoke and fire are very useful for explaining this topic. Oh, I put too big a fire in the pot so you can see it! That is not *gok gyur*, hidden, for you. But if I put the incense deeper in the pot you can only see the smoke directly, *ngön gyur*. After following that apprehension of smoke, you realize that there must be fire. There is a difference between saying "must be" and "there is." One you gain by inference and the other you realize directly. When we say "must be," the situation has not been definitely decided. However, it is a kind of unerring judgment. Therefore, *pak pa* means to judge or to make a correct guess. *Tse ma*, pramāṇa in Sanskrit, means correct cognition.

Since this definition of inferential valid cognition is lacking the negative particle "*ma*," saying *tak yang dak la ten ne*, instead of *tak yang dak la <u>ma</u> ten par*, this indicates that inferential valid cognitions are based on correct reasons and so get at their hidden objects in an indirect way. For example, what do you see rising here? Smoke. Why is there smoke coming from here? Because something is burning in that container. Smoke, in this case, is *tak yang dak*, a good reason or sign, to prove that there is fire in that container. Using smoke as a reason or sign, you can realize there must be fire in that container. The mind that perceives this is *je pak tse ma*, inferential valid cognition, which depends upon a correct reason to gain access to its object. Your knowledge, being that perception of fire, is an infallible mind.

What is the correct reason upon which this cognition is based in this case? The smoke that you see directly. *Rang gi shel ja*, Its object, is fire, which is *gok gyur*, a hidden phenomenon, because you cannot perceive it directly. Since it is hidden from your direct perception, you can only perceive it indirectly through good reasons. That cognition which perceives that there must be fire in that container is a kind of infallible knowledge due to the infallible relationship between fire and smoke.

What kind of mind is it that can see smoke? Eye consciousness. That eye consciousness is *ngön sum tse ma*, direct perception. When you see smoke, you have perceived it. You don't have to rely on good reasons to find it. What is *je pak kyi shel ja*, the object of this inferential mind? Fire. And what is *ngön sum gyi shel ja*, the object of direct valid [sense] cognition, in this case? Smoke.

Is this clear? Just a little clear or crystal clear? Crystal clear? I'm glad.

three classifications

དབྱེ་ན། དངོས་སྟོབས་རྗེས་དཔག ཡིད་ཆེས་རྗེས་དཔག གྲགས་པའི་རྗེས་དཔག་གསུམ་ཡོད།

ye na, ngö tob je pak, yi che je pak, trak pe je pak sum yö

When inferential valid cognition is classified there are three types: inferential valid cognition by the power of the fact, inferential valid cognition based on trust, and inferential valid cognition based on conventional usage.

The first two kinds of inferential valid cognition—*ngö tob je pak* and *yi che je pak*—are the most important. The third one, *trak pe je pak*, however, is the easiest one to explain and understand.

a) inferential valid cognition by the power of the fact

The first, *ngö tob je pak*, means inference based on the power of the fact. *Ngö* is short for *ngö po*, causally effective thing. *Tob* means some kind of power of that causally effective thing. We call this *ngö po tob shuk kyi rik pa*,[20] a reason that proceeds from the power of the fact, which is a very useful term in the field of logic. *Tob* and *shuk* both mean power. We often use these two words to describe very strong people who lift huge weights, calling them *tob shuk chen po*. A way to describe this kind of inference is as follows. Smoke, as a causally effective thing, has the power of actuality. An example of *ngö po tob shuk kyi rik pa*, reason by the power of the fact, is that used in the statement: *du wa tak la ten ne me yö par tok pe tse ma*, the valid cognition that realizes that there is fire based on the sign of there being smoke. By reason of perceiving smoke you can realize that there is fire. The very actuality of smoke has the power to produce an inferential valid cognition that realizes the presence of fire through the presence of that smoke due to their intimate cause and effect relationship. This is expressed below.

> བྱས་པའི་རྟགས་ལ་བརྟེན་ནས་སྒྲ་མི་རྟག་རྟོགས་པའི་གསར་དུ་མི་སླུ་
> བའི་ཞེན་རིག་དང་པོ་དང་།
>
> *che pe tak la ten ne dra mi tak tok pe sar du mi lu we shen rik dang po dang*
>
> An example of the first (inferential valid cognition by the power of the fact) is a new, infallible conceptual mind that realizes that sound is impermanent based on the reason of its being produced.

A common example of *ngö tob je pak*, inferential valid cognition by the power of the fact, is the inference used in the logical statement: *dra chö chen, mi tak te, che pe chir*, consider sound, it is

---

[20] དངོས་པོ་སྟོབས་ཞུགས་ཀྱི་རིགས་པ་

impermanent, because it is a product. *Dra*, Sound, is the basis. *Mi tak pa*, Impermanent, is *drup che chö*, the quality to be proved, in the thesis proving that sound is impermanent. *Che pa*, Product or produced, is the reason given to prove the thesis. With this reason you can prove that sound is impermanent. What is the definition of sound? *Nyen ja dra'i tsen nyi*, Object of hearing is the definition of sound. What is the definition of *mi tak pa*, impermanence? *Ke chik ma mi tak pe tsen nyi*, Momentary is the definition of impermanence. *Ke chik ma* means disappearing and arising from one moment to the next. From this we can understand that that which has the nature of impermanence cannot remain for more than an instant. The period of duration within one fingersnap is classified into sixty-four smaller parts, with one sixty-fourth part being the smallest *ke chik ma*, period of momentary time, and one *kal pa*, eon, being the longest.

Now, if you are trying to prove that sound is *mi tak pa*, impermanent, how are you going to do that? You might use this reason: *che pa yin pe chir*, because it is a product. What is the definition of *che pa*, product? *Gyu kyen le kye pa che pe tsen nyi*,[21] That which is produced by causes and conditions is the definition of product. *Gyu* is a main cause; *kyen* refers to secondary causes. Together these make a product. If something is produced by causes and conditions it must be impermanent. Consequently, sound must be impermanent. This is the meaning of the phrase above that says *che pe tak la ten ne*, based on the reason of its being produced. *Dra mi tak tok* means you realized that sound is impermanent by your inferential cognition through using the reason of its being produced. *Sar du*, Newly, means you just realized it now and not before. *Mi lu wa* means infallible. *Shen rik* refers to a kind of mind that cognizes things other than itself as opposed to *rang rik*, self-cognizing mind [or the mind that cognizes mind itself].

Inferential knowledge can be useful in many ways for your practice. For example, it may help you to realize that if you collect bad deeds in this life, in your future lives you will be reborn as a hell being in the hells. However, if you practice morality, you will have an excellent life in the higher realms. Keeping morality has the power to give you a birth in the higher realms. Bad deeds, such as

---

[21] རྒྱུ་རྐྱེན་ལས་སྐྱེས་པ་བྱས་པའི་མཚན་ཉིད།

taking other beings' lives, for instance, have the power to give you a hell being's life. This relationship between an action and its result is infallible. However, we cannot see the power of either of these directly. The relationship between good deeds and their results, and bad deeds and their results, are not immediately apparent. Nevertheless, both of them exist, even though we cannot see them. Well then, if we don't have the power to perceive such things as subtle impermanence and the workings of karma, how can we be certain that they exist? For that we must rely on the second kind of inferential valid cognition known as *yi che je pak*, inference based on trust.

b) inferential valid cognition based on trust

> དཔྱད་གསུམ་གྱི་དག་པའི་ལུང་གི་རྟགས་ལས་སྦྱིན་པས་ལོངས་སྤྱོད་
> ཁྲིམས་ཀྱི་བདེ། ཞེས་སོགས་ཀྱི་ལུང་རང་གི་བསྟན་བྱའི་དོན་ལ་
> གསར་དུ་མི་སླུ་བའི་ཞེན་རིག་གཉིས་པ་ཡིན།
>
> *che sum gyi dak pe lung gi tak le chin pe long chö trim kyi de she sok kyi lung rang gi ten je dön la sar du mi lu we shen rik nyi pa yin*
>
> An example of the second (inferential valid cognition based on trust) is a new, infallible conceptual mind with regard to the meaning taught in scripture such as the passage: "From giving comes wealth; from keeping morality comes happiness," which is tested by the three examinations.

Che pa sum gyi dak pe lung yin pe chir means it is scripture that is tested by the three examinations. *She pe*, Says, in this case indicates a scriptural quotation. *Rang gi ten je dön la* means the meaning of what it teaches, or its subject matter. *Sar du* means newly. *Mi lu wa* means it is unerring or infallible. *Shen rik* as mentioned above, refers to a kind of mind that cognizes things other than its own mind.

Yi che je pak means inference through trust. This is very important knowledge for Dharma practitioners. How can we gain this kind of inference based on trust? We can gain it, for example, through the scriptural teachings such as: "*jin pe long chö trim gyi de*," "if we practice the perfection of giving in this life, in our future life we will be very rich." *Trim* is short for *tsul trim*, morality. *De* is short for *de wa* meaning happiness, referring to a happy life in one of the three higher realms—human realm, demigod realm, and god realm—in the future. However, the happiness of nirvana and Buddhahood are the principal goals or main happiness.

Buddha spent many, many kalpas practicing restraint from telling lies and he completely abandoned long ago the ten bad deeds consisting of three by body, four by speech, and three by mind, and he achieved the ultimate goal. After having achieved that goal, what need would there be for him to tell us lies? Through the practice of different kinds of virtues you will have different good results. He taught about this in detail. Therefore, we can trust the words of his teachings. We can have *yi che je pak*, inferential cognition based on trust, through what Buddha said. The object of that trust is infallible. The relationship between causes and their results are all perfect. Therefore, we can gain inferential valid cognition based on trust through listening to and reading Buddha's teachings.

By following *yi che je pak*, inference based on trust, at some point we will be able to perceive such things directly. For example, it is not too difficult to perceive one's own former and future lives as well as the former and future lives of others. Sometimes we can see one hundred or a thosand previous lifetimes or even a hundred thousand lifetimes in the future. In order to have that kind of perception, first we have to have gained *shi ne*, calm abiding. Without developing calm abiding, such achievement is impossible.

There are many descriptions of such kinds of knowledge. For instance, when Naropa had finished his monastic studies in eastern India, he went to a retreat place to meditate. At that time Tilopa was living in western India. For a long time while in retreat Naropa couldn't gain any results. Finally, at one point he heard a voice saying to him, "You shouldn't sit there anymore. Go meet your Lama who is residing in western India. His name is Tilopa." He heard this coming from the sky. This is but one example revealing such extraordinary experiences derived from the cultivation of the mind.

After achieving calm abiding you have to do special practices to gain the five wisdom eyes and the six clairvoyances. These are not very difficult to achieve. What is difficult to achieve, however, is the first step—calm abiding. Now you can understand how *yi che je pak*, inference based on trust, is not just some kind of blind faith.

This topic, regarding the profundity of the teachings and their validity as words to be trusted, can be explained using many reasons that show how Buddha's teachings are infallible. By way of illustration we can express this scriptural statement logically as follows: *jin pe long chö trim gyi de she pe lung chö chen, rang gi ten che dön la mi lu wa yin te, che pa sum gyi dak pe lung yin pe chir*, consider the subject, the scripture that states "by giving comes wealth, by morality comes happiness," the subject that it teaches is infallible, because it is scripture that is tested by the three examinations. What are *che pa sum*, these three examinations?[22]

1) *Tong wa ngön gyur ten pe cha la ngön sum tse me nö pa me pa*, [It is scripture] that is not harmed [by being contradicted] by direct valid cognition. *Tong wa ngön gyur* refers to any object of the direct sense consciousnesses, such as visible things, audible things, and so forth. This means that it should in no way be contradictory to any direct valid cognition. No one can say, "I see something wrong with your statement because it doesn't comply with reality." No one can properly argue with it.

2) *Chung tse gok gyur ten pe cha la je pak tse me nö pa me pa*, [It is scripture] that is not harmed [by being contradicted] by inferential valid cognition in regard to those things that are slightly hidden. For example, according to scripture in the future you will get good results by practicing the perfection of giving. Can you see those future good results right now? No, ordinary people cannot see them. However, Aryas, high Bodhisattvas, and Buddhas do have the

---

[22] དཔྱད་པ་གསུམ། 1) མཐོང་བ་མངོན་གྱུར་ལ་མངོན་སུམ་ཚད་མས་གནོད་པ་མེད་པ་ 2) ཅུང་ཟད་ལྐོག་གྱུར་ལ་རྗེས་དཔག་ཚད་མས་གནོད་པ་མེད་པ་ 3) ཤིན་ཏུ་ལྐོག་གྱུར་ལ་ལུང་ཚད་མས་གནོད་པ་མེད་པ་

capacity to see them. That condition is *gok gyur*, hidden, from ordinary persons. It is because we cannot see them directly that we have to use *je pak tse ma*, inferential valid cognition, to verify the truth of this statement. An example of something that is *chung tse gok gyur*, slightly hidden, is the perfection of giving practice toward a poor person. The result is that you will be rich and in good health in the future.

3) *Shin tu gok gyur ten pe cha la yi che je pak nö pa me pa*, [It is scripture] that is not harmed [by being contradicted] by inferential valid cognition based on trust in regard to those things that are extremely hidden. This implies that the beginning of a scriptural passage, for example, should not contradict the latter part, and vice versa; that is, it requires that the meanings not be internally self-contradictory. *Shin tu gok gyur* refers to extremely hidden objects. This indicates that we cannot argue about those objects since they are very hidden to us. Therefore, we have to rely upon *yi che je pak tse ma*, inferential valid cognition based on trust, to realize them. With this kind of inference we cannot find anything wrong with such a statement. As an example we can offer Buddha's teachings on the Four Noble Truths. If we investigate these closely and apply them to our own condition we will discover their truth and will be able to determine whether they pertain to infallible speech or not.

c) inferential valid cognition based on conventional usage

རྟོག་ཡུལ་ན་ཡོད་པའི་རྟགས་ལས་རི་བོང་ཅན་ལ་ཟླ་སྒྲས་བརྗོད་རུང་དུ་
རྟོགས་པའི་གསར་དུ་མི་སླུ་བའི་རིག་པ་དེ་གསུམ་པ་ཡིན།

tok yul na yö pe tak le ri bong chen la da dre jö rung du tok pe sar du mi lu we rik pa de sum pa yin

An example of the third is a new, infallible conceptual mind that realizes the suitability of calling the "rabbit-possessor" by the name "moon," by reason of its existing among objects of conception.

The third kind of inferential cognition is *trak pe je pak*, inferential valid cognition based on conventional usage, which is a kind of knowledge gained through names. *Trak pa* means well known, as when we say, "Everybody calls something such and such." *Tok yul na yö pe chir* means because it exists among objects of conception. In the field of conceptual objects, you can give things any name you wish since there is no restriction for doing so other than that based on convention. *Ri bong chen la* means to the "rabbit-possessor," (the moon), *da dre jö rung*, it is suitable to give the name *da*, "moon."

In the poetry of the East, the moon is often called *ri bong chen*, the rabbit-possessor. When we look up at the moon we can see the figure of a rabbit. That is how poets came to give the moon that name. There is also a very beautiful story regarding how this image came to be there.

In logic we give the following reason: *ri bong chen chö chen, da dre jö rung yin te, tok yul na yö pe chir,*[23] consider the "rabbit-possessor," it is suitable to call it "moon," because it exists among objects of conception. Since people perceive it that way, it is valid to give it such a name.

---

[23] རི་བོང་ཅན་ཆོས་ཅན། ཟླ་སྒྲས་བརྗོད་རུང་ཡིན་ཏེ། རྟོག་ཡུལ་ན་ཡོད་པའི་ཕྱིར།

B. Non-Valid Cognition
five classifications

གསར་དུ་མི་སླུ་བ་མ་ཡིན་པའི་རིག་པ། ཚད་མིན་གྱི་བློའི་མཚན་ཉིད།

sar du mi lu wa ma yin pe rik pa, tse min gyi lo'i tsen nyi

The definition of non-valid cognition is an awareness that is neither new nor infallible.

This is the opposite of correct cognition since these minds are not *tse ma*, valid mind. The classifications are as follows:

དབྱེ་ན། བཅད་ཤེས།[24] ཐེ་ཚོམ། ཡིད་དཔྱོད། ལོག་ཤེས། སྣང་ལ་མ་ངེས་དང་ལྔ།

ye na, che she, te tsom, yi chö, lok she, nang la ma nge dang nga

When classified there are five: subsequent cognition, doubt, analytical speculation, wrong consciousness, and inattentive perception.

These are the five classes of non-valid cognition.

[24] There are two spellings of this word in Tibetan: ***bcad shes*** and ***dpyad shes***.

III. Subsequent cognition

རང་གི་ཉེར་ལེན་དུ་གྱུར་པའི་ཚད་མ་སྔ་མས་རྟོགས་ཟིན་པའི་དོན་ལ་
མནན་ནས་འཛིན་པའི་རིག་པ། བཅད་ཤེས་ཀྱི་མཚན་ཉིད།

rang gi nyer len du gyur pe tse ma nga me tok sin pe dön la nen ne dzin pe rik pa, che she kyi tsen nyi

The definition of subsequent cognition is a mind that firmly holds its object, which has been previously realized by valid cognition, its substantial cause.

There are many *yik cha*, monastic manuals, that deal with these logic topics. Some of them add *tok sin tok pe*, realizing what has already been realized, to the definition. Some definitions are abbreviated and others are very detailed. Nevertheless, the meaning is the same.

Do you remember what came out of this incense box a while ago? "Yes, smoke." You can say, "I saw smoke." How did you see it? "I saw it with my eye consciousness." Do you remember it? "Yes." Is that memory of smoke eye consciousness or not? "No, it is not eye consciousness." However, that recollection was produced by an eye consciousness that saw smoke previously and therefore is the main or substantial cause of the subsequent mind realizing that smoke. That is the meaning of *rang gi nyer len du gyur pe*, having become its main substantial cause.

There are different kinds of causes. For example, if you plant rice seeds, rice sprouts will eventually grow. What do those rice sprouts grow from? Seeds. Those seeds are *nyer len gyi gyu*, the substantial cause, of that rice. Heat, water, fertilizer, and dirt are secondary causes. So, in this case, the mind that is your memory has a previous eye consciousness, which saw that smoke, serving as its substantial cause.

Tse ma nga me means perceived by a previous valid cognition. *Tok sin* means perceived already. *Dön la* means with regard to that object, for example, the smoke you saw previously. *Nen ne dzin pa* is another way of saying to hold or retain a perception; that is, you still remember the object and are focusing the recollecting mind on that smoke. *Rik pa* is a kind of mind.

two classifications

> དབྱེ་ན། རྟོག་པ་བཅད་ཤེས། མངོན་སུམ་བཅད་ཤེས་གཉིས།
>
> *ye na, tok pa che she, ngön sum che she nyi*
>
> When subsequent cognition is classified there are two types: conceptual subsequent cognition and direct [non-conceptual] subsequent cognition.

Ngön sum means direct cognition; *tok pa* means conceptual or indirect cognition, referring here to *je pak tse ma*, inferential valid cognition. To use our previous example, you had both kinds of valid mind regarding the smoke that you saw earlier.

Tok pa che she, Conceptual subsequent cognition, can be explained this way. Did you realize before that there was fire in the incense holder because smoke was rising from there? Yes. Through using smoke as a reason or a sign to realize the existence of fire in that holder you gained *je pak tse ma*, inferential valid cognition. Do you still remember the result of that reasoning—realizing the existence of fire in that holder? Yes. The realization you acquired from that reasoning is an example of *tok pa che she*, conceptual subsequent cognition.

Ngön sum che she, Direct [non-conceptual] cognition, can be explained as follows. Do you remember the smoke that you saw a while ago? The memory of the smoke that you perceived directly at a previous time is *ngön sum che she*, direct subsequent cognition. Therefore, you had both kinds of minds previously in regard to that smoke and fire.

Now, below are examples from the text.

ཚུར་མཐོང་གི་རྒྱུད་ཀྱི་སྔོན་འཛིན་མིག་ཤེས་ཀྱིས་དྲངས་པའི་སྔོན་པོ་
དོན་མཐུན་དུ་ངེས་པའི་ངེས་ཤེས་དེ་དང་པོ་དང་།

tsur tong gi gyu kyi ngön dzin mik she kyi drang pe ngön po dön tun du nge pe nge she de dang po dang

An example of the first, conceptual subsequent cognition, is an ascertaining consciousness in the mind of an ordinary person perceiving the color blue, which was elicited by his eye consciousness apprehending the color blue, as being in accord with the fact.

Tsur tong, meaning literally "seeing this side," is a synonym for an ordinary person, or non-Arya, one who has not attained the Path of Insight. In the Vinaya Sūtra they are also called *chi pa*, immature persons, or *tse pa.* The first period of a human being's life is known as the stage of *chi pa*, an immature person, referring to the period of mental and physical immaturity from birth up to the age of twenty years old. By analogy this is also a description of *tsur tong*, a non-Arya. So, before perceiving the real nature of all phenomena directly and thereby achieving the Arya's path, a person is considered a *chi pa* or *tsur tong. Tsur tong gi gyu kyi* means the eye consciousness in the mind of that kind of person who has perceived the actual color blue. *Drang pe* means induced or having a memory of what produced that mind, in this case, a memory of a blue color. *Dön tun* means unerringly. *Nge she* means that recollecting mental consciousness.

སྔོན་འཛིན་མིག་ཤེས་སྐད་ཅིག་གཉིས་པ་གཉིས་པ་ཡིན།

ngön dzin mik she ke chik nyi pa nyi pa yin

An example of the second, direct subsequent cognition, is the second moment of an eye consciousness apprehending a blue color.

IV. Doubt

རང་གི་དམིགས་པ་ལ་མཐའ་གཉིས་སུ་དོགས་པའི་སེམས་པ། ཐེ་ཚོམ་གྱི་མཚན་ཉིད།

rang gi mik pa la ta nyi su dok pe sem pa, te tsom gyi tsen nyi

The definition of doubt is a mind [mental derivative] that oscillates in two ways with regard to its object.

Te tsom, Doubt, is a kind of mind that we are all very familiar with. *Rang gi mik pa la* means focusing on its object. *Ta nyi su* means in two ways. *Dok pa* means having misgivings or being indecisive about the object. *Sem pa* refers to a mental derivative.

two (or three) classifications

དབྱེ་ན། དོན་འགྱུར་གྱི་ཐེ་ཚོམ། དོན་མི་འགྱུར་གྱི་ཐེ་ཚོམ་གཉིས་ཡོད།

ye na, dön gyur gyi te tsom, dön mi(n) gyur gyi te tsom nyi yö

When doubt is classified there are two kinds: doubt tending toward the fact and doubt tending away from the fact.

Some logic textbooks list a third kind, *cha nyam pe te tsom*,[25] equal doubt or equally undecided doubt, but here it gives the two most important ones. *Dön gyur* means a kind of doubt that is closer to the correct object. Such a mind, though not sure, is inclined toward the correct object. *Dön mi(n) gyur* means a kind of doubt that gets farther away from the right object, inclining in the opposite direction.

---

[25] ཆ་མཉམ་པའི་ཐེ་ཚོམ་

The text gives illustrations of these kinds of doubt as follows.

སྒྲ་རྟག་གམ་མི་རྟག་ཕལ་ཆེར་མི་རྟག་སྙམ་དུ་འཛིན་པའི་ཐེ་ཚོམ་དང་པོ་དང་། སྒྲ་རྟག་གམ་མི་རྟག་ཕལ་ཆེར་རྟག་སྙམ་དུ་འཛིན་པའི་ཐེ་ཚོམ་གཉིས་པ་ཡིན།

dra tak gam mi tak pel cher mi tak nyam du dzin pe te tsom dang po dang, dra tak gam mi tak pel cher tak nyam du dzin pe te tsom nyi pa yin

An example of the first [doubt tending toward the fact] is like the doubt in the mind of someone who in wondering whether sound is impermanent or permanent thinks that maybe it is impermanent. An example of the second [doubt tending away from the fact] is like the doubt in the mind of someone who in wondering whether sound is impermanent or permanent thinks that maybe it is permanent.

Pel cher means maybe. *Nyam du* means thinking that way. *Dzin pe* means holding that position.

V. Speculative assumption

མྱོང་བ་དང་རང་གི་རྟགས་ཡང་དག་ལ་མ་བརྟེན་པར་རང་ཡུལ་བདེན་པ་མཐའ་གཅིག་གསར་དུ་ངེས་པའི་ཞེན་རིག རང་ཉིད་ཡིད་དཔྱོད་ཀྱི་མཚན་ཉིད།

nyong wa dang rang gi tak yang dak la ma ten par rang yul den pa ta chik sar du nge pe shen rik, rang nyi yi chö kyi tsen nyi

The definition of speculative assumption is a conceptual cognition that newly and unwaveringly ascertains its true object without relying on either experience or a perfect reason.

To illustrate what this means: if I were to present to you the statement, *dra chö chen, mi tak te, che pe chir*, consider sound, it is impermanent, because it is produced, just by hearing those words you can gain some knowledge. This kind of knowledge is *yi chö*, speculative assumption, since you neither have any experience about the meaning of that statement nor do you have *tse ma*, valid cognition, gained by means of a correct sign. Even though the statement may give the correct sign as a reason, still you don't know why it is a correct sign. Nevertheless, just by hearing the correct reason given in that statement you gain some knowledge about the impermanence of sound.

Another definition for speculative assumption may be found in the *Yongdzin Dura*:

རང་ཡུལ་ལ་ཞེན་པའི་སླུ་བའི་ཞེན་རིག་དོན་མཐུན་ཡིད་དཔྱོད་ཀྱི་མཚན་ཉིད།

rang yul la shen pe lu we shen rik dön tun yi chö kyi tsen nyi

> The definition of speculative assumption is a fallible, conceptual mind that is consistent with reality in relation to the object of its belief.

Rang yul la means with regard to its object. *Shen pa* means a kind of conception or belief about something. Even though you cannot perceive the object directly, or even apprehend it indirectly through reasoning, nevertheless, you still maintain some kind of belief toward that object. This implies that not only do you hold a belief but that you are also attached to that belief in some way, as expressed by "I like it," or "I don't like it." *Lu wa*, Fallible, means that such a belief is not always correct, since the belief pertaining to analytical speculation can sometimes be wrong. In general, *lu wa* means cheating; so, if you follow that erroneous object, you will be cheated out of the truth of that object. *Shen rik* is a conceiving cognition or believing mind with regard to its object. *Dön tun* generally means its mode of perception is okay implying that it accords with reality; for instance, perceiving yellow as yellow, red as red, and so forth, and not perceiving white as blue.

two (or five) classifications

> དེ་ལ་རྒྱུ་མཚན་ཅན་གྱི་ཡིད་དཔྱོད་རྒྱུ་མཚན་མེད་པའི་ཡིད་དཔྱོད་
> གཉིས།
>
> *de la gyu tsen chen gyi yi chö gyu tsen me pe yi chö nyi*
>
> [In general] there are two kinds of speculative assumption: speculative assumption with a reason and speculative assumption lacking a reason.

The example given above where the statement about sound is qualified by a perfect reason illustrates the first kind of speculative assumption. An example of the second is as follows. Is sound impermanent or not? You may have heard that sound is impermanent, but can you give me a good reason why it is impermanent? If you cannot supply a correct reason why sound is impermanent because you're not really sure why it has that nature, this is an example of *gyu tsen me pe yi chö*, speculative assumption lacking a reason.

There is another way of classifying speculative assumption into five kinds. This rendition is found in the *Yongdzin Dura* as follows.

> དེ་ལ་དབྱེ་ན། རྒྱུ་མཚན་མེད་པའི་ཡིད་དཔྱོད། རྒྱུ་མཚན་དང་འགལ་བའི་ཡིད་དཔྱོད། རྒྱུ་མཚན་མ་ངེས་པའི་ཡིད་དཔྱོད། རྒྱུ་མཚན་མ་གྲུབ་པའི་ཡིད་དཔྱོད། རྒྱུ་མཚན་ཡོད་ཀྱང་གཏན་ལ་མ་ཕེབས་པའི་ཡིད་དཔྱོད་དང་ལྔ།
>
> *de la ye na, gyu tsen me pe yi chö, gyu tsen dang gel we yi chö, gyu tsen ma nge pe yi chö, gyu tsen ma drup pe yi chö, gyu tsen yö kyang ten la ma pep pe yi chö dang nga*
>
> When speculative assumption is classified there are five kinds: 1) speculative assumption without reasons, 2) speculative assumption that uses contradictory reasons, 3) speculative assumption that uses indefinite reasons, 4) speculative assumption that uses unestablished reasons, and 5) speculative assumption that lacks well-founded reasons.

By understanding these five classifications, you can learn the main quality of speculative assumption.

1) *Gyu tsen me pe yi chö*, speculative assumption without reasons, means gaining this kind of mind without using reasons.

2) *Gyu tsen dang gel we yi chö*, speculative assumption that uses contradictory reasons, means gaining this kind of mind through some kind of wrong or contradictory reasoning.

3) *Gyu tsen ma nge pe yi chö*, speculative assumption that uses indefinite reasons, means you have seen or heard some reason but you have not realized or verified it. "I heard a reason, but I'm not too sure about it." "I saw something, but wasn't sure whether it was

smoke or a cloud." This kind of mind only assumes something that it has not verified by itself.

4) *Gyu tsen ma drup pe yi chö*, speculative assumption that uses unestablished reasons, means you gained a mind of speculative assumption through using a reason but that reason cannot prove the subject correctly.

5) *Gyu tsen yö kyang ten la ma pep pe yi chö*, speculative assumption that lacks well-founded reasons, means you do have some reason but you're not sure whether or not it correctly proves that subject since it doesn't firmly establish it. Consequently, there is still some potential error regarding the object of engagement.

As speculative minds, none of these is correct and infallible, since they are *lu wa*, fallible, with respect to their objects. Examples of these are given below.

དང་པོ་ནི། སྒྲ་མི་རྟག་ཅེས་པའི་ངག་ཙམ་ལ་བརྟེན་ནས་སྒྲ་མི་རྟག་
པར་འཛིན་པའི་བློ་ལྟ་བུ་སྟེ། སྒྲ་མི་རྟག་ཅེས་པའི་ངག་དེས་སྒྲ་མི་རྟག་
པའི་དམ་བཅའ་བརྗོད་ཀྱི། རྒྱུ་མཚན་མ་བརྗོད་པའི་ཕྱིར།

dang po ni, dra mi tak che pe ngak tsam la ten ne dra mi tak par dzin pe lo ta bu te, dra mi tak che pe ngak de dra mi tak pe dam ja jö kyi, gyu tsen ma jö pe chir

An example of the first [speculative assumption without reasons] is like the mind that believes sound to be impermanent through relying strictly on some statement that says: "Sound is impermanent." Swearing that sound is impermanent because [you heard the statement] "sound is impermanent" is making a statement without giving any reason to support it.

This example is like blind faith. If someone were to say to you, "Sound is impermanent," and you believe what they say strictly on the basis of their saying it, in this way you are holding sound to be impermanent without giving any reason save the mere speech of someone else. This is an assumption because you didn't gain that knowledge by means of good reasons. Even if you were to hear the statement: *dra chö chen, mi tak te, che pe chir*, consider sound, it is impermanent, because it is produced [by its causes], although this statement is using a perfect reason to prove it, that is, that sound must be impermanent because it was produced from causes, it is still a speculative mind, since you have not validated this reason for yourself. This is why *yi chö*, analytical speculation, is close to *je pak tse ma*, inferential valid cognition. By using *che pa*, produced, as a reason, you can gain a valid inferential cognition about the impermanence of sound. However, just hearing such a reason is not enough to establish it validly to oneself. Just hearing something and establishing it to your own mind are very different! So, this reveals that there is a significant difference between analytical speculation and inferential valid cognition. If you find a good reason, you can establish it to your mind.

Dra mi tak par dzin pe lo, A mind that holds sound as impermanent, is not necessarily *tse ma*, a valid mind. Though true, it may not be established through using good reasons to substantiate it and may be *ngak tsam*, mere speech.

Dra mi tak che pe ngak te means saying the statement "sound is impermanent." *Dam ja* means swearing or saying firmly what you believe, such as "I believe that sound is impermanent." Such a belief can either be with or without a good reason. For example, *dra chö chen, mi tak te, che pa yin pe chir*, consider sound, it is impermanent, because it is produced, "being produced" is a good reason that can validate the impermanence of sound. But if you say, *dra chö chen, mi tak te*, consider sound, it is impermanent, you are making that statement without putting forth a reason to prove it. *Gyu tsen ma jö pe chir* means because you are not stating the reason why sound is impermanent. If you say "*dra mi tak pa*, sound is impermanent," this indicates some kind of belief about the nature of sound without showing any reason why it is impermanent to support it. As such this is an example of *gyu tsen me pe yi chö*, analytical speculation without reasons.

Most simple statements qualify as assertions induced by this kind of mind. For example, if someone were to say, "The car is moving," you can understand such a simple statement without having reasons to prove it. You may not know whether the engine has been recently fixed or not, or whether the car has a brand new engine, or whether the car just got new juice put in the gas tank or not. Since no reason is put forth to qualify the statement that "The car is moving," you just take it at face value.

གཉིས་པ་ནི། དོན་བྱེད་ནུས་སྟོང་གི་རྟགས་ལས་སྒྲ་མི་རྟག་པར་འཛིན་པའི་བློ་ལྟ་བུ་སྟེ། དོན་བྱེད་ནུས་སྟོང་མི་རྟག་པ་དང་འགལ་བ་ཡིན་པའི་ཕྱིར།

> *nyi pa ni, dön che nu tong gi tak le dra mi tak par dzin pe lo ta bu te, dön che nu tong mi tak pa dang gel wa yin pe chir*
>
> An example of the second, (speculative assumption that uses contradictory reasoning) is the mind maintaining that sound is impermanent because of being empty of the ability to effect something. Being empty of the ability effect something is the opposite of [the nature of] impermanence.

This second one is a speculative mind that is gained through a contradictory reason. *Dön che nu pa*, The ability to effect something, that is, [something that produces results], is the definition of *ngö po*, causally effective thing. *Dön che* means usage. *Nu pa* means you can use it so that it will function and give a result. *Dön che nu tong* means void of the ability to give results, which is the opposite of a causally effective thing. Therefore, *dön che nu tong ngö me kyi tsen nyi*,[26] the definition of a non-causally effective thing is that which does not have the ability to effect something. What is the opposite of a causally effective thing? *Tak pa*, A permanent entity. Well then, what about a hare's horn? Wouldn't you say that it too qualifies as *dön che nu tong*, void of being able to effect something? Yes, it is void of being able to effect something, yet it is not a permanent entity because it doesn't exist. Why is a hare's horn not a permanent entity? This can be explained by examining the two parts of the definition of *tak pa*, permanent or unchanging. *Chö dang ke chik ma*

---

[26] དོན་བྱེད་ནུས་སྟོང་དངོས་མེད་ཀྱི་མཚན་ཉིད།

ma yin pe shi tun pa tak pe tsen nyi,[27] The definition of permanent is that which is both a phenomenon and non-momentary. This definition emphasizes that a permanent entity must be *chö*, a phenomenon or an existent. *Ke chik ma* means it changes with each passing instant. If something is *shi tun pa*, that combination, it must be *tak pa*, permanent, as well. A permanent entity can't be something that changes with every instant nor can it be non-existent. It must be both a phenomenon [or existent] and something that doesn't change from moment to moment. Therefore, a hare's horn, not being a phenomenon, cannot be a permanent entity. Did you understand?

The word *tong*, void, is used with the term *tong pa nyi*, emptiness. It is also used in the phrase *rang shin gyi drup pe tong pa*, empty of being inherently established. Here *dön che nu pe tong wa* means empty of being able to be used; that it, not being able to function to create results.

When we make the statement *dra chö chen, mi tak te*, consider sound, it is impermanent, we are wondering whether sound is impermanent or not. *Dra*, Sound, is the basis of debate. *Mi tak pa*, Impermanence, is *drup che chö*, the quality to be proved. If we say "sound is impermanent" and give a contradictory reason to prove why it is impermanent, such as saying *dön che nu tong yin pe chir*, because it is void of being able to effect something, your mind would hold sound as permanent based on that reason. The reason given, *dön che nu tong*, because it is void of effecting something, is wrong, because it is giving a reason that is completely contradictory. If it is *dön che nu tong*, void of effecting something, it cannot be *mi tak pa*, impermanent, because *mi tak pa* and *dön che nu tong* are opposites. That is why this is an example of *gyu tsen dang gel we yi chö*, speculative assumption that uses a contradictory reason.

Definitions are very important in logic as well as for general knowledge. They make your knowledge sharp and decisive. What is the definition of *gel wa*, the contradictory? *Ta te gang shik shi tun mi si pa gel we tsen nyi,* The definition of contradictory is two distinct entities whose combination is not possible.[28] Since they are

---

[27] ཆོས་དང་སྐད་ཅིག་མ་མ་ཡིན་པའི་གཞི་མཐུན་པ་རྟག་པའི་མཚན་ཉིད།

[28] ཐ་དད་གང་ཞིག་གཞི་མཐུན་མི་སྲིད་པ་འགལ་བའི་མཚན་ཉིད།

distinct, you cannot find one thing that is both of them. *Chik* means one or single. *Ta te* means different, individual, or separate phenomena. For example, how many moons do we have? *Chik*, Only one. However, the sun and moon are *ta te*, [two] separate entities.

What about wood and a pillar, are they two things or one? Generally, wood and pillar are *ta te*, separate things. However, there can be one thing that is both of them, a wooden pillar, for instance, which is *shi tun si pa*, a possible existent that is a combination of both things. Although the example above—being impermanent and empty of the ability to effect something—has the first qualification of being *ta te*, separate, it doesn't satisfy the second qualification, which is the impossibility of one thing being both of them. That is why this kind of reason is called *gyu tsen dang gel we yi chö*, speculative assumption that uses contradictory reasoning, because the example in the text above satisfies the definition of the contradictory.

གསུམ་པ་ནི། གཞལ་བྱའི་རྟགས་ལས་སྒྲ་མི་རྟག་པར་འཛིན་པའི་བློ་ལྟ་བུ་སྟེ། གཞལ་བྱ་དེ་དེ་སྒྲུབ་ཀྱི་མ་ངེས་པའི་གཏན་ཚིགས་ཡིན་པའི་ཕྱིར།

sum pa ni, shel je tak le dra mi tak par dzin pe lo ta bu te, shel ja de de drup kyi ma nge pe ten tsik yin pe chir

An example of the third (speculative assumption that uses indefinite reasons) is like the mind that holds sound to be impermanent because it is an object of comprehension. By using "object of comprehension" as a reason, this kind of reasoning is what is known as an indefinite reason in a proof.

Shel je tak le means by reason of being an object of comprehension. *Dra mi tak par dzin pe lo ta bu* means like the mind that holds sound as impermanent. *Shel ja de de drup kyi ma nge pe ten tsik yin pe chir*, Giving "object of comprehension" as a reason, exemplifies a speculative mind based on an indefinite reason.

Reasons are classified into perfect reasons and false reasons. False reasons are further classified into three main types: 1) a contradictory reason in a particular proof, 2) an indefinite reason in a particular proof, and 3) an unestablished reason in a particular proof. The reason given above is an example of this second kind of false reason.

This example appears in "*Chok chö kor lo*," "The Wheel of Reasons" (found at the end of Part III, *Analysis of Reasons*, in the present volume). It is stated as *dra chö chen, mi tak te, shel ja yin pe chir*, consider sound, it is impermanent, because it is an object of comprehension.

What is the definition of *shel ja*? *Tse me shel war ja wa shel je tsen nyi,*[29] The definition of object of comprehension is that object comprehended by valid cognition. A comprehensible object is the object of *tse ma*, valid cognition. *Shel ja, yö pa, she ja,* and *shi drup* are synonyms for existent. Though sound is in fact an object of comprehension, it is not an appropriate reason to verify the statement, *dra chö chen, mi tak te, shel ja yin pe chir*, consider sound, it is impermanent, because it is an object of comprehension. What is the nature of sound? Sound is impermanent. Why? Now, you have to use your logic. In order for this reason to qualify as a correct reason to prove the impermanence of sound, we would have to be able to make the following pervasion: *shel ja yin na mi tak pa yin pe kyap*, if it is an object of comprehension it must be impermanent, but there is no pervasion since *shel ja yin na mi tak pa yin pe ma kyap*, whatever is an object of comprehension is not necessarily an impermanent entity. Why? Because not all objects of comprehension are impermanent entities—take uncomposed space, for instance. Therefore, in this statement of proof, *shel ja*, object of comprehension, does not qualify as *tak yang dak*, a perfect reason. However, in the statement, *che pa yin na mi tak pa yin pe kyab*, if it is produced it must be impermanent, *che pa*, produced, is a perfect reason.

Let's confirm our understanding of what has just been discussed.

---

[29] ཚད་མས་གཞལ་བར་བྱ་བ་གཞལ་བྱའི་མཚན་ཉིད།

***

—*Shel ja yin na mi tak pa yin pe ma kyap ka re shak*, What would you posit as something that is an object of comprehension but is not necessarily an impermanent entity?

—*Nam ka chö chen*, Consider space, or *tak pa chö chen*, consider permanent entity, or *she ja chö chen*, consider object of knowledge.

—Now, is object of comprehension a permanent entity or a causally effective thing?

—It can be both.

—*Shel ja*, Object of comprehension, can be classified into two: permanent and impermanent. Therefore, in compliance with the logic rule, *tak ngö nyi ke cha yö pe chö yin na tak pa yin pe kyap*, whatever exists that consists of both permanent and impermanent entities, itself is classified as a permanent entity. From this we can understand how object of comprehension is a permanent entity since it consists of both kinds of entities.

བཞི་པ་ནི། མིག་ཤེས་ཀྱི་གཟུང་བྱའི་རྟགས་ལས་སྒྲ་མི་རྟག་པར་འཛིན་པའི་བློ་ལྟ་བུ་སྟེ། མིག་ཤེས་ཀྱི་གཟུང་བྱ་དེ་དེ་སྒྲུབ་ཀྱི་མ་གྲུབ་པའི་གཏན་ཚིགས་ཡིན་པའི་ཕྱིར།

shi pa ni, mik she kyi sung je tak le dra mi tak par dzin pe lo ta bu te, mik she kyi sung ja de de drup kyi ma drup pe ten tsik yin pe chir

An example of the fourth [speculative assumption that uses an unestablished reason] is like the mind that maintains that sound is impermanent due to the fact of its being an object held by the visual consciousness.

What is *mik she kyi sung ja*? This is the definition of the form-source of perception or form āyatana. *Mik she kyi sung ja suk kyi kye che kyi tsen nyi,*[30] The definition of form-source is that which is held by the visual consciousness. The twelve āyatanas [the six sense powers and their objects] are referred to negatively in the *Heart Sutra* where it states: *mik me, na wa me, na me, che me, lu me, yi me*, no eye, no ear, no nose, no tongue, no body, no mind; their objects respectively, *suk me, dra me, dri me, ro me, rek ja me, chö me*, no form, no sound, no smell, no taste, no tactile sensation, no phenomenon. Knowledge of these is very useful in the field of logic. The system of study in our monastery is unbelievable. Our kind of study is invaluable for keeping Buddha's teachings fresh, nice, and correct. This is why we have to establish everything with reasoning.

Now if we try to prove that sound is impermanent by using the reason "because it is the object of the visual consciousness," this is what is known as *gyu tsen ma drup pe ten tsik*, an unestablished reason. Since sound is an object of the ear consciousness and not of the eye consciousness, this reason is not a correct reason because it is unestablished. However, even though you cannot use this as a reason to prove that sound is impermanent, why would this not be considered a complete contradiction?

Let's take these flowers for example. They are *mik she kyi sung ja*, objects of the eye consciousness. Are they impermanent or permanent? They are impermanent. The fact that these flowers are objects of the eye consciousness does not contradict the fact that they are impermanent entities. A flower can be both impermanent and an object of the eye consciousness. Therefore, sound and eye consciousness do share a common quality; i.e., their impermanent nature. So we say this reason is unestablished rather than contradictory.

The second reason given above, i.e., that sound is impermanent because it is empty of being able to effect something, however, is completely contradictory. There is nothing that can be a combination of being empty of the ability to effect something and being impermanent since these are opposites.

---

30 མིག་ཤེས་ཀྱི་གཟུང་བྱ་གཟུགས་ཀྱི་སྐྱེ་མཆེད་ཀྱི་མཚན་ཉིད།

ལྔ་པ་ནི། སྒྲ་བྱས་པ་དང་། བྱས་ན་མི་རྟག་པས་ཁྱབ་པ་ཚད་མས་མ་
ངེས་པར་བྱས་རྟགས་ལས་སྒྲ་མི་རྟག་པར་འཛིན་པའི་བློ་ལྟ་བུ་སྟེ། བྱས་
པ་སྒྲ་མི་རྟག་པར་སྒྲུབ་པའི་རྟགས་ཡང་དག་ཡིན་ཀྱང་གང་ཟག་དེས་
གཏན་ལ་མ་ཕེབས་པའི་ཕྱིར།

nga pa ni, dra che pa dang, che na mi tak pe kyap pa tse me ma nge par che tak le dra mi tak par dzin pe lo ta bu te, che pa dra mi tak par drup pe tak yang dak yin kyang gang sak de ten la ma pep pe chir

An example of the fifth (speculative assumption that lacks a well-founded reason) is like the mind that holds sound to be impermanent because it is produced, however, without ascertaining by valid cognition the pervasion that whatever is produced must be impermanent. Although "being produced" is a perfect reason proving that sound is impermanent, that person has not firmly established it in his own mind.

This kind of reason qualifies as a type of *ma drup pe ten tsik*, unestablished reasons, known as *göl wa la tö ne ma drup pe ten tsik*, an unestablished reason dependent upon the opponent in debate. This means that your opponent's belief may be a little strange or simply not mature.

This can be briefly explained. First it is important to understand the characteristics of a perfect reason, which is a critical part of the logic system. *Tsul sum yin pa tak yang dak gyi tsen nyi*,[31] The definition of a perfect reason is that which is the three modes. These three modes are known as *chok chö*, the quality of the reason in the subject, *je kyap*, positive pervasion, and *dok kyap*, reverse pervasion. If all of these are not perfectly understood by the person you are debating with, then the reason you give him cannot be a perfect

---

[31] ཚུལ་གསུམ་ཡིན་པ་རྟགས་ཡང་དག་གི་མཚན་ཉིད།

reason. In regard to the statement: consider sound, it is impermanent, because it is produced, in order to have *chok chö*, the quality of the reason in the subject, the opponent should have perceived by his valid cognition that sound is produced. Also, the opponent should perceive that whatever is produced must necessarily be impermanent. This is *je kyap*, positive pervasion. If he has no realization of that pervasion through his valid cognition, then that reason cannot be a perfect reason for him. If *je kyap*, positive pervasion, is present, definitely *dok kyap* is present as well. We say, *je kyap drup na dok kyap drup pe kyap*, if it is established by positive pervasion, it is also necessarily established by reverse pervasion.

If all these qualifications are met and exist relative to that opponent, then all three modes are present. Consequently, that debater should perceive by means of his valid cognition that sound is produced. If he hasn't perceived that, he is lacking *chok chö nge pe tse ma*, valid cognition that ascertains the quality of the reason in the subject. *Chok*, The subject, is *dra*, sound. *Chö* means its particular or characteristic, which in this case is *che pa*, being produced. Therefore, "being produced" should be the quality of sound and the opponent should have perceived this through his *je pak tse ma*, inferential valid cognition.

If all these qualifications are met for that opponent, when making the statement, *dra chö chen, mi tak te, che pa yin pe chir*, consider sound, it is impermanent, because it is produced, being produced will serve as *tak yang dak*, a perfect reason, for him and prove that statement. Why? Because it complies with the three modes. There is *chok chö*, the quality of the reason in the subject, because he knows that sound is produced; there is *je kyap*, positive pervasion, because he perceives by his inferential valid cognition that whatever is produced has to be impermanent; and there is *dok kyap*, reverse pervasion, because the opponent perceives by inferential valid cognition that whatever is permanent must not be produced. However, to a person who does not have these qualifications, such a reason is not a perfect reason. Therefore, as it states above, *che pa dra mi tak par drup pe tak yang dak yin kyang*, although "being produced" is a perfect reason proving that sound is impermanent, *gang sak de de la ma pep pe chir*, that person has not firmly established this reason in his own mind. This is an example of *ten la ma pep pe yi chö*, analytical speculation that lacks a well-founded reason.

VI. Wrong cognition

རང་གི་ཞེན་ཡུལ་ལ་འཁྲུལ་བའི་རིག་པ། ལོག་ཤེས་ཀྱི་མཚན་ཉིད།

rang gi shen yul la trul we rik pa, lok she kyi tsen nyi

The definition of wrong cognition is a mind that is mistaken with regard to its conceived object.

For example, previously in India, there were many, many tenets. According to the tenets of some non-Buddhist school systems, the gods in general have an impermanent nature; they are born and they die. However, Brahma, the king of the gods of the Form Realm, and Indra, the king of the gods of the Desire Realm, are said to have a permanent nature and can stay forever without changing. The kind of view that believes in such a nature is *lok ta*, a wrong view. *Shen yul* means the conceived object and refers to the object of that wrong view. *Trul wa* means erroneous or mistaken.

Do you believe in karma and its results? "I don't know." That kind of answer is a little bit better than saying straight out, "No, I don't believe in them." Such a belief is a kind of *lok ta*, wrong view. Do you believe in previous and future lives in samsara? "No, they don't exist." This is another kind of *lok ta.* Do you believe in nirvana and Buddhahood? "No, I don't believe in them." In this way the degrees of wrong view get worse and worse.

two classifications

དབྱེ་ན། རྟོག་པ་ལོག་ཤེས་དང་། རྟོག་མེད་ལོག་ཤེས་གཉིས་ཡོད།
གང་ཟག་གི་བདག་འཛིན་ལྟ་བུ་དང་པོ་དང་། ཟླ་གཅིག་ཟླ་གཉིས་སུ་
སྣང་བའི་དབང་ཤེས་གཉིས་པ་ཡིན།

ye na, tok pa lok she dang, tok me lok she nyi yö, gang sak gi dang dzin ta bu dang po dang, da chik da nyi su nang we wang she nyi pa yin

> When wrong cognition is classified there are two kinds: conceptual wrong cognition and non-conceptual wrong cognition. An example of the first is grasping at the self of person. An example of the second is the sense consciousness to which one moon appears as two.

Gang sak gi dang dzin means holding yourself as an independent, self-existent person and is the main cause of samsara. Here it is given as an example of *tok pa lok she*, conceptual wrong cognition. An example of *tok me lok she*, non-conceptual wrong cognition, is given as the perception of two moons when looking at a single moon. Some people can have certain eye problems such that when they look at the moon they see two moons. However, this faulty condition in itself is not a wrong view, but the *belief* that there are in fact two moons when you mistakenly see two instead of one is a non-conceptual wrong cognition.

VII. Non-ascertaining perception

རང་ཡུལ་མངོན་སུམ་དུ་སྣང་ཡང་ངེས་པ་འདྲེན་མི་ནུས་པའི་རིག་པ།
སྣང་ལ་མ་ངེས་ཀྱི་བློའི་མཚན་ཉིད། ཡིད་གཟུགས་མཛེས་ལ་ལྷག་པར་
ཆགས་བཞིན་པའི་གང་ཟག་གི་རྒྱུད་ཀྱི་སྒྲ་འཛིན་ཉན་ཤེས་ལྟ་བུ་ཡིན་ནོ།

rang yul ngön sum du nang yang nge pa dren mi nu pe rik pa, nang la ma nge kyi lo'i tsen nyi, yi sung dze la hlak par chak shin pe gang sak gi gyu kyi dra dzin nyen she ta bu yin no

The definition of non-ascertaining perception is a mind that, although its object appears directly to it, that mind is not able to elicit ascertainment [of what it is perceiving]. An example of such a mind is the ear consciousness perceiving a sound in the mind of a person whose attention [eye consciousness] is completely engrossed in a beautiful form.

This kind of mind is very obvious. For example, when you go to the theater and view something very interesting that is being presented, your mind focuses single-pointedly on what is happening on the stage. If somebody should say something to you while you are watching the performance, since your mind is so absorbed in that visual object, even though you heard them speaking to you, you can't tell for certain what it was they had said. *Nang* means appears to your consciousness. *Yi* means your mind. *Sung dze* means some beautiful or attractive form such as that performance. *Hlak par* means extremely. *Chak shin pe* means while focusing on something with very strong attraction. *Gang sak kyi gyu kyi* means in that person's mind. *Dra dzin nyen she* means an ear consciousness grasping sound. That ear consciousness is *nang la ma nge pa*, a non-ascertaining perception: "I heard him say something but I'm not sure what it was."

PART III

རྟགས་རིགས་

ANALYSIS OF REASONS

Analysis of Reasons, The Essence of Scriptural Authority and Logical Reasoning:

A Presentation of Reasoning to Delight Scholars

INTRODUCTION

THE MAIN PURPOSE OF THIS section on *Analysis of Reasons*[1] is to determine what does and what does not qualify as a good reason to prove a thesis. In this text we will make use of a certain proof statement—proving the impermanence of sound by reason of its being produced—as a template to help clarify the various forms of reasoning and parts of a logical statement being presented throughout. It is the following: *dra chö chen, mi tak te, che pa yin pe chir*, consider sound, it is impermanent, because it is produced. What does *che pa* mean in this statement? *Che pa*, Produced, means something that was made by causes. For example, who made this table? Someone made it. What are the other causes of this table? There are many causes. First of all, one of you, an enthusiastic "master" carpenter built it with his not so good tools. He used some wood and glue and some sharp screws and nails, which you can still feel here when you try to pick it up from underneath to move it. All of these materials, gathered together, compose this table. Therefore, this table is *che pa*, produced, due to its causes coming together and producing a result. Every...thing—from machines to paper to books, etc.—are *che pa*, produced, since their causes have combined together to bring about their result. The causes of their causes are also *che pa*, produced, since they likewise came from their own causes.

Mi tak pa, Impermanent, means that because its nature is made from causes this table cannot stay for more than a moment without changing. At the very beginning this table could stand on its four legs pretty nicely, but look, now it's not too good. See, one leg is a little bent and another is nearly detaching itself, which makes it lean over and wobble when you put anything on it. I asked another student to try to fix it, but he brought it back roughly in the same condition, since there wasn't much he could do to rescue it. In this

---

[1] རྟགས་རིགས་

way, the table shows its quality of *mi tak pa*, impermanence. Its nature is also such that eventually it will get worse and worse. *Mi* is a negative; *tak pa* means unchanging, therefore, *mi tak pa* means "not unchanging." Therefore, *che pa*, produced, can be used as a perfect reason to prove that this table is impermanent. We can explain why as follows.

The statement presented above is what is known in logic as *rang shin gyi tak*, a reason of same nature. There are three parts to this statement: 1) *dra*, sound, is *tsö shi*, the subject of debate, 2) *mi tak pa*, impermanent, is *drup che chö*, the predicate or quality to be proved, and 3) *che pa*, produced, is *tak*, the reason. In brief, we call these parts *tak chö dön sum*, the three—reason, quality, and subject.

Dra, Sound, is *shen dö chö chen*, the subject about which there is doubt; *mi tak pa*, impermanent, is *drup che chö*, the quality to be proved; *che pa*, produced, is *tak*, the reason. Each part of the statement of proof should be different from the other two. If two of the parts are the same, then the statement cannot represent a perfect reason. For instance, if the reason and the quality to be proved are not two different things, it is not a perfect reason. In this case, *dra*, sound, is the subject we are investigating and as such serves as the basis of debate. *Mi tak pa*, Impermanent, is *drup che chö*, the quality we are seeking to prove about sound. If sound is impermanent, how are we going to prove it? To prove it we have to use *che pa*, produced, as a reason. If sound is produced, then it must certainly be impermanent.

Have you heard of *tsul sum*, the three modes—*chok chö, je kyap,* and *dok kyap*? Generally, *tsul* means way or mode. These three will be explained individually in this section on the *Analysis of Reasons*. What "way" can we use to prove that sound is impermanent? One way is to use *che pa*, produced, as a reason.

Dra, Sound, is *chö chen*, but more specifically, *shen dö chö chen*, the basis about which we are debating. If I am trying to prove to you that sound is impermanent, it is not enough that sound be the subject of debate; it must also be *shen dö chö chen*, or the subject of debate about which you have some doubt. *Shen dö* means doubt. Even though you know what sound is, do you know about all its characteristics? You might say, for instance, "Sure, I know what sound is...there are all kinds of sounds—pleasant sounds, unpleasant sounds and so on." Well, if you know everything about sound, what then do you know about the real nature of sound? By investigating the nature of sound you will come to understand that sound has many characteristics, some of which may cause you to have some doubt about it. Therefore, even though you know about sound, you might have some doubt as to whether sound is *mi tak pa*, changing, or not. In some non-Buddhist schools, there are scholars who, although they are very skilled in logic, still describe sound as *tak pa*, an unchangeable phenomenon. If they continue studying wrong tenets in this regard and make their belief firm, this can turn into a wrong view that can almost calcify in their mind.

Therefore, you have to know two of our main enemies: *lok tok* (***log rtog***), wrong belief, and *te tsom* (***the tshom***), [bad] doubt. If someone holds a wrong belief such as "sound is an unchanging entity," that belief is erroneous. Even if you were to present them with the statement: *dra chö chen, mi tak te, che pe chir*, consider sound, it is impermanent, because it is produced, rather than convince them of the true nature of sound, it would fail to remove that *lok tok*, wrong view, from their mind. Why? Because their belief is too strong. This is why you have to first begin by transforming their wrong belief into doubt. "I believed that sound is permanent, just as our texts describe it, but now, having been presented with these good reasons, it seems that sound might not be permanent after all." Such thinking shows that an opponent's *lok tok*, wrong belief, has been changed into doubt. Once his wrong belief has turned into doubt and lost some of its strength, should he be presented once again with that same proof statement, it should convince him of the true nature of sound since he will gain understanding through being offered a good reason.

Therefore, first you have to remove *lok tok*, wrong belief. Next, you have to remove the traces of *te tsom*, doubt. Once you remove their doubt, the person to whom you are presenting logical arguments can gain *je pak tse ma*, indirect valid cognition. *Je* means after. After what? After being given good reasons. *Pak* means perceiving or understanding something: "I realize that sound is impermanent because of that perfect reason." *Tse ma* means unerring perception, a kind of mind, in this case, that perceives its object unerringly by means of a good reason.

Now, in order to remove their wrong view, we have to use *ten gyur yang dak*,[2] a perfect "consequential" reason. *Prasaṅga* is the Sanskrit term for *tel(n) gyur* or [absurd] consequence. *Ten gyur yang tak, tak yang dak, ten tsik yang dak, jor wa yang dak* are synonyms meaning a perfect reason. In the statement used above: *dra chö chen, mi tak te, che pe chir*, the particle "*te*" indicates a statement of belief and shows that a reason is to follow. The reason used here is "because sound is produced." The style pertaining to *ten gyur*,[3] however, is to prove something in the reverse; that is, by using absurd consequences derived from the opponent's own statements. A statement of absurd consequence might be expressed as follows: *dra chö chen, ma che par tel, tak pa yin pe chir*, consider sound, it is not produced, because it is unchanging. That "*tel*," or consequence, is capable of changing the opponent's belief by using a contradictory reason of absurdity. *Gyur* in the term "*tel(n) gyur*" means "to change," referring to bringing about a change in the opponent's wrong belief through the use of that consequence. *Ma che par tel*, It is not produced, is a question that is posed in direct opposition to his wrong belief. (On the debate ground, to economize, we use as few words as possible to express such statements.) That is, "It follows then from what you say that sound is not produced!?" Of course the debater will know that sound is produced. [The absurdity of the statement implies that the rational conclusion will be obvious to the opponent.]

The correct answer to this statement is "*chi chir*," which means, "Why?" as in "Why would you say that sound is not produced from its causes?" At this point the opponent is given the absurd reason that he himself had originally posited: "Because (you believe that) sound is *tak pa*, permanent and unchanging." Such a response is certain to hurt his wrong belief. He will think: "I can't say that sound is not produced." If scholars (who are most often learned and knowledgeable people) are presented with good reasons, of course they will accept it, since they are not crazy.

---

2 ཐལ་འགྱུར་ཡང་དག་

3 ཐལ་འགྱུར་

The statement: *dra chö chen, ma che par tel, tak pa yin pe chir*, consider sound, it is not produced, because it is unchanging, is *tel gyur*, or a statement of absurd consequence. In order for a statement to be logically perfect, it should have *kyap pa yang dak*, perfect pervasion. This can be expressed as: *tak pa yin na, ma che pe kyap*, if it is unchanging, it must not be produced, which is a correct pervasion. Since the opponent has already responded with "*chi chir*," "Why not?," meaning "Why wouldn't it [sound] be produced?" this indicates that he believes sound to be made from causes. If sound is *che pa*, produced, then it cannot be *tak pa*, unchanging. So if it is *tak pa*, unchanging, we can put forth the pervasion: *tak pa yin na, ma che pe kyap*, whatever is permanent cannot be produced. That is the meaning of *kyap pa yang dak*, perfect pervasion. It is evident that the absurd consequence presented above has hurt his wrong belief and will most likely cause him to think: "Maybe sound is not *tak pa*, an unchanging entity, after all. It may very possibly be *mi tak pa*, changing." This kind of thinking reveals the opponent's *te tsom*, doubt or hesitation.

What is the definition of doubt? *Rang yul la ta nyi su dok pe sem jung te tsom gyi tsen nyi*,[4] A mental factor that oscillates in two ways with regard to its object. *Yul la* means to its object; *ta nyi su dok pa* means "maybe yes, maybe not" showing hesitation while focusing on two alternative views with regard to its object. *Sem jung* is a mental derivative [as opposed to a main mind]. If the debater has this kind of doubt, he has already lost his wrong belief due to that *ten gyur*, absurd consequence, which transformed his wrong belief into *te tsom*, doubt.

There are three classifications of *te tsom*: *dön gyur gyi te tsom*, doubt tending toward the fact, *dön mi(n) gyur gyi te tsom*, doubt tending away from the fact or going in the wrong direction, and *cha nyam pe te tsom*, doubt standing in the middle between two beliefs about a single object. This knowledge is very important in the logic field. The one described above, that is, the kind of doubt to which it is preferable to sway an opponent in debate, is *dön gyur gyi te tsom*, doubt leaning toward the truth.

---

[4] རང་ཡུལ་ལ་མཐའ་གཉིས་སུ་དོགས་པའི་སེམས་བྱུང་ཐེ་ཚོམ་གྱི་མཚན་ཉིད།

Dön is the word in Tibetan for "meaning"; *gyur* means changing. *Dön* in this case refers to the thesis *dra mi tak pa*, the impermanence of sound. Since his doubt is approaching closer to the correct way things are, the opponent has lost that *lok tok*, wrong view, and has gained *dön gyur gyi te tsom*, doubt tending toward the fact, and is just about ready to attain *je pak tse ma*, inferential valid cognition, with regard to the nature of sound.

Now we have to investigate the meaning of *shen dö chö chen*, a subject about which someone has doubt. *Shen dö* is the same as *te tsom* or doubt; *shuk pa* means to have doubt while engaging in something. *Dra*, Sound, has turned into *shen dö chö chen*, a subject about which there is doubt, for the opponent. If you are such a person who has doubt about the nature of sound, you have become *chir göl yang dak*, a perfect person with whom to debate. There is a difference between *chir göl*, a debater or opponent in debate, and *chir göl yang dak*, a perfect person with whom to debate. *Chir göl yang dak* should have *ten gyur gyi te tsom*, doubt precipitated by being presented with a wrong consequence elicited from his own statements, and not someone with a firm *lok ta*, wrong view.

When presenting an opponent with the following statement: *dra chö chen, mi tak te, che pa yin pe chir*, consider sound, it is impermanent, because it is produced, we are using a correct reason (this is *jor wa yang dak* or *ten tsik yang dak*, a statement of proof, and not *ten gyur*, an absurd consequence) to prove to him that sound is impermanent. From this he can gain *je pak tse ma*, valid inferential cognition. "Now I've realized that sound is impermanent because it is produced. I can accept that sound is impermanent because I have already accepted sound as something produced." When did he realize that? When he answered forcefully with "*chi chir*, why would you say that?" to "*ma che par tel*," "it follows from what you say that it is not produced," as an absurd consequence elicited from his own belief in response to *ten gyur*, an absurd consequence, expressed as: *dra chö chen, ma che par tel, tak pa yin pe chir*, consider sound, it follows that it is not produced, because it is a permanent entity. Now, having accepted that sound is *che pa*, produced, he understands the following *jor wa*, statement of reason: *che pa yin na, mi tak pa yin pe kyap*, if something is produced, it must be impermanent. Finally, the main purpose of debate is to bring an opponent from a state of wrong belief at least to a point of doubt tending toward the truth.

Now, what is the purpose of studying *Analysis of Reasons*? The purpose is to understand how to use correct reasoning. To do this, you have to become familiar with the various kinds of reasons. There are three general classifications of reasons: *dre tak yang dak, rang shin gyi tak yang dak, ma mik pe tak yang dak*, reasons of effect, reasons of nature, and reasons of non-observation. As mentioned in the line from glorious Dharmakīrti's *Commentary to (Dignāga's) "Compendium of Valid Cognition"*:

> །གཏན་ཚིགས་དེ་ནི་རྣམ་གསུམ་ཉིད།
>
> *ten tsik de ni nam sum nyi*
>
> Those three [alone] are perfect reasons.

First, why is it important to study *dre tak*, reasons of effect? Of course, from samsara up to Buddhahood, on both sides, there are many levels of causes and effects. All results are related to their causes. Without a cause not even the slightest result can come out. So by studying these kinds of reasons you will learn more about the relationship between causes and effects. Although outer causes and effects are definitely important, it is far more important to concentrate on inner causes and effects, learning about them and developing your *je pak tse ma*, inferential valid cognition, and even your *ngön sum tse ma*, direct valid cognition, in regard to them. If you realize by valid cognition the relationship of cause and effect, both outer and inner, it will serve as the main tool to subdue your mind and bring you knowledge.

For example, there is a reason that smoke appears; it appears because there is fire. When you see smoke, you can use that as a reason to understand that there must be fire. That smoke, being related to fire, can give you direct cognition. You can also understand indirectly or incidentally that without fire, smoke cannot exist. In a similar way you can gain an understanding of the nature of karma and its results through this study of causes and effects.

Once you learn them nicely, you have to practice continuously. You have to think about karma and its results all the time—try to reduce bad results and increase good results—take great pains to improve your situation. That is the purpose of studying *dre tak*, reasons of effect or result signs.

Through studying the second kind of reason, *rang shin gyi tak*, reason of nature, we can gain a better understanding of the nature of things. An example of this kind of reason is the one we have already used several times so far: *dra chö chen, mi tak te, che pa yin pe chir*, consider sound, it is impermanent, because it is produced. *Rang shin gyi tak* can be explained as follows. When *che pa*, being produced, exists, it is related to *mi tak pa*, impermanence, because they are of the same nature. Once you've gained an understanding of outer things, you have to change the subject of the statement and apply the thesis to your own mind, to all your five heaps. All of these are impermanent because they are produced. When they exist, they necessarily exist with an impermanent nature. Scrutinize your own nature, day by day, hour by hour, moment by moment and see how it is changing. It cannot stay in one state for long because it is *che pa*, produced, and *mi tak pa*, impermanent. Once you begin to realize impermanence relating to inner things, you have to practice using this knowledge in relation to the system of karma, which is less evident.

Now, if you want to practice karma unerringly, you have to understand the third kind of reason: *ma mik pe tak*, reason of non-observation. You cannot say there is no karma or karma's result. Why? Because you don't have valid cognition perceiving that such does not exist. Were you to perceive through direct or indirect valid cognition that karma did not exist, since these minds are infallible, karma could not exist. It would be the same case with bodhichitta, renunciation, and right view. Can you say definitively that they exist or not? Do you have valid cognition to perceive them or not? If you don't have *ngön sum tse ma*, direct valid cognition, or *je pak tse ma*, inferential valid cognition, would it be correct for you to decide whether or not they exist? Did you have a former life? Will you have a future life? Do you have valid cognition in your mind about their existence? Can you decide whether or not they exist determined by your inability to perceive them? Matters such as these are investigated in this book through the use of reasoning. In this regard the great pandit Dharmakīrti says in his commentary: *tse ma nam ni min juk pa me la min juk*, meaning "if you don't have valid cognition about something, you shouldn't engage in saying that such does not exist."

Can you determine whether or not there is a ghost staying on this table listening happily to what we are saying? Can you tell? You cannot say either way, "yes" or "no." If you say, "No, there isn't a ghost on this table because I cannot see it," that would not serve as correct proof. Are there Buddhas on this table or not? Again, you cannot say either way whether there are or not because you don't have valid cognition in that regard. If you say either way, you have committed yourself to having some kind of valid cognition. This is why you have to learn about *ma mik pe tak*, reasons of non-observation. These are very beautiful parts of logic. Logic is unbelievable, so detailed and clear.

REASONS

general explanation

༄༅། །རྟགས་རིགས་ཀྱི་རྣམ་བཞག་ལུང་རིགས་ཀྱི་སྙིང་པོ་བསྡུས་པ་མཁས་པ་
དགྱེས་བྱེད་ཅེས་བྱ་བ་བཞུགས་སོ། །གཉིས་པ་རྟགས་རིགས་ཀྱི་རྣམ་གཞག་
རྒྱས་པར་ནི་གཞན་དུ་བཤད་ཟིན་ཅིང་འདིར་མདོར་བསྡུས་མཚོན་ཙམ་ཞིག་
བཤད་པར་བྱ་སྟེ། དེ་ནི།

tak rik kyi nam shak lung rik kyi nying po du pa ke pa gye che je ja wa shuk so, nyi pa tak rik kyi nam shak gye par ni shen du she sin ching dir dor du tsön tsam shik she par ja te, de ni

Analysis of Reasons, The Essence of Scriptural Authority and Logical Reasoning: A Presentation of Reasoning to Delight Scholars. Having given a more extensive explanation of signs and reasoning elsewhere,[5] here I shall just give a brief presentation.

To introduce this subject of logic, the author[6] begins with a quotation from *The Entryway to Valid Reasoning*[7] by the great scholar Dignāga who, in the Indian Buddhist tradition was the first teacher, virtually the inventor of the logical method of valid cognition, following the teachings of the Buddha. Previously in the Sanskrit system there were five major

[5] *Extensive Explanation of the Path of Reason concerning Signs and Reasoning to Open the Eye of Intelligence* (T: ***rtags rigs kyi rnam gzhag rgyas pa rigs lam blo gros mig 'byed***). This will be referred to hereafter as the *Extensive Explanation.*

[6] Chone Lama Drakpa Shedrup (***Co ne bla ma grags pa bshad sgrub***)

[7] T: ***tshad ma rigs par 'jug pa'i sgo***

sciences,[8] which included *ten tsik rik pa*, logic or logical reasoning, also called *tse ma rik pa.* It is within this context that the study of valid reasoning figures.

ཚད་མ་རིགས་སྒོ་ལས། གཏན་ཚིགས་ནི་ཚུལ་གསུམ་མོ། །ཚུལ་གསུམ་གང་
ཞེ་ན། ཕྱོགས་ཀྱི་ཆོས་ཉིད་དང་། མཐུན་པའི་ཕྱོགས་ཉིད་ལ་ཡོད་པར་ངེས་པ་
དང་། མི་མཐུན་པའི་ཕྱོགས་ཉིད་ལ་མེད་པ་ཉིད་དུ་ངེས་པར་ཡོད་དོ། །ཞེས་
དང་།

tse ma rik go le, ten tsik ni, tsul sum mo, tsul sum gang she na, chok kyi chö nyi dang, tun pe chok nyi la yö par nge pa dang, mi tun pe chok nyi la me pa nyi du nge par yö do, she dang

From *The Entryway to Valid Reasoning*: "A perfect reason is the three modes. What are those three? They are: 1) the reason's relevance to the subject, 2) that which is ascertained to exist in only the class [of entities] compatible with the subject, and 3) what is verified as not existing at all in the class [of entities] incompatible with the subject.

Tse ma in the title *tse ma rik go*, means infallible cognition or that which is non-deceptive. How many types of valid cognition are there? There are two: *ngön sum tse ma*, direct valid cognition, and *je pak tse ma*, inferential valid cognition. The field of reasoning dealt with in this short text is concerned primarily with inferential valid

---

8 *Rik pe ne nga* (***rig pa'i gnas lnga***) the five sciences: 1) *ten tsik rik pa* (***gtan tshig rig pa***) logical reasoning; 2) *dra rik pa* (***sgra rig pa***) grammar and rhetoric, 3) *so rik pa* (***gso rig pa***) medicine, 4) *so rik pa* (***bzo rig pa***) arts and craftsmanship, and 5) *nang dön rik pa* (***nang don rig pa***) philosophy and religion.

cognition. *Go* means door, referring to entry into these great sciences, which is Dignāga's main purpose for writing this work.

Here the present author briefly identifies the three logical modes—*chok chö, je kyap, dok kyap sum*—by quoting the great pandit Dharmakīrti from his *Commentary on (Dignāga's) "Compendium of Valid Cognition"*:

ཕྱོགས་ཆོས་དེ་ཆས་ཁྱབ་པ་ཡི། །གཏན་ཚིགས་ཤེས་པས་མདོར་བསྟན་ཏེ།

chok chö de che kyap pa yi, ten tsik she pe dor ten te

> This quotation teaches in an abbreviated way the modes of a perfect reason: "A [perfect] reason is the reason's relevance to the subject and its [positive and reverse] pervasions."

The first mode is *chok chö*, the reason's relevance to the subject [of debate]. *De che kyap*, Pervaded by those parts, explicitly indicates *je kyap*, positive pervasion, which is described as that which is perceived as having a nature compatible with the quality to be proved, and implicitly indicates *dok kyap*, reverse pervasion, which is described as that which is perceived as not existing at all among those entities incompatible in nature with the reason and the quality to be proved about the subject [of debate]. *Ten tsik*, A perfect reason, must comprise these *tsul sum*, three modes.

འདི་ལ་གསུམ་ རྟགས་ཀྱི་མཚན་ཉིད། དབྱེ་བ། འཕྲོས་དོན་བཤད་པའོ།

di la sum, tak kyi tsen nyi, ye wa, trö dön she pa'o

> This section consists of three parts: the definition of a reason, its classifications, and supplementary explanations.

།དང་པོ་ནི། རྟགས་སུ་བཀོད་པ། རྟགས་ཀྱི་མཚན་ཉིད།

dang po ni, tak su kö pa tak gi tsen nyi

The first: the definition of a reason is anything you put forth as a reason.

Dang po ni means the first, that is, regarding the definition of a reason. *Tak* means reason. *Kö pa* means positing or stating a reason verbally. What is the definition of a reason? It is that which you give as a reason.

Here we can rely on the method used in debate to check and confirm our understanding. This method, as follows, is especially useful in verifying definitions.

***

—*Tak gi tsen nyi shak gyu me pe chir*, I bet you can't give me the definition of a reason.
—*Tak ma drup*, It's not true that I can't give you the definition of a reason. (This implies *shak gyu yö*, I do have the definition.)
—*Tak gi tsen nyi shak gyu yö par tel*, So you can give me the definition of a reason?
—*Dö*, Yes.
—*Sho!*, Well then, tell me what it is!
—*Tak su kö pa*, That which is put forth as a reason.

You have to repeat this template several times substituting different definitions in order to learn it well. Now repeat it. Make your lips move. If you just sit there in silence without saying a peep on the debate ground everybody will call you *hlak pa ka gyen*, "windblocker," which means that all you do is block the cold winds that come rolling down from the mountains.

དེ་སྒྲུབ་ཀྱི་རྟགས་སུ་བཀོད་པ། དེ་སྒྲུབ་ཀྱི་རྟགས་ཀྱི་མཚན་ཉིད།

de drup kyi tak su kö pa, de drup kyi tak kyi tsen nyi

The definition of a reason in a proof is what is stated as the reason in that proof.

In the definition of a reason given above it says only "what you put forth as a reason," and does not specify under what circumstances. Here, however, the definition qualifies the situation and says more specifically *de drup kyi*, in a particular proof, which means the reason you give within a specific context.

ཡོད་མེད་གང་རུང་ཡིན་ན། དེ་སྒྲུབ་ཀྱི་རྟགས་ཡིན་པས་ཁྱབ་སྟེ།

yö me gang rung yin na, de drup kyi tak yin pe kyap te

Whether it exists or not, it can be used as a reason in a proof.

Yö means exists; *me* means does not exist. *Gang rung* means either of them. Whether the reason exists or not, *de drup kyi tak yin pe kyap*, it may always be put forth in an attempt to prove something. For example, *am jo ye yön gang rung yin na, am jo yin pe kyap*, your left ear or your right ear, whichever it is, it must still be an ear. Or again, *lak pa ye yön gang rung yin na, lak pa yin pe kyap*, whether it's a right hand or a left hand, it's still a hand. *Kyap te* means "Why must it be that way?" and shows that a reason follows.

དེ་ཡིན་ན། དེ་སྒྲུབ་ཀྱི་རྟགས་སུ་བཀོད་པས་ཁྱབ་པའི་ཕྱིར་ཏེ།

de yin na, de drup kyi tak su kö pe kyap pe chir te

Whatever it is, it can be stated as a reason in a proof. Because …

De yin na means no matter which it is, existent or nonexistent. *Te drup kyi* means in a particular proof. *Tak su kö pa* means it may be stated as a reason to prove that statement. *Te* means why is that so?

རི་བོང་རྭ་དེ། དེ་ཆོས་ཅན། མི་རྟག་སྟེ། རི་བོང་རྭ་ཡིན་པའི་ཕྱིར་ཞེས་པའི་

རྟགས་སུ་བཀོད་པའི་ཕྱིར།

> *ri bong ra de, de chö chen, mi tak te, ri bong ra yin pe chir, she pe tak su kö pe chir*
>
> [Even] a hare's horn can be given as a reason in a proof. Consider "that" [anything], it is impermanent, because it is a hare's horn.

De chö chen is referring to anything as the subject. You can use a hare's horn as a reason to prove that anything is impermanent because it is a hare's horn. Up to this point in the presentation, it doesn't matter whether you use a correct reason or an incorrect reason. The logic gradually becomes more specific. *She pe* means making that statement.

> སྒྲ་མི་རྟག་པར་སྒྲུབ་པར་བྱེད་པའི་རྟགས་སུ་བཀོད་པ། སྒྲ་མི་རྟག་པར་སྒྲུབ་པར་བྱེད་པའི་རྟགས་ཀྱི་མཚན་ཉིད། དེ་བཞིན་དུ་གཞན་ལ་སྦྱོར་ཚུལ་འགྲེའོ།
>
> *dra mi tak par drup par che pe tak su kö pa, dra mi tak par drup par che pe tak kyi tsen nyi, de shin du shen la jor tsul dre'o*
>
> The definition of a reason used to prove that sound is impermanent is that which is used as a reason to prove that sound is impermanent. In a similar way, you can apply this to other proofs.

Dra chö chen, mi tak te, ri bong ra yin pe chir, Consider sound, it is impermanent, because it is a hare's horn. This example shows that you can use anything as a reason in a statement. The point being made here is that the reason given does not necessarily have to be *tak yang dak*, a correct reason. We can say, for instance, *gyap chi go lok yin pe chir.*[9] *Gyap chi go lok mi tak par drup par che pe tak su*

---

[9] Rinpoche is referring to Drölma, the temple dog, who is in the habit of doing the exact opposite of what he asks her to do. He tells her to come and she walks in the opposite direction. As the phrase translates: "because she turns her back and goes in the opposite direction."

kö pa, gyap chi go lok mi tak par drup par che pe tak gi tsen nyi, The definition of a reason used to prove that [Drölma's] being contrary is impermanent is what is given as the reason used to prove that her being contrary is impermanent. *Te shin du,* In the same way, means you can apply this reasoning to other proofs as well.

།བྱས་པའི་རྟགས་ཀྱིས་སྒྲ་མི་རྟག་པར་སྒྲུབ་པར་བྱེད་པའི་རྟགས་སུ་བཀོད་པ།
བྱས་པའི་རྟགས་ཀྱིས་སྒྲ་མི་རྟག་པར་སྒྲུབ་པར་བྱེད་པའི་རྟགས་ཀྱི་མཚན་ཉིད་
ཡིན་ཀྱང་དེ་ཡིན་ན་བྱས་པ་དང་གཅིག་ཡིན་པས་ཁྱབ་པ་ཡིན་ནོ།

che pe tak kyi dra mi tak par drup par che pe tak su kö pa, che pe tak kyi dra mi tak par drup par che pe tak kyi tsen nyi yin kyang de yin na che pa dang chik yin pe kyap pa yin no

Although the definition of a reason that is used to prove that sound is impermanent by the reason "because it is produced" is what is presented as the reason that is used to prove that sound is impermanent by the reason "because it is produced," in order for it to qualify as a perfect reason, it [the reason] must be only what is produced [i.e., it must be one and the same as what is produced].

In order to understand this we have to apply it to the model proof to which this refers as follows:

།སྒྲ་ཆོས་ཅན། མི་རྟག་སྟེ། བྱས་པའི་ཕྱིར་ཞེས་བཀོད་པའི་ཚེ་སྒྲ་རྩོད་གཞི།
མི་རྟག་པ་བསྒྲུབ་བྱའི་ཆོས། སྒྲ་མི་རྟག་པ་བསྒྲུབ་བྱ། བྱས་པ་རྟགས་ཡང་དག
།རྟག་པ་དགག་བྱའི་ཆོས། སྒྲ་རྟག་པ་དགག་བྱར་འཇོག་སྟེ། གཞན་ལ་སྦྱོར་ཚུལ་
ཤེས་པར་བྱའོ།

dra chö chen, mi tak te, che pe chir, she kö pe tse, dra tsö shi, mi tak pa drup che chö, dra mi tak pa drup ja, che pa tak yang dak, tak pa gak je chö, dra tak pa ga jar jok te, shen la jor tsul she par ja'o

In the statement: Consider sound, it is impermanent, because it is produced, sound is the basis of debate; the impermanence of sound is the quality to be proved [or the predicate]; [that] sound is impermanent is the thesis; [because it is] produced is a perfect reason; the permanence of sound is the quality to be refuted; [that] sound is permanent is the thesis to be refuted. This can be applied to other cases in a similar way.

What is *tak*, the reason, in this case? *Che pa*, Product. To be a product implies that it was produced. How was it produced? By *gyu dang kyen*, causes and conditions, gathering together. Therefore,

དེ་ཡིན་ན་བྱས་པ་དང་གཅིག་ཡིན་པས་ཁྱབ་པ་ཡིན་ནོ།

de yin na che pa dang chik yin pe kyap pa yin no

For it to be a [perfect reason], it must necessarily be one with product.

Is the quality of being produced one or many? It is only one; that is, product is product. Product is *dak chik*, one nature, with product. What does *de*, that, refer to here? It refers to *tak yang dak*, a perfect reason. So, *de drup kyi tak yang dak yin na*, for it to be a perfect reason in that proof, it must be one with *che pa*, product.

།གཉིས་པ་ལ་གཉིས། རྟགས་ཡང་དག་བཤད་པ་དང་། རྟགས་ལྟར་སྣང་བཤད་པའོ།

nyi pa la nyi, tak yang dak she pa dang tak tar nang she pa'o

> The second (classification of reasons) itself has two parts: an explanation of perfect reasons and an explanation of false reasons.

Reasons can be [nominally] divided into two categories: perfect reasons and false reasons. Later on, this text makes many distinctions and qualifications concerning these two, which potentially allows for a lot of debate, but a simple explanation will suffice for now.

PERFECT REASONS

།དང་པོ་ལ་གསུམ། དེའི་སྟོས་གཞི་དང་། མཚན་ཉིད། དབྱེ་བའོ།

dang po la sum, de'i tö shi dang, tsen nyi ye wa'o

Regarding the first (a perfect reason), there are three parts: 1) its bases of relation, 2) definition, and 3) classifications.

De'i means its, referring to *tak yang dak*, perfect reasons. When describing perfect reasons there are three categories: 1) *tak yang dak gyi tö shi*, the bases of relation of a perfect reason, 2) *tak yang dak gyi tsen nyi*, the definition of a perfect reason, and 3) *tak yang dak gyi ye wa*, the classifications of a perfect reason. We begin with *tö shi*, bases of relation, which has two categories.

bases of relation

།དང་པོ་ལ་གཉིས། ཕྱོགས་ཆོས་ཀྱི་ལྟོས་གཞི་དང་། ཁྱབ་པའི་ལྟོས་གཞིའོ།

dang po la nyi, chok chö kyi tö shi dang, kyap pe tö shi'o

The first one (bases of relation) has two parts: the basis of relation of the property of the subject [referring to the relationship between the subject and the reason] and the basis of relation of pervasion [both positive and reverse, referring to the relationship between the reason and the predicate].

What are *tsul sum*, the three modes [for a perfect reason]? *Chok chö, je kyap, dok kyap sum*, the three—reason's relevance to the subject or the property of the subject, positive pervasion, and reverse pervasion.

In a given syllogism such as our model, *dra chö chen, mi tak te, che pa yin pe chir*, consider sound, it is impermanent, because it is produced: *Chok chö ka re shak*, What is the reason's relevance to the subject? *Je kyap ka re shak*, What is the positive pervasion? *Dok kyap ka re shak*, What is the reverse pervasion? *Che pa*, Being produced, applies to all of them. Therefore, *che pe dra mi tak par drup par che pe chok chö*, [being produced] is the reason's relevance to the subject serving to prove that sound is impermanent by reason of its "being produced"; *che pe dra mi tak par drup par che pe je kyap*, [being produced] satisfies the positive pervasion serving to prove that sound is impermanent by reason of its "being produced"; *che pe dra mi tak par drup par che pe dok kyap*, [being produced] satisfies the reverse pervasion serving to prove that sound is impermanent by reason of its "being produced." Since *che pa*, being produced, satisfies all of these, it is a perfect reason in this proof.

Chok chö kyi tö shi refers to the relationship between the subject of debate and the reason. *Tö* means to rely on or depend upon; *shi* means basis. What does *chok chö* rely on? What does *je kyap* rely on? What does *dok kyap* rely on? In this case, they all rely on *che pa*, product. Therefore, *chok chö kyi tö shi*, the basis of relation between the property of the subject and the reason here is *che pa*, product.

basis of relation of the
property of the subject

།དང་པོ་ལ་གསུམ། ཤེས་འདོད་ཆོས་ཅན་སྐྱོན་མེད་ཀྱི་མཚན་ཉིད་དང་། མཚན་
གཞི་དང་། སྒྲུབ་བྱེད་དོ།

dang po la sum, shen dö chö chen kyön me kyi tsen nyi dang, tsen shi dang, drup che do

The first (basis of relation of the property of the subject or the reason's relevance to the subject) has three parts: 1) the definition of a faultless subject about which there is doubt, 2) an illustration, and 3) a proof.

To understand this first basis of relation it is important to learn the definition of *shen dö chö chen kyön me*, a faultless subject about which there is doubt, and its illustration, which reveals how something qualifies as that. [There are certain requirements for this relationship between the subject of debate and the reason in order for it to hold up. One of these is factual validity; that is, the sign or reason must be related to or be present in the subject. Another requirement is that it be contextually "faultless" insofar as there is an appropriate person who has some doubt about the thesis and consequently is investigating the matter. The parameters of these requirements are detailed in the following definitions and explanation.]

> །དང་པོ་ནི་མཚོན་ན།
>
> *dang po ni tsön na*
>
> Regarding the first one (the definition of a faultless subject about which there is doubt) is illustrated by an example.

The first quality of *shen dö chö chen kyön me*, a faultless subject about which there is doubt:

> ཁྱོད་བྱས་པས་རྟགས་ཀྱིས་སྒྲ་མི་རྟག་པར་སྒྲུབ་པར་བྱེད་པའི་ཆོས་ཅན་དུ་
> གཟུང་བ་ཡང་ཡིན།
>
> *kyö che pe tak kyi dra mi tak par drup par che pe chö chen du sung wa yang yin*
>
> It is a combination of being what is considered the subject of debate when proving that sound is impermanent by reason of its "being produced" and…

Kyö, generally meaning "you," in the field of logic most commonly means "it," acting as a relative pronoun referring to the subject, which in this case is *dra*, sound, or the present subject under discussion.

ཁྱོད་བྱས་པར་ཚད་མས་ངེས་ནས་

kyö che par tse me nge ne

It [sound] has been perceived [by the opponent] as something produced,

མི་རྟག་པ་ལ་ཤེས་འདོད་ཞུགས་པའི་གང་ཟག་སྲིད་པ་ཡང་ཡིན་པའི་

mi tak pa la shen dö shuk pe gang sak si pa yang yin pe

… regarding its impermanence, there is a possible person who has doubt about it [and therefore wants to know],

Sound's impermanence is *drup che chö*, the predicate or the quality to be proved, about the subject [in that proof]. *Shen dö* is a verb meaning to doubt and refers here to someone having doubt about sound's impermanence.

གཞི་མཐུན་པར་དམིགས་པ་དེ། ཁྱོད་བྱས་པའི་རྟགས་ཀྱིས་སྒྲ་མི་རྟག་པར་
སྒྲུབ་པར་བྱེད་པའི་ཤེས་འདོད་ཆོས་ཅན་སྐྱོན་མེད་ཀྱི་མཚན་ཉིད།

shi tun par mik pa de, kyö che pe tak kyi dra mi tak par drup par che pe shen dö chö chen kyön me kyi tsen nyi

… [and] it is perceived as having a combination of both qualities [stated above], is the definition of a faultless subject about which someone has doubt used to prove that sound is impermanent by reason of its being produced.

In brief, this means that the opponent with whom you are debating has perceived *dra*, sound, and has perceived *che pa*, produced or product, by his valid cognition. This person has also perceived by valid cognition that sound—the subject in question—is a produced entity. However, it is possible that there is a kind of person who has doubt about whether or not sound is impermanent even though they have a valid perception of its production. For such a person *dra*, sound ['s impermanence], is *shen dö chö chen*, a subject about which he has doubt, [and *kyön me*, faultless, insofar as there is someone who has doubt about the thesis and consequently trying to gain new knowledge]. Nevertheless, this subject is not *shen dö chö chen* for everyone, not even for Drölma. She doesn't know anything—except her favorite food and drink—Chicken Nuggets and Tibetan tea. Therefore, the reason—"sound's being a produced thing"—is not *tak yang dak*, a perfect reason, for her when trying to prove to her that sound is impermanent. It is not *shen dö chö chen kyön me*, a faultless subject about which she has doubt, because she doesn't qualify as a suitable recipient of that logical statement. One can only use this reason in a statement when made to the kind of person fitting the description as outlined in this definition. [To reiterate: The definition of a faultless subject about which someone has doubt in [a proof] proving the impermanence of sound by reason of its being produced is perceived as a combination of being that which is considered the subject in that proof proving sound's impermanence by reason of its being produced, and (the fact that) there is potentially someone who has doubt regarding the impermanence (of sound) after having perceived by valid cognition that (sound) is produced.] Such is the definition of *shen dö chö chen kyön me* in regard to proving the impermanence of sound.

དེ་སྒྲུབ་ཀྱི་རྩོད་གཞི་ཡིན་ན། དེ་སྒྲུབ་ཀྱི་ཤེས་འདོད་ཆོས་ཅན་ཡིན་པས་མ་ཁྱབ་ཀྱང་།

de drup kyi tsö shi yin na, de drup kyi shen dö chö chen yin pe ma kyap kyang

Whatever is the subject of dispute in a particular proof is not necessarily a subject about which someone has doubt in that proof; nevertheless...

De drup kyi tsö shi, The subject of dispute in this particular proof, is *dra*, sound. What is the above statement trying to prove about sound? That it is impermanent. Therefore, it uses *tak*, the reason, of sound's being produced to prove that it is impermanent. Now the text says, "Whatever is the subject of dispute in that proof is not necessarily the subject about which someone has doubt in that proof." Why is this?

The opposing party in a debate is called *göl wa*[10] in Tibetan. For a specific debater, *dra de drup kyi tsö shi yin*, sound may be the subject of dispute in a proof, and *dra de drup kyi shen dö chö chen kyön me yin*, sound may be a faultless subject [about whose nature of impermanence] he has doubt. Now, using our example, *dra chö chen, mi tak te, che pe chir*, consider sound, it is impermanent, because it is produced, would we be correct in saying that the thesis—sound is impermanent—is both *de drup kyi tsö shi*, a subject of debate in this proof, and *de drup kyi shen dö chö chen kyön me*, a faultless subject about which there is doubt, for the Buddha? Would both of these apply in regard to the Buddha or not? Would sound be a subject of debate for the Buddha were he sitting right here in front of us? Yes, it would be *tsö shi*, a subject of debate, but it would definitely not be *shen dö chö chen kyön me*, a faultless subject about which the Buddha has doubt, because Buddha doesn't have any doubt about whether or not sound is impermanent. That is the meaning expressed above when it states: *de drup kyi tsö shi yin na, de drup kyi shen dö chö chen yin pe ma kyap*, whatever is a subject of dispute in that proof is not necessarily a subject about which someone has doubt in that proof. However…

> ཕྱི་མ་ཡིན་ན་སྔ་མ་ཡིན་པས་ཁྱབ་བོ།
>
> *chi ma yin na nga ma yin pe kyap bo*
>
> Whatever is the latter [a subject about which someone has doubt], must necessarily be the former [a subject of dispute].

The text below further illustrates the case of a subject that is not a subject about which someone has doubt in a proof.

---

10 རྒོལ་བ་

དེ་ཡང་ཡིན་ཏེ།

de yang yin te

It is that way because...

སྒྲ་སྒྲར་སྒྲུབ་པའི་ཆོས་ཅན་ཡིན་ཀྱང་དེ་སྒྲུབ་ཀྱི་ཤེས་འདོད་ཆོས་ཅན་མ་ཡིན་པའི་ཕྱིར།

dra drar drup pe chö chen yin kyang de drup kyi shen dö chö chen ma yin pe chir

Although [sound] may be the subject in a proof seeking to establish that sound is sound, it is not a subject about which someone has doubt in that proof.

དེར་ཐལ། སྒྲ་ཚད་མས་ངེས་ནས་སྒྲ་སྒྲ་ཡིན་མིན་ཐེ་ཚོམ་ཟ་བའི་གང་ཟག་མེད་པའི་ཕྱིར་རོ།

der tel, dra tse me nge ne dra dra yin min te tsom sa we gang sak me pe chir ro

This is the case because once someone has perceived sound by valid cognition he would not have any doubt as to whether sound is in fact sound.

If we make the statement, *dra chö chen, dra yin te, che pa yin pe chir*, consider sound, it is sound, because it is produced, what is *tsö shi*, the basis of debate? *Dra*, Sound. What is *de drup kyi drup che chö*, the quality to be proved in that proof? Also *dra*, sound. Therefore, it says, "Although there may be a subject in a proof proving that sound is sound, it is not necessarily a subject about which someone has doubt in that proof." Why? For example, if I know you, it would be ridiculous for me to say, "I know you very well, but I don't know you." If I know you, I don't have any doubt about whether I know you or not. Because I know you it's not necessary to use reason to prove that I know you. This kind of situation is what is being expressed above. Nevertheless, this doesn't stop anyone from making such a statement.

> །འོན་ཀྱང་བྱས་པའི་རྟགས་ཀྱིས་སྒྲ་མི་རྟག་པར་སྒྲུབ་པར་བྱེད་པའི་ཤེས་འདོད་ཆོས་ཅན་དང་། དེ་སྒྲུབ་ཀྱི་རྩོད་གཞི་དང་། དེ་སྒྲུབ་ཀྱི་དཔག་གཞི་གསུམ་དོན་གཅིག་གོ
>
> *wön kyang che pe tak kyi dra mi tak par drup par che pe shen dö chö chen dang, de drup kyi tsö shi dang, de drup kyi pak shi sum dön chik go*
>
> In any case, the three—the subject about which someone has doubt in a proof, the basis of dispute in that proof, and the basis of inference in that proof—used to prove that sound is impermanent by reason of [sound's] being produced, are equivalent in meaning.
>
> །གཉིས་པ་མཚན་གཞི་ནི་སྒྲ་དེའོ།
>
> *nyi pa tsen shi ni dra de'o*
>
> The second part, an illustration, [for a subject about which someone has doubt in that given proof] is sound.

Sound, in our logical statement is *shen dö chö chen kyön me,* the faultless subject about which someone has doubt, *tsö shi*, the basis of dispute, and *pak shi*, the basis of inference. Why does sound qualify as all of these? The proof statement below gives the reason.

> །གསུམ་པ་སྒྲུབ་བྱེད་ནི། སྒྲ་ཆོས་ཅན། ཁྱོད་བྱས་པའི་རྟགས་ཀྱིས་སྒྲ་མི་རྟག་པར་སྒྲུབ་པར་བྱེད་པའི་ཤེས་འདོད་ཆོས་ཅན་སྐྱོན་མེད་ཡིན་ཏེ། མཚན་ཉིད་

བ་ཤད་པ་ལྟར་ཡིན་པའི་ཕྱིར་ཞེས་བྱའོ།

sum pa drup che ni, dra chö chen, kyö che pe tak kyi dra mi tak par drup par che pe shen dö chö chen kyön me yin te, tsen nyi she pa tar yin pe chir she ja'o

The third part, a correct proof, is: Consider sound, it is a faultless subject about which there is doubt in a proof establishing the impermanence of sound by reason of its "being produced," because it so much as exempifies the definition.

This means that sound in the proof statement above fits the definition of *shen dö chö chen kyön me*, a faultless subject about which there is doubt.

Now,

།སྒྲ་མ་ཡིན་པ་ལས་ལོག་པ་དང་མཉན་བྱ་གཉིས་རེ་རེ་ནས་དེ་མ་ཡིན་ཏེ།

dra ma yin pa le lok pa dang nyen ja nyi re re ne de ma yin te

Neither the opposite of non-sound nor an object of hearing is that.

In order to explain this concept, let's consider Drölma. Is she *mi*, a human, or *mi ma yin pa*, a non-human? She's *mi ma yin pa*, a non-human. How about you, are you *mi ma yin pa le lok pa*, the opposite of being non-human, or not? You are *mi ma yin pa le lok pa*, the opposite of being non-human. *Ka wa*, Pillar, and *ka wa ma yin pa le lok pa*, the opposite of non-pillar, are the same. *Bum pa ma yin pa le lok pa*, The opposite of non-pot, is *bum pa*, pot. *Dra ma yin pa le lok pa*, The opposite of non-sound, is *dra*, sound. *Dra ma yin pa le lok pa yin na dra yin pe kyap*, Whatever is the opposite of non-sound is necessarily sound. Therefore, sound and the opposite of non-sound are *dön chik*, equivalent in meaning or synonyms. If they are synonyms, why bother saying this at all? What is the difference between *dra*, sound, and *dra ma yin pa le lok pa*, the opposite of non-sound? The difference is that one is a positive entity and one is a negative entity; that is, one is getting at its object in a negative way. In the Tibetan grammar poem it says:[11] "The particles *ma, mi, min,* and *me* are negative particles known [in Tibetan] as *gak dra*. *Ma* and *mi* precede the word they negate, while *min* and *me* follow the word they negate." *Rang gi ngö ming gi tar me min sok gak tsik chi rik jar we chö gak tsik gi tsen nyi,*[12] The definition of a negative is a phenomenon that is created by joining an actual name with any of the negative particles such as "*me*" or "*min*" to negate it. Of course it's not necessary to use all of these negative particles to negate one subject, but you have to use at least one of them appropriately.

The main point here, as mentioned, is that what distinguishes *dra* from *dra ma yin pa le lok pa* is that one presents the subject as *drup pa*, a positive, and one as *gak pa*, a negative. *Dra*, Sound, is *drup pa*, a positive. *Dra ma yin pa le lok pa*, The opposite of non-sound, is *gak pa*, a negative. If you apply a negative particle to a noun it becomes *gak pa*, a negative. Because *dra ma yin pa le lok pa*, the opposite of non-sound, uses *gak dra*, a negative particle (*ma*), after the noun, the phrase becomes negative.

Now, can we use *dra ma yin pa le lok pa*, the opposite of non-sound, as *chö chen*, a subject of debate, in place of *dra*, sound, in the statement: *dra chö chen, mi tak te, che pa yin pe chir*, consider the subject sound, it is impermanent, because it is produced? [That is,

---

[11] This is a reference to the grammar poem, *The Divine Tree* (T: ***sum cu pa'i snying po'i don gsal byed legs bshad ljon pa'i dbang po***), written by *Ngulchuwa Yangchen Drup Pe Dorje* (***dngul cu ba dbyangs chen grub pa'i rdo rje***), based on the grammar root text, *The Thirty Verses* (T: ***sum cu pa***), composed by Thönmi Sambhota (***thun mi sam bho ta***).

།མ་མི་མིན་མེད་དགག་སྒྲ་སྟེ། །མ་མི་ཐོག་མ་མིན་མེད་འཇུག །

[12] རང་གི་དངོས་མིང་གི་མཐར་མེད་མིན་སོགས་དགག་ཚིག་སྤྱི་རིགས་སྦྱར་བའི་ཆོས་དགག་ཚིག་གི་མཚན་ཉིད།

dra ma yin pa le lok pa chö chen, mi tak te, che pa yin pe chir, consider the opposite of non-sound, it is impermanent, because it is produced.] No, we cannot use it because *dra ma yin pa le lok pa*, the opposite of non-sound, is not *drup pa*, a positive, but *gak pa*, a negative. The purpose of this statement is to prove that sound is a positive entity and not a negative entity, as it mentions below.

> སྒྲ་མ་ཡིན་པ་ལས་ལོག་པ་དེ་སྒྲ་སྒྲུབ་པར་སྒྲུབ་པར་བྱེད་པའི་ཤེས་འདོད་ཆོས་ཅན་སྐྱོན་མེད་མ་ཡིན་པའི་ཕྱིར་ཏེ། དེ་སྒྲུབ་པ་མ་ཡིན་པའི་ཕྱིར།
>
> *dra ma yin pa le lok pa de dra drup par drup par che pe shen dö chö chen kyön me ma yin pe chir te, de drup pa ma yin pe chir*
>
> The opposite of non-sound is not a faultless subject about which someone has doubt used in proving sound as a positive entity, because it [that subject] is not a positive [but a negative] entity.

Drup par drup par in the statement above means to prove sound as a positive entity. This is why *dra ma yin pa le lok pa shen dö chö chen ma yin*, the opposite of non-sound [a negative entity] is not the subject of debate about which someone has doubt [i.e., no one has doubt in this case about whether or not the opposite of non-sound has the quality of impermanence]. Similarly, *nyen ja*, object of hearing, *de drup kyi shen dö chö chen ma yin*, is not the subject about which someone has doubt in this proof [i.e., no one has doubt in this case about whether or not sound is the object of an ear consciousness].

> གཞན་ཡང་། དེ་ཆོས་ཅན། དེ་སྒྲུབ་ཀྱི་ཤེས་འདོད་ཆོས་ཅན་མ་ཡིན་པར་ཐལ། དེ་སྒྲུབ་ཀྱི་ཕྱོགས་ཆོས་ཡིན་པའི་ཕྱིར།

> *shen yang de [dra ma yin pa le lok pa] chö chen, de drup kyi shen dö chö chen ma yin par tel, de drup kyi chok chö yin pe chir*
>
> Furthermore, consider that subject [the opposite of non-sound], it follows that such is not a subject about which someone has doubt in that proof, because it [the opposite of non-sound] is the property of the subject [*chok chö*] in that proof.

The author offers a quotation to explain this.

> །རྣམ་འགྲེལ་ལས། ཆོས་ཅན་གཏན་ཚིགས་དངོས་གྱུར་ནི།
>
> །ཤེས་བྱེད་ཉིད་དུ་མ་གྲུབ་ཕྱིར། །ཞེས་གསུངས་པའི་ཕྱིར་རོ།
>
> *nam drel le, chö chen ten tsik ngö gyur ni,*
> *she che nyi du ma drup chir, she sung pe chir ro*
>
> As it says in the *Commentary to (Dignāga's) "Compendium of Valid Cognition"*: "The subject being [also] used as the logical mark, it does not serve as a perfect reason [in a proof]."

She che nyi means perfect reason. If you use *chö chen*, the subject of debate, as *ten tsik*, the reason or logical mark, then the subject will not be *shen dö chö chen kyön me*, a faultless subject about which there is doubt. Consequently, that reason will not qualify as *tak yang dak*, a perfect reason. Why? In the proof, *dra chö chen, mi tak te, dra ma yin pa le lok pa yin pe chir*, consider sound, it is impermanent, because it is the opposite of non-sound, if *dra ma yin pa le lok pa*, the opposite of non-sound, [that is, "sound"] is *ten tsik*, the reason, it cannot also be *chö chen*, the subject of debate. [This is equivalent to saying sound as a positive entity (*dra*), is impermanent, because it is the opposite of non-sound, or sound as a negative entity (*dra ma yin pa le lok pa*).]

།མཉན་བྱ་དེ་དེ་མ་ཡིན་ཏེ། དེ་སྒྲ་མཚོན་བྱར་སྒྲུབ་པའི་ཤེས་འདོད་ཆོས་ཅན་སྐྱོན་མེད་མ་ཡིན་པའི་ཕྱིར་ཏེ། དེ་མཚོན་བྱ་མ་ཡིན་པའི་ཕྱིར།

nyen ja de de ma yin te, de dra tsön jar drup pe shen dö chö chen kyön me ma yin pe chir te, de tsön ja ma yin pe chir

Object of hearing is not [a subject about which there is doubt in that proof], because it is not a faultless subject about which there is doubt in proving sound as an object to be defined. Such is the case because "object of hearing" is not an object to be defined.

Nyen ja, Object of hearing, is not *tsön ja*, an object to be defined, but *tsen nyi*, a definition; more precisely, it is the definition of sound.

གཞན་ཡང་། དེ་དེ་སྒྲུབ་ཀྱི་ཤེས་འདོད་ཆོས་ཅན་མ་ཡིན་པར་ཐལ། དེ་དེ་སྒྲུབ་ཀྱི་ཕྱོགས་ཆོས་ཡིན་པའི་ཕྱིར། དེར་ཐལ། དེ་དེ་སྒྲུབ་ཀྱི་ཐུན་མོང་མ་ཡིན་པའི་མ་ངེས་པའི་གཏན་ཚིགས་ཡིན་པའི་ཕྱིར་རོ།

shen yang de de drup kyi shen dö chö chen ma yin par tel, de de drup kyi chok chö yin pe chir, der tel, de de drup kyi tun mong ma yin pe ma nge pe ten tsik yin pe chir ro

Moreover, it follows that it [object of hearing] is not a subject about which there is doubt [regarding its impermanence] in that proof, because it is the property of the subject in that proof. That follows because it is a unique indefinite reason in that proof.

Tun mong ma yin pa ma nge pe ten tsik, A unique indefinite reason, is represented in the center of the chart known as *chok chö kyi kor lo*, "Wheel of [Nine] Reasons," derived from a short text by Acharya Dignāga. (This chart can be found at the end of this present text.) The example used there is *dra chö chen, tak te, nyen ja yin pe chir*, consider sound, it is permanent, because it is an object of hearing. This can be explained through the general definition of *ma nge pe ten tsik*, an indefinite reason, as it is given below.

ཁྱོད་ཀྱི་རྟགས་ཀྱིས་དེ་སྒྲུབ་ཀྱི་ཁྱབ་པའི་ཚུལ་གཉིས་རྣམ་པར་མ་ངེས་པ། དེ་སྒྲུབ་ཀྱི་མ་ངེས་པའི་གཏན་ཚིགས་ཀྱི་མཚན་ཉིད།

kyö kyi tak kyi, de drup kyi kyap pe tsul nyi nam par ma nge pa, de drup kyi ma nge pe ten tsik kyi tsen nyi

The definition of an indefinite reason in a proof is what has two modes of pervasion, which are indefinite in that proof when using it as a reason.

This means that *kyap pe tsul nyi*, the two modes of pervasion [positive and reverse] in that proof are imperfect. A more complete definition of an indefinite reason is given in the *Extensive Explanation* as:

ཁྱོད་དེ་སྒྲུབ་ཀྱི་ཕྱོགས་ཆོས་གང་ཞིག ཁྱོད་ཀྱི་རྟགས་ཀྱིས་དེ་སྒྲུབ་ཀྱི་ཁྱབ་པའི་ཚུལ་གཉིས་རྣལ་མར་ཡང་མ་ངེས། ཁྱོད་ཀྱི་རྟགས་ཀྱིས་དེ་སྒྲུབ་ཀྱི་ཁྱབ་པའི་ཚུལ་གཉིས་ཕྱིན་ཅི་ལོག་ཏུ་ཡང་མ་ངེས་པ་དེ། ཁྱོད་དེ་སྒྲུབ་ཀྱི་མ་ངེས་པའི་གཏན་ཚིགས་ཀྱི་མཚན་ཉིད།

kyö de drup kyi chok chö gang shik, kyö kyi tak kyi de drup kyi kyap pe tsul nyi nel mar yang me nge, kyö kyi tak kyi de drup kyi kyap pe tsul nyi chin chi lok tu yang ma nge pa de kyö de drup kyi ma nge pe ten tsik kyi tsen nyi

The definition of an indefinite reason in a proof is that which is the property of the subject in that proof [reason's relevance to the subject], whose two modes of pervasion are indefinite in that proof when using it as a reason, and which is also erroneous in its two modes of pervasion in that proof when using it as a reason.

Both *nyen ja*, object of hearing, and *yö pa*, being existent, are examples of unique indefinite reasons in the respective proofs: *dra chö chen, mi tak te, nyen ja yin pe chir*, consider sound, it is impermanent, because it is an object of hearing. And again, *dra chö chen, mi tak te, yö pe chir*, consider sound, it is impermanent, because it is an existent. Regarding this last proof, the following rule applies to show how it is *kyap pe tsul nyi nam par ma nge pa*, indefinite in its two modes of pervasion. *Yö pa yin na mi tak pa yin pe yang ma kyap, ma yin pe yang ma kyap*, If something is an existent, it is not necessarily an impermanent entity and not necessarily <u>not</u> an impermanent entity. That is, there is not complete entailment.

།དེ་སྒྲུབ་ཀྱི་ཤེས་འདོད་ཆོས་ཅན་ཡོད་ན། དེ་སྒྲུབ་ཀྱི་ཕྱོགས་ཆོས་ཡོད་པས་
མ་ཁྱབ་སྟེ།

de drup kyi shen dö chö chen yö na, de drup kyi chok chö yö pe ma kyap te

If there is a subject about which there is doubt in a proof, there does not necessarily exist a property of the subject in that proof.

For example, *dra chö chen, mi tak te, dra yin pe chir, she gö pe tse, de drup kyi shen dö chö chen yö kyang, de drup kyi chok chö me pe chir*, when we make the statement, "Consider sound, it is impermanent, because it is sound," although there is a subject about which there is doubt in that proof [concerning sound's impermanence], there is not a property of the subject in that proof. Why? Because *chö chen*, the subject of debate, is sound and *tak*, the reason, is also sound. Since sound is sound, there is no *chok chö*, property of the subject or [the reason's relevance to the subject, necessarily implying the other qualifications of the definition]. The text offers this same example.

> །སྒྲའི་རྟགས་ཀྱིས་སྒྲ་མི་རྟག་པར་སྒྲུབ་པར་བྱེད་པའི་ཤེས་འདོད་ཆོས་ཅན་ཡོད་ཀྱང་། དེའི་རྟགས་ཀྱིས་དེ་སྒྲུབ་ཀྱི་ཕྱོགས་ཆོས་མེད་པའི་ཕྱིར།
>
> *dra'i tak kyi dra mi tak par drup par che pe shen dö chö chen yö kyang, de'i tak kyi de drup kyi chok chö me pe chir*
>
> Although there is a subject of doubt in a proof establishing the impermanence of sound by reason of its being sound, there is no property of the subject in that proof when using that reason.

The author doesn't give a reason to explain this because it is obvious. The kind of statement being used here is what is known as *ma drup pe ten tsik*, an unestablished reason, whose definition is given below.

> དེ་སྒྲུབ་ཀྱི་ཕྱོགས་ཆོས་མ་ཡིན་པར་དམིགས་པ་དེ། དེ་སྒྲུབ་ཀྱི་མ་གྲུབ་པའི་གཏན་ཚིགས་ཀྱི་མཚན་ཉིད།
>
> *de drup kyi chok chö ma yin par mik pa de, de drup kyi ma drup pe ten tsik kyi tsen nyi*
>
> The definition of an unestablished reason in a proof is that which is perceived as what is not the property of the subject in that proof.

There are nine kinds of *ma drup pe ten tsik*, unestablished reasons. For example, *dra chö chen, mi tak te, dra yin pe chir, she kö pe tse, de drup kyi shen dö chö chen yö, chok chö me*, when we make the statement, "Consider sound, it is impermanent, because it is sound," there is a subject about which there is doubt in that proof [sound's impermanence], but there is no property of the subject in that proof [since sound is sound, given that the subject and the reason are the same].

What is *tsö shi*, the basis of dispute, in this statement? *Dra*, Sound. What is *tak*, the reason? Also *dra*, sound. In particular, this is an example of *shi tak ta te me ne ma drup pe tak*,[13] an unestablished reason through the lack of difference between the basis of debate and the reason.

basis of relation of pervasion

གཉིས་པ་ཁྱབ་པའི་ལྟོས་གཞི་ལ་གཉིས། བསྒྲུབ་བྱའི་ཆོས་དང་། མཐུན་ཕྱོགས་དང་མི་མཐུན་ཕྱོགས་སོ།

nyi pa kyap pe tö shi la nyi, drup je chö dang, tun chok dang mi tun chok so

The second, the basis of relation of pervasion, has two parts: 1) the quality to be proved, and 2) the similar and dissimilar classes.

[Basis of relation of pervasion refers to the relationship between the reason and the predicate in a proof.] There are two parts to *kyap pe tö shi*, basis of relation of pervasion: 1) *drup che chö*, the quality to be proved or predicate, and 2) *tun chok*, the similar class, and *mi tun chok*, the dissimilar class. *Tun chok kyi tö shi*, Basis of relation of the similar class, refers to *je kyap kyi tö shi*, the basis of relation of positive pervasion; *mi tun chok kyi tö shi*, the basis of relation of the dissimilar class, refers to *dok kyap kyi tö shi*, the basis of relation of reverse pervasion.

In order to understand this it is helpful to refer to the model template. In the statement, *dra chö chen, mi tak te, che pa yin pe chir*, consider sound, it is impermanent, because it is produced, *dra*,

---

13 གཞི་རྟགས་ཐ་དད་མེད་ནས་མ་གྲུབ་པ་

sound, is *chok chö kyi tö shi*, the basis of relation of the property of the subject. *Mi tak pa*, Impermanence, as *drup che chö*, the quality to be proved or predicate, is *kyap pe tö shi*, the basis of relation of positive pervasion. What is *tun chok*, the similar class, in relation to this proof? Everything that is *mi tak pa*, impermanent. *Tun* means the same class [of entities] as the quality to be proved. Examples of these are pitchers, pillars, mountains, rivers, trees, etc., all being *tun chok*, of a similar class, with the quality of *mi tak pa*, impermanence. This can be stated as: *dra chö chen, mi tak te, che pa yin pe chir, she gö pe tse, tun chok bum pa ta bu*, in the proof that states, "Consider sound, it is impermanent, because it is produced," there is that which is of a similar class [with the class of impermanent entities] like a pitcher. Since impermanence is *drup che chö*, the quality to be proved, in this proof, things such as pillars, pitchers, trees, and so forth, being impermanent entities belong to the similar class of the quality to be proved in this proof. They are *te drup kyi tun chok*, of a similar class [with the quality to be proved] in this proof (also referred to as *tun pe* [**mthun dpe**] or examples of the similar class).

On the other hand, all *tak pa*, permanent entities, are *mi tun chok*, belonging to the dissimilar class, in relation to *mi tak pa*, the impermanent. An example of something belonging to this dissimilar class is *du ma che kyi nam ka*, uncomposed space. This can be stated as: *dra chö chen, mi tak te, che pa yin pe chir, she gö pe tse, mi tun chok nam ka ta bu*, in the proof that states, "Consider sound, it is impermanent, because it is produced," there is that which is of a dissimilar class [with the class of impermanent entities] like space. Space, along with all other permanent entities, *te drup kyi mi tun chok*, [pertains to] the dissimilar class in this proof. Since *tak pa*, permanence, is *mi tun chok*, pertaining to the dissimilar class, in this proof, it is *de drup kyi gak che chö*, the quality to be refuted in this proof. *Du ma che kyi nam ka*, Uncomposed space, is *gak ja dang tun pa*, of a compatible nature with that which is to be refuted. As a phenomenon belonging to the dissimilar class, uncomposed space also serves as *mi tun pe*, an example of that dissimilar class.

quality to be proved [or predicate]

།དང་པོ་ལ་གསུམ། མཚན་ཉིད། དབྱེ་བ། སྒྲུབ་བྱེད་དོ། །བསྒྲུབ་བྱའི་ཆོས་སུ་
གཟུང་བར་བྱ་བ་དེ། བསྒྲུབ་བྱའི་ཆོས་ཀྱི་མཚན་ཉིད།

dang po la sum, tsen nyi, ye wa, drup che chö, drup che chö su sung war ja wa de, drup che chö kyi tsen nyi

The first (quality to be proved) has three parts: its definition, divisions, and a correct proof. The definition of the quality to be proved is that which is held as the quality to be proved.

To understand why something qualifies as *drup che chö*, a quality to be proved, you have to learn the definition, divisions, and proofs. The definition given above means that any statement used in the position of the quality to be proved is a quality to be proved. An example is *mi tak pa*, impermanence, which is used in the second position of the statement: *dra chö chen, mi tak te, che pa yin pe chir*, consider sound, it is impermanent, because it is produced. Now, the definition becomes more precise.

དེ་སྒྲུབ་ཀྱི་བསྒྲུབ་བྱའི་ཆོས་སུ་གཟུང་བར་བྱ་བ། དེ་སྒྲུབ་ཀྱི་བསྒྲུབ་བྱའི་ཆོས་
ཀྱི་མཚན་ཉིད།

de drup kyi drup che chö su sung war ja wa, de drup kyi drup che chö kyi tsen nyi

The definition of the quality to be proved in a proof is what is held as the quality to be proved in that proof.

The phrase "*de drup kyi*" means in a particular proof, which is added in order to base the statement in a specific context.

བདག་མེད་ཡིན་ན། དེ་སྒྲུབ་ཀྱི་བསྒྲུབ་བྱའི་ཆོས་ཡིན་པས་ཁྱབ་སྟེ།

dak me yin na, de drup kyi drup je chö yin pe kyap te

Whatever is selfless is necessarily a quality to be proved in a proof.

Since this text is based on the view of the lower schools, when the term *dak me*, selflessness, is used, it is referring to either *gang sak tak chik rang wang chen gyi tong pa*,[14] being empty of a permanent, single, independent person, or to *gang sak rang kya tub pe dze yö kyi tong pa*,[15] being empty of a self-sufficient, substantially existent person. *Me* in the term *dak me*, is a negative particle rejecting *dak*, self.

What is the difference between the following terms for selflessness: *dak me*, *den me*, and *rang ngö ne ma drup pa*? It depends on the school. *Dak me*, Selflessness, here is referring mostly to the view held by those belonging to the Śrāvakakayāna (Listener Vehicle)[16] and Pratyekabuddhayāna (Solitary Realizer Vehicle)[17] systems. Although the higher schools will also accept that interpretation of *dak me*, it is still *rak pa*, rough, and not subtle enough for them.

The general definition of *gang sak*, person, is *rang gi pung po nga po gang rung la ten ne tak pe kye bu gang sak gi tsen nyi*,[18] the definition of person is that which is ascribed to [at least four] of the five aggregates. This is also a little bit subtle. *Rang gi pung po nga po gang rung* means any [four] of its five aggregates: *suk*, form, *tsor wa*, feeling, *du she*, conception, *du che*, formations, and *nam par she pa*, consciousness. It doesn't say *tun mong nga la tak pe kye bu*, a

---

14 གང་ཟག་རྟག་གཅིག་རང་དབང་ཅན་གྱི་སྟོང་པ་

15 གང་ཟག་རང་རྐྱ་ཐུབ་པའི་རྫས་ཡོད་ཀྱི་སྟོང་པ་

16 ཉན་ཐོས་ཀྱི་ཐེག་པ་

17 རང་རྒྱལ་གྱི་ཐེག་པ་

18 རང་གི་ཕུང་པོ་ལྔ་པོ་གང་རུང་ལ་བརྟེན་ནས་བཏགས་པའི་སྐྱེ་བུ་གང་ཟག་གི་མཚན་ཉིད།

person ascribed on the common five aggregates. Well then, what kind of person could there be who doesn't have all five aggregates? *Suk me kam pa*, Persons of the formless realm. Of the three realms—desire realm, form realm, and formless realm—the beings of this third realm don't have the form aggregate. *La ten ne tak pa* means the basis of ascribing a person on those aggregates. However, this only applies when debating in the Sūtra field. When we debate in the Tantric field, the situation is very different.

Gang sak means person or individual. *Dak dang gang sak ngö su che we dak*, The self that actually acts, or the conventional self and conventional person, do exist. However, *dak mi che pe dak*, a self that does not act, implying an inherently existent self, is non-existent. *Yö pe dak*, Existent self, and *me pe dak*, a non-existent self, are different. For instance, an eater, drinker, worker, student, practitioner are all *dak* or *gang sak*, and do exist; but *rang kya tub pe gang sak*, a self-sufficient, independent person, does not exist. *Rang* means itself. *Kya tub pa* means not relying on anything else; "anything else" in this context refers to *pung po la ma tö pa*, not relying on its heaps. *Rang kya wa tub pa* means to exist independently and implies that the heaps are used by that *gang sak* who is their owner.

According to the view of the lower schools, when they have a direct perception of this kind of selflessness, they can achieve Hinayāna nirvana. But according to the view of the higher schools one does not achieve nirvana this way because that wisdom is not subtle enough. In this system, *gang sak rang kya tub pa dze yö*, an independent, substantial person, is *gak ja*, the object to be refuted. If anything exists it should be *dak me*, selfless. If that *dak* is what is to be refuted, then everything should be *dak me*, selfless. This is why it states in the text above: *dak me yin na, de drup kyi drup che chö yin pe kyap*, whatever is selfless must necessarily be a quality to be proved in that proof. Since everything is *dak me*, selfless, you can use anything as *drup che chö*, a quality to be proved, in a proof. Did you get the idea? This is just a rough explanation and enough for rookies.

The text gives an example below.

རི་བོང་རྭ་དེ་རི་བོང་གི་རར་སྒྲུབ་པར་བྱེད་པའི་བསྒྲུབ་བྱའི་ཆོས་སུ་གཟུང་བྱ་ཡིན་པའི་ཕྱིར་ཏེ། དེ་ཆོས་ཅན། རི་བོང་རྭ་ཡིན་ཏེ། དེ་ཡིན་པའི་ཕྱིར་ཞེས་པའི་བསྒྲུབ་བྱའི་ཆོས་ཡིན་པའི་ཕྱིར།

ri bong ra de ri bong gyi rar drup par che pe drup je chö su sung ja yin pe chir te, de chö chen, ri bong ra yin te, de yin pe chir she pe drup je chö yin pe chir

Because a hare's horn is what is held as the quality to be proved when proving a hare's horn is a hare's horn in the statement, "Consider a hare's horn, it is a hare's horn, because it is a hare's horn." A hare's horn is that quality to be proved.

[This is to comply with the logic rule: *yö me gang rung yin na, dak me yin pe kyap*, whether it exists or not, it must be selfless. Therefore, even a non-existent such as a hare's horn is selfless and can be used as the quality to be proved in this proof.]

དེས་ན་བསྒྲུབ་བྱའི་ཆོས་ཡིན་ན། ཆོས་ཡིན་པས་མ་ཁྱབ་བོ།

de na drup je chö yin na, chö yin pe ma kyap bo

Therefore, if such is the case, whatever is a quality to be proved is not necessarily a phenomenon.

The definition of a phenomenon is that which holds its own essence, *rang gi ngo wo dzin pa chö kyi tsen nyi*.[19] *Ngo wo* means nature, essence, or identity. For example, if someone were to ask you, "Do you have a piece of chalk?" "Yes, here's one." That piece of chalk already holds its own identity, *ngo wo*, but it cannot speak. If it could, it would say, "I am a piece of chalk." Again, "Do you

---

[19] རང་གི་ངོ་བོ་འཛིན་པ་ཆོས་ཀྱི་མཚན་ཉིད།

know what a cup is?" "Sure, this is a cup." You can say that. If everything were not *rang gi ngo wo dzin pa*, holding its own identity, you would not be able to find things and name them. Why can you find them so easily? Precisely because each thing holds its own quality. So, when the text states, "Whatever is a quality to be proved is not necessarily a phenomenon," it means that the quality to be proved does not have to possess the characteristic described by the definition of a phenomenon.

།སྒྲ་མི་རྟག་པར་སྒྲུབ་པར་བྱེད་པའི་བསྒྲུབ་བྱའི་ཆོས་སུ་གཟུང་བར་བྱ་བ་དེ། སྒྲ་མི་རྟག་པར་སྒྲུབ་པར་བྱེད་པའི་བསྒྲུབ་བྱའི་ཆོས་ཀྱི་མཚན་ཉིད། མི་རྟག་པ་དེ་དེའི་མཚན་གཞིའོ།

dra mi tak par drup par che pe drup che chö su sung war ja wa de, dra mi tak par drup par che pe drup che chö kyi tsen nyi, mi tak pa de de'i tsen shi'o

The definition of the quality to be proved used to prove that sound is impermanent is what is held as the quality to be proved in proving that sound is impermanent. Impermanent is an example of a quality to be proved [in that proof].

Since this statement is trying to prove that sound is impermanent, *mi tak pa*, impermanent, is what is used as the quality to be proved about sound.

At this point, the text presents the model template (cited previously) used to identify the various parts of a syllogism. You should memorize this template so that you have a firm understanding of the function of each of its parts. This will help you to recognize them when they are referred to throughout this text.

།སྒྲ་ཆོས་ཅན། མི་རྟག་སྟེ། བྱས་པའི་ཕྱིར་ཞེས་བཀོད་པའི་ཚེ་སྒྲ་རྩོད་བཞི། མི་རྟག་པ་བསྒྲུབ་བྱའི་ཆོས། སྒྲ་མི་རྟག་པ་བསྒྲུབ་བྱ། བྱས་པ་རྟགས་ཡང་དག །

།རྟག་པ་དགག་བྱའི་ཆོས། སྒྲ་རྟག་པ་དགག་བྱར་འཇོག་སྟེ། གཞན་ལ་སྦྱོར་
ཚུལ་ཤེས་པར་བྱའོ།

dra chö chen, mi tak te, che pe chir she kö pe tse dra tsö shi, mi tak pa drup che chö, dra mi tak pa drup ja, che pa tak yang dak, tak pa gak che chö, dra tak pa gak jar jok te, shen la jor tsul she par ja'o

In the statement, "Consider sound, it is impermanent, because it is produced," sound is the basis of debate; being impermanent is the quality to be proved [about sound]; [that] sound is impermanent is the thesis; being produced is the perfect reason; [sound's] permanence is the quality to be refuted; [that] sound is permanent is the thesis to be refuted. This [paradigm] can be applied similarly to other examples.

Dra, Sound, is *tsö shi*, the basis of dispute, *pak shi,* the basis of inference, *chö chen*, the subject of debate, and, in this case, *shen du chö chen kyön me*, the faultless subject about which there is doubt. *Pak* is short for *je pak*, which means to guess or infer. What is the object of your inference? The basis of debate, which in this case is sound. What are you inferring about it? What is the quality you are trying to prove about sound? "I think sound is impermanent." *Mi tak pa*, Impermanence, is *drup che chö*, the quality to be proved [about sound]. Why is sound impermanent? *Che pe chir*, Because it is produced. *Che pa*, Product, is *tak yang dak*, a perfect reason. *Gak che chö*, The quality to be rejected, is *tak pa*, [that sound is] permanent. *Gak ja*, The object to be negated, is *dra tak pa*, permanent sound. What is it exactly that you are rejecting? You cannot reject *tak pa*, permanence itself, unless you are crazy, because permanent entities do exist. However, you can reject the fact that sound is permanent because sound is not a permanent entity. Therefore, *dra tak pa gak ja*, permanent sound is the object to be negated. *Shen la jor tsul she par ja'o* means all logical statements should be like that. In this way you can learn what a good reason is, what it is you are rejecting, what the basis of debate is, and so forth.

གཉིས་པ་དེ་ལ་དབྱེ་ན། དེའི་དངོས་ཀྱི་བསྒྲུབ་བྱའི་ཆོས་དང་། ཤུགས་ཀྱི་བསྒྲུབ་བྱའི་ཆོས་གཉིས་ཡོད་པའི་མི་རྟག་པ་དེ་དང་པོ་དང་སྐད་ཅིག་མ་ནི་ཕྱི་མའོ།

nyi pa de la ye na, de'i ngö kyi drup che chö dang, shuk kyi drup che chö nyi yö pe mi tak pa de dang po dang ke chik ma ni chi ma'o

The second part, the classifications (of the quality to be proved), has two divisions: 1) the explicit quality to be proved, and 2) the implicit quality to be proved. In the model statement, "impermanent" is an example of this first, and "momentary" is an example of the second.

In the statement, *dra chö chen, mi tak te, che pa yin pe chir*, consider sound, it is impermanent, because it is produced, *ngö gyi drup che chö*, the explicit quality to be proved, is *mi tak pa*, impermanent. *Shuk kyi drup che chö*, The implicit quality to be proved, is *ke chik ma*, momentary, which is the general definition of *mi tak pa*, impermanent.

བྱས་པའི་རྟགས་ཀྱིས་སྒྲ་མི་རྟག་པར་སྒྲུབ་པར་བྱེད་པའི་བསྒྲུབ་བྱའི་ཆོས་ལའང་དེའི་དངོས་ཀྱི་བསྒྲུབ་བྱའི་ཆོས་དང་། དེའི་ཤུགས་ཀྱི་བསྒྲུབ་བྱའི་ཆོས་གཉིས། མི་རྟག་པ་དང་སྐད་ཅིག་མ་གཉིས་རེ་རེ་ནས་དང་པོ་དང་། དེ་གཉིས་མ་ཡིན་པ་ལས་ལོག་པ་གཉིས་རེ་རེ་ནས་གཉིས་པ་ཡིན་ནོ།

che pe tak kyi dra mi tak par drup par che pe drup che chö la'ang de'i ngö kyi drup che chö dang, de'i shuk kyi drup che'i chö nyi, mi tak pa dang ke chik ma nyi re re ne dang po dang, de nyi ma yin pa le lok pa nyi re re ne nyi pa yin no

> Also, regarding the quality to be proved in a proof establishing the impermanence of sound by using "being produced" as a reason, impermanent and momentary can each serve as the first, i.e., the explicit quality to be proved, and the opposite of non-impermanent and the opposite of non-momentary respectively can serve as the implicit qualities to be proved [in that proof].

To state this using the method of debate:

***

—*Dra chö chen, mi tak te, che pa yin pe chir, she gö pe tse, ngö gyi drup che chö ka re shak*, Tell me, what is the explicit quality to be proved in the statement, "Consider sound, it is impermanent, because it is produced"?
—*Mi tak pa shak*, Impermanent.
—*Shuk kyi drup che chö ka re shak*, Can you tell me what the implicit quality to be proved is in this proof?
—*Ke chik ma shak*, Momentary.

When using *che pe chir*, because it is produced, as a reason to prove that sound is impermanent, it can be implicitly understood that while sound is produced it is also momentary.

In a proof, when *mi tak pa*, impermanent, is stated as *ngö kyi drup che chö*, the explicit quality to be proved, *mi tak pa ma yin pa le lok pa*, the opposite of non-impermanent, becomes *shuk kyi drup che chö*, the implicit quality to be proved. Similarly, when *ke chik ma*, momentary, is stated as *ngö kyi drup che chö*, the explicit quality to be proved, in a proof, *ke chik ma ma yin pa le lok pa*, the opposite of non-momentary, becomes *shuk kyi drup che chö*, the implicit quality to be proved. *Mi tak pa ma yin pa le lok pa* and *ke chik ma ma yin pa le lok pa* are both *gak pa*, negatives. However, in the proof, *dra chö chen, mi tak te, che pa yin pe chir*, consider sound, it is impermanent, because it is produced, the reason, *che pa*, being produced, is *drup pa*, a positive entity, used to prove that sound is impermanent, implying that it is not proving sound as *gak pa*, a negative entity. Do you understand?

Dra ma yin pa le lok pa, The opposite of non-sound, is *dra*, sound, nevertheless, it is a negative entity, since it incorporates the negative particle "*ma*" in the phrase. *Mi tak ma ma yin pa le lok pa*, The opposite of non-impermanent, is *mi tak pa*, impermanent. *Ke chik ma ma yin pa le lok pa*, The opposite of non-momentary is *ke chik ma*, momentary. *Tak pa*, Permanent [entities], such as space are not *ke chik ma*, momentary, but rather *ke chik pa ma yin pa*, non-momentary. *Lok pa* means that it is the opposite or void of that quality. *Mi ma yin pa le lok pa*, The opposite of non-human, is human. *Kyi*, Dog, is *mi ma yin pa*, not a human. *Kyi ma yin pa le lok pa*, The opposite of non-dog, is *kyi*, dog. This is how the logic system works.

གསུམ་པ་སྒྲུབ་བྱེད་ནི། མི་རྟག་པ་ཆོས་ཅན། ཁྱོད་སྒྲ་མི་རྟག་པར་སྒྲུབ་པར་བྱེད་པའི་བསྒྲུབ་བྱའི་ཆོས་ཡིན་ཏེ། མཚན་ཉིད་དེའི་ཕྱིར་རོ།

sum pa drup che ni, mi tak pa chö chen, kyö dra mi tak par drup par che pe drup che chö yin te, tsen nyi de'i chir ro

The third section concerns a correct proof. Consider impermanence, it is the quality to be proved in a proof seeking to establish sound's impermanence, because it satisfies the definition of a quality to be proved.

To understand this it is important to recall the definition of *drup che chö*, the quality to be proved, which is:

དེ་སྒྲུབ་ཀྱི་བསྒྲུབ་བྱའི་ཆོས་སུ་གཟུང་བར་བྱ་བ། དེ་སྒྲུབ་ཀྱི་བསྒྲུབ་བྱའི་ཆོས་ཀྱི་མཚན་ཉིད།

de drup kyi drup che chö su sung war ja wa, de drup kyi drup che chö kyi tsen nyi

> The definition of a quality to be proved in that proof is what is held as the quality to be proved in that proof.
>
> །སྐད་ཅིག་མ་ཆོས་ཅན། སྒྲ་མི་རྟག་པར་སྒྲུབ་པར་བྱེད་པའི་དངོས་ཀྱི་བསྒྲུབ་བྱའི་ཆོས་མ་ཡིན་ཏེ།
>
> *ke chik ma chö chen, dra mi tak par drup par che pe ngö kyi drup che chö ma yin te*
>
> Consider the momentary, it is not the explicit quality to be proved used in the proof establishing sound's impermanence…

Previously it stated *ngö kyi drup che chö nyi re re ne*, each of these—impermanent and momentary—were the explicit qualities to be proved in that proof, but here it is saying that momentary is not the explicit quality to be proved. What is the difference? It is not the explicit quality to be proved in this particular proof because the reason [the critical third part of the syllogism] has not been stated yet. If one makes the statement, *ke chik ma te, dra mi tak par drup par che pe ngö kyi drup che chö ma yin te, dra chö chen, mi tak pa yin te*, momentary is not the explicit quality to be proved in the proof proving the impermanence of sound [where only part of the statement is made saying], "Consider sound, it is impermanent, because…." Since the reason in that proof is yet to be stated, it does not qualify as the explicit quality to be proved until you complete the statement by offering a reason. For example, when you include *che pe tak kyi*, by reason of its being produced, you have made a complete proof, which allows for momentary, in this case, to become a potential explicit quality to be proved in this proof.

Also, when making only a partial statement such as *dra chö chen, mi tak te*, consider sound, it is impermanent, we could not call *ke chik ma*, momentary, the explicit quality to be proved because there is a chance that when completing the statement, *ke chik ma*, momentary, may be used as the reason in that proof, as mentioned below.

དེ་སྒྲུབ་ཀྱི་རྟགས་ཡང་དག་ཡིན་པའི་ཕྱིར།

de drup kyi tak yang dak yin pe chir

because it [may be used as] a perfect reason in that proof.

For example, we might say: *dra chö chen, mi tak te, ke chik ma yin pe chir*, consider sound, it is impermanent, because it is momentary. Therefore, it may or may not be the explicit quality to be proved depending on whether or not you have completed the proof. That is why it says above, *ngö kyi drup che chö ma yin te, de drup kyi tak yang dak yin pe chir*, it is not the explicit quality to be proved [in this case], because it may be used as a perfect reason in that proof.

དེར་ཐལ། དེ་སྒྲུབ་ཀྱི་ཐ་སྙད་འབའ་ཞིག་སྒྲུབ་ཀྱི་རྟགས་ཡང་དག་ཡིན་པའི་ཕྱིར།

der tel, de drup kyi ta nye ba shik drup kyi tak yang dak yin pe chir

This follows, because it is a perfect reason that proves only a term in that proof.

Between the two kinds of perfect reason, *ta nye ba shik drup kyi tak yang dak*, a perfect reason proving only a term, and *dön ba shik drup kyi tak yang dak*, a perfect reason proving only a meaning, here it is referring to the first, *ta nye ba shik drup kyi tak yang dak*. This kind of reason only proves a term by giving the definition of that term as a reason; the second only proves a meaning by giving the term or object to be defined as a reason. *Dön*, The meaning, is only *tsen nyi*, the definition; *ta nye*, the term, is only *tsön ja*, that which is to be defined. The statement above is referring to *ta nye*, term, since *mi tak pa*, impermanent, the quality to be proved in that proof, is a term and not a definition. For example, when we say, *dra chö chen, mi tak te, ke chik ma yin pe chir*, consider sound, it is impermanent, because it is momentary, only *mi tak pa* and not *ke chik ma*, is *ngö kyi drup che chö*, the explicit quality to be proved, since *ke chik ma*, the definition of impermanence, is being used as the reason in this statement.

Furthermore, if it is used as the reason in that proof, it cannot also be used as the quality to be proved in that proof. *Tak*, The reason, must be different from *tsö shi*, the basis of debate. Why? Generally, such a reason would qualify as *de drup kyi tak tar nang*, a false reason in that proof; specifically, it would be *tak chö ta te me ne ma drup pe ten tsik*, an unestablished reason through lack of difference between the reason and the quality to be proved.

དེ་བྱས་པའི་རྟགས་ཀྱིས་དེ་སྒྲུབ་ཀྱི་དངོས་ཀྱི་བསྒྲུབ་བྱའི་ཆོས་ཡིན་ཏེ། བྱས་པའི་རྟགས་ཀྱིས་དེ་སྒྲུབ་ཀྱི་དངོས་ཀྱི་བསྒྲུབ་བྱའི་ཆོས་སུ་གྱུར་པའི་མཚན་མཚོན་གཉིས་ཀ་ཡོད་པའི་ཕྱིར།

de che pe tak kyi de drup kyi ngö kyi drup che chö yin te, che pe tak kyi de drup kyi ngö kyi drup che chö su gyur pe tsen tsön nyi ka yö pe chir

Both [impermanent and momentary] can be the explicit qualities to be proved in the proof that uses "produced" as a reason, because by using "produced" as the [perfect] reason in that proof, both the definition [momentary] and what is defined [impermanent] can become the explicit quality to be proved in that proof.

Both the definition of impermanence, *ke chik ma*, momentary, and object to be defined, *mi tak pa*, impermanence, can become the explicit quality to be proved in that proof when a perfect reason, in this case, *che pa*, produced, is used to prove the impermanence of sound.

དེར་ཐལ། བྱས་པ་དེ་སྒྲ་མི་རྟག་པར་སྒྲུབ་པར་བྱེད་པའི་དོན་དང་ཐ་སྙད་
གཉིས་ཀ་སྒྲུབ་པར་བྱེད་པའི་རྟགས་ཡང་དག་ཡིན་པའི་ཕྱིར་རོ།

der tel, che pa te dra mi tak par drup par che pe dön dang ta nye nyi ka drup par che pe tak yang dak yin pe chir ro

It follows that both [can be used as the explicit quality to be proved in that proof] because "being produced" is a perfect reason that serves to prove both the definition and the term in proving the impermanence of sound.

As mentioned previously, *dön*, meaning, refers to *tsen nyi*, the definition, and *ta nye*, term, refers to *tsön ja*, that which is to be defined. For example, *dra chö chen, mi tak te, che pa yin pe chir, she gö pe tse,* when we make the statement, "Consider sound, it is impermanent, because it is produced," *che pa*, produced, is *te drup kyi dön dang ta nye nyi ka drup pe tak yang dak*, a perfect reason that proves both the definition and that which is to be defined in that proof. *Dön*, The meaning, is *ke chik ma*, momentary, the definition of *mi tak pa*, impermanent; *ta nye*, term, is *mi tak pa*, impermanent. *Che pa*, Produced, is a perfect reason that proves both of them [the definition and the term]. If the statement is *dra chö chen, mi tak te, ke chik ma yin pe chir*, consider sound, it is impermanent, because it is momentary, *ke chik ma*, momentary, the definition of impermanence, is *dön*, the meaning, and is used here as the reason to prove only *ta nye*, the term, or *tsön ja*, that which is to be defined, and as the text previously mentioned, qualifies as *de drup kyi ta nye ba shik drup kyi tak yang dak*, a perfect reason that proves only a term in that proof.

།གཉིས་པ་མཐུན་ཕྱོགས་དང་མི་མཐུན་ཕྱོགས་ལ་གཉིས། དངོས་དང་།
དཔེ་གཉིས་བཤད་པའོ།

nyi pa tun chok dang mi tun chok la nyi, ngö dang, pe nyi she pa'o

The second, similar class and dissimilar class, has two parts: an explanation of actual [similar and dissimilar classes] and examples.

Ngö means actual, referring here to both *tun chok*, similar class, and *mi tun chok*, dissimilar class. A description of these is presented below.

།དང་པོ་ལ་བཞི། མཚན་ཉིད། དབྱེ་བ། སྒྲ་དོན། སྒྲུབ་བྱེད་དོ།

dang po la shi, tsen nyi, ye wa, dra dön, drup che do

Regarding the first (similar and dissimilar classes), the definitions, classifications, meaning of the terms, proof statements.

similar class

།དང་པོ་ནི། དེ་སྒྲུབ་ཀྱི་བསྒྲུབ་བྱའི་ཆོས་ཀྱི་འགོད་ཚུལ་དང་མཐུན་པར་ཡོད་པ་དེ། དེ་སྒྲུབ་ཀྱི་མཐུན་ཕྱོགས་ཀྱི་མཚན་ཉིད། དེ་ལ་ཡིན་འགོད་དང་ཡོད་འགོད་གཉིས།

dang po ni, de drup kyi drup je chö kyi gö tsul dang tun par yö pa de, de drup kyi tun chok kyi tsen nyi, de la yin gö dang yö gö nyi

Regarding the first (the definition of the similar class): the definition of the similar class in a proof is that which exists in accord with the way the quality to be proved [predicate] is stated in that proof. There are two ways in which a proof may be stated: as a predicative statement and as a statement of existence.

This is expressed more specifically as applied to an example.

སྒྲ་མི་རྟག་པར་སྒྲུབ་པར་བྱེད་པའི་བསྒྲུབ་བྱའི་ཆོས་ཀྱི་འགོད་ཚུལ་དང་མཐུན་པར་ཡོད་པ་དེ། དེ་སྒྲུབ་ཀྱི་མཐུན་ཕྱོགས་ཀྱི་མཚན་ཉིད། དེ་དང་མི་རྟག་པ་གཉིས་དོན་གཅིག

dra mi tak par drup par che pe drup je chö kyi gö tsul dang tun par yö pa de, de drup kyi tun chok kyi tsen nyi, de dang mi tak pa nyi dön chik

The definition of the similar class in a proof is that which exists in accord with the way the quality to be proved is stated when used in a proof proving sound's impermanence. What is of a similar class and the impermanent are synonymous [when applied to this proof].

dissimilar class

།དེ་སྒྲུབ་ཀྱི་བསྒྲུབ་ཀྱི་བསྒྲུབ་བྱའི་ཆོས་ཀྱི་འགོད་ཚུལ་དང་མཐུན་པར་མེད་པ་དེ། དེ་སྒྲུབ་ཀྱི་མི་མཐུན་ཕྱོགས་ཀྱི་མཚན་ཉིད། དེ་བཞིན་དུ་སྒྲ་མི་རྟག་པར་སྒྲུབ་པར་བྱེད་པའི་མི་མཐུན་ཕྱོགས་ཀྱི་མཚན་ཉིད་དང་སྦྱར་ན། དེ་དང་མི་རྟག་པ་མ་ཡིན་པ་གཉིས་དོན་གཅིག

de drup kyi drup kyi drup je chö kyi gö tsul dang tun par me pa de, de drup kyi mi tun chok kyi tsen nyi, de shin du dra mi tak par drup par che pe mi tun chok kyi tsen nyi dang jar na, de dang mi tak pa ma yin pa nyi dön chik

The definition of the dissimilar class in a proof is that which does not exist in accord with the way the quality to be proved is stated in that proof. In like manner, when we apply the definition of dissimilar class to a proof proving sound's impermanence, what is of a dissimilar class and the non-impermanent are synonymous.

three types of dissimilar class

།གཉིས་པ་དབྱེ་ན་གསུམ་སྟེ་དེ་སྒྲུབ་ཀྱི་མེད་པ་མི་མཐུན་ཕྱོགས། གཞན་པ་
མི་མཐུན་ཕྱོགས། འགལ་ཟླ་མི་མཐུན་ཕྱོགས་སོ། །དང་པོ་ནི་རི་བོང་གི་རྭ་
ལྟ་བུ། གཉིས་པ་ནི་ཤེས་བྱ་ལྟ་བུ། གསུམ་པ་ནི་རྟག་པ་ལྟ་བུའོ།

nyi pa ye na sum te de drup kyi me pa mi tun chok, shen pa mi tun chok, gel(n) da mi tun chok so, dang po ni ri bong gi ra ta bu, nyi pa ni she ja ta bu, sum pa ni tak pa ta bu'o

When this second (dissimilar class) is classified there are three types: 1) the dissimilar class consisting of non-existents, 2) the dissimilar class of overextension, and 3) the dissimilar class of the contradictory.

In our example, *dra chö chen, mi tak te, che pa yin pe chir*, consider sound, it is impermanent, because it is produced, three different kinds of *mi tun chok*, dissimilar class, are possible: 1) *de drup kyi me pa mi tun chok*, the dissimilar class of non-existents, 2) *de drup kyi shen pa mi tun chok*, the dissimilar class of overextension, or 3) *de drup kyi gel(n) da mi tun chok*, the dissimilar class of the contradictory.

The first, the dissimilar class of non-existents, can be illustrated as follows. *Me pa* means non-existent. A classic example of a non-existent is *ri bong ra*, a hare's horn. For example: *dra chö chen, mi tak te, che pa yin pe chir, she gö pe tse ri bong ra ta bu*, when we make this statement, "Consider sound, it is impermanent, because it is produced, like a hare's horn," a hare's horn is *de drup kyi me pa mi tun chok*, of a dissimilar class [through being] a non-existent ["member" of the dissimilar class] in that proof, because it is not *tun chok*, of a similar class [of existents being proved in the proof, which includes all entities that are *mi tak pa*, impermanent].

Regarding the second, *shen pa mi tun chok*, the dissimilar class of overextension. *Shen pa* means other or different and refers to those phenomena that belong to a category that exceeds, or consists of qualities not pertaining to, the similar class and consequently includes other phenomena belonging to the dissimilar class as well. The example used here is *she ja*, object of knowledge: *dra chö chen, mi tak te, che pa yin pe chir, she gö pe tse she ja ta bu*, when we make the statement, "Consider sound, it is impermanent, because it is produced, like an object of knowledge," object of knowledge is *de drup kyi shen pa mi tun chok*, of a dissimilar class [relative to the quality to be proved i.e., *mi tak pa*, impermanent] in this proof. Why is *she ja*, object of knowledge, different from *mi tak pa*, impermanent? Because not all *she ja*, objects of knowledge, are impermanent entities, since the "class" of objects of knowledge also includes permanent entities. So, relative to impermanent entities, they are *shen pa mi tun chok*, a dissimilar class of overextension [i.e., including more than the quality of impermanence].

An example of the third kind, *de drup kyi gel(n) da mi tun chok*, the dissimilar class of the contradictory in this proof, is *tak pa*, a permanent entity. To illustrate: *dra chö chen, mi tak te, che pa yin pe chir, she gö pe tse, tak pa ta bu*, when we make the statement, "Consider sound, it is impermanent, because it is produced, like permanent entity," permanent entity is an example [of a dissimilar class of entities contradictory to the quality to be proved (*mi tak pa*, impermanent) in this proof]. This is so because *tak pa* and *mi tak pa* are *gel wa*, contradictory. When proving that sound is *mi tak pa*, impermanent, all permanent entities are *gel wa*, contradictory, to the quality to be proved in that proof. You will understand this when you learn the definition of contradictory: *ta te gang shik shi tun mi si pa gel we tsen nyi,*[20] The definition of being contradictory is two different things whose combination in one thing is impossible.

To express one example using the method of debate:

***

—*Tak pa chö chen, dra mi tak pa drup par che pe tak kyi dra mi tak par drup par che pe drup che chö gel(n) da yin par tel,* Consider what is permanent, does it follow that it belongs to the contradictory quality to be proved in that proof establishing the impermanence of sound by using the reason "being produced" to prove that sound is impermanent?

—*Dö*, Yes.

—*Gel(n) da mi tun chok yin te*, It pertains to the dissimilar class of contradictory entities because...

—*Ke chik ma ma yin pe chir*, It is non-momentary [and therefore the opposite of impermanent].

Now, *dra cho chen, mi tak te, che pa yin pe chir, she gö pe tse*, when we make the statement, "Consider sound, it is impermanent, because it is produced," what is *de drup kyi tun chok*, those things that are concordant with the quality to be proved in that proof? Everything that is *mi tak pa*, impermanent, such as *bum pa*, pitcher, and *ka wa*, pillar. Conversely, whatever is *tak pa*, permanent, is *mi tun chok*, incompatible with the quality to be proved in that proof. Permanent entities, in this case, are *gel(n) da mi tun chok*, incompatible through being directly contradictory.

---

[20] ཐ་དད་གང་ཞིག་གཞི་ཐུན་མི་སྲིད་པ་འགལ་བའི་མཚན་ཉིད།

།གསུམ་པ་སྒྲ་དོན་ནི། དེ་སྒྲུབ་ཀྱི་མཐུན་ཕྱོགས་དང་མི་མཐུན་ཕྱོགས་གཉིས་ལ་སྒྲ་བཤད་འཇུག་པའི་མུ་གསུམ་རེ་ཡོད་དེ། བསྡུས་ནས་བརྗོད་ན། བུམ་པ་དེ་སྒྲ་མི་རྟག་པར་སྒྲུབ་པར་བྱེད་པའི་མཐུན་ཕྱོགས་དང་དེའི་སྒྲ་བཤད་དུ་ཡོད་པའི་མུ་དང་། སྒྲ་རྟག་པར་སྒྲུབ་པར་བྱེད་པའི་དེ་གཉིས་ཀ་མ་ཡིན་པའི་མུ་དང་། སྒྲ་མི་རྟག་པར་སྒྲུབ་པར་བྱེད་པའི་མི་མཐུན་ཕྱོགས་དང་དེའི་སྒྲ་བཤད་དུ་ཡོད་པ་གཉིས་ཀ་མ་ཡིན་པའི་མུ་ཡིན་ཏེ། དེ་མི་རྟག་པ་ཡིན། དེ་སྒྲ་དང་མི་རྟག་པར་ཆོས་མཐུན་ཞིང་དེ་སྒྲ་དང་རྟག་པར་ཆོས་མི་མཐུན་པ་ཡིན་པའི་ཕྱིར། འདུས་མ་བྱས་ཀྱི་ནམ་མཁའ་དེ་སྒྲ་མི་རྟག་པར་སྒྲུབ་པར་བྱེད་པའི་མཐུན་ཕྱོགས་དང་དེའི་སྒྲ་བཤད་དུ་ཡོད་པ་གཉིས་ཀ་མ་ཡིན་པའི་མུ་དང་། སྒྲ་རྟག་པར་སྒྲུབ་པར་བྱེད་པའི་མཐུན་ཕྱོགས་ཡིན་ལ་དེའི་སྒྲ་བཤད་དུ་མེད་པའི་མུ་དང་། དེ་སྒྲུབ་ཀྱི་མི་མཐུན་ཕྱོགས་ཀྱི་སྒྲ་བཤད་དུ་ཡོད་ལ་དེ་སྒྲུབ་ཀྱི་མི་མཐུན་ཕྱོགས་མ་ཡིན་པའི་མུ་དང་། སྒྲ་མི་རྟག་པར་སྒྲུབ་པར་བྱེད་པའི་མི་མཐུན་ཕྱོགས་དང་དེའི་སྒྲ་བཤད་དུ་ཡོད་པའི་མུ་ཡིན་ཏེ། དེ་རྟག་པ་ཡིན། དེ་སྒྲ་དང་རྟག་པར་ཆོས་མི་མཐུན། དེ་སྒྲ་དང་མི་རྟག་པར་ཆོས་མི་མཐུན་པ་ཡིན་པའི་ཕྱིར།

sum pa dra dön ni, de drup kyi tun chok dang mi tun chok nyi la dra she juk pe mu sum re yö de, du ne jö na, bum pa de dra mi tak par drup par che pe tun chok dang de dra she du yö pe mu dang, dra tak par drup par che pe de nyi ka ma yin pe mu dang, dra mi tak par drup par che pe mi tun chok dang de dra she du yö pa nyi ka ma yin pe mu yin te, de mi tak pa yin, de dra dang mi tak par chö tun shing de dra dang tak par chö mi tun pa yin pe chir, du ma che kyi nam ka de dra mi tak par drup par che pe tun chok dang de dra she du yö pa nyi ka ma yin pe mu dang, dra tak par drup par che pe tun chok yin la de dra she du me pe mu dang, de drup kyi mi tun chok kyi dra she du yö la de drup kyi mi tun chok ma yin pe mu dang, dra mi tak par drup par che pe mi tun chok dang de dra she du yö pe mu yin te, de tak pa yin, de dra dang tak par chö mi tun, de dra dang mi tak par chö mi tun pa yin pe chir

The third part [concerns] the meaning of the terms. When applying the meaning of the term to the similar class in a proof and the dissimilar class in a proof, there are three logical possibilities for each of these. This is presented briefly as follows: 1) a pot is an example of the logical possibility of being both a member of the similar class and complying with the meaning of the term of "similar class" in the proof proving sound as impermanent; 2) a pot is an example of the logical possibility of something that is neither a member of the similar class nor complies with the meaning of the term "similar class" in the proof proving sound as permanent; 3) a pot is an example of the logical possibility of something that is neither a member of the dissimilar class nor does it comply with the explanation of the term "dissimilar class" in the proof of sound as impermanent. This is so because a pot is impermanent and as such has a nature that is compatible with sound and impermanence. It is also the case since it is incompatible in nature with sound as a permanent entity; 4) uncomposed space is an example of the logical possibility of something that is neither a member of the similar class nor does it comply with the meaning of the term "similar class" in the proof proving sound as impermanent; and 5) uncomposed space is an example of the logical possibility of being something that is a member of the similar class in the proof of sound as permanent, but does not comply with the meaning of the term "similar class," as well as being an example of the logical possibility of something that complies with the meaning of the term "dissimilar class," but is not a member of the dissimilar class in the proof proving sound as permanent; 6) uncomposed space is an example of the logical possibility of something that is a member of the dissimilar class and complies with the meaning of the term "dissimilar class" in the proof proving sound as impermanent. This is so because uncomposed space is a permanent entity and since sound and what is permanent are incompatible, [uncomposed space] is incompatible with sound as an impermanent entity.

First, you have to understand the meaning of *dra she du yö pa*, existing [in accord with] the meaning of the term. To borrow an example from poetry, the name of a lotus is *chö kye*, a flower that grows in water, also sometimes called *tso kye*, a lake-grown flower. Now, if someone were to ask you, "Do all lotuses grow in water?" Don't be shy. Say something. Don't be afraid. Nobody will beat you if you talk. There are several kinds of lotuses, yet not all of them come from a lake. Some we call *kam le kye pe padma*, lotuses that grow on dry land. *Kam*, Dryness, of course is the opposite of water. Nevertheless, we still call such flowers *tso kye*, lake-grown, because that is the general name given to a lotus. However, somebody might argue with that and say, "They are not *tso kye*, lake-grown, because they didn't grow in a lake but rather they grew in your own garden!" Therefore, they are not *dra she*, the meaning of the word in accord with the literal explanation of that term. That is why the usage of this word is qualified by the expression "*dra juk du yö*," which means you can call them by the name "lotus" or "lake-grown," even though the term doesn't apply to them literally. It is in this sense that the terms "*tun chok* and *mi tun chok*" are being investigated here; that is, through using the system of distinguishing possibilities of relationship between being a member of the similar class or dissimilar class and complying with the meaning of the term of each of these.

།བཞི་པ་སྒྲུབ་བྱེད་ནི། རི་བོང་ར་སོགས་གསུམ་པོ་དེ་ཆོས་ཅན། སྒྲ་མི་རྟག་པར་སྒྲུབ་པར་བྱེད་པའི་མི་མཐུན་ཕྱོགས་ཡིན་ཏེ། དེ་སྒྲུབ་ཀྱི་བསྒྲུབ་བྱའི་ཆོས་ཀྱི་འགོད་ཚུལ་དང་མི་མཐུན་པའི་ཕྱིར་ཏེ། དངོས་མེད་ཡིན་པའི་ཕྱིར། བུམ་པ་ཆོས་ཅན། སྒྲ་མི་རྟག་པར་སྒྲུབ་པར་བྱེད་པའི་མཐུན་ཕྱོགས་ཡིན་ཏེ། དེ་ལྟར་སྒྲུབ་པའི་འགོད་ཚུལ་དང་མཐུན་པའི་ཕྱིར་ཏེ། མི་རྟག་པ་ཡིན་པའི་ཕྱིར་རོ།

shi pa drup che ni, ri bong ra sok sum po te chö chen, dra mi tak par drup par che pe mi tun chok yin te, de drup kyi drup che chö kyi gö tsul dang mi tun pe chir te, ngö me yin pe chir, bum pa chö chen, dra mi tak par drup par che pe tun chok yin te, de tar drup pe gö tsul dang tun pe chir te, mi tak pa yin pe chir ro

The fourth part, correct proofs: Consider the three, a hare's horn, and so forth, they belong to the dissimilar class of entities relative to the proof proving the impermanence of sound, because they are incompatible with the way of stating the quality to be proved in that proof, as well as being non-causally effective things. On the other hand, consider a pitcher, it is compatible with the proof of sound as impermanent, because it is compatible with the way of stating such a proof, as well as being an impermanent entity.

Sum po te, The three, refers to the following: *ri bong ra*, a hare's horn, *she ja*, object of knowledge, and *tak pa*, the permanent [examples of the dissimilar class mentioned previously]. *Ngö me* means *ngö po ma yin*, that which is not a causally effective thing. Non-causally effective phenomena and permanent phenomena are synonymous.

གཉིས་པ་དཔེ་གཉིས་ལས་ཆོས་མི་མཐུན་སྦྱོར་གྱི་སྒྲུབ་ངག་གི་མི་མཐུན་དཔེ་ནི་

nyi pa pe nyi le chö mi tun jor gyi drup ngak gi mi tun pe ni

The second, between the two kinds of examples (of similar and dissimilar classes), an example of incompatibility in a verbal proof that applies to the dissimilar class.

There are two kinds of *drup ngak*, verbal proofs: *chö tun jor gyi drup ngak*,[21] a verbal proof that applies to a similar class, and *chö mi tun jor gyi drup ngak*,[22] a verbal proof that applies to a dissimilar class. *Drup ngak*, Verbal proof, means the style of proving something by making a statement of proof. This is distinguished from another style of proof known as *tel(n) gyur*,[23] as mentioned previously, wherein the debater uses the statements of his opponent to elicit absurd logical consequences.

An example illustrating *mi tun jor*, a verbal proof that applies to a dissimilar class, is as follows:

གང་རྟག་ན་མ་བྱས་པས་ཁྱབ། དཔེར་ན་འདུས་མ་བྱས་ཀྱི་ནམ་མཁའ་བཞིན།

སྒྲ་ནི་བྱས་སོ། ཞེས་པའི་ངག་ལྟ་བུ་དང་།

gang tak na ma che pe kyap, per na du ma che kyi nam ka shin, dra ni che so

"Whatever is permanent must be uncomposed; for example, uncomposed space. Sound, however, is composed," as this verbal proof states.

Ni is a grammar particle that shows disjunction in this case and indicates the exclusion of one thing from another. *Dra ni*, Sound however, means that sound is different from, and consequently excluded from, permanent things, because sound is impermanent. This kind of statement is an example of a verbal proof showing an

---

21 ཆོས་མཐུན་སྦྱོར་གྱི་སྒྲུབ་ངག་

22 ཆོས་མི་མཐུན་སྦྱོར་གྱི་སྒྲུབ་ངག་

23 ཐལ་འགྱུར་

incompatible quality [or a quality that is incompatible in nature with the quality to be proved].

ཆོས་མཐུན་སྦྱོར་གྱི་སྒྲུབ་ངག་གི་དཔེ་ནི་གང་བྱས་ན་མི་རྟག་པས་ཁྱབ།

དཔེར་ན་བུམ་པ་བཞིན། སྒྲ་ཡང་བྱས་སོ་ཞེས་པ་ལྟ་བུ་སྟེ།

chö tun jor gyi drup ngak gi pe ni gang che na mi tak pe kyap, per na bum pa shin, dra yang che so she pa ta bu te

An example of a verbal proof applying to a similar class, is: "Whatever is produced must be impermanent; for example, a pot. Sound is also produced," as this statement says.

Yang is a grammar particle that shows inclusion and here indicates that not only is pitcher impermanent but sound is as well since it is something that is produced.

སྤྱིར་མི་མཐུན་ཕྱོགས་ཀྱི་དཔེ་མེད་དེ། གཞི་གྲུབ་ན། སྒྲ་གང་ཟག་གི་བདག་མེད་དུ་

སྒྲུབ་པར་བྱེད་པའི་མཐུན་དཔེ་ཡིན་དགོས་པའི་ཕྱིར་རོ།

chir mi tun chok kyi pe me de, shi drup na, dra gang sak gi dak me du drup par che pe tun pe yin gö pe chir ro

In general, an example of the dissimilar class doesn't exist because whatever exists must be an example of the similar class of entities compatible with the selfless in proving the selflessness of sound.

This is a rule of logic, which can be explained as follows. Because *shi drup na tak yang dak yin pe kyap*, whatever is a basic existent must be a perfect reason [in some proof], *tak tar nang me*, false reasons do not exist. However, *de drup kyi tak tar nang yö*, false reasons do exist in statements of proof. In a similar way, because *shi drup na tun chok yin pe kyap*, whatever is a basic existent must belong to the similar class [of all existents], *chö mi tun chok me*, phenomena pertaining to the dissimilar class do not exist. Nevertheless, *de drup kyi mi tun chok yö*, phenomena pertaining to the dissimilar class <u>in</u> <u>a</u> <u>particular</u> <u>proof</u> do exist.

PERFECT REASON
definition

།གཉིས་པ་ནི། ཚུལ་གསུམ་ཡིན་པ། རྟགས་ཡང་དག་གི་མཚན་ཉིད།

nyi pa ni, tsul sum yin pa, tak yang dak gi tsen nyi

The second: the definition of a perfect reason is that which is the three modes.

If "that which is the three modes" is the definition of a perfect reason, can you also say, *tsul sum tsang wa tak yang dak gi tsen nyi*, the definition of a perfect reason is that which *fulfills* the three modes? No, this is not correct, because there is a difference between *tsul sum yin pa*, being those three modes, and *tsul sum tsang wa*, fulfilling those three modes. Why? For example, *dra tak pa tsul sum tsang wa*, "permanent sound" fulfills those three modes; however, *dra tak pa tsul sum yin pa*, "permanent sound" being those three modes, does not exist. *Dra chö chen, tak te, che pa yin pe chir, she gö pe tse*, When we make the statement, "Consider sound, it is permanent, because it is produced," does such a statement have *tsul sum gang rung*, any of those three modes? Yes, there is *chok chö*, the property of the subject [the reason's relevance to the subject]. *Dra chö chen, tak te, chö dang ke chik ma ma yin pe shi tun pa yin pe chir, she gö pe tse*, When we make the statement, "Consider sound, it is permanent, because it is the combination of being a phenomenon and non-momentary," again is there any of those three modes? Yes, this statement has *je kyap*, positive pervasion, since the reason given is the definition of a permanent entity, which is defining the predicate of the statement. That is, whatever is a combination of being a phenomenon and non-momentary must be a permanent entity. It also has *dok kyap*, reverse pervasion, because whatever is not permanent is necessarily not a combination of being a phenomenon and non-momentary.

So, we can say, *dra tak pa drup pe tsul sum yö*, *tsul sum yin pa me*, the statement proving that sound is permanent has the three modes, but there doesn't exist anything that *is* those three modes. That is why *tsul sum yin pa*, what is those three modes, is the definition of a perfect reason and not *tsul sum tsang wa*, fulfilling the three modes. These examples are given to show the importance of stating the definition of a perfect reason in this manner.

What are those *tsul sum*, three modes?

the three modes (*tsul sum*)

> ཚུལ་གསུམ་ནི། ཕྱོགས་ཆོས། རྗེས་ཁྱབ། ལྡོག་ཁྱབ་བོ།
>
> *tsul sum ni, chok chö, je kyap, dok kyap bo*
>
> The three modes are: the property of the subject [reason's relevance to the subject], positive pervasion, and reverse pervasion.
>
> །ཚུལ་གསུམ་སོ་སོ་ལ་མཚན་ཉིད། སྒྲུབ་བྱེད་ཀྱི་ཚད་མ་དང་རྗེས་སུ་འགྲོ་ལྡོག་ངེས་བྱེད་སོགས་ལས།
>
> *tsul sum so so la tsen nyi, drup che kyi tse ma dang je su dro(n) dok nge che sok le*
>
> The definitions of each of these [three modes], valid proofs, ascertaining the positive and reverse pervasions and the like. Among these…

Drup che kyi tse ma means valid proof and is synonymous with *tse ma yang dak*, perfect validity, and *rik pa yang dak*, perfect reasoning.

Dra chö chen, mi tak te, che pa yin pe chir, she gö pe tse, When we make the statement, "Consider sound, it is impermanent, because it is produced," *che pa*, product, *de drup kyi tsul sum ka*, is those three modes in that proof. That is, *de drup kyi chok chö*, it is the property of the subject in that proof; *de drup kyi je kyap*, it is the positive pervasion in that proof; and *de drup kyi dok kyap*, it is the reverse pervasion in that proof.

Je su dro(n) dok refers to positive pervasion and reverse pervasion. For example, *je kyap*, positive pervasion, may be stated as, *che pa yin na mi tak pa yin pe kyap*, whatever is produced must necessarily be impermanent; and *dok kyap*, reverse pervasion, may be stated as, *tak pa yin na ma che pa yin pe kyap*, whatever is a permanent entity must necessarily not be produced.

> དང་པོ་ནི།
>
> *dang po ni*
>
> Regarding the first one, (*chok chö*, the property of the subject)…

property of the subject [*chok chö*]

> དེ་སྒྲུབ་ཀྱི་ཤེས་འདོད་ཆོས་ཅན་སྐྱོན་མེད་ཀྱི་སྟེང་དུ་འགོད་ཚུལ་དང་མཐུན་པར་ཡོད་པ་ཉིད་དུ་ཚད་མས་ངེས་པ། དེ་སྒྲུབ་ཀྱི་ཕྱོགས་ཆོས་ཀྱི་མཚན་ཉིད།
>
> *de drup kyi shen dö chö chen kyön me kyi teng du gö tsul dang tun par yö pa nyi du tse me nge pa, de drup kyi chok chö kyi tsen nyi*
>
> The definition of the property of the subject in a particular proof is that which is perceived by valid cognition to only exist in accord with the way the assertion is made in that proof relative to a faultless subject about which someone has doubt in that proof.

You should be able to give this definition even in your dreams and have it ready so that you can recite it automatically, as easily as reciting OM MANI PADME HUM. We can explain this definition by analyzing each part.

De drup kyi means in this specific proof or context, and implies "I am using *che pa*, product, to prove that sound is impermanent."

Shen dö means doubt. *Chö chen* means the subject of debate. Therefore, *shen dö chö chen* means a subject about which there is doubt. However, if something is *chö chen*, a subject, it is not necessarily *shen dö chö chen kyön me*, a faultless subject about which there is doubt in that debate. For example, as mentioned before, if I make the statement: *dra chö chen, dra yin te, che pa yin pe chir*, consider sound, it is sound, because it is produced, although sound is the subject of debate, it is not a faultless subject about which there is doubt because no one doubts that sound is sound. With regard to our model statement, we are trying to prove to an opponent by using good reasons that sound is impermanent with the goal of inducing in him an inferential valid cognition perceiving that sound is in fact impermanent. Briefly, we are trying to remove the doubt he has regarding the impermanence of sound. One can do this by using *che pa*, being produced, as the reason to prove sound's impermanence.

Teng du means with regard to and here applies to sound. *Gö tsul* means the way of making a statement. *Dang tun par* means in accord with. *Gö tsul dang tun par*, In accord with the way of stating the proof, can be explained using the following statement: *shen dö chö chen kyön me gyi teng du gö tsul dang tun par, dra chö chen, mi tak te, che pa yin pe chir, she gö pe tse*, when we make the statement, "Consider sound, it is impermanent, because it is produced," a debater has faultless doubt about the subject in accord with the way it is stated. *Gö tsul dang tun par yö pa* means that *che pa*, being produced, *dra'i teng du*, exists with or relative to the subject sound; that is, the quality of being produced is being predicated as a quality of sound, since the statement uses the word "*yin*," meaning "it *is* that quality of being produced." *Yö pa nyi* means existing necessarily as a quality of sound according to the way it is stated in that proof.

Now, *dra chö chen, mi tak te, ri bong ra yin pe chir, she gö pe tse, ri bong ra te dra'i teng du*, when we make the statement, "Consider sound, it is impermanent, because it is a hare's horn," relative to sound, does a hare's horn exist or not? No, it does not exist because a hare's horn is a non-existent. Or *dra chö chen, mi tak te, dung dra yin pe chir, she gö pe tse*, when we make the statement, "Consider the subject, sound, it is impermanent, because it is the sound of a conch shell," does *dung dra dra'i teng du yö pa nyi*, the sound of a conch shell exist relative to [all] sounds? No, because not all sounds are the sound of a conch shell.

To explain this further let me ask you, does the quality of *che pa*, being produced, pertain to sound? Is it a quality of sound? Be silent and calm, okay? That way when you finish your Geshe degree you will get a *calm* Geshe degree! Don't hesitate in answering! Yes, being produced is a quality of sound. Why? Because *che pa*, being produced, is *de drup kyi chok chö*, the property of the subject or the reason's relevance to the subject in this statement. Contrarily, if I were to make the statement: *dra chö chen, mi tak te, mik she kyi sung ja yin pe chir*, consider sound, it is impermanent, because it is the object of the eye consciousness, since ear consciousness cannot perceive shapes and colors (which are the objects of eye consciousness), such a reason is not *chok chö*, the property of the subject, because this quality [of being an object of the eye consciousness] does not apply to sound. *Yö pa*, It exists, refers to this. Therefore, *yö pa*, it exists [relative to sound], is missing in the statement I just gave you; that is, we cannot say [*mik she kyi sung ja*, the object of the eye consciousness] *yö pa dra'i teng du*, exists in relation to sound [as one of its qualities].

Nyi is synonymous with *ko na* meaning "only" or "necessarily," indicating that it is an essential quality pertaining to its referent. We can explain this by contrasting it with cases in which some quality is not essential. For example, *tsöl jung*, arising from effort, applies to some sounds but not to all sounds, since the sound of a waterfall, for instance, does not arise from [human] effort. Therefore, *tsöl jung*, arising from effort, is not an essential quality pertaining to sound. When the definition above states *yö pa nyi*, exists necessarily, this refers to the fact that such a quality exists relative to the subject without any exceptions. *Nyi du*, Just that way, shows an all-inclusive requirement, referring to the fact that every sound, for instance, must have the quality of being produced. It is not the case that some sounds are produced and some are not. Or again, in this regard we can say that *che pa*, being produced, is a quality that exists in relation to all sounds and not to just some sounds. For this reason it is described as *yö pa nyi*, existing necessarily, as a quality of sound, since all sounds—without exception—are produced.

We can give another example to explain *nyi*. *Jön shing* means trees, which have *lo ma*, leaves, and *yel ga*, branches, and so forth; that is, those characteristics pertaining to a healthy tree. But *chir röl pa*, non-Buddhists, with whom most of the Buddhist scholar logicians debated in previous times, made such statements as: *jön shing chö chen, sem den yin te, tsen mo lo ma kum den nyel we chir*, consider trees, they have mind, because their leaves curl up at night when they sleep.[24] Here in the West some people say that trees have mind. What do you think? Some say that not only do trees have *sok*, life, but they have mental consciousness as well. With regard to this statement, "Trees have a mind because their leaves curl up at night as they sleep," does this quality of their leaves curling up at night "as they sleep" (*tsen mo lo ma kum den nyel wa*) exist relative to *jön shing*, Ashoka trees, or not? Yes, of course. Their leaves shrink up and they stay there all night like that. So, when some *chir röl pa*, non-Buddhists, make this statement, can we say that this quality exists relative to *jön shing*, Ashoka trees? Yes. But *yö pa nyi ma yin*, this quality is not an essential quality specific to all existent trees. Does this quality of *tsen mo lo ma kum den nyel wa*, leaves curling up at night as they sleep, exist relative to juniper trees or pine trees, for example? No. Why? Don't they also have leaves? Aren't those nettles leaves? Don't such trees have branches and a trunk and some kind of fruit or seeds, and so forth?

The logical idea is that although that quality does exist for some trees, *yö pa nyi ma yin*, it doesn't apply to each and every tree. We can make the logical statement: *jön shing teng du yö pa nyi yin na jön shing ta dak la yö gö*, if it is an essential quality that necessarily exists relative to trees, then it must exist relative to each and every tree. Therefore, in this case, every single tree should have the quality of their leaves curling up at night when they sleep, however, not

---

24 མཚན་མོ་ལོ་མ་འཁུམས་ནས་ཉལ་བས་ལྗོན་ཤིང་སེམས་ལྡན་དུ་སྒྲུབ་པ་བཞིན་ནོ།

tsen mo lo ma kum ne nyel we jön shing sem den du drup pa shin no

It is like trying to prove that trees have consciousness because their leaves curl up at night when they "sleep."

every tree does. That is why it says, *yö pa nyi ma yin*, it is not a case of necessary existence.

Tse me nge pa means that it is ascertained by valid cognition to be that way and that someone is not just making up that statement of *yö pa nyi*, essential to that existent. If all cases have that quality in question, the subject and reason must be *chok chö*, the quality of the reason in the subject. Otherwise, if there is even one exception, it cannot qualify as *chok chö.*

To further explain *tse me nge pa*, ascertained by valid cognition, we need to introduce the definition of *chir göl yang dak*, a perfect opponent to debate with. First you have to recall the difference between *chir göl*, a debater, and *chir göl yang dak*, a perfect opponent to debate with.[25] The first is the general term for a debater or opponent in debate, without specifying the circumstances or relationship between the two opponents. However, *de drup kyi chir göl yang dak*, a perfect opponent in debate relative to a specific proof, indicates the relationship and the circumstances of a debate. This you can learn from the definition as follows: *tak chö dön sum tse me nge shing drup ja la shen dö shuk pe göl wa kab kyi chir göl yang dak kyi tsen nyi*,[26] the definition of a perfect opponent with whom to debate is someone who has perceived all three modes by valid cognition but has doubt about the thesis of the proof in question. Therefore, you can see how not every opponent qualifies as *chir göl yang dak. Kab kyi* means when debating and refers to the qualifications of the opponent at the time of a debate; that is, someone who qualifies as *chir göl yang dak*, a perfect opponent, relative to a specific debate. For example, there might be a debater who does not have *tse ma*, valid cognition, about sound [the subject of debate], and therefore, sound cannot qualify as *chok chö*, the property of the reason in that subject. Some debaters might still have doubt as to whether or not sound is produced and so "being

[25] ཕྱི་རྒོལ་དང་ཕྱི་རྒོལ་ཡང་དག

[26] རྟགས་ཆོས་དོན་གསུམ་ཚད་མས་ངེས་ཤིང་བསྒྲུབ་བྱ་ལ་ཤེས་འདོད་ཞུགས་པའི་རྒོལ་བ་སྐབས་ཀྱི་ཕྱི་རྒོལ་ཡང་དག་གི་མཚན་ཉིད།

produced" in the model statement would not qualify as *tak yang dak*, a perfect reason, for them.

Tak chö dön sum tse me nge shing tak che pa drup che chö mi tak pa, chö chen dra tse me nge, The opponent ascertains the reason [being produced] by valid cognition; the quality to be proved [impermanent]; and the subject of debate [sound]. *Tse me nge*, Ascertains by valid cognition, refers to a valid mind that can certify things, and not the kind of mind that thinks: "Maybe it's like this or maybe it's like that." Just thinking that something is so is not enough to verify it; you have to be completely sure about it in so far as you ascertain it.

Drup ja la dra mi tak pa yin min la shen dö shuk pe göl wa, That opponent is one who wonders whether or not sound is impermanent. In regard to the subject sound, *shen dö shuk pe kyön me*, he has faultless doubt as to whether sound is impermanent or not. *Chir göl*, An opponent in debate, in this case, is one who has that kind of doubt about the subject. To qualify as *chir göl yang dak*, a perfect opponent in debate, he must be a person satisfying all of these requirements.

Now, to continue, the definition of the property of the subject [reason's relevance to the subject] is given more extensively through being applied to a proof.

སྒྲ་མི་རྟག་པར་སྒྲུབ་པར་བྱེད་པའི་ཤེས་འདོད་ཆོས་ཅན་སྐྱོན་མེད་ཀྱི་སྟེང་དུ་འགོད་ཚུལ་དང་མཐུན་པར་ཡོད་པ་ཉིད་དུ་ཚད་མས་ངེས་པ་དེ། སྒྲ་མི་རྟག་པར་སྒྲུབ་པར་བྱེད་པའི་ཕྱོགས་ཆོས་ཀྱི་མཚན་ཉིད།

dra mi tak par drup par che pe shen dö chö chen kyön me kyi teng du gö tsul dang tun par yö pa nyi du tse me nge pa de, dra mi tak par drup par che pe chok chö kyi tsen nyi

The definition of the property of the subject in a proof proving sound's impermanence is that [reason] which is ascertained by valid cognition to exist only in accord with the way the assertion is made in that proof relative to a faultless subject about which there is doubt [in that proof] proving sound's impermanence.

And further,

དེ་བཞིན་དུ་བྱས་པའི་རྟགས་ཀྱིས་སྒྲ་མི་རྟག་པར་སྒྲུབ་པར་བྱེད་པའི་ཕྱོགས་
ཆོས་ཀྱི་མཚན་ཉིད་སོགས་ལ་སྦྱར་ཚུལ་འགྲེའོ།

te shin du che pe tak kyi dra mi tak par drup par che pe chok chö kyi tsen nyi sok la jar tsul dre'o

Just as with the proof establishing sound's impermanence by using the reason of its being produced, in like manner one can apply the definition of the property of the subject to other proofs as well.

This is explained in more detail with an illustration below from the *Extensive Explanation*.

མཚན་གཞི་ནི། བྱས་པ་ལྟ་བུ། བྱས་པ་ཆོས་ཅན། སྒྲ་མི་རྟག་པར་སྒྲུབ་པར་བྱེད་
པའི་ཕྱོགས་ཆོས་ཡིན་ཏེ། ཁྱོད་ཀྱི་རྟགས་ཀྱིས་སྒྲ་མི་རྟག་པར་སྒྲུབ་པར་བྱེད་
པའི་ཤེས་འདོད་ཆོས་ཅན་སྐྱོན་མེད་ཡོད་པ་གང་ཞིག ཁྱོད་དེ་སྒྲུབ་ཀྱི་ཤེས་
འདོད་ཆོས་ཅན་གྱི་སྟེང་དུ་འགོད་ཚུལ་དང་མཐུན་པར་ཡོད་པ་ཉིད་དུ་ཚད་མས་
ངེས་པའི་ཕྱིར།

tsen shi ni, che pa ta bu, che pa chö chen, dra mi tak par drup par che pe chok chö chen kyön me yö pa gang shik, kyö de drup kyi shen dö chö chen gyi teng du gö tsul dang tun par yö pa nyi du tse me nge pe chir

"Being produced" is an illustration. Consider "being produced," it is the property of the subject in the proof proving sound's impermanence, because there exists a faultless subject about which there is doubt in that proof proving sound's impermanence using ["being produced"] as a reason, and it [the reason] is ascertained by valid cognition to only exist in accord with the way the assertion is made relative to the subject about which there is doubt in that proof.

དང་པོ་གྲུབ་སྟེ། སྒྲ་དེ་དེ་ཡིན་པའི་ཕྱིར། མ་གྲུབ་ན། སྒྲ་ཆོས་ཅན། ཁྱོད་བྱས་པའི་རྟགས་ཀྱིས་དེ་སྒྲུབ་ཀྱི་ཤེས་འདོད་ཆོས་ཅན་སྐྱོན་མེད་ཡིན་པར་ཐལ། ཁྱོད་དེ་སྒྲུབ་ཀྱི་ཤེས་འདོད་ཆོས་ཅན་དུ་གཟུང་བ་གང་ཞིག ཁྱོད་བྱས་པར་ཚད་མས་ངེས་ནས་མི་རྟག་པ་ཡིན་པ་ལ་ཤེས་འདོད་ཞུགས་པའི་གང་ཟག་ཡོད་པའི་ཕྱིར།

dang po drup te, dra de de yin pe chir, ma drup na, dra chö chen, kyö che pe tak kyi de drup kyi shen dö chö chen kyön me yin par tel, kyö de drup kyi shen dö chö chen du sung wa gang shik, kyö che par tse me nge ne mi tak pa yin pa la shen dö shuk pe gang sak yö pe chir

The first part is true because sound complies with the qualifications expressed by that definition. If someone responds again by saying "This is not true," we say, "It is true," because: Consider sound, it follows that it [sound] is a faultless subject about which there is doubt in that proof, which is using the reason "being produced" to prove it, since what is held as the subject about which there is doubt in that proof is that, and there exists a person who, having first ascertained by valid cognition that sound is produced, has doubt about whether or not sound is impermanent.

There are two types of statements used in expressing the property of the subject: *yin gö*, a predicative statement or a statement of being [a certain nature or quality], and *yö gö*, a statement of existence, or existential statement. Using *dre tak*, a reason of effect, as an example we can make the following statement: *du den gyi la la chö chen, me yö te, du wa yö pe chir*, consider smoke rising from a mountain pass, there must be fire there, because there is smoke. *Tak*, The reason, is *yö pe chir*, because "there is" [a statement of existence], instead of *yin pe chir*, because "it is" [a predicative statement]. The kind of statement used here is *yö gö*, an existential statement, not *yin gö*, a predicative statement. If it were *yin gö*, a predicative statement, the meaning would be: Consider smoke on a mountain pass, there is fire, because it [smoke] is smoke.

However, in the model statement proving the impermanence of sound by using the reason of its being produced, this is *yin gö*, a predicative statement, because sound *is* something that has that quality. *Che pa*, Being produced, is a quality of *dra*, sound. In fact, sound is a product. [The statement is trying to prove sound's quality of impermanence, not the *existence* of sound.]

positive pervasion (*je kyap*)

A detailed definition of *je kyap*, positive pervasion [the second of the three modes] is given in the *Extensive Explanation* as follows:

དེ་སྒྲུབ་ཀྱི་མཐུན་ཕྱོགས་ཁོ་ན་ལ་འགོད་ཚུལ་དང་མཐུན་པར་ཡོད་པ་ཉིད་དུ་ཚད་མས་ངེས་པ་དེ། དེ་སྒྲུབ་ཀྱི་རྗེས་ཁྱབ་ཀྱི་མཚན་ཉིད། གཞི་ལ་སྦྱར་ན། སྒྲ་མི་རྟག་པར་སྒྲུབ་པར་བྱེད་པའི་མཐུན་ཕྱོགས་ཁོ་ན་ལ་འགོད་ཚུལ་དང་མཐུན་པར་ཡོད་པ་ཉིད་དུ་ཚད་མས་ངེས་པ་དེ། སྒྲ་མི་རྟག་པར་སྒྲུབ་པར་བྱེད་པའི་རྗེས་ཁྱབ་ཀྱི་མཚན་ཉིད།

de drup kyi tun chok ko na la gö tsul dang tun par yö pa nyi du tse me nge pa de, de drup kyi je kyap kyi tsen nyi, shi la jar na, dra mi tak par drup par che pe tun chok ko na la gö tsul dang

> *tun par yö pa nyi du tse me nge pa de, dra mi tak par drup par che pe je kyap kyi tsen nyi*
>
> The definition of positive pervasion in a proof is that [reason] which is ascertained by valid cognition only to exist in the similar class in accord with the way the assertion is made in that proof. The following is an example when applied to a particular case. The definition of positive pervasion used to prove sound's impermanence is that [reason] which is ascertained by valid cognition to only exist in the similar class [of that proof] proving sound's impermanence in accord with the way the assertion is made in that proof.

Je kyap, Positive pervasion, is the second of the three modes. Positive pervasion in this case can be expressed as, *che na mi tak pe kyap*, whatever is produced must be impermanent. Applying the definition to our model statement: *dra chö chen, mi tak te, che pe chir*, consider sound, it is impermanent, because it is produced, all entities that are impermanent are *tun chok*, (pertaining to or compatible with) the similar class [of the quality to be proved in that proof]. All permanent entities are *mi tun chok*, (or incompatible with) the similar class [of the quality to be proved in that proof]. Now if I make the statement: *dra chö chen, tak te, che pa yin pe chir*, consider sound, it is permanent, because it is produced, is *che pa*, being produced, *tun chok ko na la gö tsul dang tun par*, compatible with the way of making the statement as existing exclusively in the similar class (of entities), or not? It is not, because *tun chok*, the similar class, in this case is the class of permanent entities. *Che pa*, Being produced, does not qualify as *je kyap*, positive pervasion, in this statement because *che pa tak pa la me pa*, what is produced does not exist (in the class of) permanent entities.

We can use another example to investigate the meaning of *yö pa nyi du*, existing exclusively. If I make the statement: *dra chö chen, mi tak te, shel ja yin pe chir*, consider sound, it is impermanent, because it is an object of comprehension, would you say that such a reason is *tun chok ko na la yö pa nyi du tse me nge pa*, ascertained by valid cognition to only exist in the similar class of entities that are impermanent, or not? You said, "No." Good. It's also a good sign that you answered quickly! Although sometimes you can make big mistakes by doing that! What is *tun chok*, similar class, in this case? All impermanent entities. *Shel ja*, Object of comprehension, however, consists of both permanent and impermanent entities. Therefore, in this case, object of comprehension also exists in the dissimilar class of entities as well. So we cannot say that it is *yö pa nyi*, existing as an exclusive quality, of sound.

Sometimes, however, in debate we can get into trouble when exploring this subject because certain problems such as the following can crop up. For example, concerning what arises from effort and what does not, someone might say, "What about rocks on the mountainside, didn't they arise from effort?" If somebody answers, "No, that's not so," the other could reply with, "What do you mean, weren't they made by the effort of beings? Of course they were. What about the quotation from the great scholar Vasubandhu's *Treasury of Higher Knowledge* that states: *le le jik ten na tsok kye*,[27] "All variety of things in the world have arisen from karma!"? All the world was made by the karma collected by beings. Therefore, those rocks were made by beings since it was their karma that produced them!" So, in this sense they too arose from the effort of beings. Although on the debate ground you have to hold your position no matter what, nevertheless, you cannot go so far as to reject what it says in those sacred texts.

reverse pervasion [*dok kyap*]

The brief definition of *dok kyap*, reverse pervasion [the third of the three modes], is.

།དེ་སྒྲུབ་ཀྱི་དངོས་ཀྱི་བསྒྲུབ་བྱའི་ཆོས་ཀྱི་དོནལྡོག་དང་འབྲེལ་སྟོབས་ཀྱིས་དེ་སྒྲུབ་ཀྱི་
མི་མཐུན་ཕྱོགས་ལ་འགོད་ཚུལ་དང་མཐུན་པར་མེད་པ་ཉིད་དུ་ཚད་མས་ངེས་པ་དེ།

[27] ལས་ལས་འཇིག་རྟེན་སྣ་ཚོགས་སྐྱེས།

དེ་སྒྲུབ་ཀྱི་ལྡོག་ཁྱབ་ཀྱི་མཚན་ཉིད།

de drup kyi ngö kyi drup che chö kyi dön dok dang drel tob kyi de drup kyi mi tun chok la gö tsul dang tun par me pa nyi du tse me nge pa de, de drup kyi dok kyap kyi tsen nyi

The definition of reverse pervasion in that proof is that [reason] which is ascertained by valid cognition to not exist at all in the dissimilar class in accord with the way the assertion is made in that proof due to its relationship with the meaning isolate of the explicit quality to be proved in that proof.

The detailed definition of *dok kyap*, reverse pervasion, is given in the *Extensive Explanation* as follows:

དེ་སྒྲུབ་ཀྱི་དངོས་ཀྱི་བསྒྲུབ་བྱའི་ཆོས་སུ་གཟུང་བྱར་འགྲོ་རྒྱུ་དང་འབྲེལ་སྟོབས་ཀྱིས་དེ་སྒྲུབ་ཀྱི་མི་མཐུན་ཕྱོགས་ལ་འགོད་ཚུལ་དང་མཐུན་པར་མེད་པ་ཉིད་དུ་ཚད་མས་ངེས་པ་དེ། དེ་སྒྲུབ་ཀྱི་ལྡོག་ཁྱབ་ཀྱི་མཚན་ཉིད། གཞི་གཞན་དང་སྦྱར་ན། སྒྲ་མི་རྟག་པར་སྒྲུབ་པར་བྱེད་པའི་དངོས་ཀྱི་བསྒྲུབ་བྱའི་ཆོས་སུ་གཟུང་བྱར་འགྲོ་རྒྱུ་དང་འབྲེལ་སྟོབས་ཀྱིས་དེ་སྒྲུབ་ཀྱི་མི་མཐུན་ཕྱོགས་ལ་འགོད་ཚུལ་དང་མཐུན་པར་མེད་པ་ཉིད་དུ་ཚད་མས་ངེས་པ་དེ། སྒྲ་མི་རྟག་པར་སྒྲུབ་པར་བྱེད་པའི་ལྡོག་ཁྱབ་ཀྱི་མཚན་ཉིད། དེ་བཞིན་དུ་བྱས་པའི་རྟགས་ཀྱིས་སྒྲ་མི་རྟག་པར་སྒྲུབ་པར་བྱེད་པ་སོགས་ལ་ཡང་སྦྱོར།

de drup kyi ngö kyi drup che chö su sung jar dro gyu dang drel tob kyi de drup kyi mi tun chok la gö tsul dang tun par me pa nyi du tse me nge pa de, de drup kyi dok kyap kyi tsen nyi, shi shen dang jar na, dra mi tak par drup par che pe ngö kyi drup je chö su sung jar dro gyu dang drel tob kyi de drup kyi mi tun chok la gö tsul dang tun par me pa nyi du tse me nge pa de, dra mi tak par drup par che pe dok kyap kyi tsen nyi, de shin du che pe tak kyi dra mi tak par drup par che pa sok la yang jor

The definition of reverse pervasion in a proof is that [reason] which is ascertained by valid cognition to not exist at all in the dissimilar class in accord with the way the assertion is made due to its necessary relationship with what is held as the explicit quality to be proved in that proof. Apply this definition to other bases such as the following: The definition of reverse pervasion used in a proof proving the impermanence of sound is that [reason] which is ascertained by valid cognition to not exist at all in the dissimilar class in accord with the way the assertion is made due to its necessary relationship with what is held as the explicit quality to be proved in proving sound's impermanence.

Dok kyap, Reverse pervasion, is the third of the three modes (*tsul sum*). Reverse pervasion in relation to our model statement can be expressed as, *tak na ma che pe kyap*, whatever is permanent must not be produced. When we make the statement, *dung dra chö chen, mi tak te, tsöl jung yin pe chir*, consider the sound of a conch shell, it is impermanent, because it arises from effort, is there *dok kyap*, reverse pervasion? Yes. What is *mi tun chok*, the dissimilar class, in this case? All permanent entities. What is the reason in this statement? *Tsöl jung*, Arising from effort. Therefore, we can say: *tsöl jung yin na tak pa ma yin pe kyap*, whatever arises from effort must necessarily not be a permanent entity.

We can review what we've just covered this way.

***

—*Tak yang dak gyi tsen nyi shak gyu me pe chir*, It's obvious you don't know the definition of a perfect reason. (*Shak gyu me pe chir* means "Can you tell me or not?")
—*Tak ma drup*, That's not true. (This implies, "I know it.")
—*Tak yang dak gyi tsen nyi shak gyu yö par tel*, Then you do know the definition of a perfect reason?

—*Dö*, Yes, I do.
—*Sho*, Well then, tell me what it is! (This requires that you respond by giving the definition as *chö chen*, a subject.)
—*Tsul sum yin pa chö chen*, The subject "That which is the three modes."
—*Tsul sum yin pa chö chen, tak yang dak gyi tsen nyi yin par tel*, You're telling me that the subject "That which is the three modes" is the definition of a perfect reason?
—*Dö*, Yes, that's right.
—*Ma yin par tel, tsul sum po te re re ne trang gyu me pe chir*, That can't be so, since you can't tell me what those three modes are one by one. (This is an expression used on the debate ground to clarify the various parts of a particular assertion or definition, and means, "You probably can't count each one of those individually, isn't that right?")
—*Tak ma drup*, No, that's not right. I can count them.
—*Tsul sum po te re re ne trang gyu yö par tel*, I'm amazed! So you can count them individually?
—*Dö*, Yes.
—*Trong sho,* Count them!
—*Chok chö, je kyap, dok kyap sum po te chö chen*, The subject, the three: the quality of the reason in the subject, positive pervasion, and reverse pervasion.
—*Chok chö, je kyap, dok kyap sum po te chö chen, tsul sum po te re re ne yin par tel*, It follows that the subject, the quality of the reason in the subject, positive pervasion, and reverse pervasion, are each of the three modes?
—*Dö*, Yes.

Now, repeat this template counting each repetition on your fingers. When you've finished begin counting using your toes. It is critical that you memorize definitions and rules and even particular "*ka chik ma*'s" or debates, as you learn. This is what we had to do in the monastery.

When I was young, about ten or eleven years old, I made a very big mistake. My main teacher had another teacher drill me in memorization so that I had to recite to him whatever texts I had learned. At first I didn't do much but only proceeded slowly, trying my best to keep the task to a minimum. As a result he only gave me short passages to memorize, which I had to recite back to him at the end of each day. However, at a certain point things didn't turn out as I had planned. During the summer, in Lhasa City we used to have picnics in some very beautiful parks. People used to go to these places and put up their tents and set out food and bring enough provisions so that they could spend three, four, or even five days there enjoying themselves. It was very pleasant, very delightful.

One day I received a message from my family at home telling me that they were going to start such a picnic the day after tomorrow and that I should ask permission from each of my teachers to be able to go with them on the picnic. Naturally I was unbelievably excited. But when I asked permission of this particular teacher, saying: "Please allow me to go on that picnic with my family tomorrow!" He said, "Okay, you can go, but first you have to memorize White Tara's ritual by tomorrow. If you recite the entire ritual without any problem, then you can go."

So, a little downtrodden, I took the text and went to my room to memorize it straightaway. I started in the morning and by early that afternoon I finished memorizing the entire text. After that I had to go to his room and "squeeze." It turns out I squeezed very nicely, reciting everything from memory without any problem whatsoever. He was very, very happy and so of course he gave me permission to go on the picnic with my family. But, ever since then he began loading me down unbelievably with many times more than what I previously had to memorize. That was a big mistake! Like that.

In *The Entryway to Valid Reasoning* it says:

།གཏན་ཚིགས་ནི་ཚུལ་གསུམ་མོ།

ten tsik ni tsul sum mo

A [perfect] reason [consists of] the three modes.

We can illustrate the use of the three modes as follows:

།བྱས་པ་དེ་སྒྲ་མི་རྟག་པར་སྒྲུབ་པར་བྱེད་པའི་ཚུལ་གསུམ་གའི་
མཚན་གཞི་ཡིན་ནོ།

che pa de dra mi tak par drup par che pe tsul sum ge tsen shi yin no

Product is an illustration of these three modes used in a proof proving sound's impermanence.

Che pa de dra mi tak par drup par che pe chok chö yin, Product is the property of the subject [the reason's relevance to the subject] used to prove that sound is impermanent. *Che pa de dra mi tak par drup par che pe je kyap yin*, Product is the positive pervasion used to prove that sound is impermanent. *Che pa de dra mi tak par drup par che pe dok kyap yin*, Product is the reverse pervasion used to prove that sound is impermanent. *Tsul sum gyi tsen shi yin*, Such is an illustration of the three modes.

You have to be aware that when actually debating, it is necessary to make various distinctions here. Is *che pa*, product, a causally effective thing or a permanent entity? It is a causally effective thing, of course. Is the statement, *che pe tak kyi dra mi tak par drup par che pe tsul sum*, the three modes used to prove that sound is impermanent, a causally effective thing or a permanent phenomenon? If you say *tsul sum*, the three modes, is *tak pa*, a permanent entity, then *che pa*, product, could not be *tsul sum,* those three modes. If *che pa*, product, were *tak pa*, a permanent entity, it could not be those three modes. If, as a permanent phenomenon, it were not those three modes, how then could it qualify as *tsen shi*, an illustration, of those three modes? This is why we have to state these three modes individually as follows: *che pa*, product, *dra mi tak par chok chö yin*, is the property of the subject proving sound's impermanence; product *dra mi tak par je kyap yin*, is the positive pervasion proving sound's impermanence; and product *dra mi tak par dok kyap yin*, is the reverse pervasion proving sound's impermanence.

The reason why "the three modes" itself is a permanent entity can be explained this way. In the Vaibhāṣhika system of logic *chi*, general category, is *tak pa*, a permanent entity, and *che drak*, particular instance, is *mi tak pa*, an impermanent entity. *Tsul sum*, The three modes, is also *chi*, a general-abstract category. However, *tsul sum gyi tsen shi*, an [actual] illustration of the three modes [i.e., something that *is* those three modes], itself must be *che drak*, a particular instance and consequently an impermanent entity.

།སྒྲུབ་བྱེད་ལ་བྱས་པ་ཆོས་ཅན། སྒྲ་མི་རྟག་པར་སྒྲུབ་པར་བྱེད་པའི་ཕྱོགས་ཆོས་ཡིན་ཏེ། ཁྱོད་ཁྱོད་ཀྱི་རྟགས་ཀྱིས་སྒྲ་མི་རྟག་པར་སྒྲུབ་པར་བྱེད་པའི་ཤེས་འདོད་ཆོས་ཅན་སྐྱོན་མེད་ཀྱི་སྟེང་དུ་འགོད་ཚུལ་དང་མཐུན་པར་ཡོད་པ་ཉིད་དུ་ཚད་མས་ངེས་པའི་ཕྱིར།

drup che la che pa chö chen, dra mi tak par drup par che pe chok chö yin te, kyö kyö kyi tak kyi dra mi tak par drup par che pe shen dö chö chen kyön me kyi teng du gö tsul dang tun par yö pa nyi du tse me nge pe chir

Consider the subject "product" in that proof statement, it qualifies as the property of the subject used to prove sound as impermanent, because it [the reason] is perceived by valid cognition to only exist in accord with the way the assertion is made in that proof in regard to a faultless subject about which there is doubt proving sound as impermanent by reason of its being a product.

This previous statement is *drup che*, a proof statement, which shows the reason why *che pa*, product, is *dra mi tak par drup par che pe chok chö*, the property of the subject proving sound as impermanent. Why? Because it complies with the definition given above of *chok chö*, the property of the subject.

དེར་ཐལ། དེ་འདྲའི་ཤེས་འདོད་ཆོས་ཅན་སྒྲའི་སྟེང་དུ་འགོད་ཚུལ་ཡིན་འགོད་དང་མཐུན་པར་ཡོད་པ་ཁོ་ན་ཡིན་ཅིང་སྐབས་ཀྱི་རྒོལ་བས་ཀྱང་རང་ཉིད་ཚད་མས་ངེས་པའི་ཕྱིར་རོ།

der tel, den dre shen dö chö chen dra'i teng du gö tsul yin gö dang tun par yö pa ko na yin ching kab kyi göl we kyang rang nyi tse me nge pe chir ro

It follows that it [the reason, "product"] does comply with the definition of a property of the subject, because that [reason] is ascertained by valid cognition by a suitably qualified opponent on this occasion to only exist in accord with the way the assertion is made [in this case a predicative statement] relative to sound about which that opponent has some doubt [regarding its impermanence].

Kab kyi göl wa, An opponent on this occasion, complies with the definition of a suitable opponent (*chir göl yang dak*) as previously explained.

Below is a proof statement qualifying the positive pervasion.

།བྱས་པ་ཆོས་ཅན། སྒྲ་མི་རྟག་པར་སྒྲུབ་པར་བྱེད་པའི་རྗེས་ཁྱབ་ཡིན་ཏེ། ཁྱོད་ཁྱོད་ཀྱི་རྟགས་ཀྱིས་སྒྲ་མི་རྟག་པར་སྒྲུབ་པར་བྱེད་པའི་མཐུན་ཕྱོགས་ཁོ་ན་ལ་ཡོད་པ་ཉིད་དུ་ཚད་མས་ངེས་པའི་ཕྱིར། དེར་ཐལ། ཁྱོད་མི་རྟག་པ་ཡིན། ཁྱོད་ཡིན་ན་མི་རྟག་པ་ཡིན་པས་ཁྱབ་པའི་ཚུལ་གྱིས་ཁྱོད་མི་རྟག་པ་ཁོ་ན་ལ་ཡོད་པ་ཉིད་དུ་ཚད་མས་ངེས་པའི་ཕྱིར།

che pa chö chen, dra mi tak par drup par che pe je kyap yin te, kyö kyö kyi tak kyi dra mi tak par drup par che pe tun chok ko na la yö pa nyi du tse me nge pe chir, der tel, kyö mi tak pa yin, kyö yin na mi tak pa yin pe kyap pe tsul gyi kyö mi tak pa ko na la yö pa nyi du tse me nge pe chir

Consider the subject, product, it is the positive pervasion used in a proof proving sound's impermanence, because it is perceived by valid cognition to only exist in the similar class when proving sound's impermanence using it [product] as a reason. It follows that such is the case, because a product is impermanent and is also perceived by valid cognition to only exist as impermanent in accord with the pervasion that whatever is produced must be impermanent.

What does *kyö* refer to here? To *che pa*, product, which is the reason in this proof. *Che pa yin na mi tak pa yin pe kyap*, Whatever is a product must be impermanent. We can say that *kyö mi tak pa ko na la yö pa*, a product exists only as an impermanent entity. *Nyi du tse me nge pe chir*, Because it is verified by valid cognition to exist exclusively that way.

Below is a proof statement qualifying the reverse pervasion.

བྱས་པ་ཆོས་ཅན། ཁྱོད་དེ་སྒྲུབ་ཀྱི་ལྡོག་ཁྱབ་ཡིན་ཏེ། ཁྱོད་དེ་སྒྲུབ་ཀྱི་བསྒྲུབ་བྱའི་ཆོས་ཀྱི་དོན་ལྡོག་དང་འབྲེལ་སྟོབས་ཀྱིས་དེ་སྒྲུབ་ཀྱི་མི་མཐུན་ཕྱོགས་ལ་འགོད་ཚུལ་དང་མཐུན་པར་མེད་པ་ཉིད་དུ་ཚད་མས་ངེས་པའི་ཕྱིར།

che pa chö chen, kyö de drup kyi dok kyap yin te, kyö de drup kyi drup je chö kyi dön dok dang drel tob kyi de drup kyi mi tun chok la gö tsul dang tun par me pa nyi du tse me nge pe chir

Consider the subject, product, it is the reverse pervasion in that proof, because due to its relationship with the meaning isolate of the quality to be proved in that proof, product is perceived by valid cognition to not exist at all in the dissimilar class in accord with the way the assertion is made in that proof.

What is the meaning of *te drup kyi drup che chö kyi dön dok*, the meaning isolate/defining property of the quality to be proved in that proof? *Dön dok*, Meaning isolate/defining property, is a phenomenon's own definition, referring here to the definition of the quality to be proved. For example, *dön che nu pa*, able to effect something, is the meaning isolate of *ngö po*, causally effective thing, since it is the definition of causally effective thing. *Che pa*, Product, *drel tob kyi*, is related, to the quality to be proved [through being of the same nature, i.e., impermanent]. Consequently, *de drup kyi mi tun chok*, the dissimilar class in this proof statement, is *tak pa*, all permanent phenomena.

> དེར་ཐལ། ཁྱོད་མི་རྟག་པ་ཡིན། ཁྱོད་ཡིན་ན་མི་རྟག་པ་ཡིན་པས་ཁྱབ།
>
> *der tel, kyö mi tak pa yin, kyö yin na mi tak pa yin pe kyap*
>
> It follows that it [product] is impermanent, because if it is produced it must be impermanent.
>
> ཁྱོད་མི་རྟག་པ་དང་འབྲེལ་ཞིང་མི་རྟག་པ་མ་ཡིན་པ་ལ་མེད་པ་ཉིད་དུ་ཚད་མས་ངེས་པའི་ཕྱིར་རོ།
>
> *kyö mi tak pa dang drel shing mi tak pa ma yin pa la me pa nyi du tse me nge pe chir ro*
>
> Product is related [by nature] to impermanent and is perceived by valid cognition not to exist at all in the class of the non-impermanent.

Che pa, Product, is *mi tak pa drel*, related to impermanence. What kind of relationship is this? *Rang shin chik pe drel wa* (also called *dak nyi chik pe drel wa*), A relationship of same nature, meaning that whatever is a product has the nature of being impermanent.

འོན་ཀྱང་མཚན་ཉིད་དང་སྒྲུབ་བྱེད་དེ་དག་ནི་གོ་བ་གཙོ་བོར་བྱས་པ་ཡིན་གྱི་
དེར་ངེས་པ་ནི་མ་ཡིན་ཏེ།

wön kyang tsen nyi dang drup che de dak ni go wa tso wor che pa yin gyi der nge pa ni ma yin te

Nevertheless, these definitions and proof statements are given here principally [as a means] to help [the reader's] understanding but are not definitive.

Go wa means to understand and here refers to the author's writing in order to help the reader understand this subject in a general way without too many details. However, to be able to use these on the debate ground, one would have to qualify them with additional points [in accord with any specific debate].

སྒྲ་དེ་སྒྲ་མི་རྟག་པར་སྒྲུབ་པར་བྱེད་པའི་མཚན་ཉིད་དེ་གསུམ་ཀ་ཡིན་ཀྱང་མཚོན་བྱ་
དེ་རྣམས་རེ་རེ་ནས་མ་ཡིན་པའི་ཕྱིར།

dra de dra mi tak par drup par che pe tsen nyi de sum ka yin kyang tsön ja de nam re re ne ma yin pe chir

Although sound is those three definitions [of *chok chö*, *je kyap*, and *dok kyap*] proving that sound is impermanent, it does not qualify as the object to be defined for each of those [definitions].

Why is sound not the object to be defined for each one of the definitions [of the three modes]? This is so because, although sound qualifies as an example that complies with the requirements of each of the definitions of these three modes, sound is not the object to be defined for each of these definitions.

THREE KINDS OF PERFECT REASONS

classification of perfect reasons by way of their nature

གསུམ་པ་དབྱེ་བ་ལ་གསུམ་ཡོད་དེ། རྣམ་འགྲེལ་ལས། དེ་ནི་རྣམ་གསུམ་ཉིད། ཅེས་གསུངས་པ་ལྟར། འབྲས་རྟགས། རང་བཞིན་གྱི་རྟགས། མ་དམིགས་པའི་རྟགས་སོ། །དང་པོ་ནི། རྣམ་འགྲེལ་ལས། རྒྱུ་ལ་རང་བཞིན་ཇི་སྙེད་ཅིག །མེད་ན་མི་འབྱུང་འབྲས་བུ་ནི། །གཏན་ཚིགས་ཡིན་ཏེ། ཞེས་སོགས་དང་། མེ་ཡི་འབྲས་བུ་དུ་བ་སྟེ། །ཞེས་པས་བསྟན་ཅིང་། འདི་ལ་གསུམ། མཚན་ཉིད། དབྱེ་བ། སྒྲུབ་བྱེད་དོ།

sum pa ye wa la sum yö de, ram drel le, de ni nam sum nyi, che sung pa tar, dre tak, rang shin gyi tak, ma mik pe tak so, dang po ni, nam drel le, gyu la rang shin ji nye chik, me na mi jung dre bu ni, ten tsik yin te, she sok dang, me yi dre bu du wa te, she pe ten ching, di la sum, tsen nyi, ye wa, drup che do

The third part, consisting of three classifications of perfect reasons, as it states in the *Commentary to (Dignāga's) "Valid Cognition"*: "The kinds [of reasons] are three." These three are: perfect reasons of effect, perfect reasons of nature, and perfect reasons of non-observation.

Concerning the first, perfect reasons of effect, it instructs in this same text, "Whatever nature the cause has, without it [as a producer] its effect will not arise." And further, "Smoke is the effect of fire," and so forth.

Regarding a perfect reason of effect, there are three parts: its definition, classifications, and proofs.

Gyal Tsab Je gives this example of a perfect reason of effect in his *Clearing the Path to Liberation*:[28]

དུ་བ་ཆོས་ཅན། དུ་ལྡན་ལ་ལ་མེ་གོ་བྱེད་ཀྱི་འབྲས་རྟགས་ཡང་དག་ཡིན་ཏེ། དེ་སྒྲུབ་ཀྱི་ཚུལ་གསུམ་གང་ཞིག མེའི་འབྲས་བུར་ངེས་པའི་ཕྱིར།

du wa chö chen, du den la la me go che kyi dre tak yang dak yin te, de drup kyi tsul sum gang shik, me'i dre bur nge pe chir

Consider smoke, it is a perfect reason of effect that causes one to understand that there is fire on a mountain pass, because it is the three modes in that proof and is ascertained to be the effect of fire.

[28] T: ***tshad ma rnam 'grel gyi tshig le'ur byas pa'i rnam bshad thar lam phyin ci ma log par gsal bar byed pa***

PERFECT REASON OF EFFECT

།དང་པོ་ནི། འབྲས་བུའི་ཚུལ་གསུམ་ཡིན་པ། འབྲས་རྟགས་ཡང་དག་གི་མཚན་ཉིད།
དེ་དང་འདུས་བྱས་གཉིས་དོན་གཅིག །དེ་སྒྲུབ་ཀྱི་འབྲས་བུའི་ཚུལ་གསུམ་ཡིན་པ།
དེ་སྒྲུབ་ཀྱི་འབྲས་རྟགས་ཡང་དག་གི་མཚན་ཉིད།

dang po ni, dre bu'i tsul sum yin pa, dre tak yang dak kyi tsen nyi, de dang du che nyi dön chik, de drup kyi dre bu'i tsul sum yin pa, de drup kyi dre tak yang dak gi tsen nyi

First, the definition of a perfect reason of effect is what is the three effect modes. The two—perfect reason of effect and composed phenomenon—are synonymous. That which is the three effect modes in a proof is the definition of a perfect reason of effect in a proof.

A classic example of a perfect reason of effect is the reason found in the following statement: *du den gyi la la chö chen, me yö te, du wa yö pe chir*, consider smoke on a mountain pass, there is fire, because there is smoke. Since smoke is the effect of fire it is a perfect reason to prove that there is fire on a mountain pass by virtue of its presence there.

གོ་བ་དང་སྦྱར་ན། ཁྱོད་དེ་སྒྲུབ་ཀྱི་རྟགས་ཡང་དག་གང་ཞིག །ཁྱོད་ཀྱི་རྟགས་
ཀྱིས་དེ་སྒྲུབ་ཀྱི་དངོས་ཀྱི་བསྒྲུབ་བྱའི་ཆོས་སུ་གཟུང་བྱའི་གཙོ་བོ་ཡང་ཡིན།
ཁྱོད་ཀྱི་རྒྱུ་ཡང་ཡིན་པའི་གཞི་མཐུན་སྲིད་པ་དེ། ཁྱོད་དེ་སྒྲུབ་ཀྱི་འབྲས་རྟགས་
ཡང་དག་གི་མཚན་ཉིད།

go wa dang jar na, <u>kyö</u> de drup kyi tak yang dak gang shik, <u>kyö</u> kyi tak kyi de drup kyi ngö kyi drup je chö su sung je tso

> *wo yang yin, kyö kyi gyu yang yin pe shi tun si pa te, kyö de drup kyi dre tak yang dak gi tsen nyi*
>
> To apply this definition to a specific example so that we can better understand it: 1) it [smoke] is a perfect reason in that proof, and 2) there is potentially something that is a combination of being the principal explicit object held as the quality to be proved in that proof having [smoke] as its sign and that which is its cause. Such is the definition of [smoke's] being a perfect effect reason in that proof.

The briefest definition of a perfect reason of effect is *dre bu'i tsul sum yin pa*, that which is the three modes of effect (as previously explained). However, sometimes we say *go wa dang jar na*, which means giving a description by applying it to a specific object to facilitate understanding.

How many *kyö*'s are there in the definition above? Four. Although *kyö* usually means "you," here it means "it," referring to *du wa*, smoke, the subject of debate. *Gang shik* shows that what precedes it is the subject as well as one quality of a definition. *Kyö kyi tak kyi* means "smoke" is being used as a reason. *De drup kyi ngö kyi drup che chö*, The explicit quality to be proved in this proof, is *me*, fire, as expressed in the proof: *du den gyi la la chö chen, me yö te, du wa yö pe chir*, consider smoke on a mountain pass, there is fire, because there is smoke.

Generally, *me yö pa*, the existence of fire, [indicating a general abstract quality] would be considered *tak pa*, a permanent entity, on the debate ground. Permanent fire cannot produce [the impermanent entity] *du wa*, smoke. But here, *de drup kyi ngö kyi drup che chö*, the explicit quality to be proved in this proof, is *me*, fire. So, instead of simply saying *me te*, fire, we have to qualify it more specifically by saying *me yö te*, there is fire.

Yang yin and *shi tun* show that there is a combination of things. *Kyö kyi gyu yang yin* means it [fire] is also smoke's cause. *Sung ja*, What is held [as the quality to be proved], in this case, is *me*, fire. *Tso wo* means principal.

To further clarify the meaning of *tso wo*, principal, we can use the example of *me ma yin pa le lok pa*, the opposite of non-fire. *Me ma yin pa le lok pa, de drup kyi ngö kyi drup je chö su sung ja yin,* [Although] the opposite of non-fire is what is held as the explicit quality to be proved, *ngö kyi drup je chö su sung ja tso wo ma yin,* it is not what is held as the *principal* quality to be proved in this proof. The word *tso wo* means main point and indicates a certain precision about what is being referred to. *Me ma yin pa le lok pa,* The opposite of non-fire, is also *me,* fire. *De drup kyi ngö kyi drup je chö su sung ja,* What is held as the explicit quality to be proved in this proof, is both *me* and *me ma yin pa le lok pa.* But *tso wo,* the precise [object to be proved], here shows that [the positive] *me,* fire, is the explicit quality to be proved in this proof, and not [the negative] *me ma yin pa le lok pa,* opposite of non-fire. Nevertheless, *me ma yin pa le lok pa,* opposite of non-fire, is *shuk kyi drup che chö,* the implicit quality to be proved.

Kyö kyi gyu, Smoke's cause, is also *ngö kyi drup che chö kyi sung je tso wo,* what is held as the principal explicit quality to be proved in this proof. *Shi tun pa* means a combination of being both the principal explicit quality to be proved in this proof and smoke's cause, which is fire.

More simply, *chö chen,* the subject of debate, is *du den gyi la la,* smoke on a mountain pass. *Ngö kyi drup che chö su sung je tso wo,* The principal explicit quality to be proved in this proof, is *me,* fire. *De drup kyi tak yang dak,* the perfect reason in this proof, is *du wa,* smoke.

འབྲས་རྟགས་ལ་དབྱེ་ན་སྤྱིར་མང་ཡང་། བསྡུ་ན་རྒྱུ་དངོས་སྒྲུབ་དང་། རྒྱུ་སྔོན་སོང་དང་། རྒྱུ་ཆོས་རྗེས་དཔོག་གི་འབྲས་རྟགས་གསུམ་ཡོད་པ་ལས།

dre tak la ye na chir mang yang, du na gyu ngö drup (kyi dre tak) dang, gyu ngön song (gi dre tak) dang, gyu chö je pok gi dre tak sum yö pa le

When classifying perfect reasons of effect, in general there are many. However, these can be succinctly condensed into three: a perfect reason of effect proving a direct cause, a perfect reason of effect proving a distant prior cause, and a perfect reason of effect inferring causal attributes.

Examples follow.

reason of effect proving a direct cause

དུ་བ་དེ། དུ་ལྡན་གྱི་ལ་ལ་མེ་ཡོད་པར་བསྒྲུབ་པའི་རྒྱུ་དངོས་སྒྲུབ་ཀྱི་འབྲས་རྟགས།

du wa te, du den gyi la la me yö par drup pe gyu ngö drup kyi dre tak

Smoke [is] that [perfect] reason of effect proving a direct cause, which is used to establish that there is fire on a smoky mountain pass.

Ngö means direct; *drup* means to prove. *Gyu ngö drup kyi dre tak* means a reason of effect that proves its own direct cause. *Du den gyi la la me yö pe chir*, There is smoke on a mountain pass because there is fire, is an example of this kind of reason. Smoke is used to prove its direct cause, which is fire.

Now, once the smoke comes from fire, it soars into the sky and remains floating there for a pretty long time. This serves as an example of the second kind of effect reason, which is *gyu ngön song gi dre tak*, a reason of effect proving a distant prior cause, illustrated below.

reason of effect proving a distant prior cause

དུ་བ་དེ། བར་སྣང་གི་དུ་བ་སྔོ་ལོང་ངོ་རང་རྒྱུ་མེ་སྔ་མ་སྔོན་སོང་དུ་བསྒྲུབ་པའི་འབྲས་རྟགས།

du wa de, bar nang gi du wa ngo long po rang gyu me nga ma ngön song du drup pe dre tak

Smoke is that [perfect] reason of effect proving a distant prior cause, which proves that fire was its prior cause, since there is still a bluish cloud of smoke rising in the air.

Bar nang means in space; *du wa* means smoke; *ngo* means a bluish color; *long po*, billowing, refers to its shape as it soars in the air; *nga ma ngön du song te* means prior or just before it. Therefore, we can make the statement: *de chö chen, rang gyu me nga ma ngön du song te, du wa yin pe chir*, consider that subject—a cloud of smoke floating in the air—fire was the prior cause that produced it, because it is smoke.

Du wa, Smoke, is *tak*, the sign, that proves its cause. Where is that smoke's cause at the time you see the cloud of smoke floating in the air? Is fire, its cause, still there or not? The implication is that fire, smoke's prior cause, has already disappeared. *Nga ma ngön du song te*, Having previously been there, implies that without fire there could not be any smoke. That is the meaning of *gyu ngön song gi dre tak*, a reason of effect proving a distant prior cause.

reason of effect inferring causal attributes

བུ་རོ་ད་ལྟ་བ་དེ། ཁ་ནང་བུ་རོ་གོང་བུའི་སྟེང་དུ་བུ་རོ་སྔ་མས་རོ་གཟུགས་ཕྱི་མ་
བསྐྱེད་པའི་ནུས་པ་ཡོད་པར་བསྒྲུབ་པའི་རྒྱུ་ཆོས་རྗེས་དཔོག་གི་འབྲས་རྟགས་སོ།

bu ro da ta wa de, ka nang bu ro gong bu'i teng du, bu ro nga me ro suk chi ma kye pe nu pa yö par drup pe gyu chö je pok gi dre tak so

The present taste of brown sugar is a perfect reason of effect inferring causal attributes since it proves that, based on the lump of brown sugar in your mouth, it has the ability to produce a later taste and form of that sugar due to the previous taste of brown sugar.

Ka nang bu ro gong bu'i teng na chö chen, bu ro nga me ro suk chi ma kye pe nu pa yö te, bu ro da ta wa yö pe chir, Consider the taste of brown sugar in your mouth, it has the ability to produce a later taste and form, because there is a present taste of brown sugar [in your mouth]. This is an example of *gyu chö je pok gi dre tak*, a reason of effect inferring causal attributes.

Bu ram is brown sugar. *Bu ro* is short for *bu ram gyi ro*, which means the taste of brown sugar. *Gong bu* means a piece or lump; *ka nang* means in your mouth; *teng du* means relative to that piece of sugar in your mouth. *Bu ram*, Lump of brown sugar, is the object we are talking about. It has a sweet taste and a specific form, which, in this case, is something felt by the body consciousness. Both of these are *kye chö*,[29] characteristics or qualities, applied to a basis [that piece of sugar]. *Teng du* means using this as a basis. *Bu ro nga me*, That sugar's previous taste [and form], have the power to produce their own next results, which refers to the taste and form of that lump of brown sugar in the next moment. Just after you have put it in your mouth, it won't disappear immediately. As you chew that lump of brown sugar and let it dissolve in your mouth, it lingers there over a good period of time...for one moment, a second moment, a third moment, and so on.

In the first moment, *bu ram gyi ro*, that taste of brown sugar, can have the power to produce both the sugar's taste and form of the next moment. *Ro* means taste. *Suk* means form. *Chi ma* means later. *Nu pa* means it has that power. Why does it have that power? *Bu ro da ta wa yö pe chir*, Because there is the present taste of sugar in your mouth. *Da ta wa*, The present [of that lump of brown sugar], produces its result of the next moment. Such is the nature of *ngö po*, a causally effective thing. *Gyu da ta wa*, Present cause, means it has the power to produce its result of the next moment.

In this example of *gyu chö je pok gi dre tak*, a reason of effect inferring causal attributes, *gyu*, the cause, is *bu ro nga ma*, a

[29] ཁྱད་ཆོས་

previous taste of brown sugar. Its *kye chö*, characteristics, are both that sugar's taste and form. Because you have the present taste and feel the form of that brown sugar in your mouth, these have the power to produce the taste and form of the next moment, their effects, since taste and form are that piece of sugar's basic characteristics. *Gyu chö*, Causal characteristics, are *bu ro nga ma*, previous taste and form of that sugar. *Je pok* is a verb meaning to infer, and implies that a later effect can prove through inference the characteristics of its prior cause.

Now, I'm not just giving a *lung* [verbal recitation of a text for oral transmission] of this text. You have to move your mouth and make the statements yourself.

***

—*Gyu ngö drup kyi dre tak gö gyu me pe chir*, You can't give me an example of a reason of effect proving a direct cause.
—*Tak ma drup*, That's not true.
—*Gyu ngö drup kyi dre tak gö gyu yö par tel*, So you can give me an example of a reason of effect proving a direct cause?
—*Dö*, Yes, I can.
—*Gö sho*, Tell me what it is!
—*Du den gyi la la chö chen, me yö te, du wa yö pe chir, she pe du wa te, gyu ngö drup kyi dre tak [yin pe chir]*, Consider the subject smoke on a mountain pass, there is fire, because there is smoke, when making that statement, smoke is an example of a reason of effect proving its direct cause.
—*Ma yin par tel, du den gyi la la chö chen, me yö te, du wa yö pe chir, she pe tak du chö chen, gyu ngö drup kyi dre tak yin par tel*, Then it follows that when you make the statement: "Consider the subject smoke on a mountain pass, there is fire, because there is smoke," smoke in this case is an example of a reason of effect proving its direct cause?
—*Dö*, Yes, that's right.

—*Ma yin par tel, gyu ngön song gyi dre tak gö gyu me pe chir,* Well then, it seems you can't give me an example of a reason of effect proving a distant prior cause.

—*Tak ma drup,* I can posit one.

—*Gyu ngön song gyi dre tak gö gyu yö par tel,* Really, you can posit one?

—*Dö,* Yes, I can.

—*Sho,* Tell me!

—*Bar nang gi du wa ngo long po chö chen, rang gyu me nga ma ngön du song te, du wa yin pe chir, gyu ngön song gyi dre tak yin pe chir,* Because the subject, a cloud of blue smoke rising in the air had fire as its previous cause, since it is smoke.

—*Bar nang gi du wa ngo long po chö chen, rang gyu me nga ma ngön du song te, du wa yin pe chir, she pe tak du chö chen, gyu ngön song gyi dre tak yin par tel,* So the reason "smoke" in the statement, the subject, a billowing cloud of blue smoke rising in the air, had fire as its distant prior cause, since it is smoke, is a reason of effect proving a distant prior cause?

—*Dö,* Yes.

—*Ma yin par tel, gyu chö je pok gi dre tak gö gyu me pe chir,* If you say that's so, then it seems you can't give me an example of a reason of effect inferring causal attributes.

—*Tak ma drup,* I can give you one.

—*Gyu chö je pok gi dre tak gö gyu yö par tel,* You can posit one?

—*Dö,* Yes.

—*Gö sho,* Tell me then!

—*Ka nang bu ro gong bu'i teng du chö chen, bu ro nga me ro suk chi ma kye pe nu pa yö te, bu ro da ta wa yö pe chir,* Consider a lump of sugar in the mouth, it has the ability to produce a later taste and form of this previous lump of sugar, because there still exists [in the mouth] a present sweet taste.

—*Ka nang bu ro gong bu'i teng du chö chen, bu ro nga me ro suk chi ma kye pe nu pa yö te, bu ro da ta wa yö pe chir, she pe tak du chö chen, gyu chö je pok kyi dre tak yin par tel,* So it follows that when you make the statement, "Consider a lump of sugar in the mouth, it has the ability to produce a later taste and

form of this previous lump of sugar, because there still exists [in the mouth] a present sweet taste," this present sweet taste of brown sugar is an example of a reason of effect inferring causal attributes?
—*Dö*, Yes, that's correct.

ཡང་དེའི་སྟེང་དུ།

yang de'i teng du

Not only that...

reason of effect proving a general cause

རེས་འགའ་སྐྱེ་པའི་དངོས་པོ་དེ་ཉེར་ལེན་གྱི་ཕུང་པོ་རང་རྒྱུ་དང་བཅས་པར་
བསྒྲུབ་པའི་རྒྱུའི་སྤྱིའམ་རང་ལྡོག་སྒྲུབ་ཀྱི་འབྲས་རྟགས་དང་།

ren ga kye pe ngö po de nyer len gyi pung po rang gyu dang che par drup pe gyu'i chi'am rang dok drup kyi dre tak dang

Those things that occasionally arise, the general causes along with [other] accompanying causes of the perpetuating aggregates, [are an example of] a perfect reason of effect proving a general cause, also called a reason of effect that proves its own distinguisher [or isolate].

Included with the three kinds of reasons of effect just discussed are two others that are not counted separately. These are known as *gyu chi drup kyi dre tak*, a reason of effect proving a general cause, and *gyu kye par drup kyi dre tak*, a reason of effect proving a particular cause. The first one is illustrated by the example given above.

Nyer len gyi pung po chö chen, rang gyu dang che pa yin te, rang gi nyer len me par mi kye pe ngö po yin pe chir, Consider the perpetuating aggregates, they are accompanied by their own causes, because they are causally effective things that would not have arisen without taking them on.

Nyer len gyi pung po chö chen, rang gyu dang che pa yin te, ren ga kye pe ngö po yin pe chir, Consider the perpetuating aggregates, they are accompanied by their own causes, because they are causally effective things that arise occasionally. *Nyer len gyi pung po* means all aggregates that are produced by karma and mental afflictions such as ours. *Nyer len gyi pung po chö chen, rang gyu dang che pa yin te* means consider the perpetuating aggregates, they have their own unique causes. *Ren ga kye pe ngö po* means a kind of causally effective thing that occurs only occasionally due to the erratic arising of certain causes and conditions. Why doesn't it arise all the time? Because its unique causes are not always present. When the causes gather together, the results come. When the causes do not gather together, the results do not arise. The perpetuating aggregates are a prime example of *ren ga kye pe ngö po*, a causally effective thing that arises sometimes and sometimes not, because they have their own unique causes. You can prove it that way.

Nyer len gyi pung po chö chen, The perpetuating aggregates, is the subject; *rang gyu dang che pa*, together with its causes, is *drup che chö*, the quality to be proved; *ren ga kye pe ngö po*, occasionally arising causally effective thing, is *tak*, the reason. This kind of reason is an example of *gyu chi drup kyi dre tak*, a reason of effect proving general causes. Why? Because *nyer len gyi pung po*, the perpetuating aggregates, have both karma and mental afflictions as their general causes, as well as specific causes such as the unique substances of one's parents. Since these causes are not counted separately they are referred to as *rang gyu dang che pa*, accompanying causes.

Rang dok[30] *drup kyi dre tak*, A reason of effect that proves its own distinguisher [or reason of effect proving a particular cause], is the fourth kind of reason of effect, which is given below.

---

[30] An example of ***rang ldog***, the self-distinguisher, of pot is pot itself.

reason of effect proving a particular cause

རང་གི་དམིགས་རྐྱེན་མེད་པར་མི་སྐྱེ་པའི་དངོས་པོ་དེ་སྔོར་སྣང་དབང་ཤེས་
རང་གི་དམིགས་རྐྱེན་དང་བཅས་པར་བསྒྲུབ་པའི་རྒྱུའི་ཁྱད་པར་སྒྲུབ་ཀྱི་འབྲས་
རྟགས་དང་ལྔར་ཕྱེའོ།

rang gi mik kyen me par mi kye pe ngö po de ngor nang wang she rang gi mik kyen dang che par drup pe gyu'i kye par drup kyi dre tak dang ngar che'o

[An example of] a reason of effect proving a particular cause is a[n eye] sense consciousness appearing as blue, a causally effective thing that could not arise without its object condition, since a[n eye] sense consciousness appearing as blue possesses its object condition [in this case, the color blue]. There are five distinct kinds.

Let's examine this in more detail. What is that in the vase on the table? A flower. What are these? The flower's petals. They are also a part of a flower. And these? Its leaves. And this? Its stem. So we may legitimately say that this flower has different parts? Yes. What is the color of the leaves? Green. This color we call *ngön po* in Tibetan, which means a bluish-green color. This term is also used for the color of the sky on a clear day. *Wang she*, Sense consciousness, here is referring to *mik kyi nam par she pa*, the eye sense consciousness. The color of this flower's leaves are appearing as a blue-green color to your eye sense consciousness. The blue-green color of these leaves is *mik kyen*, the object condition, of that eye sense consciousness. This is one of the four kinds of conditions, which include: *gyu kyen*, causal condition, *mik kyen*, object condition, *dak kyen*, governing condition, and *de ma tak kyen*, immediately preceding condition. These *kyen*, conditions, are also a kind of *gyu*, cause. *Mik kyen*, Object condition, in this case, is comprised of the flower's colors and shape. The color of the leaves is blue-green and the color of the petals is red.

Ngor nang wang she, [Eye] sense consciousness appearing as blue-green, means that the visual sense consciousness is focusing on the blue-green color of the leaves in this case [causing the consciousness to take on the aspect of blue-green]. We can express this with the following statement: *ngön dzin mik she chö chen, rang gi mik kyen dang che pa yin te, rang gi mik kyen me par mi kye pe ngö po yin pe chir*, consider an eye consciousness apprehending a blue-green color, it possesses an object condition, because it is a causally effective thing that could not arise without such an object condition.

When we focus our attention on a flower, we see the blue-green color of its leaves and the red color of its petals. Those are the flower's *kye par*, characteristics. Here they are being used as examples of *gyu'i kye par*, the characteristics of a specific cause. *Ngor nang wang she*, A[n eye] sense consciousness appearing as blue-green, arises only when perceiving a blue-green color. In order for that to occur, there must be *mik kyen*, an object condition, to produce it. What is *mik kyen*, the object condition, in this case? A characteristic of the flower; specifically, the blue-green color of the flower's leaves. Without *mik kyen*, an object condition, you cannot have *ngön dzin mik she*, an eye consciousness apprehending a blue-green color. *Ngön dzin mik she* and *ngor nang wang she* are the same. *Gyu*, The cause, is your object of focus, which in this case is the flower. *Kye par*, The characteristic, is the blue-green color of the flower's leaves. This is an example of *gyu'i kye par drup kyi dre tak*, a reason of effect proving a particular cause.

other classifications of reasons of effect

།ཡང་དེ་ལ་དབྱེ་ན་གཉིས་ཡོད་དེ།

yang de la ye na nyi yö de

There is also a way of classifying reasons of effect into two.

In addition to the classifications given above, there is another way in which reasons of effect can be classified into two.

reason of effect that engages
the similar class as a pervader

དུ་བ་དེ་དུ་ལྡན་ལ་ལ་དུ་བའི་དངོས་རྒྱུ་ཡོད་པར་སྒྲུབ་པའི་མཐུན་ཕྱོགས་ལ་ཁྱབ་བྱེད་དུ་འཇུག་པའི་འབྲས་རྟགས་དང་། དུ་བ་དེ་དུ་ལྡན་ལ་ལ་མེ་ཡོད་པར་སྒྲུབ་པའི་མཐུན་ཕྱོགས་ལ་རྣམ་གཉིས་སུ་འཇུག་པའི་འབྲས་རྟགས་ཡིན་པའི་ཕྱིར།

du wa de du den la la du we ngö gyu yö par drup pe tun chok la kyap che du juk pe dre tak dang, du wa de du den la la me yö par drup pe tun chok la nam nyi su juk pe dre tak yin pe chir

Smoke is 1) a reason of effect that engages the similar class as a pervader in proving the existence of the direct cause of smoke on a mountain pass that has smoke, and 2) smoke is also a reason of effect that engages the similar class in two ways in proving that there is fire on a mountain pass that has smoke.

Here, as seen before, the very important phrase in logic, *de drup kyi*, in a [specific] proof, is used in order to specify the circumstance in which the statement is made and qualifies statements in order to distinguish the general category from specific instances. Because there are so many different kinds of *tak yang dak*, perfect reasons, and *tak tar nang*, false reasons, you have to use this phrase to clarify your statements.

Du wa, Smoke, can be *de drup kyi tun chok la kyap je du juk pe dre tak*, a reason of effect that engages the similar class as a pervader, or it can be *de drup kyi tun chok la nam nyi su drup che dre tak*, a reason of effect that engages the similar class in two ways. Which one it is depends upon the current *drup che chö*, quality to be proved.

Du den gyi la la chö chen, me yö te, du wa yö pe chir, Consider smoke on a mountain pass, there is fire, because there is smoke. What is *de drup kyi tak*, the reason in this proof? *Du wa*, Smoke. What is *de drup kyi drup che chö*, the quality to be proved in this proof? *Me*, Fire. What is *de drup kyi tun chok*, the similar class in this proof? Things compatible with the quality to be proved in this proof [which is fire]. What is *de drup kyi mi tun chok*, the dissimilar class in this proof? Things incompatible with the quality to be proved in this proof, or *me ma yin pa*, things that are not [of the same class as] fire.

> དེ་སྒྲུབ་ཀྱི་མཐུན་ཕྱོགས་ལ་ཁྱབ་བྱེད་དུ་འཇུག་པའི་དོན་ནི། དུ་བའི་དངོས་རྒྱུ་ཡོད་ན་དུ་བ་ཡོད་པས་ཁྱབ་པའི་དོན་དང་།
>
> *de drup kyi tun chok la kyap che du juk pe dön ni, du we ngö gyu yö na du wa yö pe kyap pe dön dang*
>
> An example illustrating the meaning of engaging the similar class as a pervader in that proof is: if there is the direct cause of smoke [fire], then there must necessarily be smoke.

To show this with a proof: *du den gyi la la chö chen, du wa ngö gyu yö te, du wa yö pe chir*, consider smoke on a mountain pass, there is the direct cause of smoke, because there is smoke. It is important to say *du wa yö pe chir*, because there is smoke, instead of saying *du we chir*, because smoke, which implies "because *it is* smoke," for reasons mentioned previously.

Kyap je, A pervader [of the similar class of the quality to be proved], means in this case, *du wa yö na*, if there is smoke, *du wa ngö gyu yö pe kyap*, there must be the direct cause of smoke. *Tun chok*, Similar class, of the quality to be proved, is *du we ngö gyu*, that which is the direct cause of smoke [which is fire].

Again, in the statement: *du den gyi la la chö chen, du we ngö gyu yö te, du wa yö pe chir*, consider smoke on a mountain pass, there is the direct cause of smoke, because there is smoke, what is *de drup kyi drup che chö*, the quality to be proved? *Du wa ngö gyu yö*, The existence of the direct cause of smoke. What is *de drup kyi tak*, the reason in this proof? *Du wa*, Smoke. Therefore, *du wa yö na*, if there is smoke, *du we ngö gyu yö pe kyap*, there must necessarily be the direct cause of smoke. This is an example of *tun chok la kyap je*, pervader of the similar class.

What is the meaning of *ngö gyu*, direct cause, in this case? For example, what is *du we ngö gyu*, the direct cause of smoke? *Me*, Fire. The direct cause means *du we ngö su kye che*, the direct producer of smoke. Between the effect and the direct cause there is absolutely no gap whatsoever. Although both the cause and effect are *ke chik ma*, momentary, just when the effect arises, there are no other *kye che*, producers or causes, between the moment of the arising of this effect and the direct cause that produces it.

reason of effect that engages the similar class in two ways

དེ་ལ་རྣམ་གཉིས་སུ་འཇུག་པའི་དོན་ནི། མེ་ཡོད་ན། དུ་བ་ཡོད་པས་མ་ཁྱབ་པའི་དོན་ཡིན་ནོ།

de la nam nyi su juk pe dön ni, me yö na, du wa yö pe ma kyap pe dön yin no

An example illustrating the meaning of engagement in two ways is: if there is fire, there is not necessarily smoke.

Nam nyi, Two ways, indicates that it may either be pervasive or non-pervasive. An example given above is: *me yö na, du wa yö pe ma kyap*, if there is fire, there is not necessarily smoke. Why? When making such a statement, instead of starting with *tak*, the reason, [*du wa yö pe chir*, because there is smoke] we started with *drup che chö*, the quality to be proved, [*me yö*, there is fire]. In this case *tun chok*, the similar class, refers to *me*, fire. When we make the statement: *me yö na, du wa yö pe ma kyap*, if there is fire, there is not necessarily smoke, it is both the case that: *me yö na, du wa yö pe yang ma kyap*, if there is fire, there is not necessarily smoke, and also, *me yö na, du wa me pe yang ma kyap*, if there is fire, there is not necessarily not smoke. *Nam nyi*, Two ways, can be expressed this way: *yö pe yang ma kyap, me pe yang ma kyap*, it does not necessarily exist, nor does it necessarily not exist.

Why is this so? *Me yö na du wa yö pe ma kyap ka re shak*, Can you give me an example of when there is fire but there is not necessarily smoke? You have to understand a crucial point about *gyu dang dre bu*, cause and effect. Which comes first, the cause or the effect? The cause comes first, of course, and the effect comes later. *Me*, Fire, comes first because it is the cause of smoke, and *du wa*, smoke, its effect, comes later. So, at the very moment of the establishment of fire, smoke does not exist yet. Therefore, we can reasonably say: *me yö na du wa yö pe ma kyap*, if there is fire, there is not necessarily smoke [because an effect cannot arise simultaneous with its cause].

However, *me yö na du wa me pe yang ma kyap*, if there is fire, it is also the case that there is not necessarily not smoke. This is the meaning of *tun chok la nam nyi su juk pa*, engagement of the similar class in two ways. That is how logic works.

སྒྲུབ་བྱེད་ནི། དུ་བ་ཆོས་ཅན། ཁྱོད་དུ་བ་དང་ལྡན་པའི་ལ་ལ་མེ་ཡོད་པར་
བསྒྲུབ་པའི་འབྲས་རྟགས་ཡིན་ཏེ། ཁྱོད་དེ་སྒྲུབ་ཀྱི་རྟགས་ཡང་དག་གང་ཞིག
།ཁྱོད་མེའི་འབྲས་བུ་ཡིན་པའི་ཕྱིར། ཞེས་པ་ནི་མཚོན་པ་ཙམ་མོ།

drup che ni du wa chö chen, kyö du wa dang den pe la la me yö par drup pe dre tak yin te, kyö de drup kyi tak yang dak gang shik, kyö me dre bu yin pe chir, she pa ni tsön pa tsam mo

A correct proof is as follows: Consider smoke, it is a [perfect] reason of effect proving there is fire on a mountain pass that has smoke, because 1) smoke is a perfect reason [sign] in that proof, and 2) smoke is the effect of fire. This is just an illustration.

དུ་བ་དེ་དུ་ལྡན་ལ་ལ་མེ་ཡོད་པར་བསྒྲུབ་པའི་རྟགས་ཡང་དག་དང་དེ་སྒྲུབ་ཀྱི་
བཀོད་ཚོད་དང་སོང་ཚོད་ཀྱི་རྟགས་གཉིས་ཀ་དང་དུ་བའི་རྟགས་ཀྱིས་དེ་སྒྲུབ་
ཀྱི་རྟགས་ཡང་དག་ཡིན།

du wa de du den la la me yö par drup pe tak yang dak dang de drup kyi kö tsö dang song tsö kyi tak nyi ka dang du we tak kyi de drup kyi tak yang dak yin

Smoke is a perfect reason proving that there is fire on a mountain pass that has smoke, and is both the stated reason and the actual reason in that proof. Therefore, the reason, smoke, is a perfect sign in that proof.

Kö tsö kyi tak means the stated reason. *Song tsö kyi tak* means the actual reason and refers to what appears to the mind. *Tak yang dak*, The perfect reason, used in this statement is *dre tak yang dak*, a perfect reason of effect, and as such must be *ngö kyi dre bu*, the direct effect, of *drup che chö*, the quality to be proved. *Du wa yö pa*, The existence of smoke, is *de drup kyi tak*, the reason in this proof. It is also *kö tsö kyi tak*, the stated reason. *Kö tsö* means using *du wa yö pe chir*, because there is smoke, as a reason. However, *du wa yö pa*, the existence of smoke, is not *song tsö kyi tak*, the actual reason. Why is this so according to logic?

དུ་བ་ཡོད་པ་དེ་དེ་སྒྲུབ་ཀྱི་རྟགས་ཡང་དག་དང་བཀོད་ཚོད་ཀྱི་རྟགས་ཡིན་ཀྱང་
།དེ་སྒྲུབ་ཀྱི་སོང་ཚོད་ཀྱི་རྟགས་དང་དུ་བའི་རྟགས་ཀྱིས་དེ་སྒྲུབ་ཀྱི་རྟགས་ཡང་
དག་མ་ཡིན།

du wa yö pa de de drup kyi tak yang dak dang kö tsö kyi tak yin kyang, de drup kyi song tsö kyi tak dang du we tak kyi de drup kyi tak yang dak ma yin

> Although the existence of smoke is a perfect reason as well as the *stated* reason in that proof, by using the reason "smoke," it is not the *actual* reason that proves that [fire], and in this sense "smoke" is not a perfect reason in that proof.

Du wa yö pa song tsö kyi tak ma yin te, The existence of smoke is not the actual reason in that proof because, if it were, it would be *me'i dre bu*, the [actual] result of fire, since it is a reason of effect. However, *du wa yö pa*, the "existence of smoke" [itself], is not the effect of fire because in the field of logic it is considered *tak pa*, a permanent phenomenon. *Tak pa*, A permanent phenomenon, cannot be *dre bu*, an effect, and consequently cannot serve as *dre tak*, a reason of effect. So, although *du wa yö pa*, the existence of smoke, is *de drup kyi kö tsö kyi tak yang dak*, the stated perfect reason in this proof, it is not *de drup kyi song tsö kyi dre tak*, the actual effect reason in this proof. *De drup kyi kö tsö kyi tak*, The stated reason in this proof, is *du wa yö pe chir*, because there is smoke; *de drup kyi song tsö kyi tak*, the actual reason in this proof, is *du wa*, smoke, because smoke is the [actual] effect of fire.

From this we can understand that *du wa yö pa la tak pa dang ngö po yin pe cha yö*, there are two factors at issue regarding *du wa yö pa*, "the existence of smoke," serving as both a permanent phenomenon [as an abstract statement] and as a causally effective thing [since smoke itself, is a causally effective thing].

> མེ་དེ་དུ་བའི་རྟགས་ཀྱིས་དེ་སྒྲུབ་ཀྱི་བསྒྲུབ་བྱའི་ཆོས་དང་བཀོད་ཚོད་དང་སོང་ཚོད་ཀྱི་བསྒྲུབ་བྱའི་ཆོས་ཡིན།
>
> *me de du we tak kyi de drup kyi drup che chö dang kö tsö dang song tsö kyi drup che chö yin*
>
> Fire is the quality to be proved in that proof using smoke as a reason and is also both the stated quality to be proved and the actual quality to be proved.

མེ་ཡོད་པ་དེ་དེ་སྒྲུབ་ཀྱི་བསྒྲུབ་བྱའི་ཆོས་དང་བཀོད་ཚོད་ཀྱི་བསྒྲུབ་བྱའི་ཆོས་དང་། དུ་བའི་རྟགས་ཀྱིས་དེ་སྒྲུབ་ཀྱི་བསྒྲུབ་བྱའི་ཆོས་ཡིན་ཀྱང་། དེ་སྒྲུབ་ཀྱི་སོང་ཚོད་ཀྱི་དེ་མ་ཡིན་ནོ།

me yö pa de de drup kyi drup che chö dang kö tsö kyi drup che chö dang, du we tak kyi de drup kyi drup che chö yin kyang, de drup kyi song tsö kyi de ma yin no

The "existence of fire" is both the quality to be proved and the stated quality to be proved in that proof. Although the quality to be proved in that proof gives smoke as a reason to prove it, the "existence of fire" is not the actual quality to be proved in that proof.

This is true because, as stated before, *me yö pa*, the existence of fire, is not *dre bu*, an effect, but rather *tak pa*, a permanent entity. *De drup kyi song tsö kyi drup che chö yin na*, If it is the actual quality to be proved in a proof, then *du we gyu yin gö*, it must be the cause of smoke. *Du we gyu yin na, ngö po yin gö*, If it is the cause of smoke, it has to be a causally effective thing. *Me yö pa*, The existence of fire, is not a causally effective thing, but a permanent phenomenon. Therefore, *me yö pa song tsö kyi drup che chö ma yin*, the "existence of fire" is not the actual quality to be proved in this proof.

།མེ་ཚད་མས་དམིགས་པ་དང་ཚ་ཞིང་སྲེག་པ་གཉིས་པོ་དེ་རེ་རེ་ནས་དུ་ལྡན་ལ་ལ་མེ་ཡོད་པར་བསྒྲུབ་པའི་དངོས་ཀྱི་བསྒྲུབ་བྱའི་ཆོས་སུ་གཟུང་བྱ་མ་ཡིན་ཏེ།

me tse me mik pa dang tsa shing sek pa nyi po de re re ne du den la la me yö par drup pe ngö kyi drup che chö su sung ja ma yin te

Neither "fire perceived by valid cognition" nor "hot and burning" are what are held as the explicit quality to be proved when proving that fire exists on a smoky mountain pass. Why?

The explicit quality to be proved in this proof is *me yö pa*, existing fire [translated to indicate its nature as a causally effective thing], or *me*, fire. *Me tse me mik pa*, Fire perceived by valid cognition, is the definition of the valid perception of fire, and as such is not the explicit quality to be proved in this proof. Similarly, *tsa shing sek pa*, hot and burning, the definition of fire, is not the explicit quality to be proved. Additionally, when we make the statement: *du den gi la la chö chen, me yö te, du wa yö pe chir*, consider smoke on a mountain pass, there is fire, because there is smoke, that reason is what is known as *tsön ja drup pe tak yang dak*, a perfect reason proving an object to be defined, which in this case is *me*, fire. It is not proving a definition such as *me tse me mik pa*, fire perceived by valid cognition, or *tsa shing sek pa*, hot and burning [the definition of fire].

དེ་སྒྲུབ་ཀྱི་རྟགས་ཡང་དག་ཡིན་པའི་ཕྱིར།

de drup kyi tak yang dak yin pe chir

Because [each of these may serve] as a perfect reason in that proof.

As mentioned above, there is a difference between the two following kinds of reasons: *ta nye ba shik drup kyi tak*, a reason proving a term, and *dön ba shik drup kyi tak*, a reason proving a meaning. For example, *me*, fire, is *ta nye*, a term, and *tsa shing sek pa*, hot and burning, [its definition] is *dön*, its meaning. *Dön* refers to *tsen nyi*, the definition, and *ta nye*, term, refers to *tsön ja*, the object to be defined. In this case, *me*, fire, is the term or the object to be defined, and *tsa shing sek pa*, hot and burning, is the meaning or the definition. So, if we were to posit the statement: *du den gyi la la chö chen, me yö te, tsa shing sek pa yin pe chir*, consider smoke on a mountain pass, there is fire, because it is hot and burning, this is an example of *ta nye ba shik drup kyi tak yang dak*, a perfect reason proving a term. However, *de drup kyi ngö kyi drup che chö*, the explicit quality to be proved in that proof, cannot be *tsa shing sek pa*, hot and burning, because it is being used here as a reason [since the quality to be proved and the reason cannot be the same in a given proof]. Again, if we were to say: *dra chö chen, mi tak te, dra yin pe chir*, consider sound, it is impermanent, because it is sound, it would not be correct to use *dra*, sound, as a reason if it is also the subject of debate in that statement. Or, *dra chö chen, mi tak te, mi tak pa yin pe chir*, consider sound, it is impermanent, because it is impermanent. Such reasons are *ma drup pe tak*, unestablished reasons, because, in the first one, the subject and the reason are the same; and in the second one, the quality to be proved and the reason are the same.

> འོན་ཀྱང་དེ་གཉིས་རེ་རེ་ནས་དུ་བའི་རྟགས་ཀྱིས་དེ་སྒྲུབ་ཀྱི་དངོས་ཀྱི་བསྒྲུབ་
> བྱའི་ཆོས་སུ་གཟུང་བྱ་ཡིན་ཏེ།
>
> *wön kyang de nyi re re ne du we tak kyi de drup kyi ngö kyi drup che chö su sung ja yin te*
>
> Nevertheless, each of these may be held as the explicit quality to be proved in that proof when using the reason smoke [to prove the thesis]...

When using *du wa*, smoke, as *tak*, the reason in that proof, *me tse me mik pa*, fire perceived by valid cognition, and *tsa shing sek pa*, hot and burning, may be held as the explicit qualities to be proved.

> དེའི་རྟགས་ཀྱིས་དེ་སྒྲུབ་ཀྱི་དངོས་ཀྱི་བསྒྲུབ་བྱའི་ཆོས་སུ་གཟུང་བྱ་ཡང་ཡིན་
> མཚན་ཉིད་ཀྱང་ཡིན་པའི་གཞི་མཐུན་པ་ཡོད་པའི་ཕྱིར་རོ།
>
> *de tak kyi de drup kyi ngö kyi drup che chö su sung ja yang yin tsen nyi kyang yin pe shi tun pa yö pe chir ro*
>
> This is so because they ["fire perceived by valid cognition" and "hot and burning"] are a combination of being both the explicit

quality to be proved in that proof when using that reason to prove it and a definition.

purpose

Now, what is the purpose of studying *dre tak*, reasons of effect? First we have to understand *gyu(n) dre gyi drel wa*, the relationship that exists between cause and effect. These two, cause and effect, are not *ngo wo chik pe drel wa*, related through being of the same nature, but rather *ngo wo ta te pe drel wa* or *de jung drel*[31] related with different natures.

Du den gyi la la chö chen, me yö te, du wa yö pe chir, she pe tak te, dre tak, Consider smoke on a mountain pass, there is fire, because there is smoke, when we make this statement, the reason used here is a reason of effect. Smoke and fire are related through *de jung drel*, a causal relationship. *Me pen dok che du me na, dre bu du wa mi jung wa*, If there is no fire to act as the producer, its result, smoke, will not arise. Therefore, smoke is related to fire through relying upon it. In any relationship that exists between a cause and its result, without *pen dok che*, a producer, no result, whether good or bad can emerge.

This explanation should reveal the essential purpose for studying this kind of reason in logic, which is to gain a firm understanding of *le dang dre*, karma and its results. These logical statements illustrate *dre tak*, reasons of effect, through using various external examples such as smoke on a mountain pass, fire, sound, and so forth. However, what are not mentioned here but only implied are examples of *dre tak*, reasons of effect, as applied to our inner condition. Inner reasons of effect are far more important than those outer ones.

---

[31] ཆོས་དེ་དང་རྫས་ཐ་དད་པའི་སྒོ་ནས་ཆོས་དེའི་འབྲས་བུའི་རིགས་སུ་གནས་པ།
དེ་བྱུང་འབྲེལ་གྱི་མཚན་ཉིད།

The definition of causal relationship is that kind of relationship of phenomena whereby a phenomenon's effect is of a different substantial entity than its cause.

Ge wa, Happiness, any happiness relies upon its own unique causes. Without its causes, or *pen dok che*, helpers, to promote it, of course a result cannot arise. For example, a sprout needs dirt, water, heat, and fertilizer as its *pen dok che*, helpers, to assist in its growth. No sprout could grow without them.

We can talk about inner attainments in a similar way; *ngön to dang nge lek*, higher realms and nirvana, for instance. What does "higher" refer to here? Higher than what? Than the three lower realms. In order to achieve a future life in the higher realms, you have to collect its unique causes. Without those unique causes, you cannot achieve it. What, then, are those unique causes? Their principal cause is none other than morality.

Nge lek, Nirvana, [in the higher school systems] refers to *tar pa dang tam che kyen pe go pang*, the status of liberation and omniscience. *Nge* means definite, perfect; *lek* means good. To achieve that status you have to practice to gain knowledge and abandon all obstacles. Therefore, the main purpose for studying *dre tak*, reasons of effect, is to realize nicely the infallibly tight relationship between inner causes and inner effects, namely, that of karma and its results.

Perfect reason of same nature

།གཉིས་པ་ནི།

nyi pa ni

The second [type of reason]:

The first reason explained is *dre tak*, a reason of effect. The second type is *rang shin gyi tak*, a reason of same nature.

རྣམ་འགྲེལ་ལས། རང་བཞིན་ཡོད་ཙམ་དང་། འབྲེལ་བ་ཅན་གྱི་ངོ་བོ་ཡང་།

།ཞེས་པས་བསྟན་ཏེ།

nam drel le, rang shin yö tsam dang, drel wa chen gyi ngo wo yang, she pe ten te

The *Commentary to (Dignāga's) "Compendium of Valid Cognition"* says: "Just by having that nature, it automatically has a perfect relationship of nature. Also…"

འདི་ལ་མཚན་ཉིད་སོགས་གསུམ་གྱི་དང་པོ།

di la tsen nyi sok sum gyi dang po

Regarding this [reason of same nature], the first of three parts: its definition, and so forth.

"The three" refer to the definition, classifications, and proofs for reasons of same nature.

རང་བཞིན་གྱི་ཚུལ་གསུམ་ཡིན་པ། རང་བཞིན་གྱི་རྟགས་ཡང་དག་གི་མཚན་

ཉིད།

rang shin gyi tsul sum yin pa, rang shin gyi tak yang dak gi tsen nyi

The definition of a perfect reason of same nature is that which is the three modes of same nature.

Or more specifically,

དེ་སྒྲུབ་ཀྱི་རང་བཞིན་གྱི་ཚུལ་གསུམ་ཡིན་པ། དེ་སྒྲུབ་ཀྱི་རང་བཞིན་གྱི་རྟགས་ཡང་དག་གི་མཚན་ཉིད།

de drup kyi rang shin gyi tsul sum yin pa, de drup kyi rang shin gyi tak yang dak gi tsen nyi

The definition of a perfect reason of same nature in that proof is that which is the three modes of same nature in that proof.

Another way to formulate the definition is as follows:

ཡང་ན་ཁྱོད་དེ་སྒྲུབ་ཀྱི་རྟགས་ཡང་དག་གང་ཞིག །ཁྱོད་ཀྱི་རྟགས་ཀྱིས་དེ་སྒྲུབ་ཀྱི་དངོས་ཀྱི་བསྒྲུབ་བྱའི་ཆོས་སུ་གཟུང་བྱ་ཡིན་ན་ཁྱོད་དང་བདག་ཉིད་གཅིག་ཡིན་དགོས་པའི་ཆ་ནས་བཞག་པ་དེ། ཁྱོད་དེ་སྒྲུབ་ཀྱི་རང་བཞིན་གྱི་རྟགས་ཡང་དག་གི་མཚན་ཉིད།

yang na kyö de drup kyi tak yang dak gang shik, kyö kyi tak kyi de drup kyi ngö kyi drup che chö su sung ja yin na kyö dang dak nyi chik yin gö pe cha ne shak pa de, kyö de drup kyi rang shin gyi tak yang dak gi tsen nyi

Or again, the definition of a perfect reason of same nature in a proof is that which is a perfect reason in that proof, and when posited, should be of the same nature as what is held as the explicit quality to be proved in that proof using that reason to prove it.

For example, *dra chö chen, mi tak te, che pa yin pe chir, she gö pe tse*, when we make the statement, consider sound, it is impermanent, because it is produced, *che pa*, produced, is *rang shin gyi tak yang dak*, a perfect reason of same nature. *De drup kyi ngö gyi drup che chö su sung ja*, What is held as the explicit quality to be proved in that statement, is *mi tak pa*, impermanent. What is *de drup kyi tak yang dak*, the perfect reason in that proof? *Che pa*, Produced. Impermanent things are *che pa*, produced, because their causes have gathered together to make them.

Now, is it the case that *mi tak pa yin na che pa yin pe kyap*, if something is impermanent must it be produced? *Kyap*, That must be the case. Consequently, you cannot find anything *mi tak pa yin che pa ma yin*, impermanent but not produced. If something exists as an impermanent entity, it must exist as an entity that has *rang shin*, the nature, of a produced thing. Produced things and impermanent things are *dak nyi chik,*[32] of the same nature. *Dak nyi chik*, *rang shin chik*, and *ngo wo chik*, of the same nature, are synonyms. Given that, we can state: *mi tak pa yin na kyö dang dak nyi chik pe cha ne shak gö pa*, if something is impermanent, [anything] you posit [as a perfect reason to prove it] must be of one nature with it. If it is not of the same nature, then it cannot be a perfect reason. *Cha ne shak pa*

---

[32] ཆོས་དེ་དང་བདག་གཅིག་འབྲེལ་གྱི་མཚན་ཉིད་ཡོད་དེ། ཁྱོད་ཆོས་དེ་དང་བདག་ཉིད་གཅིག་པའི་སྒོ་ནས་ཐ་དད། ཆོས་དེ་མེད་ན་ཁྱོད་མེད་དགོས་པའི་ཆོས་དེ་དེ་ཡིན་པའི་ཕྱིར།

chö de dang dak chik drel gyi tsen nyi yö de, kyö chö de dang dak nyi chik pe go ne ta te, chö de me na kyö me gö pe chö de de yin pe chir

The definition of a relationship of nature is [a relationship of] two different phenomena with one and the same nature such that if the one phenomenon did not exist, the other would necessarily not exist.

means to establish it. That is, in order for it to serve as a perfect reason it should be established that way.

In the statement: *du den gyi la la chö chen, me yö te, du wa yö pe chir*, consider smoke on a mountain pass, there must be fire, because there is smoke, the main relationship between the quality to be proved, in this case *me*, fire, and the reason in that proof used to prove it, *du wa*, smoke, is not *dak nyi chik*, of one nature, but rather *dak nyi ta te pe drel wa*, a relationship of different natures, or *de jung drel*, a causal relationship, and as such is a perfect reason of effect and not a reason of same nature.

དབྱེ་ན། དེར་གྱུར་པའི་ཁྱད་པར་ལྟོས་པ་བའི་དེ་དང་། ཁྱད་པར་དགག་པ་བའི་དེ་
གཉིས་སོ། །དང་པོ་ལ་དེར་གྱུར་པའི་རང་གི་བྱེད་ཆོས་དངོས་སུ་འཕངས་པ་དང་།
ཤུགས་ལ་འཕངས་པ་གཉིས།

ye na, der gyur pe kye par tö pa we de dang, kye par dak pa we de nyi so, dang po la der gyur pe rang gi che chö ngö su pang pa dang, shuk la pang pa nyi

(Reasons of same nature) can be classified into two types: 1) reasons of same nature suggesting an agent, and 2) reasons of same nature not suggesting an agent. This first one also has two kinds consisting of 1) those that indicate an agent directly, and 2) those that indicate an agent indirectly.

Kye par means quality or characteristic. For example, *dra*, sound, is *kye shi*, the basis, and *dra'i mi tak pa*, sound's impermanence, is *dra'i kye par* or *dra'i kye chö*, sound's quality. *Rang gi che chö ngö su pang pa* means indicating its quality directly; *rang gi che chö shuk la pang pa* means indicating its quality indirectly.

reason of same nature suggesting an agent directly

དང་པོ་ནི། སྒྲ་ཆོས་ཅན། མི་རྟག་སྟེ། སྐྱེས་པ་ཡིན་པའི་ཕྱིར་ཞེས་བཀོད་པའི་ཚེ་
སྐྱེས་པ་ལྟ་བུ།

dang po ni, dra chö chen, mi tak te, kye pa yin pe chir, she kö pe tse kye pa ta bu

The first: Consider sound, it is impermanent, because it is created, when we make this statement, "being created" is an example (of a reason of same nature suggesting an agent directly).

In the statement above *kye pa*, created, shows *kye chö*, a characteristic, of sound, which is indicated directly in this statement. Although *kye pa*, created, and *che pa*, produced, are very close in meaning, *kye pa*, however, is slightly stronger and implies something or someone involved in the act of creation. *What* produced it? *Who* produced it? *Gyu dang kyen*, Causes and conditions, are sound's producers since sound is impermanent. *Kye pa*, Being created, as *kye chö*, a quality of sound, also possesses this nature of impermanence. What is the main characteristic of a created thing or a produced thing? *Ke chik ma*, Being momentary.

reason of same nature suggesting an agent indirectly

གཉིས་པ་ནི། དེ་ཆོས་ཅན། མི་རྟག་སྟེ། བྱས་པའི་ཕྱིར་ཞེས་བཀོད་པའི་ཚེ་བྱས་
པ་ལྟ་བུ།

nyi pa ni, de chö chen, mi tak te, che pe chir, she kö pe tse che pa ta bu

> The second (reason of same nature suggesting an agent indirectly) is "produced" in the statement: Consider sound, it is impermanent, because it is produced.

Dra chö chen, mi tak te, che pa yin pe chir, she gö pe tse, che pa dang shuk la pang pa, When we make the statement, consider sound, it is impermanent, because it is produced, being produced is a quality that is indicated indirectly. *Che pa*, Produced, is not as strong a word as *kye pa*, created. *Che pa*, Produced, as a weaker term than *kye pa*, created, indicates its quality indirectly, since it does not specify by what or in what manner the subject was produced. This is the meaning of *shuk la pang pa*, indicating indirectly.

reason of same nature not suggesting an agent

དགག་པ་བ་ནི། དེ་ཆོས་ཅན། མི་རྟག་སྟེ། དངོས་པོ་ཡིན་པའི་ཕྱིར་ཞེས་པའི་རྟགས་ལྟ་བུ།

dak pa wa ni, de chö chen, mi tak te, ngö po yin pe chir, she pe tak ta bu

> Regarding a reason of same nature not suggesting an agent, [an example is] the reason used in the statement: Consider something, it is impermanent, because it is a causally effective thing.

In the statement above *ngö po*, causally effective thing, is *dak pa wa*, a nature not suggesting an agent. If something is a causally effective thing, it must be impermanent since that is its nature. *Mi tak pa*, Impermanent, and *ngö po*, causally effective thing, are virtually synonymous.

སྐད་ཅིག་མ་དེ་སྒྲ་མི་རྟག་པར་སྒྲུབ་པར་བྱེད་པའི་ཤུགས་ཀྱི་བསྒྲུབ་བྱའི་ཆོས་
སུ་གཟུང་བྱ་ཡིན་གྱི།

ke chik ma de dra mi tak par drup par che pe shuk kyi drup che chö su sung ja yin gyi

Momentary is what is held as the implicit quality to be proved in proving sound as impermanent, but...

Ke chik ma, Momentary, is the definition of *mi tak pa*, impermanent, which is *tsön ja*, the object to be defined [by that definition]. As a definition, it is what is implied when the object to be defined is being used as a quality to be proved. When we make the statement: *dra chö chen, mi tak te, ke chik ma yin pe chir*, consider sound, it is impermanent, because it is momentary, this *tak*, reason, is *ta nye drup kyi tak yang dak*, a perfect reason establishing a term. *Kye chö*, The quality, [of the subject, sound] is *mi tak pa*, impermanent, and as such is *ta nye*, the term, or *tsön ja*, object to be defined. Because the definition of impermanent is used as a perfect reason in this proof, it [the definition] cannot also be used as *drup che chö*, the quality to be proved, in this proof.

དངོས་ཀྱི་བསྒྲུབ་བྱའི་ཆོས་སུ་གཟུང་བྱ་མིན་ལ་དེའི་དངོས་ཀྱི་བསྒྲུབ་བྱའི་ཆོས་
ལ་ནི་མི་རྟག་པ་ཉིད་འཇོག་ཅིང་།

ngö kyi drup che chö su sung ja min la de ngö kyi drup che chö la ni mi tak pa nyi jok ching

...it is not what is held as the explicit quality to be proved since only impermanent itself is what is posited as the explicit quality to be proved in that proof.

འོན་ཀྱང་དེའི་དངོས་ཀྱི་བསྒྲུབ་བྱའི་ཆོས་ནི་མི་རྟག་པར་བཞག་ཏུ་མི་རུང་ངོ་།

> *wön kyang de ngö kyi drup che chö ni mi tak par shak tu mi rung ngo*
>
> Nevertheless, it is not suitable to put forth impermanent as its explicit quality to be proved.

Why is this so? This is explained by a general logic rule. *Mi tak pa*, Impermanent, is *ngö kyi drup che chö*, the explicit quality to be proved. However, it is not suitable to posit *mi tak pa*, impermanent, as *de'i ngö kyi drup che chö*, the explicit quality to be proved in that proof, because *ngö kyi drup che chö* ["explicit quality to be proved," the abstract quality] is *tak pa*, a permanent entity. Why? Because *tak chö dön sum tak pa yin*, the reason, quality, and the subject [as an abstract group] are permanent phenomena. Although *ngö kyi drup che chö yin na mi tak pa yin pe kyap*, whatever *is* the quality to be proved [in that proof] must necessarily be an impermanent phenomenon, nevertheless, *ngö kyi drup che chö*, "the explicit quality to be proved," itself, is *tak pa*, a permanent phenomenon, and not *mi tak pa*, impermanent. That is why it says above, "it is not suitable to posit it as impermanent." Now, you'll have to stay in retreat for at least three weeks to think about this.

It is for this same reason that *me yö pa*, the existence of fire, is *ngö kyi drup che chö su sung ja yin*, the explicit object held as the quality to be proved [in that proof], but *ngö kyi drup che chö ma yin*, not the explicit quality to be proved. *Ngö kyi drup che chö*, The explicit quality to be proved, is *me*, fire. The explicit quality to be proved should be *rang shin chik*, of the same nature, with the reason. However, if the abstraction "explicit quality to be proved" itself is *tak pa*, a permanent entity, it cannot be *che pa*, a produced thing, since permanent and impermanent entities are contradictory and definitely not of the same nature.

reason of same nature that engages
the similar class as a pervader
and
reason of same nature that engages
the similar class in two ways

ཡང་དེ་ལ་མཐུན་ཕྱོགས་ལ་ཁྱབ་བྱེད་དུ་འཇུག་པའི་དེ་དང་མཐུན་ཕྱོགས་ལ་རྣམ་གཉིས་སུ་འཇུག་པའི་དེ་གཉིས་ཡོད་དེ། བྱས་པ་དེ་སྒྲ་མི་རྟག་པར་སྒྲུབ་པར་བྱེད་པའི་དང་པོ་དང་། བྱས་པའི་བྱེ་བྲག་དེ་དེ་སྒྲུབ་ཀྱི་གཉིས་པ་ཡིན་པའི་ཕྱིར།

yang de la tun chok la kyap che du juk pe de dang tun chok la nam nyi su juk pe de nyi yö de, che pa de dra mi tak par drup par che pe dang po dang, che pe che drak de de drup kyi nyi pa yin pe chir

There is also another way of classifying reasons of same nature into two: 1) that which engages the similar class as a pervader, and 2) that which engages the similar class in two ways. An example of the first is the reason "produced" that is used to prove sound as impermanent. An example of the second is any particular of product that is used as a reason in that proof.

སྒྲུབ་བྱེད་ནི་རང་བཞིན་གྱི་རྟགས་ཡང་དག་གི་མཚན་ཉིད་གོ་བ་དང་སྦྱར་ནས་བཞག་པ་དེས་ཤེས་པར་བྱའོ།

drup che ni rang shin gyi tak yang dak gi tsen nyi go wa dang jar ne shak pa de she par ja'o

A correct proof can be understood through a presentation and application of the definition of a perfect reason of same nature.

A correct proof may be presented this way. *Che pa chö chen, dra mi tak par drup par che pe rang shin gyi tak yang dak yin te, kyö de drup kyi tak yang dak gang shik, kyö kyi tak kyi ngö kyi drup che chö su sung je tso wo yin*, Consider product, it is a perfect reason of same nature that proves that sound is impermanent, because 1) it is a perfect reason in that proof, and 2) through using it as a sign, it is the principal object held as [being of the same nature as] the explicit quality to be proved. For this reason, when proving sound as impermanent, *che pa*, product, is a perfect reason of same nature used to prove it.

PERFECT REASON OF NON-OBSERVATION

།གསུམ་པ་མ་དམིགས་པའི་རྟགས་ཡང་དག་ལ་མཚན་ཉིད་དང་དབྱེ་བ་གཉིས།

sum pa ma mik pe tak yang dak la tsen nyi dang ye wa nyi

The third section, perfect reason of non-observation, has two parts: its definition and classifications.

Of the three perfect reasons—reasons of effect, reasons of same nature, and reasons of non-observation—this is the third. In his autocommentary to the *Commentary to* (*Dignāga's*) *"Compendium of Valid Cognition,"* the great Dharmakīrti states:

།དེ་ལ་གཉིས་ནི་དངོས་པོ་བསྒྲུབ་པ་ཡིན་ལ། །གཅིག་ནི་དགག་པའི་གཏན་ཚིགས་སོ།

de la nyi ni ngö po drup pa yin la, chik ni gak pe ten tsik so

Two reasons prove positive entities and one proves a negative entity.

This means that *dre tak*, reasons of effect, and *rang shin gyi tak*, reasons of same nature, are *drup tak yang dak*, perfect positive reasons, whereas *ma mik pe tak*, reasons of non-observation, are *gak tak yang dak*, perfect negative reasons. This accords with the following definition.

དང་པོ་ནི། ཁྱོད་དེ་སྒྲུབ་ཀྱི་རྟགས་ཡང་དག་གང་ཞིག །ཁྱོད་ཀྱི་རྟགས་ཀྱིས་དེ་སྒྲུབ་ཀྱི་དངོས་ཀྱི་བསྒྲུབ་བྱའི་ཆོས་སུ་གཟུང་བྱ་ཡང་ཡིན། དགག་པ་ཡང་ཡིན་

པའི་གཞི་མཐུན་སྲིད་པ་དེ། ཁྱོད་དེ་སྒྲུབ་ཀྱི་མ་དམིགས་པའི་རྟགས་ཡང་དག་
གི་མཚན་ཉིད།

dang po ni, kyö de drup kyi tak yang dak gang shik, kyö kyi tak kyi de drup kyi ngö kyi drup che chö su sung ja yang yin, gak pa yang yin pe shi tun si pa de, kyö de drup kyi ma mik pe tak yang dak gi tsen nyi

The first: the definition of a perfect reason of non-observation in a proof is something that is a possible combination of a perfect reason in that proof and what is held as the explicit quality to be proved in that proof using that reason to prove it is a negative phenomenon.

དབྱེ་ན་མི་སྣང་བ་མ་དམིགས་པའི་རྟགས་ཡང་དག་དང་། སྣང་རུང་མ་
དམིགས་པའི་རྟགས་ཡང་དག་གོ

ye na mi nang wa ma mik pe tak yang dak dang nang rung ma mik pe tak yang dak go

When classifying perfect reasons of non-observation there are two: 1) a perfect reason of non-observation of the non-appearing, and 2) a perfect reason of non-observation of the suitable to appear.

To examine the material just covered:

***

—*Mi nang wa ma mik pe tak la ye na ka tsö yö*, When classifying reasons of non-observation, how many are there?
—*Nyi yö*, Two.
—*Nyi me par tel, nyi po te re re ne trang gyu me pe chir*, There are not two, since I'm sure you can't count each one. (If there is only one, then you must say "*shak gyu me pe chir*"; if there are

more than one, you have to say "*trang gyu me pe chir.*" This means, "Can you count them?")

—*Tak ma drup*, That's not true. Of course I can count them.

—*Nyi po te re re ne trang gyu yö par tel*, So you can count each one of them?

—*Dö*, Yes.

—*Trong shok*, Okay, count them!

—*Mi nang wa ma mik pe tak yang dak dang nang rung ma mik pe tak yang dak nyi*, A perfect reason of non-observation of the non-appearing and a perfect reason of non-observation of the suitable to appear.

[Such an exchange may be used as a template for identifying and listing various classifications by substituting the subject where appropriate.]

---

reason of non-observation of the non-appearing

དང་པོ་ནི། མདོ་ལས། གང་ཟག་གིས་གང་ཟག་གི་ཚོད་གཟུང་བར་མི་བྱ་སྟེ། ཉམས་པར་གྱུར་ཏ་རེ། ཞེས་རང་ལ་མི་སྣང་བ་ཙམ་གྱིས་གཞན་ལ་ཡོན་ཏན་དེ་ལྟ་བུ་མེད་ཅེས་འཆད་མི་རིགས་པའི་དོན་སྟོན་པ་ལ།

dang po ni, do le, gang sak gi gang sak gi tsö sung war mi ja te, nyam par gyur ta re, she rang la mi nang wa tsam gyi shen la yön ten de ta bu me je che mi rik pe dön tön pa la

This first (a perfect reason of non-observation of the non-appearing) is referred to in Sūtra: "You should not judge the qualities of another person. If you do, you will fall." This passage is teaching the impropriety of thinking that just because the good qualities of another person are not apparent to you, that person doesn't have those good qualities.[33]

རྣམ་འགྲེལ་ལས། ཚད་མ་རྣམས་ནི་མི་འཇུག་པ། །མེད་ལ་མི་འཇུག་འབྲས་བུ་ཅན། །ཞེས་སོགས་ཀྱིས་བསྟན་ཏེ་

nam drel le, tse ma nam ni mi juk pa me la mi juk dre bu chen, she sok kyi ten te

As it says in the *Commentary to (Dignāga's) "Compendium of Valid Cognition"*: "Without having valid cognition[s], it's a perfect reason to prove that you don't have it [subsequent cognition]."

This passage is rooted in Sūtra. However, this text by Dharmakīrti, which expresses such meanings very succinctly, is the main source for the explication of reasons of non-observation.

---

33 Regarding this, Gyaltsab Je, in his work *Clearing the Path to Liberation* (***rnam 'grel thar lam gsal byed***), further explains this quotation from Sūtra:

མདོ་ལས། ངའམ་ང་དང་འདྲ་བས་གང་ཟག་གི་ཚོད་བཟུང་གི་གང་ཟག་གིས་གང་ཟག་གི་ཚོད་མི་བཟུང་སྟེ། ཉམས་པར་འགྱུར་ཏ་རེ་ཞེས་གསུངས་པའི་དོན་ཡིན་པས་རྒྱུ་མཚན་མ་མཐོང་བཞིན་དུ་གང་ཟག་འདི་སྐྱོན་འདི་དག་དང་བཅས་སོ། །ཡོན་ཏན་ཙུང་ཟད་ཀྱང་མེད་དོ་ཞེས་སམ་འདི་དང་འདི་ལས་གཞན་མེད་དོ་ཞེས་ཙུང་ཟད་ཀྱང་སྨྲ་བར་མི་བྱ་འོ་ཞེས་པའི་དོན་ནོ།

"In Sūtra, Buddha said: 'I alone or someone like me can guess the quality of another person. However, if someone is not me or not like me, they shouldn't try to guess another person's level. Why? Because they will fall.' Reasons of non-observation are used to teach the impropriety of thinking, 'This person has such and such faults; he doesn't even have the slightest good qualities.' Or, 'He has no other qualities than such and such.' It is improper to even mention such things."

འདི་ལ་བཞི། མཚན་ཉིད། འཇུག་དུས། དབྱེ་བ། དགོས་པ་སོགས་ལས།

di la shi, tsen nyi, juk du, ye wa, gö pa sok le

There are four parts (to the explanation of reasons of non-observation of the non-appearing): its definition, when to use it, classifications, purpose for using it, and so forth. Among these…

མི་སྣང་བ་མ་དམིགས་པའི་ཚུལ་གསུམ་ཡིན་པ། མི་སྣང་བ་མ་དམིགས་པའི་རྟགས་ཡང་དག་གི་མཚན་ཉིད། དེ་སྒྲུབ་ཀྱི་མི་སྣང་བ་མ་དམིགས་པའི་ཚུལ་གསུམ་ཡིན་པ། དེ་སྒྲུབ་ཀྱི་མི་སྣང་བ་མ་དམིགས་པའི་རྟགས་ཡང་དག་གི་མཚན་ཉིད།

mi nang wa ma mik pe tsul sum yin pa, mi nang wa ma mik pe tak yang dak gi tsen nyi, de drup kyi mi nang wa ma mik pe tsul sum yin pa, de drup kyi mi nang wa ma mik pe tak yang dak gi tsen nyi

The definition of a perfect reason of non-observation of the non-appearing is that which is the three modes of non-observation of the non-appearing. The definition of a perfect reason of non-observation of the non-appearing in a proof is that which is the three modes of non-observation of the non-appearing in that proof.

གོ་བ་དང་སྦྱར་བ་ནི་སྒྲ་བཤད་ཀྱིས་ཤེས་ལ། འཇུག་དུས་ནི། དགག་གཞི་སྣང་རུང་ཡིན་ཡང་དེ་སྒྲུབ་ཀྱི་དགག་བྱའི་ཆོས་སུ་བཏགས་པའི་དོན་དེ་རྒོལ་བ་དེའི་ངོར་སྣང་དུ་མི་རུང་ན། མི་སྣང་བ་མ་དམིགས་པའི་རྟགས་སུ་འཇོག་ཅིང།

དེའི་སྒོ་ནས་སྒྲ་བཤད་ཀྱང་ཤེས་པར་བྱའོ།

> *go wa dang jar wa ni dra she kyi she la, juk du ni, gak shi nang rung yin yang de drup kyi gak che chö su tak pe dön de göl wa te ngo wor nang du mi rung na, mi nang wa ma mik pe tak su jok ching, de go ne dra she kyang she par ja'o*
>
> One can understand and apply [this reason] through explaining the term. Let's consider occasions when it is used. Although it is a basis of negation that is suitable to appear, if the object ascribed as the quality to be refuted in that proof is essentially not something that is suitable to appear to [a particular] opponent, one must posit a reason of non-observation of the non-appearing. It is in this way that one should understand this term.

Now, we will explain a perfect reason of non-observation of the non-appearing using a classic example as follows. *Dun gyi shi dir chö chen, sha sa kel dön du song we gang sak gi gyu la de nge che gyi che she dön tun me de, gang sak de gyu la de sha sa mik che kyi tse ma me pe chir*, Consider this place in front, there doesn't exist a factually concordant subsequent cognition that remembers a ghost in the mind of a person who has doubt about the existence of ghosts, because in the mind of that person there was no valid cognition perceiving a ghost [in the first place].

Can you see any ghosts on this table? No. In Tibetan we call ghosts *sha sa*, *bar do wa*, *si pa bar ma*, or *dri sa.*[34] If you can't see any ghosts on this table, do you doubt whether or not there are ghosts here? Maybe there are, maybe there aren't. *Kel dön* means a kind of doubt or skepticism toward that which is beyond a person's perceptual powers; that is, what is not perceptible to *that* person is what is being called into question. [This term is explained in more detail later.]

Although you may have doubt about whether or not there are ghosts on this table, Buddha, on the other hand, doesn't have any

---

[34] ཤ་ཟ། བར་དོ་བ། སྲིད་པ་བར་མ། དྲི་ཟ།

doubt. Also, there are some people who have *ngön she*, clairvoyance, special kinds of awareness that allow them to perceive beings like ghosts. If there are ghosts on this table, they are able to see them. If there are no ghosts on this table, they won't see them nor will they have any doubt in this regard.

Dun gyi shi dir means in this place in front. *Kel dön du song we gang sak* means any person who has some doubt or uncertainty. *Gang sak*, *dak*, *kye bu* are all synonyms for person. *Sha sa mik che kyi tse ma* means the valid cognition that has perceived a ghost. *Nge che* in the phrase *sha sa nge che kyi che she dön tun*[35] means factually concordant or true recollection. To express this sometimes we say such things as: "I heard it, I saw it, I remember it." These are different from "I hear it, I see it," and so forth, in so far as the former reveal that something has been previously perceived as opposed to something being presently perceived.

Che she means subsequent cognition. *Rang gi nyer len du gyur pe tse ma nga me tok sin tok pe dön la nen ne dzin pe rik pa che she kyi tsen nyi*,[36] The definition of subsequent cognition is a mind that holds firmly to an object previously realized by valid cognition, which acts as its substantial cause. The abbreviated definition of subsequent cognition is *tok sin tok pe rik pa*, realizing what has previously been realized. *Nyer len* means substantial cause, in this case referring to mind as a producer. *Tse ma nga me*, By previous valid cognition, can be direct valid cognition or inferential valid cognition. *Tok sin tok pe* means "having already perceived its object" and is the producer of this subsequent mind through perceiving [a mental image of] that same object again. *Nen ne dzin pa* means holding it steadily. *Rik pa* means mind or something mental. Therefore, this kind of mind had a previous *tse ma*, valid cognition, and is holding it.

---

[35] *Dön tun* (**don mthun**) is a term that implies a certain concordance with reality insofar as, were you to try to find your object, it would be findable.

[36] རང་གི་ཉེར་ལེན་དུ་གྱུར་པའི་ཚད་མ་སྔ་མས་རྟོགས་ཟིན་རྟོགས་པའི་དོན་ལ་མནན་ནས་འཛིན་པའི་རིག་པ། བཅད་ཤེས་ཀྱི་མཚན་ཉིད།

What is the definition of *tse ma*, valid cognition? *Sar du mi lu we rik pa tse me tsen nyi*,[37] The definition of valid cognition is a new, infallible mind. This is the definition of valid cognition according to the Vaibhāṣhika, Sautrāntika, Chittamātra, and Svātantrika schools. However, the Prāsaṅgikas do not accept this as a definition for valid cognition. Instead, they render the definition as *rang gi dzin tang gyi yul gyi tso wo la mi lu we rik pa tse me tsen nyi*,[38] the definition of valid cognition is a mind that is infallible with regard to its principal object according to the way of apprehending it. Why do they say this? Because in the Prāsaṅgika school, *che she*, subsequent cognition, is considered a kind of valid cognition. This qualification of subsequent cognition as a kind of valid cognition is one of the eighteen unique tenets of this school, which holds that a realization does not have to be *sar du*, "new," in order for it to qualify as valid cognition.[39]

A person who has doubt as to whether or not there is a ghost in the space in front of him is *chir göl yang dak*, a suitable recipient of this logical statement. Such a person's mind cannot have a factually concordant subsequent cognition that corresponds to a previous valid cognition of a ghost in the space in front of him, because he didn't have a prior valid perception of a ghost in front of him. This is the kind of person who is rejecting the fact that there is a ghost on this table. As previously mentioned, the definition of a perfect opponent to debate with on this occasion [with respect to this specific logical statement] is a debater who ascertains by valid cognition the reason, the quality to be proved, and the subject of debate, but has doubt about the thesis.

Gak shi, A basis of negation, can be this table, for instance. Can you see this table? Yes. Why? *Nang rung yin pe chir*, Because it is fitting that it appears to you. *Yin yang* means but. *De drup gyi gak*

---

[37] གསར་དུ་མི་སླུ་བའི་རིག་པ། ཚད་མའི་མཚན་ཉིད།

[38] རང་གི་འཛིན་སྟངས་ཀྱི་ཡུལ་གྱི་རྩོ་བོ་ལ་མི་སླུ་བའི་རིག་པ། ཚད་མའི་མཚན་ཉིད།

[39] This hinges on the fact that this school interprets the Sanskrit prefix "*pra*" of *pramāṇa*, valid cognition, as "most excellent" (***rab***) or "superior" (***mchog***) rather than as "new" or "fresh" (***gsar du***).

che chö su tak pe dön, The object ascribed as the quality to be refuted in this proof, is *sha sa*, a ghost, on this basis i.e., this table. In general, we can say that *gak che chö*, the quality to be refuted, is *sha sa*, a ghost, but we should say more specifically *sha sa yö pa*, the existence of a ghost [on this table]. *Göl wa te ngo wo nang du mi rung na, mi nang wa ma mik pe tak su jok*, If the nature of that object is not suitable to appear to that person [i.e., he doesn't have the "fortune" (***bskal***) or perceptual capacity to perceive it], then one should posit a reason of non-observation of the non-appearing. Would such a reason be *tak yang dak*, a perfect reason, for Buddha? No. That is why something is qualified as a perfect reason relative to the person whom you are trying to convince. So, Buddha in this case would definitely not be *chir göl yang dak*, a perfect person to debate with.

What's the difference between *dre*, demons, and *sha sa*, ghosts? Ghosts only lack physical form. Do demons have a physical form or not? Although there are many kinds of demons, in general, they can be classified into two: *mi dang mi ma yin pa*, human and non-human. Their main function and wish is to hinder Dharma practitioners from practicing. That is their *bak chak*, karmic propensity.

You have to review all of these points. This is a very good chance to learn this material. When you hear somebody talking about this subject in the kitchen, for example, now you can say, "Yes, I know, I know," and maybe even correct them when they get something wrong. You can say, "No, it's not like that, it's like this!"

དེས་ན། ཁྱོད་དེ་སྒྲུབ་ཀྱི་མ་དམིགས་པའི་རྟགས་ཡང་དག་གང་ཞིག །ཁྱོད་དེ་
སྒྲུབ་པ་ལ་ཕྱོགས་ཆོས་ཅན་དུ་སོང་བའི་གང་ཟག་ལ་དགག་བྱའི་ཆོས་སུ་བཏགས་
པའི་དོན་བསྐལ་དོན་ཡང་ཡིན་པའི་གཞི་མཐུན་པ་དེ། ཁྱོད་དེ་སྒྲུབ་ཀྱི་མི་སྣང་བ་
མ་དམིགས་པའི་རྟགས་ཡང་དག་གི་མཚན་ཉིད།

de na, kyö de drup kyi ma mik pe tak yang dak gang shik, kyö de drup pa la chok chö chen du song we gang sak la gak che chö su tak pe dön kel dön yang yin pe shi tun pa de, kyö de drup kyi mi nang wa ma mik pe tak yang dak gi tsen nyi

The definition of a perfect reason of non-observation of the non-appearing in that proof is a combination of being 1) a perfect reason of non-observation in that proof, and 2) what is ascribed as the object to be refuted in that proof is something beyond that appropriate opponent's ability [or fortune] to perceive it and that same person qualifies as a holder of the property of the subject [reason's relevance to the subject] in that proof.

Mi nang wa ma mik pe tak, A reason of non-observation of the non-appearing, and *nang rung ma mik pe tak*, a reason of non-observation of the suitable to appear, are both *ma mik pe tak*, reasons of non-observation, as well as perfect reasons. *Kyö*, It, refers to the reason being defined. *De drup la* means in that proof. *Chok chö chen du song we gang sak* is implying *chir göl yang dak*, a person suitable to debate with.

Gak che chö su tak pe dön, The object ascribed as the quality to be refuted, is *sha sa*, a ghost. *Kel dön*, Doubt, here refers to the doubt in the mind of a person concerning the existence of ghosts, which is why he cannot say whether or not there is a ghost in front of him. *Yang yin pe shi tun pa* means it is a combination of the various qualities [listed in the definition]. *Mi nang wa* means it doesn't appear to him, i.e., he cannot see it. Such a person doesn't have *sha sa mik che kyi tse ma*, a valid cognition that has previously perceived a ghost. If there is no cause, there cannot be any result. For this reason, there cannot possibly be *che she dön tun*, a factually concordant subsequent cognition, because such a mind can only be the result of valid cognition.

དབྱེ་ན། དེར་གྱུར་པའི་འབྲེལ་ཟླ་མ་དམིགས་པའི་རྟགས་དང་། འགལ་ཟླ་
དམིགས་པའི་རྟགས་གཉིས་ལས།

ye na, der gyur pe drel(n) da ma mik pe tak dang gel(n) da mik pe tak nyi le

When classified there are two: 1) reason of non-observation of a related object, and 2) reason of observation of a contradictory object. Of these two…

reason of non-observation of a related object

དང་པོ་ནི། དེ་སྒྲུབ་ཀྱི་མི་སྣང་བ་མ་དམིགས་པའི་རྟགས་ཡང་དག་གང་ཞིག །རང་གི་དངོས་མིང་གི་མཐར་མེད་མིན་སོགས་དགག་ཚིག་ཅི་རིགས་སྦྱར་བའི་ཆོས་དེ། དེ་སྒྲུབ་ཀྱི་མི་སྣང་བའི་འབྲེལ་ཟླ་མ་དམིགས་པའི་རྟགས་ཡང་དག་གི་མཚན་ཉིད།

dang po ni, de drup kyi mi nang wa ma mik pe tak yang dak gang shik, rang gi ngö ming gi tar me min sok gak tsik chi rik jar we chö de, de drup kyi mi nang we drel(n) da ma mik pe tak yang dak gi tsen nyi

Regarding the first (the definition of a perfect reason of non-observation of a non-appearing related object in a proof) is 1) a perfect sign of non-observation of the non-appearing in that proof, as well as 2) a phenomenon to which is applied one of the negative particles such as "*me*" [མེད་] or "*min*" [མིན་] after it in that phrase.

For example, *me* [མེ་] is fire. *Me me pa*, The non-existence of fire is a negative phrase because of the presence of the negative particle "*me* [མེད་]." Or again, we apply "*mi*" before *tak pa*, permanent, to negate it, forming the word *mi tak pa*, meaning <u>*im*</u>permanent.

དེ་ལ་དབྱེ་ན། དེར་གྱུར་པའི་རྒྱུ་མ་དམིགས་པའི་དེ་དང་། ཁྱབ་བྱེད་མ་
དམིགས་པའི་དེ་དང་། རང་བཞིན་མ་དམིགས་པའི་རྟགས་དང་གསུམ་སྟེ།

de la ye na, der gyur pe gyu ma mik pe de dang kyap che ma mik pe de dang rang shin ma mik pe tak dang sum te

When (reasons of non-observation of a non-appearing related object) are classified there are three: 1) a reason of non-observation of the cause, 2) a reason of non-observation of a pervader, and 3) a reason of non-observation of the same nature.

reason of non-observation of the cause

ཁྱད་པར་རྒྱས་པར་ནི་གཞན་དུ་ཤེས་པར་བྱ་ཞིང་མཚོན་ཙམ་ནི། མདུན་གྱི་
གཞི་འདིར་ཆོས་ཅན། ཤ་ཟ་བསྐལ་དོན་དུ་སོང་བའི་གང་ཟག་གི་རྒྱུད་ལ་དེ་
ངེས་པའི་དཔྱད་ཤེས་དོན་མཐུན་མེད་དེ། གང་ཟག་དེའི་རྒྱུད་ལ་དེ་དམིགས་
བྱེད་ཀྱི་ཚད་མ་མེད་པའི་ཕྱིར། ཞེས་པའི་རྟགས་དེ་ལྟ་བུ་དང་པོ་དང་།

kye par gye par ni shen du she par ja shing tsön tsam ni, dun gyi shi dir chö chen, sha sa kel dön du song we gang sak gi gyu la de nge pe che she dön tun me de, gang sak de gyu la de mik che kyi tse ma me pe chir, she pe tak de ta bu dang po dang

If you wish to have a more detailed explanation concerning these, you should consult other texts [such as the *Extensive Explanation* by the same author]. Here, we will only give examples. An example of the first (a reason of non-observation of the cause [of the non-appearing]) is as follows: Consider the place in front, there doesn't exist a factually concordant subsequent cognition that [remembers] a ghost in the mind of a person who has doubt about the existence of ghosts, because in that person's mind there was no valid cognition that perceived [a ghost in the first place].

The cause in this case is *sha sa mik che gyi tse ma*, a valid cognition perceiving a ghost. That person's not having the cause just mentioned is being used as a reason to prove that he cannot have [the effect] a subsequent cognition of a ghost. If he has a subsequent cognition, he should have a memory of having perceived a ghost, which is impossible without having perceived a ghost with his valid cognition in the first place. *Che she dön tun* means a perfect subsequent cognition that is free of any error. It cannot be the result of a mistaken perception like the kind we have when seeing a scarecrow standing at the corner of a field and think, "I wonder who that skinny fellow is over there picking corn."

reason of non-observation of a pervader

མདུན་གྱི་གཞི་འདིར་ཆོས་ཅན། ཤ་ཟ་བསྐལ་དོན་དུ་སོང་བའི་གང་ཟག་གིས་
དེ་ཡོད་ཅེས་དམ་བཅའ་མི་རིགས་ཏེ། །གང་ཟག་དེའི་རྒྱུད་ལ་ཤ་ཟ་དམིགས་
བྱེད་ཀྱི་ཚད་མ་མེད་པའི་ཕྱིར་ཞེས་པ་ལྟ་བུ། དེའི་རྟགས་དེ་གཉིས་པ་དང་།

dun gyi shi dir chö chen, sha sa kel dön du song we gang sak gi de yö che dam ja mi rik te, gang sak de gyu la sha sa mik che kyi tse ma me pe chir she pa ta bu

Consider the place in front, it is improper for a person who has doubt about the existence of ghosts to swear that such a ghost exists there, because in that person's mind there was no [previous] valid perception perceiving a ghost. This is an example of the second (reason of non-observation of a pervader).

Dam ja means to swear the way one does when taking an oath. In the statement above the debater who has doubt about the subject cannot swear that there is a ghost in front of him. If someone were to ask him whether or not there is a ghost on the table, he could not say with certainty whether there is or not. *Yö che* means saying verbally that a ghost does exist. *Dam ja mi rik te* means it is not proper to swear to such a perception. Why? He cannot testify to having perceived the cause [the perception of a ghost] by his valid cognition, because its corresponding result—a subsequent cognition remembering that correct perception—does not exist in his mind. *Dam ja* can be a strong wish, like the wish we have to achieve paradise. On top of making a decision in our mind, we swear by a verbal oath and set out to do something with determination. Similarly, the person who has perceived something by valid cognition should be able to swear with conviction to what he has perceived since he would have perfect *che she*, subsequent cognition, as a result of that perception. "I can swear that I saw a ghost on this table. It was even talking to me."

reason of non-observation of same nature

དེ་ཆོས་ཅན། དེའི་རྒྱུད་ལ་དེ་ངེས་བྱེད་ཀྱི་དཔྱད་ཤེས་དོན་མཐུན་མེད་དེ། དེས་དེ་འདྲ་བ་དེ་ཚད་མས་མ་དམིགས་པའི་ཕྱིར། ཞེས་བཀོད་པའི་ཚེ་རྟགས་དེ་ལྟ་བུ་གསུམ་པའོ།

de'i tak de nyi pa dang, de chö chen, de'i gyu la de nge che kyi che she dön tun me de, de de dra wa de tse me ma mik pe chir, she kö pe tse tak de ta bu sum pa'o

An example of the third (a reason of non-observation of same nature) is the reason given in the statement: Consider the place in front, there doesn't exist a definitive factually concordant subsequent cognition regarding a ghost in the mind of that person, because that person did not perceive such an object [a ghost] by his valid cognition [in the first place].

De chö chen is referring to *dun gyi shi*, the place in front. *De'i gyu la* means in that debater's mind. *Nge che kyi che she dön tun me de* means there cannot be a definitive factually concordant subsequent cognition in his mind. That debater also cannot swear that he had a factually concordant perception of a ghost in the space in front of him, because he doesn't have *che she dön tun*, a factually concordant subsequent cognition, due to the fact of his not having previously perceived a ghost there by his valid cognition. This is an illustration of the third kind of reason of non-observation—*rang shin ma mik pe tak*, a reason of non-observation of same nature [referring to the similar mental nature of valid cognition and subsequent cognition]. *Sha sa mik pe tse ma*, Valid cognition perceiving a ghost, is the basis upon which is applied *sha sa mik che gyi che she dön tun*, a factually concordant subsequent cognition of the perception of a ghost. Because these two factors [valid cognition and subsequent cognition] are *rang shin chik*, of the same nature, what is not observed on this occasion can be used as *rang shin ma mik pe tak*, a reason of non-observation of same nature.

purpose

དགོས་པ་ནི།

gö pa ni

The purpose is explained as follows:

Why study reasons of non-observation?

མདུན་གྱི་གཞི་འདིར་ལྷའི་བར་སྲིད་དང་། ཤ་ཟ་ཡོད་མེད་ཐེ་ཚོམ་ཟ་བའི་བློ་
ནས་བསྐལ་དོན་དུ་སོང་བའི་གང་ཟག་གིས་གཞི་འདིར་དེ་གཉིས་ཡོད་ཅེས་

སམ་མེད་ཅེས་ཐག་གཅོད་དུ་མི་རུང་བ་དཔེར་མཛད་ནས། དོན་ལ་གང་ཟག་
གང་དང་གང་གི་སྐྱོན་ཡོན་རང་གི་ཚད་མས་མ་ངེས་བཞིན་དུ་སྒྲོ་སྐུར་བྱར་མི་
རུང་བར་ཤེས་པའི་ཆེད་དོ།

dun gyi shi dir hla'i bar si dang, sha sa yö me te tsom sa we go ne kel dön du song we gang sak gi shi dir de nyi yö che sam me che tak chö du mi rung wa per dze ne, dön la gang sak gang dang gang gi kyö yön rang gi tse me ma nge shin du dro kur jar mi rung war she pe che do

These examples show that it is improper for a person who has doubt about such things to say, for instance, that there exists either a celestial's bardo being or a ghost in the space in front of him. The purpose for giving these examples is to make one understand that, given that one lacks the capacity to ascertain by valid cognition either the faults or the virtues of another person, it is improper either to exaggerate or underestimate that other person's qualities.

Dun gyi shi dir means here in the space in front. *Hla'i bar si*, The bardo being of a god, is another name for a ghost. *Yö me te tsom sa we* means having doubt about whether or not there is such a ghost in front of him. *Kel dön du song we gang sak* means a person who has doubt about that subject. *De nyi*, Those two, is referring to both a celestial's bardo being and a ghost. *Yö che sam me che tak chö du mi rung wa* means it is not appropriate for him to decide whether or not there are such beings in front of him. *Per dze* means examples. *Dön la* means the main purpose or meaning for using such a reason in a statement like the one above. *Gang sak gang dang gang gi* means any person whatsoever. *Kyön* means faults. In Tibetan this word implies every nature of fault including obstacles, mental afflictions, bad deeds and the like, so the English word "fault" may limit the meaning of this word somewhat. Learning the specific meanings of such words is critical to gaining a more profound understanding of this material. *Yön*, short for *yön ten*, comprises a variety of meanings such as good qualities, knowledge, virtue, excellent manners, and so forth. *Rang gi tse me ma nge shin du* means while [that person] did not ascertain by his valid cognition. *Dro* is short for *dro(n) dok*, which means being false through exaggeration. An example would be praising someone for their excellent qualities when in fact that person lacks such qualities. *Kur* is short for *kur(n) deb*, which means being false through underestimation. An example of this would be putting down or denigrating someone by saying that they lack certain excellent qualities, which they do in fact possess. *Char mi rung* means it is improper to do it. *She pe che do* means the purpose for establishing such reasons is to help you understand this point and shows how useful logic can be.

In short, the main purpose for using reasons of non-observation is in reference to other persons. If someone without valid perceptions perceives faults (*kyön*) in another person, when in fact that other person does not possess those faults, this is an instance of *kur(n) deb*, or putting down that person. Conversely, if someone without valid perceptions perceives good qualities (*yön ten*) in someone who in fact does not possess those qualities, this is an instance of *dro(n) dok*, exaggeration or overestimation. Combined these are known as "*dro kur*."

Now, there should be a great difference between what you are learning here and what you learn by studying other subjects. Here you should gain an understanding of the logical style and the ideas logic engages as well as its general system. This will be very useful for you. If there is no sun, there can be no sunlight.

དེ་སྒྲུབ་ཀྱི་དགག་བྱའི་ཆོས་སུ་བཏགས་པའི་དོན་ཡིན་ན། དེ་སྒྲུབ་ཀྱི་དགག
བྱའི་ཆོས་ཡིན་པས་མ་ཁྱབ་སྟེ། མདུན་གྱི་གཞི་འདིར་ཤ་ཟ་བསྐལ་དོན་དུ་སོང་
བའི་གང་ཟག་གི་རྒྱུད་ལ་ཤ་ཟ་དེས་བྱེད་ཀྱི་དཔྱད་ཤེས་དོན་མཐུན་ཡོད་པ་དེ
དེ་འདྲའི་དཔྱད་ཤེས་དོན་མཐུན་མེད་པར་བསྒྲུབ་པའི་དགག་བྱའི་ཆོས་སུ

བཏགས་པའི་དོན་དང་དེའི་དགག་བྱའི་ཆོས་གཉིས་ཀ་ཡིན་ཀྱང་༑ཤ་ཟ་དང་དེ་
འདྲའི་དཔྱད་༑ཤེས་དོན་མཐུན་གཉིས་རེ་རེ་ནས་དེ་སྒྲུབ་ཀྱི་དགག་བྱའི་ཆོས་སུ་
བཏགས་པའི་དོན་ཡིན་ཀྱང་དེའི་དགག་བྱའི་ཆོས་མ་ཡིན་པའི་ཕྱིར།

de drup kyi gak che chö su tak pe dön yin na, de drup kyi gak che chö yin pe ma kyap te, dun gyi shi dir sha sa kel dön du song we gang sak gi gyu la sha sa nge che kyi che she dön tun yö pa de de(n) dre che she dön tun me par drup pe gak che chö su tak pe dön dang de gak che chö nyi ka yin kyang sha sa dang de(n) dre che she dön tun nyi re re ne de drup kyi gak che chö su tak pe dön yin kyang de gak che chö ma yin pe chir

Whatever is an object ascribed as the quality to be refuted in a proof is not necessarily the quality to be refuted in that proof. [For instance], that there exists a definitive factually concordant subsequent cognition of a ghost in the mind of a person who has doubt about the existence of a ghost in front of him is the object ascribed as the quality to be refuted when proving that there exists no such factually concordant subsequent cognition. Now, although a ghost and the factually concordant subsequent cognition of a ghost are both the ascribed objects of refutation, the object, in this case, [the existence of] ghosts in general, is not what is being refuted.

(*Dun gyi shi dir chö chen*), *sha sa kel dön du song we gang sak gi yul la sha sa nge che kyi che she dön tun yö pa de*, (Consider in the space in front), there does not exist a definitive factually concordant subsequent cognition of a ghost in the mind of a person who has doubt about the existence of ghosts, is *de drup kyi drup che chö*, the quality to be proved in that proof. *Yö pa*, There being [a factually concordant subsequent cognition in such a person's mind], is *de drup kyi gak che chö*, the quality to be refuted in that proof.

The above can be illustrated using the model proof: *dra chö chen, mi tak te, che pa yin pe chir*, consider sound, it is impermanent, because it is produced, the permanence of sound is the quality to be refuted in this proof, and not "permanence" in general, because permanent entities do exist. Well then, do ghosts exist or not? Yes, they do. Does *sha sa che she dön tun*, a factually concordant subsequent cognition of a ghost, exist or not? This depends upon whether or not there was a valid cognition [in that person's mind] of a ghost prior to this cognition. If the valid cognition exists, then the factually concordant subsequent cognition must exist as well. What is *gak che chö*, the quality to be refuted, in the proof above? Is it *sha sa mik che kyi tse me yö pa*, the existence of a valid cognition of a ghost? No, because there are some beings who do have such valid cognitions and so those cognitions do exist. Therefore, a definitive factually concordant subsequent cognition of a ghost in the mind of a person who has doubt about the existence of ghosts, is the quality to be refuted, while *drup che chö*, the quality to be proved, is the non-existence of such a cognition in that person's mind [not the existence of ghosts in general]. The nature of the perceiver is emphasized by including the words *kel dön du song we gang sak gi gyu la*, in the mind of a person who has certain doubts about the subject. Generally, *sha sa*, a ghost, is *yö pa*, an existent, and as such is perceivable by valid cogntion, complying with the definition of an existent. If it exists, then it cannot be refuted [as to its existence].

དང་པོ་སླ།

dang po la

The first is easy.

This means that the first part of the statement given above is easy to establish should anyone try to take up issue with it.

ཕྱི་མ་མ་གྲུབ་ན། ཤ་ཟ་དང་དེ་འདྲའི་དཔྱད་ཤེས་དོན་མཐུན་གཉིས་རེ་རེ་ནས་
དེ་སྒྲུབ་ཀྱི་དགག་བྱའི་ཆོས་སུ་བཏགས་པའི་དོན་ཡིན་ཏེ། དེ་སྒྲུབ་ཀྱི་ཕྱི་རྒོལ་
ཡང་དག་དེས་མདུན་གྱི་གཞི་འདིར་ཤ་ཟ་ཡོད་མེད་ཐེ་ཚོམ་ཟ་བའི་ཕྱིར་དང་།
དེས་དེ་འདྲ་བའི་དཔྱད་ཤེས་དོན་མཐུན་ཡོད་མེད་ཐེ་ཚོམ་ཟ་བའི་ཕྱིར། དེ་
གཉིས་རེ་རེ་ནས་དེ་སྒྲུབ་ཀྱི་དགག་བྱའི་ཆོས་མ་ཡིན་ཏེ། སྤྱིར་ཤ་ཟ་ཡོད་པའི་
ཕྱིར་དང་། དུ་བ་དེ་མཚན་མོའི་རྒྱ་མཚོར་དུ་བ་མེད་པར་བསྒྲུབ་པའི་དགག་
བྱའི་ཆོས་མ་ཡིན་པའི་ཕྱིར།

chi ma ma drup na, sha sa dang de(n) dre che she dön tun nyi re re ne de drup kyi gak che chö su tak pe dön yin te, de drup kyi chir göl yang dak de dun gyi shi dir sha sa yö me te tsom sa we chir dang, de de(n) dra we che she dön tun yö me te tsom sa we chir, de nyi re re ne de drup kyi gak che chö ma yin te, chir sha sa yö pe chir dang, du wa de tsen mö gya tsor du wa me par drup pe gak je chö ma yin pe chir

If someone were to say that the latter assertion is not true, a ghost and the factually concordant subsequent valid cognition of such are both the objects ascribed as the quality to be refuted in that proof, because an appropriate debater has doubt about whether or not there is a ghost in the place in front of him and there is doubt as to whether or not there exists a factually concordant subsequent cognition in the mind of such a person. However, neither of these *is* the quality to be refuted in that proof, because ghosts do exist in general as does smoke, which is [also] not the quality to be refuted [in the statement] proving that there is no smoke on a lake at night.

reason of observation of an object
contradictory to the non-appearing

ཁྱོད་དེ་སྒྲུབ་ཀྱི་མི་སྣང་བ་མ་དམིགས་པའི་རྟགས་ཡང་དག་གང་ཞིག །མ་ཡིན་དགག་དང་སྒྲུབ་པ་གང་རུང་ཡང་ཡིན་པའི་གཞི་མཐུན་པ་དེ། ཁྱོད་དེ་སྒྲུབ་ཀྱི་མི་སྣང་བའི་འགལ་ཟླ་དམིགས་པའི་རྟགས་ཡང་དག་གི་མཚན་ཉིད། ཡོད་པ་དེ་མདུན་གྱི་གཞི་འདིར་ཤ་ཟ་བསྐལ་དོན་དུ་སོང་བའི་གང་ཟག་གི་རྒྱུད་ལ་དེ་ངེས་བྱེད་ཀྱི་དཔྱད་ཤེས་དོན་མཐུན་མེད་པར་བསྒྲུབ་པའི་མི་སྣང་བའི་འགལ་ཟླ་དམིགས་པའི་རྟགས་ཡང་དག་ཡིན་ནོ།

kyö de drup kyi mi nang wa ma mik pe tak yang dak gang shik, ma yin gak dang drup pa gang rung yang yin pe shi tun pa de, kyö de drup kyi mi nang we gel(n) da mik pe tak yang dak gi tsen nyi yö pa de dun gyi shi dir sha sa kel dön du song we gang sak gi gyu la de nge che kyi che she dön tun me par drup pe mi nang we gel(n) da mik pe tak yang dak yin no

The definition of a perfect reason of observation of an object contradictory to the non-appearing in a proof is a combination of being a perfect reason of non-observation of the non-appearing in a proof and is either an implicating negative [*ma yin gak*] or a positive phenomenon [*drup pa*]. That existent [ghost] is a perfect reason of observation of an object contradictory to the non-appearing, which serves to prove that there is no definitive factually concordant subsequent cognition in the mind of a person who has doubt about the existence of ghosts in the space in front of him.

three types of doubt (fortune) related to mind

།བློ་ལ་ལྟོས་པའི་བསྐལ་དོན་ལ་གསུམ་ཡོད་དེ། ཡུལ་དང་དུས་དང་ངོ་བོའི་བསྐལ་དོན་གསུམ་ཡོད་པའི་ཕྱིར། དང་པོ་ནི། རང་དང་ཕྱོགས་ཐག་ཤིན་ཏུ་རིང་བ་ན་ཡོད་པའི་སྣོད་བཅུད་ཀྱི་ཁྱད་པར་ལྟ་བུ། གཉིས་པ་ནི། བསྐལ་པ་འདས་ཟིན་པ་དང་འབྱུང་བའི་དུས་ན་ཛི་འདྲ་བྱུང་བ་དང་འབྱུང་བའི་ཁྱད་པར་ལྟ་བུ་སྟེ། དེ་རྣམས་ནི་སྤྱིར་བསྐལ་དོན་མིན་ཡང་རང་གི་བློ་ལ་ལྟོས་པའི་བསྐལ་དོན་ནོ། །གསུམ་པ་ནི། རང་དང་ཉེ་བ་ན་ཡོད་ཀྱང་ངོ་བོ་ཕྲ་བའི་དབང་གིས་བསྐལ་དོན་དུ་སོང་བ་མདུན་གྱི་ཤ་ཟ་ལྟ་བུ་དང་། ལྷ་མིའི་བར་སྲིད་པ་རྣམས་དང་དེའི་བུམ་པ་ལྟ་བུའོ།

lo la tö pe kel dön la sum yö de, yul dang du dang ngo wö kel dön sum yö pe chir, dang po ni, rang dang chok tak shin tu ring wa na yö pe nö chu kyi kye par ta bu, nyi pa ni, kel pa de sin pa dang jung we du na jin dra jung wa dang jung we kye par ta bu te, de nam ni chir kel dön min yang rang gi lo la tö pe kel dön no, sum pa ni, rang dang nye wa na yö kyang ngo wo tra we wang gi kel dön du song wa dun gyi sha sa ta bu dang, hla mi bar si pa nam dang de bum pa ta bu'o

There are three ways in which doubt [or fortune] (*kel dön*) is produced relative to the mind of an observer: 1) with regard to the object, 2) with regard to time, and 3) with regard to its nature.

With respect to the first, we can use the example of [judging the quality] of a vessel that is placed at a great distance from us whereby, due to the distance of the object, it is beyond our perceptual power of discernment.

With respect to the second, [judging] the quality of something that existed an eon ago, due to time, is beyond our power of discernment.

Although the previous two examples are not beyond our powers of perception in general, [that is, they are not beyond the power of discernment of every being], relative to the mind of a specific person, they may be beyond their power of perception and thereby cause them to have doubt about the subject.

An example of the third is as follows. Even though such beings as ghosts, the bardo being of a god or human, or even the pots those beings are holding, may be close to us, due to their very subtle nature, they are beyond our power of perception.

reason of non-observation of the suitable to appear

།གཉིས་པ་སྣང་རུང་མ་དམིགས་པའི་རྟགས་ནི། རྣམ་འགྲེལ་ལས། གཏན་ཚིགས་བྱེ་བྲག་ལ་ལྟོས་ནས། །འགའ་ཞིག་མེད་ཤེས་འབྲས་བུ་ཅན། །ཞེས་སོགས་ཀྱིས་བསྟན་ཏེ་ལ་གསུམ།

nyi pa nang rung ma mik pe tak ni, nam drel le, ten tsik che drak la tö ne, ga shik me she dre bu chen, she sok kyi ten te la sum

The second reason, a reason of non-observation of the suitable to appear, is mentioned in the *Commentary to (Dignāga's) "Valid Cognition"*: "It is a reason that, in reliance upon a quality [of being suitable to appear if it were present], has the effect [of bringing] knowledge of something's not being present there."[40]

---

[40] Geshe Yeshe Wangchuk in "Ornament of '*The Valid's*' True Intent" comments on these lines as follows:

Nang rung ma mik pe tak, A reason of non-observation of the suitable to appear, can be examined this way. Can you see a rabbit on this table? No. Can you see an elephant here? No. If there were a rabbit or an elephant on this table, would you be able to see them? Yes, you would. This is the meaning of *nang rung*, suitable to appear. In contrast, if there were a ghost on this table, would you be able to see it? No, because you don't have the perceptual capacity to perceive it and so *mi nang wa*, it does not appear, to you. Now, if there were an animal on the table, would you be able to see it? "Yes." Could there be a rabbit on this table but no animal? "No." So if there is no animal on this table, there cannot be a rabbit on this table? "That's right." You can use that as a reason to prove that there is no rabbit on this table. Such a proposition can be stated this way: *dun gyi shi dir chö chen, ri bong me te, du(n) dro me pe chir*, consider this place in front of us, there is no rabbit, because there is no animal [here]. This is the main idea and the way to use reasoning to prove it.

Some *drup che chö*, qualities to be proved, may refer to the absence of something. *Dre bu chen*, Having a result, means that one can gain some knowledge from the [non-appearance of a] result.

འདི་ལ་གསུམ། མཚན་ཉིད། དབྱེ་བ། ཞར་བྱུང་ངོ་།

di la sum, tsen nyi, ye wa, shar jung ngo

Regarding this (a perfect reason of non-observation of the suitable to appear) there are three parts: its definition, classifications, and incidental explanations.

དེས་ཆོས་གང་ཡིན་ཡང་རང་ལ་སྣང་རུང་དུ་ཡོད་པ་དེ་རང་གིས་མ་དམིགས་ན་དེ་མེད་པར་བསྒྲུབ་ནུས་པའི་སྣང་རུང་མ་དམིགས་པའི་རྟགས་བསྟན།

What these lines indicate is that if someone does not perceive a quality that is suitable to appear to that person, [were that quality present] a reason of non-observation of the suitable to appear is able to prove the non-presence of that quality.

།དེའི་དང་པོ་ནི། སྣང་རུང་མ་དམིགས་པའི་ཚུལ་གསུམ་ཡིན་པ། སྣང་རུང་མ་
དམིགས་པའི་རྟགས་ཡང་དག་གི་མཚན་ཉིད། དེ་སྒྲུབ་ཀྱི་སྣང་རུང་མ་དམིགས་
པའི་ཚུལ་གསུམ་ཡིན་པ། དེ་སྒྲུབ་ཀྱི་སྣང་རུང་མ་དམིགས་པའི་རྟགས་ཡང་
དག་གི་མཚན་ཉིད།

de dang po ni, nang rung ma mik pe tsul sum yin pa, nang rung ma mik pe tak yang dak gi tsen nyi, te drup kyi nang rung ma mik pe tsul sum yin pa, de drup kyi nang rung ma mik pe tak yang dak gi tsen nyi

The first of these (the definition of a perfect reason of non-observation of the suitable to appear) is what is the three modes of a reason of non-observation of the suitable to appear. That which is the three modes of a reason of non-observation of the suitable to appear in a proof is the definition of a reason of non-observation of the suitable to appear in a proof.

།གོ་བ་དང་སྦྱར་ན། ཁྱོད་དེ་སྒྲུབ་ཀྱི་མ་དམིགས་པའི་རྟགས་ཡང་དག་གང་ཞིག
ཁྱོད་ཀྱི་རྟགས་ཀྱིས་དེ་སྒྲུབ་ཀྱི་དགག་བྱའི་ཆོས་སུ་བརྟགས་པའི་དོན་དེ་ཡོད་
ན། ཁྱོད་དེ་སྒྲུབ་ལ་ཕྱོགས་ཆོས་ཅན་དུ་སོང་བའི་གང་ཟག་གི་ཚད་མ་ལ་སྣང་
རུང་ཡིན་དགོས་པ། ཁྱོད་དེ་སྒྲུབ་ཀྱི་སྣང་རུང་མ་དམིགས་པའི་རྟགས་ཡང་
དག་གི་མཚན་ཉིད།

go wa dang jar na, kyö de drup kyi ma mik pe tak yang dak gang shik, kyö kyi tak kyi de drup kyi gak che chö su tak pe dön de yö na, kyö de drup la chok chö chen du song we gang

> *sak gi tse ma la nang rung yin gö pa, kyö de drup kyi nang rung ma mik pe tak yang dak gi tsen nyi*
>
> When applying this definition to a specific case to enhance understanding, it is a perfect reason of non-observation in that proof and, whatever exists as an object ascribed as the quality to be refuted in that proof using that reason [to prove it] must be suitable to appear to the valid cognition of a person who qualifies as an appropriate person [having doubt about the subject, and so forth]. Such is the definition of a perfect reason of non-observation of the suitable to appear in that proof.

De drup kyi, In a proof, makes the statement more specific by situating it within a specified context. *Ma mik pe tak yang dak* means a perfect reason of non-observation. *Gang shik* indicates the first quality of the defintion. *Kyö kyi tak kyi* means using that reason to prove the thesis. *De drup kyi gak che chö su tak pe dön yö na* means if there exists what is ascribed as the quality to be refuted in that proof. For example, in the statement: On a lake at night where there is no fire, there is no smoke, because there is no fire, the presence of smoke is what is ascribed as the quality to be refuted. *Kyö de drup pa la chok chö chen du song we gang sak gyi* is referring to *chir göl yang dak*, a proper opponent to debate with, about this subject and means that the object must be suitable to appear to the valid cognition of a person who is an appropriate recipient of that proof. *Chir göl te tse ma la nang rung yin gö pa* means the opponent must be able to perceive by his valid cognition what is suitable to appear to him.

Gak che chö su tak pe dön, The object ascribed as the quality to be refuted, is, for example, the presence of a rabbit on this table. If there were a rabbit on this table your opponent would be able to see it. That is the meaning of *nang rung yin pa*, something that is suitable to appear [to him]. *Tse ma*, Valid cognition, in this case, is referring to *wang pö ngön sum tse ma*, direct valid sense cognition, yet more specifically, to *mik gyi wang po ngön sum gyi tse ma*, direct valid eye cognition. *Yin gö pa* means that he should be able to perceive it with his direct valid cognition. Therefore, if it is a perfect reason of non-observation of the suitable to appear, it should have all of the characteristics mentioned above.

གཉིས་པ་དེ་ལ་དབྱེ་ན་སྣང་རུང་གི་འབྲེལ་ཟླ་མ་དམིགས་པ་དང་། འགལ་ཟླ་

དམིགས་པའི་རྟགས་གཉིས།

nyi pa de la ye na nang rung gi drel(n) da ma mik pa dang gel(n) da mik pe tak nyi

When this second (a perfect reason of non-observation of the suitable to appear) is classified there are two: 1) a reason of non-observation of a related object that is suitable to appear, and 2) a reason of observation of the contradictory [that is suitable to appear].

reason of non-observation of a related object that is suitable to appear

དང་པོ་ནི། དེ་སྒྲུབ་ཀྱི་སྣང་རུང་མ་དམིགས་པའི་རྟགས་ཡང་དག་ཀྱང་ཡིན།

མེད་དགག་ཀྱང་ཡིན་པའི་གཞི་མཐུན་པ་དེ། དེ་སྒྲུབ་ཀྱི་དང་པོའི་མཚན་ཉིད།

dang po ni, de drup kyi nang rung ma mik pe tak yang dak kyang yin, me gak kyang yin pe shi tun pa de, de drup kyi dang pö tsen nyi

The definition of the first is something that is a combination of being both 1) a perfect reason of non-observation of the suitable to appear in that proof, and 2) a non-implicating negation [*me gak*].

དེ་ལ་སྣང་རུང་གི་རྒྱུ། ཁྱབ་བྱེད། རང་བཞིན། དངོས་འབྲས་མ་དམིགས་པའི་

རྟགས་དང་བཞི།

de la nang rung gi gyu, kyap che, rang shin, ngön dre ma mik pe tak dang shi

(A reason of non-observation of a related object itself is classified into four kinds): 1) the cause of a related object that is suitable to appear, 2) a related pervader that is suitable to appear, 3) a related object of [same] nature that is suitable to appear, and 4) a reason of non-observation of its direct effect.

When verbally stating these, the phrase *nang rung gi drel(n) da*, "a related object that is suitable to appear," has to precede each one. For example, we must say *nang rung gi drel(n) de'i gyu*, the cause of a related object that is suitable to appear, and so forth.

reason of non-observation of the cause of a related object that is suitable to appear

དང་པོ་ནི། མེ་མེད་པའི་མཚན་མོའི་རྒྱ་མཚོར་ཆོས་ཅན། དུ་བ་མེད་དེ། མེ་མེད་པའི་ཕྱིར་ཞེས་བཀོད་པའི་ཚེ་མེ་མེད་པ་ལྟ་བུ།

dang po ni, me me pe tsen mö gya tsor chö chen, du wa me de, me me pe chir she kö pe tse me me pa ta bu

An example of the first (the non-observation of the cause of a related object that is suitable to appear) is the reason used in the statement: Consider on a lake at night where there is no fire, there is no smoke, because there is no fire.

Nang rung gi drel(n) de'i gyu ma mik pe tak, A reason of non-observation of the cause of a related object that is suitable to appear, is the reason used in the statement above. The non-existing fire in that place serves as an example. *Me me pa*, The absence of fire, is *de drup kyi tak yang dak*, a perfect reason in this proof. *Du wa me pa*, The absence of smoke, is *de drup kyi ngö kyi drup che chö*, the explicit quality to be proved in this proof. What is *lok chok*, the opposite of this quality to be proved? *Du wa*, Smoke. Why? Smoke is related to fire. *Drel(n) da* means the partners of a relationship such as smoke and fire. *Me me pa*, The absence of fire, is related to *du wa me pa*, the absence of smoke, through a causal relationship [that is, if there is no fire—the cause, there can be no smoke—the effect]. Due to this causal relationship it can be used as *drel(n) de'i gyu ma mik pe tak*, a reason of non-observation of the cause of a related object [that is suitable to appear]. This is a combination of *gyu ma mik pa*, non-observation of a cause, and *drel(n) da ma mik pa*, non-observation of a related object. In the example given, neither *du we gyu*, the cause of smoke (fire), is observed nor is smoke (the effect of fire).

Du wa me pa, The absence of smoke, must be *de drup kyi ngö kyi drup che chö su sung je tso wo*, the principal explicit quality to be proved in this proof. Because *du we drel yul*, the related object to smoke, is fire and *me du we gyu*, fire is the cause of smoke, *ma mik pe tak su gö pa*, one must use a reason of non-observation to prove it. The reason of non-observation used above is *me me pe chir*, because of the absence of fire [that is, through not observing fire where it is suitable that it appear were it present, is a perfect sign that its effect, smoke, will not be present either].

When we go outside at night, it is easy to determine that there is no smoke, because we cannot see any fire. Without fire, its effect, smoke, cannot arise. If there were fire, we would see it. Therefore, to prove that there is no smoke we can use *drel(n) de'i gyu ma mik pe tak*, a reason of non-observation of the cause of a related object, due to their cause and effect relationship.

reason of non-observation of a related
pervader that is suitable to appear

གཉིས་པ་ནི། ཤིང་མེད་པའི་བྲག་རྫོང་ན་ཆོས་ཅན། ཤ་པ་མེད་དེ། ཤིང་མེད་
པའི་ཕྱིར་ཞེས་པའི་རྟགས་དེ་ལྟ་བུ།

nyi pa ni, shing me pe drak dzong na chö chen, sha pa me de, shing me pe chir, she pe tak te ta bu

An example of the second (a perfect reason of non-observation of a related pervader that is suitable to appear) is the reason used in the statement: Consider on a treeless rocky cliff, there are no Ashoka trees, because there are no trees.

These words sound very pleasant to my ears and are unbelievably special for me. Just hearing them makes me think of the time when the monasteries of Tibet would gather to debate the *Pramāṇavārttika* for three months out of each year. When I hear these examples I immediately think: "Oh, I must go to the debates next year!"

Shing, Tree, is a general category. *Sha pa*, Ashoka tree, is a particular or specific kind of tree. The Ashoka is a small tree that only exists in very specific places. A barren desert can also be considered as *shing me pe drak tsong*, a rocky, treeless place. We can use that as an example: Consider in a barren desert, there are no Ashoka trees, because there are no trees. Why? *Shing*, Tree, is *chi*, a general category. The general category covers or pervades those particular instances that pertain to it. *Kyap pa* means covering. Therefore, that barren desert cannot have any Ashoka trees, because it doesn't have any trees at all. How do you know this? If *kyap je*, the pervader, is not present, then *kyap ja*, the pervaded, i.e., its particular instances, cannot be present. If the general category is not present, its particular instances cannot be present either. General trees in this case are *kyap je*, the pervader, and Ashoka tree is *kyap ja*, what is pervaded. Without *kyap je*, the pervader, there is no *kyap ja*, the pervaded. That is why this is known as *drel(n) da kyap je ma mik pe tak*, a reason of non-observation of a related object as a pervader.

What is *de drup kyi ngö kyi drup che chö*, the explicit quality to be proved in this proof? *Sha pa me pa*, The absence of Ashoka trees. What is its *lok chok*, opposite object? *Sha pa*, Ashoka tree. Therefore, an Ashoka tree, the pervaded, cannot exist in that barren place, because there is no pervader, or trees in general. That is the meaning of this kind of reason.

reason of non-observation of a related object
of same nature that is suitable to appear

གསུམ་པ་ནི། བུམ་པས་དབེན་པའི་ས་ཕྱོགས་ཆོས་ཅན། བུམ་པ་མེད་དེ། བུམ་པ་
ཚད་མས་མ་དམིགས་པའི་ཕྱིར་ཞེས་པའི་རྟགས་དེ་ལྟ་བུ།

sum pa ni, bum pe wen pe sa chok chö chen, bum pa me de, bum pa tse me ma mik pe chir, she pe tak de ta bu

The third: Consider the place that is absent of a pot, there is no pot there, because no pot is perceived by valid cognition to be [present] in that place.

This is an example of *drel(n) da rang shin ma mik pe tak*, a reason of non-observation of a related object of same nature [that is suitable to appear]. *Bum pa* means pot. *Wen pa* means excluding or being absent of something. *Sa chok* means a place. These words are used quite often in the field of logic. *Bum pe wen pa* means being absent of a pot. *Bum pa tse me ma mik pe chir* means because a pot is not perceived by valid cognition [to be in that place].

What is *de drup kyi ngö kyi drup che chö*, the explicit quality to be proved in this proof? *Bum pa me pa*, The absence of a pot. What is *lok chok*, the opposite object? *Bum pa yö pa*, The presence of a pot, or simply a pot. Is a pot *yö pa*, an existent, or *me pa*, a non-existent? It's *yö pa*, an existent. Therefore, it is *tse me mik pa*, perceivable by valid cognition, which is the definition of an existent. *Bum pa yö pa*, An existent pot, and *bum pa tse me mik pa*, a pot perceived by valid cognition, are *rang shin chik*, of one nature. We can state it this way: *bum pa yö na bum pa tse me mik pa yin gö*, if a pot exists it must be a pot that is perceived by valid cognition. Similarly, *che pa yin na ngö po yin gö, mi tak pa yin gö*, if a product exists it must be a causally effective thing as well as an impermanent entity. They are *rang shin chik*, of one nature. This is the meaning of *rang shin ma mik pa*, non-observation of a related object of the same nature [that is suitable to appear].

reason of non-observation of the direct
effect of the suitable to appear

བཞི་པ་ནི། དུ་བས་དབེན་པའི་ས་ཕྱོགས་ཆོས་ཅན། དུ་བའི་དངོས་རྒྱུ་མེད་དེ། དུ་བ་མེད་པའི་ཕྱིར་ཞེས་པའི་རྟགས་དེ་ལྟ་བུ།

shi pa ni, du we wen pe sa chok chö chen, du we ngö gyu me de, du wa me pe chir, she pe tak de ta bu

The fourth: Consider a place where there is no smoke, the direct cause of smoke doesn't exist in that place, because there is no smoke.

The fourth reason is *ngön dre ma mik pe tak*, a reason of non-observation of the [related] direct effect [of the suitable to appear]. What is *de drup kyi ngö kyi drup che chö*, the explicit quality to be proved in this proof? *Du we ngö gyu me pa*, The absence of the direct cause of smoke. In order to understand this, first you have to know something about *gyu dang dre bu*, cause and effect, in general, and *ngö gyu*, direct cause, and *ngön dre*, direct effect, in particular. If there is a cause there must be a direct cause. For example, if you plant some seeds of grain in a field, sprouts will not arise automatically, since the process takes time, not to mention the possibility of crops not being produced at all due to those seeds having been eaten by birds or pigs. If animals have eaten those seeds this relationship of cause and effect won't exist between them and, needless to say, the seeds won't be able to generate any sprouts.

Ngö gyu refers to the direct cause of a sprout, which is the seed that is just about to ripen and put forth a sprout. At the time of *ngö gyu*, direct cause, the seed is just ready to grow into a sprout. The seed that is just ready to give a sprout is *ngö gyu*, direct cause, and the sprout that comes out immediately after is *ngön dre*, its direct effect. There should be no gap between them. Therefore, there is a big difference between cause and effect and *direct* cause and *direct* effect. Above it says, *du we ngö gyu me de*, there is no direct cause of smoke. If there is the direct cause of smoke, which is fire, there should also be the direct effect, which is smoke. So, *de drup kyi ngö kyi drup che chö*, the explicit quality to be proved in this proof, is *du we ngö gyu me pa*, the absence of the direct cause of smoke. *Lok chok*, The opposite object, is *du we ngö gyu yö pa*, the presence of the direct cause of smoke. *Du we ngö gyu me te, du wa me pe chir*, Without the presence of the direct cause of smoke, smoke cannot exist, due to the causal relationship between fire and smoke.

reason of observation of the contradictory

གཉིས་པ་འགལ་ཟླ་དམིགས་པའི་རྟགས་ལ། མཚན་ཉིད་ནི། དེ་སྒྲུབ་ཀྱི་སྣང་རུང་མ་དམིགས་པའི་རྟགས་ཡང་དག་གང་ཞིག །མ་ཡིན་དགག་དང་སྒྲུབ་པ་གང་རུང་ཡང་ཡིན་པའི་གཞི་མཐུན་པ་དེ་དེའི་མཚན་ཉིད།

nyi pa geln da mik pe tak la, tsen nyi ni, de drup kyi nang rung ma mik pe tak yang dak gang shik, ma yin gak dang drup pa gang rung yang yin pe shi tun pa de de tsen nyi

Regarding the second, the definition of a [perfect] reason of observation of the contradictory, is that which is a combination of being both 1) a perfect reason of non-observation of the suitable to appear in that proof, and 2) is either an implicating negation [*ma yin gak*] or a positive entity [*drup pa*].

A reason of non-observation of the suitable to appear, is *me gak*, a non-implicating negation, whereas the reason presented here, a reason of observation of the contradictory is either *ma yin gak*, an implicating negation, or *drup pa*, a positive entity. There is a lot of debate about this on the debate ground, but since you won't have to go there, it's easier.

དབྱེ་ན། ལྷན་ཅིག་མི་གནས་འགལ་གྱི་དེ་དང་། ཕན་ཚུན་སྤངས་འགལ་གྱི་དེ་གཉིས།

ye na, hlen chik mi ne gel gyi de dang, pen tsun pang gel gyi de nyi

When (perfect reasons of observation of the contradictory) are classified there are two: 1) a reason of non-abiding opposites, and 2) a reason of mutually contradictory opposites.

reason of observation of non-abiding opposites

དང་པོ་ལ་འགལ་བའི་རང་བཞིན་དམིགས་པ་བཞི། འབྲས་བུ་དམིགས་པ་བཞི་ཁྱབ་བྱ་དམིགས་པ་བཞི་སྟེ་བཅུ་གཉིས་སོ། །དེ་དག་གི་དབྱེ་བ་རྒྱས་པར་ནི་གཞན་དུ་བལྟ་ལ།

dang po la gel we rang shin mik pa shi, dre bu mik pa shi, kyap ja mik pa shi te chu nyi so, de dak gi ye wa gye par ni shen du ta la

In regard to the first (a reason of observation of non-abiding opposites), all in all there are twelve kinds consisting of: four reasons of observation of a contradictory nature; four reasons of observation of the effect; and four reasons of observation of the pervader. For a more detailed explanation, one should consult the other more detailed text.[41]

མཚན་གཞི་ཙམ་ནི། རང་བཞིན་དང་འགལ་བའི་རང་བཞིན་དམིགས་པ། རྒྱུ་དང་འགལ་བའི་རང་བཞིན་དམིགས་པ། ཁྱབ་བྱེད་དང་འགལ་བའི་རང་

[41] Referring to the *Extensive Reasoning* (***rtag rigs brgyas pa***), by the same author.

བཞིན་དམིགས་པ། རང་བཞིན་དང་འགལ་བའི་འབྲས་བུ་དམིགས་པ། རྒྱུ་
དང་འགལ་བའི་འབྲས་བུ་དམིགས་པའི་རྟགས་ཡང་དག་ལྔ་ལས།

tsen shi tsam ni, rang shin dang gel we rang shin mik pa, gyu dang gel we rang shin mik pa, kyap che dang gel we rang shin mik pa, rang shin dang gel we dre bu mik pa, gyu dang gel we dre bu mik pe tak yang dak nga le

Just illustrations of the five kinds of observed opposites will be given here: 1) a perfect reason of observation of a contradictory nature of non-abiding opposites, 2) a perfect reason of observation of a nature contradictory to the cause, 3) a perfect reason of observation of a nature that is contradictory to the pervader, 4) a perfect reason of observation of an effect that is contradictory with its nature, and 5) a perfect reason of observation of an effect that is contradictory to another cause.

reason of observation of a contradictory nature of non-abiding opposites

དང་པོ་ནི། མེ་སྟོབས་ཆེན་པོས་ཁྱབ་པར་གནོན་པའི་ཤར་གྱི་དངོས་པོ་ཆོས་ཅན།
གྲང་རེག་རྒྱུན་ཆགས་སུ་གནས་པ་མེད་དེ། མེ་སྟོབས་ཆེན་པོས་ཁྱབ་པར་
གནོན་པའི་དངོས་པོ་ཡིན་པའི་ཕྱིར་ཞེས་པའི་རྟགས་དེ་ལྟ་བུའོ།

dang po ni, me tob chen pö kyap par nön pe shar gyi ngö po chö chen, trang rek gyun chak su ne pa me de, me tob chen pö kyap par nön pe ngö po yin pe chir she pe tak de ta bu'o

An example of the first (a perfect reason of observation of a contradictory nature of non-abiding opposites) is the reason used in the following statement: Consider a place in the east that is covered by a great raging fire, there does not exist a

> continuous sensation of cold there, because it is a place covered by a great raging fire.

This *tak*, reason, a place where there is a raging fire, is being used because it is contradictory to the nature of *gak che chö*, the quality to be refuted, which in this case is *trang rek gyun chak su ne pa yö*, the existence of an abiding feeling of cold. *Trang rek su ne pa dang tsa rek dang gel wa*, An abiding cold sensation and a hot sensation are contradictory [and non-abiding opposites].

reason of observation of a nature [of a non-abiding opposite] contradictory to the cause

> གཉིས་པ་ནི། དེ་ཆོས་ཅན། གྲང་འབྲས་སྤུ་ལོང་བྱེད་རྒྱུན་ཆགས་སུ་གནས་
> པ་མེད་དེ། དེ་འདྲའི་དངོས་པོ་ཡིན་པའི་ཕྱིར་ཞེས་པའི་རྟགས་ལྟ་བུ།
>
> *nyi pa ni, de chö chen, trang dre pu long che gyun chak su ne pa me de, de(n) dre ngö po yin pe chir she pe tak ta bu*
>
> The second (a perfect reason of observation of a nature [of a non-abiding opposite] contradictory to the cause), is the reason used in the following statement: Consider a place in the east that is covered by a great raging fire, there doesn't exist an abiding cold sensation that produces goose bumps—an effect of being cold—because there is a great raging fire in that place.

Trang dre pu long che means emerging goose bumps. Why does one get goose bumps? When do they arise? They arise upon contact with the cold. Therefore, in order for goose bumps to arise, their cause, the cold, has to be present. However, cold cannot be present where there is a great raging fire. So the observation of a contradictory condition to cold, such as a great raging fire, serves as an example of *gyu dang gel we rang shin mik pa*, a perfect reason of observation of a nature [of a non-abiding opposite] contradictory to the cause.

reason of observation of a nature [of a non-abiding opposite] contradictory to the pervader

གསུམ་པ་ནི། དེ་ཆོས་ཅན། ཁ་བའི་རེག་པ་རྒྱུན་ཆགས་སུ་གནས་པ་མེད་དེ། དེ་འདྲའི་དངོས་པོ་ཡིན་པའི་ཕྱིར་ཞེས་པའི་རྟགས་ལྟ་བུ།

sum pa ni, de chö chen, ka we rek pa gyun chak su ne pa me de, de(n) dre ngö po yin pe chir she pe tak ta bu

The third (a perfect reason of observation of a nature [of a non-abiding opposite] contradictory to the pervader) is the reason used in the following statement: Consider a place in the east that is covered by a great raging fire, there does not exist a continuously abiding tangible sensation of snow, because there is a great raging fire in that place.

Ka we rek pa means the tangible sensation of snow, which is used here as an example, because whenever you touch snow the kind of sensation it gives you is a cold feeling.

reason of observation of an effect that is [a non-abiding opposite] contradictory with its nature

བཞི་པ་ནི། དུ་བ་དྲག་ཕྱུར་བས་ཁྱབ་པར་གནོན་པའི་ཤར་གྱི་དངོས་པོ་ཆོས་ཅན། གྲང་རེག་རྒྱུན་ཆགས་སུ་གནས་པ་མེད་དེ། དེས་ཁྱབ་པར་གནོན་པའི་དངོས་པོ་ཡིན་པའི་ཕྱིར་ཞེས་པའི་རྟགས་ལྟ་བུ།

shi pa ni, du wa drak chur we kyap par nön pe shar gyi ngö po chö chen, trang rek gyun chak su ne pa me de de kyap par nön pe ngö po yin pe chir she pe tak ta bu

The fourth (a perfect reason of observation of an effect that is [a non-abiding opposite] contradictory with its nature), is illustrated by the reason in the following statement: Consider a place in the east that is covered by a thick cloud of smoke, there does not exist an abiding cold sensation, because it is a place covered like that [with smoke].

reason of observation of an effect that is [a non-abiding opposite] contradictory to another cause

ལྔ་པ་ནི། དེ་ཆོས་ཅན། གྲང་འབྲས་སྤུ་ལོང་བྱེད་རྒྱུན་ཆགས་སུ་གནས་པ་མེད་དེ། དེ་འདྲའི་དངོས་པོ་ཡིན་པའི་ཕྱིར་ཞེས་པའི་རྟགས་ལྟ་བུའོ། །དེ་ཡང་རྩོད་པའི་ཚེ་རྟགས་སུ་གང་འགྲོ་རྒྱུ་དེ་སྨོས་ནས་འཇོག་དགོས་སོ།

nga pa ni, de chö chen, trang dre pu long che gyun chak su ne pa me de, den dre ngö po yin pe chir she pe tak ta bu'o, de yang tsö pe tse tak su gang dro gyu de mö ne jok gö so

The fifth (a perfect reason of observation of an effect that is [a non-abiding opposite] contradictory to another cause), is illustrated by the reason in the following statement: Consider a place in the east that is covered by a thick cloud of smoke, there cannot exist continually abiding goose bumps—the effect of feeling cold, because of its being a causally effective thing such as that. When debating, however, one must posit whatever reason is appropriate in accord with the way the debate progresses.

reason of observation of mutually contradictory opposites

> གཉིས་པ་ཕན་ཚུན་སྤངས་འགལ་ནི།
>
> *nyi pa pen tsun pang gel ni*
>
> The second [kind of reason] is a reason of observation of mutually contradictory opposites.

Whereas, *tsa rek*, the sensation of heat, and *trang rek*, the sensation of cold, are *hlen chik mi ne gel*, non-abiding contradictory entities, *tak pa*, permanent entities, and *ngö po*, causally effective entities, are *pen tsun pang gel*, mutually exclusive entities. Mutual exclusivity means that if you accept something as being one thing, you have to reject it as being the other. One thing cannot be both since their natures are diametrically opposed. For example, in the statement: *dra chö chen*, *mi tak te*, *che pa yin pe chir*, consider sound, it is impermanent, because it is produced, if you accept sound as impermanent, using "produced" as a reason, *gak che chö*, the quality to be rejected, is the permanence (of sound). *Dra tak pa*, Permanent sound, is *gak ja*, the thesis you are rejecting. That is, if you accept sound as impermanent, you cannot also accept it as being permanent, because their natures are *pen tsun pang gel*, of a mutually exclusive contradictory nature.

> སྒྲ་ཆོས་ཅན། རྟག་པས་སྟོང་སྟེ། བྱས་པ་ཡིན་པའི་ཕྱིར་ཞེས་པའི་རྟགས་དེ་ལྟ་བུའོ།
>
> *dra chö chen, tak pe tong te, che pa yin pe chir, she pe tak de ta bu'o*
>
> Consider sound, it is void of permanence, because it is produced; it is like that reason used in such a statement.

Tak pe tong, Being empty of permanence, and *mi tak pa*, impermanence, are the same. Being something and being empty of something represent two qualities that are mutually contradictory.

> དེས་ན། རྭ་ཅན་དེ་མདུན་གྱི་གོང་བུ་རྭ་ཅན་རྟ་མ་ཡིན་པར་སྒྲུབ་པའི་ཕན་ཚུན་
> སྤངས་འགལ་ལ་བརྟེན་པའི་འགལ་དམིགས་ཀྱི་རྟགས་ཡང་དག་ཡིན།
>
> *de na, ra chen de dun gyi gong bu ra chen ta ma yin par drup pe pen tsun pang gel la ten pe gel mik kyi tak yang dak yin*
>
> Also, something that possesses horns is a perfect reason of observation of the [mutually] contradictory that relies on mutual exclusion when proving that the mass in front [of you] possessing horns is not a horse.

An example of *ra chen*, something possessing horns, is a bull. Horses, however, do not have horns. *Dun gyi gong bu ra chen*, A mass in front of you with horns, is *chö chen*, the subject of debate. *Dun gyi gong bu ra chen chö chen, ta ma yin te, ra chen yin pe chir*, Consider a mass in front of you with horns, it is not a horse, because it has horns. The reason may be explained this way. *Ra chen yin na, ta ma yin pe kyap*, If something has horns, it is necessarily not a horse. Why? *Ra chen dang ra chen ma yin pa nyi gel wa*, The two, that which has horns and that which does not have horns are [mutually] contradictory. This statement is using *ra chen ma yin pe gel wa*, the opposite of what does not have horns [meaning that which has horns], to prove something that does not have horns: *dun gyi gong bu ra chen chö chen, ta ma yin te, ra chen yin pe chir*, consider a mass in front of you with horns, it is not a horse, because it has horns. Unless you are crazy, you cannot accept one thing as being both a horse and a creature that has horns. That is the meaning of mutual exclusion.

reason of observation of mutually contradictory opposites that rejects being definitive due to dependence

> དབྱེ་བ་ལ། ལྟོས་པས་ངེས་པ་འགོག་པའི་དེ་དང༌། ངེས་པས་ལྟོས་པ་འགོག་པའི་དེ་གཉིས་ཡོད། དང་པོ་ནི། སྣམ་བུ་དཀར་པོ་ཆོས་ཅན། རང་གྲུབ་ཙམ་ནས་ཚོན་ཅན་དུ་མ་ངེས་ཏེ། རང་ཉིད་ཚོན་ཅན་དུ་འགྱུར་བ་རང་ལས་ཕྱིས་འབྱུང་གི་རྒྱུ་ལ་ལྟོས་པའི་ཕྱིར་ཞེས་པའི་རྟགས་ལྟ་བུ།
>
> *ye wa la, tö pe nge pa gok pe de dang, nge pe tö pa gok pe de nyi yö, dang po ni, nam bu kar po chö chen, rang drup tsam ne tsön chen du ma nge te, rang nyi tsön chen du gyur wa rang le chi jung gi gyu la tö pe chir she pe tak ta bu*
>
> When (perfect reasons of observation of mutually contradictory opposites) are classified there are two: 1) a reason that rejects being definitive due to dependence, and 2) a reason that rejects dependence due to being definitive. An example of the first is the reason used in the statement: Consider white wool, it is not ascertained as having a color from the very beginning, because it relies on a cause occurring later to give it [that] color.

Tö pe means it relies upon something and is here used as *tak*, a reason. It is rejecting the fact of something's being non-reliant from the beginning, and is positing that such reliance depends upon later causes. *Nam bu kar po* means white wool. Usually, wool is dyed to give it [another] color. It says here that white wool, *rang drup tsam ne*, from the very beginning, *tsön chen du ma nge*, is ascertained as not having any color [other than white]. This means, for example, that if somebody were to show you a bolt of wool, you might say that you wouldn't be able to make clothes with it because the wool is lacking in color. In order to be usable for clothes, it will have to be dyed another color later to give it a color that is usable for clothing. That is, from the beginning it does not possess that dyed color, since you have to dye it whatever color you want—whether blue, red, black, and so forth—in order to get it that color. Conversely, fire, for example, is an orangish-yellow color from the beginning and smoke is a blue-gray color; they don't have to rely on anything else [later causes] to give them their color.

reason of observation of mutually contradictory opposites that rejects dependence due to being definitive

གཉིས་པ་ནི། བྱས་པ་ཆོས་ཅན། རང་ཉིད་འཇིག་པ་རང་ལས་ཕྱིས་འབྱུང་གི་རྒྱུ་ལ་མི་ལྟོས་ཏེ། རང་ཉིད་གྲུབ་ཙམ་ནས་འཇིག་ངེས་ཡིན་པའི་ཕྱིར་ཞེས་པའི་རྟགས་ལྟ་བུ།

nyi pa ni, che pa chö chen, rang nyi jik pa rang le chi jung gi gyu la mi tö te, rang nyi drup tsam ne jik nge yin pe chir she pe tak ta bu

The second (a reason that rejects dependence due to being definitive): Consider a product, it does not rely on later causes to make it have the nature of disintegrating, because it has always had a disintegrating nature.

Here *che pa*, a product, is being used as the subject of the proof, but it is far better for the mind of practitioners to use *nyer len gyi pung po*, the appropriated heaps, as a subject to illustrate this reason.

How many heaps do you have? Five. Yet, some people who have a lot of hair on their face have an extra heap. Those five heaps are *nyer len gyi pung po*, appropriated heaps, which means *nyer len gyi gyu la ten ne*, they were obtained through relying on perpetuating causes—mental afflictions and karma. Based on these causes, good karma or bad karma, different heaps are created.

We can make this statement: *nyer len gyi pung po chö chen, rang nyi jik pa rang le chi jung gi gyu la mi tö te, rang nyi drup tsam ne jik nge yin pe chir,* consider the appropriated heaps, they don't rely on the arising of later causes other than their own perishable nature, because their nature is perishable from the very beginning. When their power is exhausted, they will perish.

incidental points: other modes of classification

གསུམ་པ་ཤར་བྱུང་ནི། རྟགས་དེ་ལ་དངོས་སྟོབས་ཀྱི་རྟགས། ཡིད་ཆེས་ཀྱི་རྟགས། གྲགས་པའི་རྟགས། དོན་སྒྲུབ་ཀྱི་རྟགས། ཐ་སྙད་སྒྲུབ་ཀྱི་རྟགས། མཐུན་ཕྱོགས་ལ་རྣམ་གཉིས་སུ་འཇུག་པ་དང་ཁྱབ་བྱེད་དུ་འཇུག་པའི་རྟགས་བདུན་ལས།

sum pa shar jung ni, tak de la ngö tob kyi tak, yi che kyi tak, trak pe tak, dön drup kyi tak, ta nye drup kyi tak, tun chok la nam nyi su juk pa dang kyap che du juk pe tak dun le

The third part consists of incidental points. Reasons can also be classified into seven types: 1) a reason by the power of the fact, 2) a reason based on trust, 3) a reason based on convention, 4) a reason establishing the meaning, 5) a reason establishing the term, 6) a reason that engages the similar class in two ways, and 7) a reason that engages the similar class as a pervader.

three classifications by way of the thesis: reason based on the power of the fact

དང་པོ་ནི། བྱས་པ་དེ། སྒྲ་མི་རྟག་པར་སྒྲུབ་པར་བྱེད་པའི་དངོས་སྟོབས་ཀྱི་རང་བཞིན་གྱི་རྟགས་དང་།

dang po ni, che pa de, dra mi tak par drup par che pe ngö tob kyi, rang shin gyi tak dang

Product is an example of the first since it is a reason of nature of the power of the fact that serves to prove sound as impermanent.

For example, in the statement: *dra chö chen, mi tak te, che pa yin pe chir*, consider sound, it is impermanent, because it is produced, just on the strength of having the nature of a causally effective thing, one can use that to prove something. Here this statement is proving that sound is impermanent because it is produced. This is an example of *rang shin gyi tak*, a reason of nature, [because sound has the nature of being a produced thing].

དུ་བ་དེ་དུ་ལྡན་ལ་ལ་མེ་ཡོད་པར་བསྒྲུབ་པའི་དངོས་སྟོབས་ཀྱི་འབྲས་རྟགས་
དང་།

du wa de du den la la me yö par drup pe ngö tob kyi dre tak dang

Smoke is an example of a reason of effect by the power of the fact proving that there is fire on a smoky mountain pass.

This is showing an effect reason by the power of the fact.

མེ་མེད་པ་དེ་མཚན་མོའི་རྒྱ་མཚོར་དུ་བ་མེད་པར་བསྒྲུབ་པའི་དེ་སྒྲུབ་ཀྱི་མ་
དམིགས་པའི་རྟགས་ཡིན།

me me pa de tsen mö gya tsor du wa me par drup pe de drup kyi ma mik pe tak yin

The absence of fire is an example of a reason of non-observation in a proof establishing that there is no smoke on a lake at night.

This is indicating a reason of non-observation as also *ngö tob kyi tak*, a reason by the power of the fact, because, if there is no fire, there cannot be any smoke since they are both perceptible by valid cognition.

reason based on trust

གཉིས་པ་ནི། དཔྱད་གསུམ་གྱིས་དག་པའི་ལུང་དེ། རང་གི་བསྟན་བྱའི་དོན་ལ་མི་སླུ་བར་སྒྲུབ་པར་བྱེད་པའི་ཡིད་ཆེས་ཀྱི་རང་བཞིན་གྱི་རྟགས་དང་། དཔྱད་གསུམ་གྱིས་དག་པའི་ལུང་དེ། སྦྱིན་པས་ལོངས་སྤྱོད་ཁྲིམས་ཀྱིས་བདེ། །ཞེས་པའི་ལུང་རང་གི་བསྟན་དོན་རྟོགས་པའི་ཚད་མ་སྔ་མ་སྔོན་དུ་སོང་བར་བསྒྲུབ་པའི་ཡིད་ཆེས་ཀྱི་འབྲས་རྟགས་དང་། དེ་དེ་འདྲའི་ལུང་རང་གི་བསྟན་བྱའི་དོན་ལ་མི་སླུ་བར་བསྒྲུབ་པའི་ཡིད་ཆེས་ཀྱི་མ་དམིགས་པའི་རྟགས་ཡིན།

nyi pa ni che sum gyi dak pe lung de, rang gi ten che dön la mi lu war drup par che pe yi che kyi rang shin gyi tak dang, che sum gyi dak pe lung de, jin pe long chö trim kyi de, she pe lung rang gi ten dön tok pe tse ma nga ma ngön du song war drup pe yi che kyi dre tak dang, de den dre lung rang gi ten che dön la mi lu war drup pe yi che kyi ma mik pe tak yin

The second, an example of a reason of same nature based on trust, is the scripture tested by the three examinations used to prove the infallibility of the meaning of what it teaches; an example of a reason of effect based on trust proving that there was a prior [source of] valid [authority] that realized the meaning of what is taught in that scripture tested by the three examinations, is the quotation: "From giving comes wealth; from morality, happiness." An example of a reason of non-observation based on trust is a scripture such as that which proves the infallibility of the meaning that is taught there.

This kind of reason is very important for Dharma practitioners. An example of scripture tested by the three examinations is: *jin pe long chö trim gyi de*, if you practice giving, you will be rich in the future; by keeping morality, in the future you will be very happy. *Rang gi ten che dön la* means that the subject of this scripture is to teach these qualities of giving, which brings wealth, and morality, which brings happiness, and so forth. *Mi lu wa yin te* means non-deceptive; that is, it cannot be false in any way. *She pe* indicates making a statement. Therefore, *rang gi ten che dön la mi lu wa yin te* means the words of this statement are perfect without any error. *Che pa sum gyi dak pe lung yin pe chir* means [it is perfect] because it is a scripture that is tested by the three examinations. *Che pa* means putting it to the test in three different ways. *Dak pe* means that statement has been made pure, or validated, by those three analyses; [that is, such teachings are not found to be erroneous in any of the three following ways].

What are these three examinations? *Che pa sum gyi*, These three examinations are: 1) *tong wa ngön gyur tön pe cha la ngön sum tse me nö pa me pa*, this scripture does not contradict those things that are perceivable by direct valid cognition; 2) *chung se gok gyur tön pe cha la je pak tse me nö pa me pa*, this scripture does not contradict slightly hidden things that are perceivable by inferential valid cognition; and 3) *shin tu gok gyur tön pe cha la yi che je pak gi nö pa me pa*, this scripture does not contradict deeply hidden things that are perceivable by inferential cognition based on trust.

These are the three types of valid cognitions used to examine such a statement. Although *tong wa* itself means to see, *tong wa ngön gyur* here indicates an object perceivable by any of our five direct sense consciousnesses, but primarily those of the eye consciousness. For example, it is possible to actually see someone giving something; you can observe someone practicing charity or taking vows. These are perceptible by the eye consciousness and perfect in so far as an unerring eye consciousness can see them. As such they cannot be rejected on the basis of not being perceptible.

Chung se gok gyur means a little bit hidden; that is, its object cannot be seen by the direct valid cognition of a *so so kye wo,* beginner or ordinary person. Since these things are hidden to them, they have to be validated through *je pak tse ma*, inferential cognition, based on good reasons. An example would be: *dra chö chen, mi tak te, che pa yin pe chir*, consider sound, it is impermanent, because it is produced. *Dra*, Sound, is *ngön gyur*, a manifest phenomenon, because you can hear sound directly with your ear consciousness. *Mi tak pa*, Impermanence, is *chung se gok gyur*, a slightly hidden phenomenon, in that it is not directly perceptible but is accessible through good reasoning. Therefore, such things must be perceived by inference.

Yi che je pak, Inference through trust, is the kind of cognition employed when dealing with things that are *shin tu gok gyur*, extremely hidden. [Such reasons, used in relation to extremely hidden phenomena, must be accessed through inferential valid cognition that is dependent upon a correct sign.] For example, the statement: *gyu ge wa chen po la tö ne dre bu de wa jung wa*, reliant upon very virtuous causes, its effect—happiness—will arise. This subtle relationship is *shin tu gok gyur*, very hidden. Nevertheless, *yi che je pak*, inference based on trust, can access it through Buddha's teachings, since those teachings are infallible. Another important factor present in this third examination is that there is no internal contradiction such as the first part of a teaching, for example, contradicting the latter part or vice versa.

reason based on convention

གསུམ་པ་ནི། རྟོག་ཡུལ་ན་ཡོད་པ་དེ། རི་བོང་ཅན་ལ་ཟླ་སྒྲ་བརྗོད་རུང་དུ་བསྒྲུབ་པར་བྱེད་པའི་གྲགས་པའི་རང་བཞིན་གྱི་རྟགས་དང་། དེ་རི་བོང་ཅན་ལ་དངོས་དབང་གིས་ཟླ་སྒྲ་བརྗོད་རུང་མ་ཡིན་པར་བསྒྲུབ་པའི་གྲགས་པའི་མ་དམིགས་པའི་རྟགས་ཡིན།

sum pa ni tok yul na yö pa de, ri bong chen la da dre jö rung du drup par che pe trak pe rang shin gyi tak dang, de ri bong chen la ngö wang gi da(n) dre jö rung ma yin par drup pe trak pe ma mik pe tak yin

> The third (a reason based on convention) is exemplified by the following: What exists among conceptual objects of thought is a reason of nature based on convention serving to prove that it is suitable to call the "rabbit-possessor" by the name "moon." It is also a reason of non-observation of convention that proves it is not suitable to call the "rabbit-possessor" by the name "moon" by the power of the fact.

Ri bong chen, The "rabbit-possessor," is a synonym for the moon and is an image used in poetry to describe the design on the surface of the moon, which appears in the shape of a rabbit. *Da(n) dre jö rung* means it is fitting to call such an object that has the image of a rabbit on its surface by the name "moon" since people commonly perceive it that way. *Da wa* means moon. *Dre* means by that term. *Jö rung* means you can ascribe that name to it and agree upon the term through conventional usage. Why? Because most everybody is familiar with this object and the way it looks.

Now, if it is *ri bong chen,* a "rabbit-possessor," you can call it by the name "moon." However, *ngö wang gi da(n) dre jö rung ma yin* means that it doesn't exist that way [by the power of the fact]. If such were the case the moon would actually have a rabbit in it. Therefore, it is only called that due to its being known popularly as such.

classifications by way of the mode of proof:
reason establishing a meaning *and*
reason establishing a term

བཞི་པ་དང་ལྡུ་པ་ལ་སྦྱོར་ན་ལྔ་ཡོད་དེ། དེ་སྒྲུབ་ཀྱི་རྟགས་ཡང་དག་གང་ཞིག

།དེ་སྒྲུབ་ཀྱི་དངོས་ཀྱི་བསྒྲུབ་བྱའི་ཆོས་སུ་བཟུང་བྱ་དང་མཚན་ཉིད་ཀྱི་གཞི་

མཐུན་སྲིད་པ་དེ། དེ་སྒྲུབ་ཀྱི་དོན་སྒྲུབ་ཀྱི་རྟགས་ཡང་དག་གི་མཚན་ཉིད། དེ་

དང་མཚོན་བྱའི་གཞི་མཐུན་སྲིད་པ་དེ། དེ་སྒྲུབ་ཀྱི་ཐ་སྙད་སྒྲུབ་ཀྱི་རྟགས་ཡང་དག་གི་མཚན་ཉིད།

shi pa dang nga pa la trö na nga yö de, de drup kyi tak yang dak gang shik, de drup kyi ngö kyi drup che chö su sung ja dang tsen nyi kyi shi tun si pa de, de drup kyi dön drup kyi tak yang dak gi tsen nyi, de dang tsön che shi tun si pa de, de drup kyi ta nye drup kyi tak yang dak gi tsen nyi

If we elaborate on the fourth and fifth [kinds of reasons] there are five in all. The definition of a perfect reason that establishes a meaning is a possible combination of 1) being a perfect reason in that proof, and 2) what is held as the explicit quality to be proved in that proof is a definition. The definition of a perfect reason that establishes a term in that proof is a possible combination of 1) a perfect reason in that proof, and 2) what is held as the quality to be proved in that proof is an object to be defined.

An example of the first is as follows. In the statement: *dra chö chen, ke chik ma yin te, che pa yin pe chir*, consider sound, it is momentary, because it is produced, *de drup kyi drup che chö dang tsen nyi shi tun pa*, in that proof there is one thing that is both an explicit quality to be proved and a definition; that is, *ke chik ma*, momentary, is the definition of *mi tak pa*, impermanent, and is the explicit quality to be proved about sound in this proof. The kind of reason used here to prove this is *de drup kyi dön drup kyi tak yang dak*, a perfect reason proving the meaning in this proof. *Dön*, Meaning, refers to the definition.

In the statement: *dra chö chen, ke chik ma yin te, mi tak pa yin pe chir*, consider sound, it is momentary, because it is impermanent, what is *de drup kyi shen dö chö chen*, the subject about which there is doubt in this proof? *Dra*, Sound. What is *de drup kyi tsö shi*, the basis of contention in this proof? *Dra*, Sound. What is *de drup kyi ngö kyi drup che chö*, the explicit quality to be proved in this proof? *Ke chik ma*, [That sound is] momentary. What is *de drup kyi tak yang dak*, the perfect reason in this proof? *Mi tak pa*, Impermanent. *Mi tak pa*, Impermanent, is also *tsön ja*, the object to be defined. *Ke chik ma*, Momentary, is *tsen nyi*, the definition. If the object to be defined is used as the reason in that proof, it cannot also be used as the explicit quality to be proved in that same proof. This is a rule of logic.

An example of the second is as follows. *Ta nye*, Term, is referring to *tsön ja*, object to be defined. In the statement: *dra chö chen, mi tak te, ke chik ma yin pe chir*, consider sound, it is impermanent, because it is momentary, *mi tak pa*, impermanence, is *ta nye*, a term, or *tsön ja*, object to be defined, that is being proved by this reason [*ke chik ma*, momentary, the definition of impermanence]. Since *ke chik ma*, momentary, is being used as a reason in this proof, it cannot also be used as the quality to be proved. This is the meaning of *ta nye drup kyi tak yang dak*, a perfect reason proving a term.

དེ་དང་མཚོན་བྱའི་གཞི་མཐུན་མི་སྲིད་ཅིང་མཚན་ཉིད་ཀྱི་གཞི་མཐུན་སྲིད་པ་དེ། དེ་སྒྲུབ་ཀྱི་དོན་འབའ་ཞིག་སྒྲུབ་ཀྱི་རྟགས་ཡང་དག་གི་མཚན་ཉིད།

de dang tsön che shi tun mi si ching tsen nyi kyi shi tun si pa de, de drup kyi dön ba shik drup kyi tak yang dak gi tsen nyi

The definition of a perfect reason proving only a meaning in a proof is a possible combination of being 1) a definition, and 2) what is never an object to be defined.

དེ་དང་མཚན་ཉིད་ཀྱི་གཞི་མཐུན་མི་སྲིད་ཅིང་མཚོན་བྱའི་གཞི་མཐུན་སྲིད་པ་དེ། དེ་སྒྲུབ་ཀྱི་ཐ་སྙད་འབའ་ཞིག་སྒྲུབ་ཀྱི་རྟགས་ཡང་དག་གི་མཚན་ཉིད།

de dang tsen nyi kyi shi tun mi si ching tsön je shi tun si pa de, de drup kyi ta nye ba shik drup kyi tak yang dak gi tsen nyi

The definition of a perfect reason proving only a term in that proof is a possible combination of being 1) an object to be defined, and 2) what is never a definition.

དེ་དང་མཚན་ཉིད་ཀྱི་གཞི་མཐུན་ཡང་སྲིད་མཚོན་བྱའི་གཞི་མཐུན་ཡང་སྲིད་པ་དེ། དེ་སྒྲུབ་ཀྱི་དོན་དང་ཐ་སྙད་གཉིས་ཀ་སྒྲུབ་ཀྱི་རྟགས་ཡང་དག་གི་མཚན་ཉིད་ཡིན་པའི་ཕྱིར།

de dang tsen nyi kyi shi tun yang si tsön che shi tun yang si pa de, de drup kyi dön dang ta nye nyi ka drup kyi tak yang dak gi tsen nyi yin pe chir

The definition of a perfect reason that can prove both a meaning and a term in that proof is what is possible to be either a definition or an object to be defined.

An example is *dra chö chen, mi tak te, che pa yin pe chir*, consider sound, it is impermanent, because it is produced.

classifications by way of the mode of engagement of the similar class:

reason that engages [the similar class] in two ways *and* reason that engages [the similar class] as a pervader

དྲུག་པ་དང་བདུན་པ་གཉིས་ནི་རིམ་པ་བཞིན། རྩོལ་བྱུང་དེ་སྒྲ་མི་རྟག་པར་སྒྲུབ་པར་བྱེད་པའི་མཐུན་ཕྱོགས་ལ་རྣམ་གཉིས་སུ་འཇུག་པའི་རྟགས། བྱས་པ་དེ་དེ་སྒྲུབ་ཀྱི་མཐུན་ཕྱོགས་ལ་ཁྱབ་བྱེད་དུ་འཇུག་པའི་རྟགས་ཡང་དག་ཡིན་ནོ།

།དེ་ཡང་གོང་གི་དང་པོ་གསུམ་ནི་སྒྲུབ་བྱའི་སྒོ་ནས་དབྱེ་བ་དང་། བཞི་པ་དང་ལྔ་པ་གཉིས་ནི་སྒྲུབ་ཚུལ་གྱི་སྒོ་ནས་དབྱེ་བ་དང་། དྲུག་པ་དང་བདུན་པ་གཉིས་ནི་མཐུན་ཕྱོགས་ལ་འཇུག་ཚུལ་གྱི་སྒོ་ནས་དབྱེ་བ་ཡིན་ནོ།

drup pa dang dun pa nyi ni rim pa shin, tsöl jung de dra mi tak par drup par che pe tun chok la nam nyi su juk pe tak, che pa de de drup kyi tun chok la kyap che du juk pe tak yang dak yin no, de yang gong gi dang po sum ni drup che go ne ye wa dang, shi pa dang nga pa nyi ni drup tsul gyi go ne ye wa dang, druk pa dang dun pa nyi ni tun chok la juk tsul gyi go ne ye wa yin no

The sixth and seventh are explained respectively. That which arises from effort is a reason that engages the similar class in two ways in a proof establishing the impermanence of sound. Product is a perfect reason that engages the similar class as a pervader in that proof. The first three reasons above are classified by way of their thesis. The fourth and fifth are classified by way of their mode of proof. The sixth and seventh are classified by way of their mode of engagement of the similar class.

Tsöl jung, Arising from effort, can be explained as follows. Sometimes when it is just about to rain there is the sound of thunder. Is it a sound made by somebody? No. What about when someone picks up a bugle and starts blowing on it—toot too too toooo, is that sound made by someone? Yes, of course. This is the meaning of *tsöl jung*, arising from somebody's efforts. *Be tsöl* means a kind of effort exerted by someone. The sound comes from somebody's making it. However, there are some sounds that don't require people to make them, like the sound of thunder. These are general sounds. So in the statement: *dra chö chen, mi tak te, tsöl jung yin pe chir*, what is the quality to be proved? *Mi tak pa*, Impermanence. What is *tun chok*, the similar class, in this case? Anything that is impermanent. Therefore, we can say: *che pa yin na mi tak pa yin pe kyap*, whatever is produced must necessarily be impermanent. However, with regard to the statement above—*dra chö chen, mi tak te, tsöl jung yin pe chir*—this statement is an example of *tun chok la kyap pa nam nyi su juk pe tak*, a reason engaging the similar class in two ways. The pervasions must be stated as follows: *mi tak pa yin na tsöl jung yin pe ma kyap*; *mi tak pa yin na tsöl jung ma yin pe yang ma kyap*, whatever is impermanent does not necessarily arise from effort, and whatever is impermanent also does not necessarily not arise from effort. Now, *ka re shak*, what would you put forth as an example of the first pervasion? *Gang ri chö chen*, The subject, a snowy mountain. This is a well-known example of something that is not made by anyone. Now, for the second pervasion: *mi tak pa yin na, tsöl jung ma yin pe ma kyap*, *ka re shak*, what would you put forth as an example of something that although impermanent is not necessarily not arisen from effort? *Dung dra chö chen*, The sound of a conch shell. If somebody doesn't apply effort to produce that sound, no sound will come from it. We can also say: *mi yin na kuk pa yin pe ma kyap*, whoever is a human being is not necessarily stupid; *mi yin na kuk pa ma yin pe yang ma kyap*, whoever is a human being is also not necessarily not stupid. This is the meaning of *nam pa nyi*, two aspects [of pervasion].

An example of *de drup gyi tun chok la kyap je du juk pe tak yang dak*, a perfect reason engaging the similar class as a pervader, given above is *che pa*, product, in the statement: *dra chö chen, mi tak te, che pa yin pe chir*, consider sound, it is impermanent, because it is a product. In this proof, the reason, product, pervades the similar class of the impermanent.

classifications by way of the quality to be proved:
perfect affirmative reason

།ཡང་དེ་ལ་བསྒྲུབ་བྱའི་ཆོས་ཀྱི་སྒོ་ནས་དབྱེ་ན་སྒྲུབ་རྟགས་ཡང་དག་དང་

དགག་རྟགས་ཡང་དག་གཉིས། དེ་སྒྲུབ་ཀྱི་རྟགས་ཡང་དག་གང་ཞིག །དེ་

སྒྲུབ་ཀྱི་དངོས་ཀྱི་བསྒྲུབ་བྱའི་ཆོས་སུ་གཟུང་བྱ་ཡང་ཡིན་སྒྲུབ་པ་ཡང་ཡིན་
པའི་གཞི་མཐུན་སྲིད་པ་དེ། དེ་སྒྲུབ་ཀྱི་དང་པོའི་མཚན་ཉིད།

yang de la drup che chö kyi go ne ye na drup tak yang dak dang gak tak yang dak nyi, de drup kyi tak yang dak gang shik, de drup kyi ngö kyi drup che chö su sung ja yang yin drup pa yang yin pe shi tun si pa de, de drup kyi dang pö tsen nyi

Also, when perfect reasons are classified according to their quality to be proved, there are two: perfect affirmative reasons and perfect negative reasons. The definition of a perfect affirmative reason in that proof is that which is a possible combination of 1) being a perfect reason in that proof, and 2) what is held as the explicit quality to be proved in that proof is a positive entity.

An example, once again, is the reason used in the statement: *dra chö chen, mi tak te, che pa yin pe chir*, consider sound, it is impermanent, because it is produced. *Che pa*, Produced, is *drup tak yang dak*, a perfect affirmative reason.

perfect negative reason

དེ་དང་དགག་པ་ཡང་ཡིན་པའི་གཞི་མཐུན་སྲིད་པ་དེ། དེ་སྒྲུབ་ཀྱི་གཉིས་པའི་
མཚན་ཉིད། འོན་ཀྱང་འདི་ལ་དཔྱད་པར་བྱ་བ་མང་ངོ།

de dang gak pa yang yin pe shi tun si pa de, de drup kyi nyi pe tsen nyi, wön kyang di la che par ja wa mang ngo

The definition of a perfect negative reason in that proof is that which is a possible combination of 1) being a perfect reason in that proof, and 2) what is held as the explicit quality to be proved in that proof is a negative entity. However, these may be analyzed in many ways.

On the debate ground we have to debate a lot about this point [concerning affirmative and negative reasons].

We can investigate some difficulties that may arise using the method of debate.

***

—*Dra chö chen, mi tak te, che pa yin pe chir, she gö pe tse che pa de chö chen, de drup gyi drup tak yang dak yin par tel,* In the posited statement: Consider sound, it is impermanent, because it is a product, does it follow that "product" is a perfect affirmative reason in this proof?
—*Dö*, Yes.
—*De drup gyi ngö kyi drup che chö su sung ja de drup pa yin par tel,* You're telling me then that what is held as the explicit quality to be proved in this proof is a positive entity?
—*Dö*, Yes.
—*Mi tak pa drup pa yin par tel,* Is "<u>im</u>permanent" a positive entity?
—*Dö*, Yes.
—*Drup pa ma yin par tel, gak pa yin pe chir,* It is *not* a positive entity, because it's a negative entity.
—*Chi chir,* Why would you say that?
—*Yin par tel, de rang gi ming gi ta mar "mi" la sok pa, yin pe chir,* It has to be a negative entity because it complies with the definition of a negative word that states: "a word is made negative when you apply [one of the four] negative particles to it," as is the case with "*<u>mi</u> tak pa*," impermanent.

There are many debates like this that are very difficult to answer. This is only a very brief example to give you some idea of what is involved in debating such problems.

།དེ་སྒྲུབ་ཀྱི་འབྲས་རང་གི་རྟགས་ཡང་དག་གཉིས་པོ་གང་རུང་ཡིན་ན། དེ་སྒྲུབ་ཀྱི་སྒྲུབ་རྟགས་ཡང་དག་ཡིན་པས་ཁྱབ་པ་དང་། དེ་སྒྲུབ་ཀྱི་མ་དམིགས་པའི་རྟགས་ཡང་དག་ཡིན་ན། དེ་སྒྲུབ་ཀྱི་དགག་རྟགས་ཡང་དག་ཡིན་པས་ཁྱབ་སྟེ། རྣམ་འགྲེལ་རང་འགྲེལ་ལས། དེ་ལ་གཉིས་ནི་དངོས་པོ་བསྒྲུབ་པ་ཡིན་ལ། །གཅིག་ནི་དགག་པའི་གཏན་ཚིགས་སོ། །ཞེས་གསུངས་པའི་ཕྱིར།

de drup kyi dre rang gi tak yang dak nyi po gang rung yin na, de drup kyi drup tak yang dak yin pe kyap pa dang, de drup kyi ma mik pe tak yang dak yin na, de drup kyi gak tak yang dak yin pe kyap te, nam drel rang drel le, de la nyi ni ngö po drup pa yin la, chik ni gak pe ten tsik so, she sung pe chir

If something is either of the two, a reason of effect or a reason of same nature, in a proof, it must necessarily be a perfect affirmative reason in that proof. Also, if something is a perfect reason of non-observation in that proof, it must necessarily be a perfect negative reason in that proof. As the great Acharya Dharmakīrti states in his autocommentary to the *Commentary to (Dignāga's) "Valid Cognition"*: "Two reasons [reason of effect and reason of same nature] prove positive entities and one [reason of non-observation] is proof of a negative entity.

Nyi ni refers to the two, *rang shin gyi tak*, a reason of same nature, and *dre tak*, a reason of effect. *Dre rang ma mik pe tak sum le*, Among [these three reasons], two of them—*dre tak*, reason of effect, and *rang shin gyi tak nyi ni*, reason of same nature—*ngö po drup pa tak yang dak yin*, are perfect reasons that are positive entities. *Chik ni gak pe ten tsik* means one of them is a negative entity, referring to *ma mik pe tak*, reason of non-observation.

classifications by way of the opponent:
perfect reasons for oneself *and*
perfect reasons for others

ཡང་དེ་ལ་རང་དོན་སྐབས་ཀྱི་རྟགས་ཡང་དག་དང་གཞན་དོན་སྐབས་ཀྱི་
རྟགས་ཡང་དག་གཉིས་ཡོད་དེ།

yang de la rang dön kab kyi tak yang dak dang shen dön kab kyi tak yang dak nyi yö de

Perfect reasons may also be classified into two other categories: perfect reasons within the context of proving something to oneself and perfect reasons within the context of proving something to others.

For example, if I make the statement: *dra chö chen, mi tak te, che pa yin pe chir*, consider sound, it is impermanent, because it is produced, this is *shen dön kab kyi tak yang dak*, a perfect reason within the context of [proving something to] others. In this case, *nga göl*, the challenger, is making this statement to *chir göl*, the defender; that is, somebody is presenting reasons to you or you to someone else. However, if another person is not present and you are investigating the nature of impermanence, you can make a similar statement to yourself using "pot," for instance, as a subject: *bum pa chö chen, mi tak te, che pa yin pe chir*, consider a pot, it is impermanent, because it is produced. Within the context of proving something to oneself in the absence of an opponent, such a reason is known as *rang dön kab gyi tak yang dak*, a perfect reason within the context of establishing something for oneself. In this case you can use your own logic and reasons to establish the truth to yourself.

དེ་གཉིས་དེ་སྒྲུབ་ཀྱི་རྟགས་ཡང་དག་ཡིན་པར་མཚུངས་ཀྱང་དེ་སྒྲུབ་ཀྱི་ཕྱི་
རྒོལ་ཡང་དག་ཡོད་མེད་ཀྱི་སྒོ་ནས་འཇོག་པའི་ཕྱིར་རོ།

de nyi de drup kyi tak yang dak yin par tsung kyang de drup kyi chir göl yang dak yö me kyi go ne jok pe chir ro

Both of these are similar in that they are perfect reasons; however, the difference only depends on whether or not a perfect second party is present.

Although they are both perfect reasons, *rang dön kab kyi tak yang dak*, a perfect reason within the context of proving something for oneself, does not require *chir göl*, a second party. *Shen dön kab kyi tak yang dak*, A perfect reason within the context of proving something for others, does require *chir göl*, a second party. This is the difference between these two.

The next kind of reason is very important for us.

།ཡང་སྐྱེ་བ་སྔ་ཕྱི་ཡོད་པར་བསྒྲུབ་པའི་རྟགས་སྦྱོར་ནི། སོ་སྐྱེ་འཆི་ཁ་མའི་སེམས་ཐ་མ་ཆོས་ཅན། ཁྱོད་ཀྱི་ཉེར་འབྲས་སུ་གྱུར་པའི་རིག་པ་ཕྱི་མ་ཡོད་དེ། ཁྱོད་ཆགས་བཅས་རྒྱུན་ལྡན་གྱི་རིག་པ་ཡིན་པའི་ཕྱིར། དཔེར་ན། ད་ལྟའི་བློ་བཞིན།

yang kye wa nga chi yö par drup pe tak jor ni, so kye chi ka me sem ta ma chö chen, kyö kyi nyern dre su gyur pe rik pa chi ma yö de, kyö chak che gyun den gyi rik pa yin pe chir, per na, da te lo shin

Also, [we can] apply perfect reasons to prove that there are previous and future rebirths. An illustrative proof is: Consider the very last moment of mind of an ordinary person just on the verge of dying, there exists a later cognitive awareness that becomes its direct effect, because it is a cognitive awareness that has a continuum infused with desire. Take our present mind as an example.

So (sö) kye (wo) means an ordinary person. *Chi ka me sem ta ma chö chen* means the very last moment of mind before dying in the mental continuum of that ordinary person. What marks the division between being an ordinary person and an Arya? The achievement of *tong lam*, the Path of Insight. It is when you reach this path that you become an Arya and cease to be an ordinary person.

After the very last moment of death of an ordinary person comes the beginning of that one's bardo or [intermediate state between this life and the next]. *Kyö kyi nyer(n) dre su gyur pe* means [this mind] becomes the direct effect of that previous life's mind. *Nyer(n) dre* means the effect that arises from its most immediate cause. *Rik pa* means mind. *Ke chik dang po* refers to the very first moment of the bardo. This moment [of mind] is *nyer(n) dre*, the direct effect, of that previous mind of an ordinary being and serves as the first mind of that one's bardo being. *Kyö chak che gyun den gyi rik pa yin pe chir* means that an ordinary person, as *kor wa pa*, a samsaric being, still has a mind that is influenced by the mental afflictions of ignorance, hatred, and desire. By the force of mental afflictions and karma, that ordinary being will be looking for his next life. For this kind of being it is *se pa*, strong craving, that induces him to look for a next life, and *len pa*, grasping, that chooses it. These are the primary forces that arrange the next life. And, given that most of the deeds of a samsaric being are non-virtuous, choosing the next life is not so much a matter of choosing but rather a matter of getting what comes first, like sticking your hand in a jar of candy and pulling out whatever it is you grasp.

However, as a Dharma practitioner, at the very last moment before death, if you are ready to abandon samsara and achieve nirvana, at that moment *kor we gyun chak pa*, you can cut the continuum of samsara, or that desirous mind, and achieve Arhatship. Therefore, *neln jor pa*, yogi practitioners, have to understand this system, know what they are doing, and learn how to stop such a mind.

Da te lo shin means like our present mind, which is constantly thinking about how to achieve the "good" things of samsara. Understanding this kind of *ma rik pa*, ignorance, is crucial in Buddhist philosophy and serves an important purpose, since it proves that there is a next life, and that life won't just vanish when we die. Once we prove future lives, we have to proceed to prove previous lives as well.

> བྱིས་པ་བཙས་མ་ཐག་པའི་བློ་ཆོས་ཅན། རང་གི་རིགས་འདྲའི་བློ་སྔ་མ་སྔོན་དུ་སོང་སྟེ། རིག་པ་ཡིན་པའི་ཕྱིར། དཔེར་ན། རྒན་པོའི་བློ་བཞིན་ཞེས་པ་ལྟ་བུའོ།
>
> *chi pa tse ma tak pe lo chö chen, rang gi ring dre lo nga ma ngön du song te, rik pa yin pe chir, per na gen pö lo shin she pa ta bu'o*
>
> Consider the mind of a freshly newborn baby, it had a prior mind that was similar in kind to the one it has at present, because it is an awareness; we can take the mind of an old person by analogy.

Chi pa means baby. *Tse ma tak* means just born, "waaa, waaaaa, waaa." That baby's mind is unbelieveable; only after nine months and ten days it can make such a noise. Just before that it was barely starting in the mother's womb.

Consider the mind of a newborn infant, *rang gi ring dre lo nga ma ngön du song te* means it has the same continuum as previously; *rik pa yin pe chir*, because it is mind. *Per na gen pö lo shin*, An old person's mind, for instance. We often hear old people say: "When I was young I did such and such…and then I went to school and learned such and such," and so forth. This indicates a certain continuity or current of mind where one memory follows another in that old person's life. It is by using such reasons that we can establish the existence of previous and future lives.

Some non-Buddhists believe in previous lives, but fail to believe in karma. Some of them also believe that when a person dies as a human being, he will definitely be reborn in the next life as a human being. Or they believe that when a donkey dies, for instance, it must be reborn in the next life as a donkey. These views are very mistaken. Most non-Buddhists don't even believe in previous lives. They believe that when a being dies its life simply goes out like *mar me*, a butterlamp. When it goes out it is extinguished and there is no next life. In their view, once it goes out it goes out forever and that's it.

False reasons

We have finished our discussion of perfect reasons. Here begins an explanation of false reasons.

།གཉིས་པ་རྟགས་ལྟར་སྣང་ནི། རྣམ་འགྲེལ་ལས། གཏན་ཚིགས་ལྟར་སྣང་དེ་
ལས་གཞན་ཞེས་སོགས་ཀྱིས་བསྟན་ཏེ། དེ་ལ་སྤྱིར་རྟགས་ལྟར་སྣང་མེད་དེ།
གཞི་གྲུབ་ན་རྟགས་ཡང་དག་ཡིན་དགོས་པའི་ཕྱིར། དེ་སྒྲུབ་ཀྱི་རྟགས་ལྟར་
སྣང་ཡོད་དེ། དེ་སྒྲུབ་ཀྱི་ཚུལ་གསུམ་མ་ཡིན་པ། དེ་སྒྲུབ་ཀྱི་རྟགས་ལྟར་སྣང་གི་
མཚན་ཉིད།

nyi pa tak tar nang ni, nam drel le, ten tsik tar nang de le shen she sok kyi ten te, de la chir tak tar nang me de, shi drup na tak yang dak yin gö pe chir, de drup kyi tak tar nang yö de, de drup kyi tsul sum ma yin pa, de drup kyi tak tar nang gi tsen nyi

This second section is regarding false reasons. In the *Commentary to (Dignāga's) "Compendium of Valid Cognition"* these are referred to in a verse that states: "Those reasons other than [perfect reasons] are false reasons." In general, false reasons do not exist, since whatever is a basic existent must be a perfect reason. But false reasons do exist when presented in a specific proof. The definition of a false reason in a proof is that which is not the three modes in that proof.

De la chir tak tar nang me de means that in general there is no such thing as [that which is] a false reason, because this does not comply with the logic rule: *shi drup na tak yang dak yin gö pe chir*, whatever is a basic existent must be a perfect reason. *De drup kyi tak tar nang yö de, de drup kyi tsul sum ma yin pa, de drup kyi tak tar nang gyi tsen nyi*, A false reason can exist in a specific proof, because that which is not the three modes in a proof is the definition of a false reason in that proof. This is further clarified by: *tak tar nang me, de drup kyi tak tar nang yö*, false reasons don't exist, but they do exist [when stated] in a particular proof.

> དབྱེ་ན་གསུམ་སྟེ། དེ་སྒྲུབ་ཀྱི་འགལ་བའི་རྟགས། མ་ངེས་པའི་རྟགས། མ་གྲུབ་པའི་རྟགས་སོ།
>
> *ye na sum te, de drup kyi gel we tak, ma nge pe tak, ma drup pe tak so*
>
> There are three [nominal] classifications of false reasons: 1) a false contradictory reason in that proof, 2) a false indefinite reason in that proof, and 3) a false unestablished reason in that proof.

This threefold classification can be abbreviated as, *de drup gyi gel ma nge ma drup pe tak sum*, three kinds of false reasons: contradictory, indefinite, and unestablished.

false contradictory reason

> །དེ་སྒྲུབ་ཀྱི་ཕྱོགས་ཆོས་གང་ཞིག །ཁྱོད་ཀྱི་རྟགས་ཀྱིས་དེ་སྒྲུབ་ཀྱི་ཁྱབ་པའི་ཚུལ་གཉིས་ཕྱིན་ཅི་ལོག་ཏུ་ངེས་པ། དེ་སྒྲུབ་ཀྱི་འགལ་རྟགས་ཀྱི་མཚན་ཉིད། མཚན་གཞི་ནི་སྒྲ་ཆོས་ཅན། རྟག་སྟེ། བྱས་པ་ཡིན་པའི་ཕྱིར་ཞེས་པའི་རྟགས་དེ་ལྟ་བུ།
>
> *de drup kyi chok chö gang shik, kyö kyi tak kyi de drup kyi kyap pe tsul nyi chin chi lok tu nge pa, de drup kyi gel tak*

> *kyi tsen nyi, tsen shi ni dra chö chen, tak te che pa yin pe chir she pe tak de ta bu*
>
> The definition of a false contradictory reason in a proof is that which is the property of the subject and what is ascertained as erroneous in two ways of pervasion in that proof when using that reason to prove it. An example is the reason used in the following statement: Consider sound, it is permanent, because it is produced.

The meaning of *kyap pe tsul nyi chin chi lok du nge pa*, ascertained as erroneous in two ways of pervasion, can be explained using the following illustration: *dra chö chen, tak te, che pa yin pe chir, she kö pe tse, che pa te de drup kyi gel tak yin*, when we make the statement: Consider sound, it is permanent, because it is a product, this is an example of a false contradictory reason in a proof. Why? *She kö pe tse, che pa te, de drup kyi chok chö*, When we make that statement, product is the property of the subject [because sound, the subject, is a product]. *Che na mi tak pe kyap*, Whatever is a product is impermanent [positive pervasion]. *Che na tak pa ma yin pe kyap*, Whatever is a product is necessarily not permanent [reverse pervasion]. *Kyap pe tsul nyi* means with regard to these two pervasions [positive and reverse], it is *chin chi lok*, erroneous since this statement is attempting to prove the opposite, i.e., that sound is permanent.

false indefinite reason

དེ་སྒྲུབ་ཀྱི་ཕྱོགས་ཆོས་གང་ཞིག །ཁྱོད་ཀྱི་རྟགས་ཀྱིས་དེ་སྒྲུབ་ཀྱི་ཁྱབ་པའི་
ཚུལ་གཉིས་རྣམ་པར་མ་ངེས་པ། དེ་སྒྲུབ་ཀྱི་མ་ངེས་པའི་གཏན་ཚིགས་ཀྱི་
མཚན་ཉིད། མཚན་གཞི་ནི། སྒྲ་ཆོས་ཅན། མི་རྟག་སྟེ། ཡོད་པའི་ཕྱིར་ཞེས་པའི་
རྟགས་དེ་ལྟ་བུ།

de drup kyi chok chö gang shik, kyö kyi tak kyi de drup kyi kyap pe tsul nyi nam par ma nge pa, de drup kyi ma nge pe ten tsik kyi tsen nyi, tsen shi ni, dra chö chen, mi tak te, yö pe chir she pe tak de ta bu

The definition of a false indefinite reason in a proof is that which is the property of the subject and what is indefinite in two ways of pervasion in that proof. To illustrate this, we can use the reason in the statement: Consider sound, it is impermanent, because it exists.

De drup kyi chok chö gang shik, Being the property of the subject, signifies that if it is *de drup kyi gel tak*, a contradictory reason in that proof, or *de drup kyi ma nge pe tak*, an indefinite reason in that proof, it must have *de drup kyi chok chö*, the property of the subject in that proof. That is the main rule. *Che pa*, Product, is *de drup kyi chok chö*, the property of the subject in this proof.

Gel tak, A false contradictory reason, is *kyap pe tsul nyi chin chi lok du nge pa*, ascertained as erroneous in both pervasions [positive and reverse]. By contrast, *ma nge pe tak*, a false indefinite reason, is *kyap pe tsul nyi nam par ma nge pa*, indefinite in two ways with regard to those pervasions. What does "indefinite" mean here? This can be explained using the example given by the text: *dra chö chen, mi tak te, yö pe chir*, consider sound, it is impermanent, because it exists. *Yö pa yin na mi tak pa yin pe yang ma kyap, ma yin pe yang ma kyap*, If it exists it is both not necessarily impermanent and it is not necessarily not impermanent since permanent entities are existents as well.

***

—*Yö pa yin na mi tak pa yin pe ma kyap ka re shak*, What would you propose as an example of something that exists but is not necessarily impermanent?

—*Du ma che kyi nam ka chö chen, tak pa shak, she ja shak*, I would put forth uncomposed space, permanent phenomenon, or object of knowledge.

—*Yö pa yin na mi tak pa ma yin pe yang ma kyap ka re shak*, Now, what would you propose as an example of something that exists but is not necessarily not impermanent?

—*Bum pa chö chen*, I would posit a pitcher.

That is the meaning of *kyap pe tsul nyi nam par ma nge pa*, indefinite in two ways in regard to its pervasions, which can be verified by the following: *yin pe yang ma kyap, ma yin pe yang ma kyap*, it is both not necessarily that and not necessarily not that.

---

false unestablished reason

དེ་སྒྲུབ་ཀྱི་ཕྱོགས་ཆོས་མ་ཡིན་པར་དམིགས་པ་དེ། དེ་སྒྲུབ་ཀྱི་མ་གྲུབ་པའི་གཏན་ཚིགས་ཀྱི་མཚན་ཉིད།

de drup kyi chok chö ma yin par mik pa de, de drup kyi ma drup pe ten tsik kyi tsen nyi

The definition of a false unestablished reason in a proof is that which is perceived as not being the property of the subject in that proof.

Unlike the two other kinds of false reasons, this kind of false reason cannot have *chok chö*, the property of the subject, at all.

> དབྱེ་ན་མང་ཡང་བསྡུ་ན་དགུ་སྟེ།
>
> *ye na mang yang du na gu te*
>
> This kind of reason has many classifications. However, these can be condensed into nine types, which are as follows:
>
> དེ་སྒྲུབ་ཀྱི་རྟགས་ཀྱི་ངོ་བོ་མེད་ནས་མ་གྲུབ་པ། དེ་བཞིན་དུ་ཆོས་ཅན་གྱི་ངོ་བོ་
> མེད་ནས་མ་གྲུབ་པ། རྩོད་གཞིའི་སྟེང་དུ་མེད་ནས་མ་གྲུབ་པ། གསུམ་དང་།
> ཞེན་འདོད་མེད་ནས་མ་གྲུབ་པ། ཆོས་ཅན་ལ་ཐེ་ཚོམ་ཟ་ནས་མ་གྲུབ་པ།
> འབྲེལ་བ་ལ་ཐེ་ཚོམ་ཟ་ནས་མ་གྲུབ་པ་གསུམ་དང་། རྟགས་ཆོས་ཐ་དད་མེད་
> ནས་མ་གྲུབ་པ། གཞི་ཆོས་ཐ་དད་མེད་ནས་མ་གྲུབ་པ། གཞི་རྟགས་ཐ་དད་མེད་
> ནས་མ་གྲུབ་པ་དང་གསུམ་སྟེ་དགུའོ།
>
> *1) de drup kyi tak kyi ngo wo me ne ma drup pa, 2) de shin du chö chen gyi ngo wo me ne ma drup pa, 3) tsö shi teng du me ne ma drup pa sum dang, 4) shen dö me ne ma drup pa, 5) chö chen la te tsom sa ne ma drup pa, 6) drel wa la te tsom sa ne ma drup pa sum dang, 7) tak chö ta te me ne ma drup pa, 8) shi chö ta te me ne ma drup pa, 9) shi tak ta te me ne ma drup pa dang sum te gu'o*
>
> 1) An unestablished reason through the lack of identity of the reason in that proof, 2) an unestablished reason through the lack of identity of the subject of debate in that proof, 3) an unestablished reason due to the non-existent nature relative to the basis of debate in that proof, those three; and 4) an unestablished reason through the lack of doubt about

the subject in that proof, 5) an unestablished reason through having misgivings about the existence of the subject of debate in that proof, 6) an unestablished reason through having misgivings about the relationship in that proof, those three; and 7) an unestablished reason through the lack of difference between the reason and the quality to be proved in that proof, 8) an unestablished reason through the lack of difference between the basis of debate and the quality to be proved in that proof, and 9) an unestablished reason through the lack of difference between the basis of debate and the reason in that proof, those three; making a total of nine.

In general, *de drup kyi chok chö*, the property of the subject, doesn't exist in false unestablished reasons. Therefore, there cannot be *shen dö chö chen kyön me*, a faultless subject about which there is doubt. For example, if we make the statement: *ri bong ra chö chen, mi tak te, ri bong ra yin pe chir*, consider a hare's horn, it is impermanent, because it is a hare's horn, there is no *chok chö*, property of the subject, because that subject, *ri bong ra*, a hare's horn, doesn't exist.

Examples to illustrate these nine kinds of false unestablished reasons are given below.

1) an unestablished reason through lack of identity of the reason in that proof

།མཚན་གཞི་ནི་རིམ་པ་བཞིན་དུ་དང་པོ་ནི། སྒྲ་ཆོས་ཅན། སྐྱེས་པ་ཡིན་ཏེ། རྒྱུ་རྟག་པ་ལས་བྱུང་བའི་ཕྱིར་ཞེས་པའི་རྟགས་དེ་ལྟ་བུའོ།

tsen shi ni rim pa shin du dang po ni, dra chö chen, kye pa yin te, gyu tak pa le jung we chir she pe tak te ta bu'o

These are the respective illustrations. The first is the reason used in the following statement: Consider sound, it is created, because it arises from a permanent cause.

This is an example of *tak kyi ngo wo me ne ma drup pa*, an unestablished reason through the lack of identity of the reason [in that proof]. *Gyu tak pa,* A permanent cause, does not exist and consequently such a reason cannot be logically applied to sound.

2) an unestablished reason through the lack of identity of the subject of debate in that proof

།གཉིས་པ་ནི། རི་བོང་གི་ར་ཆོས་ཅན། ཡོད་དེ། ར་ཡིན་པའི་ཕྱིར། ཞེས་པའི་
རྟགས་དེ་ལྟ་བུ།

nyi pa ni, ri bong gi ra chö chen, yö de, ra yin pe chir, she pe tak de ta bu

An example of the second is the reason used in the statement: Consider a hare's horn, it exists, because it is a horn.

This is an example of *chö chen kyi ngo wo me ne ma drup pa*, an unestablished reason through the lack of identity of the subject of debate [in that proof], because *chö chen*, the subject of debate, in this case, a hare's horn, does not exist.

3) an unestablished reason due to the non-existent nature relative to the basis of debate in that proof

གསུམ་པ་ནི། སྒྲ་ཆོས་ཅན། དངོས་པོ་ཡིན་ཏེ། མིག་གིས་མཐོང་བའི་ཕྱིར། ཞེས་
པའི་རྟགས་དེ་ལྟ་བུ་དང་།

sum pa ni, dra chö chen, ngö po yin te, mik gi tong we chir, she pe tak de ta bu dang

> An example of the third is that reason used in the statement: Consider sound, it is a causally effective thing, because it is perceived by the eye.

This is an example of *tsö shi teng du me ne ma drup pa*, an unestablished reason through the non-existent nature relative to the basis of debate [in that proof], because sound is obviously not something that can be perceived by the eye. *Mik she kyi sung ja*, The object of eye consciousness, does not exist relative to *tsö shi*, the basis of debate, which in this case is *dra*, sound.

4) an unestablished reason through the lack of doubt about the subject in that proof

བཞི་པ་ནི། དེ་ཆོས་ཅན། མཉན་བྱ་ཡིན་ཏེ། མི་རྟག་པ་ཡིན་པའི་ཕྱིར་ཞེས་པའི་རྟགས་ལྟ་བུ།

shi pa ni, de chö chen, nyen ja yin te, mi tak pa yin pe chir she pe tak ta bu

> An example of the fourth is the reason used in the statement: Consider sound, it is an object of ear [consciousness], because it is impermanent.

This is an example of *shen dö me ne ma drup pa*, an unestablished reason due to the lack of doubt about the subject [in that proof]. The meaning of *shen dö* can be illustrated by this example: *dra chö chen, mi tak te, che pa yin pe chir, chir göl te, dra che pa yin pa tse me nge, che pa yin na mi tak pa yin pe kyap pa tse me nge, dra mi tak pa yin min la te tsom sa*, consider sound, it is impermanent, because it is a product; that opponent has ascertained sound as being a product; he knows that if it is a product it must be impermanent; yet he has doubt as to whether or not sound [the subject of debate] is impermanent. However, *dra nyen ja yin pa shen dö shuk gang sak me*, there doesn't exist a person who has doubt as to whether or not sound is an object of the ear consciousness.

5) an unestablished reason through having misgivings about the existence of the subject of debate in that proof

ལྔ་པ་ནི། དྲི་ཟ་བསྐལ་དོན་དུ་སོང་བའི་གང་ཟག་གི་ངོ་བོར་དྲི་ཟའི་གླུ་དབྱངས་ཆོས་ཅན། མི་རྟག་སྟེ། བྱས་པའི་ཕྱིར་ཞེས་པའི་རྟགས་དེ་ལྟ་བུ།

nga pa ni, dri sa kel dön du song we gang sak gi ngo wor dri se lu yang chö chen, mi tak te, che pe chir she pe tak de ta bu

An example of the fifth is the reason used in the statement: Consider the song of a ghost in the presence of a person who has doubt about the existence of ghosts, it is impermanent, because it is produced.

This is an example of *chö chen la te tsom sa ne ma drup pa*, an unestablished reason through having misgivings about the existence of the subject of debate [in that proof]. The subject in this statement is the song of a ghost relative to a person who has doubt about the existence of ghosts in general. That debater cannot know anything about ghosts. If that's the case, what is he going to respond to you when you begin asking him about the song of a ghost?

6) an unestablished reason through having misgivings about the relationship in that proof

དྲུག་པ་ནི། དེ་ཆོས་ཅན། ཡོད་དེ། དྲི་ཟའི་ཚད་མས་གྲུབ་པའི་ཕྱིར། ཞེས་པའི་རྟགས་དེ་ལྟ་བུ་དང་།

druk pa ni, de chö chen, yö de, dri se tse me drup pe chir, she pe tak de ta bu dang

An example of the sixth is the reason used in the statement: Consider the song of a ghost in the presence of a person who has doubt about the existence of ghosts, it exists, because it is perceived by the valid cognition of a ghost.

The sixth is an example of *drel wa la te tsom sa ne ma drup pa*, an unestablished reason due to doubt about the relationship [in that proof]. Here the subject is the same as the one above. Giving the reason "because it is established by the valid cognition of a ghost" to *chir göl*, an opposing debater, who doesn't know anything about ghosts, how can he know anything about what a ghost perceived by its valid cognition? That's not possible.

7) an unestablished reason through the lack of difference between the reason and the quality to be proved in that proof

བདུན་པ་ནི། སྒྲ་ཆོས་ཅན། མི་རྟག་སྟེ། མི་རྟག་པའི་ཕྱིར། ཞེས་པའི་རྟགས་དེ་ལྟ་བུ།

dun pa ni, dra chö chen, mi tak te, mi tak pe chir, she pe tak de ta bu

An example of the seventh is the reason used in the statement: Consider sound, it is impermanent, because it is impermanent.

The seventh is an example of *tak chö ta te me ne ma drup pa*, an unestablished reason through the lack of difference between the reason and the quality to be proved [in that proof].

8) an unestablished reason through the lack of difference between the basis of debate and the quality to be proved in that proof

བརྒྱད་པ་ནི། སྒྲ་ཆོས་ཅན། སྒྲ་ཡིན་ཏེ། མི་རྟག་པའི་ཕྱིར། ཞེས་པའི་རྟགས་དེ་ལྟ་བུ།

gye pa ni, dra chö chen, dra yin te, mi tak pe chir, she pe tak de ta bu

An example of the eighth is the reason used in the statement: Consider sound, it is sound, because it is impermanent.

The eighth is an example of *shi chö ta te me ne ma drup pa*, an unestablished reason through the lack of difference between the basis of debate and the quality to be proved [in that proof].

9) an unestablished reason through the lack of difference between the basis of debate and the reason in that proof

དགུ་པ་ནི། སྒྲ་ཆོས་ཅན། མི་རྟག་སྟེ། སྒྲ་ཡིན་པའི་ཕྱིར་ཞེས་བཀོད་པའི་ཚེ་རྟགས་དེ་ལྟ་བུའོ།

gu pa ni, dra chö chen, mi tak te, dra yin pe chir she kö pe tse tak de ta bu'o

An example of the ninth is the reason used in the statement: Consider sound, it is impermanent, because it is sound.

This is an illustration of the ninth kind of unestablished reason, namely, *shi tak ta te me ne ma drup pa*, an unestablished reason through the lack of difference between the basis of debate and the reason [in that proof].

We can review this way.

***

—*Tak tar nang la ye na ka tsö yö*, When false reasons are classified, how many are there?

—*Sum yö*, Three.

—Ha! *Ri bong la ye na ka tsö yö*, If you classify a hare's horns, how many would you say there are? That is why you have to add the phrase *de drup kyi*, in a particular proof, to your reply because false reasons only exist relative to particular proofs and not otherwise.

—*De drup kyi gel tak gyi tsen nyi shak gyu me pe chir*, I bet you don't know the definition of a false contradictory reason in a proof.

—*Tak ma drup*, That's not true.

—*De drup kyi gel tak gyi tsen nyi shak gyu yö par tel*, So you do know the definition of a false contradictory reason in a proof?

—*Dö*, Sure I do.

—*Sho*, Tell me what it is!

—*Kyö de drup gyi chok chö gang shik, kyö kyi tak kyi de drup kyi kyap pe tsul nyi chin chi lok tu nge pa, de drup kyi gel tak kyi tsen nyi*, The definition of a false contradictory reason in a proof is the property of the subject in that proof and what is ascertained as erroneous in two ways of pervasion.

—*De drup kyi gel tak gyi tsen shi kyi sho*, Give me an example illustrating a false contradictory reason!

—*Dra chö chen, tak te, che pe chir*, Consider sound, it is permanent, because it is a product. *Che pa*, Product, is *de drup kyi chok chö*, the property of the subject in this proof. *Kyap pe tsul nyi chin chi lok du nge pa yin te*, [Product] is ascertained as being erroneous in two ways of pervasion, because *che na tak pa ma yin pe kyap*, if it is a product, it is necessarily not a permanent entity. Therefore, when making the statement: *dra chö chen, tak te, che pa yin pe chir, she kö pe tse che pa te, de drup kyi gel(n) tak*, consider sound, it is permanent, because it is produced, this is an example of a contradictory reason in that proof.

—*De drup kyi ma nge pe ten tsik kyi tsen nyi shak gyu me pe chir*, I bet you don't know the definition of a false indefinite reason in a proof?

—*Tak ma drup*, That's not true.

—*De drup kyi ma nge pe ten tsik kyi tsen nyi shak gyu yö par tel*, So you do know the definition of a false indefinite reason in a proof.

—*Dö*, Yes, of course.

—*Sho*, If that's so, then tell me what it is!

—*Kyö de drup kyi chok chö gang shik, kyö kyi tak kyi de drup kyi kyap pe tsul nyi nam par ma nge pa, de drup kyi ma nge pe ten tsik kyi tsen nyi*, The definition of a false indefinite reason in a proof is the property of the subject in that proof and what is indefinite in two ways of pervasion in that proof.

—*De drup kyi ma nge pe ten tsik gyi tsen shi kyi sho*, Give me an example illustrating a false indefinite reason!

—*Dra chö chen, mi tak te, yö pe chir*, Consider sound, it is impermanent, because it exists. That is, *de drup kyi chok chö gang shik, de drup kyi kyap pe tsul nyi nam par ma nge pa*, It has the property of the subject in that proof as well as being indefinite in two ways of pervasion in that proof. *Yö na, mi tak pa yin pe yang ma kyap, yö na mi tak pa ma yin pe yang ma kyap*, If it exists, it is not necessarily an impermanent phenomenon and, if it exists it is not necessarily not an impermanent phenomenon. That is the meaning of *kyap pe tsul nyi nam par ma nge pa*, being indefinite in two ways of pervasion.

—*Yö na, mi tak pa yin pe ma kyap ka re shak*, What can you posit as an example of something that exists but is not necessarily an impermanent phenomenon?

—*Du ma che kyi nam ka chö chen*, Uncomposed space.

—*Yö na, mi tak pa ma yin pe yang ma kyap ka re shak*, What can you posit as an example of something that exists but is not necessarily not an impermanent phenomenon?

—*Ka wa chö chen*, A pillar.

—*De drup kyi ma drup pe ten tsik gyi tsen nyi shak gyu me pe chir*, I bet you don't know the definition of a false unestablished reason in a proof.
—*Tak ma drup*, Of course I do.
—*De drup kyi ma nge pe ten tsik gyi tsen nyi shak gyu yö par tel*, You really do know the definition of a false unestablished reason in a proof?
—*Dö*, Yes.
—*Sho*, Tell me what it is then!
—*Kyö de drup kyi chok chö ma yin par mik pa de, de drup kyi ma drup pe ten tsik kyi tsen nyi*, The definition of a false unestablished reason in a proof is that which is perceived as not being the property of the subject in that proof.
—*De drup kyi ma drup pe ten tsik gyi tsen shi kyi sho*, Give me an example illustrating a false unestablished reason.
—There are many, but if you abbreviate them, they may be classified into nine different kinds. [These have already been cited above.]

།ཕྱོགས་ཆོས་འཁོར་ལོ།

།སྒྲ་ཆོས་ཅན། །རྟག་སྟེ། །གཞལ་བྱ་ཡིན་པའི་ཕྱིར།	།སྒྲ་ཆོས་ཅན། །མི་རྟག་སྟེ། །བྱས་པ་ཡིན་པའི་ཕྱིར།	།དུང་སྒྲ་ཆོས་ཅན། །རྩོལ་བྱུང་ཡིན་ཏེ། །མི་རྟག་པ་ཡིན་པའི་ཕྱིར།
།སྒྲ་ཆོས་ཅན། །རྟག་པ་ཡིན་ཏེ། །བྱས་པ་ཡིན་པའི་ཕྱིར།	།སྒྲ་ཆོས་ཅན། །རྟག་པ་ཡིན་ཏེ། །མཉན་བྱ་ཡིན་པའི་ཕྱིར།	།དུང་སྒྲ་ཆོས་ཅན། །རྟག་པ་ཡིན་ཏེ། །རྩོལ་བྱུང་ཡིན་པའི་ཕྱིར།
།དུང་སྒྲ་ཆོས་ཅན། །རྩོལ་བྱུང་མ་ཡིན་ཏེ། །མི་རྟག་པ་ཡིན་པའི་ཕྱིར།	།དུང་སྒྲ་ཆོས་ཅན། །མི་རྟག་སྟེ། །རྩོལ་བྱུང་ཡིན་པའི་ཕྱིར།	།སྒྲ་ཆོས་ཅན། །རྟག་པ་ཡིན་ཏེ། །རེག་བྱ་ཅན་མ་ཡིན་པའི་ཕྱིར།

Wheel of Reasons

Consider sound, it is permanent, because it is an object of comprehension.	Consider sound, it is impermanent, because it is produced.	Consider the sound of a conch shell, it has arisen from effort, because it is impermanent.
Consider sound, it is permanent, because it is produced.	Consider sound, it is permanent, because it is an object of hearing.	Consider the sound of a conch shell, it is permanent, because has arisen from effort.
Consider the sound of a conch shell, it has arisen from effort, because it is impermanent.	Consider the sound of a conch shell, it is impermanent, because it has arisen from effort.	Consider sound, it is permanent, because it does not possess tangibility.

༄༅ སྒྲ་དང་སྒྲ་དང་དུང་སྒྲ་དང་། །སྒྲ་དང་སྒྲ་དང་དུང་སྒྲ་དང་།
།དུང་སྒྲ་དུང་སྒྲ་སྒྲ་དང་བཅས། །རྟག་དང་མི་རྟག་རྩོལ་བྱུང་ཡིན།
།རྟག་དང་རྟག་དང་རྟག་པ་དང་། །རྩོལ་བྱུང་མིན་དང་མི་རྟག་རྟག
།གཞལ་བྱ་བྱས་དང་མི་རྟག་དང་། །བྱས་དང་མཉན་བྱ་རྩོལ་ལས་བྱུང་།
།མི་རྟག་རྩོལ་བྱུང་རེག་བྱ་མིན།

།སྟེང་འོག་གཉིས་ལ་ཡང་དག་དང་། །ལོག་གཉིས་འགལ་བའི་གཏན་
ཚིགས་དང་། །ཟུར་བཞི་དངོས་ཀྱི་མ་ངེས་པ། །དབུ་ན་ཐུན་མོང་མིན་པའོ།

dra dang dra dang dung dra dang,
dra dang dra dang dung dra dang,
dung dra dung dra dra dang che,
tak dang mi tak tsöl jung yin,
tak dang tak dang tak pa dang,
tsöl jung min dang mi tak tak,
shel ja che dang mi tak dang,
che dang nyen ja tsöl le jung,
mi tak tsöl jung rek ja min

teng wok nyi la yang dak dang,
lok nyi gel we ten tsik dang,
sur shi ngö kyi ma nge pa,
u na tun mong min pa'o

Sound, sound, and the sound of a conch shell; sound, sound, and the sound of a conch shell; the sound of a conch shell, the sound of a conch shell together with sound; permanent, impermanent, and arisen from effort; permanent, permanent, and permanent; not arisen from effort, impermanent, and permanent, object of comprehension, composed entity, and impermanent; composed entity, object of hearing, and arisen from effort; impermanent, arisen from effort, and that which is intangible.

The top and the bottom are perfect reasons, the two sides are contradictory reasons, the four corners are indefinite reasons regarding actual evidence, and the middle one is a unique indefinite reason.

།རྟགས་ཡང་དག་པའི་གོལ་ས་རྣམས།
།ཤེས་ཕྱིར་གཏན་ཚིགས་ལྟར་སྣང་བསྟན།
།ཡང་དག་དང་ནི་ལྟར་སྣང་གི
།རྣམ་དབྱེ་ལེགས་པར་ཕྱེ་བའི་ཆེད།
།ཕྱོགས་ཆོས་ཅན་གྱི་གཏན་ཚིགས་དགུའི།
།རྣམ་གཞག་གཏན་ལ་ཕབ་པ་ཡིན།
།དེས་ན་སྐལ་བཟང་ཐར་འདོད་རྣམས།
།ཡང་དག་རིགས་པའི་རྗེས་འབྲངས་ཏེ།
།གླང་དོར་ཚུལ་བཞིན་རབ་ཕྱེ་ནས།
།སྐུ་གསུམ་གླིང་དུ་བགྲོད་པར་མཛོད།

tak yang dak pe göl sa nam
she chir ten tsik tar nang ten
yang dak dang ni tar nang gi
nam ye lek par che we che
chok chö chen gi ten tsik gu'i
nam shak ten la pab pa yin

de na kel sang tar dö nam
yang dak rik pe je drang te
lang dor tsul shin rab ye ne
ku sum ling du drö par dzö

In order to clearly distinguish between perfect reasons and false reasons,
And to discern well the nature of those contrary reasons,
This "Wheel of Reasons" is presented here.

How fortunate those followers of perfect reasoning,
Since they alone will know what to abandon
And what to pursue on their desired path of liberation to the
Land of the Three Kayas.

Göl sa nam means opposite. When we say *lam gyi göl sa*, this means *lam lok pa*, going the opposite way of the path. Here it is referring to the opposite of a perfect reason, which is *tak tar nang*, a false reason. *She chir* means in order to learn about these. *Ten tsik tar nang ten* means it teaches these false reasons. *Yang dak dang ni tar nang gi, nam ye lek par che we che* means for the purpose of learning clearly and nicely about perfect and false reasons. *Chok chö chen gyi ten tsik gu* means the text is presenting nine kinds of reasons by way of this "Wheel of Reasons." *Nam shak ten la pab pa yin* means that such is its purpose. *Kel sang tar dö nam* means that for this reason logicians are very lucky. *Lang dor tsul shin rab che ne* means properly knowing what is wrong and what is correct, what to get rid of and what to take up. *Ku sum ling du drö par dzö* means that once you've done that, you have to achieve the three bodies—dharmakāya, sambhogakāya, and nirmāṇakāya. That is why you have to follow this system of perfect reasoning.

Okay, we will leave it here. Now we have finished *"thak" rik*.[42]

[42] Rinpoche is making fun of our pronunciation of *tak* (***rtag***), reason, and pronouncing it as *thak* (***thag***), which means rope.

Root Text

བློ་རིག་

Types of Mind

༄༅ དང་པོ་ལ། གསལ་ཞིང་རིག་པ། བློའི་མཚན་ཉིད། དེ་ལ་དབྱེ་ན་ཚད་མ་དང་། ཚད་མིན་གྱི་བློ་གཉིས། གསར་དུ་མི་སླུ་བའི་རིག་པ། ཚད་མའི་མཚན་ཉིད། དབྱེ་ན་མངོན་སུམ་གྱི་ཚད་མ་དང་རྗེས་སུ་དཔག་པའི་ཚད་མ་གཉིས། རང་གི་རྟེན་རྟགས་ལ་མ་བརྟེན་པར་རང་གི་གཞལ་བྱ་ལ་རྟོག་པ་དང་བྲལ་བའི་གསར་དུ་མི་སླུ་བའི་རིག་པ། དང་པོའི་མཚན་ཉིད། དེ་ལ་དབྱེ་ན་དབང་པོའི་མངོན་སུམ་གྱི་ཚད་མ། ཡིད་ཀྱི་མངོན་སུམ་གྱི་ཚད་མ། རང་རིག་མངོན་སུམ་གྱི་ཚད་མ། རྣལ་འབྱོར་མངོན་སུམ་གྱི་ཚད་མ་དང་བཞི། རང་གི་ཐུན་མོང་མ་ཡིན་པའི་བདག་རྐྱེན་དབང་པོ་གཟུགས་ཅན་པ་ལ་བརྟེན་ནས་སྐྱེས་པའི་རང་གི་གཞལ་བྱ་ལ་རྟོག་པ་དང་བྲལ་བའི་མངོན་སུམ་གྱི་ཚད་མ། དང་པོའི་མཚན་ཉིད། དབྱེ་ན། གཟུགས་འཛིན་དབང་པོའི་མངོན་སུམ་གྱི་ཚད་མ་ནས། རེག་འཛིན་དབང་པོའི་མངོན་སུམ་གྱི་ཚད་མའི་བར་ལྔ་ཡོད། རང་གི་ཐུན་མོང་མ་ཡིན་པའི་བདག་རྐྱེན་མིག་དབང་ལ་བརྟེན་ནས་རང་གི་གཞལ་བྱ་ལ་རྟོག་པ་དང་བྲལ་བའི་གསར་དུ་མི་སླུ་བའི་དབང་པོའི་མངོན་སུམ་གྱི་ཚད་མ། དང་པོའི་མཚན་ཉིད། དེ་བཞིན་དུ་འོག་མ་རྣམས་ལ་ཤེས་པར་བྱའོ། རང་གི་ཐུན་མོང་མ་ཡིན་པའི་བདག་རྐྱེན་ཡིད་དབང་ལ་བརྟེན་ནས་རང་གི་གཞལ་བྱ་ལ་རྟོག་པ་དང་བྲལ་ཞིང་གསར་དུ་མི་སླུ་བའི་མངོན་སུམ་གྱི་ཚད་མ། ཡིད་ཀྱི་མངོན་སུམ་ཚད་མའི་མཚན་ཉིད། རང་གི་གཞལ་བྱ་ལ་རྟོག་པ་དང་བྲལ་

ཞེང་མ་འཁྲུལ་བའི་གསར་དུ་མི་སླུ་བའི་འཛིན་རྣམ། རང་རིག་མངོན་སུམ་གྱི་ཚད་མའི་མཚན་ཉིད། རང་གི་ཐུན་མོང་མ་ཡིན་པའི་བདག་རྐྱེན་ཞི་ལྷག་ཟུང་འབྲེལ་གྱི་ཏིང་ངེ་འཛིན་ལ་བརྟེན་ནས་རང་གི་གཞལ་བྱ་ཡང་དག་པའི་དོན་ལ་རྟོག་པ་དང་བྲལ་ཞིང་གསར་དུ་མི་སླུ་བའི་མངོན་སུམ་ཚད་མ། རྣལ་འབྱོར་མངོན་སུམ་གྱི་ཚད་མའི་མཚན་ཉིད། དེ་ལ་རྟེན་གྱི་སྒོ་ནས་དབྱེ་ན། ཉན་ཐོས་འཕགས་པ། རང་རྒྱལ་འཕགས་པ། བྱང་སེམས་འཕགས་པ། སངས་འཕགས་ཀྱི་རྒྱུད་ཀྱི་རྣལ་འབྱོར་མངོན་སུམ་དང་བཞི་ཡོད། ཡུལ་གྱི་སྒོ་ནས་དབྱེ་ན་ཇི་སྙེད་པ་རྟོགས་པའི་དེ། ཇི་ལྟ་བ་རྟོགས་པའི་རྣལ་འབྱོར་མངོན་སུམ་གཉིས་ཡོད། རང་གི་རྟེན་རྟགས་ལ་བརྟེན་ནས་རང་གི་གཞལ་བྱ་ལྐོག་གྱུར་ལ་གསར་དུ་མི་སླུ་བའི་ཞེན་རིག །རྗེས་སུ་དཔག་པའི་ཚད་མའི་མཚན་ཉིད། དབྱེ་ན། དངོས་སྟོབས་རྗེས་དཔག །ཡིད་ཆེས་རྗེས་དཔག །གྲགས་པའི་རྗེས་དཔག་གསུམ་ཡོད། བྱས་པའི་རྟགས་ལ་བརྟེན་ནས་སྒྲ་མི་རྟག་རྟོགས་པའི་གསར་དུ་མི་སླུ་བའི་ཞེན་རིག་དང་པོ་དང་། དཔྱད་གསུམ་གྱི་དག་པའི་ལུང་གི་རྟགས་ལས་སྦྱིན་པས་ལོངས་སྤྱོད་ཁྲིམས་ཀྱི་བདེ། ཞེས་སོགས་ཀྱི་ལུང་རང་གི་བསྟན་བྱའི་དོན་ལ་གསར་དུ་མི་སླུ་བའི་ཞེན་རིག་གཉིས་པ་ཡིན། རྟོག་ཡུལ་ན་ཡོད་པའི་རྟགས་ལས་རི་བོང་ཅན་ལ་ཟླ་སྒྲས་བརྗོད་རུང་དུ་རྟོགས་པའི་

གསར་དུ་མི་སླུ་བའི་རིག་པ་དེ་གསུམ་པ་ཡིན། གསར་དུ་མི་སླུ་བ་མ་ཡིན་པའི་རིག་པ། ཚད་མིན་གྱི་བློའི་མཚན་ཉིད། དབྱེ་ན། བཅད་ཤེས། ཐེ་ཚོམ། ཡིད་དཔྱོད། ལོག་ཤེས། སྣང་ལ་མ་ངེས་དང་ལྔ། རང་གི་ཉེར་ལེན་དུ་གྱུར་པའི་ཚད་མ་སྔ་མས་རྟོགས་ཟིན་པའི་དོན་ལ་མནན་ནས་འཛིན་པའི་རིག་པ། བཅད་ཤེས་ཀྱི་མཚན་ཉིད། དབྱེ་ན། རྟོག་པ་བཅད་ཤེས། མངོན་སུམ་བཅད་ཤེས་གཉིས། ཚུར་མཐོང་གི་རྒྱུད་ཀྱི་སྔོན་འཛིན་མིག་ཤེས་ཀྱིས་དྲངས་པའི་སྔོན་པོ་དོན་མཐུན་དུ་ངེས་པའི་ངེས་ཤེས་དེ་དང་པོ་དང་། སྔོན་འཛིན་མིག་ཤེས་སྐད་ཅིག་གཉིས་པ་གཉིས་པ་ཡིན། རང་གི་དམིགས་པ་ལ་མཐའ་གཉིས་སུ་དོགས་པའི་སེམས་པ། ཐེ་ཚོམ་གྱི་མཚན་ཉིད། དབྱེ་ན། དོན་འགྱུར་གྱི་ཐེ་ཚོམ། དོན་མི་འགྱུར་གྱི་ཐེ་ཚོམ་གཉིས་ཡོད། སྒྲ་རྟག་གམ་མི་རྟག་ཕལ་ཆེར་མི་རྟག་སྙམ་དུ་འཛིན་པའི་ཐེ་ཚོམ་དང་པོ་དང་། སྒྲ་རྟག་གམ་མི་རྟག་ཕལ་ཆེར་རྟག་སྙམ་དུ་འཛིན་པའི་ཐེ་ཚོམ་གཉིས་པ་ཡིན། སྒྱོང་བ་དང་རང་གི་རྟགས་ཡང་དག་ལ་མ་བརྟེན་པར་རང་ཡུལ་བདེན་པ་མཐའ་གཅིག་གསར་དུ་ངེས་པའི་ཞེན་རིག །རང་ཉིད་ཡིད་དཔྱོད་ཀྱི་མཚན་ཉིད། དེ་ལ་རྒྱུ་མཚན་ཅན་གྱི་ཡིད་དཔྱོད། རྒྱུ་མཚན་མེད་པའི་ཡིད་དཔྱོད་གཉིས། རང་གི་ཞེན་ཡུལ་ལ་འཁྲུལ་བའི་རིག་པ། ལོག་ཤེས་ཀྱི་མཚན་ཉིད། དབྱེ་ན། རྟོག་པ་ལོག་ཤེས་དང་། རྟོག་མེད་ལོག་ཤེས་གཉིས་ཡོད། གང་ཟག་གི་བདག་

འཛིན་ལྟ་བུ་དང་པོ་དང་། ཟླ་གཅིག་ཟླ་གཉིས་སུ་སྣང་བའི་དབང་ཤེས་གཉིས་པ་ཡིན། རང་ཡུལ་མངོན་སུམ་དུ་སྣང་ཡང་ངེས་པ་འདྲེན་མི་ནུས་པའི་རིག་པ། སྣང་ལ་མ་ངེས་ཀྱི་བློའི་མཚན་ཉིད། ཡིད་གཟུགས་མཛེས་ལ་ལྷག་པར་ཆགས་བཞིན་པའི་གང་ཟག་གི་རྒྱུད་ཀྱི་སྒྲ་འཛིན་ཉན་ཤེས་ལྟ་བུ་ཡིན་ནོ།

Root Text

རྟགས་རིགས་

Analysis of Reasons

༄། །རྟགས་རིགས་ཀྱི་རྣམ་བཞག་ལུང་རིགས་ཀྱི་སྙིང་པོ་བསྡུས་པ་
མཁས་པ་དགྱེས་བྱེད་ཅེས་བྱ་བ་བཞུགས་སོ། །

ANALYSIS OF REASONS,
THE ESSENCE OF SCRIPTURAL AUTHORITY AND LOGICAL REASONING:
A PRESENTATION TO DELIGHT SCHOLARS

༄༅། །གཉིས་པ་རྟགས་རིགས་ཀྱི་རྣམ་གཞག་རྒྱས་པར་ནི་གཞན་དུ་བཤད་ཟིན་ཅིང་
འདིར་མདོར་བསྡུས་མཚོན་ཙམ་ཞིག་བཤད་པར་བྱ་སྟེ། དེ་ནི། ཚད་མ་རིགས་སྒོ་ལས།
གཏན་ཚིགས་ནི་ཚུལ་གསུམ་མོ། །ཚུལ་གསུམ་གང་ཞེ་ན། ཕྱོགས་ཀྱི་ཆོས་ཉིད་དང་
། མཐུན་པའི་ཕྱོགས་ཉིད་ལ་ཡོད་པར་ངེས་པ་དང་། མི་མཐུན་པའི་ཕྱོགས་ཉིད་ལ་མེད་པ་
ཉིད་དུ་ངེས་པར་ཡོད་དོ། ། ཞེས་དང་། རྣམ་འགྲེལ་ལས། ཕྱོགས་ཆོས་དེ་ཆས་ཁྱབ་པ་ཡི།
།གཏན་ཚིགས་ཞེས་པས་མདོར་བསྟན་ཏེ་འདི་ལ་གསུམ། རྟགས་ཀྱི་མཚན་ཉིད། དབྱེ་བ།
འཕྲོས་དོན་བཤད་པའོ། །དང་པོ་ནི། རྟགས་སུ་བཀོད་པ། རྟགས་ཀྱི་མཚན་ཉིད། དེ་སྒྲུབ་
ཀྱི་རྟགས་སུ་བཀོད་པ། དེ་སྒྲུབ་ཀྱི་རྟགས་ཀྱི་མཚན་ཉིད། ཡོད་མེད་གང་རུང་ཡིན་ན། དེ་
སྒྲུབ་ཀྱི་རྟགས་ཡིན་པས་ཁྱབ་སྟེ། དེ་ཡིན་ན། དེ་སྒྲུབ་ཀྱི་རྟགས་སུ་བཀོད་པས་ཁྱབ་པའི་
ཕྱིར་ཏེ། རི་བོང་རྭ་དེ། དེ་ཆོས་ཅན། མི་རྟག་སྟེ། རི་བོང་རྭ་ཡིན་པའི་ཕྱིར་ཞེས་པའི་རྟགས་
སུ་བཀོད་པའི་ཕྱིར། སྒྲ་མི་རྟག་པར་སྒྲུབ་པར་བྱེད་པའི་རྟགས་སུ་བཀོད་པ། སྒྲ་མི་རྟག་
པར་སྒྲུབ་པར་བྱེད་པའི་རྟགས་ཀྱི་མཚན་ཉིད། དེ་བཞིན་དུ་གཞན་ལ་སྦྱོར་ཚུལ་འགྲེའོ།
།བྱས་པའི་རྟགས་ཀྱིས་སྒྲ་མི་རྟག་པར་སྒྲུབ་པར་བྱེད་པའི་རྟགས་སུ་བཀོད་པ། བྱས་པའི་
རྟགས་ཀྱིས་སྒྲ་མི་རྟག་པར་སྒྲུབ་པར་བྱེད་པའི་རྟགས་ཀྱི་མཚན་ཉིད་ཡིན་ཀྱང་དེ་ཡིན་ན་
བྱས་པ་དང་གཅིག་ཡིན་པས་ཁྱབ་པ་ཡིན་ནོ། །གཉིས་པ་ལ་གཉིས། རྟགས་ཡང་དག་
བཤད་པ་དང་། རྟགས་ལྟར་སྣང་བཤད་པའོ། །དང་པོ་ལ་གསུམ། དེའི་ལྡོས་གཞི་དང་།

མཚན་ཉིད། དབྱེ་བའོ། །དང་པོ་ལ་གཉིས། ཕྱོགས་ཆོས་ཀྱི་ལྟོས་གཞི་དང་། ཁྱབ་པའི་ལྟོས་གཞིའོ། །དང་པོ་ལ་གསུམ། ཤེས་འདོད་ཆོས་ཅན་སྐྱོན་མེད་ཀྱི་མཚན་ཉིད་དང་། མཚན་གཞི་དང་། སྒྲུབ་བྱེད་དོ། །དང་པོ་ནི་མཚོན་ན། ཁྱོད་བྱས་པས་རྟགས་ཀྱིས་སྒྲ་མི་རྟག་པར་སྒྲུབ་པར་བྱེད་པའི་ཆོས་ཅན་དུ་བཟུང་བ་ཡང་ཡིན་ཁྱོད་བྱས་པར་ཚད་མས་ངེས་ནས་མི་རྟག་པ་ལ་ཤེས་འདོད་ཞུགས་པའི་གང་ཟག་སྲིད་པ་ཡང་ཡིན་པའི་གཞི་མཐུན་པར་དམིགས་པ་དེ། ཁྱོད་བྱས་པའི་རྟགས་ཀྱིས་སྒྲ་མི་རྟག་པར་སྒྲུབ་པར་བྱེད་པའི་ཤེས་འདོད་ཆོས་ཅན་སྐྱོན་མེད་ཀྱི་མཚན་ཉིད། དེ་སྒྲུབ་ཀྱི་རྩོད་གཞི་ཡིན་ན། དེ་སྒྲུབ་ཀྱི་ཤེས་འདོད་ཆོས་ཅན་ཡིན་པས་མ་ཁྱབ་ཀྱང་། ཕྱི་མ་ཡིན་ན་སྔ་མ་ཡིན་པས་ཁྱབ་བོ། །དེ་ཡང་ཡིན་ཏེ། སྒྲ་སྒྲར་སྒྲུབ་པའི་ཆོས་ཅན་ཡིན་ཀྱང་དེ་སྒྲུབ་ཀྱི་ཤེས་འདོད་ཆོས་ཅན་མ་ཡིན་པའི་ཕྱིར། དེར་ཐལ། སྒྲ་ཚད་མས་ངེས་ནས་སྒྲ་སྒྲ་ཡིན་མིན་ཐེ་ཚོམ་ཟ་བའི་གང་ཟག་མེད་པའི་ཕྱིར་རོ། །འོན་ཀྱང་བྱས་པའི་རྟགས་ཀྱིས་སྒྲ་མི་རྟག་པར་སྒྲུབ་པར་བྱེད་པའི་ཤེས་འདོད་ཆོས་ཅན་དང་། དེ་སྒྲུབ་ཀྱི་རྩོད་གཞི་དང་། དེ་སྒྲུབ་ཀྱི་དཔག་གཞི་གསུམ་དོན་གཅིག་གོ། །གཉིས་པ་མཚན་གཞི་ནི་སྒྲ་དེའོ། །གསུམ་པ་སྒྲུབ་བྱེད་ནི། སྒྲ་ཆོས་ཅན། ཁྱོད་བྱས་པའི་རྟགས་ཀྱིས་སྒྲ་མི་རྟག་པར་སྒྲུབ་པར་བྱེད་པའི་ཤེས་འདོད་ཆོས་ཅན་སྐྱོན་མེད་ཡིན་ཏེ། མཚན་ཉིད་བ་ཤད་པ་ལྟར་ཡིན་པའི་ཕྱིར་ཞེས་བྱའོ། །སྒྲ་མ་ཡིན་པ་ལས་ལོག་པ་དང་མཐུན་བྱ་གཉིས་རེ་རེ་ནས་དེ་མ་ཡིན་ཏེ། སྒྲ་མ་ཡིན་པ་ལས་ལོག་པ་དེ་སྒྲ་སྒྲུབ་པར་སྒྲུབ་པར་བྱེད་པའི་ཤེས་འདོད་ཆོས་ཅན་སྐྱོན་མེད་མ་ཡིན་པའི་ཕྱིར་ཏེ། དེ་སྒྲུབ་པ་མ་

ཡིན་པའི་ཕྱིར། གཞན་ཡང་། དེ་ཆོས་ཅན། དེ་སྒྲུབ་ཀྱི་ཤེས་འདོད་ཆོས་ཅན་མ་ཡིན་པར་ཐལ། དེ་སྒྲུབ་ཀྱི་ཕྱོགས་ཆོས་ཡིན་པའི་ཕྱིར། ཁྱབ་སྟེ། རྣམ་འགྲེལ་ལས། ཆོས་ཅན་གཏན་ཚིགས་དངོས་གྱུར་ནི། །ཤེས་བྱེད་ཉིད་དུ་མ་གྲུབ་ཕྱིར། །ཞེས་གསུངས་པའི་ཕྱིར་རོ། །མཚན་བྱ་དེ་དེ་མ་ཡིན་ཏེ། དེ་སྒྲ་མཚོན་བྱར་སྒྲུབ་པའི་ཤེས་འདོད་ཆོས་ཅན་སྐྱོན་མེད་མ་ཡིན་པའི་ཕྱིར་ཏེ། དེ་མཚོན་བྱ་མ་ཡིན་པའི་ཕྱིར། གཞན་ཡང་། དེ་དེ་སྒྲུབ་ཀྱི་ཤེས་འདོད་ཆོས་ཅན་མ་ཡིན་པར་ཐལ། དེ་དེ་སྒྲུབ་ཀྱི་ཕྱོགས་ཆོས་ཡིན་པའི་ཕྱིར། དེར་ཐལ། དེ་དེ་སྒྲུབ་ཀྱི་ཐུན་མོང་མ་ཡིན་པའི་མ་ངེས་པའི་གཏན་ཚིགས་ཡིན་པའི་ཕྱིར། རོ། །དེ་སྒྲུབ་ཀྱི་ཤེས་འདོད་ཆོས་ཅན་ཡོད་ན། དེ་སྒྲུབ་ཀྱི་ཕྱོགས་ཆོས། །ཡོད་པས་མ་ཁྱབ་སྟེ། སྒྲའི་རྟགས་ཀྱིས་སྒྲ་མི་རྟག་པར་སྒྲུབ་པར་བྱེད་པའི་ཤེས་འདོད་ཆོས་ཅན་ཡོད་ཀྱང་། དེའི་རྟགས་ཀྱིས་དེ་སྒྲུབ་ཀྱི་ཕྱོགས་ཆོས་མེད་པའི་ཕྱིར། གཉིས་པ་ཁྱབ་པའི་ལྟོས་གཞི་ལ་གཉིས། བསྒྲུབ་བྱའི་ཆོས་དང་། མཐུན་ཕྱོགས་དང་མི་མཐུན་ཕྱོགས་སོ། །དང་པོ་ལ་གསུམ། མཚན་ཉིད། དབྱེ་བ། སྒྲུབ་བྱེད་དོ། །བསྒྲུབ་བྱའི་ཆོས་སུ་གཟུང་བར་བྱ་བ་དེ། བསྒྲུབ་བྱའི་ཆོས་ཀྱི་མཚན་ཉིད། དེ་སྒྲུབ་ཀྱི་བསྒྲུབ་བྱའི་ཆོས་སུ་གཟུང་བར་བྱ་བ། དེ་སྒྲུབ་ཀྱི་བསྒྲུབ་བྱའི་ཆོས་ཀྱི་མཚན་ཉིད།བདག་མེད་ཡིན་ན། དེ་སྒྲུབ་ཀྱི་བསྒྲུབ་བྱའི་ཆོས་ཡིན་པས་ཁྱབ་སྟེ། རི་བོང་རྭ་དེ་རི་བོང་གི་རར་སྒྲུབ་པར་བྱེད་པའི་བསྒྲུབ་བྱའི་ཆོས་སུ་གཟུང་བྱ་ཡིན་པའི་ཕྱིར་ཏེ། དེ་ཆོས་ཅན། རི་བོང་རྭ་ཡིན་ཏེ། དེ་ཡིན་པའི་ཕྱིར་ཞེས་པའི་བསྒྲུབ་བྱའི་ཆོས་ཡིན་པའི་ཕྱིར། དེས་ན་བསྒྲུབ་བྱའི་ཆོས་ཡིན་ན། ཆོས་ཡིན་པས་མ་

ཁྱབ་བོ། །སྒྲ་མི་རྟག་པར་སྒྲུབ་པར་བྱེད་པའི་བསྒྲུབ་བྱའི་ཆོས་སུ་གཟུང་བར་བྱ་བ་དེ། སྒྲ་མི་རྟག་པར་སྒྲུབ་པར་བྱེད་པའི་བསྒྲུབ་བྱའི་ཆོས་ཀྱི་མཚན་ཉིད། མི་རྟག་པ་དེ་དེའི་མཚན་གཞིའོ། །སྒྲ་ཆོས་ཅན། མི་རྟག་སྟེ། བྱས་པའི་ཕྱིར་ཞེས་བཀོད་པའི་ཚེ་སྒྲ་རྩོད་གཞི། མི་རྟག་པ་བསྒྲུབ་བྱའི་ཆོས། སྒྲ་མི་རྟག་པ་བསྒྲུབ་བྱ། བྱས་པ་རྟགས་ཡང་དག །རྟག་པ་དགག་བྱའི་ཆོས། སྒྲ་རྟག་པ་དགག་བྱར་འཇོག་སྟེ། གཞན་ལ་སྦྱོར་ཚུལ་ཤེས་པར་བྱའོ། །གཉིས་པ་དེ་ལ་དབྱེ་ན། དེའི་དངོས་ཀྱི་བསྒྲུབ་བྱའི་ཆོས་དང་། ཤུགས་ཀྱི་བསྒྲུབ་བྱའི་ཆོས་གཉིས་ཡོད་པའི་མི་རྟག་པ་དེ་དང་པོ་དང་སྐད་ཅིག་མ་ནི་ཕྱི་མའོ། །བྱས་པའི་རྟགས་ཀྱིས་སྒྲ་མི་རྟག་པར་སྒྲུབ་པར་བྱེད་པའི་བསྒྲུབ་བྱའི་ཆོས་ལའང་དེའི་དངོས་ཀྱི་བསྒྲུབ་བྱའི་ཆོས་དང་། དེའི་ཤུགས་ཀྱི་བསྒྲུབ་བྱའི་ཆོས་གཉིས། མི་རྟག་པ་དང་སྐད་ཅིག་མ་གཉིས་རེ་རེ་ནས་དང་པོ་དང་། དེ་གཉིས་མ་ཡིན་པ་ལས་ལོག་པ་གཉིས་རེ་རེ་ནས་གཉིས་པ་ཡིན་ནོ། །གསུམ་པ་སྒྲུབ་བྱེད་ནི། མི་རྟག་པ་ཆོས་ཅན། ཁྱོད་སྒྲ་མི་རྟག་པར་སྒྲུབ་པར་བྱེད་པའི་བསྒྲུབ་བྱའི་ཆོས་ཡིན་ཏེ། མཚན་ཉིད་དེའི་ཕྱིར་རོ། །སྐད་ཅིག་མ་ཆོས་ཅན། སྒྲ་མི་རྟག་པར་སྒྲུབ་པར་བྱེད་པའི་དངོས་ཀྱི་བསྒྲུབ་བྱའི་ཆོས་མ་ཡིན་ཏེ། དེ་སྒྲུབ་ཀྱི་རྟགས་ཡང་དག་ཡིན་པའི་ཕྱིར། དེར་ཐལ། དེ་སྒྲུབ་ཀྱི་ཐ་སྙད་འབའ་ཞིག་སྒྲུབ་ཀྱི་རྟགས་ཡང་དག་ཡིན་པའི་ཕྱིར། དེ་བྱས་པའི་རྟགས་ཀྱིས་དེ་སྒྲུབ་ཀྱི་དངོས་ཀྱི་བསྒྲུབ་བྱའི་ཆོས་ཡིན་ཏེ། བྱས་པའི་རྟགས་ཀྱིས་དེ་སྒྲུབ་ཀྱི་དངོས་ཀྱི་བསྒྲུབ་བྱའི་ཆོས་སུ་གྱུར་པའི་མཚན་མཚོན་གཉིས་ཀ་ཡོད་པའི་ཕྱིར། དེར་ཐལ། བྱས་པ་དེ་སྒྲ་མི་རྟག་པར་སྒྲུབ་པར་

བྱེད་པའི་དོན་དང་ཐ་སྙད་གཉིས་ཀ་སྒྲུབ་པར་ བྱེད་པའི་རྟགས་ཡང་དག་ཡིན་པའི་ཕྱིར་རོ། །གཉིས་པ་མཐུན་ཕྱོགས་དང་མི་མཐུན་ཕྱོགས་ལ་གཉིས། དངོས་དང་། དཔེ་གཉིས་བཤད་པའོ། །དང་པོ་ལ་བཞི། མཚན་ཉིད། དབྱེ་བ། སྒྲ་དོན། སྒྲུབ་བྱེད་དོ། །དང་པོ་ནི། དེ་སྒྲུབ་ཀྱི་བསྒྲུབ་བྱའི་ཆོས་ཀྱི་འགོད་ཚུལ་དང་མཐུན་པར་ཡོད་པ་དེ། དེ་སྒྲུབ་ཀྱི་མཐུན་ཕྱོགས་ཀྱི་མཚན་ཉིད། དེ་ལ་ཡིན་འགོད་དང་ཡོད་དགོད་གཉིས། སྒྲ་མི་རྟག་པར་སྒྲུབ་པར་བྱེད་པའི་བསྒྲུབ་བྱའི་ཆོས་ཀྱི་འགོད་ཚུལ་དང་མཐུན་པར་ཡོད་པ་དེ། དེ་སྒྲུབ་ཀྱི་མཐུན་ཕྱོགས་ཀྱི་མཚན་ཉིད། དེ་དང་མི་རྟག་པ་གཉིས་དོན་གཅིག། དེ་སྒྲུབ་ཀྱི་བསྒྲུབ་བྱའི་ཆོས་ཀྱི་འགོད་ཚུལ་དང་མཐུན་པར་མེད་པ་དེ། དེ་སྒྲུབ་ཀྱི་མི་མཐུན་ཕྱོགས་ཀྱི་མཚན་ཉིད། དེ་བཞིན་དུ་སྒྲ་མི་རྟག་པར་སྒྲུབ་པར་བྱེད་པའི་མི་མཐུན་ཕྱོགས་ཀྱི་མཚན་ཉིད་དང་སྦྱར་ན། དེ་དང་མི་རྟག་པ་མ་ཡིན་པ་གཉིས་དོན་གཅིག། གཉིས་པ་དབྱེ་ན་གསུམ་སྟེ་དེ་སྒྲུབ་ཀྱི་མེད་པ་མི་མཐུན་ཕྱོགས། གཞན་པ་མི་མཐུན་ཕྱོགས། འགལ་བ་ཟླ་མི་མཐུན་ཕྱོགས་སོ། །དང་པོ་ནི་རི་བོང་གི་རྭ་ལྟ་བུ། གཉིས་པ་ནི་ཤེས་བྱ་ལྟ་བུ། གསུམ་པ་ནི་རྟག་པ་ལྟ་བུའོ། །གསུམ་པ་སྒྲ་དོན་ནི། དེ་སྒྲུབ་ཀྱི་མཐུན་ཕྱོགས་དང་མི་མཐུན་ཕྱོགས་གཉིས་ལ་སྒྲ་བཤད་འཇུག་པའི་རྒྱུ་གསུམ་རེ་ཡོད་དེ། བསྡུས་ནས་བརྗོད་ན། བུམ་པ་དེ་སྒྲ་མི་རྟག་པར་སྒྲུབ་པར་བྱེད་པའི་མཐུན་ཕྱོགས་དང་དེའི་སྒྲ་བཤད་དུ་ཡོད་པའི་རྒྱུ་དང་། སྒྲ་རྟག་པར་སྒྲུབ་པར་བྱེད་པའི་དེ་གཉིས་ཀ་མ་ཡིན་པའི་རྒྱུ་དང་། སྒྲ་མི་རྟག་པར་སྒྲུབ་པར་བྱེད་པའི་མི་མཐུན་ཕྱོགས་དང་དེའི་སྒྲ་བཤད་དུ་ཡོད་པ་གཉིས་ཀ་མ་ཡིན་པའི་

སྒྲུ་ཡིན་ཏེ། དེ་མི་རྟག་པ་ཡིན། དེ་སྒྲ་དང་མི་རྟག་པར་ཆོས་མཐུན་ཞིང་དེ་སྒྲ་དང་རྟག་པར་ཆོས་མི་མཐུན་པ་ཡིན་པའི་ཕྱིར། འདུས་མ་བྱས་ཀྱི་ནམ་མཁའ་དེ་སྒྲ་མི་རྟག་པར་སྒྲུབ་པར་བྱེད་པའི་མཐུན་ཕྱོགས་དང་དེའི་སྒྲ་བ་ཤད་དུ་ཡོད་པ་གཉིས་ཀ་མ་ཡིན་པའི་སྒྲུ་དང་། སྒྲ་རྟག་པར་སྒྲུབ་པར་བྱེད་པའི་མཐུན་ཕྱོགས་ཡིན་ལ་དེའི་སྒྲ་བ་ཤད་དུ་མེད་པའི་སྒྲུ་དང་། དེ་སྒྲུབ་ཀྱི་མི་མཐུན་ཕྱོགས་ཀྱི་སྒྲ་བ་ཤད་དུ་ཡོད་ལ་དེ་སྒྲུབ་ཀྱི་མི་མཐུན་ཕྱོགས་མ་ཡིན་པའི་སྒྲུ་དང་། སྒྲ་མི་རྟག་པར་སྒྲུབ་པར་བྱེད་པའི་མི་མཐུན་ཕྱོགས་དང་དེའི་སྒྲ་བ་ཤད་དུ་ཡོད་པའི་སྒྲུ་ཡིན་ཏེ། དེ་རྟག་པ་ཡིན། དེ་སྒྲ་དང་རྟག་པར་ཆོས་མི་མཐུན། དེ་སྒྲ་དང་མི་རྟག་པར་ཆོས་མི་མཐུན་པ་ཡིན་པའི་ཕྱིར། བཞི་པ་སྒྲུབ་བྱེད་ནི། རི་བོང་རྭ་སོགས་གསུམ་པོ་དེ་ཆོས་ཅན། སྒྲ་མི་རྟག་པར་སྒྲུབ་པར་བྱེད་པའི་མི་མཐུན་ཕྱོགས་ཡིན་ཏེ། དེ་སྒྲུབ་ཀྱི་བསྒྲུབ་བྱའི་ཆོས་ཀྱི་འགོད་ཚུལ་དང་མི་མཐུན་པའི་ཕྱིར་ཏེ། དངོས་མེད་ཡིན་པའི་ཕྱིར། བུམ་པ་ཆོས་ཅན། སྒྲ་མི་རྟག་པར་སྒྲུབ་པར་བྱེད་པའི་མཐུན་ཕྱོགས་ཡིན་ཏེ། དེ་ལྟར་སྒྲུབ་པའི་འགོད་ཚུལ་དང་མཐུན་པའི་ཕྱིར་ཏེ། མི་རྟག་པ་ཡིན་པའི་ཕྱིར་རོ། །དེ་སྒྲུབ་ཀྱི་མཐུན་ཕྱོགས་ཞེས་པའི་ཕྱོགས་དེ་ཡིན་ན་དེ་སྒྲུབ་ཀྱི་བསྒྲུབ་བྱའི་ཆོས་ཡིན་པས་མ་ཁྱབ་ཏེ། སྒྲ་མི་རྟག་པར་སྒྲུབ་པར་བྱེད་པའི་མཐུན་ཕྱོགས་ཞེས་པའི་ཕྱོགས་དེ་དང་དེ་སྒྲུབ་ཀྱི་མཐུན་ཕྱོགས་ལ་ཡོད་མེད་ཅེས་པའི་ཕྱོགས་གཉིས་མི་འདྲ་བར་འཇོག་དགོས་པའི་ཕྱིར། མ་ཁྱབ་ན་སླ། མ་གྲུབ་ན་དེར་ཐལ། སྒྲ་མི་རྟག་པར་སྒྲུབ་པར་བྱེད་པའི་སྐབས་ཀྱི་རྗེས་སུ་དཔག་བྱའམ་ཕྱོགས་ཀྱི་སྒྲའི་འཇུག་གཞི་དེ་ལ་གསུམ་ཡོད་པ་ལས། དེ་སྒྲུབ

ཀྱི་ཕྱོགས་ཆོས་ཞེས་པའི་ཕྱོགས་དེ་དེ་སྒྲུབ་ཀྱི་ཤེས་འདོད་ཆོས་ཅན་ལ་བྱེད། དེ་སྒྲུབ་ཀྱི་མཐུན་ཕྱོགས་ལ་ཡོད་མེད་ཅེས་པའི་ཕྱོགས་དེ་དང་དེ་སྒྲུབ་ཀྱི་ཁྱབ་པའི་འབྲེལ་ཡུལ་གྱི་ཕྱོགས་དེ་གཉིས་དེ་སྒྲུབ་ཀྱི་བསྒྲུབ་བྱའི་ཆོས་སམ་མི་རྟག་པའི་སྤྱི་ལྡོག་ལ་བྱེད་ཀྱང་དེ་སྒྲུབ་ཀྱི་མཐུན་ཕྱོགས་ཞེས་པའི་ཕྱོགས་དེ་ལ་མི་རྟག་པའི་སྤྱི་ལྡོག་དང་གཞི་ལྡོག་ཐམས་ཅད་འཛོག་དགོས་པའི་ཕྱིར། དང་པོ་གྲུབ་སྟེ། འཐད་ལྡན་ཆེ་བ་ལས། རྗེས་སུ་དཔག་པའི་ཐ་སྙད་ནི་གསུམ་སྟེ། སྒྲུབ་བྱེད་ཀྱིས་བསྒྲུབ་པར་བྱ་བའི་ཆོས་དང་ཆོས་ཅན་གྱི་སྤྱི་ལ་དངོས་དང་ཁྱབ་པའི་ཡུལ་གྱི་བསྒྲུབ་པར་བྱ་བའི་ཆོས་དང་གཏན་ཚིགས་ཀྱི་ཡུལ་ཆོས་ཅན་ལ་བཏགས་ནས་སོ། །ཞེས་གསུངས་པའི་ཕྱིར། གཉིས་པ་དེར་ཐལ། རྣམ་འགྲེལ་རང་འགྲེལ་ལས། ཕྱོགས་ནི་ཆོས་ཅན་ནོ། །ཞེས་དང་། རིགས་ཐིགས་ལས། རྗེས་སུ་དཔག་པར་བྱ་བ་ནི་འདིར་ཤེས་པར་འདོད་པའི་བྱེ་བྲག་དང་ལྡན་པའི་ཆོས་ཅན་ནོ། །ཞེས་གསུངས་པའི་ཕྱིར། གསུམ་པ་དེར་ཐལ། ཚད་མ་མདོར། རྗེས་དཔག་བྱ་དང་དེ་མཐུན་ལ། །ཡོད་མེད་ཉིད་ལ་མེད་པའོ། །ཞེས་དང་། དེའི་རང་འགྲེལ་ལས་ཕྱོགས་ཞེས་བྱ་སྟེ། དེ་ཡང་བསྒྲུབ་བྱའི་ཆོས་ཞེས་བྱའོ། །ཞེས་དང་། འཐད་ལྡན་ལས། ཁྱབ་པའི་ཡུལ་ནི་སྒྲུབ་པར་བྱ་བའི་ཆོས་དང་། ཞེས་གསུངས་པའི་ཕྱིར། བཞི་པ་དེར་ཐལ། བུམ་པ་ལ་སོགས་པའི་འདུས་བྱས་རྣམས་དེ་སྒྲུབ་ཀྱི་བསྒྲུབ་བྱའི་ཆོས་སུ་གཟུང་རྒྱུའི་མི་རྟག་པ་སྤྱི་ལྡོག་དེ་དང་དོན་མཐུན་པའི་ཕྱོགས་ཡིན་པས་ན་དེ་སྒྲུབ་ཀྱི་མཐུན་ཕྱོགས་ཞེས་བཤད་པའི་ཕྱིར། མ་ཁྱབ་ན་སླ། མ་གྲུབ་ན་དེར་ཐལ། རིགས་ཐིགས་ལས། བསྒྲུབ་པར་བྱ་བའི་ཆོས་ཀྱི་སྤྱིའི་དོན

མཐུན་པ་ནི་མཐུན་པའི་ཕྱོགས་སོ། །ཞེས་པ་དང་། འཐད་ལྡན་ཆུང་བ་ལས། ཕྱི་ཞེས་སྨོས་པ་ནི་བྱེ་བྲག་བཀར་བའི་དོན་ཏེ། བསྒྲུབ་པར་བྱ་བ་ཡང་ཡིན། ཕྱི་ཡང་ཡིན་པས་ན་ཕྱི་སྟེ། དེ་དང་དོན་མཐུན་པ་ནི་མཐུན་པའི་ཕྱོགས་སོ། །ཞེས་གསུངས་པའི་ཕྱིར། སྤྲོས་ཏེ་དཔྱད་པར་བྱའོ། །སྒྲ་མི་རྟག་པ་སྒྲུབ་པར་བྱེད་པའི་མི་མཐུན་ཕྱོགས་ཡོད་ཀྱང་ཕྱིར་མི་མཐུན་ཕྱོགས་མེད་དེ། བདག་མེད་ཡིན་ན་མཐུན་ཕྱོགས་ཡིན་པས་ཁྱབ་པའི་ཕྱིར། དེར་ཐལ། དེ་ཡིན་ན། སྒྲ་གང་ཟག་གི་བདག་མེད་དུ་སྒྲུབ་པར་བྱེད་པའི་མཐུན་ཕྱོགས་ཡིན་པས་ཁྱབ་པའི་ཕྱིར། དེ་ལ་ཁོ་ན་རེ། མི་མཐུན་ཕྱོགས་ཡོད་པར་ཐལ། ཆོས་མི་མཐུན་སྦྱོར་གྱི་སྒྲུབ་ངག་ཡོད་པའི་ཕྱིར་ཟེར་ན་མ་ཁྱབ་བོ། །གཉིས་པ་དཔེ་གཉིས་ལས། ཆོས་མི་མཐུན་སྦྱོར་གྱི་སྒྲུབ་ངག་གི་མི་མཐུན་དཔེ་ནི། གང་རྟག་ན་མ་བྱས་པས་ཁྱབ། དཔེར་ན་འདུས་མ་བྱས་ཀྱི་ནམ་མཁའ་བཞིན། སྒྲ་ནི་བྱས་སོ་ཞེས་པའི་ངག་ལྟ་བུ་དང་། ཆོས་མཐུན་སྦྱོར་གྱི་སྒྲུབ་ངག་གི་དཔེ་ནི་གང་བྱས་ན་མི་རྟག་པས་ཁྱབ། དཔེ་ན་བུམ་པ་བཞིན། སྒྲ་ཡང་བྱས་སོ་ཞེས་པ་ལྟ་བུ་སྟེ། ཕྱིར་མི་མཐུན་ཕྱོགས་ཀྱི་དཔེ་མེད་དེ། གཞི་གྲུབ་ན། སྒྲ་གང་ཟག་གི་བདག་མེད་དུ་སྒྲུབ་པར་བྱེད་པའི་མཐུན་དཔེ་ཡིན་དགོས་པའི་ཕྱིར་རོ།

།གཉིས་པ་ནི། ཚུལ་གསུམ་ཡིན་པ། རྟགས་ཡང་དག་གི་མཚན་ཉིད། ཚུལ་གསུམ་ནི། ཕྱོགས་ཆོས། རྗེས་ཁྱབ། ལྡོག་ཁྱབ་བོ། །ཚུལ་གསུམ་སོ་སོ་ལ་མཚན་ཉིད། སྒྲུབ་བྱེད་ཀྱི་ཚད་མ་དང་རྗེས་སུ་འགྲོ་ལྡོག་ངེས་བྱེད་སོགས་ལས། དང་པོ་ནི། དེ་སྒྲུབ་ཀྱི་ཤེས་འདོད་ཆོས་ཅན་སྐྱོན་མེད་ཀྱི་སྟེང་དུ་འགོད་ཚུལ་དང་མཐུན་པར་ཡོད་པ་ཉིད་དུ་ཚད་

མས་ངེས་པ། དེ་སྒྲུབ་ཀྱི་ཕྱོགས་ཆོས་ཀྱི་མཚན་ཉིད། སྒྲ་མི་རྟག་པར་སྒྲུབ་པར་བྱེད་པའི་ཤེས་འདོད་ཆོས་ཅན་སྐྱོན་མེད་ཀྱི་སྟེང་དུ་འགོད་ཚུལ་དང་མཐུན་པར་ཡོད་པ་ཉིད་དུ་ཚད་མས་ངེས་པ་དེ། སྒྲ་མི་རྟག་པར་སྒྲུབ་པར་བྱེད་པའི་ཕྱོགས་ཆོས་ཀྱི་མཚན་ཉིད། དེ་བཞིན་དུ་བྱས་པའི་རྟགས་ཀྱིས་སྒྲ་མི་རྟག་པར་སྒྲུབ་པར་བྱེད་པའི་ཕྱོགས་ཆོས་ཀྱི་མཚན་ཉིད་སོགས་ལ་སྦྱར་ཚུལ་འགྲེའོ། །དེ་སྒྲུབ་ཀྱི་མཐུན་ཕྱོགས་ཁོ་ན་ལ་འགོད་ཚུལ་དང་མཐུན་པར་ཡོད་པ་ཉིད་དུ་ཚད་མས་ངེས་པ་དེ། དེ་སྒྲུབ་ཀྱི་རྗེས་ཁྱབ་ཀྱི་མཚན་ཉིད། དེ་བཞིན་དུ་སྒྲ་མི་རྟག་པར་སྒྲུབ་པར་བྱེད་པའི་རྗེས་ཁྱབ་ཀྱི་མཚན་ཉིད་དང་། བྱས་པའི་རྟགས་ཀྱིས་སྒྲ་མི་རྟག་པར་སྒྲུབ་པར་བྱེད་པའི་རྗེས་ཁྱབ་ཀྱི་མཚན་ཉིད་སོགས་ལ་སྦྱར་བར་བྱའོ། །དེ་སྒྲུབ་ཀྱི་དངོས་ཀྱི་བསྒྲུབ་བྱའི་ཆོས་ཀྱི་དོན་ལྡོག་དང་འབྲེལ་སྟོབས་ཀྱིས་དེ་སྒྲུབ་ཀྱི་མི་མཐུན་ཕྱོགས་ལ་འགོད་ཚུལ་དང་མཐུན་པར་མེད་པ་ཉིད་དུ་ཚད་མས་ངེས་པ་དེ། དེ་སྒྲུབ་ཀྱི་ལྡོག་ཁྱབ་ཀྱི་མཚན་ཉིད་དང་གཞི་ལ་སྦྱར་ན། སྒྲ་མི་རྟག་པར་སྒྲུབ་པར་བྱེད་པའི་ལྡོག་ཁྱབ་དང་། བྱས་པའི་རྟགས་ཀྱིས་སྒྲ་མི་རྟག་པར་སྒྲུབ་པར་བྱེད་པའི་ལྡོག་ཁྱབ་ཀྱི་མཚན་ཉིད་ཀྱང་དེས་རིགས་འགྲེའོ། །བྱས་པ་དེ་སྒྲ་མི་རྟག་པར་སྒྲུབ་པར་བྱེད་པའི་ཚུལ་གསུམ་གའི་མཚན་གཞི་ཡིན་ནོ། །སྒྲུབ་བྱེད་ལ་བྱས་པ་ཆོས་ཅན། སྒྲ་མི་རྟག་པར་སྒྲུབ་པར་བྱེད་པའི་ཕྱོགས་ཆོས་ཡིན་ཏེ། ཁྱོད་ཁྱོད་ཀྱི་རྟགས་ཀྱིས་སྒྲ་མི་རྟག་པར་སྒྲུབ་པར་བྱེད་པའི་ཤེས་འདོད་ཆོས་ཅན་སྐྱོན་མེད་ཀྱི་སྟེང་དུ་འགོད་ཚུལ་དང་མཐུན་པར་ཡོད་པ་ཉིད་དུ་ཚད་མས་ངེས་པའི་ཕྱིར། དེར་ཐལ། དེ་འདྲའི་ཤེས་འདོད་ཆོས་ཅན་སྒྲའི་སྟེང་དུ་འགོད་ཚུལ་

ཡིན་འགོད་དང་མཐུན་པར་ཡོད་པ་ཁོ་ན་ཡིན་ཅིང་སྐབས་ཀྱི་རྩོལ་བས་ཀྱང་རང་ཉིད་ཚད་མས་ངེས་པའི་ཕྱིར་རོ། །བྱས་པ་ཆོས་ཅན། སྒྲ་མི་རྟག་པར་སྒྲུབ་པར་བྱེད་པའི་རྗེས་ཁྱབ་ཡིན་ཏེ། ཁྱོད་ཁྱོད་ཀྱི་རྟགས་ཀྱིས་སྒྲ་མི་རྟག་པར་སྒྲུབ་པར་བྱེད་པའི་མཐུན་ཕྱོགས་ཁོ་ན་ལ་ཡོད་པ་ཉིད་དུ་ཚད་མས་ངེས་པའི་ཕྱིར། དེར་ཐལ། ཁྱོད་མི་རྟག་པ་ཡིན། ཁྱོད་ཡིན་ན་མི་རྟག་པ་ཡིན་པས་ཁྱབ་པའི་ཚུལ་གྱིས་ཁྱོད་མི་རྟག་པ་ཁོ་ན་ལ་ཡོད་པ་ཉིད་དུ་ཚད་མས་ངེས་པའི་ཕྱིར། བྱས་པ་ཆོས་ཅན། ཁྱོད་དེ་སྒྲུབ་ཀྱི་ལྡོག་ཁྱབ་ཡིན་ཏེ། ཁྱོད་དེ་སྒྲུབ་ཀྱི་བསྒྲུབ་བྱའི་ཆོས་ཀྱི་དོན་ལྡོག་དང་འབྲེལ་སྟོབས་ཀྱིས་དེ་སྒྲུབ་ཀྱི་མི་མཐུན་ཕྱོགས་ལ་འགོད་ཚུལ་དང་མཐུན་པར་མེད་པ་ཉིད་དུ་ཚད་མས་ངེས་པའི་ཕྱིར། དེར་ཐལ། ཁྱོད་མི་རྟག་པ་ཡིན། ཁྱོད་ཡིན་ན་མི་རྟག་པ་ཡིན་པས་ཁྱབ། ཁྱོད་མི་རྟག་པ་དང་འབྲེལ་ཞིང་མི་རྟག་པ་མ་ཡིན་པ་ལ་མེད་པ་ཉིད་དུ་ཚད་མས་ངེས་པའི་ཕྱིར་རོ། །འོན་ཀྱང་མཚན་ཉིད་དང་སྒྲུབ་བྱེད་དེ་དག་ནི་གོ་བ་གཙོ་བོར་བྱས་པ་ཡིན་གྱི་དེར་ངེས་པ་ནི་མ་ཡིན་ཏེ། སྒྲ་དེ་སྒྲ་མི་རྟག་པར་སྒྲུབ་པར་བྱེད་པའི་མཚན་ཉིད་དེ་གསུམ་ཀ་ཡིན་ཀྱང་མཚོན་བྱ་དེ་རྣམས་རེ་རེ་ནས་མ་ཡིན་པའི་ཕྱིར། དེས་ན་མཚན་ཉིད་དང་པོའི་འགོར། ཁྱོད་སྒྲ་དང་ཕན་ཚུན་ཐ་དད་པའི་ཚུལ་གྱིས། ཞེས་སྦྱོར་བ་དང་། མཚན་ཉིད་ཕྱི་མ་གཉིས་ཀྱི་འགོར། ཁྱོད་ཀྱི་རྟགས་ཀྱིས་སྒྲ་མི་རྟག་པར་སྒྲུབ་པར་བྱེད་པའི་རྟགས་ཆོས་གཉིས་ལྡན་གྱི་མཐུན་དཔེ་ཡང་དག་ཡོད། ཁྱོད་མི་རྟག་པ་ལ་འབྲེལ། ཞེས་སྦྱོར་བར་བྱའོ། །གསུམ་པ་དབྱེ་བ་ལ་གསུམ་ཡོད་དེ། རྣམ་འགྲེལ་ལས། དེ་ནི་རྣམ་གསུམ་ཉིད། ཅེས་གསུངས་པ་ལྟར། འབྲས་

རྟགས། རང་བཞིན་གྱི་རྟགས། མ་དམིགས་པའི་རྟགས་སོ། །དང་པོ་ནི། རྣམ་འགྲེལ་ལས། རྒྱུ་ལ་རང་བཞིན་ཇི་སྙེད་ཙམ། །མེད་ན་མི་འབྱུང་འབྲས་བུ་ནི། །གཏན་ཚིགས་ཡིན་ཏེ། ཞེས་སོགས་དང་། མེ་ཡི་འབྲས་བུ་དུ་བ་སྟེ། །ཞེས་པས་བསྟན་ཅིང་། འདི་ལ་གསུམ། མཚན་ཉིད། དབྱེ་བ། སྒྲུབ་བྱེད་དོ། །དང་པོ་ནི། འབྲས་བུའི་ཚུལ་གསུམ་ཡིན་པ། འབྲས་རྟགས་ཡང་དག་གི་མཚན་ཉིད། དེ་དང་འདུས་བྱས་གཉིས་དོན་གཅིག །དེ་སྒྲུབ་ཀྱི་འབྲས་བུའི་ཚུལ་གསུམ་ཡིན་པ། དེ་སྒྲུབ་ཀྱི་འབྲས་རྟགས་ཡང་དག་གི་མཚན་ཉིད། གོ་བ་དང་སྦྱར་ན། ཁྱོད་དེ་སྒྲུབ་ཀྱི་རྟགས་ཡང་དག་གང་ཞིག །ཁྱོད་ཀྱི་རྟགས་ཀྱིས་དེ་སྒྲུབ་ཀྱི་དངོས་ཀྱི་བསྒྲུབ་བྱའི་ཆོས་སུ་གཟུང་བྱའི་གཙོ་བོ་ཡང་ཡིན། ཁྱོད་ཀྱི་རྒྱུ་ཡང་ཡིན་པའི་གཞི་མཐུན་སྲིད་པ་དེ། ཁྱོད་དེ་སྒྲུབ་ཀྱི་འབྲས་རྟགས་ཡང་དག་གི་མཚན་ཉིད། འབྲས་རྟགས་ལ་དབྱེ་ན་སྤྱིར་མང་ཡང་། བསྡུ་ན་རྒྱུ་དངོས་སྒྲུབ་དང་། རྒྱུ་སྔོན་སོང་དང་། རྒྱུ་ཆོས་རྗེས་དཔོག་གི་འབྲས་རྟགས་གསུམ་ཡོད་པ་ལས། དུ་བ་དེ། དུ་ལྡན་གྱི་ལ་ལ་མེ་ཡོད་པར་བསྒྲུབ་པའི་རྒྱུ་དངོས་སྒྲུབ་ཀྱི་འབྲས་རྟགས། དུ་བ་དེ། བར་སྣང་གི་དུ་བ་སྔོ་ལོང་པོ་རང་རྒྱུ་མེ་སྔ་མ་སྔོན་སོང་དུ་བསྒྲུབ་པའི་འབྲས་རྟགས། བུ་རོ་ད་ལྟ་བ་དེ། ཁ་ནང་བུ་རོ་གོང་བུའི་སྟེང་དུ་བུ་རོ་སྔ་མས་རོ་གཟུགས་ཕྱི་མ་བསྐྱེད་པའི་ནུས་པ་ཡོད་པར་བསྒྲུབ་པའི་རྒྱུ་ཆོས་རྗེས་དཔོག་གི་འབྲས་རྟགས་སོ། །ཡང་དེའི་སྟེང་དུ། རེས་འགའ་སྐྱེ་བའི་དངོས་པོ་དེ་ཉེར་ལེན་གྱི་ཕུང་པོ་རང་རྒྱུ་དང་། །བཅས་པར་བསྒྲུབ་པའི་རྒྱུའི་སྤྱི་འམ་རང་ལྡོག་སྒྲུབ་ཀྱི་འབྲས་རྟགས་དང་།

རང་གི་དམིགས་རྐྱེན་མེད་པར་མི་སྐྱེ་བའི་དངོས་པོ་དེ་སྔོར་སྣང་དབང་ཤེས་རང་གི་དམིགས་རྐྱེན་དང་བཅས་པར་བསྒྲུབ་པའི་རྒྱུའི་ཁྱད་པར་སྒྲུབ་ཀྱི་འབྲས་རྟགས་དང་ལྔར་ཕྱེའོ། །ཡང་དེ་ལ་དབྱེ་ན་གཉིས་ཡོད་དེ། དུ་བ་དེ་དུ་ལྡན་ལ་ལ་དུ་བའི་དངོས་རྒྱུ་ཡོད་པར་བསྒྲུབ་པའི་མཐུན་ཕྱོགས་ལ་ཁྱབ་བྱེད་དུ་འཇུག་པའི་འབྲས་རྟགས་དང་། དུ་བ་དེ་དུ་ལྡན་ལ་ལ་མེ་ཡོད་པར་བསྒྲུབ་པའི་མཐུན་ཕྱོགས་ལ་རྣམ་གཉིས་སུ་འཇུག་པའི་འབྲས་རྟགས་ཡིན་པའི་ཕྱིར། དེ་སྒྲུབ་ཀྱི་མཐུན་ཕྱོགས་ལ་ཁྱབ་བྱེད་དུ་འཇུག་པའི་དོན་ནི། དུ་བའི་དངོས་རྒྱུ་ཡོད་ན་དུ་བ་ཡོད་པས་ཁྱབ་པའི་དོན་དང་། དེ་ལ་རྣམ་གཉིས་སུ་འཇུག་པའི་དོན་ནི། མེ་ཡོད་ན། དུ་བ་ཡོད་པས་མ་ཁྱབ་པའི་དོན་ཡིན་ནོ། །སྒྲུབ་བྱེད་ནི། དུ་བ་ཆོས་ཅན། ཁྱོད་དུ་བ་དང་ལྡན་པའི་ལ་ལ་མེ་ཡོད་པར་བསྒྲུབ་པའི་འབྲས་རྟགས་ཡིན་ཏེ། ཁྱོད་དེ་སྒྲུབ་ཀྱི་རྟགས་ཡང་དག་གང་ཞིག །ཁྱོད་མེའི་འབྲས་བུ་ཡིན་པའི་ཕྱིར། ཞེས་པ་ནི་མཚོན་པ་ཙམ་མོ། །དུ་བ་དེ་དུ་ལྡན་ལ་ལ་མེ་ཡོད་པར་བསྒྲུབ་པའི་རྟགས་ཡང་དག་དང་དེ་སྒྲུབ་ཀྱི་བཀོད་ཚོད་དང་སོང་ཚོད་ཀྱི་རྟགས་གཉིས་ཀ་དང་དུ་བའི་རྟགས་ཀྱིས་དེ་སྒྲུབ་ཀྱི་རྟགས་ཡང་དག་ཡིན། དུ་བ་ཡོད་པ་དེ་དེ་སྒྲུབ་ཀྱི་རྟགས་ཡང་དག་དང་བཀོད་ཚོད་ཀྱི་རྟགས་ཡིན་ཀྱང་། དེ་སྒྲུབ་ཀྱི་སོང་ཚོད་ཀྱི་རྟགས་དང་དུ་བའི་རྟགས་ཀྱིས་དེ་སྒྲུབ་ཀྱི་རྟགས་ཡང་དག་མ་ཡིན། མེ་དེ་དུ་བའི་རྟགས་ཀྱིས་དེ་སྒྲུབ་ཀྱི་བསྒྲུབ་བྱའི་ཆོས་དང་བཀོད་ཚོད་དང་སོང་ཚོད་ཀྱི་བསྒྲུབ་བྱའི་ཆོས་ཡིན། མེ་ཡོད་པ་དེ་དེ་སྒྲུབ་ཀྱི་བསྒྲུབ་བྱའི་ཆོས་དང་བཀོད་ཚོད་ཀྱི་བསྒྲུབ་བྱའི་ཆོས་དང་། དུ་བའི་རྟགས་ཀྱིས་དེ་སྒྲུབ་ཀྱི་བསྒྲུབ་བྱའི་ཆོས་ཡིན་ཀྱང་།

དེ་སྒྲུབ་ཀྱི་སོང་ཚོད་ཀྱི་དེ་མ་ཡིན་ནོ། །མི་ཚད་མས་དམིགས་པ་དང་ཚ་ཞིང་བསྲེག་པ་
གཉིས་པོ་དེ་རེ་རེ་ནས་དུ་ལྡན་ལ་ལ་མི་ཡོད་པར་བསྒྲུབ་པའི་དངོས་ཀྱི་བསྒྲུབ་བྱའི་ཆོས་
སུ་གཟུང་བྱ་མ་ཡིན་ཏེ། དེ་སྒྲུབ་ཀྱི་རྟགས་ཡང་དག་ཡིན་པའི་ཕྱིར། འོན་ཀྱང་དེ་གཉིས་རེ་
རེ་ནས་དུ་བའི་རྟགས་ཀྱིས་དེ་སྒྲུབ་ཀྱི་དངོས་ཀྱི་བསྒྲུབ་བྱའི་ཆོས་སུ་གཟུང་བྱ་ཡིན་ཏེ།
དེའི་རྟགས་ཀྱིས་དེ་སྒྲུབ་ཀྱི་དངོས་ཀྱི་བསྒྲུབ་བྱའི་ཆོས་སུ་གཟུང་བྱ་ཡང་ཡིན་མཚན་ཉིད་
ཀྱང་ཡིན་པའི་གཞི་མཐུན་པ་ཡོད་པའི་ཕྱིར་རོ། །གཉིས་པ་ནི། རྣམ་འགྲེལ་ལས། རང་
བཞིན་ཡོད་ཙམ་དང་། འབྲེལ་བ་ཅན་གྱི་ངོ་བོ་ཡང་། །ཞེས་པས་བསྟན་ཏེ། འདི་ལ་མཚན་
ཉིད་སོགས་གསུམ་གྱི་དང་པོ་རང་བཞིན་གྱི་ཚུལ་གསུམ་ཡིན་པ། རང་བཞིན་གྱི་རྟགས་
ཡང་དག་གི་མཚན་ཉིད། དེ་སྒྲུབ་ཀྱི་རང་བཞིན་གྱི་ཚུལ་གསུམ་ཡིན་པ། དེ་སྒྲུབ་ཀྱི་རང་
བཞིན་གྱི་རྟགས་ཡང་དག་གི་མཚན་ཉིད། ཡང་ན་ཁྱོད་དེ་སྒྲུབ་ཀྱི་རྟགས་ཡང་དག་གང་
ཞིག །ཁྱོད་ཀྱི་རྟགས་ཀྱིས་དེ་སྒྲུབ་ཀྱི་དངོས་ཀྱི་བསྒྲུབ་བྱའི་ཆོས་སུ་གཟུང་བྱ་ཡིན་ན་ཁྱོད་
དང་བདག་ཉིད་གཅིག་ཡིན་དགོས་པའི་ཆ་ནས་བཞག་པ་དེ། ཁྱོད་དེ་སྒྲུབ་ཀྱི་རང་བཞིན་
གྱི་རྟགས་ཡང་དག་གི་མཚན་ཉིད། དབྱེ་ན། དེར་གྱུར་པའི་ཁྱད་པར་ལྟོས་པ་བའི་དེ་དང་།
ཁྱད་པར་དག་པའི་དེ་གཉིས་སོ། །དང་པོ་ལ་དེར་གྱུར་པའི་རང་གི་བྱེད་ཆོས་དངོས་སུ་
འཕངས་པ་དང་། ཤུགས་ལ་འཕངས་པ་གཉིས། དང་པོ་ནི། སྒྲ་ཆོས་ཅན། མི་རྟག་སྟེ། སྐྱེས་
པ་ཡིན་པའི་ཕྱིར་ཞེས་བཀོད་པའི་ཚེ་སྐྱེས་པ་ལྟ་བུ། གཉིས་པ་ནི། དེ་ཆོས་ཅན། མི་རྟག་སྟེ།
བྱས་པའི་ཕྱིར་ཞེས་བཀོད་པའི་ཚེ་བྱས་པ་ལྟ་བུ། དགག་པ་བ་ནི། དེ་ཆོས་ཅན། མི་རྟག་སྟེ།

དངོས་པོ་ཡིན་པའི་ཕྱིར་ཞེས་པའི་རྟགས་ལྟ་བུ། སྐད་ཅིག་མ་དེ་སྒྲ་མི་རྟག་པར་སྒྲུབ་པར་བྱེད་པའི་ཤུགས་ཀྱི་བསྒྲུབ་བྱའི་ཆོས་སུ་གཟུང་བྱ་ཡིན་གྱི། དངོས་ཀྱི་བསྒྲུབ་བྱའི་ཆོས་སུ་གཟུང་བྱ་མིན་ལ་དེའི་དངོས་ཀྱི་བསྒྲུབ་བྱའི་ཆོས་ལ་ནི་མི་རྟག་པ་ཉིད་འཛོག་ཅིང་། འོན་ཀྱང་དེའི་དངོས་ཀྱི་བསྒྲུབ་བྱའི་ཆོས་ནི་མི་རྟག་པར་བཞག་ཏུ་མི་རུང་ངོ་། །ཡང་དེ་ལ་མཐུན་ཕྱོགས་ལ་ཁྱབ་བྱེད་དུ་འཇུག་པའི་དེ་དང་མཐུན་ཕྱོགས་ལ་རྣམ་གཉིས་སུ་འཇུག་པའི་དེ་གཉིས་ཡོད་དེ། བྱས་པ་དེ་སྒྲ་མི་རྟག་པར་སྒྲུབ་པར་བྱེད་པའི་དང་པོ་དང་། བྱས་པའི་བྱེ་བྲག་དེ་དེ་སྒྲུབ་ཀྱི་གཉིས་པ་ཡིན་པའི་ཕྱིར། སྒྲུབ་བྱེད་ནི་རང་བཞིན་གྱི་རྟགས་ཡང་དག་གི་མཚན་ཉིད་གོ་བ་དང་སྦྱར་ནས་བཞག་པ་དེས་ཤེས་པར་བྱའོ། །གསུམ་པ་མ་དམིགས་པའི་རྟགས་ཡང་དག་ལ། མཚན་ཉིད་དང་དབྱེ་བ་གཉིས། དང་པོ་ནི། ཁྱོད་དེ་སྒྲུབ་ཀྱི་རྟགས་ཡང་དག་གང་ཞིག །ཁྱོད་ཀྱི་རྟགས་ཀྱིས་དེ་སྒྲུབ་ཀྱི་དངོས་ཀྱི་བསྒྲུབ་བྱའི་ཆོས་སུ་གཟུང་བྱ་ཡང་ཡིན། དགག་པ་ཡང་ཡིན་པའི་གཞི་མཐུན་སྲིད་པ་དེ་ཁྱོད་དེ་སྒྲུབ་ཀྱི་མ་དམིགས་པའི་རྟགས་ཡང་དག་གི་མཚན་ཉིད། དབྱེ་ན་མི་སྣང་བ་མ་དམིགས་པའི་རྟགས་ཡང་དག་དང་། སྣང་རུང་མ་དམིགས་པའི་རྟགས་ཡང་དག་གོ། དང་པོ་ནི། མདོ་ལས། གང་ཟག་གིས་གང་ཟག་གི་ཚོད་གཟུང་བར་མི་བྱ་སྟེ། ཉམས་པར་གྱུར་ཏ་རེ། ཞེས་རང་ལ་མི་སྣང་བ་ཙམ་གྱིས་གཞན་ལ་ཡོན་ཏན་དེ་ལྟ་བུ་མེད་ཅེས་འཆད་མི་རིགས་པའི་དོན་སྟོན་པ་ལ། རྣམ་འགྲེལ་ལས། ཚད་མ་རྣམས་ནི་མི་འཇུག་པ། །མེད་ལ་མི་འཇུག་འབྲས་བུ་ཅན། །ཞེས་སོགས་ཀྱིས་བསྟན་ཏེ་འདི་ལ་བཞི། མཚན་ཉིད། འཇུག་དུས། དབྱེ་

བ། དགོས་པ་སོགས་ལས། མི་སྣང་བ་མ་དམིགས་པའི་ཚུལ་གསུམ་ཡིན་པ། མི་སྣང་བ་མ་
དམིགས་པའི་རྟགས་ཡང་དག་གི་མཚན་ཉིད། དེ་སྒྲུབ་ཀྱི་མི་སྣང་བ་མ་དམིགས་པའི་
ཚུལ་གསུམ་ཡིན་པ། དེ་སྒྲུབ་ཀྱི་མི་སྣང་བ་མ་དམིགས་པའི་རྟགས་ཡང་དག་གི་མཚན་
ཉིད། གོ་བ་དང་སྦྱར་བ་ནི་སྒྲུབ་ཤད་ཀྱིས་ཤེས་ལ། འཇུག་དུས་ནི། དགག་གཞི་སྣང་རུང་
ཡིན་ཡང་དེ་སྒྲུབ་ཀྱི་དགག་བྱར་ཆོས་སུ་བཏགས་པའི་དོན་དེ་རྩོལ་བ་དེའི་ངོ་བོར་སྣང་དུ་
མི་རུང་ན། མི་སྣང་བ་མ་དམིགས་པའི་རྟགས་སུ་འཇོག་ཅིང་། དེའི་སྒོ་ནས་སྒྲུབ་ཤད་ཀྱང་
ཤེས་པར་བྱའོ། །དེས་ན། ཁྱོད་དེ་སྒྲུབ་ཀྱི་མ་དམིགས་པའི་རྟགས་ཡང་དག་གང་ཞིག
།ཁྱོད་དེ་སྒྲུབ་ལ་ཕྱོགས་ཆོས་ཅན་དུ་སོང་བའི་གང་ཟག་ལ་དགག་བྱའི་ཆོས་སུ་བཏགས་
པའི་དོན་བསྐལ་དོན་ཡང་ཡིན་པའི་གཞི་མཐུན་པ་དེ། ཁྱོད་དེ་སྒྲུབ་ཀྱི་མི་སྣང་བ་མ་
དམིགས་པའི་རྟགས་ཡང་དག་གི་མཚན་ཉིད། དབྱེ་ན། དེར་གྱུར་པའི་འབྲེལ་ཟླ་མ་
དམིགས་པའི་རྟགས་དང་། འགལ་ཟླ་དམིགས་པའི་རྟགས་གཉིས་ལས། དང་པོ་ནི། དེ་
སྒྲུབ་ཀྱི་མི་སྣང་བ་མ་དམིགས་པའི་རྟགས་ཡང་དག་གང་ཞིག །རང་གི་དངོས་མིང་གི་
མཐར་མེད་མིན་སོགས་དགག་ཚིག་ཅི་རིགས་སྦྱར་བའི་ཆོས་དེ། དེ་སྒྲུབ་ཀྱི་མི་སྣང་བའི་
འབྲེལ་ཟླ་མ་དམིགས་པའི་རྟགས་ཡང་དག་གི་མཚན་ཉིད། དེ་ལ་དབྱེ་ན། དེར་གྱུར་པའི་
རྒྱུ་མ་དམིགས་པའི་དེ་དང་། ཁྱབ་བྱེད་མ་དམིགས་པའི་དེ་དང་། རང་བཞིན་མ་དམིགས་
པའི་རྟགས་དང་གསུམ་སྟེ། ཁྱད་པར་རྒྱས་པར་ནི་གཞན་དུ་ཤེས་པར་བྱ་ཞིང་མཚོན་ཙམ་
ནི། མདུན་གྱི་གཞི་འདིར་ཆོས་ཅན། ཤ་ཟ་བསྐལ་དོན་དུ་སོང་བའི་གང་ཟག་གི་རྒྱུད་ལ

དེ་ངེས་པའི་དཔྱད་ཤེས་དོན་མཐུན་མེད་དེ། གང་ཟག་དེའི་རྒྱུད་ལ་དེ་དམིགས་བྱེད་ཀྱི་ཚད་མ་མེད་པའི་ཕྱིར། ཞེས་པའི་རྟགས་དེ་ལྟ་བུ་དང་པོ་དང་། མདུན་གྱི་གཞི་འདིར་ཆོས་ཅན། ཤ་ཟ་བསྐལ་དོན་དུ་སོང་བའི་གང་ཟག་གིས་དེ་ཡོད་ཅེས་དམ་བཅའ་མི་རིགས་ཏེ། །གང་ཟག་དེའི་རྒྱུད་ལ་ཤ་ཟ་དམིགས་བྱེད་ཀྱི་ཚད་མ་མེད་པའི་ཕྱིར་ཞེས་པ་ལྟ་བུ། འདིའི་རྟགས་དེ་གཉིས་པ་དང་། དེ་ཆོས་ཅན། དེའི་རྒྱུད་ལ་དེ་ངེས་བྱེད་ཀྱི་དཔྱད་ཤེས་དོན་མཐུན་མེད་དེ། ངེས་དེ་འདྲ་བ་དེ་ཚད་མས་མ་དམིགས་པའི་ཕྱིར། ཞེས་བཀོད་པའི་ཚེ་རྟགས་དེ་ལྟ་བུ་གསུམ་པའོ། །དགོས་པ་ནི། མདུན་གྱི་གཞི་འདིར་ལྷའི་བར་སྲིད་དང་། ཤ་ཟ་ཡོད་མེད་ཐེ་ཚོམ་ཟ་བའི་བློ་ནས་བསྐལ་དོན་དུ་སོང་བའི་གང་ཟག་གིས་གཞི་འདིར་དེ་གཉིས་ཡོད་ཅེས་སམ་མེད་ཅེས་ཐག་གཅོད་དུ་མི་རུང་བ་དཔེར་མཚོན་ནས། དོན་ལ་གང་ཟག་གང་དང་གང་གི་སྐྱོན་ཡོན་རང་གི་ཚད་མས་མ་ངེས་བཞིན་དུ་སྒྲོ་སྐུར་བྱར་མི་རུང་བར་ཞེས་པའི་ཆེད་དོ། །དེ་སྒྲུབ་ཀྱི་དགག་བྱའི་ཆོས་སུ་བཏགས་པའི་དོན་ཡིན་ན། དེ་སྒྲུབ་ཀྱི་དགག་བྱའི་ཆོས་ཡིན་པས་མ་ཁྱབ་སྟེ། མདུན་གྱི་གཞི་འདིར་ཤ་ཟ་བསྐལ་དོན་དུ་སོང་བའི་གང་ཟག་གི་རྒྱུད་ལ་ཤ་ཟ་ངེས་བྱེད་ཀྱི་དཔྱད་ཤེས་དོན་མཐུན་ཡོད་པ་དེ་དེ་འདྲའི་དཔྱད་ཤེས་དོན་མཐུན་མེད་པར་བསྒྲུབ་པའི་དགག་བྱའི་ཆོས་སུ་བཏགས་པའི་དོན་དང་དེའི་དགག་བྱའི་ཆོས་གཉིས་ཀ་ཡིན་ཀྱང་ཤ་ཟ་དང་དེ་འདྲའི་དཔྱད་ཤེས་དོན་མཐུན་གཉིས་རེ་རེ་ནས་དེ་སྒྲུབ་ཀྱི་དགག་བྱའི་ཆོས་སུ་བཏགས་པའི་དོན་ཡིན་ཀྱང་དེའི་དགག་བྱའི་ཆོས་མ་ཡིན་པའི་ཕྱིར། དང་པོ་སླ། ཕྱི་མ་མ་གྲུབ་ན། ཤ་ཟ་དང་དེ་འདྲའི་དཔྱད་

ཞེས་དོན་མཐུན་གཉིས་རེ་རེ་ནས་དེ་སྒྲུབ་ཀྱི་དགག་བྱའི་ཆོས་སུ་བཏགས་པའི་དོན་ཡིན་ཏེ། དེ་སྒྲུབ་ཀྱི་ཕྱི་རྒོལ་ཡང་དག་དེས་མདུན་གྱི་གཞི་འདིར་ཤ་ཟ་ཡོད་མེད་ཐེ་ཚོམ་ཟ་བའི་ཕྱིར་དང་། དེས་དེ་འདྲ་བའི་དཔྱད་ཞེས་དོན་མཐུན་ཡོད་མེད་ཐེ་ཚོམ་ཟ་བའི་ཕྱིར། དེ་གཉིས་རེ་རེ་ནས་དེ་སྒྲུབ་ཀྱི་དགག་བྱའི་ཆོས་མ་ཡིན་ཏེ། སྤྱིར་ཤ་ཟ་ཡོད་པའི་ཕྱིར་དང་། དུ་བ་དེ་མཚོན་མོའི་རྒྱ་མཚོར་དུ་བ་མེད་པར་བསྒྲུབ་པའི་དགག་བྱའི་ཆོས་མ་ཡིན་པའི་ཕྱིར། ཁྱོད་དེ་སྒྲུབ་ཀྱི་མི་སྣང་བ་མ་དམིགས་པའི་རྟགས་ཡང་དག་གང་ཞིག །མ་ཡིན་དགག་དང་སྒྲུབ་པ་གང་རུང་ཡང་ཡིན་པའི་གཞི་མཐུན་པ་དེ། ཁྱོད་དེ་སྒྲུབ་ཀྱི་མི་སྣང་བའི་འགལ་ཟླ་དམིགས་པའི་རྟགས་ཡང་དག་གི་མཚན་ཉིད། ཡོད་པ་དེ་མདུན་གྱི་གཞི་འདིར་ཤ་ཟ་བསྐལ་དོན་དུ་སོང་བའི་གང་ཟག་གི་རྒྱུད་ལ་དེ་དེས་བྱེད་ཀྱི་དཔྱད་ཞེས་དོན་མཐུན་མེད་པར་བསྒྲུབ་པའི་མི་སྣང་བའི་འགལ་ཟླ་དམིགས་པའི་རྟགས་ཡང་དག་ཡིན་ནོ། །བློ་ལ་ལྟོས་པའི་བསྐལ་དོན་ལ་གསུམ་ཡོད་དེ། ཡུལ་དང་དུས་དང་ངོ་བོའི་བསྐལ་དོན་གསུམ་ཡོད་པའི་ཕྱིར། དང་པོ་ནི། རང་དང་གྲོགས་ཐག་ཤིན་ཏུ་རིང་བ་ན་ཡོད་པའི་སྣོད་བཅུད་ཀྱི་ཁྱད་པར་ལྟ་བུ། གཉིས་པ་ནི། བསྐལ་པ་འདས་ཟིན་པ་དང་འབྱུང་བའི་དུས་ན་ཇི་འདྲ་བྱུང་བ་དང་འབྱུང་བའི་ཁྱད་པར་ལྟ་བུ་སྟེ། དེ་རྣམས་ནི་སྤྱིར་བསྐལ་དོན་མིན་ཡང་རང་གི་བློ་ལ་ལྟོས་པའི་བསྐལ་དོན་ནོ། །གསུམ་པ་ནི། རང་དང་ཉེ་བ་ན་ཡོད་ཀྱང་ངོ་བོ་ཕྲ་བའི་དབང་གིས་བསྐལ་དོན་དུ་སོང་བ་མདུན་གྱི་ཤ་ཟ་ལྟ་བུ་དང་། ལྷ་མིའི་བར་སྲིད་པ་རྣམས་དང་དེའི་བུམ་པ་ལྟ་བུའོ། །གཉིས་པ་སྣང་རུང་མ་དམིགས་པའི་རྟགས་ནི།

རྣམ་འགྲེལ་ལས། གཏན་ཚིགས་བྱེ་བྲག་ལ་ལྟོས་ནས། །འགའ་ཞིག་མེད་ཤེས་འབྲས་བུ་ཅན། །ཞེས་སོགས་ཀྱིས་བསྟན་ཏེ་འདི་ལ་གསུམ། མཚན་ཉིད། དབྱེ་བ། ཞར་བྱུང་ངོ། །དེའི་དང་པོ་ནི། སྣང་རུང་མ་དམིགས་པའི་ཚུལ་གསུམ་ཡིན་པ། སྣང་རུང་མ་དམིགས་པའི་རྟགས་ཡང་དག་གི་མཚན་ཉིད། དེ་སྒྲུབ་ཀྱི་སྣང་རུང་མ་དམིགས་པའི་ཚུལ་གསུམ་ཡིན་པ། དེ་སྒྲུབ་ཀྱི་སྣང་རུང་མ་དམིགས་པའི་རྟགས་ཡང་དག་གི་མཚན་ཉིད། གོ་བ་དང་། །སྦྱར་ན། ཁྱོད་དེ་སྒྲུབ་ཀྱི་མ་དམིགས་པའི་རྟགས་ཡང་དག་གང་ཞིག ཁྱོད་ཀྱི་རྟགས་ཀྱིས་དེ་སྒྲུབ་ཀྱི་དགག་བྱའི་ཆོས་སུ་བཏགས་པའི་དོན་དེ་ཡོད་ན། ཁྱོད་དེ་སྒྲུབ་ལ་ཕྱོགས་ཆོས་ཅན་དུ་སོང་བའི་གང་ཟག་གི་ཚད་མ་ལ་སྣང་རུང་ཡིན་དགོས་པ། ཁྱོད་དེ་སྒྲུབ་ཀྱི་སྣང་རུང་མ་དམིགས་པའི་རྟགས་ཡང་དག་གི་མཚན་ཉིད། གཉིས་པ་དེ་ལ་དབྱེ་ན་སྣང་རུང་གི་འབྲེལ་ཟླ་མ་དམིགས་པ་དང་། འགལ་ཟླ་དམིགས་པའི་རྟགས་གཉིས། དང་པོ་ནི། དེ་སྒྲུབ་ཀྱི་སྣང་རུང་མ་དམིགས་པའི་རྟགས་ཡང་དག་ཀྱང་ཡིན། མེད་དགག་ཀྱང་ཡིན་པའི་གཞི་མཐུན་པ་དེ། དེ་སྒྲུབ་ཀྱི་དང་པོའི་མཚན་ཉིད། དེ་ལ་སྣང་རུང་གི་རྒྱུ། ཁྱབ་བྱེད། རང་བཞིན། དངོས་འབྲས་མ་དམིགས་པའི་རྟགས་དང་བཞི། དང་པོ་ནི། མེ་མེད་པའི་མཚན་མོའི་རྒྱ་མཚོར་ཆོས་ཅན། དུ་བ་མེད་དེ། མེ་མེད་པའི་ཕྱིར་ཞེས་བཀོད་པའི་ཚེ་མེད་པ་ལྟ་བུ། གཉིས་པ་ནི། ཤིང་མེད་པའི་བྲག་རྫོང་ན་ཆོས་ཅན། ཤ་པ་མེད་དེ། ཤིང་མེད་པའི་ཕྱིར་ཞེས་པའི་རྟགས་དེ་ལྟ་བུ། གསུམ་པ་ནི། བུམ་པས་དབེན་པའི་ས་ཕྱོགས་ཆོས་ཅན། བུམ་པ་མེད་དེ། བུམ་པ་ཚད་མས་མ་དམིགས་པའི་ཕྱིར་ཞེས་པའི་རྟགས་དེ་ལྟ་བུ། བཞི་པ་ནི། དུ་

བས་དབེན་པའི་ས་ཕྱོགས་ཆོས་ཅན། དུ་བའི་དངོས་རྒྱུ་མེད་དེ། དུ་བ་མེད་པའི་ཕྱིར་ཞེས་པའི་རྟགས་དེ་ལྟ་བུ། གཉིས་པ་འགལ་ཟླ་དམིགས་པའི་རྟགས་ལ། མཚན་ཉིད་ནི། དེ་སྒྲུབ་ཀྱི་སྣང་རུང་མ་དམིགས་པའི་རྟགས་ཡང་དག་གང་ཞིག །མ་ཡིན་དགག་དང་སྒྲུབ་པ་གང་རུང་ཡང་ཡིན་པའི་གཞི་མཐུན་པ་དེ་དེའི་མཚན་ཉིད། དབྱེ་ན། ལྷན་ཅིག་མི་གནས་འགལ་གྱི་དེ་དང་། ཕན་ཚུན་སྤངས་འགལ་གྱི་དེ་གཉིས། དང་པོ་ལ་འགལ་བའི་རང་བཞིན་དམིགས་པ་བཞི། འབྲས་བུ་དམིགས་པ་བཞི། ཁྱབ་བྱ་དམིགས་པ་བཞི་སྟེ་བཅུ་གཉིས་སོ། །དེ་དག་གི་དབྱེ་བ་རྒྱས་པར་ནི་གཞན་དུ་བལྟ་ལ། མཚན་གཞི་ཙམ་ནི། །རང་བཞིན་དང་འགལ་བའི་རང་བཞིན་དམིགས་པ། རྒྱུ་དང་འགལ་བའི་རང་བཞིན་དམིགས་པ། ཁྱབ་བྱེད་དང་འགལ་བའི་རང་བཞིན་དམིགས་པ། རང་བཞིན་དང་འགལ་བའི་འབྲས་བུ་དམིགས་པ། རྒྱུ་དང་འགལ་བའི་འབྲས་བུ་དམིགས་པའི་རྟགས་ཡང་དག་ལྔ་ལས། དང་པོ་ནི། མེ་སྟོབས་ཆེན་པོས་ཁྱབ་པར་གནོན་པའི་ཤར་གྱི་དངོས་པོ་ཆོས་ཅན། གྲང་རེག་རྒྱུན་ཆགས་སུ་གནས་པ་མེད་དེ། མེ་སྟོབས་ཆེན་པོས་ཁྱབ་པར་གནོན་པའི་དངོས་པོ་ཡིན་པའི་ཕྱིར་ཞེས་པའི་རྟགས་དེ་ལྟ་བུའོ། །གཉིས་པ་ནི། དེ་ཆོས་ཅན། གྲང་འབྲས་སྤུ་ལོང་བྱེད་རྒྱུན་ཆགས་སུ་གནས་པ་མེད་དེ། དེ་འདྲའི་དངོས་པོ་ཡིན་པའི་ཕྱིར་ཞེས་པའི་རྟགས་ལྟ་བུ། གསུམ་པ་ནི། དེ་ཆོས་ཅན། ཁ་བའི་རེག་པ་རྒྱུན་ཆགས་སུ་གནས་པ་མེད་དེ། དེ་འདྲའི་དངོས་པོ་ཡིན་པའི་ཕྱིར་ཞེས་པའི་རྟགས་ལྟ་བུ། བཞི་པ་ནི། དུ་བ་དྲག་ཕྱུར་བས་ཁྱབ་པར་གནོན་པའི་ཤར་གྱི་དངོས་པོ་ཆོས་ཅན། གྲང་རེག་རྒྱུན་ཆགས་སུ་གནས་པ་མེད་དེ། དེས་

ཁྱབ་པར་གནོན་པའི་དངོས་པོ་ཡིན་པའི་ཕྱིར་ཞེས་པའི་རྟགས་ལྟ་བུ། ལྔ་པ་ནི། དེ་ཆོས་ཅན། གྲང་འབྲས་སྤུ་ལོང་བྱེད་རྒྱུན་ཆགས་སུ་གནས་པ་མེད་དེ། དེ་འདྲའི་དངོས་པོ་ཡིན་པའི་ཕྱིར་ཞེས་པའི་རྟགས་ལྟ་བུའོ། །དེ་ཡང་རྟོད་པའི་ཚེ་རྟགས་སུ་གང་འགྲོ་རྒྱུ་དེ་སྨོས་ནས་འཇོག་དགོས་སོ། ། གཉིས་པ་ཕན་ཚུན་སྤངས་འགལ་ནི། སྒྲ་ཆོས་ཅན། རྟག་པས་སྟོང་སྟེ། བྱས་པ་ཡིན་པའི་ཕྱིར་ཞེས་པའི་རྟགས་དེ་ལྟ་བུའོ། ། དེས་ན། རྭ་ཅན་དེ་མདུན་གྱི་གོང་བུ་རྭ་ཅན་རྟ་མ་ཡིན་པར་བསྒྲུབ་པའི་ཕན་ཚུན་སྤངས་འགལ་ལ་བརྟེན་པའི་འགལ་དམིགས་ཀྱི་རྟགས་ཡང་དག་ཡིན། དབྱེ་བ་ལ། ལྟོས་པས་ངེས་པ་འགོག་པའི་དེ་དང་། ངེས་པས་ལྟོས་པ་འགོག་པའི་དེ་གཉིས་ཡོད། དང་པོ་ནི། སྣམ་བུ་དཀར་པོ་ཆོས་ཅན། རང་གྲུབ་ཙམ་ནས་ཚོན་ཅན་དུ་མ་ངེས་ཏེ། རང་ཉིད་ཚོན་ཅན་དུ་འགྱུར་བ་རང་ལས་ཕྱིས་འབྱུང་གི་རྒྱུ་ལ་ལྟོས་པའི་ཕྱིར་ཞེས་པའི་རྟགས་ལྟ་བུ། གཉིས་པ་ནི། བྱས་པ་ཆོས་ཅན་རང་ཉིད་འཇིག་པ་རང་ལས་ཕྱིས་འབྱུང་གི་རྒྱུ་ལ་མི་ལྟོས་ཏེ། རང་ཉིད་གྲུབ་ཙམ་ནས་འཇིག་ངེས་ཡིན་པའི་ཕྱིར་ཞེས་པའི་རྟགས་ལྟ་བུ། གསུམ་པ་ཞར་བྱུང་ནི། རྟགས་དེ་ལ་དངོས་སྟོབས་ཀྱི་རྟགས། ཡིད་ཆེས་ཀྱི་རྟགས། གྲགས་པའི་རྟགས། དོན་སྒྲུབ་ཀྱི་རྟགས། ཐ་སྙད་སྒྲུབ་ཀྱི་རྟགས། མཐུན་ཕྱོགས་ལ་རྣམ་གཉིས་སུ་འཇུག་པ་དང་ཁྱབ་བྱེད་དུ་འཇུག་པའི་རྟགས་བདུན་ལས། དང་པོ་ནི། བྱས་པ་དེ། སྒྲ་མི་རྟག་པར་སྒྲུབ་པར་བྱེད་པའི་དངོས་སྟོབས་ཀྱི་རང་བཞིན་གྱི་རྟགས་དང་། དུ་བ་དུ་ལྡན་ལ་ལ་མེ་ཡོད་པར་བསྒྲུབ་པའི་དངོས་སྟོབས་ཀྱི་འབྲས་རྟགས་དང་། མེ་མེད་པ་དེ་མཚན་མོའི་རྒྱ་མཚོར་དུ་བ་མེད་པར་བསྒྲུབ་

པའི་དེ་སྒྲུབ་ཀྱི་མ་དམིགས་པའི་རྟགས་ཡིན། གཉིས་པ་ནི། དཔྱད་གསུམ་གྱིས་དག་པའི་ལུང་དེ། རང་གི་བསྟན་བྱའི་དོན་ལ་མི་སླུ་བར་སྒྲུབ་པར་བྱེད་པའི་ཡིད་ཆེས་ཀྱི་རང་བཞིན་གྱི་རྟགས་དང་། དཔྱད་གསུམ་གྱིས་དག་པའི་ལུང་དེ། སྦྱིན་པས་ལོངས་སྤྱོད་ཁྲིམས་ཀྱིས་བདེ། །ཞེས་པའི་ལུང་རང་གི་བསྟན་དོན་རྟོགས་པའི་ཚད་མ་སྔ་མ་སྔོན་དུ་སོང་བར་བསྒྲུབ་པའི་ཡིད་ཆེས་ཀྱི་འབྲས་རྟགས་དང་། དེ་དེ་འདྲའི་ལུང་རང་གི་བསྟན་བྱའི་དོན་ལ་མི་སླུ་བར་བསྒྲུབ་པའི་ཡིད་ཆེས་ཀྱི་མ་དམིགས་པའི་རྟགས་ཡིན། གསུམ་པ་ནི། །རྟོག་ཡུལ་ན་ཡོད་པ་དེ། རི་བོང་ཅན་ལ་ཟླ་སྒྲས་བརྗོད་རུང་དུ་བསྒྲུབ་པར་བྱེད་པའི་གྲགས་པའི་རང་བཞིན་གྱི་རྟགས་དང་། དེ་རི་བོང་ཅན་ལ་དངོས་དབང་གིས་ཟླ་སྒྲས་བརྗོད་རུང་མ་ཡིན་པར་བསྒྲུབ་པའི་གྲགས་པའི་མ་དམིགས་པའི་རྟགས་ཡིན། བཞི་པ་དང་ལྔ་པ་ལ་སྤྲོས་ན་ལྔ་ཡོད་དེ། དེ་སྒྲུབ་ཀྱི་རྟགས་ཡང་དག་གང་ཞིག །དེ་སྒྲུབ་ཀྱི་དངོས་ཀྱི་བསྒྲུབ་བྱའི་ཆོས་སུ་བཟུང་བྱ་དང་མཚན་ཉིད་ཀྱི་གཞི་མཐུན་སྲིད་པ་དེ། དེ་སྒྲུབ་ཀྱི་དོན་སྒྲུབ་ཀྱི་རྟགས་ཡང་དག་གི་མཚན་ཉིད། དེ་དང་མཚོན་བྱའི་གཞི་མཐུན་སྲིད་པ་དེ། དེ་སྒྲུབ་ཀྱི་ཐ་སྙད་སྒྲུབ་ཀྱི་རྟགས་ཡང་དག་གི་མཚན་ཉིད། དེ་དང་མཚོན་བྱའི་གཞི་མཐུན་མི་སྲིད་ཅིང་མཚན་ཉིད་ཀྱི་གཞི་མཐུན་སྲིད་པ་དེ། དེ་སྒྲུབ་ཀྱི་དོན་འབའ་ཞིག་སྒྲུབ་ཀྱི་རྟགས་ཡང་དག་གི་མཚན་ཉིད། དེ་དང་མཚན་ཉིད་ཀྱི་གཞི་མཐུན་མི་སྲིད་ཅིང་མཚོན་བྱའི་གཞི་མཐུན་སྲིད་པ་དེ། དེ་སྒྲུབ་ཀྱི་ཐ་སྙད་འབའ་ཞིག་སྒྲུབ་ཀྱི་རྟགས་ཡང་དག་གི་མཚན་ཉིད།

དེ་དང་མཚན་ཉིད་ཀྱི་གཞི་མཐུན་ཡང་སྲིད་མཚོན་བྱའི་གཞི་མཐུན་ཡང་སྲིད་པ་དེ། དེ་སྒྲུབ་ཀྱི་དོན་དང་ཐ་སྙད་གཉིས་ཀ་སྒྲུབ་ཀྱི་རྟགས་ཡང་དག་གི་མཚན་ཉིད་ཡིན་པའི་ཕྱིར། དེ་རེ་རེ་ལ་འང་འབྲས་རང་མ་དམིགས་པའི་རྟགས་གསུམ་རེ་ཡོད། དེ་ཡང་དང་པོ་གཉིས་ཀྱི་གསུམ་རེ་དང་ལྔ་པའི་གསུམ་པོ་དེ་གོང་གི་དངོས་སྟོབས་ཀྱི་རྟགས་གསུམ་པོ་འདོན་པ་བསྒྱུར་ནས་འཇོག་ལུགས་ཤེས་པར་བྱ་ཞིང་། གསུམ་པའི་གསུམ་ནི། བྱས་པའི་འབྲས་བུ་དེ་བྱས་པའི་འབྲས་བུར་གྱུར་པའི་གཟུགས་སྐད་ཅིག་མར་བསྒྲུབ་པའི་དོན་འབའ་ཞིག་སྒྲུབ་ཀྱི་འབྲས་རྟགས་དང་། །བྱས་པ་དེ་སྒྲ་སྐད་ཅིག་མར་སྒྲུབ་པར་བྱེད་པའི་དོན་སྒྲུབ་ཀྱི་རང་བཞིན་གྱི་རྟགས་དང་། བྱས་པ་དེ་སྒྲ་སྐད་ཅིག་མ་མ་ཡིན་པ་ལས་ལོག་པར་བསྒྲུབ་པའི་དོན་འབའ་ཞིག་སྒྲུབ་ཀྱི་མ་དམིགས་པའི་རྟགས་ཡིན། བཞི་པའི་གསུམ་ནི། བྱས་པའི་འབྲས་བུར་གྱུར་པའི་སྐད་ཅིག་མ་དེ་བྱས་པའི་འབྲས་བུར་གྱུར་པའི་གཟུགས་མི་རྟག་པར་བསྒྲུབ་པའི་ཐ། །སྙད་འབའ་ཞིག་སྒྲུབ་ཀྱི་འབྲས་རྟགས་དང་། སྐད་ཅིག་མ་དེ། སྒྲ་མི་རྟག་པར་སྒྲུབ་པར་བྱེད་པའི་ཐ་སྙད་འབའ་ཞིག་སྒྲུབ་ཀྱི་རང་བཞིན་གྱི་རྟགས་དང་། སྐད་ཅིག་མ་དེ་སྒྲ་མི་རྟག་པ་མ་ཡིན་པ་ལས་ལོག་པར་བསྒྲུབ་པའི་ཐ་སྙད་འབའ་ཞིག་སྒྲུབ་ཀྱི་མ་དམིགས་པའི་རྟགས་ཡིན། དྲུག་པ་དང་བདུན་པ་གཉིས་ནི་རིམ་པ་བཞིན། རྩོལ་བྱུང་དེ་སྒྲ་མི་རྟག་པར་སྒྲུབ་པར་བྱེད་པའི་མཐུན་ཕྱོགས་ལ་རྣམ་གཉིས་སུ་འཇུག་པའི་རྟགས། བྱས་པ་དེ་དེ་སྒྲུབ་ཀྱི་མཐུན་ཕྱོགས་ལ་ཁྱབ་བྱེད་དུ་འཇུག་པའི་རྟགས་ཡང་དག་ཡིན་ནོ། །དེ་ཡང་གོང་གི་དང་པོ་གསུམ་ནི་སྒྲུབ་བྱའི་སྒོ་ནས་དབྱེ་བ་དང་། བཞི་པ

དང་ལྔ་པ་གཉིས་ནི་སྒྲུབ་ཚུལ་གྱི་སྒོ་ནས་དབྱེ་བ་དང་། དྲུག་པ་དང་བདུན་པ་གཉིས་ནི་མཐུན་ཕྱོགས་ལ་འཇུག་ཚུལ་གྱི་སྒོ་ནས་དབྱེ་བ་ཡིན་ནོ། །ཡང་དེ་ལ་བསྒྲུབ་བྱའི་ཆོས་ཀྱི་སྒོ་ནས་དབྱེ་ན་སྒྲུབ་རྟགས་ཡང་དག་དང་དགག་རྟགས་ཡང་དག་གཉིས། དེ་སྒྲུབ་ཀྱི་རྟགས་ཡང་དག་གང་ཞིག །དེ་སྒྲུབ་ཀྱི་དངོས་ཀྱི་བསྒྲུབ་བྱའི་ཆོས་སུ་གཟུང་བྱ་ཡང་ཡིན་སྒྲུབ་པ་ཡང་ཡིན་པའི་གཞི་མཐུན་སྲིད་པ་དེ། དེ་སྒྲུབ་ཀྱི་དང་པོའི་མཚན་ཉིད། དེ་དང་དགག་པ་ཡང་ཡིན་པའི་གཞི་མཐུན་སྲིད་པ་དེ། དེ་སྒྲུབ་ཀྱི་གཉིས་པའི་མཚན་ཉིད། འོན་ཀྱང་འདི་ལ་དཔྱད་པར་བྱ་བ་མང་ངོ་། །དེ་སྒྲུབ་ཀྱི་འབྲས་རང་གི་རྟགས་ཡང་དག་གཉིས་པོ་གང་རུང་ཡིན་ན། དེ་སྒྲུབ་ཀྱི་སྒྲུབ་རྟགས་ཡང་དག ཡིན་པས་ཁྱབ་པ་དང་། དེ་སྒྲུབ་ཀྱི་མ་དམིགས་པའི་རྟགས་ཡང་དག་ཡིན་ན། དེ་སྒྲུབ་ཀྱི་དགག་རྟགས་ཡང་དག་ཡིན་པས་ཁྱབ་སྟེ། རྣམ་འགྲེལ་རང་འགྲེལ་ལས། དེ་ལ་གཉིས་ནི་དངོས་པོ་བསྒྲུབ་པ་ཡིན་ལ། །གཅིག་ནི་དགག་པའི་གཏན་ཚིགས་སོ། །ཞེས་གསུངས་པའི་ཕྱིར། ཡང་དེ་ལ་རང་དོན་སྐབས་ཀྱི་རྟགས་ཡང་དག་དང་གཞན་དོན་སྐབས་ཀྱི་རྟགས་ཡང་དག་གཉིས་ཡོད་དེ། དེ་གཉིས་དེ་སྒྲུབ་ཀྱི་རྟགས་ཡང་དག་ཡིན་པར་མཚུངས་ཀྱང་དེ་སྒྲུབ་ཀྱི་ཕྱི་རྒོལ་ཡང་དག་ཡོད་མེད་ཀྱི་སྒོ་ནས་འཇོག་པའི་ཕྱིར་རོ། །ཡང་སྐྱེ་བ་སྔ་ཕྱི་ཡོད་པར་བསྒྲུབ་པའི་རྟགས་སྦྱོར་ནི། སོ་སྐྱེ་འཆི་ཁ་མའི་སེམས་ཐ་མ་ཆོས་ཅན། ཁྱོད་ཀྱི་ཉེར་འབྲས་སུ་གྱུར་པའི་རིག་པ་ཕྱི་མ་ཡོད་དེ། ཁྱོད་ཆགས་བཅས་རྒྱུན་ལྡན་གྱི་རིག་པ་ཡིན་པའི་ཕྱིར། དཔེར་ན། ད་

ལྟའི་བློ་བཞིན། བྱིས་པ་བཙས་མ་ཐག་པའི་བློ་ཆོས་ཅན། རང་གི་རིགས་འདྲའི་བློ་སྔ་མ
སྔོན་དུ་སོང་སྟེ། རིག་པ་ཡིན་པའི་ཕྱིར། དཔེར་ན། རྒན་པོའི་བློ་བཞིན་ཞེས་པ་ལྟ་བུའོ།
།གཉིས་པ་རྟགས་ལྟར་སྣང་ནི། རྣམ་འགྲེལ་ལས། གཏན་ཚིགས་ལྟར་སྣང་དེ་ལས་གཞན་
ཞེས་སོགས་ཀྱིས་བསྟན་ཏེ། དེ་ལ་སྤྱིར་རྟགས་ལྟར་སྣང་མེད་དེ། གཞི་གྲུབ་ན་རྟགས་ཡང་
དག་ཡིན་དགོས་པའི་ཕྱིར། དེ་སྒྲུབ་ཀྱི་རྟགས་ལྟར་སྣང་ཡོད་དེ། དེ་སྒྲུབ་ཀྱི་ཚུལ་གསུམ
མ་ཡིན་པ། དེ་སྒྲུབ་ཀྱི་རྟགས་ལྟར་སྣང་གི་མཚན་ཉིད། དབྱེ་ན་གསུམ་སྟེ། དེ་སྒྲུབ་ཀྱི་
འགལ་བའི་རྟགས། མ་ངེས་པའི་རྟགས། མ་གྲུབ་པའི་རྟགས་སོ། །དེ་སྒྲུབ་ཀྱི་ཕྱོགས་ཆོས་
གང་ཞིག །ཁྱོད་ཀྱི་རྟགས་ཀྱིས་དེ་སྒྲུབ་ཀྱི་ཁྱབ་པའི་ཚུལ་གཉིས་ཕྱིན་ཅི་ལོག་ཏུ་ངེས་པ།
དེ་སྒྲུབ་ཀྱི་འགལ་རྟགས་ཀྱི་མཚན་ཉིད། མཚན་གཞི་ནི་སྒྲ་ཆོས་ཅན། རྟག་སྟེ། བྱས་པ་
ཡིན་པའི་ཕྱིར་ཞེས་པའི་རྟགས་དེ་ལྟ་བུ། དེ་སྒྲུབ་ཀྱི་ཕྱོགས་ཆོས་གང་ཞིག །ཁྱོད་ཀྱི་
རྟགས་ཀྱིས་དེ་སྒྲུབ་ཀྱི་ཁྱབ་པའི་ཚུལ་གཉིས་རྣམ་པར་མ་ངེས་པ། དེ་སྒྲུབ་ཀྱི་མ་ངེས་པའི་
གཏན་ཚིགས་ཀྱི་མཚན་ཉིད། མཚན་གཞི་ནི། སྒྲ་ཆོས་ཅན། མི་རྟག་སྟེ། ཡོད་པའི་ཕྱིར་
ཞེས་པའི་རྟགས་དེ་ལྟ་བུ། དེ་སྒྲུབ་ཀྱི་ཕྱོགས་མ་ཡིན་པར་དམིགས་པ་དེ། དེ་སྒྲུབ་ཀྱི་མ
གྲུབ་པའི་གཏན་ཚིགས་ཀྱི་མཚན་ཉིད། དབྱེ་ན་མང་ཡང་བསྡུ་ན་དགུ་སྟེ། དེ་སྒྲུབ་ཀྱི་
རྟགས་ཀྱི་ངོ་བོ་མེད་ནས་མ་གྲུབ་པ། དེ་བཞིན་དུ་ཆོས་ཅན་གྱི་ངོ་བོ་མེད་ནས་མ་གྲུབ་པ།

རྩོད་གཞིའི་སྟེང་དུ་མེད་ནས་མ་གྲུབ་པ། གསུམ་དང་། ཤེས་འདོད་མེད་ནས་མ་གྲུབ་པ། ཆོས་ཅན་ལ་ཐེ་ཚོམ་ཟ་ནས་མ་གྲུབ་པ། འབྲེལ་བ་ལ་ཐེ་ཚོམ་ཟ་ནས་མ་གྲུབ་པ་གསུམ་དང། རྟགས་ཆོས་ཐ་དད་མེད་ནས་མ་གྲུབ་པ། གཞི་ཆོས་ཐ་དད་མེད་ནས་མ་གྲུབ་པ། གཞི་རྟགས་ཐ་དད་མེད་ནས་མ་གྲུབ་པ་དང་གསུམ་སྟེ་དགུའོ། །མཚན་གཞི་ནི་རིམ་པ་བཞིན་དུ་དང་པོ་ནི། སྒྲ་ཆོས་ཅན། སྐྱེས་པ་ཡིན་ཏེ། རྒྱུ་རྟག་པ་ལས་བྱུང་བའི་ཕྱིར་ཞེས་པའི་རྟགས་དེ་ལྟ་བུའོ། །གཉིས་པ་ནི། རི་བོང་གི་རྭ་ཆོས་ཅན། ཡོད་དེ། རྭ་ཡིན་པའི་ཕྱིར། ཞེས་པའི་རྟགས་དེ་ལྟ་བུ། གསུམ་པ་ནི། སྒྲ་ཆོས་ཅན། དངོས་པོ་ཡིན་ཏེ། མིག་གིས་མཐོང་བའི་ཕྱིར། ཞེས་པའི་རྟགས་དེ་ལྟ་བུ་དང་། བཞི་པ་ནི། དེ་ཆོས་ཅན། མཉན་བྱ་ཡིན་ཏེ། མི་རྟག་པ་ཡིན་པའི་ཕྱིར་ཞེས་པའི་རྟགས་ལྟ་བུ། ལྔ་པ་ནི། དྲི་ཟ་བསྐལ་དོན་དུ་སོང་བའི་གང་ཟག་གི་ངོ་བོར་དྲི་ཟའི་གླུ་དབྱངས་ཆོས་ཅན། མི་རྟག་སྟེ། བྱས་པའི་ཕྱིར་ཞེས་པའི་རྟགས་དེ་ལྟ་བུ། དྲུག་པ་ནི། དེ་ཆོས་ཅན། ཡོད་དེ། དྲི་ཟའི་ཚད་མས་གྲུབ་པའི་ཕྱིར། ཞེས་པའི་རྟགས་དེ་ལྟ་བུ་དང་། བདུན་པ་ནི། སྒྲ་ཆོས་ཅན། མི་རྟག་སྟེ། མི་རྟག་པའི་ཕྱིར། ཞེས་པའི་རྟགས་དེ་ལྟ་བུ། བརྒྱད་པ་ནི། སྒྲ་ཆོས་ཅན། སྒྲ་ཡིན་ཏེ། མི་རྟག་པའི་ཕྱིར། ཞེས་པའི་རྟགས་དེ་ལྟ་བུ། དགུ་པ་ནི། སྒྲ་ཆོས་ཅན། མི་རྟག་སྟེ། སྒྲ་ཡིན་པའི་ཕྱིར་ཞེས་བཀོད་པའི་ཚེ་རྟགས་དེ་ལྟ་བུའོ། །གསུམ་པ་འཁྲུལ་དོན་ལ་གཉིས། སྒྲུབ་ངག་བཤད་པ་དང་། འཁྲུལ་དོན་གཞན་བཤད་པའོ། །དང་པོ་ལ་གཉིས། ཡང་དག་དང་ལྟར་སྣང་ངོ། །དང་པོ་ལ།

དབྱེ་ན། འབྲས་རང་མ་དམིགས་པའི་སྒྲུབ་ངག་གསུམ། དང་པོ་ལ་ཆོས་མཐུན་སྦྱོར་དང་། ཆོས་མི་མཐུན་སྦྱོར་གྱི་སྒྲུབ་ངག་གཉིས་ལས། དང་པོ་ནི། སྦྱོར་བ་བཀོད་རྗེས་སུ། དུ་བ་ཡོད་ན། མེ་ཡོད་པས་ཁྱབ། དཔེར་ན། ཚང་མང་བཞིན། དུ་ལྡན་གྱི་ལ་ལ་ཡང་དུ་བ་ཡོད་དོ་ཞེས་པ་ལྟ་བུ། གཉིས་པ་ནི། མེ་མེད་ན། དུ་བ་མེད་པས་ཁྱབ། དཔེར་ན། ཆུ་ཀླུང་བཞིན། དུ་ལྡན་གྱི་ལ་ལ་དུ་བ་ཡོད་དོ་ཞེས་པ་ལྟ་བུའོ། །གཉིས་པ་རང་བཞིན་གྱི་སྒྲུབ་ངག་ལ་ཆོས་མཐུན་མི་མཐུན་གཉིས་ཡོད་པ་ལས་དང་པོ་ནི། བྱས་ན། མི་རྟག་པས་ཁྱབ། དཔེར་ན། བུམ་པ་བཞིན། སྒྲ་ཡང་བྱས་སོ་ཞེས་པ་ལྟ་བུ། གཉིས་པ་ནི། རྟག་ན། མ་བྱས་པས་ཁྱབ། དཔེར་ན། འདུས་མ་བྱས་ཀྱི་ནམ་མཁའ་བཞིན། སྒྲ་ནི་བྱས་སོ་ཞེས་པ་ལྟ་བུའོ།། གསུམ་པ་མ་དམིགས་པའི་སྒྲུབ་ངག་ལ་གཉིས་ལས། དང་པོ་ནི། ཤིང་མེད་ན། ཤུག་པ་མེད་པས་ཁྱབ། དཔེར་ན། ཤིང་མེད་པའི་ཐང་བཞིན། ཤིང་མ་དམིགས་པའི་བྲག་ངོས་ན་ནི་ཤིང་མེད་དོ་ཞེས་པ་ལྟ་བུ། གཉིས་པ་ནི། ཤུག་པ་ཡོད་ན། ཤིང་ཡོད་པས་ཁྱབ། དཔེར་ན། ནགས་ཚལ་བཞིན། ཤིང་མ་དམིགས་པའི་བྲག་ངོས་ན་ནི་ཤིང་མེད་དོ་ཞེས་པ་ལྟ་བུའོ། །སྤྱིར་སྒྲུབ་ངག་ཡང་དག་ལ། ཚུལ་གསུམ་དཔེ་དང་བཅས་པ་ལྷག་ཆད་མེད་པར་སྟོན་པ་ཞིག་དགོས་ཏེ། མཚོན་ཙམ་བརྗོད་ན། སྒྲ་ཆོས་ཅན། མི་རྟག་སྟེ། བྱས་པའི་ཕྱིར་ཞེས་བཀོད་ནས། བྱས་ན་མི་རྟག་པས་ཁྱབ། དཔེར་ན་བུམ་པ་བཞིན། སྒྲ་ཡང་བྱས་སོ་ཞེས་པའི་ངག་འདིའི་བྱས་ན་མི་རྟག་པས་ཁྱབ་ཅེས་པས་རྗེས་ཁྱབ་དངོས་སུ་བརྗོད་ནས་ལྡོག་ཁྱབ་ཤུགས་ལ་འཕེན་ཅིང་། སྒྲ་ཡང་བྱས་ཞེས་པས་ཆོས་ཅན་དང་འབྲེལ་བའི་ཕྱོགས་ཆོས་

དངོས་སུ་བརྗོད་དེ། དཔེར་ན་བུམ་པ་བཞིན་ཞེས་པས་མཐུན་དཔེ་དངོས་སུ་བརྗོད་པ་ལྟ་བུ་ཡིན་པའི་ཕྱིར། ཕྱོགས་ཆོས་དང་། །ལྡོག་ཁྱབ་དངོས་སུ་བརྗོད་ནས་རྗེས་ཁྱབ་ཤུགས་ལ་འཕེན་པ་ནི། རྟག་ན་མ་བྱས་པས་ཁྱབ། དཔེར་ན། ནམ་མཁའ་བཞིན། སྒྲ་ནི་བྱས་སོ་ཞེས་པ་ལྟ་བུའོ། །འོན་ཀྱང་། བྱས་ན་མི་རྟག་པས་ཁྱབ་པ་དང་།རྟག་ན་མ་བྱས་པས་ཁྱབ་པ་གཉིས་ནི། སྦྱོར་བ་དེའི་རྗེས་ཁྱབ་དང་ལྡོག་ཁྱབ་མ་ཡིན་གྱི། བྱས་པ་ཉིད་དེའི་རྗེས་ཁྱབ་དང་ལྡོག་ཁྱབ་ཡིན་ཞིང་། ཕྱོགས་ཆོས་ཀྱང་ཡིན་ཏེ། དེའི་ཚུལ་གསུམ་ཡིན་པའི་ཕྱིར་རོ།

།གཉིས་པ་འཕྲོས་དོན་གཞན་ལ། འོ་ན། གཞི་མ་གྲུབ་པ་ཆོས་ཅན་དུ་བཟུང་བའི་རྟགས་ཡང་དག་ཡོད་དམ་མེད། ཡོད་ན་དེའི་ཕྱོགས་ཆོས་ཇི་ལྟར་གྲུབ། མེད་ན་ནི། རི་བོང་རྭ་ཆོས་ཅན། བདག་མེད་ཡིན་ཏེ། ཡོད་མེད་གང་རུང་ཡིན་པའི་ཕྱིར་ཞེས་པ་འདི་རྟགས་སྦྱོར་ཡང་དག་ཇི་ལྟར་ཡིན་ཞེ་ན་འདི་ལ་བཞེད་པ་མི་མཐུན་པ་ཡོད་ ཀྱང་རྒྱལ་ཚབ་རིན་པོ་ཆེས་ནི་སྒྲུབ་རྟགས་ལ་གཞི་མ་གྲུབ་པ་རྩོད་གཞིར་བཟུང་བའི་རྟགས་ཡང་དག་མེད་ཀྱང་། དགག་རྟགས་ལ་དེ་ཡོད་པར་བཤད་པས་དཔྱད་རྒྱུ་མང་ཡང་བཞག་གོ

ཡང་དབུ་མའི་ལུགས་ཀྱི་རྟེན་འབྲེལ་གྱི་རྟགས་དང་། ཆ་ཅན་གྱི་རྟགས། གཅིག་དུ་བྲལ་གྱི་རྟགས། མུ་བཞི་སྐྱེ་འགོག་གི་རྟགས་རྣམས་སྔར་བཤད་པའི་རྟགས་ གསུམ་གང་རུང་དུ་འདུས་སམ་མ་འདུས་ཞེ་ན། སྤྱིར་རྟགས་ཡང་དག་ཐམས་ཅད་འབྲས་རང་མ་དམིགས་པའི་རྟགས་གསུམ་དུ་འདུས་ལ། འབྲས་རང་གི་རྟགས་གཉིས་ནི་གཙོ་བོར་སྒྲུབ་རྟགས་

ཡིན་ཞིང་། མ་དམིགས་པའི་རྟགས་ལ་དགག་རྟགས་གཙོ་ཆེ་ཡང་། དེ་སྒྲུབ་ཀྱི་དགག་རྟགས་ཡིན་ན། དགག་པ་ཡིན་མི་དགོས་ཏེ། བྱས་པ་དེ་སྒྲུབ་པ་ཡིན་ཀྱང་དེ་སྒྲ་མི་རྟག་པར་སྒྲུབ་པར་བྱེད་པའི་རང་བཞིན་གྱི་རྟགས་ཡང་དག་དང་། སྒྲ་རྟག་སྟོང་དུ་སྒྲུབ་པར་བྱེད་པའི་མ་དམིགས་པའི་རྟགས་ཡང་དག་ཡིན་པའི་ཕྱིར། ཕྱི་མ་གྲུབ་སྟེ། དེ་དེ་སྒྲུབ་ཀྱི་འགལ་ཟླ་དམིགས་པའི་རྟགས་ཡང་དག་ཡིན་པའི་ཕྱིར་ཏེ། སྒྲ་ཆོས་ཅན། རྟག་པས་སྟོང་སྟེ། བྱས་པ་ཡིན་པའི་ཕྱིར་ཞེས་བཀོད་པའི་ཚེ་ན་དེ་ལྟར་ཡིན་པའི་ཕྱིར། དབུ་མའི་ལུགས་ཀྱི་རྟེན་འབྲེལ་གྱི་རྟགས་ནི། དེའི་ལུགས་ལ་དངོས་པོ་བདེན་མེད་དུ་བསྒྲུབ་པའི་ འགལ་ཟླ་དམིགས་པའི་རྟགས་ཡིན་པར་རྗེ་ཉིད་ཀྱིས་བཤད་ཅིང་། ཆ་བཅས་ཀྱི་རྟགས་ ཀྱང་དེ་དང་འདྲའོ། །གཅིག་དུ་བྲལ་གྱི་རྟགས་ནི་དབུ་མ་རྒྱན་ལས། བདེན་མེད་བསྒྲུབ་པའི་ཁྱབ་བྱེད་མ་དམིགས་པའི་རྟགས་སུ་བཤད་ཅིང་། འདིའི་རིགས་པས་དེ་སྒྲུབ་ཀྱི་བདེན་མེད་བསྒྲུབ་པའི་རྟགས་ཡང་དག་ཐམས་ཅད་ཀྱང་དེ་སྒྲུབ་ཀྱི་མ་དམིགས་པའི་རྟགས་སུ་འགྱུར་ ཏེ། དེ་ཡང་སྣང་རུང་མ་དམིགས་པའི་རྟགས་གཙོ་ཆེའོ། །མཚོན་ན། བུམ་པ་ཆོས་ཅན། བདེན་པར་མེད་དེ། བདེན་པར་ཚད་མས་མ་དམིགས་པའི་ཕྱིར་ཞེས་པའི་རྟགས་འདི་ལྟ་བུ་རང་བཞིན་མ་དམིགས་པའི་རྟགས་དང་། བུམ་པས་དག་པའི་ས་ཕྱོགས་ཆོས་ཅན། གསེར་བུམ་མེད་དེ། བུམ་པ་མེད་པའི་ཕྱིར་ཞེས་པའི་རྟགས་འདི་ལྟ་བུ་ཁྱབ་བྱེད་མ་དམིགས་པའི་རྟགས་དང་། མེས་དབེན་པའི་རྩིག་སྐོར་ན་ཆོས་ཅན། དུ་བ་མེད་དེ། མེ་མེད་པའི་ཕྱིར་ཞེས་པའི་རྟགས་འདི་ལྟ་བུ་རྒྱུ་མ་དམིགས་པའི་རྟགས་དང་། མྱུ་གུ་ཆོས་ཅན། བདེན་པས་སྟོང་སྟེ།

རྟེན་འབྲེལ་ཡིན་པའི་ཕྱིར། ཞེས་པའི་རྟགས་འདི་ལྟ་བུ་འགལ་ཟླ་དམིགས་པའི་རྟགས་ཡང་དག་ཡིན་པ་དེ་བཞིན་དུ་གཞན་ལ་སྦྱར་ནས་ཤེས་པར་བྱའོ། །གཞི་གཅིག་ལ་ལྟོས་པའི་རྟགས་གསུམ་འགལ་ཡང་སྒྲུབ་གཞི་སོ་སོ་ལ་ལྟོས་ནས་མི་འགལ་ཏེ། མཚོན་ན། སྐྱེས་པ་དེ། སྨྱུ་གུ་རང་གི་རྒྱུ་ལས་བྱུང་བར་སྒྲུབ་པར་བྱེད་པའི་འབྲས་རྟགས་ཡང་དག་ཡིན་ཀྱང་། །སྨྱུ་གུ་མི་རྟག་པར་བསྒྲུབ་པའི་རང་བཞིན་གྱི་རྟགས་དང་། དེ་གང་ཟག་གི་བདག་མེད་དུ་སྒྲུབ་པར་བྱེད་པའི་མ་དམིགས་པའི་རྟགས་ཡང་དག་ཡིན་པའི་ཕྱིར་རོ། །བྱས་པའི་རྟགས་ཀྱིས་སྒྲ་མི་རྟག་པར་བསྒྲུབ་པའི་རྟགས་ཆོས་དོན་གསུམ་པོ་སྤྱི་མཚན་རྟོག་པས་བཏགས་ཙམ་ཡིན་ཡང་། དེ་སྒྲུབ་ཀྱི་རྟགས་ཆོས་དོན་གསུམ་པོ་གང་རུང་ཡིན་ན། རང་མཚན་ཡིན་དགོས་ཏེ། དེ་ཡིན་ན། དངོས་པོ་ཡིན་དགོས་པའི་ཕྱིར་ཏེ། དེ་སྒྲུབ་ཀྱི་དོན་རྩོད་གཞི་ཡིན་ན་སྒྲ་ཡིན་དགོས་ཤིང་། དངོས་ཀྱི་བསྒྲུབ་བྱའི་ཆོས་ཡིན་ན་མི་རྟག་པ་ཡིན་དགོས། རྟགས་ལ་བྱས་པ་ཉིད་དགོས་པའི་ཕྱིར་རོ། །དེས་ན་དེ་སྒྲུབ་ཀྱི་རྟགས་ཆོས་དོན་གསུམ་ནི་དེ་སྒྲུབ་ཀྱི་རྟགས་དོན་གསུམ་མིན་ཞེས་བྱ་སྟེ། དེ་བཞིན་དུ་གཞན་ལ་ཡང་སྦྱར་ནས་ཤེས་པར་བྱ་དགོས་སོ། །སྨྲས་པ། རིགས་གཞུང་རྒྱ་གཏེར་ཆེན་པོ་ལས་འཁྲུངས་པའི། །རིགས་ཚུལ་སྙིང་པོ་བསྡུས་པའི་ཆ་ཙམ་ཞིག །རིགས་པ་དོན་གཉེར་ཅན་ལ་ཕན་པའི་ཆེད། །རིགས་པའི་ལམ་ནས་དྲངས་ཏེ་བདག་གིས་བཀོད། །འོན་ཀྱང་སྦྱངས་མཁས་བློ་ཡི་མེ་ལོང་ངོས། །ཚུལ་འདིའི་ཟབ་དོན་གཟུགས་བརྙན་གསལ་འཆར་ཡང་། །མ་སྦྱངས་མི་མཁས་བློ་གྲོས་རྡེག་ངོས་སུ། །འཆར་དཀའ་ཆོས་ཉིད་ཡིན་ཕྱིར་བདག་ལྟས་ཅི།

།ཞེས་པ་འདི་ཡང་ཡར་རིས་རབ་འབྱམས་པ་བློ་བཟང་རྒྱལ་མཚན་ཞེས་བྱ་བ་དགེ་
བཤེས་སུ་གྲགས་པ་དེས་བསྐུལ་བ་ལ་བརྟེན་ནས། ཤཱཀྱའི་དགེ་སློང་གྲགས་པ་བཤད་
སྒྲུབ་ཀྱིས་ཙོ་ནེའི་དགོན་ཉིད་དུ་སྦྱར་བའོ། ॥

TIBETAN DEFINITIONS FROM *ANALYSIS OF REASONS* (*rtags rigs*)

[Definitions and classifications to facilitate study and debate.]

1 རྟགས་སུ་བཀོད་པ། རྟགས་ཀྱི་མཚན་ཉིད།

2 དེ་སྒྲུབ་ཀྱི་རྟགས་སུ་བཀོད་པ། དེ་སྒྲུབ་ཀྱི་རྟགས་ཀྱི་མཚན་ཉིད།

3 རྟགས་ལ་དབྱེ་ན་གཉིས་ཡོད། རྟགས་ཡང་དག་དང་རྟགས་ལྟར་སྣང་།

4 ཁྱོད་བྱས་པས་རྟགས་ཀྱིས་སྒྲ་མི་རྟག་པར་སྒྲུབ་པར་བྱེད་པའི་ཆོས་ཅན་དུ་གཟུང་བ་ཡང་ཡིན། ཁྱོད་བྱས་པར་ཚད་མས་ངེས་ནས་མི་རྟག་པ་ལ་ཤེས་འདོད་ཞུགས་པའི་གང་ཟག་སྲིད་པ་ཡང་ཡིན་པའི་གཞི་མཐུན་པར་དམིགས་པ་དེ། ཁྱོད་བྱས་པའི་རྟགས་ཀྱིས་སྒྲ་མི་རྟག་པར་སྒྲུབ་པར་བྱེད་པའི་ཤེས་འདོད་ཆོས་ཅན་སྐྱོན་མེད་ཀྱི་མཚན་ཉིད།

5 དེ་སྒྲུབ་ཀྱི་བསྒྲུབ་བྱའི་ཆོས་སུ་གཟུང་བར་བྱ་བ། དེ་སྒྲུབ་ཀྱི་བསྒྲུབ་བྱའི་ཆོས་ཀྱི་མཚན་ཉིད།

6 དེ་སྒྲུབ་ཀྱི་བསྒྲུབ་བྱའི་ཆོས་ཀྱི་འགོད་ཚུལ་དང་མཐུན་པར་ཡོད་པ་དེ། དེ་སྒྲུབ་ཀྱི་མཐུན་ཕྱོགས་ཀྱི་མཚན་ཉིད།

7 དེ་སྒྲུབ་ཀྱི་བསྒྲུབ་བྱའི་ཆོས་ཀྱི་འགོད་ཚུལ་དང་མཐུན་པར་མེད་པ་དེ། དེ་སྒྲུབ་ཀྱི་མི་མཐུན་ཕྱོགས་ཀྱི་མཚན་ཉིད།

8 ཚུལ་གསུམ་ཡིན་པ། རྟགས་ཡང་དག་གི་མཚན་ཉིད།

9 དེ་སྒྲུབ་ཀྱི་ཤེས་འདོད་ཆོས་ཅན་སྐྱོན་མེད་ཀྱི་སྟེང་དུ་འགོད་ཚུལ་དང་མཐུན་པར་ཡོད་པ་ཉིད་དུ་ཚད་མས་ངེས་པ། དེ་སྒྲུབ་ཀྱི་ཕྱོགས་ཆོས་ཀྱི་མཚན་ཉིད།

10 དེ་སྒྲུབ་ཀྱི་མཐུན་ཕྱོགས་ཁོ་ན་ལ་འགོད་ཚུལ་དང་མཐུན་པར་ཡོད་པ་ཉིད་དུ་ཚད་མས་ངེས་པ་དེ། དེ་སྒྲུབ་ཀྱི་རྗེས་ཁྱབ་ཀྱི་མཚན་ཉིད།

11 དེ་སྒྲུབ་ཀྱི་དངོས་ཀྱི་བསྒྲུབ་བྱའི་ཆོས་ཀྱི་དོན་ལྡོག་དང་འབྲེལ་སྟོབས་ཀྱིས་དེ་སྒྲུབ་ཀྱི་མི་མཐུན་ཕྱོགས་ལ་འགོད་ཚུལ་དང་མཐུན་པར་མེད་པ་ཉིད་དུ་ཚད་མས་ངེས་པ་དེ། དེ་སྒྲུབ་ཀྱི་ལྡོག་ཁྱབ་ཀྱི་མཚན་ཉིད།

12 (or) དེ་སྒྲུབ་ཀྱི་དངོས་ཀྱི་བསྒྲུབ་བྱའི་ཆོས་སུ་གཟུང་བྱར་འགྱུར་རྒྱུ་དང་འབྲེལ་སྟོབས་ཀྱིས་དེ་སྒྲུབ་ཀྱི་མི་མཐུན་ཕྱོགས་ལ་འགོད་ཚུལ་དང་མཐུན་པར་མེད་པ་ཉིད་དུ་ཚད་མས་ངེས་པ་དེ། དེ་སྒྲུབ་ཀྱི་ལྡོག་ཁྱབ་ཀྱི་མཚན་ཉིད།

13 རྟགས་ཡང་དག་ལ་དབྱེ་ན་གསུམ་ཡོད། འབྲས་རྟགས། རང་བཞིན་གྱི་རྟགས། མ་དམིགས་པའི་རྟགས།

14 འབྲས་བུའི་ཚུལ་གསུམ་ཡིན་པ། འབྲས་རྟགས་ཡང་དག་གི་མཚན་ཉིད།

15 དེ་སྒྲུབ་ཀྱི་འབྲས་བུའི་ཚུལ་གསུམ་ཡིན་པ། དེ་སྒྲུབ་ཀྱི་འབྲས་རྟགས་ཡང་དག་གི་མཚན་ཉིད།

16 ཁྱོད་དེ་སྒྲུབ་ཀྱི་རྟགས་ཡང་དག་གང་ཞིག ཁྱོད་ཀྱི་རྟགས་ཀྱིས་དེ་སྒྲུབ་ཀྱི་དངོས་ཀྱི་བསྒྲུབ་བྱའི་ཆོས་སུ་གཟུང་བྱའི་གཙོ་བོ་ཡང་ཡིན། ཁྱོད་ཀྱི་རྒྱུ་ཡང་ཡིན་པའི་གཞི་མཐུན་སྲིད་པ་དེ། ཁྱོད་དེ་སྒྲུབ་ཀྱི་འབྲས་རྟགས་ཡང་དག་གི་མཚན་ཉིད།

17 འབྲས་རྟགས་ཡང་དག་ལ་དབྱེ་ན་ལྔ་ཡོད། རྒྱུ་དངོས་སྒྲུབ་ཀྱི་འབྲས་རྟགས། རྒྱུ་སྔོན་སོང་གི་འབྲས་རྟགས། རྒྱུ་སྤྱི་སྒྲུབ་ཀྱི་འབྲས་རྟགས། རྒྱུའི་ཁྱད་པར་སྒྲུབ་ཀྱི་འབྲས་རྟགས། རྒྱུ་ཆོས་རྗེས་དཔོག་གི་འབྲས་རྟགས་དང་ལྔ་ཡོད།

18 དེ་སྒྲུབ་ཀྱི་རང་བཞིན་གྱི་ཚུལ་གསུམ་ཡིན་པ། དེ་སྒྲུབ་ཀྱི་རང་བཞིན་གྱི་རྟགས་ཡང་དག་གི་མཚན་ཉིད།

19 ཁྱོད་དེ་སྒྲུབ་ཀྱི་རྟགས་ཡང་དག་གང་ཞིག །ཁྱོད་ཀྱི་རྟགས་ཀྱིས་དེ་སྒྲུབ་ཀྱི་དངོས་ཀྱི་བསྒྲུབ་བྱའི་ཆོས་སུ་གཟུང་བྱ་ཡིན་ན་ཁྱོད་དང་བདག་ཉིད་གཅིག་ཡིན་དགོས་པའི་ཆ་ནས་བཞག་པ་དེ། ཁྱོད་དེ་སྒྲུབ་ཀྱི་རང་བཞིན་གྱི་རྟགས་ཡང་དག་གི་མཚན་ཉིད།

20 རང་བཞིན་གྱི་རྟགས་ཡང་དག་ལ་དབྱེ་ན་གཉིས་ཡོད། དེར་གྱུར་པའི་ཁྱད་པར་ལྟོས་པ་བའི་དེ་དང་། ཁྱད་པར་དག་པ་བའི་དེ་གཉིས་ཡོད།

21 ཁྱོད་དེ་སྒྲུབ་ཀྱི་རྟགས་ཡང་དག་གང་ཞིག །ཁྱོད་ཀྱི་རྟགས་ཀྱིས་དེ་སྒྲུབ་ཀྱི་དངོས་ཀྱི་བསྒྲུབ་བྱའི་ཆོས་སུ་གཟུང་བྱ་ཡང་ཡིན། དགག་པ་ཡང་ཡིན་པའི་གཞི་མཐུན་སྲིད་པ་དེ། ཁྱོད་དེ་སྒྲུབ་ཀྱི་མ་དམིགས་པའི་རྟགས་ཡང་དག་གི་མཚན་ཉིད།

22 མ་དམིགས་པའི་རྟགས་ཡང་དག་ལ་དབྱེ་ན་གཉིས་ཡོད། མི་སྣང་བ་མ་དམིགས་པའི་རྟགས་ཡང་དག་དང་། སྣང་རུང་མ་དམིགས་པའི་རྟགས་ཡང་དག་གཉིས་ཡོད།

23 ཁྱོད་དེ་སྒྲུབ་ཀྱི་མི་སྣང་བ་མ་དམིགས་པའི་རྟགས་ཡང་དག་གང་ཞིག །མ་ཡིན་དགག་དང་སྒྲུབ་པ་གང་རུང་ཡང་ཡིན་པའི་གཞི་མཐུན་པ་དེ། ཁྱོད་དེ་སྒྲུབ་ཀྱི་མི་སྣང་བའི་འགལ་ཟླ་དམིགས་པའི་རྟགས་ཡང་དག་གི་མཚན་ཉིད།

24 ཁྱོད་དེ་སྒྲུབ་ཀྱི་མ་དམིགས་པའི་རྟགས་ཡང་དག་གང་ཞིག །ཁྱོད་ཀྱི་རྟགས་ཀྱིས་དེ་སྒྲུབ་ཀྱི་དགག་བྱའི་ཆོས་སུ་བརྟགས་པའི་དོན་དེ་ཡོད་ན། ཁྱོད་དེ་སྒྲུབ་ལ་

ཕྱོགས་ཆོས་ཅན་དུ་སོང་བའི་གང་ཟག་གི་ཚད་མ་ལ་སྣང་རུང་བ། ཁྱོད་དེ་སྒྲུབ་ཀྱི་སྣང་རུང་མ་དམིགས་པའི་རྟགས་ཡང་དག་གི་མཚན་ཉིད།

25 སྣང་རུང་མ་དམིགས་པའི་རྟགས་ཡང་དག་ལ་དབྱེ་ན་གཉིས་ཡོད། སྣང་རུང་གི་འབྲེལ་ཟླ་མ་དམིགས་པའི་རྟགས་དང་། འགལ་ཟླ་དམིགས་པའི་རྟགས་གཉིས་ཡོད།

26 དེ་སྒྲུབ་ཀྱི་སྣང་རུང་མ་དམིགས་པའི་རྟགས་ཡང་དག་ཀྱང་ཡིན། མེད་དགག་ཀྱང་ཡིན་པའི་གཞི་མཐུན་པ་དེ། དེ་སྒྲུབ་ཀྱི་སྣང་རུང་གི་འབྲེལ་ཟླ་མ་དམིགས་པའི་རྟགས་ཡང་དག་གི་མཚན་ཉིད།

27 སྣང་རུང་གི་འབྲེལ་ཟླ་མ་དམིགས་པའི་རྟགས་ཡང་དག་ལ་དབྱེ་ན་བཞི་ཡོད། སྣང་རུང་གི་རྒྱུ། ཁྱབ་བྱེད། རང་བཞིན། དངོས་འབྲས་མ་དམིགས་པའི་རྟགས་དང་བཞི་ཡོད།

28 དེ་སྒྲུབ་ཀྱི་སྣང་རུང་མ་དམིགས་པའི་རྟགས་ཡང་དག་གང་ཞིག །མ་ཡིན་དགག་དང་སྒྲུབ་པ་གང་རུང་ཡང་ཡིན་པའི་གཞི་མཐུན་པ་དེ། འགལ་ཟླ་དམིགས་པའི་རྟགས་ཡང་དག་གི་མཚན་ཉིད།

29 འགལ་ཟླ་དམིགས་པའི་རྟགས་ཡང་དག་ལ་དབྱེ་ན་གཉིས་ཡོད། ལྷན་ཅིག་མི་གནས་འགལ་གྱི་འགལ་ཟླ་དམིགས་པའི་རྟགས་ཡང་དག་དང་། ཕན་ཚུན་སྤངས་འགལ་གྱི་འགལ་ཟླ་དམིགས་པའི་རྟགས་ཡང་དག་གཉིས་ཡོད།

30 དེ་སྒྲུབ་ཀྱི་ཚུལ་གསུམ་མ་ཡིན་པ། དེ་སྒྲུབ་ཀྱི་རྟགས་ལྟར་སྣང་གི་མཚན་ཉིད།

31 དེ་སྒྲུབ་ཀྱི་རྟགས་ལྟར་སྣང་ལ་དབྱེ་ན་གསུམ་ཡོད། དེ་སྒྲུབ་ཀྱི་འགལ་བའི་རྟགས། །དེ་སྒྲུབ་ཀྱི་མ་ངེས་པའི་རྟགས། དེ་སྒྲུབ་ཀྱི་མ་གྲུབ་པའི་རྟགས་དང་གསུམ།

32 ཁྱོད་ཀྱི་རྟགས་ཀྱིས་དེ་སྒྲུབ་ཀྱི་ཁྱབ་པའི་ཚུལ་གཉིས་ཕྱིན་ཅི་ལོག་ཏུ་ངེས་པ། དེ་སྒྲུབ་ཀྱི་འགལ་རྟགས་ཀྱི་མཚན་ཉིད།

33 ཁྱོད་ཀྱི་རྟགས་ཀྱིས་དེ་སྒྲུབ་ཀྱི་ཁྱབ་པའི་ཚུལ་གཉིས་རྣམ་པར་མ་ངེས་པ། དེ་སྒྲུབ་ཀྱི་མ་ངེས་པའི་རྟགས་ཀྱི་མཚན་ཉིད།

34 དེ་སྒྲུབ་ཀྱི་ཕྱོགས་ཆོས་མ་ཡིན་པར་དམིགས་པ་དེ། དེ་སྒྲུབ་ཀྱི་མ་གྲུབ་པའི་གཏན་ཚིགས་ཀྱི་མཚན་ཉིད།

35 མ་གྲུབ་པའི་གཏན་ཚིགས་ལ་དབྱེ་ན་དགུ་ཡོད། དེ་སྒྲུབ་ཀྱི་རྟགས་ཀྱི་ངོ་བོ་མེད་ནས་མ་གྲུབ་པ། དེ་བཞིན་དུ་ཆོས་ཅན་གྱི་ངོ་བོ་མེད་ནས་མ་གྲུབ་པ། རྩོད་གཞིའི་སྟེང་དུ་མེད་ནས་མ་གྲུབ་པ། ཤེས་འདོད་མེད་ནས་མ་གྲུབ་པ། ཆོས་ཅན་ལ་ཐེ་ཚོམ་ཟ་ནས་མ་གྲུབ་པ། འབྲེལ་བ་ལ་ཐེ་ཚོམ་ཟ་ནས་མ་གྲུབ་པ། རྟགས་ཆོས་ཐ་དད་མེད་ནས་མ་གྲུབ་པ། གཞི་ཆོས་ཐ་དད་མེད་ནས་མ་གྲུབ་པ། གཞི་རྟགས་ཐ་དད་མེད་ནས་མ་གྲུབ་པ།

List of Terms

ENGLISH TO TIBETAN

TIBETAN TO ENGLISH

LIST OF TERMS

ENGLISH TO TIBETAN

A

abandon, discard སྤོང་བ་

(non-interfering) active cause བྱེད་རྒྱུ་

actual reason སོང་ཚོད་ཀྱི་རྟགས་

actual object being negated དགག་བྱའི་ཆོས་སུ་བཏགས་པའི་དོན་

air (element) རླུང་

appearance, appear སྣང་བ་

apprehended aspect, གཟུང་རྣམ་
objective aspect

apprehending aspect, འཛིན་རྣམ་
subjective aspect (def: of self-cognizing
cognition or apperceptive cognition)

appropriated heaps ཉེར་ལེན་གྱི་ཕུང་པོ་

arisen from effort རྩོལ་བྱུང་

Arya, exalted one འཕགས་པ་

ascertain, ascertainment, ངེས་པ་
definite

aspect, kind རྣམ་པ་

assistant, helper ཕན་འདོགས་བྱེད་

Ashoka tree ཤ་པ་

B

basic existent གཞི་གྲུབ་

basis of dispute, subject of debate རྩོད་གཞི་

basis of inference དཔག་གཞི་

basis of relation between the subject and the reason ཕྱོགས་ཆོས་ཀྱི་ལྟོས་གཞི་

basis of relation of pervasion or concomitance (between the reason and quality to be proved) ཁྱབ་པའི་ལྟོས་གཞི་

basis, place གཞི་

be able to, have the ability ནུས་པ་

be possible, samsaric existence སྲིད་པ་

because it is ཡིན་པའི་ཕྱིར་

because there is/are; exists ཡོད་པའི་ཕྱིར་

being, person སྐྱེས་བུ་

blue, blue-green སྔོན་པོ་

body sense power ལུས་ཀྱི་དབང་པོ་

brown sugar, molasses བུ་རམ་

busyness, distraction, noise འདུ་འཛི་

but, at any rate, nevertheless, "I disagree" འོན་ཀྱང་

butterlamp, lamp flame མར་མེ་

C

calm abiding, *shamatha* ཞི་གནས་

causal relationship དེ་འབྱུང་འབྲེལ་

causally effective thing དངོས་པོ་

cause རྒྱུ་

cause of similar fortune སྐལ་མཉམ་གྱི་རྒྱུ་

challenger, questioner, initiator in a debate སྔ་རྒོལ་

characteristic, quality ཁྱད་ཆོས་

clairvoyance མངོན་ཤེས་

class generality རིགས་སྤྱི་

classification དབྱེ་བ་

be clear, lucid གསལ་

co-arising cause, concurrent cause ལྷན་ཅིག་འབྱུང་བའི་རྒྱུ་

cold གྲང་

collective generality ཚོགས་སྤྱི་

combination, one thing that is both གཞི་མཐུན་

combined, bring together སྡོམས་

common, shared ཐུན་མོང་

complete, comprise ཚང་བ་

composed entity, compounded འདུས་བྱས་

conception, conceptual cognition རྟོག་པ་

conceptual subsequent cognition རྟོག་པ་བཅད་ [དཔྱད་] ཤེས་

conceptual wrong consciousness རྟོག་པ་ལོག་ཤེས་

concomitant cause མཚུངས་ལྡན་གྱི་རྒྱུ་

concrete phenomenon རང་མཚན་

condition རྐྱེན་

consciousness, mind ཤེས་པ་

contaminated, defiled (by mental afflictions) ཟག་བཅས་

contaminated heaps ཟག་བཅས་ཀྱི་ཕུང་པོ་

contaminated virtue དགེ་བ་ཟག་བཅས་

continuum, continuity, stream རྒྱུན་

contradictory འགལ་བ་

contradictory reason འགལ་བའི་གཏན་ཚིགས་

co-operating cause ལྷན་ཅིག་བྱེད་རྐྱེན་

correct consequence ཐལ་འགྱུར་ཡང་དག་

count!, enumerate! སྒྲོངས་ཞོག་

created སྐྱེས་པ་

crop, harvest ལོ་ཏོག་

D

debater, opponent in debate རྒོལ་བ་

decide, determine ཐག་གཅོད་

definition, characteristic མཚན་ཉིད་

deprecation, underestimation སྐུར་འདེབས་

desire realm འདོད་ཁམས་

desirous attachment འདོད་ཆགས་

determinative knower, conceptual knower, conceiving cognition ཞེན་རིག་

devoid of, solitary place, isolated place དབེན་

different ཐ་དད་

direct cause དངོས་རྒྱུ་

direct cognition མངོན་སུམ་

direct effect དངོས་འབྲས་

direct valid cognition མངོན་སུམ་ཚད་མ་

direct valid mental cognition ཡིད་ཀྱི་མངོན་སུམ་གྱི་ཚད་མ་

direct valid self-cognizing cognition རང་རིག་མངོན་སུམ་གྱི་ཚད་མ་

direct valid sense cognition དབང་པོ་མངོན་སུམ་གྱི་ཚད་མ་

direct valid yogic cognition རྣལ་འབྱོར་མངོན་སུམ་གྱི་ཚད་མ་

directly suggesting its agent རང་གི་ཁྱད་ཆོས་དངོས་སུ་འཕངས་པ་

directly suggestive དངོས་སུ་འཕངས་པ་

discursive thought, superstition རྣམ་རྟོག་

dispelling remaining doubts རྩོད་པ་སྤོང་བ་

dissimilar class comprised of non-existents མེད་པ་མི་མཐུན་ཕྱོགས་

dissimilar class of overextension གཞན་པ་མི་མཐུན་ཕྱོགས་

dissimilar class of the contradictory འགལ་ཟླ་མི་མཐུན་ཕྱོགས་

dissimilar, disharmonious, incompatible མི་མཐུན་ཕྱོགས་

dominant condition བདག་པོའི་འབྲས་བུ་

doubt ཐེ་ཚོམ་

doubt tending away from the fact དོན་མི་འགྱུར་གྱི་ཐེ་ཚོམ་

doubt tending toward the fact དོན་འགྱུར་གྱི་ཐེ་ཚོམ་

doubt, fortune, beyond one's perceptual capacity, having misgivings about something, entertaining doubts བསྐལ་དོན་(དུ་སོང་བ་)

doubt, wanting to know ཤེས་འདོད་

E

each and every, individually རེ་རེ་ནས་

ear sense power རྣ་བའི་དབང་པོ་

earth (element) ས་

effect correspondent with its cause རྒྱུ་མཐུན་གྱི་འབྲས་བུ་

effect of human effort སྐྱེས་བུ་བྱེད་པའི་འབྲས་བུ་

effect of liberation བྲལ་བའི་འབྲས་བུ་

effect, result, fruit འབྲས་བུ་

Eight Doors of Pervasion ཁྱབ་པ་རྣམ་པ་སྒོ་བརྒྱད་

either one, whichever, whatever གང་རུང་

emptiness, voidness, *shūnyatā* སྟོང་པ་ཉིད་

engage, operate, signify, apply to, refer to, enter འཇུག་པ་

equally pervasive ཡིན་ཁྱབ་མཉམ་

equally undecided doubt ཆ་མཉམ་པའི་ཐེ་ཚོམ་

equivalent, same meaning, synonymous དོན་གཅིག་

essence, entity, identity ངོ་བོ་

etymology, explanation of a word or term སྒྲ་བཤད་

exaggeration, overestimation སྒྲོ་འདོགས་

example དཔེ་

example of the dissimilar class མི་མཐུན་དཔེ་

example of the similar class མཐུན་དཔེ་

excitement, mental agitation རྒོད་པ་

existent ཡོད་པ་

explicit quality to be proved དངོས་ཀྱི་བསྒྲུབ་བྱའི་ཆོས་

express, proclaim, mention, describe བརྗོད་པ་

extremely hidden phenomenon ཤིན་ཏུ་ལྐོག་གྱུར་

eye sense power མིག་གི་དབང་པོ་

F

factually concordant mind, in accord with reality, correct བློ་དོན་མཐུན་

fallible སླུ་བ་

false reason གཏན་ཚིགས་ལྟར་སྣང་

false reason རྟགས་ལྟར་སྣང་

farmer ཞིང་པ་

fault སྐྱོན་

faultless སྐྱོན་མེད་

faultless subject of debate about which someone has doubt ཤེས་འདོད་ཆོས་ཅན་སྐྱོན་མེད་

feeling ཚོར་བ་

fire (element) མེ་

five similarities, five accompanying aspects མཚུངས་ལྡན་རྣམ་པ་ལྔ་

for example དཔེར་ན་

form གཟུགས་

form realm གཟུགས་ཁམས་

formless realm གཟུགས་མེད་ཁམས་

four great elements འབྱུང་བ་བཞི་

free from, separate from དང་བྲལ་བ་

future (time) མ་འོངས་པ་

G

general abstract phenomenon སྤྱི་མཚན་

general category སྤྱི་

generally སྤྱིར་

ghost, flesh eater, demon ཤ་ཟ་

god, deity ལྷ་

good qualities ཡོན་ཏན་

goose bumps སྤུ་ལོང་

governing condition བདག་རྐྱེན་

grasp ལེན་པ་

great, advanced ཆེ་བ་

H

happiness, bliss བདེ་བ་

hare's horn རི་བོང་རྭ་

(classic example of a non-existent)

have, possess ལྡན་

heap, aggregate, *skandha* ཕུང་པོ་

"Hearer," "Listener," *Shrāvaka* ཉན་ཐོས་

help, benefit, assist ཕན་འདོགས་

hidden phenomenon ལྐོག་གྱུར་

higher realm, fortunate birth བདེ་འགྲོ་

hold, perceive, apprehend འཛིན་པ་

how many? how much? ག་ཚོད་

human being མི་

I

I accept, I agree འདོད་

if someone says ཟེར་ན་

if someone says ཁ་ཅིག་ན་རེ་

illustration, example མཚན་གཞི་

immediately preceding condition དེ་མ་ཐག་རྐྱེན་

impermanent, changing, transitory མི་རྟག་པ་

implicating negative, affirming negative, མ་ཡིན་དགག་
a negative that implies a positive

implicit quality to be proved ཤུགས་ཀྱི་བསྒྲུབ་བྱའི་ཆོས་

impute, ascribe, designate བཏགས་པ་

in a particular proof དེ་སྒྲུབ་ཀྱི་

incidental, supplementary, ancillary ཞར་བྱུང་

indefinite reason མ་ངེས་པའི་གཏན་ཚིགས་

independent, substantially existent རང་རྐྱ་ཐུབ་པའི་རྫས་ཡོད་

indirect cause བརྒྱུད་རྒྱུ་

indirect effect བརྒྱུད་འབྲས་

indirectly suggesting its agent རང་གི་ཁྱད་ཆོས་ཤུགས་ལ་འཕངས་པ་

infallible མི་སླུ་བ་

inference རྗེས་དཔག་

inference for oneself རང་དོན་རྗེས་དཔག་

inference for others གཞན་དོན་རྗེས་དཔག་

inferential valid cognition རྗེས་དཔག་ཚད་མ་

inferential valid cognition based on conventional usage གྲགས་པའི་རྗེས་དཔག་

inferential valid cognition based on trust ཡིད་ཆེས་རྗེས་དཔག་

inferential valid cognition by the power of the fact དངོས་སྟོབས་རྗེས་དཔག་

"it," an indefinite pronoun referring to the subject ཁྱོད་

J

juniper tree ཤུགས་པ་

just, merely, only ཙམ་

L

lake, ocean རྒྱ་མཚོ་

leaf ལོ་མ་

like, for example ལྟ་བུ་

logical consequence, ཐལ་བ་
it logically follows that …

logical consequence, *prasaṅga* ཐལ་འགྱུར་

logical possibility, permutation མུ་

logically inadmissible, incorrect, unreasonable མི་འཐད་

lower realm, unfortunate birth ངན་འགྲོ་

M

main mind གཙོ་སེམས་

manifest phenomenon མངོན་གྱུར་

matter བེམ་པོ་

meaning generality, general mental image arising from meaning དོན་སྤྱི་

meaning, purpose, object, goal དོན་

meditative equipoise མཉམ་བཞག་

mental affliction ཉོན་མོངས་

mental and physical flexibility, pliability, extreme ease ཤིན་ཏུ་སྦྱངས་པ་

mental consciousness ཡིད་ཤེས་

mental derivative, mental factor, secondary mind སེམས་བྱུང་

mental sense power ཡིད་དབང་

mental sinking བྱིང་བ་

method, manner, mode, way, how to… ཚུལ་

mind སེམས་

mind, cognition རིག་པ་

mind stream, *tantra* རྒྱུད་

mistaken འཁྲུལ་པ་

mistaken consciousness འཁྲུལ་ཤེས་

mistaken consciousness འཁྲུལ་ཤེས་

mode of positing, way of stating འགོད་ཚུལ་

moment, instant སྐད་ཅིག་མ་

moon ཟླ་བ་

moral discipline, morality ཚུལ་ཁྲིམས་

mountain pass, grammar particle ལ་

multiplicity of things (referring to relative truth) ཇི་སྙེད་པ་

mutually exclusive contradiction ཕན་ཚུན་སྤང་འགལ་

N

nature, identity རང་བཞིན་

negative དགག་པ་

new(ly), fresh གསར་དུ་

night, at night མཚན་མོ་

non-abiding contradiction ལྷན་ཅིག་མི་གནས་འགལ་

non-implicating negative མེད་དགག་

non-ascertaining perception སྣང་ལ་མ་ངེས་པའི་བློ་

non-associated formations ལྡན་མིན་འདུ་བྱེད་

non-conceptual subsequent cognition རྟོག་མེད་བཅད་ཤེས་

non-conceptual wrong consciousness རྟོག་མེད་ལོག་ཤེས་

non-existent མེད་པ་

non-valid cognition ཚད་མིན་གྱི་བློ་

non-valid consciousness ཚད་མིན་གྱི་ཤེས་པ་

non-virtue མི་དགེ་བ་

nose sense power སྣའི་དབང་པོ་

not suggesting an agent, sign free of qualification ཁྱད་པར་དག་པ་བ་

noun, proper name དངོས་མིང་

O

object ཡུལ་

object assisted ཕན་འདོགས་བྱ་

object condition དམིགས་རྐྱེན་

object of comprehension གཞལ་བྱ་

object of hearing གཉན་བྱ་

object of knowledge, knowable entity ཤེས་བྱ་

object of negation, what is to be negated or rejected དགག་བྱ་

object pervaded ཁྱབ་བྱ་

object to be defined མཚོན་བྱ་

occasional, occurring sometimes རེས་འགའ་

old person རྒན་པོ་

omnipresent cause ཀུན་འགྲོའི་རྒྱུ་

on this occasion, in this context སྐབས་འདིར་

one, same, single གཅིག་

only, just, sole ཁོ་ན་

opposite class, opposite of a perfect reason ལྡོག་ཕྱོགས་

opposite from, differentiated from ལས་ལྡོག་པ་

oral transmission ལུང་

ordinary being, non-*Arya* སོ་སོའི་སྐྱེ་བོ་

other knower, knower of things other than the perceiver itself, non-apperceptive cognition གཞན་རིག་

our own system རང་ལུགས་

P

part, portion, factor ཆ་

particular, specific བྱེ་བྲག་

particularity, distinguishing feature, difference ཁྱད་པར་

past (time) འདས་པ་

path ལམ་

path wisdom, exalted wisdom མཁྱེན་པ་

penetrative insight, *vipashyanā* ལྷག་མཐོང་

perfect negative reason དགག་རྟགས་ཡང་དག་

perfect opponent in debate, appropriate respondent ཕྱི་རྒོལ་ཡང་དག་

perfect positive reason སྒྲུབ་རྟགས་ཡང་དག་

perfect reason རྟགས་ཡང་དག་

perfect reason on the occasion of proving something to oneself རང་དོན་སྐབས་ཀྱི་རྟགས་ཡང་དག་

perfect reason on the occasion of proving something to others གཞན་དོན་སྐབས་ཀྱི་རྟགས་ཡང་དག་

perfect reason proving only a meaning དོན་འབའ་ཞིག་སྒྲུབ་ཀྱི་རྟགས་ཡང་དག་

perfect reason proving only an object to be defined ཐ་སྙད་འབའ་ཞིག་སྒྲུབ་ཀྱི་རྟགས་ཡང་དག་

permanent, unchanging རྟག་པ་

person གང་ཟག་

pervader ཁྱབ་བྱེད་

pervasion, entailment, concomitance, major premise ཁྱབ་པ་

phenomenon, *Dharma* ཆོས་

physical sense power དབང་པོ་གཟུགས་ཅན་པ་

pillar ཀ་བ་

place, region ས་ཕྱོགས་

place in front མདུན་གྱི་གཞི་

posit (something)! ཞོག་

posit, place གཞག་པ་

posit, place, put བཀོད་པ་ འགོད་པ་

positing our own system's views རང་ལུགས་གཞག་པ་

positive, affirmative སྒྲུབ་པ་

positive and reverse pervasions རྗེས་སུ་འགྲོ་ལྡོག་

positive pervasion རྗེས་ཁྱབ་

pot, pitcher བུམ་པ་

power, strength སྟོབས་

prasaṅga, logical consequence ཐལ་འགྱུར་

preceding, earlier སྔ་རོལ་

predicative statement, "is" statement ཡིན་འགོད་

present (time) ད་ལྟ་བ་

principal, main གཙོ་བོ་

produced, product བྱས་པ་

producer སྐྱེད་བྱེད་

proof, correct proof སྒྲུབ་བྱེད་

proof statement སྒྲུབ་ངག་

propensity, habitual tendency བག་ཆགས་

property of the reason in the subject, the reason's relevance to the subject ཕྱོགས་ཆོས་

purpose, necessity; to require དགོས་པ་

Q

quality to be negated or refuted, predicate to be negated དགག་བྱའི་ཆོས་

quality to be proved བསྒྲུབ་བྱའི་ཆོས་

quotation markers ཞེས་ / ཅེས་

R

realization རྟོགས་པ་

reason གཏན་ཚིགས་

reason of effect འབྲས་རྟགས་

reason of effect inferring causal attributes རྒྱུ་ཆོས་རྗེས་དཔོག་གི་འབྲས་རྟགས་

reason of effect proving a direct cause རྒྱུ་དངོས་སྒྲུབ་ཀྱི་འབྲས་རྟགས་

reason of effect proving a distant prior cause རྒྱུ་སྔོན་སོང་གི་འབྲས་རྟགས་

reason of effect proving a particular cause རྒྱུའི་ཁྱད་པར་སྒྲུབ་ཀྱི་འབྲས་རྟགས་

reason of effect proving causation in general རྒྱུ་སྤྱི་སྒྲུབ་ཀྱི་འབྲས་རྟགས་

reason of effect proving its own distinguisher རང་ལྡོག་སྒྲུབ་ཀྱི་འབྲས་རྟགས་

reason of non-observation མ་དམིགས་པའི་རྟགས་

reason of non-observation of a cause རྒྱུ་མ་དམིགས་པའི་རྟགས་

reason of non-observation of a related object that is suitable to appear སྣང་རུང་གི་འབྲེལ་ཟླ་མ་དམིགས་པའི་རྟགས་

reason of non-observation of the directly related non-appearing མི་སྣང་བའི་འབྲེལ་ཟླ་མ་དམིགས་པའི་རྟགས་

reason of non-observation of the non-appearance of a related object འབྲེལ་ཟླ་མ་དམིགས་པའི་རྟགས་

reason of non-observation of the non-appearing མི་སྣང་བ་མ་དམིགས་པའི་རྟགས་

reason of non-observation of the non-appearing cause དེར་གྱུར་པའི་རྒྱུ་མ་དམིགས་པའི་རྟགས་

reason of non-observation of the non-appearing pervader དེར་གྱུར་པའི་ཁྱབ་བྱེད་མ་དམིགས་པའི་རྟགས་

reason of non-observation of the non-appearing same nature དེར་གྱུར་པའི་རང་བཞིན་མ་དམིགས་པའི་རྟགས་

reason of non-observation of the suitable to appear སྣང་རུང་མ་དམིགས་པའི་རྟགས་

reason of observation of the contradictory of the non-appearing མི་སྣང་བའི་འགལ་ཟླ་དམིགས་པའི་རྟགས་

reason of observation of the contradictory that is suitable to appear སྣང་རུང་གི་འགལ་ཟླ་དམིགས་པའི་རྟགས་

reason of observation of the mutually contradictory ལྡོས་པས་ངེས་པ་འགོག་པའི་ཕན་ཚུན་སྤངས་འགལ་དམིགས་པའི་རྟགས་

that rejects being definitive due to dependence

reason of observation of the mutually contradictory that rejects dependence due to being definitive ངེས་པས་ལྟོས་པ་འགོག་པའི་ཕན་ཚུན་སྤངས་འགལ་དམིགས་པའི་རྟགས་

reason of observation of the mutually exclusive contradictory ཕན་ཚུན་སྤངས་འགལ་དམིགས་པའི་རྟགས་

reason of observation of the non-abiding contradictory ལྷན་ཅིག་མི་གནས་འགལ་ཟླ་དམིགས་པའི་རྟགས་

reason of same nature རང་བཞིན་གྱི་རྟགས་

reason of same nature not suggesting an agent དེར་གྱུར་པའི་དག་པ་བའི་རང་བཞིན་གྱི་རྟགས་

reason of same nature suggesting an agent དེར་གྱུར་པའི་ཁྱད་པར་ལྟོས་པ་བའི་རང་བཞིན་གྱི་རྟགས་

reason that engages the similar class as a pervader མཐུན་ཕྱོགས་ལ་ཁྱབ་བྱེད་དུ་འཇུག་པའི་རྟགས་

reason that engages the similar class in two ways མཐུན་ཕྱོགས་ལ་རྣམ་གཉིས་སུ་འཇུག་པའི་རང་བཞིན་གྱི་རྟགས་

reason, class, kind, family རིགས་

reason, logical sign or mark རྟགས་

reason, sign རྒྱུ་མཚན་

reason, logical reason གཏན་ཚིགས་

recollecting consciousness དྲན་ཤེས་

refuting others' views གཞན་ལུགས་དགག་པ་

related, connected འབྲེལ་བ་

related by being of the same nature བདག་གཅིག་འབྲེལ་

relative truth phenomena ཀུན་རྫོབ་པའི་ཆོས་

reverse pervasion ལྡོག་ཁྱབ་

ripened effect རྣམ་སྨིན་གྱི་འབྲས་བུ་

ripening cause རྣམ་སྨིན་གྱི་རྒྱུ་

rocky cliff བྲག་རྫོང་

root, basic རྩ་བ་

rough, coarse རགས་པ་

S

Sautrāntika, one of the four major Buddhist tenet systems མདོ་སྡེ་པ་

scripture, text གཞུང་

section of debate, someone ཁ་ཅིག་མ་

seed ས་བོན་

self-distinguisher, self-isolate རང་ལྡོག་

self-grasping བདག་འཛིན

selflessness བདག་མེད་

selflessness of person གང་ཟག་གི་བདག་མེད་

sense consciousness དབང་ཤེས་

sense power, sense faculty དབང་པོ་

sentient being སེམས་ཅན་

seven kinds of mind བློ་རིགས་བདུན་

similar aspect རྣམ་པ་མཚུངས་པ་

similar basis རྟེན་མཚུངས་པ་

similar object of reference དམིགས་པ་མཚུངས་པ་

similar substance རྫས་མཚུངས་པ་

similar time or duration དུས་མཚུངས་པ་

similar, harmonious, compatible མཐུན་ཕྱོགས་

similar, like, coincident མཚུངས་པ་

single-pointed concentration, *samādhi* ཏིང་ངེ་འཛིན་

slightly hidden phenomenon ཅུང་ཟད་ལྐོག་གྱུར་

small, beginner ཆུང་ངུ་

smell དྲི་

smoke དུ་བ་

snow ཁ་བ་

solitary realizer, *pratyekabuddha* རང་རྒྱལ་

something to posit གཞག་བྱ་

sound generality, general mental image arising from a term སྒྲ་སྤྱི་

sound, term སྒྲ་

sound of a conch དུང་སྒྲ་

space (intermediate), atmosphere བར་སྣང་

space, sky ནམ་མཁའ་

speak, speech སྨྲ་བ་

speculative assumption ཡིད་དཔྱོད་

speculative assumption that uses contradictory reasons རྒྱུ་མཚན་འགལ་བའི་ཡིད་དཔྱོད་

speculative assumption that uses indefinite reasons རྒྱུ་མཚན་མ་ངེས་པའི་ཡིད་དཔྱོད་

speculative assumption that uses not well-founded reasons རྒྱུ་མཚན་ཡོད་ཀྱང་གཏན་ལ་མ་ཕེབས་པའི་ཡིད་དཔྱོད་

speculative assumption that uses unestablished reasons རྒྱུ་མཚན་མ་གྲུབ་པའི་ཡིད་དཔྱོད་

speculative assumption without reasons རྒྱུ་མཚན་མེད་པའི་ཡིད་དཔྱོད་

sprout མྱུ་གུ་

stated reason བཀོད་ཚོད་ཀྱི་རྟགས་

stated verbally, speaking terminologically, nominally སྒྲས་བརྗོད་རིགས་ཀྱི་སྒོ་ནས་

statement of existence, "exist" statement ཡོད་འགོད་

subject of debate, logical subject ཆོས་ཅན་

subject (as holder of an object), object possessor ཡུལ་ཅན་

subsequent cognition བཅད་ཤེས་ / དཔྱད་ཤེས་

substantial cause ཉེར་ལེན་གྱི་རྒྱུ་

substantial entity རྫས་

subtle, fine ཕྲ་མོ་

suggesting an agent, sign involving a qualification ཁྱད་པར་ལྟོས་པ་བ་

suitable, be fitting རུང་བ་

supplementary explanation འཕྲོས་དོན་

swear, make a pledge དམ་བཅའ་བ་

syllogism, logical proof སྦྱོར་བ་

T

taste རོ་

tenet system གྲུབ་མཐའ་

term, expression, designation ཐ་སྙད་

term, name མིང་

that does not pervade, that does not entail ཁྱབ་པ་མ་བྱུང་

that's not true, the reason is not established རྟགས་མ་གྲུབ་

the one, (denoting one quality གང་ཞིག་
of a definition)
thesis བསྒྲུབ་བྱ་
thesis of a consequence, བསལ་བ་
remove, eliminate
things as they are (referring ཇི་ལྟ་བ་
to ultimate truth)
three examinations, tests དཔྱད་པ་གསུམ་
three modes, three criteria ཚུལ་གསུམ་
to be contradictory འགལ་བ་
tongue sense power ལྕེའི་དབང་པོ་
touch, tangible object རེག་བྱ་
tree ཤིང་

U

ultimate truth phenomenon དོན་དམ་པའི་ཆོས་
uncomposed space འདུས་མ་བྱས་ཀྱི་ནམ་མཁའ་
uncontaminated, undefiled (by mental afflictions) ཟག་མེད་
understand གོ་བ་
undesired consequence, ཐལ་འགྱུར་ལྟར་སྣང་
refutable consequence
unestablished reason མ་གྲུབ་པའི་གཏན་ཚིགས་
unestablished reason འབྲེལ་བ་ལ་ཐེ་ཚོམ་ཟ་ནས་མ་གྲུབ་པའི་གཏན་ཚིགས་
through having misgivings about the
relationship (in that proof)
unestablished reason ཆོས་ཅན་ལ་ཐེ་ཚོམ་ཟ་ནས་མ་གྲུབ་པའི་གཏན་ཚིགས་
through having misgivings about the

subject of debate (in that proof)

unestablished reason through the lack of doubt about the subject (in that proof) ཤེས་འདོད་མེད་ནས་མ་གྲུབ་པའི་གཏན་ཚིགས་

unestablished reason due to the non-existent nature relative to the basis of debate (in that proof) རྩོད་གཞིའི་སྟེང་དུ་མེད་ནས་མ་གྲུབ་པའི་གཏན་ཚིགས་

unestablished reason due to the non-existent nature of the reason (in that proof) ངོ་བོ་མེད་ནས་མ་གྲུབ་པའི་གཏན་ཚིགས་

unestablished reason through the lack of identity of the subject of debate (in that proof) ཆོས་ཅན་གྱི་ངོ་བོ་མེད་ནས་མ་གྲུབ་པའི་གཏན་ཚིགས་

unestablished reason through the lack of difference between the reason and the quality to be proved (in that proof) རྟགས་ཆོས་ཐ་དད་མེད་ནས་མ་གྲུབ་པའི་གཏན་ཚིགས་

unestablished reason through the lack of difference between the basis of debate and the quality to be proved (in that proof) གཞི་ཆོས་ཐ་དད་མེད་ནས་མ་གྲུབ་པའི་གཏན་ཚིགས་

unestablished reason through the lack of difference between the basis of debate and the reason (in that proof) གཞི་རྟགས་ཐ་དད་མེད་ནས་མ་གྲུབ་པའི་གཏན་ཚིགས་

unique , not shared ཐུན་མོང་མ་ཡིན་

unique governing condition ཐུན་མོང་མ་ཡིན་བདག་རྐྱེན་

unique indefinite reason ཐུན་མོང་མ་ཡིན་པའི་མ་ངེས་པའི་གཏན་ཚིགས་

unmistaken མ་འཁྲུལ་བ་

unspecified, neutral ལུང་མ་བསྟན་

unsuitable མི་རུང་བ་

V

valid cognition ཚད་མ་

valid referent impression དཔྱད་ (བཅད་) ཤེས་དོན་མཐུན་

verbal proof that applies to a dissimilar class ཆོས་མི་མཐུན་སྦྱོར་གྱི་སྒྲུབ་ངག་

verbal proof that applies to a similar class ཆོས་མཐུན་སྦྱོར་གྱི་སྒྲུབ་ངག་

virtue དགེ་བ་

W

water (element) ཆུ་

what, which, who, whatever གང་

what is produced སྐྱེད་བྱ་

what? ག་རེ་

white color དཀར་པོ་

why? ཅིའི་ཕྱིར་

wrong cognition ལོག་ཤེས་

List of Terms

TIBETAN TO ENGLISH

ཀ་

ཀ་བ་ pillar

ཀུན་འགྲོའི་རྒྱུ་ omnipresent cause

ཀུན་རྫོབ་པའི་ཆོས་ relative truth phenomena

དཀར་པོ་ white color

བཀོད་པ་ འགོད་པ་ posit, place, put

བཀོད་ཚོད་ཀྱི་རྟགས་ stated reason

རྐྱེན་ condition

ལྐོག་གྱུར་ hidden phenomenon

སྐད་ཅིག་མ་ moment, instant

སྐབས་འདིར་ on this occasion, in this context

སྐལ་མཉམ་གྱི་རྒྱུ་ cause of similar fortune

སྐུར་འདེབས་ deprecation, underestimation

སྐྱེད་བྱ་ what is produced

སྐྱེད་བྱེད་ producer

སྐྱེས་པ་ created

སྐྱེས་བུ་ being, person

སྐྱེས་བུ་བྱེད་པའི་འབྲས་བུ་ effect of human effort

སྐྱོན་ fault

སྐྱོན་མེད་ faultless

བསྐལ་དོན་(དུ་སོང་བ་) doubt, fortune, beyond one's perceptual capacity, having misgivings about something, entertaining doubts

ཁ་

ཁ་བ་ snow

ཁ་ཅིག་ན་རེ་ if someone says

ཁ་ཅིག་ someone, a certain person

ཁོ་ན་ only, just, sole

ཁྱད་ཆོས་ characteristic, quality

ཁྱད་པར་ particularity, distinguishing feature, difference

ཁྱད་པར་ལྟོས་པ་བ་ suggesting an agent, sign involving a qualification

ཁྱད་པར་དག་པ་བ་ not suggesting an agent, sign free of qualification

ཁྱབ་པ་ pervasion, entailment, concomitance, major premise

ཁྱབ་པ་རྣམ་པ་སྒོ་བརྒྱད་ Eight Doors of Pervasion

ཁྱབ་པའི་ལྟོས་གཞི་ basis of relation of pervasion or concomitance

ཁྱབ་པ་མ་བྱུང་ that does not pervade, that does not entail

ཁྱབ་བྱ་ object pervaded

ཁྱབ་བྱེད་ pervader

ཁྱོད་ "it," an indefinite pronoun referring to the subject

མཁྱེན་པ་ path wisdom, exalted wisdom

འཁྲུལ་པ་ mistaken

འཁྲུལ་ཤེས་ mistaken consciousness

ག་

ག་རེ་ what?

ག་ཚོད་ how many? how much?

གང་ what, which, who, whatever

གང་ཞིག་ the one, (denoting one quality in a definition)

གང་ཟག་ person

གང་ཟག་གི་བདག་མེད་ selflessness of person

གང་རུང་ either one, whichever, whatever, any

གོ་བ་ understand

གྲགས་པའི་རྗེས་དཔག་ inferential valid cognition based on conventional usage

གྲང་ cold

གྲུབ་མཐའ་ tenet system

དགག་རྟགས་ཡང་དག་ perfect negative reason

དགག་པ་ a negative

དགག་བྱ་ object of negation, what is to be negated or rejected

དགག་བྱའི་ཆོས་ quality to be negated or refuted, predicate to be negated

དགག་བྱའི་ཆོས་སུ་བརྟགས་པའི་དོན་ actual object being negated

དགེ་བ་ virtue

དགེ་བ་ཟག་བཅས་ contaminated virtue

དགོས་པ་ purpose, necessity; to require

འགལ་བ་ contradictory

འགལ་བའི་གཏན་ཚིགས་ contradictory reason

འགལ་ཟླ་མི་མཐུན་ཕྱོགས་ dissimilar class of the contradictory

འགོད་ཚུལ་ mode of positing, way of stating

རྒན་པོ་ old person

རྒོད་པ་ excitement, mental agitation

རྒོལ་བ་ debater, opponent in debate

རྒྱ་མཚོ་ lake, ocean

རྒྱུ་ cause

རྒྱུ་དངོས་སྒྲུབ་ཀྱི་འབྲས་རྟགས་ reason of effect proving a direct cause

རྒྱུ་སྔོན་སོང་གི་འབྲས་རྟགས་ reason of effect proving a distant prior cause

རྒྱུ་ཆོས་རྗེས་དཔོག་གི་འབྲས་རྟགས་ reason of effect inferring causal attributes

རྒྱུ་མཐུན་གྱི་འབྲས་བུ་ effect correspondent with its cause

རྒྱུ་སྤྱི་སྒྲུབ་ཀྱི་འབྲས་རྟགས་ reason of effect proving a direct cause

རྒྱུ་མ་དམིགས་པའི་རྟགས་ reason of non-observation of a cause

རྒྱུ་མཚན་ reason, sign

རྒྱུ་མཚན་འགལ་བའི་ཡིད་དཔྱོད་ speculative assumption that uses contradictory reasons

རྒྱུ་མཚན་མ་གྲུབ་པའི་ཡིད་དཔྱོད་ speculative assumption that uses unestablished reasons

རྒྱུ་མཚན་མ་ངེས་པའི་ཡིད་དཔྱོད་ speculative assumption that uses indefinite reasons

རྒྱུ་མཚན་མེད་པའི་ཡིད་དཔྱོད་ speculative assumption without reasons

རྒྱུ་མཚན་ཡོད་ཀྱང་གཏན་ལ་མ་ཕེབས་པའི་ཡིད་དཔྱོད་ speculative assumption that uses not well-founded reasons

རྒྱུའི་ཁྱད་པར་སྒྲུབ་ཀྱི་འབྲས་རྟགས་ reason of effect proving a particular cause

རྒྱུད་ mind stream, *tantra*

རྒྱུན་ continuum, continuity, stream

སྒྲ་ sound, term

སྒྲ་སྤྱི་ sound generality, general mental image arising from a term

སྒྲ་བཤད་ etymology, explanation of a word or term

སྒྲས་བརྗོད་རིགས་ཀྱི་སྒོ་ནས་ stated verbally, speaking terminologically, nominally

སྒྲུབ་ངག་ proof statement

སྒྲུབ་པ་ positive, affirmative

སྒྲུབ་བྱེད་ proof, correct proof

སྒྲོ་འདོགས་ exaggeration, overestimation

སྒྲོངས་ཤོག་ count!, enumerate!

བརྒྱུད་རྒྱུ་ indirect cause

བརྒྱུད་འབྲས་ indirect effect

སྒྲུབ་རྟགས་ཡང་དག་ perfect positive reason

བསྒྲུབ་བྱ་ thesis

བསྒྲུབ་བྱའི་ཆོས་ quality to be proved

ང་

ངན་འགྲོ་ lower realm, unfortunate birth

ངེས་པ་ ascertain, ascertainment, definite

ངེས་པས་ལྟོས་པ་འགོག་པའི་ཕན་ཚུན་སྤངས་འགལ་དམིགས་པའི་རྟགས་ reason of observation of the mutually contradictory that rejects dependence due to being definitive

ངོ་བོ་ essence, entity, identity

ངོ་བོ་མེད་ནས་མ་གྲུབ་པའི་གཏན་ཚིགས་ unestablished reason due to the non-existent nature of the reason in that proof

དངོས་ཀྱི་བསྒྲུབ་བྱའི་ཆོས་ explicit quality to be proved

དངོས་རྒྱུ་ direct cause

དངོས་སྟོབས་རྗེས་དཔག་ inferential valid cognition by the power of the fact

དངོས་པོ་ causally effective thing

དངོས་འབྲས་ direct effect

དངོས་མིང་ noun, proper name

དངོས་སུ་འཕངས་པ་ directly suggestive

མངོན་གྱུར་ manifest phenomenon

མངོན་ཤེས་ clairvoyance

མངོན་སུམ་ direct cognition

མངོན་སུམ་ཚད་མ་ direct valid cognition

སྔ་རྒོལ་ challenger, questioner or initiator in debate

སྔ་རོལ་ preceding, earlier

སྔོན་པོ་ blue, blue-green

ཅ་

ཅིའི་ཕྱིར་ why?

ལྕེའི་དབང་པོ་ tongue sense power

ཅུང་ཟད་ལྐོག་གྱུར་ slightly hidden phenomenon

ཅེས་ quotation marker

གཅིག་ one, same, single

བཅད་ཤེས་ / དཔྱད་ཤེས་ subsequent cognition

ཆ་

ཆ་ part, portion, factor

ཆ་མཉམ་པའི་ཐེ་ཚོམ་ equally undecided doubt

ཆུ་ water (element)

ཆུང་ངུ་ small, beginner

ཆེ་བ་ great, advanced

ཆོས་ phenomenon, *Dharma*

ཆོས་ཅན་ subject of debate, logical subject

ཆོས་ཅན་གྱི་ངོ་བོ་མེད་ནས་མ་གྲུབ་པའི་གཏན་ཚིགས་ unestablished reason through the lack of identity of the subject of debate (in that proof)

ཆོས་ཅན་ལ་ཐེ་ཚོམ་ཟ་ནས་མ་གྲུབ་པའི་གཏན་ཚིགས་ unestablished reason through having misgivings about the subject of debate in that proof

ཆོས་མཐུན་སྦྱོར་གྱི་སྒྲུབ་ངག་ verbal proof that applies to a similar class

ཆོས་མི་མཐུན་སྦྱོར་གྱི་སྒྲུབ་ངག་ verbal proof that applies to a dissimilar class

ཇ་

ཇི་སྙེད་པ་ multiplicity of things (referring to relative truth)

ཇི་ལྟ་བ་ things as they are (referring to ultimate truth)

འཇུག་པ་ engage, operate, signify, apply to, refer to, enter

རྗེས་ཁྱབ་ positive pervasion

རྗེས་དཔག་ inference

རྗེས་དཔག་ཚད་མ་ inferential valid cognition

རྗེས་སུ་འགྲོ་ལྡོག་ positive and reverse pervasions

བརྗོད་པ་ express, proclaim, mention, describe

ཉ་

ཉན་ཐོས་ "Hearer," "Listener," *Shrāvaka*

ཉེར་ལེན་གྱི་རྒྱུ་ substantial cause

ཉེར་ལེན་གྱི་ཕུང་པོ་ appropriated heaps

ཉོན་མོངས mental affliction

གཉན་བྱ་ object of hearing

མཉམ་བཞག་ meditative equipoise

ཏ་

ཏིང་ངེ་འཛིན་ single-pointed concentration, *samādhi*

གཏན་ཚིགས་ logical reason, reason

གཏན་ཚིགས་ལྟར་སྣང་ false reason

བཏགས་པ་ impute, ascribe, designate

རྟག་པ་ permanent, unchanging

རྟགས་ reason, logical sign or mark

རྟགས་ཆོས་ཐ་དད་མེད་ནས་མ་གྲུབ་པའི་གཏན་ཚིགས་ unestablished reason through the lack of difference between the reason and the quality to be proved (in that proof)

རྟགས་ལྟར་སྣང་ false reason

རྟགས་མ་གྲུབ་ that's not true, the reason is not established

རྟགས་ཡང་དག་ perfect reason

རྟེན་མཚུངས་པ་ similar basis

རྟོག་པ་ conception, conceptual cognition

རྟོག་པ་བཅད་ཤེས་ conceptual subsequent cognition

རྟོག་པ་ལོག་ཤེས་ conceptual wrong consciousness

རྟོག་མེད་བཅད་ཤེས་ non-conceptual subsequent cognition

རྟོག་མེད་ལོག་ཤེས་ non-conceptual wrong consciousness

རྟོགས་པ་ realization

ལྟ་བུ་ like, for example

ལྟོས་པས་ངེས་པ་འགོག་པའི་ཕན་ཚུན་སྤངས་འགལ་དམིགས་པའི་རྟགས་ reason of observation of the mutually contradictory that rejects being definitive due to dependence

སྟོང་པ་ཉིད་ emptiness, voidness, *shūnyatā*

སྟོབས་ power, strength

ཐ་

ཐ་སྙད་ term, expression, designation

ཐ་སྙད་འབའ་ཞིག་སྒྲུབ་ཀྱི་རྟགས་ཡང་དག་ perfect reason proving only an object to be defined

ཐ་དད་ different

ཐག་གཅོད་ decide, determine

ཐལ་འགྱུར་ logical consequence, *prasaṅga*

ཐལ་འགྱུར་ལྟར་སྣང་ undesired consequence, refutable consequence

ཐལ་འགྱུར་ཡང་དག་ correct consequence

ཐལ་བ་ logical consequence, it logically follows that…

ཐུན་མོང་ in common, shared

ཐུན་མོང་མ་ཡིན་ not in common, unique

ཐུན་མོང་མ་ཡིན་པའི་བདག་རྐྱེན་ unique governing condition

ཐུན་མོང་མ་ཡིན་པའི་མ་ངེས་པའི་གཏན་ཚིགས་ unique indefinite reason

ཐེ་ཚོམ་ doubt

མཐུན་དཔེ་ example of the similar class

མཐུན་ཕྱོགས་ similar, harmonious, compatible

མཐུན་ཕྱོགས་ལ་ཁྱབ་བྱེད་དུ་འཇུག་པའི་རྟགས་ reason that engages the similar class as a pervader

མཐུན་ཕྱོགས་ལ་རྣམ་གཉིས་སུ་འཇུག་པའི་རང་བཞིན་གྱི་རྟགས་ reason that engages the similar class in two ways

ད

ད་ལྟ་བ་ present (time)

དང་བྲལ་བ་ free from, separate from

དམ་བཅའ་བ་ swear, make a pledge

དུ་བ་ smoke

དུང་སྒྲ་ sound of a conch

དུས་མཚུངས་པ་ similar time or duration

དེ་སྒྲུབ་ཀྱི་ in a particular proof

དེ་འབྱུང་འབྲེལ་ causal relationship

དེ་མ་ཐག་རྐྱེན་ immediately preceding condition

དེར་གྱུར་པའི་ཁྱད་པར་ལྟོས་པ་བའི་རང་བཞིན་གྱི་རྟགས་ reason of same nature suggesting an agent

དེར་གྱུར་པའི་ཁྱབ་བྱེད་མ་དམིགས་པའི་རྟགས་ reason of non-observation of the non-appearing pervader

དེར་གྱུར་པའི་རྒྱུ་མ་དམིགས་པའི་རྟགས་ reason of non-observation of the non-appearing cause

དེར་གྱུར་པའི་དགག་པ་བའི་རང་བཞིན་གྱི་རྟགས་ reason of same nature not suggesting an agent

དེར་གྱུར་པའི་རང་བཞིན་མ་དམིགས་པའི་རྟགས་ reason of non-observation of the non-appearing of the same nature

དོན་ meaning, purpose, object, goal

དོན་འགྱུར་གྱི་ཐེ་ཚོམ་ doubt tending toward the fact

དོན་གཅིག་ equivalent, same meaning, synonymous

དོན་དམ་པའི་ཆོས་ ultimate truth phenomenon

དོན་སྤྱི་ meaning generality, general mental image arising from meaning

དོན་འབའ་ཞིག་སྒྲུབ་ཀྱི་རྟགས་ཡང་དག་ perfect reason proving only a meaning

དོན་མི་འགྱུར་གྱི་ཐེ་ཚོམ་ doubt tending away from the fact

དྲི་ smell

དྲན་ཤེས་ recollecting consciousness

བདག་རྐྱེན་ governing condition

བདག་གཅིག་འབྲེལ་ related by being of the same nature

བདག་པོའི་འབྲས་བུ་ dominant condition

བདག་མེད་ selflessness

བདག་འཛིན་ self-grasping

བདེ་འགྲོ་ higher realm, fortunate birth

བདེ་བ་ happiness, bliss

མདུན་གྱི་གཞི་ place in front

མདོ་སྡེ་པ་ *Sautrāntika*, one of the four major Buddhist tenet systems

འདས་པ་ past (time)

འདུ་འཛི་ busyness, distraction, noise

འདུས་བྱས་ composed entity, compounded

འདུས་མ་བྱས་ཀྱི་ནམ་མཁའ་ uncomposed space

འདོད་ I accept, I agree

འདོད་ཁམས་ desire realm

འདོད་ཆགས་ desirous attachment

ལྡན་ have, possess

ལྡན་མིན་འདུ་བྱེད་ non-associated formations

ལྡོག་ཁྱབ་ reverse pervasion

སྡོམས་ combined, bring together

ན་

ནམ་མཁའ་ space, sky

ནུས་པ་ be able to, have the ability

རྣ་བའི་དབང་པོ་ ear sense power

རྣམ་རྟོག་ discursive thought, superstition

རྣམ་པ་ aspect, kind

རྣམ་པ་མཚུངས་པ་ similar aspect

རྣམ་སྨིན་གྱི་རྒྱུ་ ripening cause

རྣམ་སྨིན་གྱི་འབྲས་བུ་ ripened effect

རྣལ་འབྱོར་མངོན་སུམ་གྱི་ཚད་མ་ direct valid yogic cognition

སྣང་བ་ appearance, appear

སྣང་རུང་གི་འགལ་ཟླ་དམིགས་པའི་རྟགས་ reason of observation of the contradictory that is suitable to appear

སྣང་རུང་གི་འབྲེལ་ཟླ་མ་དམིགས་པའི་རྟགས་ reason of non-observation of a related object that is suitable to appear

སྣང་རུང་མ་དམིགས་པའི་རྟགས་ reason of non-observation of the suitable to appear

སྣང་ལ་མ་ངེས་པའི་བློ་ non-ascertaining perception

སྣའི་དབང་པོ་ nose sense power

པ་

དཔག་གཞི་ basis of inference

དཔེ་ example

དཔེར་ན་ for example

དཔྱད་པ་གསུམ་ three examinations, three tests

དཔྱད་ཤེས་ subsequent cognition

དཔྱད་ (བཅད་) ཤེས་དོན་མཐུན་ valid referent impression

སྤུ་ལོང་ goose bumps

སྤོང་བ་ abandon, discard

སྤྱི་ general category

སྤྱི་མཚན་ general abstract phenomenon

སྤྱིར་ generally

ཕ་

ཕན་འདོགས་ help, benefit, assist

ཕན་འདོགས་བྱ་ object assisted

ཕན་འདོགས་བྱེད་ assistant, helper

ཕན་ཚུན་སྤངས་འགལ་ mutually exclusive contradiction

ཕན་ཚུན་སྤངས་འགལ་དམིགས་པའི་རྟགས་ reason of observation of the mutually exclusive contradictory

ཕུང་པོ་ heap, aggregate, *skandha*

ཕྱི་རྒོལ་ཡང་དག་ perfect opponent in debate, appropriate respondent

ཕྱོགས་ཆོས་ property of the reason in the subject, the reason's relevance to the subject

ཕྱོགས་ཆོས་ཀྱི་ལྟོས་གཞི་ basis of relation between the subject and the reason

ཕྲ་མོ་ subtle, fine

འཕགས་པ་ *Arya*, exalted one

འཕྲོས་དོན་ supplementary explanation

བ་

བག་ཆགས་ propensity, habitual tendency, karmic traces

བར་སྣང་ space (intermediate), atmosphere

བུ་རམ་ brown sugar, molasses

བུམ་པ་ pot, pitcher

བེམ་པོ་ matter

བྱས་པ་ produced, product

བྱིང་བ་ mental sinking

བྱེ་བྲག་ particular, specific

བྱེད་རྒྱུ་ (non-interfering) active cause

བྲག་རྫོང་ rocky cliff

བྲལ་བའི་འབྲས་བུ་ effect of liberation

དབང་པོ་ sense power, sense faculty

དབང་པོ་མངོན་སུམ་གྱི་ཚད་མ་ direct valid sense cognition

དབང་པོ་གཟུགས་ཅན་པ་ physical sense power

དབང་ཤེས་ sense consciousness

དབེན་ devoid of, solitary place, isolated place

དབྱེ་བ་ classification, division

འབྱུང་བ་བཞི་ four great elements

འབྲེལ་བ་ related, connected

འབྲེལ་བ་ལ་ཐེ་ཚོམ་ཟ་ནས་མ་གྲུབ་པའི་གཏན་ཚིགས་ unestablished reason through having misgivings about the relationship (in that proof)

འབྲེལ་ཟླ་མ་དམིགས་པའི་རྟགས་ reason of non-observation of the non-appearance of a related object

འབྲས་རྟགས་ reason of effect

འབྲས་བུ་ effect, result, fruit

སྦྱོར་བ་ syllogism, logical proof

མ་

མ་འཁྲུལ་བ་ unmistaken

མ་གྲུབ་པའི་གཏན་ཚིགས་ unestablished reason

མ་ངེས་པའི་གཏན་ཚིགས་ indefinite reason

མ་དམིགས་པའི་རྟགས་ reason of non-observation

མ་འོངས་པ་ future (time)

མ་ཡིན་དགག་ implicating negative, affirming negative, a negative that implies a positive

མར་མེ་ butterlamp, lamp flame

མི་ human being

མི་དགེ་བ་ non-virtue

མི་རྟག་པ་ impermanent, changing, transitory

མི་མཐུན་དཔེ་ example of the dissimilar class

མི་མཐུན་ཕྱོགས་ dissimilar, disharmonious, incompatible

མི་འཐད་ logically inadmissible, incorrect, unreasonable

མི་སྣང་བ་མ་དམིགས་པའི་རྟགས་ reason of non-observation of the non-appearing

མི་སྣང་བའི་འབྲེལ་ཟླ་མ་དམིགས་པའི་རྟགས་ reason of non-observation of the directly related non-appearing

མི་རུང་བ་ unsuitable

མི་སླུ་བ་ infallible

མིག་གི་དབང་པོ་ eye sense power

མིང་ term, name

མུ་ logical possibility, permutation

མེ་ fire (element)

མེད་དགག་ non-implicating negative

མེད་པ་ non-existent

མེད་པ་མི་མཐུན་ཕྱོགས་ dissimilar class comprised of non-existents

མྱུ་གུ་ sprout

དམིགས་རྐྱེན་ object condition

དམིགས་པ་མཚུངས་པ་ similar object of reference

སྨྲ་བ་ speak, speech

ཙ་

ཙམ་ just, merely, only

གཙོ་བོ་ principal, main

གཙོ་སེམས་ main mind

རྩ་བ་ root, basic

རྩོད་པ་སྤོང་བ་ dispelling remaining doubts

རྩོད་གཞི་ basis of dispute, subject of debate

རྩོད་གཞིའི་སྟེང་དུ་མེད་ནས་མ་གྲུབ་པའི་གཏན་ཚིགས་ unestablished reason due to the non-existent nature relative to the basis of debate (in that proof)

རྩོལ་བྱུང་ arisen from effort

ཚ་

ཚང་བ་ complete, comprise

ཚད་མ་ valid cognition

ཚད་མིན་གྱི་བློ་ non-valid cognition

ཚད་མིན་གྱི་ཤེས་པ་ non-valid consciousness

ཚུལ་ method, manner, mode, way, how to…

ཚུལ་ཁྲིམས་ moral discipline, morality

ཚུལ་གསུམ་ three modes, three criteria

ཚོགས་སྤྱི་ collection generality

ཚོར་བ་ feeling

མཚུངས་ལྡན་གྱི་རྒྱུ་ concomitant cause

མཚུངས་ལྡན་རྣམ་པ་ལྔ་ five similarities, five accompanying aspects

མཚུངས་པ་ similar, like, coincident

མཚན་ཉིད་ definition, characteristic

མཚན་མོ་ night, at night

མཚན་གཞི་ illustration, example

མཚོན་བྱ་ object to be defined

ཛ་

འཛིན་པ་ hold, perceive, apprehend

འཛིན་རྣམ་ apprehending aspect, subjective aspect (def: self-cognizing cognition or apperceptive cognition)

རྫས་ substantial entity

རྫས་མཚུངས་པ་ similar substance

ཞ་

ཞར་བྱུང་ incidental, supplementary, ancillary

ཞི་གནས་ calm abiding, *shamatha*

ཞིང་པ་ farmer

ཞེན་རིག་ conceiving cognition, determinative knower, conceptual knower

ཞེས་ / ཅེས་ quotation markers

ཞོག་ posit (something)!

གཞག་རྒྱུ་ something to posit

གཞག་པ་ posit, place

གཞན་དོན་སྐབས་ཀྱི་རྟགས་ཡང་དག་ perfect reason on the occasion of proving something to others

གཞན་པ་མི་མཐུན་ཕྱོགས་ dissimilar class of overextension

གཞན་དོན་རྗེས་དཔག་ inference for others

གཞན་རིག་ other knower, knower of things other than the perceiver itself, non-apperceptive cognition

གཞན་ལུགས་དགག་པ་ refuting others' views

གཞལ་བྱ་ object of comprehension

གཞི་ basis, place

གཞི་གྲུབ་ basic existent

གཞི་ཆོས་ཐ་དད་མེད་ནས་མ་གྲུབ་པའི་གཏན་ཚིགས་ unestablished reason through the lack of difference between the basis of debate and the quality to be proved (in that proof)

གཞི་རྟགས་ཐ་དད་མེད་ནས་མ་གྲུབ་པའི་གཏན་ཚིགས་ unestablished reason through the lack of difference between the basis of debate and the reason (in that proof)

གཞི་མཐུན་ combination, one thing that is both

གཞུང་ scripture, text

ཟ་

ཟག་བཅས་ contaminated, defiled (by mental afflictions)

ཟག་བཅས་ཀྱི་ཕུང་པོ་ contaminated heaps

ཟག་མེད་ uncontaminated, undefiled (by mental afflictions)

ཟེར་ན་ if someone says

ཟླ་བ་ moon

གཟུགས་ form

གཟུགས་ཁམས་ form realm

གཟུགས་མེད་ཁམས་ formless realm

གཟུང་རྣམ་ apprehended aspect, objective aspect

འ་

འོན་ཀྱང་ but, at any rate, nevertheless, "I disagree"

ཡ་

ཡིད་ mind

ཡིད་ཀྱི་མངོན་སུམ་གྱི་ཚད་མ་ direct valid mental cognition

ཡིད་ཆེས་རྗེས་དཔག་ inferential valid cognition based on trust

ཡིད་དཔྱོད་ speculative assumption

ཡིད་དབང་ mental sense power

ཡིད་ཤེས་ mental consciousness

ཡིན་ཁྱབ་མཉམ་ equally pervasive

ཡིན་འགོད་ predicative statement, "is" statement

ཡིན་པའི་ཕྱིར་ because it is

ཡུལ་ object

ཡུལ་ཅན་ subject (as holder of an object), object possessor

ཡོད་འགོད་ statement of existence, "exist" statement

ཡོད་པ་ existent

ཡོད་པའི་ཕྱིར་ because there is/are; exists

ཡོན་ཏན་ good qualities

ར་

རགས་པ་ rough, coarse

རང་རྐྱ་ཐུབ་པའི་རྫས་ཡོད་ independent, substantially existent

རང་གི་ཁྱད་ཆོས་དངོས་སུ་འཕངས་པ་ directly suggesting its agent

རང་གི་ཁྱད་ཆོས་ཤུགས་ལ་འཕངས་པ་ indirectly suggesting its agent

རང་རྒྱལ་ solitary realizer, *pratyekabuddha*

རང་དོན་སྐབས་ཀྱི་རྟགས་ཡང་དག་ perfect reason on the occasion of proving something to oneself

རང་དོན་རྗེས་དཔག་ inference for oneself

རང་ལྡོག་ self-distinguisher, self-isolate

རང་ལྡོག་སྒྲུབ་ཀྱི་འབྲས་རྟགས་ reason of effect proving its own distinguisher

རང་མཚན་ concrete phenomenon

རང་བཞིན་ nature, identity

རང་བཞིན་གྱི་རྟགས་ reason of same nature

རང་རིག་མངོན་སུམ་གྱི་ཚད་མ་ direct valid self-cognizing cognition

རང་ལུགས་ our own system

རང་ལུགས་གཞག་པ་ positing our own system’s views

རི་བོང་རྭ་ hare’s horn (classic example of a non-existent)

རིག་པ་ mind, cognition

རིགས་ reason, class, kind, family

རིགས་སྤྱི་ class generality

རུང་བ་ suitable, be fitting

རེ་རེ་ནས་ each and every, individually

རེག་བྱ་ touch, tangible object

རེས་འགའ་ occasional, occurring sometimes

རོ་ taste

ལ་

ལ་ mountain pass, grammar particle

ལམ་ path

ལས་ལོག་པ་ opposite from, differentiated from

ལུང་ oral transmission

ལུང་མ་བསྟན་ unspecified, neutral

ལུས་ཀྱི་དབང་པོ་ body sense power

ལེན་པ་ grasp

ལོ་ཏོག་ crop, harvest

ལོ་མ་ leaf

ལོག་ཕྱོགས་ opposite class, opposite of a perfect reason

ལོག་ཤེས་ wrong cognition

བློ་དོན་མཐུན་ factually concordant mind, mind in accord with reality, correct mind

བློ་རིགས་བདུན་ seven kinds of mind

རླུང་ air (element)

སླུ་བ་ fallible

ཤ་

ཤ་པ་ *Ashoka* tree

ཤ་ཟ་ ghost, flesh eater, demon

ཤིང་ tree

ཤིན་ཏུ་ལྐོག་གྱུར་ extremely hidden phenomenon

ཤིན་ཏུ་སྦྱངས་པ་ mental and physical flexibility, pliability, extreme ease

ཤེས་འདོད་ doubt, wanting to know

ཤེས་འདོད་ཆོས་ཅན་སྐྱོན་མེད་ faultless subject of debate about which someone has doubt

ཤེས་འདོད་མེད་ནས་མ་གྲུབ་པའི་གཏན་ཚིགས་ unestablished reason through the lack of doubt about the subject (in that proof)

ཤེས་པ་ consciousness, mind

ཤེས་བྱ་ object of knowledge, knowable entity

ཤུགས་ཀྱི་བསྒྲུབ་བྱའི་ཆོས་ implicit quality to be proved

ཤུགས་པ་ juniper tree

ས་

ས་ earth (element)

ས་ཕྱོགས་ place, region

ས་བོན་ seed

སྲིད་པ་ be possible, samsaric existence

སེམས་ mind

སེམས་ཅན་ sentient being

སེམས་བྱུང་ mental derivative, mental factor, secondary mind

སོ་སོའི་སྐྱེ་བོ་ ordinary being, non-*Arya*

སོང་ཚོད་ཀྱི་རྟགས་ actual reason

གསར་དུ་ new(ly), fresh

གསལ་ be clear, lucid

བསལ་བ་ thesis of a consequence, remove, eliminate

ཧ་

ལྷ་ god, deity

ལྷག་མཐོང་ penetrative insight, *vipashyanā*

ལྷན་ཅིག་བྱེད་རྐྱེན་ co-operating cause

ལྷན་ཅིག་འབྱུང་བའི་རྒྱུ་ co-arising cause, concurrent cause

ལྷན་ཅིག་མི་གནས་འགལ་ non-abiding contradiction

ལྷན་ཅིག་མི་གནས་འགལ་ཟླ་དམིགས་པའི་རྟགས་ reason of observation of the non-abiding contradictory

Dedication

By the immeasurable merit of the teachings thus imparted may all beings quickly attain the unsurpassable happiness of Buddhahood. May all beings meet a precious Lama. May the pure teachings of the Victor benefit all beings until samsara's end. May all good things arise and increase.